Time Out
New Orleans

Penguin Books

PENGUIN BOOKS

Published by the Penguin Group
Penguin Books Ltd, 27 Wrights Lane, London W8 5TZ, England
Penguin Books USA Inc., 375 Hudson Street, New York, New York 10014, USA
Penguin Books Australia Ltd, Ringwood, Victoria, Australia
Penguin Books Canada Ltd, 10 Alcorn Avenue, Toronto, Ontario, Canada M4V 3B2
Penguin Books (NZ) Ltd, 182-190 Wairau Road, Auckland 10, New Zealand

Penguin Books Ltd, Registered Offices: Harmondsworth, Middlesex, England

First published 1998
Second edition 2000
10 9 8 7 6 5 4 3 2 1

Colour reprographics by Westside Digital Media, 9 Bridle Lane, London W1
and Precise Litho, 34-35 Great Sutton Street, London EC1
Printed and bound by Cayfosa-Quebecor, Ctra. de Caldes, Km 3 08 130 Sta, Perpètua de Mogoda, Barcelona, Spain

Edited and designed by
Time Out Guides Limited
Universal House
251 Tottenham Court Road
London W1P 0AB
Tel + 44 (0)20 7813 3000
Fax+ 44 (0)20 7813 6001
Email guides@timeout.com
www.timeout.com

Editorial

Editors Ruth Jarvis, Caroline Taverne
Consultant Editor Harriet Swift
Deputy Editor Sophie Blacksell
Listings Editors Linda Keels, Lauren Swinney
Copy Editing Richard Lines, Cath Phillips
Proofreader Tamsin Shelton
Indexer Jackie Brind

Editorial Director Peter Fiennes
Series Editor Ruth Jarvis
Deputy Series Editor Jonathan Cox
Editorial Assistant Jenny Noden

Design

Art Director John Oakey
Art Editor Mandy Martin
Senior Designer Scott Moore
Designers Benjamin de Lotz, Lucy Grant
Scanning/Imaging Dan Conway
Picture Editor Kerri Miles
Deputy Picture Editor Olivia Duncan-Jones
Picture Admin Kit Burnet
Ad Make-up Glen Impey

Advertising

Group Advertisement Director Lesley Gill
Sales Director Mark Phillips
Advertisement Director, North American Guides Liz
Howell (1-808 732 4661/1-888 333 5776 US only)
Advertising in the US co-ordinated by *Time Out New York*
*Alison Tocci (Publisher), Tom Oesau (Advertising
Production Manager), Claudia Pedala (Assistant to the
Publisher)*

Administration

Publisher Tony Elliott
Managing Director Mike Hardwick
Financial Director Kevin Ellis
Marketing Director Christine Cort
General Manager Nichola Coulthard
Production Manager Mark Lamond
Production Controller Sam Furniss

Features in this guide were written and researched by:

Introduction Harriet Swift. **History** John Kemp, Harriet Swift. **New Orleans Today** Harriet Swift. **Mardi Gras** Harriet Swift.
Architecture Doug MacCash, Harriet Swift. **Literary New Orleans** Harriet Swift. **City of the Dead** Harriet Swift. **Sightseeing**
Roberts Batson, Christi Daugherty, Ruth Jarvis, Keith Marshall, Alex Rawls, Harriet Swift. **Accommodation** Harriet Swift.
Restaurants & Cafés Scott Simmons, Maria Wisdom. **Bars** Alex Oliver. **Shops & Services** Patti Saik. **By Season** Harriet
Swift. **Children** Margaret Woodward. **Film** Rick Barton. **Galleries** Keith Marshall. **Gay & Lesbian** Roberts Batson. **Music**
Alex Oliver. **The Performing Arts** Christi Daugherty, Harriet Swift. **Sport & Fitness** Alex Rawls. **Trips Out of Town** Harriet
Swift. **Directory** Harriet Swift.

The Editor would like to thank:

Scott Aiges, Pati D'Amico, Margie Brooke, Jane Ellen Cason, John Church, Bill Warren, Lily Dunn, Will Fulford-Jones, Karen
Gildea, Johnny Hall, Sara Hare, Jon Hildreth, Jimmy and Allane Hybart (Alabama Gulf Coast), John Kaine, Diana Ketcham,
Marilyn King (Mississippi Gulf Coast), Elisabeth Kirchner, Elaine Kolp, Michael Marshall, Sue Millon, Peggy
Critchfield Moffett, Ed McCaughan, Patric Powell & Martha Harrison (Grand Isle), Janet Rudolph, Diana Smith, Susan
Tucker, Dottie Waldrup, Wade Welch, Rich Wilson.

Ruth Jarvis flew to New Orleans with United Airlines (0845 844 4777 UK/1-800 241 6522 US/www.ual.com).

Maps by JS Graphics, 17 Beadles Lane, Old Oxted, Surrey RH8 9JG.

Photography by Paul Avis except: page 11 AKG; page 15 Louisiana Office of Tourism; page 22, 25, 213 John J Hall; page
101 Kevin Westenberg; page 123, 137, 239, 242 Ruth Jarvis; page 176 Ellis Anderson; page 176 Gail Blank; page 190,
266 Patricia Saik; page 193 Girard Mouton III; page 214 Ambush Magazine; page 245 Don Putnam; page 6, 9, 10, 12,
14, 21, 23, 26, 249, 255, 262, 267 Corbis; page 257 nouveau photeau; page 264 Russell MacMasters; page 265
Mississippi Gulf Coast CVB.
The following photographs were supplied by the featured establishments: pages 202, 206, 207, 245, 246, 258, 270.

Contents

Introduction

However you arrive in New Orleans, it's obvious that you have left the Western, industrialised world behind for an altogether different time zone. Conventional wisdom suggests turning your watch back by several decades – or throwing it away altogether.

First of all, you notice that everything looks different from most US cities. If you fly in, your initial view is of flat, dreary-looking spaces – swamps, as it turns out – that couldn't possibly support human life. Driving in from the east, you pass languid landscapes of dense, low-lying trees and bush that gradually give way to street signs for places like 'Elysian Fields', 'Piety' and 'Desire'. If you come from the west, you traverse seemingly uninhabited bayous and tiny patches of solid ground. For the few who come by boat, winding down the Mississippi River, the world seems to have turned to water.

Once in New Orleans, the sense of otherness is continually reinforced by architecture, climate, sounds and attitude. The city's medieval cast of mind always overcomes the puny symbols of the 21st century, such as high-rise buildings, mobile phones, road rage and even the calendar. New Orleans moves to a cycle of festivals, feasts and the weather. The imposed influences of the outer world are tolerated and even performed as business meetings are held, corporate plans are laid, students study for exams and public officials make a show of striving for efficiency. But then it's time for Mardi Gras or Jazz Fest, or a hurricane threatens to blow in from the Gulf of Mexico, and everything gets back to normal.

You're here to experience 'normal' New Orleans. This means that you will almost always find a festival going on somewhere in the city. Aside from the biggies, Carnival and

Jazz Fest, there are dozens of smaller events, all with the inevitable stamp of the city upon them: non-stop music, spontaneous dancing in the street, great food. While there are impressive cultural and intellectual sites and forums to behold here, it is the city's unquenchable urge to party that makes New Orleans such great fun and so endlessly fascinating.

Like any large metropolitan area, New Orleans has its problems (though crime rates, at least, are declining), but here they never seem completely hopeless because of this ingrained sense of *joie de vivre*. And it's infectious. Numerous would-be tourists have been known to drop their maps into the bin and simply stake out a barstool in the French Quarter for their entire holiday. Others soldier on with serious sightseeing agendas but will often find themselves oddly reluctant to get off the streetcar or will notice they are always carrying a 'go cup' of their favourite cocktail (which they quickly learn to smuggle into museums and such, just like the natives).

Prince Achille Murat, a minor French nobleman, counted New Orleans the highlight of his 1832 trip to the US. The city, he said, presented a 'striking contrast to other large cities' on his tour. He found no stimulating intellectual conversation, even in the best circles. Further, the bookstores and libraries were terrible. But, Murat explained, in New Orleans, 'ample means are afforded for eating, playing, dancing and making love'. Happily, little has changed since 1832. Abandon plans and pressures and forget the world beyond the levee. Immerse yourself in New Orleans and learn to do nothing and to feel everything. In the Cajun phrase, 'laissez les bon temps rouler': let the good times roll. And they will. They will.

ABOUT THE TIME OUT CITY GUIDES

The *Time Out New Orleans Guide* is one of an expanding series of *Time Out* City Guides, now numbering over 30, produced by the people behind London and New York's successful listings magazines. Our guides are all written and updated by resident experts who have striven to provide you with all the most up-to-date information you'll need to explore the city or read up on its background whether you're a local or a first-time visitor.

THE LOWDOWN ON THE LISTINGS

Above all, we've tried to make this book as useful as possible. Addresses, telephone numbers, websites, transport information, opening times, admission prices and credit card details are all included in our listings.

There is an online version of this guide, as well as weekly events listings for over 30 international cities, at www.timeout.com.

And, as far as possible, we've given details of facilities, services and events, all checked and correct as we went to press. However, owners and managers can change their arrangements at any time. Before you go out of your way, we'd advise you to telephone and check opening times, ticket prices and other particulars. While every effort has been made to ensure the accuracy of the information contained in this guide, the publishers cannot accept responsibility for any errors it may contain.

PRICES & PAYMENT
We have noted where venues such as shops, hotels and restaurants accept the following credit cards: American Express (**AmEx**), Diners Club (**DC**), Discover (**Disc**) MasterCard (**MC**) and Visa (**V**). Many businesses will also accept other cards, including Switch or Delta and JCB. Virtually all shops, restaurants and attractions will accept dollar travellers' cheques issued by a major financial institution (such as American Express).

THE LIE OF THE LAND
All our addresses include cross streets, so you can find your way around more easily, as well as websites or email addresses. We've also included zip codes for any organisation or venue you might want to write to. Map references indicate the page and square on which a central New Orleans address will be found on our comprehensive street maps at the back of the book (starting on page 306).

TELEPHONE NUMBERS
The area code for New Orleans is 504. All telephone numbers given in this guide take this code unless otherwise stated, though a new code is to be introduced by 2001 for out-of-town 504 numbers (*see page 240*). Numbers preceded by 1-800, 1-888 and 1-877 can be called free of charge from within the US and most can be dialled (at usual international rates) from the UK. We have stipulated where numbers are charged at non-standard rates. For more details of phone codes and charges, *see page 286*. The international dialling code for the US is 1.

ESSENTIAL INFORMATION
For all the practical information you might need for visiting the city, including visa and customs information, advice on disabled facilities and access, emergency telephone numbers and local transport, turn to the **Directory** chapter at the back of the guide. It starts on page 274.

MAPS
The map section at the back of this book includes useful orientation and overview maps of the the area and city, a large-scale locality

map for planning trips out of town and full street maps for the whole of central New Orleans, with a comprehensive street index. The first map starts on page 302.

LET US KNOW WHAT YOU THINK
We hope you enjoy the *Time Out New Orleans Guide*, and we'd like to know what you think of it. We welcome tips for places that you consider we should include in future editions and take note of your criticism of our choices. There's a reader's reply card at the back of this book for your feedback – or you can email us on neworleansguide@timeout.com.

Sponsors & advertisers

We would like to stress that no establishment has been included in this guide because it has advertised in any of our publications and no payment of any kind has influenced any review. The opinions given in this book are those of *Time Out* writers and entirely independent.

TimeOut

'THE GREATEST LONDON AUTHORITY'

In Context

Feature boxes

The Battle of New Orleans.

History

From the opportunism of its founding to the problems of the present,
New Orleans – naturally – has a garishly colourful past.

A New York journalist once described New Orleans as the northernmost Caribbean city, a cross between Port-au-Prince, Haiti, and Paterson, New Jersey, with a culture not unlike that of Genoa, Marseilles or Egyptian Alexandria. Although geographically closer to the British colonies, French and Spanish New Orleans was very much a part of the French and Spanish Caribbean. Its earliest populations consisted of lesser French and Spanish gentry, criminals, soldiers, debtors, tradesmen, merchants, prostitutes, priests and nuns, farmers from the fields of France and Germany, Acadian exiles from Canada, Canary Islanders, American Indians, Africans, Englishmen, Irish, and Anglo-Americans from the British colonies (later American states) along the Atlantic seaboard. Others came – Sicilians, Greeks, Eastern Europeans, Cubans, Central Americans, Chinese and Vietnamese.

For almost three centuries, New Orleans has survived yellow fever epidemics, Indian wars, slave revolts, economic depressions, conspiracies, hurricanes, floods, the American and French Revolutions, Civil War and Reconstruction, race riots and oppression, political corruption and, alas, Americanisation. Today, its jazz, French Quarter, cuisine and Mardi Gras are world famous.

Actually, the lower Mississippi River Valley came within weeks of being a British rather than a French colony, and New Orleans was founded on the insistence of a Scotsman who practically ruled the economy of early 18th-century France.

COLONIAL BEGINNINGS

It all began in 1682 when a French Canadian, Robert Cavelier, Sieur de La Salle, descended the Mississippi River to its mouth and claimed the entire Mississippi Valley for Louis XIV of France. La Salle, however, failed to establish a colony and was eventually assassinated by his own men. Colonisation was left to two other French Canadians.

In the early 1690s prominent Canadians (still governed by France) convinced Louis XIV that a strong colony in Louisiana was in his interest. They had good reasons: to protect and expand France's colonial possessions; to block the

British who were moving west from the Atlantic seaboard; and, finally, to capitalise on prosperous Spanish trade in the Gulf of Mexico.

In September 1698 the French government dispatched the Canadian Pierre Le Moyne, Sieur d'Iberville, with his younger brother, Jean Baptiste Le Moyne, Sieur de Bienville, and five small ships. After a brief encounter with the Spanish in nearby Pensacola, Florida, the expedition dropped anchor at the mouth of the Mississippi on 3 March 1699. It was Mardi Gras day and New Orleanians have been celebrating ever since.

France wasted little time in building a series of posts along the Mississippi and Gulf Coast, including Mobile, Alabama and Biloxi, Mississippi. By 1718, French officials knew they had to establish a permanent settlement on the river to protect their claim. From the beginning, however, Louisiana had been a drain on the royal purse.

> **'New Orleans became a commercial centre, connecting Europe and the West Indies with the upper regions of the Mississippi.'**

Enter John Law, an adventurous Scotsman, with a new scheme. In 1716 Law created the Banque Générale de France and then convinced Philippe, Duc d'Orleans, regent for young Louis XV, that Louisiana had potential for great wealth. Law formed a joint stock company to develop the colony and sold shares to the Duke and other investors. The Crown then granted Law's company an exclusive charter to Louisiana.

Law, a master at public relations, flooded southern Germany, France and Switzerland with posters encouraging farmers to emigrate to Louisiana. Thousands grabbed at the opportunity to make a fresh start in the New World. Most settled upriver from New Orleans in an area that to this day is called the Côte des Allemands (the German Coast). During the first four years of Law's control, the colony's population grew from about 400 to 8,000, including African slaves.

In building his city on the river, Law again showed himself to be a masterful politician. Working through Bienville in the colony, Law named the city 'Nouvelle Orleans' in honour of the Duc d'Orleans. He gave instructions that the streets of the new city be named after members of the royal family, their ancestors and cousins (including bastards), patron saints and major stockholders in the company. Law's bold

venture did not last long: by the early 1720s, the company had gone bust; Law eventually fled to France, narrowly escaping a good stoning in the streets. He died in complete obscurity.

IMPERIAL SQUABBLES

The history of New Orleans is inseparable from its port. France had hoped to reap great riches from the interior of North America, but gold and silver did not pour from the wilderness. Tobacco, lumber, indigo, animal hides and other goods were floated downriver on flatboats to the new city, where ships from France, Spanish Florida, the West Indies and the British colonies waited to trade with spices, cloth, wine and other items. New Orleans became a commercial centre, connecting Europe and the West Indies with the upper regions of the Mississippi.

But international storms were brewing. For over a century, the three major European colonial powers (France, Spain and Britain) had been at each others' throats in North America. By the early 1750s, both France and Britain had staked a claim to the Ohio River Valley. In 1754 war broke out in North America (started by the young British-American militia officer George Washington) and quickly spread to Europe. Called 'The French and Indian War' in the British-American colonies and the 'Seven Years War' in Europe, the conflict was to eliminate France as a colonial power in America. Despite an alliance with Spain a year before the war ended, France was finally defeated in 1763. It ceded all of Canada and French territory east of the Mississippi River to Britain. France also lost India to Britain and Spain ceded both East and West Florida to Britain.

New Orleans and Louisiana west of the Mississippi, however, were not included in the package. In 1762 Louis XV, realising that he was losing the war, convinced his cousin, King Carlos III of Spain, to enter the war on the side of France. As a token of appreciation, Louis gave Louisiana to his cousin. The colony was costing him his royal shirt. Carlos III, however, accepted Louisiana, as a buffer to keep the British away from nearby Mexico.

Louisiana Frenchmen were not happy about the deal. They brooded for almost six years, while petitioning the king to revoke the gift, but Louis refused. Hope received a further knock when Don Antonio de Ulloa, a military officer and respected scientist, was appointed governor. He arrived in 1766 and met a cool reception. Two years later, the colonists staged a bloodless coup and drove Ulloa from the colony. Again they begged the French Crown to take them back and again Louis refused.

Spain's retaliation was quick and complete. In July 1769 Spanish forces arrived under the command of General Alexander O'Reilly, an Irishman in Spanish service. O'Reilly crushed the short-lived rebellion, set up a new government and executed the coup's ringleaders.

REVOLUTION

Spanish New Orleans played a major role in the American Revolution against the British Crown. Through the Louisiana colony, the Spanish sent supplies and munitions to the American rebels and allowed American raiding parties to launch forays into British West Florida. While the British were busy with their upstart American colonials, the Spanish Governor, Bernardo de Galvez, drove the British from East and West Florida.

> ### 'By the end of the 18th century, New Orleans was a major North American port.'

Galvez and his successors practised an open immigration policy that gave refuge to both loyal and rebel British-Americans fleeing the Revolution, and to the Acadians driven from Nova Scotia by the British after they refused to renounce their Catholic faith and pledge allegiance to England. (Their descendants are Louisiana's French-speaking Cajuns.) Canary Islanders settled in the swamps and bayous to the south of New Orleans, where their descendants live today, many still speaking an archaic Spanish dialect.

During the final decades of the 18th century, Spanish New Orleans prospered despite fires, plagues, rebellions, pressure from Americans expanding westward and the French Revolution. While the Revolution in France was in progress, mobs of French New Orleanians roamed the streets calling Spanish Governor Carondelet a *cochon de lait* (suckling pig). Carondelet kept the mobs in hand and then, diplomatically, gave refuge to French aristocrats fleeing the Revolution.

Carondelet also had troubles with restless Americans heading west. During the American Revolution, the Continental Congress assured the Spanish that it had no designs on Louisiana. After the war, however, pressure and tension mounted between the infant United States and Spain as American commerce on the Mississippi River grew. Americans wanted free navigation of the river, and Spain, which controlled both sides of the river below Natchez, prevented free trade. Spanish officials seized American flatboats and Americans clamoured for an invasion of Louisiana. War was averted in 1795, but the tensions remained.

By the end of the 18th century, New Orleans had become a major North American port with a population of almost 10,000. Unfortunately, three fires in the 1780s and early 1790s almost destroyed the old colonial city. Most buildings in today's French Quarter were constructed during the Spanish colonial days and after the 1803 Louisiana Purchase.

Consequently, the French Quarter of the city has a fascinating mixture of 19th-century architectural styles.

THE LOUISIANA PURCHASE

In the early 1800s political events in Europe once again drifted up the Mississippi. In 1800 Napoleon forced Spain to return Louisiana to France. The news did not sit well with US president Thomas Jefferson, who feared that a war with France was inevitable. The issue concerning him most was free navigation of the Mississippi from the Ohio and Illinois territory to New Orleans. To solve the problem, he wanted to buy New Orleans and a portion of Spanish West Florida bordering the Mississippi. This would put the entire east bank of the river in American hands, but Napoleon had a better deal in mind. Needing money to fight Britain and knowing he could not hold on to the colony when war came, Napoleon decided to sell not only New Orleans, but the entire Louisiana colony. In other words, in 1803, for $15 million, the USA bought the entire central section of North America from the mouth of the Mississippi north to Canada and west to the Rockies.

VICTORY OVER THE BRITISH

The first decade or so of the American era has been described by one historian as one of 'excitement, uproar, flux, boom and bust, disasters, disappointments, and achievements': thousands of people died in the yellow fever epidemics and American and foreign sailors frequently slugged it out on the river levees and in taverns, while the Creoles saved their contempt for Anglo-Americans. Statehood came in 1812, as did the first steamboat, the *New Orleans*, captained by Nicholas Roosevelt, an ancestral kinsman of two American presidents.

The year 1812 also brought war with Great Britain. It was not a popular war in New Orleans, especially when US commander Andrew Jackson made it clear he would burn the city down before losing it to the British. Fortunately, Jackson's ragamuffin army prevailed in the 1814-15 battle and New Orleans was untouched. The irony of the battle was that a peace treaty had been signed two weeks before it was fought, but word only reached America a month later.

The battlefield is now at the edge of the town of Chalmette, in St Bernard Parish, about a 20-minute drive from the French Quarter. A hulking industrial smokestack looms to the south and oil refineries dot the river landscape, but it's easy to imagine the battlefield as it appeared to Jackson and the British commander, Major General Sir Edward Pakenham (Wellington's brother-in-law). Pakenham brought his 10,000 battle-tested redcoats downriver of New Orleans through an overland route and planned to march into the city. Jackson checked the British juggernaut with a daring night-time attack on 23 December 1814.

The two armies faced each other nine miles (14.5 kilometres) south of the city, amid sugarcane fields and swamps. Jackson established a fortified line at a natural bottleneck on the Rodriguez Canal. With the river on one side and cypress swamp on the other, the Americans lined up behind a mud rampart and carefully placed artillery.

The British attacked on 8 January 1815, counting on superior numbers, strong artillery and disciplined troops to overwhelm the Americans. Instead, the assault was a disaster, with confusion on the field and the death of key commanders. British losses were more than 2,000, while the Americans reported only 13 killed. British troops on the West Bank did put the Americans to rout but Jackson had clearly carried the day. In retrospect, the battle seems pathetically futile but historians count it as an important notch in the US quest for sovereignty, emphasising that Americans could repel European armies.

ANTEBELLUM PROSPERITY

The five decades between the Battle of New Orleans and the American Civil War were the city's golden years. It pulsated with the energy of commerce, business, change and expansion. This period also saw heightening tensions between newly arriving Anglo-Americans and Creoles. Competition and rivalry existed not only among merchants and other fortune seekers, but also between two radically different cultures. By the early 1830s the city was divided into two well-defined sections: the American Sector upriver of Canal Street and the French Quarter below Canal Street.

Prosperity and the competitive spirit between the two sections dramatically changed the landscape of New Orleans. Americans, wanting to emulate other prosperous cities on the East Coast, and Creoles, with their eyes to their

Since 1839 crowds have taken to the streets for the **Mardi Gras** parades.

beloved France and to their own architectural heritage, built antebellum New Orleans. Above Canal Street stood Gallier Hall, a Greek Revival temple facing Lafayette Square (*see page 89*); blocks of three-storeyed, red-brick row houses; and the new Customs House at the foot of Canal Street. Below Canal Street, Creoles boasted of the newly rebuilt St Louis Cathedral (*see page 77*) and the magnificent Pontalba Buildings facing the Place d'Armes (*see page 89*).

The arts also flourished during these years. New Orleans had one of the first opera houses in the USA. Blacks and whites, rich and poor, strictly segregated, could hear a Bellini, a Meyerbeer or a Donizetti opera at one of several opera houses in the city. Patrons filled the St Charles Theater in the American Sector and the Théâtre d'Orleans in the French Quarter and later the new French Opera House on fashionable Bourbon Street (destroyed by fire in 1919).

Without question, the city's most famous pastime came once a year: Mardi Gras. Mardi Gras balls are as old as the city itself, but Mardi Gras parades, for which the city is so well known, didn't arrive on the scene until the 1820s. They were pleasant, colourful events featuring costumed and masked Creoles who made their way through the streets from the opera house to some grand salon for an evening ball. These 'cavalcades' gradually degenerated into packs of masked thugs who roamed the streets throwing flour into unsuspecting faces. The first parade using vehicles or 'floats' was in 1839 when an odd assortment of wagons and carriages paraded through the American and Creole sections of the city. By the end of the 19th century, Mardi Gras was celebrated by everyone: white, black, American, Creole, as well as new immigrants from Europe, Catholics, even Protestants. For more details, *see chapter* **Mardi Gras**.

New Orleans was indeed a place where one could make a fortune and enjoy life's pleasures. But poverty and disease were never far away. Yellow fever took thousands of lives. In 1856 alone, more than 2,700 people died of the fever, more than 1,000 from cholera, and 652 from tuberculosis. By far the most devastating yellow fever epidemic hit the city in the summer of 1853. Upwards of 8,000 men, women and children died. Hardest hit were the destitute Irish and German immigrants just arriving in America. The Irish had survived the potato

famine and a treacherous Atlantic crossing only to end up in shallow mud graves along the levee. They died in such staggering numbers that open wagons rode through the streets picking up heat-swollen bodies. In stacks of 50 or more they were carted to cemeteries and shallow graves.

In the decades immediately preceding the Civil War, Irish and German immigrants arrived in the city by the thousands. Most came by ship from Liverpool, Le Havre, Bremen and Hamburg, on voyages lasting up to six weeks. Packed into steerage, many did not survive the crossing. By 1860 the Irish population in the city had reached 25,000. Both Irish and Germans found homes in the newly emerging political parties. Pitched street battles between the anti-immigrant Native American Party (former Whigs) or 'Know-Nothings', as they were called, and Democrats were common. A section of Uptown New Orleans is still called the Irish Channel for its once large concentration of Irish immigrants and their descendants, and every year the descendants of those Irish immigrants take to the streets with their New Orleans-style St Patrick's Day parade, an exuberant spectacle that belies the view that New Orleans Irish have disappeared in the great American melting pot.

New Orleans, in fact, was a melting pot unlike any other in America. Different races and nationalities retained their identities in unusual ways – perhaps the key to New Orleans's singular culture. Two segments of the New Orleans population were unique to south Louisiana and exerted a tremendous influence on the region's culture: Creoles and 'free people of colour'. In colonial times, the term Creole (from the Spanish *criollo*) meant a person of European ancestry born in the colonies. The term altered as times changed from a purely racial definition to mean anyone descended from European colonists, black or white. This shift in meaning created the overlapping and confusing castes of Creoles, Creoles of colour and free people of colour (not necessarily Creoles). With the changeover to US government, the designation took on a new edge, separating the Creoles from the arriviste Americans.

A souvenir from the **World's Industrial and Cotton Centennial Exposition** of 1884-85.

Within the New Orleans community the free people of colour included tradesmen, shopkeepers, cabinet-makers, plantation owners, artists, journalists, land speculators and investors. One such was Norbert Rillieux, a Paris-educated engineer who revolutionised the sugar industry with a brilliant invention that simplified the transformation of sugarcane into sugar crystals. Rillieux was also a cousin of the French Impressionist painter Edgar Degas. Degas' mother was born in New Orleans and later lived in France, where she met and married Degas' father. One of her uncles had a long-lasting liaison with a free woman of colour that produced Norbert Rillieux and other children, all of whom became prominent in their own fields. The lifestyles of the free blacks paralleled that of their white counterparts and relatives. Some were slave owners themselves and enlisted in the Confederacy during the early years of the Civil War.

THE CIVIL WAR

New Orleans was riding high on a wave of prosperity by the end of the 1850s: banks were strong, cotton and sugar crops were setting new records and British textile mills were buying all the cotton they could get. The nation, however, was racing towards civil war. New Orleans's adherence to the Southern cause was a bit confusing. Not only had it prospered under the economic protection of the US, but its commercial and family connections with the north-east (Boston and New York) were greater

What they say about New Orleans

'They [citizens of New Orleans and the Louisiana territory] are uninformed, indolent, luxurious – in a word illy fitted to be useful citizens of a Republic... I have seen, Sir, in this city many youths to whom nature has been apparently liberal, but... have no other accomplishments to recommend them but dancing with elegance and ease. The same observation will apply to the young females, with additional remark, that they are the most handsome women in America.'
– **William CC Claiborne**, first US governor of Louisiana, writing to President Thomas Jefferson, 1804.

'As to the morals of this city, the word is obsolete. On the Sunday we arrived, a balloon, with a live lamb in the car, and aerial fireworks, were to be exhibited by permission of the mayor... Duels are very fashionable, if they can contrive an affront such as: "How dared you to spit as I was passing?"; "How dared you to pass as I was spitting?" or, "You shall not sneeze where I am!"'
– **Arthur Singleton**, *Letters from the South & West*, 1824.

'One does nothing here, it lies in the climate... Manet would see lovely things here, even more than I do... the beautiful, refined Indian women behind their half opened green shutters, and the old women with their big bandanna kerchiefs going to market... The orange gardens and the painted houses attract too and the children all dressed in white...'
– **Edgar Degas**, 1873, during the visit when he painted *The Cotton Exchange* (pictured).

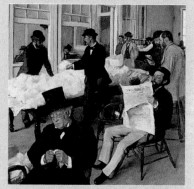

'We went to another bar... the place was seething with people who seemed soaked in alcohol; but vice and drunkenness wore light colours here. The atmosphere was not heavy; on the contrary it seemed fresh and gay... Gradually the nightclubs closed but we didn't feel like going to sleep, we felt so alive.'
– **Simone de Beauvoir**, *America Day by Day*, 1953.

'New Orleans is Blanche DuBois, and that mix of knowledge, denial, hunger, and experience is precisely what makes her so attractive to outsiders. Those who are not outsiders and who know her only too well have mixed feelings.'
– **Andrei Codrescu**, Introduction to 20th Anniversary edition of *A Confederacy of Dunces*, 2000.

than in any other Southern city. However, by the time the Civil War came in 1861, most New Orleanians fully supported the Confederacy and in January of that year Louisiana seceded from the Union. Less than three months later, war began when Southern troops under the command of New Orleans-born General Pierre Gustave Toutant Beauregard opened fire on Fort Sumter in Charleston, South Carolina. A month later the Union fleet blockaded the mouth of the Mississippi River.

New Orleans remained in the Confederacy for little more than a year. In April 1862 Union warships, commanded by 'Damn the Torpedoes' David Glasgow Farragut, came up the river, bypassing the two protecting forts, and dropped anchor in front of the city. Farragut trained his guns on the city and demanded its surrender. When city officials refused, Farragut sent a detachment ashore, cut down the rebel flag and hoisted the Stars and Stripes. For the remainder of the war, New Orleans was under military rule.

The most colourful character to emerge from this era was the Yankee military commander Major General Benjamin 'Silver Spoons' or 'Beast' Butler, a politician turned army general. New Orleanians hated him and accused him of stripping private homes of valuable possessions, which he shipped back home to Massachusetts (hence the 'Spoons' sobriquet). His lasting fame, however, came from General Order 28, which decreed that any woman who insulted a Federal soldier or officer was to be treated as a criminal, specifically as a common prostitute. New Orleans women had been waging guerrilla warfare on the Union soldiers with tactics ranging from snubbing friendly advances to dumping chamber pots from upper storey windows on passing columns of troops. Butler's angry response became one of the Confederacy's greatest publicity tools, and he was denounced in the US Congress and the British Parliament.

Despite the anger and humiliation of white New Orleanians at the quick US takeover, they suffered less than many other Southerners from wartime privations and the city emerged physically intact. New Orleans had the distinction of being under Reconstruction longer than any other Southern city. The process began in May 1862 and lasted until April 1877, when the last Union soldier withdrew from the city. Bitterness over the South's defeat and rage over continuing Federal occupation led to a poisonous atmosphere that erupted into violence on several occasions. In 1874 there was an armed battle in the streets between native whites organised into the 'White League' (no apologies for the politically incorrect name in that era) and the black and white Metropolitan Police. Order was restored only when waves of US troops arrived.

The defeated ruling class, which meant whites of every background, was not reconciled to racial equality on any level. Freed slaves and free people of colour, however, were eager to take advantage of the new social, political and economic opportunities that US rule allowed, and despite native white opposition, full civil rights were extended to black males by the 15th amendment in 1870. (Women, of course, would not vote or hold public office until well into the 20th century).

While the new post-slavery society took shape, New Orleans soon resumed its old *joie de vivre*: the French Opera House and the St Charles Theater played to large audiences and gambling halls and saloons were full, while temperance societies continued their pre-war struggle against the demon rum. Mardi Gras, too, became even grander: Rex, the grandest of all Mardi Gras parades even today, first rolled in 1871 in honour of the Russian Grand Duke Alexis's visit to New Orleans.

With the withdrawal of Federal troops in April 1877, one of the most romanticised periods in the city's history was over.

THE GILDED AGE
The 1880s and 1890s in New Orleans was an era of boom and bust, corruption and reform, racial retrenchment and labour unrest among former slaves, native whites and newly arriving immigrants. No longer backed by Federal

Controversial segregation laws led to **riots** in the 1950s and 1960s.

troops, blacks lost most of the civil rights gained during Reconstruction. The US Supreme Court in its famous Plessy vs Ferguson decision upheld the state's 'separate but equal' segregation laws and the state's 1898 constitution effectively removed most black voters from the rolls. White and black New Orleanians would live together but apart for almost half a century until the civil rights movement in the late 1950s and 1960s finally ended legal segregation.

With a population of more than 216,000, the Crescent City was still the South's largest conurbation and officials worked hard at selling it to the nation's business community. The World's Industrial and Cotton Centennial Exposition of 1884-5, held on the site of today's Audubon Park, showed how far the city had come since Reconstruction.

Despite real social and racial problems, New Orleans was booming. There was a conscious air of boosterism. Grand mansions sprang up along the major avenues; the visual and literary arts flourished; Carnival emerged bigger than ever; government reformers created Storyville, the red-light district, in a successful attempt to contain prostitution (although it was later closed down by US authorities in 1917 for its supposedly harmful effects on World War I-bound sailors and soldiers); and the old American Sector above Canal Street began its transformation into a modern American city.

The Gilded Age also brought tensions on a familiar theme: immigration. Thousands of poor Sicilians entered the city through its port in the 1880s and 1890s, and by 1890 the Sicilian population had reached 30,000. While most of these immigrants laboured hard along the docks and in other jobs, a new menace emerged from their ranks, the Mafia.

Violence erupted in October 1890 with the murder of New Orleans Police Chief David Hennessy, who had declared war on the secret crime society. With his last dying breath, Hennessy reportedly said he had been shot by the 'Dagoes'. On the night of the shooting, the city's mayor ordered the arrest of every Sicilian and Italian found on the streets of New Orleans. A total of nineteen were brought in, but only ten were actually charged. Nine others were indicted as accessories.

When a trial failed to convict any of the Sicilians, outraged newspapers urged New Orleanians to turn out in force and avenge the murder of Chief Hennessy. Gangs led by prominent citizens stormed the city jail, where they shot and hanged more than a dozen Sicilians, including those who had been acquitted by the jury.

'During the period between 1900 and World War I, jazz was born in the bordellos of Storyville.'

New Orleans newspapers generally praised the day's work, but there was widespread publicity beyond Louisiana where the crowds' blind bigotry was not applauded. The Italian Government registered strong protests (several of the murdered men were Italian citizens) and was eventually paid $25,000 by the US Government in reparations. In May 1891 a New Orleans grand jury concluded that the Mafia did exist in New Orleans, and that it had murdered Hennessy. Contemporary historians are dubious, however, seeing the incident as a worst-case scenario of American xenophobia.

THE 20TH CENTURY

New Orleans entered the 20th century with an air of optimism: the nation had just defeated Spain in the Spanish-American War, and at home in Louisiana the white supremacy Democrats had become the dominant political party. But even by the late 1890s, New Orleans had begun to fall behind other US cities. Its national standing by population dropped from ninth to 12th in 1900 and to 16th by 1918.

During this period between 1900 and World War I, jazz was born in the bordellos of Storyville and in the music halls along the city's lakefront. World War II boosted the city's economy, especially in shipbuilding. The famous Higgins landing boat that put millions of Allied troops on beaches from Normandy to Saipan was invented and built at the Higgins Shipyard in New Orleans. After the war, the city assumed a leading role in the nation's petrochemical industry.

In the early 1960s New Orleans began to change. The civil rights movement hit New Orleanians square in the face in 1960 when a federal court finally ordered the city's public schools to desegregate. Six years earlier, the US Supreme Court had declared the 'separate but equal' doctrine unconstitutional, but the city, and the rest of the South, resisted for years.

In November 1960 four black children, escorted by US federal marshals, broke the colour line for the first time since Reconstruction. The most poignant scene in that dramatic episode was the picture of little six-year-old Ruby Bridges, escorted by federal marshals and holding her mother's hand, walking with great dignity past a screaming, hysterical mob.

Civil rights also extended to the ballot box. Beginning in the early 1970s, political power in the city slowly shifted to black voters as their numbers grew. In 1977 in a dramatic break with the past, New Orleanians elected their first black mayor, long-time civil rights advocate Ernest N 'Dutch' Morial. Dutch's son, Marc Morial, was elected to the same office in 1994 and was re-elected in 1998 with hopes of changing the city charter to run for a third term. The 1960s and 1970s also saw major changes in the city's demographics as middle-class white and black families moved to the suburbs. New techniques in draining the surrounding marshlands, a new interstate highway system connected to the nearby countryside and new housing opened vast tracts of undeveloped land for city dwellers. Coupled with racial tension and rising crime, this led to more and more families moving to the 'burbs, leaving the inner city mostly to the poor.

At the same time, however, some young and affluent families remained behind to buy and renovate the 'gingerbread' Victorian cottages Uptown. Gay couples spread out of the French Quarter to the Faubourg Marigny, sowing the same kind of neighbourhood renewal. Since then, entire neighbourhoods have given way to the restoration movement.

THE OIL BOOM AND BUST
Throughout the 1970s and early 1980s, the city's port and its petroleum industry primed New Orleans's economic pump. Good times were ahead, or so its population thought. The

Jazz maestro **Louis Armstrong**.

Louisiana Superdome had been built; Poydras Avenue attracted new high-rise office buildings and hotels; oil companies moved into their corporate offices; and the 1984 Louisiana World Exposition, 'The World of Rivers', managed the intensity of a six-month-long Mardi Gras.

Unfortunately, the optimism of the early 1980s crashed and was burnt out by 1986. The state's rich petrochemical industries collapsed when OPEC dramatically increased oil production, sending prices plummeting. The 1984 World Exposition was an artistic success but a financial flop. The dramatic increase in inner-city crime and crack cocaine chased even more middle-income families to the suburbs. Every day, newspaper headlines told depressing stories of a dwindling population, poverty, corrupt police, record-breaking murder rates, gambling controversies, shady politicians and cronyism.

Another event struck at the heart of New Orleans. In 1992 the city council passed a tough anti-discrimination ordinance, denying parade permits to carnival and social organisations that were not open to all races, genders or ethnic groups. While impressive as a strike at the heart of the city's de facto segregation and a well-deserved smack in the face of the moneyed, privileged networks of family and friends who really own the city, the ordinance was another cross to bear for an already dispirited city. The Mardi Gras krewes are a complex parallel universe that mystifies outsiders. There are white krewes, black krewes, female krewes, free-for-all krewes, all with their own tribal-like ideas of who is in and who is out. The prospect of losing Mardi Gras parades was far more disturbing to most New Orleanians of all races than embedded class, race and gender issues. In the end, the ordinance was softened, a bi-racial commission formed, and compromises struck. Yet, the city's oldest and most prestigious carnival krewes – Comus, Momus and Proteus – refused to open their membership books or secret meetings, and cancelled all parades. Only Rex made token efforts to recruit black members and continued its parade. (Proteus finally made the move in 2000.)

1990S RENAISSANCE
By late 1996 and early 1997, the New Orleans and Louisiana economies had begun to make a strong comeback. Tourism and employment were up, crime was down, manufacturing increased, oil and gas prices rose sharply and other industries showed healthy growth.

Despite the city's darker side of life, its bizarre characters and reprobates, its crime and poverty, New Orleans has awoken during the past few years to its own creative spirit. It will never be the largest city in the South again, but it has reclaimed its position as a leading centre

Local Girl Makes Good

When Micaela Almonester, aged 15, was married in St Louis Cathedral to her distant cousin, Celestin de Pontalba, all of New Orleans approved of the match. 'After all,' said some local wag, 'the bridegroom is beautiful and the bride is rich'.

Indeed, in 1811, the year of her marriage, Micaela was known as the richest girl in Louisiana, the only child of an elderly father who died when she was two and he was 70. Micaela went quietly into her arranged marriage, probably bowled over by her handsome and, by all accounts, docile fiancé. After all, he would inherit a title and she would become a baroness in France.

Educated by nuns, married off and resettled in France, Micaela doubtless expected to live a quiet, upper-class life. Instead she became one of the most notorious women in France by repeatedly suing for divorce and fighting her husband's family for control of her fortune, and later returned to New Orleans to leave an impressive architectural legacy.

Micaela's story has all the ingredients of a Hitchcock thriller. Her psychopathic father-in-law tried for 20 years to force her to abandon her husband. Women had almost no rights under the law and lost all of them, including their money and property, if they left their husbands. Frustrated over his failure to gain complete control, the elder Pontalba finally shot Micaela in the family chateau, then turned the gun on himself. He died but she survived.

Micaela was finally able to wrest control of her fortune for herself after several infamous trials in the 1830s. She turned out to have a brilliant talent for making money, soon increased her holdings and launched a major building project, a new mansion in Paris.

Designed by Napoleon III's fave architect, Louis Visconti, the villa is now the official residence of the US ambassador to France.

In 1850 Micaela returned to New Orleans, determined to apply her new-found passion (and, in her view, her expertise) for architecture to her home town. She commissioned the **Pontalba Buildings** – the magnificent apartment blocks that frame Jackson Square – often acting as her own contractor. Micaela drove the construction workers mad with her micro-management style but the results of her obsession are a gift to New Orleans for all time (see page 75). Her father had paid for the rebuilding of St Louis Cathedral and the Presbytère and Cabildo buildings that flank it. Micaela completed the space with handsome brick buildings that echoed the townhouse/shopping blocks she had seen in Paris.

Although she suffered from the effects of the shooting for the rest of her life, she died a quiet death at home in Paris aged 78, richer than ever, thanks to her own efforts, and adored by her children and grandchildren: a rare happy ending for a girl who was rich but not beautiful and had been raised to be the pawn of others.

for the arts. Typically for New Orleans, it is a case of the arts done 'the way we do things here'.

The city has at last fully embraced its music, giving it pride of place in any list of New Orleans achievements. Celebrating the city's tricentennial in 1999, the official symbol was an image of Louis Armstrong and the legend, 'New Orleans, 1699-1999, The Birthplace of Jazz'. The annual New Orleans Jazz and Heritage Festival (*see page 192*), begun in 1970, is second only to Mardi Gras as the city's signature event. It brings in more than $200 million and almost 200,000 visitors. The city schools, whatever their problems, are committed to music programmes, understanding that music

is the language of New Orleans. While the city isn't as unconditional in its affection for newer music successes like rapper Master P and his ilk, there is an understanding that the New Orleans genius manifests itself in a variety of ways.

In 1817 geographer and surveyor William Darby wrote about his experiences in Louisiana and the Gulf South, most of it dispassionate description and observation. About New Orleans, however, he was unambiguous and decisive: 'There are few places where human life can be enjoyed with more pleasure,' he said, a pronouncement that continues to define the city today.

Key events

COLONIAL BEGINNINGS

1682 French Canadian Robert Cavelier, Sieur de La Salle, arrives at the mouth of the Mississippi River and claims the territory for France. He names it Louisiana in honour of Louis XIV, King of France.
1699 French Canadian Pierre Le Moyne, Sieur d'Iberville, arrives with a small fleet and begins French colonisation of the region.
1718 New Orleans founded and named after France's regent, Philippe, Duc d'Orleans.
1719 Large groups of African slaves and German and Swiss families begin arriving.
1722 Hurricane destroys much of the early city.
1727 Ursuline nuns open a school for girls, a tradition that continues to this day.
1751 Jesuits introduce sugarcane to Louisiana.

IMPERIAL SQUABBLES

1762 In the Treaty of Fontainebleau, France cedes New Orleans and all of Louisiana west of the Mississippi River to Spain.
1763 France cedes Louisiana east of the Mississippi to Britain.
1768 French Louisiana colonists rebel and drive Spanish governor from Louisiana.
1769 New Spanish governor Alexander O'Reilly executes rebel leaders.

REVOLUTION

1777 Spanish governor Bernardo de Galvez aids the American effort against the British.
1788, '92 & '94 Much of New Orleans destroyed by fire.
1794 St Louis Cathedral dedicated.

THE LOUISIANA PURCHASE

1800 Spain cedes Louisiana back to France.
1803 France sells Louisiana to the United States for $15 million.

VICTORY OVER THE BRITISH

10 January 1812 The steamboat *New Orleans*, arrives in New Orleans, signalling the rise of the city as a major US port.
30 April 1812 Louisiana becomes the 18th state of the Union.
1815 US forces under Andrew Jackson defeat British at the Battle of New Orleans.

ANTEBELLUM PROSPERITY

1832 Yellow fever and cholera kill more than 5,000 New Orleanians.
1839 First Mardi Gras parade held.
1853 Yellow fever epidemic kills more than 8,000.

THE CIVIL WAR

1861 Louisiana secedes from the US and later joins the Confederacy.
1862 US fleet captures New Orleans during the Civil War.
1865 Civil War ends.
1868 Louisiana rejoins the Union.
1874 Street battle between White League and Metropolitan Police on Canal Street.
1877 Reconstruction ends in New Orleans as Federal troops withdraw.

THE GILDED AGE

1878 Yellow fever epidemic kills more than 5,000 in Louisiana.
1891 Gang of New Orleanians lynches Italian immigrants in aftermath of the murder of Police Chief Hennessy.
1897 Storyville red-light district is created.

THE 20TH CENTURY

1915 New Orleans devastated by hurricane and flood.
1929 Great Depression begins.
1941 World War II brings prosperity to New Orleans's shipbuilding industry.
1960 New Orleans's schools desegregated.
1965 Hurricane Betsy devastates the city.
1970 First Jazz Fest held.
1975 New Orleans Superdome completed.
1978 Ernest N 'Dutch' Morial becomes New Orleans's first black mayor.

THE OIL BOOM AND BUST

1984 New Orleans's world's fair, 'The World of Rivers', is held.
1991 Legalised gambling returns to New Orleans when voters approve a new state lottery.
1992 Three of the city's oldest carnival organisations boycott Mardi Gras when the City Council passes an anti-discrimination law.
1994 Marc Morial, son of former Mayor Dutch Morial, is elected Mayor.
1995 Harrah's casino, the only non-floating casino in the city, abruptly closes.

1990S RENAISSANCE

1998 Marc Morial re-elected as Mayor.
1999 New Orleans celebrates its tricentennial.
1999 Harrah's reopens in a new casino building on Canal Street.
2000 Proteus rejoins the Mardi Gras parade line-up.

New Orleans Today

How the Big Easy does it.

At the beginning of the millennium, New Orleans was struggling with the ills and evils that beset most large US cities. The infrastructure was in dire need of massive, expensive repairs, while the public schools were in sharp decline and the crime rate very bad. Yet the city had an air of hope and expectancy as 2000 began. After a particularly bad decade, violent crime was declining, services improving, employment rates moving upward and, best of all, no New Orleans police officer had been indicted and/or convicted in months.

ANY NEWS IS GOOD NEWS

New Orleans is a city that takes good news wherever it can find it. Built on a swamp, at the mercy of floods and hurricanes, it's a place where fatalism is a birthright. But there are times when even fatalists have to try to alter the course of events. The 1990s was just such a time. The city's economy was still in shock from the oil bust of the 1980s, adding to the poverty that had long put New Orleans at the bottom of prosperity lists, and crime was escalating. For several years New Orleans led

the US in murder statistics as youthful thugs became ever more insistent on using guns to settle the most minuscule disagreements, and drug use and trade boomed.

At the same time, the police department was imploding from mismanagement, indifference to corruption and a high-profile series of crimes among its officers, from drug-running to murder. Public schools, largely given over to the blacks who were too poor to send their children to Catholic schools or flee to the working-class suburbs, were barely under control, requiring on-campus police officers and metal detectors.

Marc Morial, the ambitious young mayor first elected in 1994, has taken most of the credit for 'rebuilding New Orleans' (his favourite slogan), hiring a strong chief of police and attacking deep-rooted problems such as concentrations of abandoned houses. Morial did bring a sense of urgency to the city's problems but he was aided by New Orleans bottoming out to such an extent that any number of outside agencies and interests began to focus on 'doing something' about New Orleans.

Power, corruption and white lies

A visiting California writer was pleased to find himself at an event with New Orleans journalists the day after former Louisiana governor Edwin Edwards was convicted of extortion, fraud, conspiracy and money-laundering.

'Some trial?' he said, eager to hear the inside story from locals.

'Well, no one was really hurt by what Edwards did,' said a radio guy.

The Californian was incredulous.

'That guy swindled millions,' he said.

'But it was from casinos,' was the response. 'And if they were stupid enough to try and pay him off…'

Others at the table rolled their eyes but the Californian couldn't quite grasp the complete absence of outrage and indignation. 'Welcome to New Orleans,' one of the local writers said.

Edwards, a wily Cajun from rural Louisiana, wasn't a native son, but New Orleans found much to like in the four-time governor, an admitted gambler, womaniser and bon vivant (he was famous for quipping that the only way he could lose an election in Louisiana was to be photographed in bed with a dead woman or a live man). Investigated by federal agencies

for decades, he was finally convicted in the spring of 2000, after hidden cameras and microphones showed him accepting hundreds of thousands of dollars from casino backers vying for state gambling licences.

The trial was held in Baton Rouge instead of New Orleans as the Big Easy was felt to be far too easy on Edwards. It's a forgiving attitude toward rogues that goes back to the city's beginnings. As a neglected outpost of European powers, New Orleans would have died without the supplies and goods brought into the port by smugglers and pirates. Left mostly on its own with impossible decrees sent over from Paris and Madrid, the colony paid lip service to all legalities while going its own way. In 1798 the official hangman found it more profitable to sell liquor to the inmates and free other convicts for a price than to carry out executions. Similarly, when gambling of all kinds was strictly forbidden in the colony by the Spanish government and denounced by the governor, New Orleans was importing more than 54,000 packs of playing cards a year, enough for every man, woman, child and visitor in the colony to have at least four decks apiece.

The exposure of police corruption was largely due to federal agents who were investigating an amazing variety of police crimes. A consortium of business and civic leaders pressed for a reorganisation of the police department, bringing in a former New York City police commissioner who introduced computerised studies of crime patterns.

Although the city's freefall has been broken, it's still far from the throbbing metropolis of commerce and civic virtue that boosters claim. In addition to making lists for the 'most obese' (No.5), 'worst city for pedestrians' (No.10), 'fastest shrinking city' (No.8 and the only Sun Belt city in the Top 10), New Orleans has yet to find a satisfactory economic base to replace the loss of oil and waterfront jobs. Tourism is the primary engine of the city's economy but most of the work is minimum-wage jobs with little hope of advancement.

THE FEELGOOD FACTOR

The bad news about New Orleans appears overwhelming when it's put on graphs and charts. It's a sad collection of ills that are familiar to many US inner cities. But New

Orleans is also on many other Top 10 lists. Travel magazine polls regularly rate it as the No.1 or No.2 favourite city in America. Individual bars, restaurants, chefs and musicians, could be singled out as world-class. A hip intellectual magazine, *Utne Reader* (akin to *Granta*) even named the Lower Garden District 'the hippest neighbourhood in America'. That hotbed of artists, musicians and bohemians may face high crime and streets almost unusable with potholes but it bubbles with creativity and *joie de vivre*.

One of the most remarkable things about the pleasure principle here is how universal it is, spreading through all classes, all races. The fabulous Mardi Gras Indians, 'tribes' of black men who parade on foot in eye-popping costumes, could be seen from a sociologist's point of view as an oppressed group's desperate need for visibility and impact. But what to make, then, of the bankers and attorneys and judges who live their lives in desperate hopes of being selected for Rex or Proteus? The pinnacle of social prestige requires that these leaders of the community wear ridiculous satin and silk costumes, don pageboy wigs

What has been called 'the New Orleans way' rubbed off on even the most puritanical visitors. General Andrew Jackson, the uncompromising hero of the Battle of New Orleans, was appalled at the suggestion that he allow Jean Lafitte and his pirates to aid in the defence of the city. New Orleanians were puzzled at his indignation. After all, the state legislature might have banned piracy but one of its most prominent members, New Orleans businessman Jean Blanque, owned many of the ships used by Lafitte. Jackson called them the 'hellish Banditti' but New Orleanians were unmoved: 'those people have their own pursuits, why interfere with it?'

Jackson soon had cause to be glad of those 'pursuits' when he realised that only Lafitte could supply cannons, ammunition, guns and experienced crews in the numbers needed to mount a serious defence.

When Alexis de Tocqueville made his famous tour of America in 1832, he heartily agreed with the French consul that business and government in New Orleans were in a constant state of 'bedlam'.

In the 20th century, New Orleans was greatly offended by populist governor Huey Long and his power-mad grabs for control over everything and everyone. Yet in retrospect it seems more a case of style over substance. Long's famous abuses of patronage were a variation on a New Orleans theme. In New Orleans power is tied to patronage, doling out jobs, contracts and access. It's all done in a straightforward manner that amazes most outsiders. A black civil rights activist said late in life his most important achievement had been in the 1940s when he was able to secure regular patronage from the city government in return for delivering the increasing black vote.

The attitude of 'those people have their pursuits' runs through New Orleans history in an unbroken line. Robert Maestri, mayor during the 1930s and early '40s, was widely known to supply mattresses to Storyville bordellos. When the houses were raided, he had a deal with the police to collect all his goods. When the madams opened up again, he resold the mattresses to their former owners. In New Orleans this was called 'the original model of perpetual motion'.

There have been periodic bursts of reformist campaigns but New Orleans has a limited interest in good government. As one longtime observer of city government has pointed out, 'For one thing we would all be bored to death.' Boredom is a far deadlier sin than greed in this city.

and elaborate crowns and parade through the streets. Carnival this scale simply couldn't happen in any other US city.

'The work ethic of New Orleans is pleasure, how to fiind it, how to maintain it.'

Mardi Gras and Jazz Fest have become two of the city's biggest economic engines, each pumping millions of dollars into New Orleans every year. The primacy of tourism has intensified the debate about how to revitalise the city. Hotel interests have been snapping up old buildings in the CBD and Warehouse District, gutting them and refurbishing them as luxury hotels. Other hotel projects seek to demolish old buildings and erect glass and steel towers in their place, putting as many rooms as possible in one building. Preservationists have mounted effective campaigns against the all-hotels-are-good steamroller, stressing that visitors come to New Orleans because of its centuries-old architecture, not to visit a high-rise hotel identical to one in Cleveland, Atlanta or Los Angeles. The preservationists have not prevailed but have had reasonable success in checking the onslaught of mindless development.

THE LITTLE DIFFICULT

Often the anti-development forces have been aided by the New Orleans way of doing business, which involves interminable and inexplicable delays, mysterious alliances and under the table bribes. National and international firms often just walk away rather than deal with New Orleans. Others find that tried and true methods won't work in the Big Easy (or 'the Little Difficult' as it's sometimes called in business circles).

Harrah's Casino has become the city's most visible clash of cultures. New Orleans finally pushed into gambling, kicking and screaming, in the early 1990s. There was widespread worry that Las Vegas-type casinos would ruin the city's other tourist and entertainment businesses. The compromise struck was that all casinos would be on riverboats, sailing on the Mississippi River and Lake Pontchartrain. But through some kind of legislative sleight of hand, a decision was made to allow one non-riverboat, or 'land-based', casino in New Orleans. Harrah's, the famous Las Vegas gambling corporation, won the contract after heated bidding and was supremely confident that the New Orleans casino would be a major player.

After the failure of an 'interim' casino and some intense and often acrimonious negotiations between Harrah's, the state and the city, the new casino was completed and opened in late 1999. By mid-2000 its future was again in doubt as its monthly $19-$21 million revenues were falling short of the projected $29 million. Unlike big gambling cities such as Las Vegas and Atlantic City (and even Biloxi on the Mississippi Gulf Coast), New Orleans has many, many other marvels besides its casinos. In fact, studies reveal most people who walk into Harrah's are basically sightseers, coming in to see just another New Orleans attraction rather than focused on gambling.

But the casino is also suffering from New Orleans's overheated expectations of an economic miracle. Exasperated Harrah's executives have been anxiously protesting the fixed $100 million annual tax to the city and state, a figure not tied to revenues. Although none of the New Orleans casinos was shown to be involved in the sprawling Edwin Edwards casino kickback schemes, conventional wisdom in the city attributed the casinos' struggles to the burden of sub-rosa payments to grease the wheels of government. Indeed, there's almost a sense of civic pride about how pervasive and yet difficult to prove public corruption is in New Orleans. 'He's too smart to get caught' is a frequent compliment paid to officials who are widely supposed to be on the take. Actually, the conviction rate is not that bad (*see page 18* **Power, corruption and white lies**).

PLUS CA CHANGE

When New Orleans does turn its attention to addressing change, even the best efforts are often comically inept. The city almost lost saviour-like police chief Richard Pennington when the city council began questioning the big-money incentives tied to his contract. The members seemed to forget that it took big bucks and benefits to lure the much-respected Pennington to the city. In the end his contract was honoured and Pennington stayed but only after he was almost lured away by other ailing cities offering bigger and better contracts.

Similarly, the city brought in a former Marine officer, Al Davis, as superintendent for the woeful public school system. Davis, an African-American high achiever, initiated his term with a five-kilometre walk/run rally that was

supposed to be a bonding for administrators, teachers, parents and students. 'And they say people don't get up in the morning in New Orleans!' said a cheerful Davis at the rally's start, surrounded by many of the people who work directly for him. New Orleanians also aren't known to frolic in the August heat, as was soon explained by dozens of people being treated for heat stroke, exacerbated by inadequate water and juice supplies (which had been promised) and parents and children standing in queues for up to an hour waiting for free school supplies – which ran out.

The incredible fact about New Orleans isn't its failures and founderings but its ability to stay focused on what it holds dear. While the traffic infrastructure cannot seem to install any left-hand turns at intersections (drivers must go through the red light to a U-turn lane a block or so away, return to the intersection and make a right turn), solve street bottlenecks or remove abandoned vehicles, it mounts a dazzling display of crowd and traffic control for big events. Mardi Gras parades move in a well-oiled procession, smartly followed by lumbering street cleaning machines and armies of men sweeping up debris. During Jazz Fest, buses, taxis and private cars transport thousands to and from the Fair Grounds daily. Even though the schools are all but penniless, music progammes stay in the curriculum and middle and high schools field high-spirited, impressive marching bands with troops of dancing girls, majorettes and flag bearers. The work ethic of New Orleans is pleasure, how to find it, how to enjoy it, how to maintain it.

Embarking on the third millennium, New Orleans is seeing its fortunes taking a modest rise. The city has emerged from the lower depths of crime statistics and economic doldrums but New Orleanians aren't too anxious to see it make giant strides toward modernity and genuine civic adulthood. More than 120 years ago writer Lafcadio Hearn mourned a New Orleans that he believed was disintegrating in front of him. 'I must speak of her decay,' he wrote. 'New Orleans is fading, moldering, crumbling – slowly but certainly… in the midst of the ruined paradise of Louisiana.' No one, not even the most ardent civic cheerleader, disputes that New Orleans is prone to decay and crumbling. The climate and terrain guarantee that houses will sag, roofs leak and streets buckle. The city's many great achievements are for the most part ephemeral – music, parades, food. What is enduring about New Orleans is its continuing triumph over the limitations of the world around it, remaining not just a ruin but a 'ruined paradise'. It's the kind of contradiction that defines New Orleans.

Mardi Gras

Carnival has been the lifeblood of New Orleans for close on two centuries. Party on, and on, and on...

Mark Twain compared explaining a joke to dissecting a frog: it can be done, but the frog dies in the process. Similar rules apply to Mardi Gras. Too much thinking ruins the fun and blinds visitors to an essential characteristic of New Orleanians: they don't think about it and they get plenty of laughs.

The facts of Carnival are almost unbelievable: a major US metropolitan area all but shuts down for a fortnight, devoting the lion's share of its public and private resources to parades, balls, street revels and partying of every kind. Economists say it's approaching the $1 billion mark in its impact on New Orleans, making it one of the city's major industries.

Although New Orleans is one of the US's most Catholic cities, Mardi Gras has gone far beyond its religious roots to become one of the most entrenched traditions in America. It is a tribute to the New Orleans genius for pleasure that Carnival has not only survived into the 21st century but grown and evolved. While the rest of the US eagerly shook off its past,

shedding as much of its Old World baggage as possible, New Orleans remains serenely uninterested in such progress.

You have to be here to understand how millions of people meld into one continuous party. Ease of movement is impossible, with parades and parade preparations closing major streets and arteries. Businesses close. Employees who don't have the day off don't show up. Restaurants are full of men in black tie and women in formal gowns dining before balls. People do incredible self-debasing acts for strings of plastic beads that they could buy for $3 in a shop. Black professionals dress in black face, grass skirts and carry spears. Carnival is a world unto itself.

Mardi Gras, Fat Tuesday, is the day before Lent, which is 47 days before Easter. Because of the vagaries of the Church calendar, Mardi Gras can be anywhere from the first week of February to the second week of March. Forthcoming dates are: 27 February 2001, 12 February 2002, 4 March 2003, 24 February 2004 and 8 February 2005.

HISTORY OF CARNIVAL

Some form of Mardi Gras celebration has been a part of New Orleans life since the early 18th century. Under French rule, masked balls were held during the pre-Lent season, though this practice was discontinued under Spanish rule. Even as an American city, masking remained illegal until 1823, when Creoles petitioned for permission to resume masked balls. The first Carnival parades evolved in the 1820s as an extension of the merriment during the journey to the ball, but they were gradually hijacked by thugs. The first parade using vehicles of 'floats' took place in 1839.

Mardi Gras Indians

Few elements of New Orleans pull together as many central themes as Mardi Gras Indians. They are rarely seen on Mardi Gras itself and they aren't actually American Indians, but tradition, secrecy, money, community, music and race all play interesting parts in the Indian story.

Their origins are a matter of conjecture, since few of the original Indians were literate and the accounts that have been passed down vary. It is generally agreed that black New Orleanians first paraded as Indians in the 1880s, when Chief Becate formed the Creole Wild West. They might have chosen to be Indians because Becate and others had Indian blood, or because of the influence of Buffalo Bill's Wild West Show, which wintered in New Orleans in 1884. There might be a West African influence derived from Caribbean carnivals. Whatever the case, working-class blacks formed tribes in their neighbourhoods and met to perform a ritualised fight, doing war dances and singing boastful songs.

Dressing as Indians gave poor blacks a way to express themselves and bring Carnival to their neighbourhoods. Every Mardi Gras, tribes set out on routes known only to the chiefs and their 'Spy Boys', who led the parades on the lookout for rival tribes, a practice that continues today. They are accompanied by the second line friends and family members, who play rhythm instruments and sing the response to the chief's songs.

The songs are largely stories of 'battles, wild nights or lost friends', but they are told in a private slang whose origins, like most Indian rituals, are now obscure. Although new songs are written, songs that have been sung for generations still make up the core of the repertoire. They are passed on as part of the tradition to younger Indians and weren't set down until the 1970s when tribes like the Wild Magnolias and the Wild Tchoupitoulas made recordings (though these aren't very representative).

Today, costumes are what the Indians are best known for – huge, elaborate explosions of colours that are best understood as folk art. Victory in ritual battles goes to the chief with the most beautiful, most elaborate costume ('beautiful' and 'elaborate' become synonyms during Mardi Gras). Every year, each Indian makes a new suit, sometimes recycling bits of beadwork or decorative patches from a previous year's suit but never re-using an old one. The size and elaborateness of a suit is determined by the rank of the member, scaling up from Spy Boy and Flag Boy to the bus stop-sized creations worn by the Big Chief.

The best time to see the Indians is when the tribes meet on the Sunday closest to St Joseph's Day (19 March) and again two Sundays later. These parades are more accessible and on safer, more reliable routes than the more neighbourhood-oriented ones on Mardi Gras day.

The city's first carnival organisation was formed not by Creoles but by a group of upper crust Anglo-American businessmen. Transplants from nearby Mobile, they felt New Orleans was lagging behind its sister Gulf city in Carnival celebrations. They decided to introduce the Mobile custom of organised parades and in 1857 founded the Mistick Krewe of Comus, adopting the spelling 'krewe' because they felt it had an Old English flavour. Comus held its first parade that year, with Milton's *Paradise Lost* as its theme. Comus became the prototypical Mardi Gras krewe, holding private, ceremonial balls and creating costumes and a different Carnival theme each year. Rex, perhaps the most famous krewe, was formed in 1872. It has defined Mardi Gras for many years, giving it many of its traditions: the king cake, the purple, gold and green colour scheme, the flag and its awful theme song, 'If Ever I Should Cease to Love'. The first satirical krewe, the Knights of Momus, formed in 1872, mocking the Reconstruction government running New Orleans and Louisiana and the DC politicians who had installed them.

Zulu, the first black krewe to parade, formed to satirise Rex in 1910 and held its first parade in 1916. Today, Rex and Zulu are the crowning events of Mardi Gras, both parading down St Charles Avenue on Fat Tuesday. In 1969 Bacchus, the first of the 'superkrewes', was formed by wealthy men brought to town by the oil boom but who were slow to be welcomed into the old line krewes. Perplexed by the Byzantine ties of marriage, family, culture and religion that defined the secretive krewes, the new rich and their local allies launched their own Mardi Gras groups, changing Carnival from a mostly regional, insular celebration into a more glamorous, high-profile event. They brought in Hollywood and TV stars to reign over their krewes and commissioned enormous, gimmicky floats that horrified the old krewes. Like Endymion and Orpheus after it, Bacchus aspired to the biggest floats, the longest parades and the most generous 'throws' (trinkets dispensed from the floats). These parades were seen by the older krewes as challenges not only to the dominance of their organisations, but to the dominance of the old money they represented in New Orleans.

In 1991 the inevitable happened: someone pointed out that a black-majority city was underwriting and sanctioning the quasi-public krewes, many of which were bastions of race and class discrimination. A black city councilwoman demanded that any Carnival organisation using city services (ie parading on city streets) must prove it did not discriminate on the basis of race, gender, handicap, sexual

Carnival crowds and Mardi Gras mayhem.

orientation or national origin. Old line krewes Momus and Comus quit parading rather than co-operate with the city ordinance. Proteus carried on for 1992, then quit. Only Rex immediately signed the affidavit (and recruited black members) and paraded without interruption. Zulu, the oldest parading black krewe, had no problems – it had welcomed white and women members for years.

Carnival of 1992 is a bad memory for everyone. Even the black-majority city council backed away from the desegregation ordinance. Polls showed that white and black New Orleanians opposed it, being more concerned about the loss of parades than aggressive implementation of equal rights. When Proteus announced it was rejoining the parade lineup in 2000 there was widespread approval. 'Welcome Back!' signs, large and small, dotted the route.

PARADE INFORMATION

Parades maintain a fairly regular schedule; for details of times and routes, check the *Times-Picayune*. Also very helpful for planning your Carnival is *Arthur Hardy's Mardi Gras Guide* ($3.95, www.mardigrasguide.com), an annual magazine with exhaustive information on parade times and routes and Carnival history.

There are an ever-growing number of websites devoted to Mardi Gras, including www.mardigras.com, www.mardigrasday. com, www.fattuesday.com, www.mardigras neworleans.com, www.kreweofbacchus.org, www.carnaval.com, www.kreweoftucks. com, www.kreweoforpheus.com and www.barkus.org.

THE FIRST WEEKEND

The Mardi Gras season can be thought of as the two weekends preceding Fat Tuesday, though there are parades almost every night between the weekends. The first weekend is a good time for families because the crowds are manageable. The party gladiators and

Come See Where
Mardi Gras is MADE!

Tour New Orleans' fascinating of carnival creations – made before your very eyes! Take the **FREE** Canal Street ferry to our **FREE** Zshuttle. Open every day from 9:30a.m. to 4:30p.m.

BLAINE KERN'S
MARDI GRAS WORLD

233 NEWTON STREET • NEW ORLEANS, LA 70114
504-361-7821 • 800-362-8213 • www.mardigrasworld.com

Winnebagos have yet to come to town and the throws are neither so spectacular nor so rare that they merit tussles over ownership.

Parades once went through the French Quarter, but that practice ended because of the fragile state of the buildings. Now the only proper parade (with floats and bands) in the Quarter is the **Krewe du Vieux Carré**, which marches a Saturday or two before the Mardi Gras season. It's an irreverent gaggle of Mardi Gras enthusiasts equally divided between purists and satirists. Floats are downscale and old-fashioned, built on wagons and grocery carts, and pulled by people and mules. Like most of the Krewe du Vieux Carré costumes, they look as if they'll come apart when the spit dries or the tape peels. The Krewe du Vieux Carré likes its satire raw and juvenile and the best throws at the parade are often the printed parody items.

Sparta, which rolls on the first Saturday night, is notable for having the old line parade feel and for being one of the parades that still uses 'flambeaux' torches despite the advent of streetlights. They are carried by white-robed black men who are thrown money as they dance. The lighting of the torches beforehand is a great spectacle.

For a completely offbeat side of Mardi Gras, take in the Sunday afternoon **Krewe of Barkus** parade. This all-dog walkathon (well, there are people, too, leading, carrying and pushing the dogs) starts in Louis Armstrong Park at around 2pm and ends at the Good Friends Bar in the French Quarter (Dauphine Street at St Anne Street). The parade is a fundraiser for the local Society for the Prevention of Cruelty to Animals and brings out the gonzo side of dog owners, who compete ferociously for costume prizes for their pooches. Barkus has a queen, king, ball and theme, all dog-related, of course. 'Joan of Bark' (in 2000) is typical. Check the website, www.barkus.org, for dates and info.

Who needs a costume?

THE SECOND WEEKEND

The second weekend is the big show, with two parades on the Friday night, two on Saturday during the day and **Endymion** at dusk in Mid City. Three parades on Sunday culminate with **Bacchus**. Friday is an easy night because **Hermes**, a traditional parade and the only one with stilt-walkers, is followed down St Charles Avenue by the new, satirical **Krewe d'Etat**, rumoured to be composed of former Momus and Comus members.

Mardi Gras by numbers

$49,706,694: Amount of taxes and other revenue paid to New Orleans and Orleans Parish from Mardi Gras in 1999.

$9.1 million: Amount spent on beads for Carnival in 1999

5,527,865: People who saw at least one Mardi Gras parade in 1999

$500,000: Cost of building a new float

1871: The first year float riders threw tokens to the crowds

$750: Annual dues for members of the Krewe of Bacchus

140 feet (43 metres): Longest king cake available from local bakeries; feeds at least 2,000 people

71: Number of Carnival balls during the Mardi Gras season

47: Number of days from Mardi Gras to Easter

10: Number of marching bands required for a parade to be certified for a permit

Saturday, however, forces some tough choices. **Iris**, the only all-women's parade in the city, is long and generous in throws to those who can get close to the floats, but those stuck at the back may find its members help reinforce the stereotypes about women and throwing. **Tucks** follows Iris and is one of the must-see parades. Its satire isn't as blue as the Krewe du Vieux Carré, but its king's throne is a toilet and the royal sceptre a toilet brush. Tucks works hard to be unlike the old line parades, generating as much undignified energy as possible, and its members' energy and enthusiasm are contagious.

Across town, **Endymion** begins to form while Tucks rolls. Actually, Endymion crowds start forming three, four, even five days before the parade. The neutral (median) grounds on Orleans Avenue have become the Mayfair and Park Lane of Endymion viewing, so suburbanites drive in and stake out plots, camping for days in advance (and irritating the locals in the process). A stage is now set up on Saturday morning so bands can entertain the growing village of police-tape interlopers, coolers, barbecues and lawn chairs. A better bet is to see Endymion on the sidewalk side of Canal Street, where the crowds aren't so thick or immobile.

Show us your...

For 2000 Mardi Gras, New Orleans officialdom announced a new get-tough plan on nudity: none. Women baring their breasts and men dropping their pants in the endless quest for beads would be arrested and taken in, unsmiling police spokesmen announced on TV. No exceptions.

Their success could be measured by a big banner in the gay area of Bourbon Street on Fat Tuesday: 'Tits next block!', it screamed, meaning that attractive young men would be asked to show something in this neighbourhood and attractive young women should move on.

In fact, the police did make some very noisy arrests at the beginning of Carnival, primarily out-of-town teens who hadn't heard about the new, clean New Orleans. By the weekend

before Mardi Gras, however, it was all over. Breasts were flashed, pants were dropped, millions of beads were awarded.

The no-show policy was a hot topic on talk radio and on the *Times-Picayune* letters page. 'If it's in the Quarter,' ran the most popular refrain, 'who cares?'. Not the police, really, or anyone else. Flashing is frowned upon on the Uptown and Mid City parade routes, which are largely the turf of families. The closer the parades get to the French Quarter side of Canal Street, the less prohibition. In the Quarter, policing is noticeably slacker as the days get closer to Fat Tuesday and the further one goes into the centre of the Vieux Carré. In the gay areas, it's all but unheard of for men showing their endowments to be busted.

Endymion and the other superkrewes put on consistently good shows, each with their own strengths. Endymion specialises in excess, never throwing one string of beads when there are 11 more in the bundle, never throwing little beads when bigger ones exist and never throwing one cup when a whole sleeve would make a bigger splash. Where other krewes boast one celebrity, Endymion has two or three, and while the other big parades last almost two hours, Endymion can stretch on into the night.

Sunday's **Bacchus** is best known for its floats, which are among the most ornate and handsome. The krewe has developed a stable of signature floats that appear every year regardless of the theme. The Bacchagator and the Baccha-Whoppa each hold more than 100 riders, while the Bacchusaurus is a significant deviation from the usual model.

The **Kong family** also rolls each year, with three floats whose riders don't throw but invite the crowd to enjoy the otherwise-illegal act of throwing their lousier beads back at a float.

LUNDI GRAS

Monday, or Lundi Gras, was once a day of rest. Then the only daytime event was the arrival of the King of Rex at Spanish Plaza at the foot of Poydras and Canal Streets. In the last few years, though, Lundi Gras has become an event all of its own. Zulu hosts an all-afternoon party at Woldenberg Park near the Aquarium, while Rex has expanded its celebration at Spanish Plaza to include more music by the likes of the Neville Brothers, Dr John and the Radiators. Since 1998 King Zulu and Rex have met during Lundi Gras, each attended by their posses. This meeting of the kings, staged like a state event in the presence of the mayor, is seen as a healing of the 1992 unpleasantness and is treated with far more reverence than the visit of any (actual) world ruler.

Uptown, Harry Connick Jr's **Orpheus** is the third superkrewe parade and, after only five years, has become one of the season's best. It features the most marching bands and has floats to rival Bacchus. Its newest float, the Leviathan, is the most elaborate and expensive to date, a rolling Las Vegas casino marquee. By any Mardi Gras standards, it's bee-you-tiful.

FAT TUESDAY

Fat Tuesday begins as early as 4 or 5am, when an Endymion-like second city springs up on the neutral grounds along St Charles Avenue. The day is officially under way when **Zulu** begins at 8.30am on Jackson Avenue. It's a matter of some debate whether Zulu has ever started on time, so smart parade-goers figure it will make it to St Charles some time after 9am, though the

lateness isn't always Zulu's fault. One year vandals deflated the tyres of the floats overnight, delaying the parade by over an hour.

When it eventually arrives, Zulu riders, black and white, male and female, are in their traditional make-up, the jungle blackface of natives in Tarzan movies. Since 1909 Zulu has parodied Rex, creating low parallels to Rex's high-class pretensions, mocking white stereotypes of blacks by wearing fright wigs and black paint. The jungle theme is continued in the most prized Zulu throw, the coconut, each of which has been hand-painted. Actually, they aren't truly throws since a law passed in 1987 banned their throwing for safety reasons, but they are intermittently handed down to those zealous and determined enough to hang on to a front row spot. Further touches include building black-painted white characters on to the front of floats: a black Heidi and a black King Arthur have both featured.

Rex begins Uptown on Napoleon Avenue and follows Zulu along St Charles, and while it is a pretty parade, its pomp and old-fashioned attitude seem too restrained after a weekend of parades that throw beads that could double as skipping ropes. Members' careful distribution of small, cheap beads and their gentlemanly demeanour are anticlimactic after the slapstick of Zulu, so many skip the event and head on to the French Quarter. Rex is followed by the truck parades: more than 300 trucks pass with groups and families in costume throwing (mainly) beads recycled from other parades.

IN THE FRENCH QUARTER

At some point, all revellers make it to the French Quarter. Bourbon Street has become the popular image of Mardi Gras, so most people have to experience at least once for themselves the joys of flat draught beer and naked breasts it promises. By Fat Tuesday, even the resolute break down, devise costumes, the worse taste, the better, and head for the Quarter. The wise will get their fill on Royal or Chartres Streets, both of which feature the usual madness but with more manageable crowds.

A wide range of artists, bohemians, young families and musicians march into the Quarter under the banner of the Society of St Ann, an illl-defined group that has been gathering in the Bywater every Mardi Gras morning for about 20 years (accounts vary). Dressed in colourful costumes and led by a brass band and banners, the group begins at Markey's Bar (640 Louisa Street, at Royal) at around 9am, making refuelling stops at bars along the way before crossing Esplanade into the Quarter. There's no membership, no rules and no agenda, making St Ann's an ideal way for visitors to join in a local

Throws to catch

Just how far should you go for a Carnival throw?

▶**Basic beads** The building blocks of Carnival hysteria; all the rest of the beads thrown are judged by how much bigger, more decorative and unusual they are against these plain janes, imported by the millions from Asia.
Flash factor: Less than zero; sometimes even little kids won't pick these up.

▶▶**Big beads** Don't look for many of these glittering prizes at parades – the big, big beads are being dangled off balconies in the French Quarter. When the elaborate beads are thrown from floats they're aimed at a rider's family or friends.
Flash factor: Total disclosure required for the fist-sized bauble necklaces: that means dropping the pants for guys, full frontal nudity for gals.

▶▶▶**Krewe symbols** A good colourful catch, with fanciful designs. Not too difficult to snag, especially at Orpheus, which covers the crowds with its pendants. Zulu's fierce warrior and Rex's tiny crown are the most sought after.
Flash factor: Big smile while screaming 'I love you Orpheus!' usually works.

▶ **Knickers** Newer krewes have panties imprinted with their logo for throwing. These will always be aimed at attractive young women. Not considered a hot throw, possibly because the panties are so cheaply made as to be unusable, even for a joke.
Flash factor: They wish.

◀ **Doubloons** Krewes strike doubloons to celebrate each year's parade. Normally, it will have the krewe's name and symbol on one side, the year and parade theme on the other.
Flash factor: Zip.

Mardi Gras tradition with welcoming companions. Even if you don't have a costume, try to wear a funny hat, cape or some other evidence that you share the spirit.

The day begins to end at Café Brasil (*see page 220*) around dusk, when would-be drummers play extended rhythm jams for anyone still able to dance. The grooves are sporadic but well meant and the scene is a nice antidote to Bourbon Street for those not bothered by the relentless pounding.

Every year, the police symbolically end Mardi Gras and close down Bourbon Street with an impressive show of force at midnight, marching horses through the streets and

forcing the remaining lost souls on to the sidewalks or into the bars for yet more beer. The party goes on all night, but those still out on the streets at this point are the equivalent of house guests who can't take a hint and go home.

SURVIVAL TIPS

First, book early. Your air ticket (and it won't be cheap), your accommodation and any restaurants you want to visit. Once you're here, the most important thing to remember is that Mardi Gras is a marathon, not a sprint. Hangovers and exhaustion will eventually become a problem anyway, so there is no need to start that fight on the very first night. After alcohol-related challenges, the biggest test for

▲ **Masks** Traditionally worn only on Mardi Gras Tuesday. Masks don't usually make good throws because they're so light, but you'll find them handed out at parties and given out at the walking parades.
Flash factor: You'll have to kiss the walking parader, usually a sweet old guy who's seriously drunk.

▼ **Zulu throws** Absolutely the most sought after items of Carnival. To snag a Zulu coconut is going home a winner. The toy spears are a close second for want-ability.
Flash factor: Handed down from the floats to the prettiest girls; traded in the French Quarter for big juicy kisses or full frontals.

►**Go cups** A brilliant innovation of a decade or so ago, plastic cups marry the New Orleans tradition of 'go cups' with Mardi Gras. Colourful, useful – especially when insulated – but problematic to carry around after a parade.
Flash factor: Good leaping ability; the cups are usually thrown in a stack

▼ **Soft throws** Stuffed animals and fuzzy toys are a staple at daytime parades when children are out in greatest numbers and are fully awake.
Flash factor: Cute little kid essential.

visitors is getting around. Streetcars, buses, cabs and bicycles (*see page 234*) are by far the best ways to travel. Everybody wants a parking spot somewhere near a parade route, so, if you're driving, allow plenty of time for the maddening hunt. Parking in or near the French Quarter is virtually impossible and illegal on many streets after the Friday before Mardi Gras, though you could go for one of the overpriced parking deals offered by homeowners. Residents cram as many cars as possible on their land for upwards of $10 to $25 a day. Better, look for a church or school with parking, where you will get access to bathrooms and, sometimes, a plate of home-cooked fried chicken for a few bucks.

Next, bring some food. Ironically, this is hard to find on Fat Tuesday, when most restaurants are closed and those that are open only have limited menus. Convenience stores are open, so junk food is readily available, but it isn't the sort of fare that will keep a drinker on his or her feet into the small hours of the night. Take water as well, to guard against the heat and any alcohol-provoked dehydration.

Tempting as it may seem, Quarter visitors should avoid starting early by stunt-drinking because the day is long and bathrooms can be hard to access. There are public toilets on Decatur Street, but for the most part the facilities in bars are the only option.

Architecture

New Orleans's many building sights.

Most visitors to New Orleans will probably be chiefly interested in the indigenous Creole architecture that developed in the oldest sections of the city: the French Quarter and its immediate suburbs, Tremé and Faubourg Marigny. Admittedly, even the most aged structures in New Orleans are youthful by Old World standards. Most French Quarter buildings date from 1795 or later. The wonder of the Vieux Carré is not its age but rather that it is a relatively intact example of a colonial New World city shaped as surely by the natural environment of south Louisiana as it was by European antecedents. The real architects of New Orleans buildings past and present are the sodden ground, the lack of bedrock (or any locally available stone, for that matter), copious rain, wilting heat, occasional hurricanes and fire. Old New Orleans structures tilt wearily on their foundations, leaning against one another at the shoulder for support; beneath them lie scores of feet of silt. Most roofs, be they tile, slate or asphalt shingle, are steeply pitched in order to shed the five or six feet (1.5-1.8 metres) of

rainfall the city routinely receives each year, though, unpractically, flatter roofs were a Spanish Colonial design vogue.

The broad overhangs that shade the streets in the older parts of town against the relentless summer sun also provided a strip of negotiable, dry ground for pedestrians at a safe distance from the sloppy, unpaved streets. The eight to ten foot- (2.4-3 metre) spaces beneath raised dwellings served as storage and utility areas, but also protected the structures from periodic flooding, a feature that became more practical as the city outgrew the natural levees of the river and the barely discernible ridges. The enormously high ceilings in New Orleans townhouses, often rising to 14 feet (4.3 metres), helped dissipate the debilitating summer heat before the days of air-conditioning, as did the tall french doors and triple-hung windows that slice through the upper storeys of dwellings, taking advantage of every faint breeze.

The force of tropical winds soon taught New Orleans colonial designers to overbuild to some extent. At least one early plan for a tall building included timber buttresses reinforcing the exterior walls against the wind, though no such structure survives. However, the attics of even modest French Quarter cottages hold webs of beams that are heavier than was necessary just to support the weight of the roof.

The rapidly spreading fires that devoured the original wooden settlement on the site of the French Quarter in 1788 and 1794 dramatically demonstrated the need to use non-combustible materials in the closely spaced community. Hence, the Spanish Colonial government decreed that all rebuilt structures were made of wooden frames, filled between the uprights with brick and coated with an inch (2.5 centimetres) of stucco.

'The French Quarter might have fallen to the wrecker's ball, like so much of early urban America.'

In the early 20th century, the French Quarter was mainly a low-income sector bordered on the river side by less-than-picturesque shipping warehouses. The area was not generally revered for its architectural significance, and without the farsightedness of a handful of preservationists, including architects Sam Wilson and Richard Koch, it might have fallen to the wrecker's ball, like so much of early urban America. However, the Vieux Carré was saved from wholesale demolition in the 1960s when the freeway, which was planned to pass through the river side of the old city, was re-routed. In 1965 the whole French Quarter became a National Historic Landmark, thereby keeping the area intact.

A relatively recent threat to the French Quarter (and to all of New Orleans's wooden architecture) is the Formosan termite, a rapacious little pest that came to the Mississippi Gulf ports in shipments of material during World War II. Many locals agree that no wooden structure in the French Quarter remains completely unaffected by the plague and even a short-term lack of vigilance can allow a building to be virtually ruined.

18TH-CENTURY SURVIVORS

Visitors don't need to be helped to find historic structures in the Vieux Carré; they're everywhere. But it may help to be steered to older buildings of particular historic and architectural significance.

Painted in a ghostly absinthe-laced grey, the **Old Ursuline Convent** (1112 Chartres Street, at Ursulines Street; *see also page 80*) almost disappears behind its protective walls into the mist on the river side of the Quarter. Built

between 1749 and 1753, this graceful two-storey structure, with its steep stepped roof terminating in a gentle flair, is the only surviving building from the French Colonial period. No longer a convent, it is now the repository of the archives of the Archdiocese of Louisiana and open for tours.

Nearby is **Madame John's Legacy** (632 Dumaine Street, between Royal and Chartres Streets; *see also page 82*), which got its name from a story by George Washington Cable, a 19th-century essayist and novelist who was one of the great myth-makers of New Orleans. The building dates from the late 1780s (later than the French Colonial period) but is reportedly a faithful replica of the original structure on the site, destroyed in the fire of 1788. A raised structure, with a deep gallery and thin columns, it is the only remaining French Quarter dwelling that echoes plantation structures from the same period. It is now the property of the Louisiana State Museum and has been respectfully restored and maintained, down to the original, odd, olive-coloured trim paint.

The exact date of construction of **Lafitte's Blacksmith Shop** (941 Bourbon Street, at St Philip Street; *see also page 153*) is not known, but it is believed to have been built in the decade before the 1788 fire and therefore is the earliest known example of one of the most common types of New Orleans building: the Creole cottage. Essentially, the Creole cottage is a more or less square building divided into four rooms of equal size without a hall. French doors and windows open directly on to the sidewalk and the steep roof is often perforated with dormer windows.

Lafitte's, which is now a bar, is a particularly good example, for two reasons. First, the surfaces of the stuccoed walls have been allowed to deteriorate sufficiently to expose the underlying diagonal beam and brick structure. Second, it is now a cool, dark, romantic saloon where you can rest and contemplate Creole building methods over a

Madame John's Legacy, now a museum.

Modern masters

No US city looks to its history more than New Orleans, but even here modernity has found a foothold. In the 1970s New Orleans enjoyed a booming oil-based economy and corporate construction exploded in the old American sector of the city, just above Canal Street. Poydras Street, in particular, became a canyon of high-rise office buildings in mirrored glass and marble, which were in large measure indistinguishable from buildings of similar vintage in Dallas, Houston or Atlanta. At either end of the new corporate row are two structures of architectural importance, both for their own characteristics and because they

define the struggle between cultural uniqueness and homogenisation in New Orleans architecture: the Louisiana Superdome and the Piazza d'Italia.

Near the river end of Poydras Street, on Commerce Street, the Piazza d'Italia was designed by Charles W Moore, Allen Eskew and Ron Filson to celebrate the contribution of the Italian (particularly the Sicilian) community to the culture of New Orleans. Completed in 1978, it is walled on one side with a series of overlapping building façades that suggest abstractly both the Italianate features of much of New Orleans architecture and genuine Old World architectural components. A fountain delivers water to a pool in the shape of Italy, surrounded by concentric tile circles implying the spread of Italian influence throughout the world. Every sort of construction material was used to decorate the plaza: brightly painted stucco, chrome, glazed tiles, marble, brick and coloured lights. The design is deliberately lively, even gaudy in its decorative excess. But there is a certain harmony in the visual racket, and above all, the Piazza certainly reflects the riotous spirit of life in New Orleans.

The architects' decoration of the plaza soon earned it a place in textbooks as an example of postmodern architectural sensibility. However, shops and restaurants did not spring up around the plaza as was originally envisioned and within a very short time (coincident with the bust in the oil industry) the Piazza d'Italia fell into disrepair. It's still creating a buzz in architectural circles but as a classic case of remove or restore. The little park is turning into a genuine ruin with its non-functioning fountain, vandalised lighting system and haphazard maintenance.

The new **NOCCA** campus.

gin and tonic. Incidentally, the building was neither a blacksmith's shop nor a meeting place for Lafitte (the pirate) and Jackson (the future president) to plot the defence of the city against its English invaders. Again, the fiction of George Washington Cable has become popular history.

Built in 1792, the **Merieult House** (533 Royal Street, at St Louis Street; *see also page 83*) is an early example of the most typical of French Quarter architecture: the Spanish Colonial-style townhouse. This two-storey

structure has a ground floor dedicated to storefronts, a deep balcony, an upper storey for living quarters and an arched carriageway that leads from the street to the stairs and rear courtyard. However, like so many other Vieux Carré structures, the Merieult House does not abide by any strict set of stylistic rules. The stepped roof, for instance, is more typical of the French Colonial period, and the lower façade was redesigned in the early 19th century in a crisp geometric style suggesting Greek Revival taste.

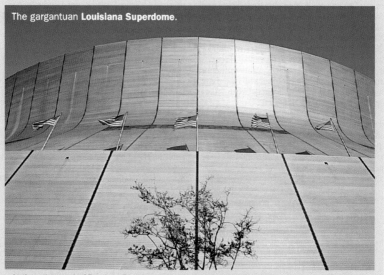

The gargantuan **Louisiana Superdome**.

At the other end of Poydras Street, springing up like a colossal mushroom, is the Louisiana Superdome. Designed by the architecture firm of Curtis and Davis and completed in 1975, it is the biggest enclosed sports arena ever built. Its white cap, 680 feet (207 metres) in diameter, with an area of 9.7 acres (3.9 hectares), is the world's largest continuous roof, unobstructed by upright supports. To stand on the playing field (as visitors are allowed to do), with the ceiling arching 273 feet (83.2 metres) above, is undeniably a humbling experience. It is equally undeniable that the Superdome has a relentlessly sterile, generic design. From the unadorned stainless-steel exterior to the grey on grey interior decor, and the impossibly green artificial playing field, the Superdome nowhere reflects the joyous character of the city it serves.

The most remarkable and encouraging addition to the cityscape in postmodern times has been a school building, the New Orleans Center for Creative Arts in the Faubourg Marigny (Chartres Street at St Ferdinand Street). Finished in 1999, the five-building campus houses an arts high school for Orleans Parish students studying music, art, theatre and creative writing. The authoritative design incorporates the remains of several 19th-century cotton warehouses while adding modern elements such as a bold red neo-factory building that is actually the school's two-storey theatre. Designed by the Mathes Group and Billes/Manning Architects, NOCCA is an exhilarating blend of New Orleans history, Creole influences and modern efficiency. The building is not open to the public during school hours but frequently opens its doors for a variety of performances and meetings.

The Merieult House was built in 1792 on the rubble of a building lost in the first conflagration and miraculously survived the second fire in 1794. Today, it is the home of the Historic New Orleans Collection, a museum and research centre. Guided tours are available around the carefully restored upper floors of the house and rear courtyards.

THE 19TH-CENTURY LEGACY

The French Quarter (which has always been a residential neighbourhood) assumed its present appearance in the early to mid-19th century,

with townhouse after townhouse lining the narrow streets (often with shared walls), displaying a variety of stylistic impulses: Spanish Colonial, French Colonial, Greek Revival, Federal and other less common fashions. Above the streets, balconies webbed with cast-and wrought-iron railings protrude from the regular, rectangular façades like beards and moustaches. At one time, the ground floors buzzed with commerce of every kind, from barber shops painted in slashes of red and white, to numerous small, corner groceries, to some light manufacturing. The rows of townhouses were punctuated here and there with cottages and, much later, the narrow-faced shotgun house, which is ubiquitous in New Orleans (*see page 35* **Shotgun houses**). Behind the townhouses, at the back of each lot, were half-buildings (which served as slave quarters in antebellum times), utility outhouses and rental apartments. You can still find these hidden buildings peeking from between taller structures throughout the Vieux Carré.

It's difficult to list the features that distinguish the Creole townhouse from the earlier Spanish-style townhouse. Perhaps the distinctions are more an issue of degree: those structures considered Creole townhouses were in many cases larger and built in greater abundance than their colonial predecessors.

'Merchant kings expressed their individuality and enormous wealth in wildly eclectic, preposterously large dwellings.'

The **Pedesclaux-Le Monnier House** (417 Royal Street, at St Peter Street), touted as a 'Creole skyscraper' by carriage-tour guides (known better for their hyperbole than their history), was (at four full storeys) the tallest townhouse in the French Quarter. The building has small shops on its ground floor, with apartments above. It was begun just after the 1794 fire but not finished until 1811. The design was started by Barthelemy Lafon and completed by Hyacinthe Laclotte, who also designed another of the French Quarter giants, the **Napoleon House** (500 Chartres Street, at St Louis Street; *see also pages 132 and 154*). This was designed as the residence of New Orleans's Mayor Nicholas Girod in 1815 and is apocryphally reported to have been offered as the New World refuge for Napoleon Bonaparte. Today, its ground floor is a bar and restaurant.

JACKSON SQUARE

Jackson Square, the centre of the French Quarter, is surrounded by the best-known buildings in New Orleans. The varied styles of these structures is a metaphor for the multi-ethnic Creole culture of the early 19th-century city.

St Louis Cathedral (*see also page 77*), the focal point of Jackson Square, was completed in 1850 from plans by JNB de Pouilly. Visitors who have beheld the great churches of Europe will certainly not be awed by this building, but its impressive, lance-like spires are taller by far than any architectural feature of the period.

The design is essentially Greek Revival, with dozens of vertical half-columns and pilasters striping the cathedral's façade, but the style is compromised by a similar number of arched windows and entrances and the towers. The checked floor was designed by Eugene Warburg, a free man of colour (the local term for the large population of free blacks who made up much of the artisan trade in antebellum New Orleans).

Flanking the cathedral at each shoulder are the **Cabildo** (on the west; *see also page 78*), designed as the seat of the Spanish Colonial government, and the **Presbytère** (on the east; *see also page 78*), envisioned as housing for priests. These imposing structures are perfect anchors for the tall cathedral that stands between them. Both were designed by Gilberto Guillemard and built just before and after the second fire: the Presbytère in 1791-1813 and the Cabildo in 1795-9. The high, rather incoherent mansard roofs were added in 1847 and serve to detract from the two-tiered horizontality of the original Spanish Colonial appearance. Both buildings are now part of the Louisiana State Museum.

The upper and lower **Pontalba Apartments**, completed in 1850, form the up- and downriver arms of the square. Built by the Baroness Pontalba (*see page 40* **Queen of the city**), who spent most of her life in France, these huge redbrick structures bear features of the classic Creole townhouse and hints of later American influence. But above all, the long, continuous apartments mirror the elegant terraced houses of 19th-century Paris. The 1850 House, one of the apartments in the Pontalba buildings, is open to the public (*see page 78*).

AMERICAN MANSIONS

St Charles Avenue is one of the best preserved, if least spectacular, of the great avenues that sprang up around the USA to demonstrate industrial-era wealth. The mercantile section of New Orleans above Canal Street was known as the 'American' sector, both to reflect the influx of business interest that followed the Louisiana Purchase and to distinguish it ethnically from the Creole enclave of the Vieux Carré.

A good place to begin investigating this more recent architecture is **Gallier Hall** (*see also page 90*), at the eastern end of St Charles Avenue at Lafayette Street. Built by Irish-born, New York-trained architect James Gallier in 1850-1 as a second city hall (to accommodate American interests), this Greek Revival temple is remarkable in the New Orleans cityscape for its size and grandeur. It packs ten Ionic columns rising to seven times the height of the average man, surmounted by a tremendous pediment.

Shotgun houses

Shotgun houses are ubiquitous throughout New Orleans. Rather than describing any undue haste on the part of their builders, the name refers to the simplicity of their structure. The rooms in these modest-framed dwellings are lined up one behind another, each opening into the next without the benefit of a hallway (though side-hall shotguns do exist). The name shotgun house is commonly credited to the notion that if you fire a shotgun through the open front door, the bullet will whoosh through the aligned interior doors and out of the open back door without hitting anything in between. Shotgun houses demand a certain immodesty from those who dwell within them, as family members and visitors alike must pass through each room to travel from one end of the house to the other.

Double shotgun houses, with twin lines of rooms side by side, are at least as common as singles. When a second floor is added to the rear rooms of a shotgun house, it becomes known as a 'camelback'. 'Raised shotguns' are shotgun houses with lower ground floors that are usually used as garages or apartments.

Shotgun houses were commonly built from the mid-1800s to the early 1900s and can be found in neighbourhoods like Bywater, the Irish Channel, Mid City and Carrollton. The neighbourhood between Esplanade and the Fair Grounds racetrack, a typical working-class enclave, is particularly enchanting, with its rows of closely spaced shotgun houses adorned with various stylistic embellishments to the façades: Italianate, Craftsman and even Gothic Revival.

The merchant, manufacturing and banking kings of New Orleans around the turn of the century expressed their individuality, their world-consciousness and, of course, their enormous wealth in the wildly eclectic, preposterously large dwellings that line St Charles further Uptown. The four-block stretch from Valence Street to Robert Street is a wonderful slice of what was New Orleans's millionaires' row. It includes the **Brown House** (4717 St Charles Avenue), built in 1905, a weighty, broad-footed Romanesque Revival mansion constructed of sandstone and roofed in red tile. The structure seems to sink into its expansive, shaded lawn, reflecting perhaps the gravity of the original occupant's self-image. On the other hand, the 1866 **Aldrich-Genella House** (at No.4801) is an airy, vertical, Second Empire construction that seems to leap from the ground with a genteel *joie de vivre*, especially as it is currently coated in candy-pink paint.

The **Rosenberg House** (No.4920) is a 1911 Colonial Revival anomaly, as stylistically suited to the south of England as south Louisiana. Designed by Emile Weil, it has an exposed wooden framework between stucco and a ground-floor stone wall that looks as though it should be circled by a moat. The mansion at 5005 St Charles Avenue, now the **Orleans Club**, was originally a residence and is of particular interest amid the mixed romanticism of the avenue. Built in 1868, it is a splendid, if austere, retelling of the American-style townhouse, with subtle Italianate flourishes and ironwork.

Unfortunately, you can't see the interiors of any of the above mansions, but both the **Columns Hotel** (No.3811; s*ee also page 64*), designed in 1883 by Thomas Sully, one of the principal architects of St Charles Avenue, and the **Milton Latter Memorial Library** (No.5120; s*ee also page 104*) were originally residences and are open to the public.

THE CREOLE AVENUE

On the other side of the French Quarter, heading towards the lake, is Esplanade Avenue, the other of the city's golden roads of the past. Esplanade is remembered as the great Creole avenue, rivalling the American avenue, St Charles. It is also rumoured to have been the road of industrial-age illicit romances: the great houses on St Charles were built for rich men's wives, the mansions on Esplanade for their mistresses. While St Charles is reasonably well-preserved, Esplanade has been allowed in large part to fall into gross disrepair. Oddly, this only adds to the shadowy road's allure.

For much of its length, Esplanade is lined with two-storey, free-standing townhouses of the American type. In addition to these typical mid- to late 19th-century homes, the street is punctuated by marvellous architectural eccentricities (sadly, the only house you can go inside is the Degas House).

About halfway between the Vieux Carré and City Park stands the somewhat dishevelled **Dufour-Baldwin House** (1707 Esplanade Avenue, at N Derbigny Street). This Greek Revival mansion was built in 1859 from a design by Henry Howard and Albert Diettel. The 16 Corinthian columns that support the broad balcony and entablature make this one of the most impressive façades on Esplanade. The forlorn grandeur of the house is only enhanced by the current mustard-yellow paint.

A typical townhouse further up Esplanade at No.2306 (at Tonti Street), built in 1854 and decorated in a popular Italianate pattern of wooden appliqué, is remarkable for two things. First, the house was the brief residence of the Impressionist master Edgar Degas on his visit to New Orleans in 1872-3, and is thus generally known as the **Degas House** (*see page 113*). The other peculiarity is that early drawings of the structure indicate that this is only half of the original house. Architectural historians (and the house's owners) now believe that the house was divided at some point in the late 19th century. The Degas House is the right side of the original. The left side is now next door at No. 2304 (and part of the Degas House B&B compound; *see page 68*).

> **'The great houses on St Charles were built for rich men's wives, the mansions on Esplanade for their mistresses.'**

The **Sharpy House** (2326 Esplanade, at N Tonti Street) is eye-catching, not only for its dramatic façade but for the peculiar, galvanised metal sculptures in the shape of shotgun houses stacked in the front yard. These large silver shapes are the satirical sculpture of artist and city planner Robert Tannen. The **Dunbar House** (No.2453, at N Dorgenois Street) is a rare, incongruous example of a mansard design, with its tall roof and elaborate dormers. This anomalous structure illustrates the Esplanade Avenue manifestation of the eclectic, cosmopolitan tastes that prevailed in the late 19th century, as does the Queen Anne-style **Cresson House** (No.2809, at N White Street).

Hiding a half-block off the Avenue at 1438 Leda Street is the **Luling Mansion** or the Jockey Club, as it is popularly if spuriously known. Designed and built in 1865, it is remembered as James Gallier's masterpiece in the Italianate style, with two wraparound balustraded balconies, arched ground-floor openings and a fourth-storey cupola.

PLACES OF WORSHIP
New Orleans is said to have more bars per capita than any other city, but also more churches. Here are a few of the best.

Touro Synagogue (4224 St Charles Avenue, at General Pershing Street) is one of the signature accomplishments of Emile Weil (who also designed the Rosenberg House on St Charles Avenue). The bone-coloured brick structure, completed in 1909, is ribboned with strips of bright ceramic tiles in geometric patterns and capped with a huge gleaming dome of reflective tiles.

St Augustine's (1200 Governor Nicholls Street, between N Rampart Street and St Claude Avenue) in Tremé is remarkable for its Italianate frame design and also as the US's first Catholic church to be built by an African-American congregation, in 1842. St Augustine's served New Orleans's free blacks before the Civil War and was the first church where slaves were allowed to worship with free men.

St Joseph's Catholic Church (1802 Tulane Avenue, at S Prieur Street), massive though it is, now seems lost in the urban wasteland of highways, parking lots and generic modern buildings that share its Mid City locale. Built in 1869-92 by two separate architects, Carl Kaiser and Patrick Keeley, this glorious Romanesque giant is the largest brick building in the city.

OTHER NEIGHBOURHOODS
Canal Street has a continuous string of 19th-century storefronts, decorated like wedding cakes with Italianate and beaux arts ornamentation. In the upper storeys of its buildings, the street provides a wonderful vision of the elegance of an earlier age; at street level, it reminds us of the gaudiness of contemporary retailing. The whole of the **Garden District**, with its glorious homes embedded in jungles of wisteria and spider lilies, is many visitors' favourite locale for architecture. The splendid residences on Prytania Street and the numbered streets (First, Second, Third and so on) are of particular note.

The city-side bank of Bayou St John (the stretch of water that skirts the eastern edge of City Park) is the location of **Pitot House** (1440 Moss Street) and the **Old Spanish Customs House** (1300 Moss Street). Built in 1805 and 1807 respectively, these two beautiful structures provide a glimpse of the plantation homes that were once scattered across the outlying areas.

Far downriver in Bywater lie two buildings that require special mention: the **Doullut Houses** (400 Egania Street, at Douglas Street), also known as the Riverboat Houses. Designed by River Captain Milton Doullut in 1905 and 1913, these charming houses have Asian-inspired roofs, decorative wooden rope strands hung above the porches and cupolas made to mimic riverboat pilot houses.

Literary New Orleans

From Mark Twain to Anne Rice, New Orleans has nurtured and fed the literary imagination.

One of the remarkable things about New Orleans's extensive literary heritage is its resonance in everyday life. People who have never seen *A Streetcar Named Desire* quote Blanche DuBois and Stanley Kowalski at the drop of a hat: 'I have always depended on the kindness of strangers', 'I have this attorney friend', and, of course, 'STELLLaaaa!'

Anne Rice, whose *Interview With the Vampire* sparked the goth-vampire revival, is as well known as a rock star, while many New Orleans visitors want dinner reservations at Antoine's restaurant (*see page 129*) purely because the title of Frances Parkinson Keyes's 1948 novel still resonates, although *Dinner at Antoine's* is long out of print. Young men in black leather jackets roar into New Orleans on cross-country road trips because that's what Jack Kerouac did in *On*

the Road. John Rechy's 1963 novel *City of Night* remains the starting point for unapologetic gay literature, while Ellen Gilchrist's insouciant stories of the 1970s and 1980s introduced a new breed of sexually exuberant women to fiction.

INSPIRATION STRIKES

Although New Orleans was one of America's richest cities before the Civil War, the concentration of wealth, a leisure class and a cosmopolitan atmosphere did not produce lasting literature at the time. Mark Twain's (1835-1910) intoxication with New Orleans began in the antebellum period when he was a steamboat pilot, but he wrote about it later in *Life on the Mississippi*. Walt Whitman (1819-92) came to New Orleans, too, before the Civil War, but although his later biographers have suggested he enjoyed the gay *demi-monde*, New Orleans was not a major influence on his poetry. Alexis de Tocqueville (1805-49) was in New Orleans during his 1831-2 pilgrimage through America. His remarks about the city in *Democracy in America* were in the context of his discussion about slavery.

New Orleans, famous for its exoticism since its earliest days, has always been a magnet for writers and artists. Many of them, however, were (and remain) 'experience tourists', alighting in the city briefly (usually in the French Quarter) to soak up material or inspiration, then moving on. Native writers and those who became permanent residents often slipped into the seductive trap of 'local colour', producing artificial, affected work in everything from novels to folklore.

'Resident writers often slipped into the seductive trap of local colour.'

There was actually a huge market for Southern writing after the Civil War. The plantation Eden with its hoop-skirted beauties and gallant cavaliers in Confederate grey were the staples of a 'belles and beaux' genre (of which Gone With the Wind is the apotheosis) that has not completely disappeared. There were plenty of writers, here and elsewhere, happy to churn out books to fill the need.

FICTION IS STRANGER THAN TRUTH

In the booming literary market of the 18th century, New Orleans did produce two fiction writers of lasting importance: George Washington Cable (1844-1925) and Kate Chopin (1851-1904). Cable was a native New Orleanian, but not a Creole. He was a staunch Presbyterian and a Confederate veteran who worked as an accountant. As a kind of hobby, he wrote sketches and essays in the local papers. Cable gradually worked his way through the ideas of the *Lost Cause* and the *Southern Way of Life* to discover that none of it made any sense. In New Orleans, with its always bizarre colour line, a society based on racism was even more absurd than in its other Southern applications.

Cable has been called the first modern Southern writer, a title that sometimes baffles today's readers, who find his *Old Creole Days* stories burdened with dialect, paternalism and sentimentality. Cable's most popular stories, such as 'Madame John's Legacy', often involve beautiful young women who are persecuted for having a drop or two of Negro blood. However, his work is underpinned by a bracing clarity in its perception of racial realities.

For spoken word events, *see p230*.

Cable's writing was praised by critics and his books were bestsellers, but he became uncomfortable in New Orleans. The polite distaste his friends and neighbours began to show towards Cable and his family eventually prompted him to move to Massachusetts, where he found continued critical acclaim and refuge in the friendship of Mark Twain.

In fact, Cable's work was so despised it impelled a young New Orleans woman, Grace King (1852-1932), to begin writing books to present a 'true' portrait of Southern life. King's version presented a genteel paradise of noble Creole aristocrats and contented, grateful black servants. Her books, such as *Balcony Stories*, sold well and King became a fairly well-known writer in the first decades of the 20th century. She made commendable efforts at recording and preserving local history, but she never wavered in her championing of white supremacy.

The writer that Grace King aspired to be, the woman who gave voice to the true New Orleans, was actually born in St Louis and married into a Louisiana Creole family, aged 21. Kate Chopin managed to write several novels and short stories, despite running a large household and giving birth to six children. She achieved some attention in her lifetime, but was ultimately assigned to the 'local colour' trashbin. Her fortunes rose again with the women's movement as women readers and feminist critics grasped that the lush New Orleans settings for her masterpiece, *The Awakening* (1889), were not mindless embroideries but the counterpoint to the heroine's arid inner life. Though not quite in the same class, Lafcadio Hearn (1850-1904) did much to enhance the city's mystique. His essays and stories about New Orleans dwelled on the Creoles, American Indians, Italians and Cajuns. A newspaperman of English–Greek extraction, Hearn spent ten years here, most of it in the French Quarter. His Creole cookbook and guide to Creole sayings, *Gombo Zhebes*, is overshadowed by his later work on Japan and his translations, but Hearn's great rubric about New Orleans is still widely quoted: 'Better to live here in sackcloth and ashes than own the whole state of Ohio.'

GREENWICH VILLAGE SOUTH

In the 1920s New Orleans showed signs of becoming a Greenwich Village South as writers, poets and artists began to gather around the Midwestern novelist Sherwood Anderson (1876-1941), author of *Winesburg, Ohio*, who had settled at the Pontalba Apartments on Jackson Square. William Faulkner (1897-1962) was part of the circle around Anderson, a melancholy young man from Mississippi whom many remembered more for his drinking than his writing. Others in and out of the city in those years included Scott Fitzgerald (1896-1940), who spent several months in New Orleans in 1920, working on the galleys of his first novel, *This Side of Paradise*. The author of *USA*, John Dos Passos (1896-1970), also lived in the city briefly. More permanent residents were novelist and anthropologist Oliver La Farge (1901-63) and local colourists Lyle Saxon (1891-1946) and Roark Bradford (1896-1948).

The literary renaissance of New Orleans was heralded through its own magazine, the *Double Dealer*, one of the famous literary 'little magazines' of the pre-World War I and 1920s period. Neither the Greenwich Village atmosphere nor the *Double Dealer* lasted very long, but both were far more influential than their short-lived careers would suggest.

Faulkner used his New Orleans experience most directly in *Pylons*, a minor novel. But New Orleans was also a revelation to Faulkner in many ways, according to Kenneth Holditch, a scholar, who has turned his encyclopedic

knowledge of New Orleans's literary history into popular books and tours (for his Literary Tour, *see page 117*). Holditch compares Faulkner's experience in New Orleans to that of the character Henry Sutpen in *Absolom, Absolom!*, Faulkner's magnum opus. Both were Mississippi men, bred in a puritan culture and then exposed to 'that city foreign and paradoxical with its atmosphere at once fatal and languorous, at once feminine and steel-hard: a place created for and by voluptuousness, the abashless and unabashed senses.'

> **'Lafcadio Hearn claimed it was better to live in New Orleans "in sackcloth and ashes than own the whole state of Ohio".'**

Faulkner lived in several apartments during his residence in the French Quarter (1924-6). One of his former homes in Pirate's Alley, behind St Louis Cathedral, now contains a bookshop, Faulkner House Books (*see page 172*). Owners Joe DaSalvo and Rosemary James have renovated the building and follow the old New Orleans custom of living over the store. DaSalvo and James are founders of the Pirate's Alley Faulkner Society and its spin-off, the Words & Music Festival in September (*see pages 42 and 194*).

STAGE STRUCK

Truman Capote (1926-84) is often linked with New Orleans, but his contact with the city was minimal. He was born there, but his young, feckless parents soon sent him away to live more or less permanently with relatives in Alabama. Capote visited the city off and on throughout his life, most importantly at the age of 20 when he was struggling with his first novel. He later said his New Orleans sojourn, in an apartment at 811 Royal Street, helped to clear his head. He gave up on a breezy novel about New York socialites and turned to his Alabama youth, producing his first major work, the Southern Gothic novella *Other Voices, Other Rooms*.

Like Capote, playwright Lillian Hellman was born in New Orleans but was not as much a daughter of the city as she liked to suggest. Her plays (*The Little Foxes, The Children's Hour, Watch on the Rhine*) have been overshadowed by revelations that she invented or seriously coloured both her memoirs and her long involvement with writer Dashiell Hammett – a revision that throws serious doubt on Hellman's ability to tell the truth.

Queens of the city Anne Rice

'Anne Rice,' announced a puckish *Times-Picayune* article, 'is single-handedly responsible for the survival of the New Orleans economy.'

Tongue in cheek, the newspaper journalist went on to demonstrate, by means of a humorous chart, how Rice has pumped life into almost every corner of New Orleans from the French Market (increased sales of garlic) to malls (demand for black clothes) to the building trades (restoration of the many properties Rice has bought). And, of course, increased tourism.

Rice, who sells millions of books, has a public presence in New Orleans and among her fans unlike any other US writer. She communicates with her legion of followers through email, voicemail and a website (522 8634, www.annerice.com). In New Orleans, she makes her opinions known through political contributions, philanthropy and full-page ads in the daily newspaper.

The author of a pile of bestsellers, beginning with *Interview With The Vampire* (1976), Rice moved back to her hometown in 1989 after more than 20 years spent in San Francisco with her husband, poet-painter Stan Rice. She comes from a working-class Irish Channel background and has close ties to her extended family. Her early output of well-received fiction has grown into a literary machine that publishes at least a book a year, all eagerly anticipated and devoured by

fanatical readers. Her fans come to New Orleans in droves, not only to catch a glimpse of their heroine but to walk in the footsteps of her characters – the witches, vampires and mortals whom Rice carefully places in the city's houses, cemeteries, churches and dark alleys.

Rice's move back to New Orleans coincided with the explosion of her popularity. She quickly changed from being a well-known writer to an international celebrity with bodyguards, several residences, a large staff and a shifting public image. Rice is not coy about her celebrity. She invites fans to tour several of her properties, including the former St Elizabeth's Orphanage, which is now an art gallery for Stan's work and a museum for Anne's extensive doll collection (see pages 105 and 209). She also has a boutique in the Rink, the upscale mini-mall in the Garden District, which sells the 'Anne Rice Collection': posters and photos of Rice and her characters as well as clothing and knick-knacks that Rice buys during her travels. Until recently, she even opened her historic Garden District home, Rosegate (see page 102), for tours one day a week.

New Orleans looks on Rice with a mixture of admiration and amusement. She refuses to do print interviews, claiming that she doesn't get fair treatment from reporters, but will do network TV. In 1997 she ignited a

---

Tennessee Williams (1911-83) is the city's genuine literary icon. His 1947 play *A Streetcar Named Desire* has fixed New Orleans in the literary and popular landscape for all time. Williams, who was born in Mississippi and raised in St Louis by Southern parents, used many Southern settings in his work, but his name is completely entwined with New Orleans. Throughout his life he referred to New Orleans as 'home', a city he came to in 1938 as a sexually and artistically frustrated young man. Escaping from a suffocating family and dead-end job in St Louis, Thomas Lanier Williams reinvented himself as 'Tennessee' in New Orleans. He acted on his sexual attraction to men and began to find his writing voice. In 1961 he confirmed his connection to the city: 'If I can be said to have a home, it is in New Orleans where I've lived off and on since 1938 and which has provided me with more material than any other part of the country.'

Williams lived in an attic room at 722 Toulouse Street during his first period in New Orleans, graduating to well-appointed hotels later in life. Later still, he bought a building at 1014 Dumaine Street; it was his longest-lasting home in New Orleans, although he sold it shortly before his death in 1983.

A contemporary of Williams, but someone he most surely never met, was Frances Parkinson Keyes (1885-1970), a one-woman publishing industry in the 1930s and 1940s. Her hackneyed romances, *Crescent Carnival, Blue Camellia* and *Steamboat Gothic*, among others, sold millions of copies, making her the Danielle Steel of her era. Keyes came to New Orleans in 1939, and eventually bought the former residence of Confederate General PGT Beauregard in the French Quarter. Keyes' literary efforts are all but forgotten now, but like Grace King she continues to be admired for her preservation efforts. She restored the Greek Revival mansion

public brawl with flamboyant restaurateur Al Copeland. Rice, like many Garden District residents, was upset by Copeland's plans for a high-profile, neon-lit restaurant on St Charles Avenue. What had been neighbourhood grumbling became a national news story when Rice took out a full-page ad in the *Times-Picayune* attacking Copeland's Straya restaurant as 'absolutely hideous'. Copeland struck back with his own ad and offered customers a discount if they brought in Rice's *Times-Picayune* screed.

The incident came not long after Rice had incensed her Catholic neighbours by buying a historic building that included their small community chapel. When chapel parishioners complained about the loss of their church, Rice took out an ad calling them 'Garden District snobs' and claiming the only reason they refused to attend the nearest Catholic church because of its location in a black neighbourhood next to the St Thomas housing project.

Anne Rice, like Grace King and Frances Parkinson Keyes before her, has a powerful urge for preservation, and has bought and improved at least seven historic properties in New Orleans. Her newspaper ads and other antics – such as arriving at book signings in a coffin – have given her a reputation as a clown with dark overtones, but this is by no means a drawback in a city that thrives on the bizarre.

in Chartres Street (now called the Beauregard-Keyes House, *see page 79*) and established a foundation for its care.

LET THE BEAT GO ON

New Orleans is usually mentioned in any discussion of the Beat poets and writers, but the city was definitely a minor outpost in the Beat world. Jack Kerouac (1922-69) and Neal Cassady (1926-68) passed through New Orleans during William Burroughs' 1948-9 stay in Algiers on the West Bank. Kerouac, in typical style, was thrilled with New Orleans: 'At dusk we were coming into the humming streets of New Orleans! The air was so sweet in New Orleans it seemed to come in soft bandannas; and you could smell the river and really smell the people, and mud, and molasses, and every kind of tropical exhalation.'

Burroughs (1914-97) was less impressed. Arrested for drugs, he left New Orleans to avoid

prosecution, and in later years described the city as 'a preserved artificial museum' and labelled the residents as 'surly'.

By the 1960s, New Orleans had several important writers in residence. In addition to the peripatetic Tennessee Williams, novelists Shirley Ann Grau, Walker Percy and John Kennedy Toole were living and working in the city. Grau, who still lives quietly in Metairie, has written a string of acclaimed novels, including *Keepers of the House*, which won the Pulitzer Prize. Walker Percy (1916-90), a non-practising doctor, was instantly recognised as a major American writer on the publication of his first book, *The Moviegoer*. Percy, a convert to Catholicism, used fiction to grapple with the big philosophical questions that absorbed him. Like the handful of novels that were to follow, *The Moviegoer* approaches the human condition with humour, compassion and a dedication to discovering principles worth living for.

The New Orleans area figures strongly in many of Percy's books, but not always the city itself, which he found a little too precious. 'The occupational hazard of the writer in New Orleans is a variety of the French flu, which might also be called the Vieux Carré syndrome,' Percy later wrote in a piece for *Esquire* magazine. 'One is apt to turn fey, potter about a patio, and write *feuilletons* and *vignettes* or catty *romans à clef*, a pleasant enough life, but for me too seductive.' Percy, whose books include *Lancelot*, *The Last Gentleman* and *Love in the Ruins*, lived contentedly with his family in suburban Covington until his death in 1990.

Unlike Grau and Percy, Toole (1937-69) laboured in obscurity. He committed suicide in 1969, partly because he could not get his novel, *A Confederacy of Dunces*, published. After his death, Toole's mother – the model for the half-mad mother of the book's amazing hero, Ignatius O'Reilly – focused all her energy on her son's neglected manuscript. In one of the great tales of American literature, she hounded Walker Percy until he agreed to read the tattered typewritten pages. Percy, shocked that the book was not only good but brilliant, became its advocate. *Confederacy* was finally brought out by Louisiana State University Press after commercial publishers rejected it. The book was a publishing triumph, a bestseller, and winner of the 1980 Pulitzer Prize. In 1997 a statue of Ignatius was put up on Canal Street, near one of his favourite haunts, the old Holmes Department Store.

Ellen Gilchrist, who lived in New Orleans during the 1960s and '70s, gained popular and critical praise for her short stories about funny, resilient Southern women with voracious appetites for sex, love and trouble. Her collection of short stories, *Victory Over Japan*, won the National Book Award in 1984. She moved to Arkansas but New Orleans continues to figure heavily in the lives of her characters.

'The city's insistence on turning every excuse into a party has created some remarkable literary events.'

In the past couple of decades, New Orleans has been home (literally and figuratively) to a wide range of well-known writers, including novelists Richard Ford and Robert Olen Butler and poet Yusef Komunyakaa – all Pulitzer Prize winners. Other notable literary figures include: Stephen Ambrose, Douglas Brinkley, Emily Toth and Christina Vella (history and biography); Tom Piazza, Jason Berry, Andrei

Cordescu, Michael Lewis, Bethany Bultman and Rodger Kamenetz (non-fiction); and Sheila Bosworth, Poppy Z Brite, Moira Crone, Louis Edwards, Tim Gatreaux and Valerie Martin (fiction). Mystery writers based in the city include Julie Smith, James Lee Burke, Jean Redmann, Tony Dunbar, Christine Wiltz, James Sallis and Tony Fennelly.

'In the Stella Shouting Contest would-be Stanleys bellow mating calls at an actress dressed as Stella.'

STELL-AARGH!

While New Orleans is light on author talks and bookstore events, it is a great place for literary festivals. The city's insistence on turning every excuse into a party has created some remarkable events. The **Tennessee Williams New Orleans Literary Festival**, held every March since 1987 (*see page 190*), is a literary lollapalooza, with workshops for scholars and aspiring writers, panel discussions featuring well-known authors and a full schedule of staged readings and productions. Anchored in Le Petit Theatre off Jackson Square, in the heart of the French Quarter, the festival is different from most literary events. Many of the discussions are held in Quarter bars, for instance, where cocktail waitresses take your drink order as speakers discuss new trends in publishing. The festival ends on Sunday in Jackson Square with the famous Stella Shouting Contest or the 'Stell-Off', when would-be Stanleys bellow mating calls at an actress dressed as Stella on a balcony. In the true spirit of Tennessee Williams, the competition is an open field. Male contestants are free to scream for Stanley (an actor, usually with beer in hand) and women often compete, dividing their attention between Stan and Stell.

Younger yet equally energetic is the **Words & Music Festival** held in September. It evolved from the annual birthday party for William Faulkner held by Faulkner House Books in the French Quarter. Director Rosemary James and her attorney-turned-bookseller husband Joe DeSalvo mount an event that brings big-name authors and musicians to New Orleans for author readings cum cocktail parties, dancing, plays and concerts.

> ▶ For details of the **literary festivals**, see chapter **By Season**, and for a bibliography see chapter **Further Reference**.

City of the Dead

The dark counterpoint to New Orleans's love affair with life.

In the spring of 2000 a quiet feature story in the *Times-Picayune* reported on the city's first gay prom. Organisers wanted gay teens to have the fun and excitement of a high-school graduation dance without fear or hypocrisy. The dance was held in the beautifully ornate rooms of an Uptown funeral parlour. For weeks afterwards the letters to the editor columns and talk radio lines were full of indignation and charges of impropriety. Of course, in deeply Catholic and Southern conservative New Orleans, the outcry was over (1) having a gay event for teenagers and (2) publicising it afterwards. No one, on any side of the fray, thought it the least bit odd to have a teen coming-of-age party in a mortuary.

The gay prom debate neatly illuminates the New Orleans attitude toward death. To outsiders, it's a very curious state of mind that is both romantic and mundane with a large infusion of the bizarre. This is a city where brass bands play at funerals, divorce settlements hinge on who gets the family tomb and vampire novels are an important component of the local economy. In New

Orleans, the most Old World of US cities, the familiarity and ease with death herald a pre-modern sensibility that daily acknowledges the inevitability of death while pondering (rather than avoiding) its mysteries.

To judge by the incredible success of Anne Rice's vampire novels (*see page 40* **Queen of the city**), the ancient attitudes of death have hit a nerve in the contemporary world. Anchored by *Interview With the Vampire*, Rice's books have sold more than 120 million copies worldwide and put the spotlight on the New Orleans culture that makes death such a vital part of everyday life.

TOMB WADERS

The obsession with death and the afterlife goes back to the beginnings of New Orleans. Since the city was built on a swamp, the first European settlers soon discovered that burials were a temporary thing. It was only possible to dig a few feet into the gooey soil before hitting water. After a steady rain, newly buried caskets would soon work their way back to the surface. During the rainy

Coffin culture: the **Backstreet Cultural Museum** explains New Orleans funerary customs.

season or a hurricane, cemeteries became ghoulish corrals of bodies and coffins bobbing in the water. Early solutions included drilling holes in the caskets, hoping they would fill with water and stay submerged, or weighting them down with a cargo of bricks and rocks. Neither was successful and there were many unhappy returns. The authorities soon insisted that burials be in above-ground mausoleums or otherwise water-safe tombs.

'Interred bodies would quickly disintegrate into ash through a process of natural cremation.'

The brick tombs became very hot under the tropical sun, and this solar heat, combined with the high humidity, caused the interred bodies to quickly disintegrate into ash through a process of natural cremation. When the authorities realised this was happening, they passed a law requiring that burial vaults remained sealed for a year after interment. One year and a day after interment, however, the door could be opened. Ashes could then be moved to the rear and a new corpse introduced, allowing many generations to use the same vault. This led to tombs becoming increasingly ornate and being handed down as family

assets. It was not unusual for exceptionally beautiful tombs to be sold after a generation or two with new marble name tablets to be affixed. Although the city is now well enough drained for in-ground burials, the old traditions continue, including the use of the brick above-ground vaults.

While many Catholic cultures have some tradition of cemetery visitation on 1 and 2 November, All Saints Day and All Souls Day, New Orleans has continued the observance with its own turns and twists. It's common now to see full-scale parties under way at the old cemeteries on All Saints Day, complete with bands and cocktails. As Louis the vampire explains in *Interview with the Vampire*, 'It is the day in New Orleans when all the faithful go to the cemeteries to care for the graves of their loved ones... It was a festival in New Orleans, a celebration of death, it might have seemed to tourists who didn't understand it, but it was a celebration of the life after.'

CEMETERY VISITS
The most important thing to remember is never to go into New Orleans's cemeteries without a group. Walking tours (*see page 119*) are not only informative, they are the safest way to visit these graveyards. St Louis Nos. 1 and 2 border marginal neighbourhoods where some young entrepreneurs look on tourists as a legitimate cash-flow source.

Beyond safety issues, the cemeteries are well worth the visit. They are villages of wonderful small-scale architecture and adaptive building. **St Louis No.1**, opened in 1789, is the city's oldest surviving burial ground. Earlier burial sites are now unmarked and lost, but the remarkable range of size, style and condition of the remaining tombs is interesting. Some family tombs are quite small, while others are large, elaborate architectural monuments. Indeed, some of the city's foremost architects designed tombs here, including JNB de Pouilly, who designed the façade of St Louis Cathedral. While most resemble little chapels in style, a few are more eccentric, such as the pyramid-shaped Varney tomb just inside the gate. Of particular note are the large 'society' tombs, constructed by groups who formed burial associations or societies. The largest of these, the Italian Benevolent Society tomb, was the site of a scene in *Easy Rider* that scandalised and angered many locals, who felt that such sanctified ground was not an appropriate place for nudity, rape and copious dope-smoking.

Among the notable New Orleanians buried in St Louis No.1 are civil rights pioneer Homer Plessy, mayors Etienne de Boré and Ernest Morial, chess genius Paul Morphy, jazz musicians Danny Barber and Barbarin and, most famously, voodoo priestess Marie Laveau (*see page 46* **Queen of the city**).

St Louis No.2, opened in 1823, is an extension of No. 1, equally absorbing and equally dicey. **St Louis No.3**, established in 1835, is one of the safer cemeteries to visit, with a quiet Mid City location, and otherwise pretty typical. You can pick up a brochure from the cemetery office near the gates.

Lafayette Cemetery No.1 was the first 'American' cemetery. It was opened in the early 1830s for the Anglos who had begun settling in the Uptown area and also contains the graves of French, German and Irish settlers. Take a tour here. Robberies are not unknown and maintenance workers sometimes lock people in by mistake. Lafayette is a frequent film location, featuring in *Interview With the Vampire* and John Woo's *Hard Target*. Anne Rice likes the place so much that she was once carried through it in a coffin in a publicity event.

Lafayette Cemetery No.1

Washington Avenue, between Prytania & Coliseum Streets. St Charles Streetcar/bus 11 Magazine. **Open** times vary.

St Louis Cemeteries No.1 & No.2

Bordered by Basin, St Louis, Iberville & North Claiborne Streets, Tremé. Bus 57 Franklin. **Open** 9am-3pm Mon-Sat; 9am-noon Sun. **Map** pp306-7 F6.

St Louis Cemetery No.3

Esplanade Avenue, between Moss Street & Leda Court, Mid City. Bus 48 Esplanade. **Open** times vary. **Map** p308 E4/5.

RITES AND RITUALS

It follows, of course, that a place where burial was so difficult would develop an elaborate ritual to ease the suffering of death and the anxieties of interment. The custom of a black-draped hearse with mannered mourners is not peculiar to New Orleans but it was enthusiastically embraced and added to here, with a marching band and other touches. The 'New Orleans funeral' came to be thought of as an African-American tradition but it was derived from many Victorian practices, and the black community continued with these for longer than the white community. A band leads mourners to the cemetery with a dirge, then accompanies the group away from the graveyard with increasingly lighthearted music, symbolising the departed's release to a better place. In contemporary New Orleans more and more families, black and white, are returning to the old customs. Several mortuaries include a 'New Orleans funeral' package in their offerings, complete with horse-drawn hearse, jazz band and a marching club to act as official mourners, leading the second line.

> **'Some locals felt that sanctified ground was not an appropriate place for nudity, rape and copious dope-smoking.'**

There's even a small museum dedicated to New Orleans funerals, the Backstreet Cultural Museum in the Tremé neighbourhood (*see page 86*). The dream of photographer and former funeral home worker Sylvester Francis, the museum is housed in a one-time black funeral home. Francis has an array of photographs and memorabilia including Mardi Gras Indian costumes on display. Francis's museum technique is hands-on and experiential rather than scholarly or historical, but the mere presence of a museum about local funerals gives a strong idea about the importance of a proper death in New Orleans.

VOODOO CHILDREN

Intertwined with the New Orleans culture of funerals, cemeteries and ritual is voodoo. There are genuine and devoted practitioners of voodoo but their voices of reverence and contemplation are drowned out by lurid media images and charlatans. Voodoo is mysterious. How it survived at all is a miracle. The roots of voodoo are in the African religions that were suppressed among slaves. Like Cuba's santeria and Brazil's condomble, voodoo fused African beliefs with Catholicism and was often practised in secret. The key element of voodoo is a belief that spirits are a part of daily life, offering help or hindrance. Rituals can convince spirits to act on one's behalf and intense dance-centred ceremonies lead to spirit possession that can change fate and fortune. Many 18th- and 19th-century travellers wrote detailed reports of visiting voodoo ceremonies where whites and blacks freely intermingled, often dancing naked amid bonfires at the edge of Lake Pontchartrain and on Bayou St John. The sheer volume and voyeuristic nature of the reports lead one to suspect a busy and savvy trade among 'voodoo priests' in supplying the demand for exotic experiences.

'New Orleanians, whatever their background, give voodoo talk a wide berth.'

This principle holds true today with everything from hamburgers to gift shops calling themselves voodoo-inspired. The reality of belief and practice of voodoo is elusive but deeply ingrained in the fabric of New Orleans life. There are regular reports of daytime cemetery workers finding dead chickens and other odd bits that suggest rituals were held the night before. Serious voodoo followers tend to disparage such events while holding a veil over their own activities. New Orleanians, whatever background, give voodoo talk a wide berth. 'No reason to stir up those folks,' they'll say when pressed, quickly changing the subject.

Queens of the city Marie Laveau

'Voodoo queen' is a phrase that inevitably follows Marie Laveau's name. She was undoubtedly a real person, a free woman of colour, probably born in 1794. She married, had at least six children, worked as a hairdresser and passed on her voodoo practice to a daughter, also called Marie Laveau. The family's small cottage still stands on St Ann Street in the French Quarter and tour groups stop in front daily, standing reverent and fascinated. The Laveau family tomb also remains in St Louis Cemetery No.1 but has been horribly desecrated by misinformed enthusiasts who scratch'X's into the façade (a practice that genuine voodoo priests insist has no connection with their rituals).

Because the writing about the Laveaus, mother and daughter, is so highly coloured (even first-hand interviews), it's difficult at this point to trace her life and work accurately. It is clear, however, that she had enormous influence in mid-19th century New Orleans among people of every class and race. As a hairdresser, she had regular entrées to the homes of rich white women. At some point she segued from helper to confidante to spiritual guide. It's a route not

unknown to today's hairdressers and surely one of the few paths to power for a woman of colour in the early 1800s.

Laveau, it was said, could bring back wandering lovers, ensure good marriages, cure diseases and punish enemies. In the uncertain times of antebellum Louisiana she probably seemed as good a chance for help as anything. Laveau presided over night-time ceremonies that were lovingly described in long newspaper reports. Like today's horror movies, the events seemed to be constructed as communal events of simulated outrage that satisfied any number of base instincts.

The Marie Laveau who died in 1881 seems to have been the mother (there is some debate) and was praised and reviled in newspaper reports of the day. One editorialist screeched that she was 'the prime mover and soul of indecent orgies' and caused the fall 'of many a virtuous woman'. Others preferred to dwell on her late-life Catholic piety and charity toward prisoners. ' Marie's name will not be forgotten in New Orleans!' promised the supportive editorial. Which remains the one indisputable fact about Marie Laveau.

Accommodation

Accommodation 48

Feature boxes

Accommodation

Shame you won't be doing much sleeping in Party City – from historic to chic, its accommodation options are almost worth staying at home for.

As a high-density tourist mecca, New Orleans is thick with hotels. In fact, many residents mutter darkly about the city becoming one big hotel. Banks, department stores, office buildings, private mansions and even schools have been converted to accommodate the visitors, while developers scheme to build high-rise boxes that strike dread into the hearts of preservationists. The French Quarter, where every first-time visitor wants to stay, strives to remain a truly residential neighbourhood by outlawing new bed and breakfasts and fighting against the proliferation of part-time residents who buy up units in condominiums but are only in town for a small part of the year.

For the traveller and tourist, the hotel wars mean you will find plenty of comfortable rooms to choose from. However, the tourist-as-cash-cow mentality means that prices are constantly on the up, often without a comparable rise in standards of service and amenities. Yet, New Orleans remains a mid-priced city for hotels. In 1999 the average hotel room in the city was $119.99 a night, rising to $143.40 in the Central Business District and $145.59 in the French Quarter. It is always possible to find good rooms in good areas for less than this, though, and during the summer low season, prices drop considerably.

WHERE TO STAY

Almost everyone wants to stay in the Quarter and for good reason. It's pretty, it feels like the centre of activity and its size makes it manageable. Those are the pluses. The major disadvantage is the price: at any time of year you will pay considerably more for less space. Other minuses include the 24-hour noise and activity, the lack of parking, the tourism-intense atmosphere and the possibility of missing out on the real New Orleans. No one should bypass the French Quarter during a visit to the city but staying there isn't always a good choice. Adopt the local attitude that the Quarter is a kind of adult theme park – great fun to visit but not the be-all and end-all of the city.

For small B&Bs, guesthouses and courtyard hotels, Marigny and Uptown are good areas to choose. The Marigny is a bit scruffy but gentrifying fast, while Uptown is the most residential neighbourhood in the city.

New Orleans has more than 30,000 hotel rooms but the range of choices is surprisingly small. The most common hotels in the city are 'limited service hotels' with 90 to 300 rooms but no restaurant. Surprisingly, New Orleans is short on those big full-service hotels with more than 1,000 rooms that usually anchor the convention trade in big meetings cities (which it is). Another surprise is its late entry into the boutique hotel boom, particularly as New Orleans seems a natural place for quirky small hotels with wildly imaginative decor and themes. A number of hotels in the city label themselves 'boutique' but the only genuine articles are the **International House**, opened in 1998, and the two **W Hotels**, in the CBD and the French Quarter, opened in 2000. For more on boutique hotels in the city, *see page 64* **Boutique chic**.

A number of hotels are due to open in late 2000, including a new Ritz Carlton in the beautiful old Maison Blanche department store building on Canal Street, the Jockey Club, a full-service luxury hotel on St Charles Avenue, and Hotel Le Cirque, a boutique hotel in the old YMCA hostel on Lee Circle.

SPECIAL EVENTS

If you have any intention at all of coming to Mardi Gras or Jazz Fest, book rooms immediately. Many of the smaller guesthouses and B&Bs are booked a year in advance for these mega-events. Even if you change your mind later and decide not to come, it's worth gambling a room deposit to secure a room; if you don't, you'll find yourself sleeping in your car or in a Motel 6 somewhere in Mississippi. Be aware, too, that all places have ' special events' rates that are applied at Carnival and Jazz Fest as well as during other major events such as New Year, the Sugar Bowl, Essence Fest and the gay Southern Decadence weekend. Rates at these times can be as much as 40 to 100 per cent higher than normal.

AND KEEP IN MIND

● Remember to factor the city's 11 per cent hotel tax into your budget. The reservations desk won't always mention it.
● Be very careful about promises of 'parking'. Almost every hotel or inn in the Quarter offers something, but frequently this means a deal on

The best Hotels

For party pals
India House, the Mid City hostel, is a relaxed, happy spot where party types like to congregate, bond and 'do' New Orleans together. See page 68.

For fitness buffs
Mackie Shilstone's famous Pro Spa makes the **Avenue Plaza** nirvana for sweat lovers. See page 63.

When money is no object
The **Soniat House** has a deceptively casual ambience, but this beautifully maintained and staffed hotel is the epitome of luxurious living with a light touch. See page 51. But if you prefer everyone to know that you have money to burn, head for the **Fairmont**, with its block-long lobby, where your entourage can make an impact. See page 59.

For voodoo
The **International House**, in its quest to embrace New Orleans culture, periodically hosts voodoo ceremonies. See page 64.

To hole up and finish that novel
The **Olivier House** is everything a French Quarter hotel should be: courtyards, odd nooks and crannies and superb personal attention from the owners. You can even bring your dog. See page 55.

For Mardi Gras
The **Hotel Inter-Continental** is minutes from the madness of the French Quarter and offers ringside seats for the downtown parades. See page 60.

For Jazz Fest
Check into the Benachi House (pictured below), part of the **Cotton Broker Houses B&B** on Esplanade and you'll be a quick stroll from the Fairgrounds. See page 68.

For romance
The **Audubon Cottages** of Maison de Ville are draped in shadow and secluded behind a high wall in the heart of the Quarter – perfect, in fact, for romantic assignations and secret trysts. See page 51.

the daily rate in a public garage that's not necessarily close to the hotel. Even places that have their own lots or garages will usually tack on a daily fee, anything from $8 to $20 a day.

● Even guesthouses and B&Bs now charge for phone use, including local calls. If you have to make a lot of calls while in town, check the hotel's phone policy. At least one hotel charges per minute even for 1-800 numbers.

● New Orleans is way behind the curve on disabled access. Historic buildings coupled with a general 'later, dawlin' attitude add up to half-hearted attempts at barrier-free access. If you need disabled access, book into a new hotel that has ramps, bathtub bars and wide doors.

● When there are few or no conventions in town, hotels often offer special deals and discounts. Always ask, or even press, the reservations desk when you're making enquiries. Nobody wants to sell the cheapest rooms first.

● Illegal guesthouses, consisting of condos and spare rooms that individuals rent out without being licensed by the city, are widespread in New Orleans and are often advertised on the Internet. While these places are often clean and comfortable, and offer some good deals, it pays to be very careful. The best rule is to never stay in a place unless you've first talked to a former guest. If the owner won't co-operate, then take your business elsewhere.

● The low season in New Orleans is summer (June until Labor Day – first Monday in September). Except for the Essence Festival on the first of July, there are no major events during this period and so there are fabulous bargains to be had. Remember, however, there's a very good reason why travel to New Orleans drops off so sharply in the summer: it's hellishly hot and humid with frequent rains and occasional floods.

ABOUT THE LISTINGS

All the places listed have air-conditioning and phones unless otherwise stated. The prices for rooms were accurate at press time but may fluctuate wildly according to the season, what's going on and the convention trade.

French Quarter

Deluxe

Hotel Maison de Ville & the Audubon Cottages

727 Toulouse Street, at Royal Street, New Orleans, LA 70130 (561 5858/1-800 634 1600/fax 528 9939/www.maisondeville.com). Bus 3 Vieux Carré. **Rates** (incl continental breakfast) $225-$245 single; $325 suite; $245-$830 cottage. **Credit** AmEx, DC, Disc, MC, V. **Map** p316 B2.

Tennessee Williams is just one of the multitude of celebrities who have stayed at this oasis of luxury and civility a block from Bourbon Street. Non-celebrities adore Maison de Ville, too, but perhaps they don't savour the quiet and discretion the way that Elizabeth Taylor, Ed Bradley, Dan Aykroyd and other famous folk do. The hotel comprises two distinct units: Maison de Ville consists of a town-house, former slave quarters, courtyard and carriage house on Toulouse Street, while the seven self-sufficient Audubon Cottages occupy a very private enclosure a few blocks away on Dauphine Street. At Maison de Ville, the rooms are on the small side but are decorated and maintained with great care. At the cottages (artist John James Audubon lived and worked in No.1 during his New Orleans stay), the rooms are larger and the furnishings grander. A stay at Maison de Ville is a serious financial investment for most travellers but has the rare virtue of a guaranteed return, paid out in dreamlike surroundings and faultless service. To cap it all, the Bistro at Maison de Ville is one of the city's best restaurants (*see p126*). Children under 12 are not allowed in the hotel.

Hotel services *Bar. Concierge. Laundry. No-smoking rooms. Parking (valet). Restaurant. Swimming pool.* **Room services** *Dataport. Minibar. Room service (11.30am-10pm). TV: VCR.*

Royal Sonesta Hotel

300 Bourbon Street, at Bienville Street, New Orleans, LA 70140 (586 0300/1-800 766 3782/fax 586 0335/www.sonestano.com). St Charles Streetcar/3 Vieux Carré, 41 Canal bus. **Rates** (incl continental breakfast) $145-$280 single; $185-$320 double; $550-$1,200 suite. **Credit** AmEx, MC, V. **Map** p316 B2.

The Royal Sonesta is a little village within the village of the French Quarter. Covering almost an entire block, bounded by Royal, Conti, Bourbon and Bienville, the majority of the 500 rooms look out on the multi-level courtyard hidden at the centre of the complex. Within the sprawling hotel are bars, restaurants, shops, meeting rooms and the lively ebb and flow of a crossroads hotel. The Royal Sonesta has an excellent business centre and all rooms have enhanced communications outlets. Staying here you have the sense of being at the heart of the Quarter, yet without the overwhelming noise, clutter and confusion that is often the reality of a big night on Bourbon Street.

Hotel services *Babysitting. Bars. Business services. Concierge. Disabled: adapted rooms (10). Gym. Laundry. No-smoking rooms. Parking. Restaurants. Swimming pool.* **Room services** *Dataport. Minibar. Room service (7am-2am). Voicemail.*

Soniat House

1133 Chartres Street, at Ursulines Street, New Orleans, LA 70116 (522 0570/1-800 544 8808/ fax 522 7208/www.soniathouse.com). Bus 3 Vieux Carré. **Rates** (incl continental breakfast) $160-$250 single/double; $275-$495 one-bedroom suite; $625 two-bedroom suite. **Credit** AmEx, MC, V. **Map** p316 C2.

Since it opened in 1983, this elegant little inn has been featured on countless 'best' lists. However, praise for its undeniably beautiful setting usually overshadows the real power of the Soniat House: its effortless, seamless service – a rarity in New Orleans. Despite its relative youth, the Soniat House has a settled, timeless feel. Comprising two 1830s-era Creole townhouses that face each other across Chartres Street, the inn is the creation of Rodney and Frances Smith, who have decorated the 25 rooms and suites with French, English and Louisiana antiques, good artwork, vintage books and a soothing palette. Each compound is entered through a flagstone carriageway that opens on to a lush, green courtyard. Although there's no café or bar, a home-made breakfast is served in guests' rooms or in the courtyard (for an extra fee) and the well-stocked honour bars take care of the cocktail hour.

Hotel services *Bar. Concierge. Laundry. No-smoking room. Parking (valet).* **Room services** *Dataport. Turndown.*

High-end

Bienville House

320 Decatur Street, at Bienville Street, New Orleans, LA 70130 (529 2345/1-800 535 7836/fax 525 6079/www.bienvillehouse.com). Bus 82 Desire, 55 Elysian Fields, 41 Canal, 11 Magazine. **Rates** (incl continental breakfast) $120-$270 single/double; $375-$650 suite. **Credit** AmEx, DC, Disc, MC, V. **Map** p316 B3.

The hotel, only a block from the Mississippi River, has several river-facing rooms with lovely views of the crescent that gave the city its moniker. A former warehouse, the building has been successfully converted into a very contemporary hotel. The Bienville is a good choice for any traveller who seeks a hotel in the Quarter that is fully accessible to the disabled (wide doors, modern elevators, etc). Rooms are stocked with more facilities, including coffeemakers and ironing boards, than is usual for this level of hotel and are decorated in soft colours.

Hotel services *Business services. Disabled: adapted rooms (3). Laundry. No-smoking floors. Parking. (valet). Swimming pool.* **Room services** *Dataport. Iron. TV: cable.*

Hotel Provincial

1024 Chartres Street, at Ursulines Street, New Orleans, LA 70116 (581 4995/1-800 535 7922/fax 581 1018/www.hotelprovincial.com). Bus 3 Vieux Carré. **Rates** $150-$175 single/double; $215 small suite; from $275 suite. **Credit** AmEx, DC, MC, V. **Map** p316 C2.

Business travellers like the Provincial because they can stay in the Quarter and still have all the necessary business facilities on hand: on-site parking, sophisticated in-room communications and meeting rooms. Non-biz travellers who want something a bit more upscale than the smaller hotels but don't want to pay top dollar for the plush places find the family-owned Provincial just right. Two storeys of

rooms encircle the inner courtyards, which are made up of pleasant sitting areas with a pool. The hotel's 105 rooms are spacious and decorated in a neo-Victorian style that mixes antiques and handsome reproductions.

Hotel services *Bar. Business services. Concierge. Laundry. No-smoking rooms. Parking. Restaurant. Swimming pool.* **Room services** *Dataport. TV: cable. Voicemail.*

Hotel Ste Hélène

508 Chartres Street, at St Louis Street, New Orleans, LA 70130 (522 5014/1-800 348 3388/fax 523 7140/www.stehelene.com). Bus 3 Vieux Carré. **Rates** (incl continental breakfast) $130 single; $150 double; $175-$225 suite. **Credit** AmEx, Disc, MC, V. **Map** p316 B2.

The Ste Hélène is a cosy little hotel next door to the Napoleon House. It's convenient for the action of the Quarter and has an appealing relaxed atmosphere. There are 26 rooms on three floors, many overlooking the interior courtyard. Rooms are pleasantly decorated but some are on the dark side (which can be useful after too many cocktails).

Hotel services *No-smoking rooms.* **Room services** *Minibar. TV: cable.*

Lafitte Guesthouse

1003 Bourbon Street, at St Philip Street, New Orleans, LA 70116 (581 2678/1-800 331 7971/fax 581 2677/www.lafitteguesthouse.com). **Rates** (incl continental breakfast) $129-$219 single/double. **Credit** AmEx, DC, Disc, MC, V. **Map** p316 C2.

Don't let the Bourbon Street address put you off; the Lafitte is located on the residential part of Bourbon in an 1849 townhouse. Some of the 14 rooms have private balconies and all are decorated with a mixture of antiques and contemporary pieces. The public rooms have the air of a 19th-century family home that's never quite caught up with the changing times. Guests are treated to complimentary continental breakfast each morning, and wine and hors d'oeuvres in the evening. **Hotel services** *Concierge. No-smoking rooms. Parking ($10 per day).* **Room services** *TV: cable.*

Monteleone Hotel

214 Royal Street, at Iberville Street, New Orleans, LA 70130 (523 3341/1-800 535 9595/fax 528 1019/ www.hotelmonteleone.com). Bus 3 Vieux Carré, 41 Canal/St Charles Streetcar. **Rates** $150-$210 single/double; $310-$400 suite. **Credit** AmEx, DC, Disc, MC, V. **Map** p316 A2.

The Monteleone is quite a big hotel (600 rooms) but it's tucked into a busy block of Royal Street in such a way that it seems cosy rather than huge. Increasingly rare in the age of big-name corporations, the hotel is a family-owned business, opened by the Monteleone family in 1886. It has been host to decades of celebrities including literary types such as Tennessee Williams, Eudora Welty and Richard Ford. A major refurbishment has shined up the place without removing the patina of age. The

The **Olivier House**. See p55.

THERE ARE HOTELS YOU STAY IN. AND ONE THAT STAYS IN YOU.

The Aveda aromatherapeutic products you find

in your shower are just another way we help you be more productive.

Not so different from our in-room faxes.

Pass the loofah please.

NEW ORLEANS

french quarter

service is slow but gracious and the hotel offers most of the amenities of the big box places including cafés, bars (check out the retro Carousel Bar, which really moves – see p150) and meeting facilities. **Hotel services** *Bars. Beauty salon. Business services. Concierge. Gym. No-smoking rooms. Parking. Restaurants (3). Swimming pool.* **Room services** *Dataport. Minibar. Phone lines (2). Room service (6am-11pm). TV: cable.*

Le Richelieu Hotel

1234 Chartres Street, at Barracks Street, New Orleans, LA 70116 (529 2492/1-800 535 9653/ fax 524 8179/www.larichelieu.com). Bus 3 Vieux Carré. **Rates**: $85-$195 single/double; from $170 one-bedroom suite; from $280 two-bedroom suite; $475 VIP suite. **Credit** AmEx, DC, Disc, MC, V. **Map** p316 D2.

Le Richelieu is on the Esplanade side of the French Quarter, housed in buildings that date from the 18th century. It's only been a hotel since 1969, but the real claim to fame is that Paul McCartney lived here with his family for two months in 1977 while recording at Sea-Saint Studios. Other celebs have checked in, too, doubtless impressed with the hotel's discretion. The hotel offers attentive service, handsome rooms and a great rarity in the Quarter: a free parking lot. **Hotel services** *Babysitting. Bar. Concierge. Free local phone calls. Interpreters. Laundry. Parking (free). Restaurants. Swimming pool.* **Room services** *Refrigerator. Room service (7am-11pm).*

Olde Victorian Inn

914 North Rampart Street, at St Philip Street, New Orleans, LA 70116 (522 2446/1-800 725 2446/ www.oldevictorianinn.com). Bus 57 Franklin. **Rates** (incl breakfast) $135-$225 single/double. **Credit** AmEx, DC, MC, V. **Map** p316 C1.

A small inn on the border of the French Quarter, the Olde Victorian offers personal service and a genuine sense of hospitality. The six rooms, with names like 'Chelsea', 'Chantilly' and 'Wedgwood', verge on frilly over-decoration but the effect is charming if you like that kind of thing. The hosts, Keith and Andre West-Harrison, greet each new arrival with just-made tea, and mornings always get off to a good start with a full cooked breakfast. **Hotel services** *Parking.* **Room services** *TV.*

Olivier House Hotel

828 Toulouse Street, at Bourbon Street, New Orleans, LA 70112 (525 8456/fax 529 2006/ www.olivierhouse1.bizonthe.net). Bus 3 Vieux Carré. **Rates** $99 single; $145 double; $165-$250 suite; $350 cottage. **Credit** AmEx, DC, MC, V. **Map** p316 B2.

The Olivier House is the kind of place that most people imagine when they try to picture a 'typical' French Quarter hotel. Housed in an 1836 Creole townhouse, it's a hands-on operation run by the amiable Danner family. The Danners are pleasantly straightforward: they keep everything running smoothly but don't feel the need to tell you how 'unique' their hotel is nor how special they are for running such a 'quaint' place. The rambling

hotel reflects their attentive care: rooms are furnished with antiques and second-hand shop finds; the garden room, a renovated stable, is full of sunlight (rare in New Orleans) and the cottage is like a Victorian dolls' house with its own tiny courtyard. The Olivier House is the French Quarter at its most authentic, unselfconscious best, and is unusual in that it accepts pets. **Hotel services** *Laundry. No-smoking rooms. Parking (free). Pets allowed. Swimming pool.* **Room services** *Kitchenette (most rooms). Minibar.*

Prince Conti Hotel

830 Conti Street, at Bourbon Street, New Orleans, LA 70112 (529 4172/1-800 366 2743/fax 581 3802/hotels@frenchquarter.com). Bus 3 Vieux Carré/St Charles Streetcar, then 10min walk. **Rates** (incl continental breakfast) $120-$170 single/double; $195 suite. **Credit** AmEx, DC, Disc, MC, V. **Map** p316 B2.

A New Orleans standby, the Prince Conti has been the favoured hotel of visiting Southerners for decades. There's an austere quality about the hotel, whose 58 rooms seem hidden behind its monotonous façade. The carpeted hallways muffle conversation and the antiques-laden rooms seem to call for bedtime sips of absinthe. The service is personal in an old-fashioned way: no one has been through a corporate training session to learn to say 'Good morning' or 'Let me take that bag for you'. The Conti tends to attract an older clientele, making it a good choice for the traveller looking for a quiet, restful hotel in the French Quarter. **Hotel services** *Bar. Business services. Concierge. Disabled: adapted rooms (3). Laundry. Parking. Restaurant.* **Room services** *Dataport. Newspaper. Room service (7am-11pm). TV.*

Mid-range

Andrew Jackson Hotel

919 Royal Street, at St Philip Street, New Orleans, LA 70117 (561 5881/1-800 654 0224/fax 596 6769/www.historicinnsneworleans.com). Bus 3 Vieux Carré. **Rates** (incl continental breakfast) $70-$129 single/double; $95-$159 double; $139-$159 suite. **Credit** AmEx, DC, Disc, MC, V. **Map** p316 C2.

Although there's no connection between the historical Andrew Jackson and the hotel, it's probably a place he would have liked. Jackson preferred a simple approach to life, and his namesake hotel is attractive and well maintained, with a minimum of fussiness. The lovely T-shaped courtyard and its fountain are the hotel's main concessions to guest luxury. The 22 rooms are decorated in an unremarkable hotel style with fully modern bathrooms. **Hotel services** *Parking (valet).* **Room services** *TV: cable.*

Bon Maison Guesthouse

835 Bourbon Street, between St Ann & Dumaine Streets, New Orleans, LA 70116 (tel/fax 561 8498/www.bonmaison.com). St Charles Streetcar, then 5min walk. **Rates** $85-$125 one-bedroom suite

(1-2 people); $135-$165 two-bedroom suite (2-4 people). **Credit** MC, V. **Map** p316 C2.

To book a room in this 1833 townhouse is to become a French Quarter resident for a few days. The managers are friendly but leave the guests alone, providing housekeeping needs and a key to the barely marked front gate. Bon Maison is a typical private Quarter compound with entry through a gated narrow entry alley that opens into a leafy brick courtyard. There are five rooms, all with private baths, some with full kitchens. Well decorated and furnished with queen-sized beds, the rooms open on to balconies that overlook the courtyard. Bon Maison is gay-oriented but straight guests are warmly welcome and will feel at home.

Room services *Kitchenette (3 rooms). TV: cable.*

Chateau Hotel

1001 Chartres Street, at St Philip Street, New Orleans, LA 70116 (524 9636/fax 525 2989/ www.chateauhotel.com). Bus 3 Vieux Carré, 41 Canal. **Rates** (incl continental breakfast) $79-$129 single; $99-$149 double; $129-$199 suite. **Credit** AmEx, DC, Disc, MC, V. **Map** p316 C2.

The open-air bar set in the middle of the courtyard, a few steps from the pool, tells you the essentials about the Chateau Hotel. It's a comfortable, attractive compound that encourages guests to relax, have a drink, sun by the pool and sink into the New Orleans state of mind. The hotel is within a few blocks of the French Market, Bourbon Street and Jackson Square, but sits on a quiet corner of Chartres. The rooms are motel comfortable, some with exposed brick and beams. This is a place where guests come back year after year and the staff get to know them by name.

Hotel services *Bar. Concierge. Parking (free). Swimming pool.* **Room services** *Dataport. TV: satellite.*

Hotel St Marie

827 Toulouse Street, at Bourbon Street, New Orleans, LA 70112 (561 8951/1-800 366 2743/fax 571 2802/hotels@frenchquarter.com). Bus 3 Vieux Carré. **Rates** $115-$150 single/double; $285 suite. **Credit** AmEx, DC, Disc, MC, V. **Map** p316 B2.

A smallish hotel (100 rooms, six suites) with all the French Quarter requisites: tropical courtyard, pool, balconies. The St Marie is owned by the same group that operates the larger Prince Conti (*see p55*). It offers few frills but reliable rooms, good front desk staff and a better than average hotel restaurant, the Northern Italian-oriented Grana. Rooms facing the courtyard are sunnier and quieter than those overlooking Toulouse Street.

Hotel services *Bar. Business services. Disabled: adapted rooms (3). Laundry. Parking (valet, $14 per night). Restaurant. Swimming pool.* **Room services** *Room service (7am-11pm). TV: cable.*

Hotel St Pierre

911 Burgundy Street, at Dumaine Street, New Orleans, LA 70116 (524 4401/1-800 225 4040/ fax 524 6800/www.historicinnsneworleans.com).

Chain reaction

Chain hotels continue to dominate the hotel business, making faint gestures of individuality and solemn promises about personal service. But the bottom line continues to be the bottom line: chains have the most rooms, usually at the cheapest prices. New Orleans is home to almost every chain that operates in the US, often with several branches. These hotels may not offer many thrills but they definitely offer reliability.

Holiday Inn

US reservations 1-800 465 4329/ UK reservations 0800 897121/ www.basshotels.com/holiday-inn.
Middle America's favourite has nine hotels in the New Orleans Metro area, including two in the French Quarter.

La Quinta Inns

reservations 1-800 531 5900/ www.laquinta.com.
Another mid-range motel chain with eight branches in the Greater New Orleans area. Most are in outlying communities, but there's one all-suites Inn in the Warehouse District.

Hilton

US reservations 1-800 445 8667/ UK reservations 0990 445866/ www.hilton.com.
There are a couple of Hiltons near the airport, one at the foot of Poydras and one opposite the convention centre.

Marriott

reservations 1-800 331 3131/ www.marriotthotels.com.
Marriott has branches in Metairie (out towards the airport) and the CBD.

Bus 3 Vieux Carré, 82 Desire. **Rates** (incl continental breakfast) $79-$109 single; $89-$129 double; $139-$159 suite. **Credit** AmEx, DC, Disc, MC, V. **Map** p316 C1.

Tucked away at the back of the Quarter, the St Pierre is a pleasing jumble of buildings that anywhere else would be a mess. But in New Orleans the elements coalesce into a pleasing compound that feels like a swinger's hideaway. Rooms, each named after a musician, vary in size and furnishings. There are a few antiques mixed with '50s tile bathrooms, exposed brick and French doors. The atmosphere borders on the boho. The staff insist they all stayed or played here when this building was a jazz club. Or was it an after-hours joint? The stories don't quite match, but so what? Continental breakfast is set out in the morning and coffee and tea are available all day. **Hotel services** *Swimming pool. Parking.* **Room services** *TV: cable.*

Hotel Villa Convento

616 Ursulines Street, at Chartres Street, New Orleans, LA 70116 (522 1793/fax 524 1902/ www.villaconvento.com). Bus 3 Vieux Carré. **Rates** (incl continental breakfast) $79-$155 single/double. **Credit** AmEx, Disc, MC, V. **Map** p316 C2.

Please disregard any mention by carriage drivers that this is the 'original House of the Rising Sun'. It's an oft-repeated myth that ranks with 'Jean Lafitte slept/schemed/swashbuckled here', which is said of every 18th-century structure in New Orleans. What you will find is a relaxed, family-run hotel that provides clean, unfussy rooms in a pleasant atmosphere and particularly helpful staff. Villa Convento is a bit dull aesthetically but has the feel of an old-fashioned boarding house with hallways and stairs leading off in several directions. Some of the rooms on the upper floors have balconies with views of the Quarter; ask to book one of these. **Hotel services** *Free local calls. Internet access (by appointment).* **Room services** *TV: cable.*

Rue Royal Inn

1006 Royal Street, at St Philip Street, New Orleans, LA 70116 (524 3900/1-800 776 3901/fax 558 0566/www.rueroyalinn.com). Bus 3 Vieux Carré. **Rates** $75-$120 single/double; $145 suite. **Credit** AmEx, DC, MC, V. **Map** p316 C2.

Resident Persian cats rule this small, friendly hotel. They allow themselves to be petted but acknowledge admirers with the barest tilt of the head. The cats are the only sniffy element of the Rue Royal, which prides itself on its helpful, accessible staff. All 17 rooms feature exposed brick walls, high ceilings and 19th-century decorative touches; most open on to the courtyard but some have balconies on Royal Street, a plus during Carnival. A better than usual continental breakfast included in the price is another bonus. **Hotel services** *Laundry. No-smoking rooms. Parking.* **Room services** *Minibar. TV: VCR (some rooms).*

St Peter House

1005 St Peter Street, at Burgundy Street, New Orleans, LA 70116 (524 9232/1-800 535 7815/fax 523 5198). Bus 3 Vieux Carré, 82 Desire. **Rates** $59-$89 single; $69-$109 double; $99-$119 one-bedroom suite; $129-$149 two-bedroom suite. **Credit** AmEx, Disc, MC, V. **Map** p316 B1.

St Peter House is the sort of place that is becoming increasingly rare in the Quarter as upscale hotels and inns threaten to take over. Located in the more residential area at the back of the Quarter, it offers more than a hostel or youth guesthouse, but remains definitely on the basics-only side of the hotel ledger. There are some Victorian furnishings but the flowers are all plastic. The inn's best feature is the broad, shaded, second-storey balcony that accommodates chairs, tables and many conversations. Be aware, though, that the hotel overlooks a loud, late-hours bar; a room facing on to Burgundy Street can mean a noisy night. Continental breakfast is included. **Room services** *TV.*

Pool your assets at the **Gallier Street Guesthouse**. *See p59.*

Ursuline Guest House

*708 Ursulines Street, at Royal Street, New Orleans,
LA 70116 (525 8509/1-800 654 2351/fax 525
8408). Bus 3 Vieux Carré.* **Rates** (incl continental
breakfast) $85-$125 single/double. **Credit** AmEx,
MC, V. **Map** p316 C2.

There are only 13 rooms in the Ursuline Guest
House, a small adults-only hotel on a quiet stretch
of Ursulines. Most rooms open on to the back
courtyard, where the jacuzzi purrs softly behind
greenery. The rooms are dark and quiet: good places
to recover from too many drinks and too much
dancing. Modern bathrooms combined with the
occasional antique create a feeling of Old French
Quarter without overdoing the cute factor. Breakfast
is served each morning and there are complimentary drinks in the evening. The Ursuline has a large
gay clientele but straight couples enjoy its easygoing, child-free atmosphere, too.

Hotel services *Jacuzzi. No-smoking rooms. Parking
(limited).* **Room services** *TV: cable.*

Marigny & Bywater

High-end

Gallier Street Guesthouse

*822 Gallier Street, at N Rampart Street, New
Orleans, LA 70117 (949 3100/1-877 949 3100/fax
949 6984/http://gallierbandb.hypermart.net). Bus 89
St Claude, 82 Desire.* **Credit** AmEx, DC, Disc, MC, V.

Even though Bywater is New Orleans's most rapidly
up-and-coming neighbourhood, the splendour of the
Gallier Street Guesthouse is a bit of a shock. Owners
Stan Barnes and Kent McIntyre have transformed
two smallish Victorian houses into elegant guesthouses decorated with English and French antiques,
rich textiles and impressive art. Interior designers
who retired to New Orleans, they set out to create a
hidden oasis of luxury and visual aesthetics and
have succeeded. The courtyard includes a hot tub
and small pool. Another big plus is the serious
breakfast, a full, gourmet meal served with style
(this is after morning coffee or tea has already been
delivered to your room).

Hotel services *No-smoking rooms. Swimming pool.*
Room services *CD-player. TV: cable. Voicemail.*

Mid-range

Sun Oak Bed & Breakfast

*2020 Burgundy Street, at Frenchmen Street, New
Orleans, LA 70116 (tel/fax 945 0322/sunoakgh
@aol.com). Bus 55 Elsyian Fields, 82 Desire.* **Rates**
(incl continental breakfast) $75-$200 single/double (2-
night minimum). **No credit cards. Map** p307 G6.

Architecture professor Eugene Cizek and art
teacher Lloyd Sensat are devoted to historic preservation through art. They teach classes, organise
seminars, travel and do a multitude of other good
works. In their private life, though, they have

restored an early-1800s Creole cottage in the
Marigny. There are only two guest rooms (both
with bath) in the compound, which includes two
gardens: one a replica of a 19th-century Creole garden, one contemporary. The four fountains and lush
plantings make this seem a hidden world. Cizek and
Sensat have used antiques and historic mementos
throughout their house to great effect. Staying at
Sun Oak is like checking into a museum with the
benefit of hosts who are two of the best-known
preservationists in Louisiana.

Hotel services *Cooking facilities. Garden. No-
smoking rooms. Parking (free).* **Room services** *TV.*

Budget

Mazant Guesthouse

*906 Mazant Street, at Burgundy Street, New
Orleans, LA 70117 (944 2662). Bus 89 St
Claude, 82 Desire, then 5min walk.* **Rates** (incl
continental breakfast) $29-$39 single/double.
No credit cards.

Popular with young Europeans and travellers of all
ages with a bohemian inclination, the Mazant offers
the basics (bed, bath, shelter from the elements)
with an unaffected congeniality. There are 11
rooms, six of which use the shared hall bathrooms.
Furniture includes some period pieces and sturdy
1950s survivors. Only the bedrooms are air-
conditioned; the rest of the house is cooled by big
windows and ceiling fans. Nearby attractions
include funky music bars such as Vaughan's (*see
p221*) and Elizabeth's Café (*see p132*).

Hotel services *Garden. Kitchen. Laundry.
No-smoking rooms. Parking. TV room.* **Room
services** *TV.*

CBD & Warehouse District

Deluxe

Fairmont Hotel

*123 Baronne Street, at Canal Street, New
Orleans 70130 (529 7111/fax 529
4775/www.fairmont.com). St Charles
Streetcar/3 Vieux Carré, 42 Canal bus.*
Rates $279-$299 single/double; $549-$950 suite.
Credit AmEx, DC, Disc, MC, V. **Map** p316 A1.

New Orleanians sometimes slip up and call this
hotel the Roosevelt even though the Fairmont chain
took it over more than 25 years ago. As the
Roosevelt, it set the standard for New Orleans
hotels and service for decades. Flamboyant
Governor Huey Long, who felt snubbed by the arch
New Orleans attitude, nonetheless loved the
Roosevelt and is said to have made sure all new
roads coming into the city went straight to it. It was
also a favourite with bestselling pulp novelist
Arthur Hailey, whose book *Hotel* is based on the
Roosevelt-Fairmont. What the rich and famous
love about the hotel is its luxurious, comforting
ambience, which is almost homey – if your home

has a block-long lobby. The marble, gilt, chandeliers and warmth of the imposing lobby make it a major crossroads and meeting place, while the Sazerac Bar (*see p156*) is one of the world's great watering holes. The hotel dates from 1893 and has been ceaselessly updated, refurbished and renewed. The high-ceilinged rooms are fussily decorated and boast elaborate bedrooms. The comfort level is enhanced by the friendly, easy service of all the staff, from doormen to housekeepers. The Fairmont makes a romantic hideaway for lovers and an impressive address for business visitors.
Hotel services *Bar. Beauty salon.*
Business services. Concierge. Gym. Laundry.
No-smoking floors. Parking (valet). Restaurants.
Swimming pool. Tennis courts (indoor). **Room**
services *Dataport. Fax. Iron. Minibar. Phone*
lines (multiple). Room service (24hrs). TV:cable/
VCR. Voicemail.

Hotel Inter-Continental

444 St Charles Avenue, at Poydras Street, New
Orleans, LA 70130 (525 5566/1-800 327 0200/
fax 523 7310/www.new-orleans.interconti.com).
St Charles Streetcar. **Rates** $210-$270 single; $230-
$290 double; $1,500 one-bedroom suite; $2,000
two-bedroom suite. **Credit** AmEx, DC, Disc, MC, V.
Map p309 C1.
The Inter-Continental is a huge, downtown hotel that is clearly aimed at the corporate and deep-pocketed tourist trade. What prevents it from being just another glass and steel big box is, oddly enough, Carnival. The Inter-Continental is strategically located on the parade route, and on Mardi Gras Day it is home to the Queen of Carnival. The Rex parade halts at the hotel's viewing stands on St Charles in order for the King of Carnival to toast his queen and her ladies-in-waiting, all of whom sit attentively in the royal box. The viewing stands are a super spot from which to watch the parades, as you get to see the float, costume design and many of the visual thrills lost to the crowds on the ground. Most importantly, you have complete, unrestricted access to the hotel's many, many bathrooms. There's also an all-day buffet in the dining room, which eliminates the need to fight your way into a crowded café or make do with junk food. The downside to all these benefits is that tickets for the viewing stand cost around $60 and the buffet is an additional $50; they are not free with your very expensive room. Yet in the madness of Mardi Gras, it is perhaps worth paying to celebrate and participate in civilised surroundings, with the freedom to hit the streets or watch from the stands, party 24 hours or take a rest from it all in high-hotel style.
Hotel services *Babysitting. Bar. Beauty salon.*
Business services. Concierge. Disabled: adapted
rooms (23). Gym. Laundry. No-smoking floors.
Parking. Restaurants. Swimming pool. **Room**
services *Dataport. Minibar. Room service (24hrs).*
TV: VCR.

International House

See p64 **Boutique chic**.

High-end

Le Pavillon Hotel

833 Poydras Street, at Baronne Street, New
Orleans, LA 70112 (581 3111/1-800 535 9095/
fax 522 5543/www.lepavilion.com). St Charles
Streetcar. **Rates** $115-$250 single; $115-$275
double; from $695 suite. **Credit** AmEx, DC, Disc,
MC, V. **Map** p309 B1.
Unlike many of the new luxury hotels in New Orleans, which were converted from department stores, banks and the like, Le Pavilion has never been anything but a grand hotel. Built in 1907, it has an impressive but welcoming lobby, with chandeliers the size of small ponies, masses of gilt and marble and gardens of fresh flowers. Single guest rooms can be on the small side but almost all of them have antiques and 18th- and 19th-century artwork. The staff, while thoroughly professional, have dispensed with haute-hotel archness. The affable attitude is perhaps best summed up by the buffet of peanut butter and jelly sandwiches set out on silver platters with elegant coolers of fresh milk each evening in the lobby. For something more substantial, head to the hotel's excellent and often overlooked dining room, the Crystal Room. The rooftop swimming pool is a beauty, too.
Hotel services *Bar. Business services.*
Concierge. Disabled: adapted rooms (4). Laundry.
No-smoking rooms. Parking. Restaurants. Swimming
pool. **Room services** *Dataport. Room service*
(24hrs). TV: cable.

Queen & Crescent Hotel

344 Camp Street, at Natchez Alley (1 block from
Poydras Street), New Orleans, LA 70130 (587 9700/
1-800 975 6652/fax 587 9701/www.queenand
crescent.com). St Charles Streetcar/11 Magazine, 41
Canal bus. **Rates** (incl continental breakfast) $99
single; $179 double. **Credit** AmEx, DC, Disc, MC, V.
Map p309 C1.
This is a good choice for the traveller who is mixing business and pleasure. The hotel is well placed in the CBD and convention centre, and the rooms are equipped with more than the usual business amenities: all have two phone lines and dataports; faxes are available on request; and, to keep you looking smart, there are full-size ironing boards and irons and shoe shines, if you ask. The hotel is also well placed for Carnival, with Canal Street parades and the French Quarter just two blocks away. The handsome building dates from 1913, when it was the headquarters of the Queen & Crescent Railroad. The rooms are attractive and comfortable, decorated with chintz and antique replicas. Rooms facing Camp Street tend to be smaller (but cost the same). The hotel provides a shuttle bus to the airport for $10.
Hotel services *Bar. Business services.*
Disabled: adapted rooms (8). Gym. Laundry.
No-smoking rooms. **Room services** *Dataport.*
Iron. Minibar. Phone lines (2). TV: cable/VCR
(on request).

Le Pavillon: You can't miss it. *See p61.*

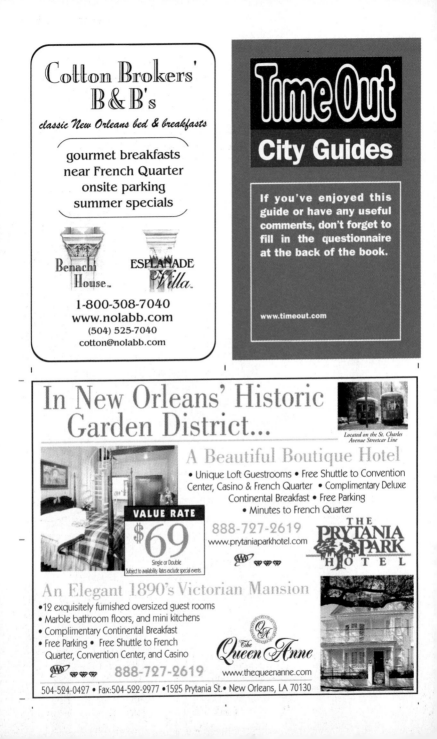

St James Hotel

330 Magazine Street, at Gravier Street, New Orleans, LA 701330 (304 4000/1-800 273 1889/fax 304 4444/www.decaturhotels.com). Bus 11 Magazine. **Rates** $179-$199 single/double. **Credit** AmEx, DC, MC, V. **Map** p309 C1.

The St James is a new hotel (1999) that is aiming for the boutique category but seems rather more like a small, old-fashioned New Orleans hotel with a cosy lobby, friendly staff and heavily decorated rooms. The hotel is on a mostly uninteresting stretch of Magazine Street, where the CBD, river and Warehouse District begin to merge, but it's well situated for getting about and offers good amenities for business travellers. Its most outstanding asset is Cuvee (*see p135*), the fashionable new restaurant next door. Hotel guests order room service from Cuvee and get priority on table reservations.
Hotel services *Business services. Concierge. Gym. No-smoking rooms. Parking (valet). Restaurant. Swimming pool.* **Room services** *Dataport. Minibar. Phone lines (2). TV: cable.*

W Hotel

See p64 **Boutique chic**.

Garden District & Uptown

High-end

McKendrick-Breaux House Bed & Breakfast

1474 Magazine Street, at Race Street, New Orleans, LA 70125 (586 1700/fax 522 7138/ www.mckendrick-breaux.com). Bus 11 Magazine. **Rates** (incl continental breakfast) *May-Sept* $95-$160. *Sept-May* $125-$195. **Credit** MC, V. **Map** p309 B3.

Located on a rapidly gentrifying stretch of Magazine Street, the McKendrick-Breaux House is preservationist in spirit and modern in practicalities. The main house is an 1860 Greek Revival townhouse, sharing a shady courtyard with a later, two-storey building. While the street still looks a bit bleak, the interior of the inn is elegant, comfortable and atmospheric, with each room decorated in individual, characterful style. The McKendrick-Breaux House is a rare B&B that makes sense for a business traveller. It provides in-room voicemail for guests, fax and modem access and ample off-street parking. All the rooms have private baths.
Hotel services *Laundry. No-smoking rooms. Parking.* **Room services** *TV: cable. Voicemail.*

Pontchartrain Hotel

2031 St Charles Avenue, at Josephine Street, New Orleans, LA 70130 (1-800 777 6193/524 0581/fax 529 1165/www.pontchartrainhotel.com). St Charles Streetcar. **Rates** $135-$225 single/double; $165-$375 suite. **Credit** AmEx, DC, Disc, MC, V. **Map** p309 B3.

The Pontchartrain sits quietly on St Charles like one of the more discreet mansions on the avenue. A New Orleans mainstay for decades, it has changed hands

several times, but many employees have been there for years, providing continuity and affable service. While the hotel is a bit on the low-tech side, the rooms have high ceilings, deep carpets, antiques and big windows. It runs a free shuttle bus to downtown, the Convention Center and the Quarter.
Hotel services *Bar. Business services. Concierge. Disabled: adapted rooms (3). Laundry. No-smoking rooms. Parking ($13 per day). Restaurant.* **Room services** *Dataport. Iron. Room service (24hrs). Turndown. TV: cable/pay movies. Voicemail.*

Mid-range

Avenue Plaza Hotel

2111 St Charles Avenue, at Jackson Street, New Orleans, LA 70130 (1-800 535 9575/566 1212/fax 525 6899). St Charles Streetcar. **Rates** $89-$249 suite. **Credit** AmEx, DC, MC, V. **Map** p309 B3.

Avenue Plaza is a favourite with business travellers for its subdued Garden District setting, parking, rooms with kitchens and other extras. A highlight is that guests have full use of Mackie Shilstone's Pro Spa, located in the hotel. Shilstone, a nationally known fitness trainer, oversees a plush gym that has something for everyone, from the massage staff to the all-out workouts that even pro athletes find challenging. The hotel is an all-suite operation with 256 rooms. All have a full (if small) kitchen. The 'junior suites' are basically one big room with kitchen

Bed in at the **McKendrick-Breaux** House.

alcove and bathroom, the 'one bedroom suites' have a bedroom and a separate sitting/dining room. **Hotel services** *Babysitting. Bar. Beauty salon. Business services. Café. Concierge. Gym. Laundry. No-smoking floors. Parking. Swimming pool.* **Room services** *Kitchenette. Voicemail.*

Columns Hotel

3811 St Charles Avenue, at General Taylor Avenue, New Orleans, LA 70115 (899 9308/fax 899 8170/ www.thecolumns.com). St Charles Streetcar. **Rates** (incl breakfast) $100-$175 single/double. **Credit** AmEx, MC, V. **Map** p306 D9.

Romantic and atmospheric, the Columns Hotel strikes most first-time visitors as eerily familiar. That's because they've probably seen it many times on film. Every movie made in New Orleans seems to have at least one scene set on its spacious veranda overlooking St Charles Avenue. In the Brooke Shields–Susan Sarandon film, *Pretty Baby*, the 1883 Italianate mansion was cast as their bordello home.

Boutique chic

New Orleans, despite its claim of being 'the city that care forgot', is really quite conservative, loth to depart from convention. This tendency is reflected in the types of accommodation on offer. Until now, New Orleans hoteliers have been firmly convinced that visitors to the city want traditional, quaint accommodation: French Quarter architecture, 19th-century furnishings, exposed brickwork, cast-iron railings and paintings of Mississippi River steamboats. The recent advent of two high-profile boutique hotels in the Central Business District, however, may change their minds. The **International House**, which opened in 1999, and the **W Hotel** (2000), have made a big splash, impressing locals and attracting steady streams of guests with an aesthetic more about contemporary design and rock 'n' roll and irony than the millennium that was.

The boutique idea appears to be gaining ground in New Orleans: a second, smaller W is now open in the Quarter, revamping an existing hotel on Royal Street, and rooms at both the Ws and International House are always full. The more pressing issue in the hotel business, however, is the onslaught of oversized, high-rise hotels, which are constantly being proposed by eager developers. While the iron-clad preservation guidelines for the Quarter prevent any new glass boxes from rising, preservationists and Quarter residents are continually fighting actions against plans for mammoth hotels on its borders. Ironically, if the boutique hotels can reinforce the idea that bigger is not better, they will have done the upholders of traditional New Orleans a great service.

International House

221 Camp Street, at Common Street, New Orleans, LA 70130 (553 9550/1-800 633 5770/fax 553 9560/www.ihhotel.com). Bus 11 Magazine. **Rates** (incl continental breakfast) $189-$289 single/double; $359-$439 suite. **Credit** AmEx, DC, MC, V. **Map** p309 C1.

When the International House opened in 1999, it signalled the belated arrival of the boutique hotel in New Orleans. The vision of young developer Sean Cummings and architect Brooks Graham, International House marries modern luxury hotel ideas to indigenous culture. Walking into the light-drenched, stylish lobby, your first thought would not be about voodoo ceremonies. The hotel, however, has held several events here and celebrates St John's Eve (late June), one of the key dates in voodoo culture.

Many boutique hotels make a trendy restaurant their cornerstone, and International House scores high here with Lemon Grass, an outstanding Vietnamese-fusion restaurant (see page 135), while the bar, called Loa after a Voodoo deity, is a popular meeting place for locals and travellers (see page 156). The guest rooms are fitted with CD-players, oversized tubs, black and white photographs of New Orleans jazz greats and plush beds with rich linens. **Hotel services** *Bar. Business services. Concierge (24hrs). Gym. No-smoking floors. Parking (valet).* **Room services** *CD-player. Dataport. Minibar. Phone lines (2). Room service (24hrs). TV: cable.*

Visitors return to the Columns year after year for its 19th-century elegance, stained glass, sweeping staircases and glowing mahogany woodwork. Guests are housed in a variety of rooms in the upper floors with handsome furnishings including huge 19th-century beds and claw-foot bathtubs. Six of the rooms have shared bathrooms. The front desk can be rigid in dealing with problems, but repeat customers give the hotel a hearty thumbs-up.

Hotel services *Bar. No-smoking rooms.*

Hampton Inn – Garden District

3626 St Charles Avenue, at Foucher Street, New Orleans, LA 70115 (899 9990/1-800 426 7866/fax 899 9908/www.hamptoninn.com). St Charles Streetcar. **Rates** (incl continental breakfast) $99-$149 single/double. **Credit** AmEx, DC, MC, V. **Map** p306 D9.

Opened in 1997, the blush-coloured Hampton Inn blends in so well with old St Charles most people don't realise it wasn't always here. It's convenient

W Hotel

333 Poydras Street, at St Peters Street, New Orleans, LA 70130 (525 9444/fax 581 7179/ www.whotels.com). Bus 10 Tchoupitoulas. **Rates** $129-$369 single/double; from $380 suite. **Credit** AmEx, DC, MC, V. **Map** p309 C1.

Opened in the spring of 2000, the W Hotel is a new luxury boutique mini-chain developed by the mega-Starwood Hotels. Ws are famous for their super-comfortable beds, which were specially developed for the hotels. In New Orleans, the hotel is a pleasing mixture of big hotel know-how with New Orleans influence. The lobby, which the staff emphatically call the 'Living Room', is a crossroads of textures, ideas and fun. The neo-Zen, semi-tropical design is home to numerous amusing nooks and crannies as well as the Whiskey

Blue bar (see p157) and Martini Bar, in the middle of the lobby. Zoe Bistrot, the upscale restaurant on the mezzanine, is another plus. Most fun of all is the rooftop pool with a real grass lawn, stepping stones and private cabanas equipped with laptop computers and phones. The service is remarkably good for New Orleans. Be on the lookout, however, for hidden charges such as the much-vaunted library of movie tapes – you pay extra. The French Quarter branch is more intimate, with no pool and a more personal atmosphere.

Hotel services *Bar. Business services. Concierge (24hrs). Gym. Laundry. No-smoking rooms. Parking. Swimming pool & spa.* **Room services** *CD-player. Dataport. Minibar. Room service (24hrs). TV: cable/VCR.*

Branch: 316 Chartres Street, at Bienville Avenue, French Quarter (581 1200).

for the St Charles Streetcar, but also offers free parking. A narrow lap pool is wedged into a small but appealing courtyard.

Hotel services *Disabled: adapted rooms (5). Free local calls. Parking. Swimming pool.* **Room services** *TV: cable. Voicemail.*

Prytania Park Hotel

1525 Prytania Street, at Terpsichore Street, New Orleans, LA 70130 (524 0427/1-800 862 1984/fax 522 2977/www.gardendistrict.com). St Charles Streetcar. **Rates** *$109 single; $119 double; $109 & $119 loft room/suite.* **Credit** AmEx, DC, Disc, MC, V. **Map** p309 B2.

The Prytania Park is a complex of old and new buildings hidden from the street. Although it's not an authentic replica of an Old New Orleans household or compound, it captures the Old New Orleans atmosphere with its open galleries, jumble of stairways, small courtyards and sense of calm and privacy. The rooms are very well furnished, which comes as no surprise when you learn that the hotel's owners also run a furniture store across the street (also the site of the very good Home Furnishings Café). Exposed brick, high ceilings, fans and warm wood tones give the Prytania's rooms a 19th-century feel, but all are equipped with new amenities such as 27-in televisions with cable, and fridges; some also have microwaves. The free shuttle bus to the French Quarter, downtown and the Convention Center (shared with other Uptown hotels) is a big plus.

Hotel services *No-smoking rooms. Parking.* **Room services** *Refrigerator. TV: cable.*

Whitney Inn

1509 St Charles Avenue, at Melpomene Street, New Orleans, LA 70130 (521 8000/fax 521 8016/ whitney.inn@worldhnet.att.net). St Charles Streetcar. **Rates** (incl continental breakfast) *$79 single; $90 double; $90-$200 suite; $250 penthouse suite.* **Credit** AmEx, MC, V. **Map** p309 B2.

Two late 19th-century townhouses have been connected to form the Whitney Inn, a back-to-basics small hotel. The inn is on a semi-commercial stretch of St Charles and fits in with the utilitarian neighbourhood. Rooms have been refitted for usefulness and easy maintenance – some have kitchenettes – and what they lack in charm, they make up for in modest prices and easy accessibility.

Hotel services *Disabled: adapted room. No-smoking rooms (2). Parking.* **Room services** *Kitchenettes (suites). Parking (free). TV: cable.*

Budget

Longpre Guest House

1726 Prytania Street, at Euterpe Street, New Orleans, LA 70130 (581 4540/www.angelfire.com/

Marquette House: no drinks allowed, but a convivial atmosphere all the same. *See p67.*

la/longprezoo). St Charles Streetcar. **Rates** $12 dormitory; $35 private room with shared bath; $40 private room with private bath. **No credit cards.** **Map** p309 B2.

When MTV came to New Orleans to film *The Real World*, the producers rented a mansion on St Charles Avenue and decorated it in the spirit of Sheryl Crowe on acid. They could have saved themselves all that trouble by merely installing cameras at the Longpre Guest House, a free-spirited hostel in an 1850 townhouse. The buildings are dingy and worn but that doesn't deter the young Europeans, Americans, Australians and Asians who fill up the dorm and private rooms. Staffers and residents proudly wear T-shirts advertising the 'Longprezoo' and the website warns that 'We try to keep everything clean but…'. There are four dorm rooms, each sleeping eight, and five private rooms.

Hotel services *Cooking facilities. No-smoking rooms. Payphone. Swimming pool. TV room.* **Room services** *No phone.*

Marquette House

2253 Carondelet Street, at Jackson Avenue, New Orleans, LA 70130 (523 3014/fax 529 5933). St Charles Streetcar. **Rates** *Dormitory* $15 members; $18.09 non-members. *Apartments* members $42.95 Mon-Fri; $46.95 Sat, Sun; non-members $45.95 Mon-Fri; $49.95 Sat, Sun. **Credit** MC, V. **Map** p309 B3.

The hostel of choice for most backpackers and under-30s. The Marquette House is a compound that includes dormitory buildings and, most interestingly, a separate building of apartments. The dorms are fine, with plenty of locker space, while the apartments represent some of the most outstanding value accommodation in New Orleans. Housed in a vaguely plantation-style, two-storey building, they offer kitchenettes, several beds and sitting areas. The decor is garage-sale utilitarian, but for the price who cares? A good portion of the Marquette House guests are greying baby boomers who just can't pass up the great deal. The atmosphere is dorm-friendly but mutterings are sometimes heard that the staff are less than accommodating.

Hotel services *Cooking facilities. No-smoking dormitories. Payphone.* **Room services** *Kitchenettes (apartments only). No phone (dormitories).*

Old World Inn

1330 Prytania Street, at Thalia Street, New Orleans, LA 70130 (566 1330/fax 566 1074/www.angelfire. com/biz/OldWorldInn). St Charles Streetcar/11 Magazine bus. **Rates** (incl continental breakfast) $39-$85 single; $49-$85 double; $69-$95 triple; $79-$85 quadruple. **Credit** MC, V. **Map** p309 B2.

A charmingly shabby inn in the grey area between the Warehouse District and the Lower Garden District, the Old World Inn is a friendly, low-key place run by musician-entertainers Charlie and Jean Matkin. The decor crosses old family pieces with yard sale bargains, but the big dining room/lounge is inviting and often the scene of impromptu music-making. The place is almost

completely no-tech: hairdryers can only be plugged into certain outlets for fear that they might overload the 100-year-old building's resources.

Hotel services *No-smoking rooms.* **Room services** *No phone.*

St Charles Guesthouse

1748 Prytania Street, at Polymnia Street, New Orleans, LA 70130 (523 6556/www.stcharles guesthouse.com). St Charles Streetcar. **Rates** (incl continental breakfast) $35 backpacker room; $65-$75 double with shared bath; $75-$85 double with private bath. **Credit** AmEx, MC, V. **Map** p309 B2.

A block away from St Charles Avenue, the St Charles Guesthouse is well worth seeking out. The rates are modest, the rooms comfortable and the atmosphere casual and genuinely friendly. Owner-manager Denis Hilton is a steady and welcome presence, chatting with guests, taking detailed phone messages and quietly making arrangements for any special needs. He also organises spontaneous parties, such as a crab boil on the last night of Jazz Fest. Hilton's philosophy is that his guests are at his hotel to see New Orleans, not to watch television or keep up with the office back home. Consequently, there are no phones in the rooms and no TVs. (He does, however, make arrangements for plugging laptops into a phone line). Europeans return year after year to the rambling old inn, often starting out as students using the clean but Spartan 'backpacker rooms', then moving up as they can afford it to the more expensive rooms with creature comforts such as double beds, old-fashioned tile bathrooms and air-conditioning.

Hotel services *No-smoking rooms. Payphone. Swimming pool.* **Room services** *No air-conditioning (backpacker rooms). No phone.*

St Charles Inn

3636 St Charles Avenue, at Foucher Street, New Orleans, LA 70115 (899 8888/fax 899 9908). St Charles Streetcar. **Rates** (incl continental breakfast) $55-$70 single; $65-$90 double. **Credit** AmEx, MC, V. **Map** p306 D9.

A big 1950s-style box on St Charles Avenue, the St Charles Inn is a good buy for the traveller who values economy over aesthetics. It's clean and well run, while the hallways and boxy rooms call up memories of early Holiday Inns. There are two restaurants on the ground floor and more eateries within a block. Another convenience is the St Charles Streetcar, which stops almost at the front door.

Hotel services *Café. Disabled: adapted room. Laundry. No-smoking rooms. Parking (free).* **Room services** *TV: cable.*

St Vincent Guesthouse

1507 Magazine Street, at Race Street, New Orleans, LA 70130 (566 1515/fax 566 1518/www. PrytaniaInns.com). Bus 11 Magazine. **Rates** (incl breakfast) $49-$59 single; $69-$79 double. **Credit** AmEx, DC, Disc, MC, V. **Map** p309 B3.

Once a Catholic orphanage, this hulking three-storey complex has been transformed into a sort of hip

Accommodation

Holiday Inn, with its own tearoom, pool and upbeat white furnishings. The redecoration and restoration are modest but have created a comfortable, affordable inn, popular with younger travellers and Europeans. St Vincent's is notable for being a historical site that is fully accessible for guests in wheelchairs, with elevators, new wide-door bathrooms and exterior ramps.

Hotel services *Disabled: adapted rooms (all). No-smoking rooms. Parking (free). Swimming pool.* **Room services** *TV.*

Mid City

High-end

Degas House Bed & Breakfast

2306 Esplanade Avenue, at North Tonti Street, New Orleans, LA 70119 (821 5009/fax 821 0870/ www.degashouse.com). Bus 48 Esplanade. **Rates** (incl continental breakfast) $125-$200 single/double. **Credit** MC, V. **Map** p308 F5.

In 1873 Edgar Degas visited his mother's Creole family in New Orleans for several months and lived here, in the Musson family's 1852 Italianate mansion. Now a bed and breakfast – and semi-shrine to Degas – the house has seven guest rooms on the second and third floors, all with private baths (one even has a jacuzzi). The bedrooms are furnished with handsome period pieces but in a minimalist style; no cosy B&B clutter here. Degas' art is everywhere in prints and reproductions. Although the original house was divided into two houses in the early 20th century, it's still possible to see the rooms that Degas used as backdrops for the handful of works he did in New Orleans.

Hotel services *No-smoking rooms.* **Room services** *TV: cable.*

Mid-range

Cotton Brokers' Houses Bed & Breakfast

Nicolas M Benachi House, 2257 Bayou Road, at Esplanade Avenue, New Orleans, LA 70119 & Esplanade Villa Bed & Breakfast, 2216 Esplanade Avenue, at Bayou Road, New Orleans, LA 70119 (both residences 1-800 308 7040/525 7040/fax 525 9760/www.nolabb.com). Bus 48 Esplanade. **Rates** (incl breakfast) *Benachi House* $105-$125 single/double. *Esplanade Villa* $125-$135 suite. **Credit** AmEx, DC, Disc, MC, V. **Map** p308 F5.

Two historic-house B&Bs face each other at the intersection of Esplanade Avenue and Bayou Road. Developed by attorney-preservationist Jim Derbes, both offer comfortable rooms, full breakfasts and beautifully restored 19th-century settings. The Nicolas M Benachi House on Bayou Road, which houses four guest rooms, is actually a mini-estate within the city limits, consisting of an 1858 Greek Revival mansion on a half-acre, landscaped lot with

a carriage house, patio and gazebo. Nearby, the 1880 Esplanade Villa consists of five suites, each with a parlour and a recreated Victorian bathroom, complete with a claw-foot tub. Guests at Esplanade walk across to the Benachi House for breakfast.

Hotel services *Laundry. No-smoking rooms. Parking (free).* **Room services** *TV: cable (most rooms).*

Budget

India House

124 South Lopez Street, at Canal Street, New Orleans, LA 70119 (821 1904/fax 821 2299/ www.indiahousehostel.com). Bus 41 Canal. **Rates** (plus $5 key deposit) $14 dormitory; $35-$60 double. **Credit** MC, V. **Map** p306-7 D/E6.

Travellers have to seek out India House, a hostel located in the marginal neighbourhood off Canal Street, but the steady stream of twentysomething backpackers, budget travellers and international tourists at this Mid City compound suggests that most people don't have much problem tracking it down. The dorm facilities (co-ed and single sex) are Spartan but well maintained, but couples may prefer to opt for the modest cabins instead. A pool and courtyard encourage guests to mingle freely and group parties are a regular feature of staying here. Public transport is nearby on Canal Street, but visitors should take care if travelling alone or late at night in the area.

Hotel services *Cooking facilities. Laundry. Parking (free). Payphone. Swimming pool. TV room: cable.* **Room services** *No phone.*

Reservation services

Several reservation services provide a helping hand for negotiating the hotel maze. Because they charge the hotels and B&Bs a fee for making bookings, travellers get their advice and help for free. For further information and guidance, also contact the **New Orleans Visitors' Bureau** (*see page 279*).

Bed & Breakfast and Beyond

3115 Napoleon Avenue, at Claiborne Street, Uptown, New Orleans, LA 70125 (896 9977/1-800 886 3709/fax 896 2482/www.nolabandb.com). Bus 24 Napoleon. **Open** 8am-10pm daily. **Map** p306 D8.

Maggie Shimon takes pride in matching the traveller to the B&B in her highly personalised service. She will also deal with other visitor requests, including booking tours and special events.

New Orleans Bed & Breakfast

PO Box 8163, New Orleans, LA 70182 (838 0071/1-888 240 0070/fax 831 0140/www. neworleans bandb.com). **Open** 9am-5pm Mon-Fri; closed Sat, Sun.

Sara-Margaret Brown represents more than 200 hosts and can recommend houses, apartments and condos for travellers who want to live like a local.

Sightseeing

Introduction

Experiencing New Orleans is less about attractions and more about just being there.

New Orleans is somehow larger than the sum of its sights. The city has museums and significant architecture and quirky localisms but those aren't what you'll remember about it. Rather, it will be the delight of a city steeped in the pursuit of pleasure amid a semi-tropical cityscape that has mostly eluded the wrecking ball of the 20th century.

Sightseeing is a way to structure your immersion into the life of New Orleans. Waiting for the St Charles Streetcar on Canal Street you might see a mini-Mardi Gras parade, even though it's September, put on for a film company or a convention or because some folks got tired of waiting for Carnival. Walking between historic house tours in the Quarter you'll pass corner bars, lone musicians and even uniformed Catholic schoolgirls. Strolling through Audubon Park you'll overhear power-walking Uptown socialites comparing notes on the new débutante crop. Looking for an address in the Marigny you'll come across the oldest gay bookstore in the South. Think of sightseeing as the stitches that pull together the rich, sometimes elusive tapestry of New Orleans. See the sights, but don't forget to look between the lines and around the corner.

ORIENTATION

New Orleans is big enough to feel like a city but small enough to get a basic orientation and visit most of the central areas in even a short stay.

How do you say that again?

New Orleanians are so accustomed to their city's nomenclature they usually don't understand the fuss that visitors make over names like Erato, Desire, Abundance, Bourbon, Piety, Mystery, Elysian Fields and Tchoupitoulas (sadly, Madmen and Amen streets have been renamed). New Orleans streets reflect the city's history as a colony of two European countries, its own history and the offbeat sense of reality that permeates it. Surely the city's most famous street is Desire, a minor throughway that weaves its way through Bywater and the Ninth Ward. The name is actually a corruption, having originally been called 'Desiree' in honour of the daughter of a large landowner. Likewise Piety Street, also in Bywater, is not a wistful hope for god-fearing attitudes but a slip from the proper name of the Piete family.

Yet there was a great deal of idealism and hope in the naming of the streets. All the streets in the French Quarter have connections with French royalty and patrons of the colony, St Louis after King Louis of France, Bourbon for his family lineage, Dumaine, Toulouse, Orleans and Chartres for royals whose titles bore those regional names.

Uptown, the 'Nine Muses' area reflects the 19th-century infatuation of the educated classes with all things Greek. Despite the difficulty Americans (including New Orleanians) have with most of the names, they have endured: Clio, Calliope, Melpomene, Terpsichore, Thalia, Euterpe, Harmony, Urania and Polyminia. Their pronunciations would mystify Greeks, with Calliope as 'callie-OPE', Melpomene as 'mel-poe-MEAN', and Euterpe as 'You-TURP'.

The flamboyant Bernard de Marigny, once the richest man in America, later destitute, gave extravagant names to the streets in his expanding suburban developments: Abundance, Treasure, Law, Agriculture, Pleasure, Elysian Fields, Music, Arts, Poets, Painters. New Orleanians don't blink at headlines that might read 'Two shot on Law Street'.

Tchoupitoulas Street (pronounced 'CHOP-a-TOO-lus') is unusual in the city in that it is an Indian name. The man who planned New Orleans, the financier John Law (see page 7), decreed that this would be a proper city, unlike earlier settlements Mobile and Biloxi where indigenous and Indian tribal names were used. Law wanted grand-sounding place names for his investors in France. It's something of a mystery how Tchoupitoulas slipped through.

Sightseeing

The bulk of Greater New Orleans lies in a rectangle between the southern bank of Lake Pontchartrain and a predominantly west–east stretch of the Mississippi River, the two approximately four to seven miles (six and a half to ten and a half kilometres) apart. The French Quarter, Central Business District (CDB) and main Uptown destinations are all to the east of the urban area. However, compass points are seldom used in New Orleans, as, thanks to a sweeping bend in the river, the street grids in many areas are not on an exact north/south orientation. Instead, New Orleanians use the terms Uptown and downtown to indicate an up- or down-river location, and lake side and river side rather than north and south.

New Orleans's best-known area is the historic **French Quarter**, a grid of shops, bars, restaurants and residences that is variously thought of as charming, overrated and untypical. Downriver from the Quarter are the developing residential areas of **Marigny**, **Tremé** and **Bywater**, and upriver, across the fallen-from-grace Canal Street, are the **CBD** and **Warehouse District**, both within walking distance of the Quarter.

From here to destinations further Uptown, including the sedate, prosperous **Garden District**, you'll need transport. The main arteries are St Charles Avenue – along which operates New Orleans's principal streetcar line – and Magazine Street, which runs parallel to the river's curving course a few blocks inland.

Moving north towards the lake, not far to the west of the French Quarter and north of Uptown, you reach **Mid City**, which has few attractions but lots of Old New Orleans atmosphere, **City Park** and the wealthy residential area of **Lakeview**.

> ▶ For more on **getting around New Orleans**, see page 274, and for **guided tours**, see page 117. For information on **safety**, see page 285 and for reviews of New Orleans's **cemeteries**, see page 43.

Sightseeing

Street names evolve in New Orleans. After the Civil War when whites had regained control, streets were named after heroes of the Lost Cause. Governor Nicholls Street is named after a former Confederate general who was the first governor after Reconstruction. Lee Circle, of course, is named for General Robert E Lee, who is iconised there. But times change. By the 1970s there was a push from the black community to name streets after civil rights heroes, resulting in Martin Luther King Boulevard, and New Orleans leaders, hence Oretha Castle Haley Boulevard and AP Tureaud Avenue. An interchange near the Xavier University campus has been named after the writer Toni Morrison. Interestingly, while the black-majority city government has renamed schools, replacing Confederate heroes (Gov Nicolls High School became Frederick Douglass High, for instance), street names have not been radically altered. A campaign to rename Claiborne Avenue after a local civil rights activist failed when African-American business owners along the route joined with historians in pointing out the logistical problems. But more than being just a triumph of practicality, the fact that Claiborne Avenue remains undisturbed demonstrates the New Orleans ethos that allows – even prefers the past to remain part of the present.

play...

French Market style

The French Quarter & Around

Ignore the tourist trappings and you'll find a multifaceted area of history and culture where the good times roll, roll and then roll some more.

The Quarter, or 'Quawduh' as the locals say, is the heart and soul of the city. And its libido, as well. It is a place of romance and sensuality, mystique and indecipherable strangeness.

For writers and artists, lovers and outcasts of all sorts, the French Quarter – officially called the Vieux Carré – has long been more than an inspiration; it has also been a refuge. Tennessee Williams called it 'the last frontier of bohemia'. Particularly for those escaping the narrow-minded parochialism of small Southern towns, the French Quarter's attitude of tolerance has provided a first safe haven.

Pleasures of the flesh abound, with opportunities ranging from the demure to the most spectacular. And, although it isn't often spoken aloud, many come to the French Quarter hoping to get laid. Like most dreams, it's often not fulfilled but there are other pleasures to be had. The Quarter provides an array of visual experiences as well, most especially architectural.

Newcomers who expect the Quarter to look like Paris are confounded by an architecture that more closely resembles Havana. This is because the early French colonial buildings, mostly modest frame cottages, were almost all consumed in the great fires of 1788 and 1794. The Spanish, then controlling Louisiana, rebuilt the town from the ground up, so the new buildings reflected their own culture rather than the styles of their French predecessors. As the Spanish administrators were mainly Creoles rather than Europeans ('creole' comes from the Spanish word 'criollo', meaning 'born in the colonies'), the new town was more Caribbean than European. What one sees today reflects that style to a large extent: plaster-over-brick buildings painted in a palette ranging from pastel to bright; decorative ironwork on the balconies that provide shelter from both tropical rains and the torrid sun of summer; and hidden patios filled with lush tropical foliage.

Everywhere there is music. From solitary saxophone players on street corners to the open doors of music clubs on Bourbon Street, music fills the air. Wander a bit further to the more

Andrew Jackson, in his Square. *See p74.*

residential areas and you'll hear a wisp of Beethoven drifting out of the window or a jazz group playing for someone's courtyard party. There have been pitched battles between full-time residents and musicians about the times and loudness of music playing but no one wants the Quarter to go completely quiet.

The French Quarter is still a residential neighbourhood, although as property values escalate it has become less affordable to the waiters, bartenders, artists and writers who have traditionally been a significant part of its

> ▶ For more on **French Quarter architecture**, see chapter **Architecture**.

Busking it...

population. However, its residents continue to defend the neighbourhood against encroaching commercial interests (with varying degrees of success), and it was this impulse that ignited the preservation movement earlier this century, which resulted in the designation of the Quarter as a historic district under the protection of the Vieux Carré Commission.

What is protected today is still a village, its street pattern very much as Adrien de Pauger, engineer of the French colony, designed it in 1722, four years after the establishment of the little settlement in the bend of the Mississippi. But what a village. From the river to North Rampart Street, the French Quarter is filled with pleasures of every sort. And surprises. It can be noisy – both maddeningly and exhilaratingly so – or serene and peaceful. And often the difference is just around a corner. Explore. This is the French Quarter and it's like nowhere else on earth.

Around Jackson Square

Map p316

Hugging the river are some of the city's oldest and newest attractions. On the downriver side of the Quarter (in the direction of Esplanade Avenue) is a series of buildings called, collectively, the **French Market**. Running from St Ann Street to Barracks Street, the market begins with the **Café du Monde**, open 24 hours a day throughout the year except

Christmas Day, and famous for coffee and square doughnuts called beignets. At the other end of the market are the open-air farmers' markets and flea markets. In between are a number of disappointingly touristy shops and restaurants. At the lower end of the Market stands the impressive **Old United States Mint** (*see page 78*).

On the upriver edge of the Quarter lie some of the area's newest additions, the riverfront **Woldenberg Park**, the **Aquarium of the Americas** and the **IMAX Theater** (*for both, see page 75*). On the upriver side of the Aquarium is the jetty for the **Canal Street–Algiers Ferry** (*see page 275*), which takes passengers over the river to Algiers Point in old-fashioned chug-alongstyle. In the middle of the Quarter, between Woldenberg Park and the Café du Monde, is a river promenade named the **Moon Walk** (in honour of former mayor Moon Landrieu), where buskers often play.

It was at this place that the city was founded. The French settled here because the bend in the river provided an excellent lookout in both directions. Near the river they laid out a public square called the Place d'Armes; its principal purpose was as an encampment and drill field for the soldiers. Later, the Spanish would call the square Plaza de Armas, and still later, Americans renamed it Jackson Square in honour of General (later US President) Andrew Jackson, hero of the Battle of New Orleans in 1815 (*see page 8*).

Facing the square and in view of the river, the French erected a simple chapel, which was promptly blown down during the settlers' first major storm. The second church on the spot burned down on Good Friday 1788. The third church, begun in 1789, designated a cathedral in 1793 and considerably enlarged and redesigned in the 1850s, is the **St Louis Cathedral**, which still stands today (*see page 77*).

The Spanish built two imposing buildings on either side of the church and today the three form one flank of the square. The **Cabildo** (*see page 78*) was the seat of government for the Spanish colony of Louisiana. On the other side, the **Presbytère** (*see page 78*) was planned as the residence for the priests of the church. Both served mainly as government buildings until they became part of the **Louisiana State Museum** system (*see page 77*). The Cabildo houses beautifully organised interlocking exhibitions that trace the development of Louisiana. The Presbytère was closed and completely reoriented as a museum devoted to Mardi Gras. Opened in spring 2000, it has been a big hit with locals and tourists.

Flanking the square, upriver and down, are the imposing redbrick **Pontalba Apartments**, built in the 1850s by one of New Orleans's most fabled women, the Baroness Michaela Almonester de Pontalba (*see page 15* **Local Girl Makes Good**). Often called the first apartment buildings in the country, they have always been used as they are today: with shops on the ground floor and residential apartments above. Of note is the elaborate cast ironwork on the balconies, thought to be the first cast-iron balconies in New Orleans. The letters 'A' and 'P' are woven into each section of the iron design after the baroness's maiden and married names. One of the apartments, the **1850 House**, is open to the public (*see page 78*).

Since the Pontalba buildings were completed – and the incongruous third floors incorporated into the Cabildo and the Presbytère – the design of the square has changed very little, making it one of the most pleasing public spaces in the US with its 19th-century scale and proportions.

Today, Jackson Square is still a starting point for the city's culture. Every day the place is filled with buskers and street performers, palm and tarot readers, and it's used as a site for civic events ranging from the **French Quarter Festival** in April (*see page 190*) to carol-singing on the Sunday before Christmas. It also serves as a sort of dividing point in the Quarter. There are exceptions, but the Canal Street half of the Quarter (known as the Upper Quarter, because it's upriver) is largely commercial, whereas the lower Quarter is quieter and more residential.

Aquarium of the Americas & IMAX Theater

1 Canal Street, at the Mississippi River (581 4629/ 1-800 774 7394/www.auduboninstitute.org). Bus 41 Canal. **Open** *Aquarium* 9.30am-6pm (last ticket sold

...on **Jackson Square**.

Sightseeing

5pm) Mon-Thur, Sun; 9.30am-7pm (last ticket sold 6pm) Fri, Sat. *IMAX* 10am-6pm daily; shows every hour. **Admission** *Aquarium* $13; $6.50-$10 concessions. *IMAX* $7.75; $5-$6.75 concessions. **Credit** AmEx, MC, V. **Map** p316 A3.
Aquariums are all the rage in American cities but it actually makes sense for New Orleans to have one. Located in a soaring glassy blue building beside the Mississippi River, the aquarium fittingly concentrates on the places close at hand: the Mississippi, the Gulf of Mexico and the Caribbean. Authenticity extends to a replica of an offshore oil rig in the Gulf of Mexico section, which green-sensitive visitors may see as a little too tolerant in its attitude to sharing the seas. The Caribbean Reef installation is spectacular: visitors walk through a 30ft (9m) glass tunnel underneath the sea world.
Next door is the IMAX Theater, a state-of-the-art film experience that virtually puts viewers on Mount Everest or at the bottom of the sea with its high-definition giant screen and multi-speaker sound system. Programmes aren't co-ordinated with the Aquarium or the Audubon Zoo (which is operated under the same auspices), but reduced-rate tickets that allow access to both attractions are available, in optional combination with a river trip.

St Louis Cathedral

725 Chartres Street, on Jackson Square (525 9585/ www.saintlouiscathedral.org). Bus 3 Vieux Carré, 55 Elysian Fields, 81 Almonaster, 82 Desire.
Open 7am-6.30pm daily. *Tours approx every 2hrs 9am-5pm Mon-Sat; 1-5pm Sun.* **Admission** free. **Map** p316 C2.
St Louis Cathedral might be modest in comparison to the great cathedrals of Europe but it is quite rightly seen as the symbol of New Orleans. Its three-steepled façade crowns Jackson Square with an uncluttered elegance. Tours are available throughout the day, arranged around masses and church activities. It is the parish church for the French Quarter. *See also p34.*

Louisiana State Museum

No institution does a better job of untangling the threads of the region's complicated past than the Louisiana State Museum (568 6968/ http://lsm.crt.state.la.us/), which is an umbrella term for six facilities in the French Quarter: the Old United States Mint on Esplanade Avenue, at the Mississippi River; the Presbytère on Jackson Square in the heart of the French Quarter; the Cabildo – a twin of the Presbytère – also on Jackson Square; the Arsenal, which is nestled behind and connected to the Cabildo; the 1850 House, in the Pontalba buildings on Jackson Square; and Madame John's Legacy, which is believed to be the oldest surviving residential building in New Orleans (*see page 81*). There is a 20 per cent discount for tickets to two or more properties.

A touching experience, and a more hands-off one, at the **Aquarium**. *See p75.*

Arsenal

619 St Peter Street, at Chartres Street. Bus 3 Vieux Carré, 55 Elysian Fields, 81 Almonaster, 82 Desire.
Open 9am-5pm Tue-Sun; closed Mon. **Admission** free with Cabildo ticket. **Map** p316 B2.
The museum in the old State Armory (built in 1839) is an extension of the Cabildo, entered from Chartres Street, not St Peter Street. But visitors should not miss going around the corner to see the façade, which is perforated by tall, broad windows to admit light, but also criss-crossed with iron straps to protect it from insurgents. The Arsenal tends to host long exhibitions. In 2000 'The Mighty Mississippi' was installed, showing ship models, navigational equipment, photographs, paintings and other artefacts describing the city's intertwined history with the river.

Cabildo

701 Chartres Street, at St Peter Street (www. gnofn.org/~fcabildo). Bus 3 Vieux Carré, 55 Elysian Fields, 81 Almonaster, 82 Desire. **Open** 9am-5pm Tue-Sun; closed Mon. **Admission** $5; $4 concessions. **Credit** MC, V. **Map** p316 C2.

Louisiana history is an aggregate of ironies, and no place exposes the unexpected aspects of the state's past better than the permanent collection at the Cabildo. For instance, the first display in the exhibit – dedicated to the Native American peoples of what would become Louisiana – is titled 'The First Families of Louisiana', a wry jab at history museum traditions of the past, which acknowledged the importance of a locale's social elite while neglecting the contributions of its first inhabitants. In another subtle commentary, the portrait of Iberville, who established the first permanent European settlement in the area, is paired with a vintage firearm, in an irresistible illustration of the adage 'might makes right'.

Louisianans of African descent are again and again featured for their role in the formation of the culture, not just for their victimhood under slavery and antebellum segregation. Here is Gabriel Gerome, a 'free man of colour' (as blacks who were not slaves were known) who fought beside Andrew Jackson to prevent the English from seizing the city during the Battle of New Orleans in 1815. Here is Norbert Rillieux, a free man of colour who invented an early

method of distilling sugarcane sap into sugar. And here is Edmund Dede, an internationally renowned composer who entertained audiences before the Civil War to great acclaim. The ironies of the New Orleans social and racial mix are poignantly emphasised in one room, in which a slave auction block in all its hideousness is juxtaposed with memorabilia from Melrose Plantation, the property of a family of free blacks who themselves owned slaves. It is this sort of collision of expectations that makes the Cabildo history display the most penetrating in the city.

1850 House

523 St Ann Street, Jackson Square (568 6968/1-800 568 6968). Bus 3 Vieux Carré, 55 Elysian Fields, 81 Almonaster, 82 Desire. **Open** 9am-5pm Tue-Sun; closed Mon. **Admission** $3; $2 concessions; free under-12s. **Credit** MC, V. **Map** p316 C2.

'House' is a little misleading for this museum as it's actually an apartment in the stately Pontalba buildings. This makes a tour all the more interesting because it's the only chance you'll have to see the residential upper floors of the Pontalbas. The ground floor houses an office and gift shop while the second and third floors have been recreated as a Victorian Creole townhouse with dining room, master bedroom and nursery.

Old United States Mint

400 Esplanade Avenue, at Decatur Street (568 6968/http://lsm.crt.state.la.us/). Bus 3 Vieux Carré, 48 Esplanade, 55 Elysian Fields, 81 Almonaster, 82 Desire. **Open** 9am-5pm Tue-Sun; closed Mon. **Admission** $5; $4 concessions. **Credit** MC, V. **Map** p316 D3.

This huge, ox blood-coloured, Greek Revival structure, built during the presidency of Andrew Jackson to produce coins for the rapidly expanding American West, served as a mint from 1838 to 1909 (you can buy examples of all the paper currency and coins once produced here). The building sits on the spot where Jackson reviewed his troops before the Battle of New Orleans. The Mint is now used as both a museum and an archive of French and Spanish colonial records (open to anyone who calls in advance to use the materials). The most interesting exhibit here is about jazz and showcases instruments such as the primitive home-made percussion kits of the first street 'spasm' bands and one of Dizzy Gillespie's signature, modified horns. But jazz pilgrims travel to the Mint to behold one relic above all: the well-worn cornet upon which the young Louis Armstrong learned to play. There's also sheet music, photographs and listening stations to hear the various eras and schools of jazz.

Presbytère

751 Chartres Street, at St Ann Street. Bus 3 Vieux Carré, 55 Elysian Fields, 81 Almonaster, 82 Desire. **Open** 9am-5pm Tue-Sun; closed Mon. **Admission** $5; $4 concessions. **Credit** MC, V. **Map** p316 C2.

The Presbytère was retooled in 2000 to be a single-theme museum, concentrating on New Orleans Mardi Gras. It was a much-needed addition to the New

In-spire-ing: **St Louis Cathedral**. *See p77.*

Carnival collectibles at the Presbytère.

Orleans museum scene and has the added advantage of being a superior installation. The curators devote ample space to almost every part of Carnival, from the crowns and robes of krewe royalty to the wildly inventive costumes seen in gay Mardi Gras celebrations. The museum knits together history, culture, myth and experience for a satisfying overview of the Carnival phenomenon. Unexpected bonuses include a screening room for films with Mardi Gras themes and restrooms that appear to be a sort of portable bathroom scattered around the city during Carnival.

Decatur & Chartres Streets

Map p316

Decatur Street separates Jackson Square from the river. Originally called Rue de la Levée, for many years it contained rough sections such as the infamous Gallatin Alley, reportedly so dangerous in the 19th century that even the police refused to enter it (the alley has since been demolished). In the 1960s it was still largely unrenovated, and became the centre for New Orleans's hippy culture. Now largely gentrified, Decatur Street is home to shops, restaurants and clubs such as **Jimmy Buffet's Margaritaville** and **House of Blues** (*see chapter* **Music: Rock, Roots &**

Jazz), as well as outposts of the **Hard Rock Café** and **Planet Hollywood** (*see page 132*).

Parallel to and north of Decatur Street is Chartres Street (pronounced 'charters'). Interrupted by St Louis Cathedral at its centre, Chartres is a mixture of galleries, shops, flats and houses. On lower Chartres stands the oldest building in the Mississippi River Valley, the **Old Ursuline Convent** (*see page 80*), now a museum of the Catholic Church. Facing the convent is the **Beauregard-Keyes House**, an 1826 Greek Revival home that is open to the public (*see below*).

Further upriver, flanking the **Hotel Ste Hélène** (*see page 52*) on Chartres Street, stands the bar, restaurant and scene of Napoleonic intrigue, the **Napoleon House** (*see pages 132 and 154*), the serious-minded **Williams Research Center** (*see page 81*) and the **New Orleans Pharmacy Museum**, site of an early 19th-century drugstore run by America's first licensed pharmacist (*see page 80*).

During the 1920s and 1930s, when the Quarter had deteriorated into little better than a slum, it attracted a number of struggling young artists and writers drawn by the charm of the area and the cheap rent. Among these were William Faulkner, who lived across from the cathedral in Pirate's Alley (in what is now **Faulkner House Books**, *see pages 41 and 172*). Novelist Sherwood Anderson lived round the corner at 708 Royal Street. Later, Tennessee Williams would live at 431 and 538 Royal Street, 722 Toulouse Street, 710 Orleans Street and 623 St Peter Street. Truman Capote wrote most of his first novel, *Other Voices, Other Rooms*, in an apartment at 811 Royal Street.

Beauregard-Keyes House

1113 Chartres Street, at Ursulines Street (523 7257). Bus 3 Vieux Carré, 55 Elysian Fields, 81 Almonaster, 82 Desire. **Open** 10am-3pm Mon-Sat (tours on the hr); closed Sun. **Admission** $5; $4 concessions; $2 under-12s. **No credit cards.** **Map** p316 C2.

This 1826 house reflects both the Creole and American building styles, with its American central hall and Creole veranda and courtyard. The house is furnished and decorated in the style of the mid-19th century. Some of the furniture and items that dress it are from the family of Confederate general PGT Beauregard, who briefly lived in the house after the Civil War. In the 1940s, the bestselling novelist Frances Parkinson Keyes (1885-1970) took over the house, then in great disrepair, gradually returning it to its old beauty, if not improving it. The back courtyard is very handsome and the side garden has been restored to a formal Creole garden. Keyes's (pronounced 'Kize', by the way) doll and costume collections are on display in the courtyard buildings where she had her offices and living

Sightseeing

If you only have two days

For the traveller on a tight schedule, New Orleans is the perfect in-and-out town. With its compact size and the easy accessibility of its best attractions, you can hit the highlights in two days and still feel that you've seen the real Big Easy. Admittedly, it may take another couple of days to recover…

DAY ONE

Aim to stay in the **French Quarter** and rise early (before 8am). Take a pre-breakfast walk around the neighbourhood and enjoy the cosy, small-town flavour of the Quarter before businesses open and tourists flood in. Shopkeepers are sweeping the sidewalks, kids with loaded-up backpacks are walking to school, often passing night-shift workers and party people as they return home. Pick a copy of the *Times-Picayune* from a street box and take a table at **Croissant d'Or** (617 Ursulines Street, 524 4663) for a leisurely breakfast of fresh-made pastries and espresso. You're right around the corner from the historic **Old Ursulines Convent** (see page 79) and **Beauregard-Keyes House** (see page 78). Both would make a good local colour stop with their manageable walk-through tours and friendly guides.

Now comes a crucial decision: where to have lunch. Good choices are **Nola** (534 St Louis Street; see page 127) for contemporary New Orleans cuisine and **Mother's** (401 Poydras Street; see page 136) for old-fashioned gumbo, po-boys, red beans and rice. Post-lunch, consider taking a walking tour. Two that originate in the Quarter are Rob Florence's **cemetery tours** and Roberts Batson's entertaining **Scandal tour** (for both, see chapter **Guided Tours**). Or you could drop by the **Historic New Orleans Collection** (533 Royal Street; see page 81) and have a do-it-yourself tour of Louisiana history in hushed, uncrowded surroundings.

For the evening's entertainment take in a jazz performance at **Snug Harbor** in the Marigny, next to the Quarter (see page 220). It will be a great show, whether it's local heroes such as Ellis Marsalis or Phillip Manuel playing or a touring star. Go early and have supper at the club. After the show, check out the other music clubs on Frenchmen Street (the real centre of New Orleans music). Don't worry about missing anything; New Orleans will still be carrying on long after you've gone to bed. Finish up with café au lait and biegnets at **Café du Monde**

---

quarters. The gift shop here is one of the few places you are likely to find Keyes's books, somewhat florid romances (*Dinner at Antoine's, Crescent Carnival* etc) that are now all out of print.

New Orleans Historic Pharmacy Museum

514 Chartres Street, at St Louis Street (565 8027/ www.pharmacymuseum.org). Bus 3 Vieux Carré, 55 Elysian Fields, 81 Almonaster, 82 Desire. **Open** 10am-5pm Tue-Sun; closed Mon. **Admission** $2; $1 concessions; free under-12s. **Credit** AmEx, MC, V. **Map** p316 B2.

This storefront museum occupies the original site of the first licensed pharmacy in the US, opened in 1823. The old wooden counters, cases and shelves have been restored to jewel-like perfection, and on display are the beautiful handmade glass vessels and ceramics that were the tools of the profession in the 19th century. The second floor includes a sick-room and library. Here, you return to a time when cocaine might have been dispensed over the counter for a toothache, a lithium potion was taken for nervousness and live leeches swam in a porcelain bowl that looked as innocent as a soup tureen – you can easily imagine Dr Jekyll having a flavoured soda water at the soda fountain. The museum is most

notable for its calm, old-fashioned approach to museumery: there are no interactive displays, no characters in costumes, no straining for relevance. The courtyard (popular with local brides) is lovely.

Old Ursuline Convent

1112 Chartres Street, at Ursulines Street (529 3040/ www.accesscom.net/ursuline). Bus 3 Vieux Carré, 55 Elysian Fields, 81 Almonaster, 82 Desire. **Open** Tours on the hour 10am-3pm Tue-Fri; 11.15am, 1pm, 2pm Sat, Sun; closed Mon. **Admission** $5; $2-$4 concessions; free under-8s. **No credit cards. Map** p316 C2.

The grande dame of New Orleans architecture, this serene-looking convent was built between 1745 and 1750, replacing an earlier compound built in the 1720s. It is the oldest surviving building in New Orleans – being one of the few structures left standing after the devastating fires of 1788 and 1794. The only complete French colonial building in New Orleans, it retains some details of the first structure. Especially lovely are the hand-hewn cypress stairs. The Ursuline nuns arrived in the city in 1727 from France and set about their work of teaching and healing. The order was prosperous and shrewd. It was notable for teaching not only the daughters of the bourgeoisie but black and Indian children as (see page 125), where you'll probably run into half the audience and most of the band members from the shows you've seen.

DAY TWO

Sleep in; this is a vacation. Besides, if you did last night properly you'll need it. For breakfast order something in from room service then walk over to the river to catch one of the **cruises** that head upriver toward Audubon Park. Sitting on the top deck, you'll get a good view of the city and a clearer understanding of how the city and the river define each other (see page 119). Leave the boat at **Audubon Zoo**. Take in the entire zoo, if you like, it's one of the best in America. But even if you're not a zoo-type, stop by the Louisiana swamp section. It's everything you would see in a swamp tour without the half-day trip (see page 108).

Leaving the zoo, walk across Audubon Park to St Charles Avenue, where you catch the streetcar heading further Uptown to Riverbend. Step off at the junction of St Charles and Carrollton, where you can have a late lunch at the **Camellia Grill**, the city's favourite (and most authentic) old-fashioned diner (see page 138). Take the streetcar back toward town. The slow-moving car with big open windows is an ideal way to see the showplaces of **St Charles Avenue** (see page 102), a textbook example of 19th-century conspicuous consumption. At the end of the line, wander back into the Quarter for cocktail hour (it's always cocktail hour in New Orleans). You'll find good company and a relaxed atmosphere at the **Napoleon House** (see pages 132 and 154). For more bar sampling, try lower Decatur Street, the ungentrified part of the Quarter where goth kids slink about and locals make the circuit of **Molly's at the Market**, the **Abbey** and **Coop's** (see chapter **Bars**).

Dress for dinner and take in one of the grand old-line New Orleans restaurants, **Antoine's**, **Galatoire's**, **Arnaud's** or maybe **Brennan's** (see chapter **Restaurants**). The food is heavy but divine, the service is courtly and the bill is huge – so you may as well linger. End the evening with a visit to **Tipitina's**, the archetypal New Orleans music club. Take a cab to the original club, the Uptown Tip's on Napoleon Avenue (see page 224). Dance, sing with the band and walk outside to get some fresh air and listen to the lonesome sound of riverboat horns a couple of blocks away. Tip's will close down at about 2 or 3am, when you can use the payphone outside to ordre a taxi to take you back to the hotel. You've done it all: music, food, history, culture, self-indulgence. It's the essence of New Orleans.

well. The convent was sold to the Church in the 19th century and used as the archbishop's residence. The adjacent St Mary's Church was built in 1845 as the archbishop's chapel. Today, the compound houses the archdiocese's archives. Visits are limited to regularly scheduled tours.

Williams Research Center of the Historic New Orleans Collection

410 Chartres Street, at Conti Street (598 7100/ www.hnoc.org). Bus 3 Vieux Carré, 55 Elysian Fields, 81 Almonaster, 82 Desire. **Open** 10am-4.30pm Tue-Sat; closed Mon, Sun. **Admission** free. **Map** p316 B2.

Housed in a gorgeously renovated turn-of-the-19th-century police station, the Williams Research Center is the newest project of the admirable HNOC. It's not a museum per se – though it always has wonderful displays of historic objects, documents and art. But its real function is as a public library and archive for serious students of any aspect of the region's culture or history. The WRC is a 'closed stack' facility; that is, visitors are not allowed to browse through the collection, but must ask research assistants for help. For details of the Historic New Orleans Collection, *see p83*.

Royal Street

Map p316

Royal Street, which runs behind the cathedral, was the main street of the original town. The banking district developed in the early 19th century around Conti Street and some historic bank buildings remain today at 334, 343, 403 and 417 Royal. The 417 Royal Street building, today the august Creole restaurant **Brennan's** (*see page 129*), was built by a grandfather of the painter Edgar Degas.

No.431 Royal Street, next door to Brennan's, was the site of possibly New Orleans's most significant contribution to civilisation. In the 1790s an apothecary named AA Peychaud operated his business there. Legend has it that Peychaud, who had concocted a mixture he called bitters, blended it with some cognac and voilà!, the first mixed drink was created. Since Peychaud had created his potion in an egg cup ('coquetière' in French) the new drink became known as a 'cocktail' by Americans, whose enthusiasm for alcoholic options exceeded their fluency in French pronunciation.

Further down the street at 533 Royal is a very early building, the **Merieult House** (1792; *see page 32*), which houses the **Historic New Orleans Collection** (*see page 83*), an important museum and archival collection of New Orleanian documents, maps, prints and artefacts (*see page 83*).

The first eight blocks of Royal Street contain some of the area's grandest Spanish-styled townhouses, displaying particularly fine examples of intricate cast-iron balconies, and at No.915 is an example of one of the city's 'cornstalk fences'. Today, most of these buildings house art galleries, antiques shops and upmarket boutiques, along with a clutch of restaurants and cafés. A few steps off Royal on St Louis Street is the famous **Antoine's Restaurant**, which has been operated by the same family since 1840 (*see page 129*). Nearby is the **Omni Royal Orleans Hotel** (621 St Louis Street, 529 5333, www.omnihotels.com), whose open-air rooftop bar provides one of the best views of French Quarter rooftops, the river and the city skyline.

Behind the cathedral is a small garden that contains a memorial to yellow fever victims and a statue of Christ with uplifted arms. Tennessee Williams, who once lived in a house that looked out on to the garden, wrote that the statue seemed to be embracing all of humankind. Less reverential passers-by have noted that the shadow cast by the statue resembles the gesture of American football referees and have dubbed it the 'Touchdown Jesus'.

Just off Royal Street, on Dumaine Street, is a rare example of early French colonial architecture. For years the house has been known as **Madame John's Legacy** (*see page 84*) after a fictional character – though most locals, used to the make-believe world of Mardi Gras, have long forgotten that there never was a Madame John, nor any such legacy. Further up Dumaine Street is the **New Orleans Historic Voodoo Museum**, perhaps not the city's most academically rigorous museum but good, scary fun nonetheless.

Further down Royal are two other famous houses. At No.1132 is the 1857 **Gallier House**

Royal Street: home of some of the city's finest balconies – and happiest crowds.

(*see below*), built by architect James Gallier Jr as his home. Open to the public for tours, it contains some interesting innovations, including Gallier's design for the first indoor plumbing system in New Orleans. Two doors down, at the corner of Governor Nicholls Street, is the **Lalaurie House** (1140 Royal Street), which is probably the most famous 'haunted house' in the city. Although the story is enthusiastically embellished by companies providing 'ghost tours', the infamy of the place is documented. Madame Lalaurie was fined for mistreating slaves, the spirits of whom are alleged to haunt the place.

Between Royal and Bourbon Streets, on Orleans Street, is the site of the old **Orleans Ballroom**, where many elegant 19th-century galas were held, including balls where white gentlemen seeking mistresses were introduced to beautiful women of colour. The ballroom, also known as the Quadroon Ballroom, has been lovingly incorporated into the design of the **Bourbon Orleans Hotel** (717 Orleans Street, 523 2222, www.wyndham.com), which occupies

most of the block. Ascend the grand double staircase to the second floor and you might be able to peer inside the ballroom.

Gallier House

1132 Royal Street, between Governor Nicholls & Ursulines Streets (525 5661/www.gnofn.org/~hggh). Bus 3 Vieux Carré, 48 Esplanade, 55 Elysian Fields, 81 Almonaster, 82 Desire. **Open** *Tours every hour 10am-3.30pm Mon-Fri; closed Sat, Sun.* **Admission** $6; $5 concessions; free under-8s. **Credit** AmEx, MC, V. **Map** p316 D2.

James Gallier Jr, son of pivotal New Orleans architect James Gallier Sr, designed this side-hall, Greek Revival townhouse. The house has been carefully restored and furnished in the style of an upper-class family of the 1860s. Furnishings change with the seasons, with mosquito netting added in summer and Christmas decorations in the winter.

Historic New Orleans Collection

533 Royal Street, at St Louis Street (523 4662/ www.hnoc.org). Bus 3 Vieux Carré, 55 Elysian Fields, 81 Almonaster, 82 Desire. **Open** *Williams Gallery 10am-4.30pm Tue-Sat; closed Mon, Sun. Louisiana History Galleries & Trapolin House tours 10am, 11am, 2pm, 3pm Tue-Sat; closed Mon, Sun.* **Admission** *Williams Gallery free. Louisiana History Galleries & Trapolin House* (by guided tour only) $4. **No credit cards. Map** p316 B2.

Low-key to the point of invisibility to the less than alert visitor, this compound of 18th- and 19th-century buildings, including the 1792 Merieult House offers art, culture and history in several attractive forms. The HNOC grew out of wealthy philanthropist Kemper Williams's interest in collecting documents and memorabilia connected to the War of 1812. His hobby expanded to include almost anything connected with Louisiana history, a passion shared by his wife, Leila. The Williamses established a foundation for their collection with an endowment to continue the work of collecting, cataloguing and studying Louisiana.

The ground-floor Williams Gallery hosts some excellent changing shows – past exhibits include photographs taken by New Orleans's mid-century Surrealist Clarence John Laughlin, and the musical memorabilia of Bill Russell, a producer and archivist of traditional jazz – while the permanent exhibits in a suite of upstairs galleries provide a detailed overview of the history of the city. Among the highlights are the documents used to negotiate the Louisiana Purchase (*see p8*); a large and detailed painting by John Antropus from 1858 of a slave funeral; and an iron ball – once manacled to a slave's leg as punishment – that visitors can lift to feel its weight. The guided tours of the 1889 Trapolin House (remodelled in the 1940s as a home for the Williamses) and the upstairs Louisiana History Galleries, given by excellent volunteer guides, are the city's best short course in local history.

Madame John's Legacy

632 Dumaine Street, at Royal Street (568 6968/ http://lsm.crt.state.la.us/). Bus 3 Vieux Carré, 55 Elysian Fields, 81 Almonaster, 82 Desire. **Open** 9am-5pm Tue-Sun; closed Mon. **Admission** $3; $2 concessions; free under-12s. **Credit** MC, V. **Map** p316 C2.

This raised Creole cottage dates from 1788, making it one of the oldest buildings in New Orleans. Its longevity renders the house one of the most architecturally and historically significant structures in Louisiana, but a writer gave the house its enduring fame and name. George Washington Cable used the house in his novella, *Madame John's Legacy*, the story of how a quadroon mistress used her inheritance from her white lover, the father of her children. Historians insist the house has no such tangled history, but it has become a symbol for the New Orleans subculture of 'shadow families'. The house, which is owned by the Louisiana State Museum, reopened to the public in 1999 after renovations. Rather than a historic house museum, Madame John's is used as a gallery and display space. Still, there are many interior details and architectural features that make it interesting to tour.

New Orleans Historic Voodoo Museum

724 Dumaine Street, at Royal Street (523 7685/ www.voodoomuseum.com). Bus 3 Vieux Carré, 55 Elysian Fields, 81 Almonaster, 82 Desire. **Open** 10am-8pm daily. **Admission** $7; $3.50-$5.50 concessions; free under-5s. **Credit** AmEx, Disc, MC, V. **Map** p316 C2.

The Voodoo Museum is hardly the spot for scholarly edification on the indigenous integration of Roman Catholicism and Afro-Caribbean religions known as voodoo – but it is a wonderfully seedy, spooky French Quarter experience nonetheless. Visitors will find room after room of weird, macabre artefacts, from a desiccated cat to baby coffins, skulls, turtle shells and alligator skins. No visit would be complete without a palm or card reading. Lots of cheesy fun, especially for kids.

Bourbon Street

Map p316

The next street north of Royal is Bourbon Street. It didn't become the famous nightlife spot and tourist trap it is today until the middle of this century. Nowadays there isn't much authentic Dixieland jazz to be heard in the clubs and bars and their offerings change quickly, so you'll hear a whole range of musical styles along the street. It's closed to traffic after 7pm, when the first eight blocks (from Canal Street to St Ann Street) become a walker's mall and most clubs leave their doors open so strollers can hear the music without even going inside.

Bourbon Street is an adult entertainment area. Among the music clubs are saloons, strip

Viewfinder

New Orleans, with its below-sea-level landscape, is not a city of dramatic vistas and surprising views. To get a bird's-eye view of the city takes a bit of thought and planning but is easily done. Here are some easy-access spots from where you can see more than usual.

● The view most recommended by locals is **Top of the Mart**, the bar on the 33rd floor of the World Trade Center on the riverfront. From the slowly revolving barroom, you can see as far as 20 miles (32 kilometres) on a clear day. Sunsets are particularly good. See page 157.

● Head for the lobby and dining room of the **Wyndham Canal Place Hotel** (100 Iberville Street, 566 7006) in the Canal Place shopping complex (see page 165). The floor-to-ceiling windows face the Mississippi River and offer sweeping views of ship traffic, the French Quarter, Algiers and further on a good day.

● The Omni Royal Orleans Hotel (621 St Louis Street, 529 5333) is one of the tallest buildings in the French Quarter (where height is severely restricted). From the rooftop bar, **La Riviera**, you get a 360-degree view of the city and the river. See page 155.

● Enjoy drinks and appetisers while you absorb the spectacular views from the **Top of the Dome** restaurant, located in the high-rise Hyatt Regency Hotel just outside the Quarter. Location markers on the walls help you recognise the sights below. See page 90.

● Travelling by river doesn't give you the panorama that you get from a tall building but it gives you a superb overview of the city and river. As New Orleans is primarily a low-rise city, the top-deck of a three-storey riverboat provides quite a good view. See chapter **Guided Tours**.

shows – and their pricey, newer incarnations, called 'Gentlemen's Clubs' – female impersonator shows and tacky T-shirt shops. The best show on the street tends to be the free one provided by its weird and wild habitués.

The street is strictly segregated by sexual orientation. The first seven blocks (to Orleans) are 'straight Bourbon' and the next two are 'gay Bourbon'. Although gay bars are scattered throughout the Quarter and the suburbs, three of the largest are in this area. Facing each other

Sightseeing

at St Ann Street are the two largest dance bars, the **Bourbon Pub & Parade Disco** and **Oz**. At the corner of Dumaine is **Café Lafitte**, one of the oldest gay bars in America, with a principally male clientele. For more on these and other venues, *see chapter* **Gay & Lesbian**.

A block further down Bourbon, at St Philip Street, is a quaint old building called **Lafitte's Blacksmith Shop** (*see page 153*), which was a gay bar in the 1940s and 1950s but now welcomes all. Although probably apocryphal, the legend still persists that the shop was a base for the privateering activities of local pirate Jean Lafitte in the 18th century.

Towards Rampart Street

Map p316

The next two streets are Dauphine and Burgundy (pronounced 'Bur-GUN-dy'). While they are pleasant parts of the Quarter and some hotels and restaurants are located here, they are mostly quiet, residential areas. On St Louis Street is the **Hermann-Grima Historic House**, with its working 1830s kitchen (*see below*). On not quite as serious a note is the **Musée Conti Wax Museum**, the inevitable tourist town attraction (*see below*).

The final street in the Quarter is Rampart Street, once the site of turn-of-the-19th-century jazz joints. Today, a few clubs offering New Orleans music have reopened, including the **Funky Butt**, and **Donna's Bar & Grill** (*for both, see page 216*), which presents New Orleans brass bands nightly.

Hermann-Grima Historic House

820 St Louis Street, between Bourbon & Dauphine Streets (525 5661/www.gnofn.org~hggh). Bus 3 Vieux Carré, 57 Franklin. **Open** *Tours* every 30min 10am-3.30pm Mon-Sat; closed Sun. **Admission** $6; $5 concessions; free under-8s. **Credit** AmEx, MC, V. **Map** p316 B2.

This Federal-style house is especially interesting for its fully restored and working 1830s kitchen. Every Thursday, from October until May, skilled volunteers cook an entire meal using the tools, foods and methods that would have been used at the time. The house is also notable for its living history programmes, during which the house is 'dressed' as it would have been in the mid-19th century for a major event such as a family funeral or wedding.

Musée Conti Wax Museum of Louisiana

917 Conti Street, at Dauphine Street (525 2605/www.get-waxed.com). Bus 3 Vieux Carré, 57 Franklin. **Open** 10am-5.30pm Mon-Sat; noon-5.30pm Sun. **Admission** $6.75; $5.75 concessions. **Credit** AmEx, MC, V. **Map** p316 B1/2.

Another somewhat anachronistic institution, the Wax Museum comprises, as you might expect, a labyrinth of dimly lit hallways bordered by kitsch tableaux played out by waxen mannequins. It doesn't rival the Cabildo or the Historic New Orleans Collection in its presentation of New Orleans's history, but it actually does a very credible job of illustrating incidents both factual and mythical that make up the city's self-image. Opened in 1964, it has a few rather dated displays – including the visit of the Duke and Duchess of Windsor to Mardi Gras in the mid-1950s – as well as a scene from the Eisenhower-era movie *Creature from the Black Lagoon*, complete with monster and shrieking female victim mired in claggy mud. But the exhibits have been kept in remarkably good shape and part of the fun is stepping back in time to an earlier sensibility.

Tremé

Map pp306-7

Across Rampart Street from the French Quarter is a section of town known as the Tremé (pronounced 'tree-may'), originally the Tremé family plantation. This is probably one of the oldest historically black neighbourhoods in America. In antebellum times, Tremé was home to many of the city's free people of colour, a vibrant, important community of artisans, workers, entrepreneurs and families. Tremé has begun to rediscover and honour that heritage in ways that make it accessible to outsiders. Although there are several institutions here and it is home to many families, Tremé can still be unsafe, at night especially. Be alert to your surroundings when visiting. One good way to get a feel for the area is to join an organised tour of St Louis Cemetery No.1 and Congo Square-Armstrong Park (*see chapter* **Guided Tours**).

The square facing Rampart Street between St Peter and St Ann Streets is called **Congo Square**. In the earliest days of the colony, this area was designated by the French Government as a place where slaves could congregate. French colonial law, as set down in the Code Noir, said that slave owners could not make their slaves work on Sunday, to encourage them to go to church services and become good Catholics. With a day off each week and a place provided where they could meet and interact, slaves in Louisiana were able to retain much more of their African language, music, dance and religion than anywhere else in North America. Elements of African culture survived long enough to become blended into European culture and with time New Orleans became the most African of North American cities.

It is this blend that created jazz. And gumbo. And voodoo. In terms of the preservation of

African culture in the New World, Congo Square is one of the most important sites in North America. Sadly, most of the surrounding neighbourhood was levelled during the first half of this century at a time when African culture wasn't appreciated. To make amends, somewhat belatedly, the resulting park was named after Louis Armstrong and a large arch erected at St Ann Street with his name on it. Also in the park is a statue of Armstrong and a bust of jazz pioneer Sidney Bechet. And the city-owned theatre in the park was recently named after native daughter Mahalia Jackson.

The newest city initiative in Tremé is the **Trème Villa Meilleur–New Orleans African-American Museum** (*see below*). Although the museum is still finding its focus, the restored 1828 mansion is a stunner with lovely surrounding gardens. A privately owned museum has also opened in Tremé, the **Backstreet Cultural Museum**, a labour of love by former mortuary worker Sylvester Francis (*see below*).

At Conti and Rampart Streets is **Our Lady of Guadeloupe Chapel** (411 N Rampart Street, 525 1551), one of the oldest in New Orleans. Now a very active Catholic parish church, it was originally built on the edge of the little town in 1826 as the mortuary chapel, to handle the great number of funerals resulting from yellow fever epidemics. To the rear of the chapel is a statue that has come to be known as 'St Expedite'. Much beloved and venerated in a neighbourhood that has historically had a vibrant African culture, St Expedite is sometimes referred to in whispers as 'the voodoo saint'. If you have never heard of St Expedite, don't rush for a copy of *Lives of the Saints*. A religious statue arrived from Europe in the 19th century with no labels or tags at all. The wooden crate was stamped 'Expedite', thus the saint received its name. Behind the chapel is **St Louis Cemetery No.1**, the oldest cemetery in New Orleans (*see page 45*).

Adjacent to the cemetery is where **Storyville**, the infamous red-light district, flourished from 1896 to 1917 (*see page 13*). Nothing remains of the grand brothels that ran from the cemetery to Canal Street. They were demolished after the district was shut down at the beginning of World War I. The only surviving building from the era is a sad little corner store at Basin and Bienville Streets, and even this lost its second floor years ago during a hurricane. The residential area behind Armstrong Park deteriorated terribly during the middle of the 20th century, although renovation and preservation efforts are beginning to make inroads into the area of Tremé near Esplanade Avenue.

Backstreet Cultural Museum

1116 St Claude Avenue, between Ursulines & Governor Nicholls Streets (525 1733). Bus 88 St Claude. **Open** 10am-5pm Tue-Sat; closed Sun. **Admission** free. **Map** pp306-7 G6.
Housed in a former mortuary on a residential street in Tremé, the museum is an odd collection of artefacts devoted to several indigenous New Orleans traditions: jazz funerals, second line and Mardi Gras Indians. Open since late 1999, it's a longtime dream of Sylvester Francis, a former funeral home employee who began photographing and videotaping jazz funerals and walking parades more than 20 years ago. The unlabelled displays of elaborate Mardi Gras Indian costumes, parade marshals' regalia and New Orleans memorabilia only make sense when explained by Francis, who owns and operates the museum. Happily, he's always on the premises and his colourful monologues are well worth the visit.

Tremé Villa Meilleur–New Orleans African-American Museum

1418 Governor Nicholls Street, at Villere Street (527 0989). **Open** 9am-5pm Mon-Sat; closed Sun. **Admission** $4; $2-$3 concessions. **No credit cards**. **Map** pp306-7 G6.
Built as a plantation residence, the Meilleur House (1828) is a beautiful example of Caribbean-antebellum US architecture. Taken over by the city in the early 1990s when it was in danger of collapsing, the house has been through a $1.5 million renovation. The museum aspect of the institution appears to be an evolving process with uneven exhibitions by local artists and changing plans for different kinds of displays. You'll probably have the place to yourself unless a school group is scheduled. The estate is off the tourist path but worth a visit for the beautiful house and soothing courtyards. Across Villere Street is a small café that is another city project, a training centre for young people headed into the restaurant business. It's a good spot for a light lunch although lessons about service don't seem to be part of the curriculum.

Faubourg Marigny & the Bywater

As Esplanade Avenue heads towards the river, it becomes the downriver boundary of the French Quarter. The old French Creole families of the 19th century hoped Esplanade would be the grandest residential avenue of the city. Wonderful homes were built here, but the more numerous – and richer – Americans in the Uptown section made St Charles Avenue even grander (*see page 102*). Today, most of the houses on Esplanade have been divided into apartments, but a few are still single homes. Most notable is the **Matilda Grey House** at 704 Esplanade. Painted what neighbours call Matilda Grey Pink, the house

Watch the **Canal Street–Algiers ferry** come and go from the riverside parks. *See p74.*

was acquired by the oil heiress earlier this century and is now one of the homes of her niece and namesake Matilda Stream.

Two hundred years ago, Esplanade Avenue marked the edge of town. On the other side was the plantation of the prominent Marigny family. Scion of this great family (his father and grandfather are buried in St Louis Cathedral), Bernard de Marigny was one of the richest men in the history of America. In around 1800 he was orphaned and inherited a fortune, then valued at $7 million. By the time Bernard came to the end of his long life, he had spent the entire fortune. He timed it well. Bernard is what Orleanians call a good role model. He lived his life fully and enjoyed what he had, though his heirs didn't see it quite that way. At some point, Bernard decided that the plantation would be more valuable as real estate than as farm land, so he sold it off as lots, creating what is often described as New Orleans's first suburb.

It is still a distinctive neighbourhood. The section between Esplanade Avenue and Elysian Fields Avenue is very much like the adjacent French Quarter. Below Elysian Fields, the properties are more modest. A less transient area than the Quarter, its residents have forged a strong neighbourhood identity. The Marigny is the site of a number of B&Bs, ranging from the **Claiborne Mansion** (2111 Dauphine Street, 949 7327), which is the most historically significant building in the neighbourhood, to

very modest establishments. (For details, *see chapter* **Accommodation**.) B&Bs have proliferated in the Marigny because they are technically illegal across Esplanade Avenue in the French Quarter.

Most of the neighbourhood is rather quiet, but three blocks on Frenchmen Street have become a very hip entertainment strip. From Esplanade to Royal are music clubs **Igor's Checkpoint Charlie**, **Café Brasil** and **Snug Harbor** (*see chapter* **Music: Rock, Roots & Jazz**) and numerous restaurants and shops. Elsewhere, the newest jazz club in New Orleans, **Sweet Lorraine's** on St Claude (*see page 220*), is another must-see. Near the music clubs is the **Faubourg Marigny Bookstore**, the oldest gay, lesbian and feminist bookstore in the South (*see page 172*). Moving eastward, you'll run across two neighbourhood hangouts, the laid-back café-deli at **Schiro's** (Royal Street, 945 4425) where you can read the *New York Times* and eat Middle Eastern delicacies, and **Café Flora**, a boho coffeehouse (2600 Royal Street, 947 8358) where you'll probably run across some interesting artwork.

The most notable new development in the Marigny is the opening of the **New Orleans Center for the Creative Arts**, a public high school devoted to the performing and creative arts. Although NOCCA has been around for 20 years (Harry Connick Jr and Wynton Marsalis are among its alumni), only in 2000 did the school get its own custom-designed campus. A former cotton warehouse was brilliantly reconceived as the centre of the campus with postmodern structures built to harmonise. The school is open to the public for events such as concerts. Be on the lookout for an excuse to go and see the campus while you're in New Orleans; this is one of the city's most impressive buildings in decades (*see page 32* **Modern masters**).

Below the Marigny is Bywater, once a working-class neighbourhood largely settled by Irish and German immigrants in the 19th century. This is the fabled Ninth Ward, where yat ('Where y'at cap?') accents are thick and everybody gets the local news by sitting on the stoop. Bywater has a growing population of artists, musicians, writers and bohemians of every stripe, drawn by the low rents and network of bars, cafés and studios. It's hardly a tourist neighbourhood but for visitors seeking out the non-trendy arts areas, this is the place. **Studio Inferno** (*see page 204*) is a seriously cool artist warehouse where you'll find several sculptors, glass artists and others at work. The studios welcome visitors and are happy to sell you artwork although they aren't primarily retail. Other art stops include photographer Christopher Porche West's hand-crafted gallery and studio (3218 Dauphine Street, 947 3880, open Sat and by appointment) and the **Waiting Room Gallery** (904 Pauline Street, 949 1805), where you'll not only see cutting edge art, but also get the chance to dance in the streets with Bywaterians at one of the opening parties.

The **Saturn Bar** (*see page 156*) and **Vaughan's** (*see page 221*) are nightspots that attract night people from all over the city, while **BJs** (on the corner of Dauphine and Lesseps Streets) and **Markey's** (640 Louisa Street, 943 0785) are classic neighbourhood bars where strangers can make new friends by the second beer. The universally popular **Elizabeth's Café** (*see page 132*) is the neighbourhood crossroads. **Lorenzo's Pizzeria** serves up great pizza and is frequently the spot for drag shows (*see page 132*). Other eateries are sprouting around the area.

Further east across the Industrial Canal Bridge is the Lower Ninth Ward, the Holy Cross and Arabi neighbourhoods, stretching into St Bernard Parish and the working-class suburb of Chalmette. Military history fans will be interested in **Jackson Barracks** in Arabi , while Chalmette has the **Chalmette Battlefield** (*for both, see below*). This was the site of the Battle of New Orleans on 8 January 1815, when Andrew Jackson and a ragtag army of frontiersmen, militiamen and pirates defeated a superior British force, led by General Sir Edward Pakenham. At the end of

the two-hour dawn battle, 2,000 British troops lay dead or dying in the field. American casualties are remembered variously from a low of nine to a high of 77. (For more information on the battle, *see page 8*.) The battlefield is now run by the National Park Service and open to the public.

A very good 30-minute video shown in the visitor centre explains the political climate that sparked the War of 1812 and gives a basic outline of the battle. Self-guided walking tours are an easy one-and-a-half-mile (two-kilometre) loop through the park. The 150-foot (48-metre) **Chalmette Monument** provides an excellent view of the battlefield but is sadly only open to visitors on rare occasions. Across the field, behind the site of the British lines, is the **National Cemetery**, a poignant Civil War burial ground lined with long rows of tiny marble headstones.

The easiest way to reach the battlefield is by car or taxi but you can also go by boat. The **Creole Queen** paddlewheeler cruise (524 0814, www.neworleansbigeasy.com), which embarks from the Riverwalk mall dock, lands at the park twice daily and is met by park rangers who give a brief talk on the battle – but these are quick on-and-off stops, with no walking about. If you go under your own steam, plan to have lunch at **Rocky & Carlo's**, the legendary Creole-Sicilian restaurant nearby (613 W St Bernard Highway, Chalmette, 279 8323).

The battle is celebrated in New Orleans every January with American and British encampments on the original site. In London, it is quietly remembered by a statue in St Paul's Cathedral of Pakenham along with his second in command, Major General Samuel Gibbs. Both are dressed in the uniforms they were wearing during the New Orleans campaign.

Chalmette Battlefield & National Cemetery

8606 W St Bernard Highway (Highway 40), Chalmette (281 0510/www.nps.gov/jela). No public transport. **Open** 9am-5pm daily. **Admission** free.

Jackson Barracks National Guard Installation & Museum

6400 St Claude Avenue, between Delery & Angela Streets (278 8242/www.la.ngb.army.mil/jbmm.htm). Bus 88 St Claude. **Open** 8am-4pm Mon-Fri; 9am-3pm Sat; closed Sun. **Admission** free.
Anyone devoted to the history of war, particularly World War II, will enjoy this out-of-the-way military museum. It has been a military installation since the 1830s and is now the headquarters of the Louisiana National Guard. The museum has weaponry from the War of 1812 as well as other 19th-century pieces, but the main focus is contemporary, with updates from the Gulf War.

CBD & Warehouse District

Business and art reign cheek by jowl in these contrasting districts.

The CBD

Map p309

The downtown section of New Orleans – stretching from Canal Street to the interstate and from Camp Street to Tulane Avenue – is known with business-like precision as the Central Business District, or CBD. It is sometimes called 'Downtown' but there's general confusion about just what that means, so stick to CBD. **Poydras Street** is the high street of the CBD, the boulevard flanked by the tall, nondescript skyscrapers built during the hazy, crazy oil boom days of the 1970s and 1980s. Fittingly for a commercial district, Poydras is a corridor between two of the city's contemporary landmarks, the **Superdome** and **Harrah's Casino** (*see page 95* **Fold 'em or hold 'em?**). The Superdome, one of the first mega-covered stadia, was built to bring professional sports to New Orleans, a debatable achievement when one considers the appalling record of the Saints football team. Likewise, Harrah's is the biggest, most sought-after casino site in Louisiana but has a troubled record despite the high spirits of its fanciful, postmodern architecture. Looking beyond the modern, however, there are a number of remnants of the city's earlier days, when architecture was grand and Gothic.

In the early 18th century, most of what is now the CBD was sugarcane plantation and **Canal Street** was a strip of dirt nearly 200 feet (61 metres) wide marking the edge of the city and the beginning of farmland. As the area's population grew, Canal Street became critical as a meeting place in a city that was divided along national lines. By the 19th century, descendants of the French lived and worked in the French Quarter, while the American residents sprawled out over what is now the CBD and the Garden District and was then known as the American Sector. Canal Street was the border between the two.

The paths of the two groups rarely crossed. In those days, the French ran the city and when the American residents wanted to meet them the meetings occurred in the middle of

Canal Street. The area was designated as a neutral ground between the two cultures and New Orleanians today still refer to the grassy space in the centre of any boulevard as a 'neutral ground'. As the city became a centre for shipping, the downtown section gradually became a business centre and the Americans moved their residences further up St Charles Avenue, forming the basis for the various neighbourhoods that exist today.

Because much of what is notable in the CBD is on **St Charles Avenue**, one of the best ways to see the area is to take the streetcar from Canal Street down St Charles to Lee Circle in the Warehouse District, and then walk back through the streets to catch the sites that aren't on the streetcar route.

On the first block of St Charles from Canal Street is the **Crescent Billiard Hall** (115 St Charles Avenue), which was built in 1826 as a rather massive structure for which the sole purpose was the playing of billiards. The building is now the home of the private Pickwick Club. Two blocks further along is the old **United Fruit Company Building** (321 St Charles Avenue), now the home of a bank. This beautiful Greek Revival building was once the local outpost of the infamous company that, with considerable help from the CIA, made a fortune in the 1940s and 1950s off the fruit and political misfortune of Central America. The company name is still emblazoned across the building.

Two blocks later is a small, somewhat dingy square surrounded by official-looking buildings. This is **Lafayette Square**, one of the oldest public squares in New Orleans and now a favourite sleeping area for the city's homeless. The buildings around it are mostly federal buildings – including the federal courthouse, which is directly across the square from the streetcar line. On the opposite side of St Charles from the square is **Gallier Hall** (*see page 90*), an 1850s structure that was used as City Hall for more than a century (it's a pity it isn't still, because the current City Hall at the edge of the CBD is a 1960s architectural nightmare).

A few blocks further down St Charles is **Julia Row**, the block of Julia Street between St Charles and Camp Street. American bigwigs occupied the 13 brick townhouses on the Uptown side between the 1830s and the Civil War, when it was one of the most fashionable areas to live. Now it's the city's most fashionable art street, hosting a number of entertaining art-centered events (*see chapters* **By Season** and **Galleries**).

Further along sits one of the city's fixtures, the decrepit **Hummingbird Hotel** (804 St Charles Avenue, 523 9165). For more than half a century the Hummingbird has thrived. Today, it is a flophouse in the 1940s style, popular with both skid-row types and backpacking college students – for years its public phone had a handmade sign above it that stated firmly, 'No talking to imaginary people'. Its $24 rooms are spare, noisy and smelly and people love them. Best of all is the grill downstairs, where the eccentric staff make some of the best fast food in the city at absurdly low prices, 24 hours a day. Breakfast, lunch or dinner will cost you less than $5 (best bets are the eggs and hamburgers). Even celebrities line up at the 'Bird – Tom Cruise and Nicole Kidman ate here while Cruise was in town filming *Interview with the Vampire*.

One significant CBD site not on St Charles Avenue is the **Church of the Immaculate Conception**, also known as the Jesuit Church (130 Baronne Street). This extraordinary structure combines a myriad of architectural influences including Moorish, Arabian and Gothic. The building is a precise 1930s replica of the original church, which stood on the site from 1857 but was demolished in 1926 because of structural weakness. It contains the furnishings of the original, including cast-iron pews and a gilt altar designed by local architect James Freret. The statue of the Virgin Mary inside the church was constructed in France for the royal chapel in the Tuileries, but the French Revolutionary War of 1848 put paid to that idea. The statue was later sold to the New Orleans church.

At the northern end of the CBD rises the hulk of the **Louisiana Superdome** (*see below; see also pages 232 and 32* **Modern Masters**), built in 1975. Encircled by elevated highways, the dome now seems as natural a part of the New Orleans skyline as any church spire. Covering 52 acres (21 hectares) and rising 27 storeys high, the structure has aged surprisingly well. It's connected to the **New Orleans Center** mall (*see page 165*) and the high-rise **Hyatt Regency** (500 Poydras Plaza, 561 1234), which offers spectacular views of the city (*see page 84* **Viewfinder**).

South of the Superdome, on the neutral ground of Loyola Avenue, is the unusual memorial-cum-art-installation known as the **Richard & Annette Bloch Cancer Survivors Plaza**. This wildly colourful sculpture and garden installation was plopped down in the middle of the busy street in 1995. Midwestern philanthropists Richard and Annette Bloch wanted to share his two-time triumph over cancer with the American public and decided to do so by honouring cancer survivors with outdoor sculptures in 54 American cities. A pavilion and fountain are linked by a group of frolicking sculptures representing presumably cancer-free men, women and children, and 14 soaring towers that carry 'positive mental attitude' aphorisms about cancer. Hardly anyone goes to the plaza because it's difficult to get to and off the beaten track, yet the sightlines down Loyola are striking and for all its earnestness there is a certain serenity about the place. A few homeless people catch some sleep on the benches, but it's a safe place to visit during the day.

Gallier Hall

545 St Charles Avenue, at Lafayette Street. St Charles Streetcar. **Map** p309 C1.
Gallier Hall is constructed of creamy-looking marble and fronted by two rows of Ionic columns. It has long been one of the city's most important buildings, where visiting heads of state are received and deceased leaders traditionally lie in state – Confederate President Jefferson Davis and Confederate General PGT Beauregard both lay in state here. Today, it is a ceremonial building, and despite not being open to the public, it's often rented out for special events. It is also the centre of all Mardi Gras activities, where every parade stops for review.

Louisiana Superdome

Sugar Bowl Drive, at Poydras Street (box office 587 3800/tour information line 587 3808/www.superdome.com). Bus 16 S Claiborne. **Open** 9am-4pm daily. *Tours* 10.30am, noon, 1.30pm on non-event days. **Admission** *Tours* $6; $4-$5 concessions. **Credit** AmEx, MC, V. **Map** p309 A/B1.
When the Superdome was completed in 1975 it was considered a modern marvel. Louisianans loved it. People drove hundreds of miles to see it, whether or not there was an event on. It's home to the New Orleans Saints football team as well as touring superstars, but is worth visiting at any time. Tours are given daily.

The Warehouse District

Map p309
Wedged in next to the river between the CBD and the Lower Garden District (*see page 97*), the Warehouse District was long the location of dozens of cavernous warehouses, designed

The **Contemporary Arts Center**. *See p94.*

were converted to public use, holding nightclubs and restaurants for the visiting fairgoers. Although the fair wasn't a financial success (falling in the middle of the recession, it was the first Worlds Fair ever to lose money), it changed the city's perspective towards the Warehouse District. Developers began seeing the rotting, window-covered behemoths for what they really were – goldmines.

The conversion process begun then continues today. Upmarket apartments and condos paved the way, with the lofts' high ceilings and enormous windows attracting scores of young professionals. The conversion of several warehouses into museums and art galleries meant the area also became known as the Arts District. Walking is the best way to see the tightly packed district, as parking spaces are at a premium and galleries are lined up virtually door to door.

Almost without planning, the Warehouse District is becoming the city's most concentrated museum district. The Contemporary Arts Center and the Confederate Museum have been an odd couple on Camp Street for years but with the addition of the $21 million **National D-Day Museum** (*see page 96*) and the **Ogden Museum of Southern Art** (moving from its temporary location in Julia Street in 2001; *see page 96*), the area achieves critical mass while adding weight to the cluster of art galleries nearby. The new Ogden Museum building will be a capstone in the development of **Lee Circle**, where the statue of Confederate General Robert E Lee has presided since 1884 (14 years after his death), atop a marble pedestal. Knowledgeable locals will point out that Lee's statue, sculpted by New Yorker Alexander Doyle, faces north, so that his back is never turned to his enemies. Lee Circle has always been a city landmark but now it's poised to become the epicentre of the burgeoning art and cultural district. While you're here, don't miss the outdoor sculptures of the **Sydney & Walda Besthoff Collection**, located on Lee Circle in K&B Plaza (*see page 96*).

Near Lee Circle on Camp Street is the rust-coloured, castle-like structure that for 100 years has housed the **Confederate Museum** (*see page 95*). Many visitors (and locals) write off the museum as a retro shrine to slavery and white supremacy without ever visiting the place, but Civil War buffs will enjoy the large collection of memorabilia – including part of General Robert E Lee's wartime silver service and flags and uniforms still dotted with 19th-century blood – in what turns out to be a restrained coverage of the War Between the States.

Across the street, the **Contemporary Arts Center** (*see page 94*) is the lynchpin of the district. It was built in an abandoned warehouse

primarily for the storage of cotton, coffee and sugar destined to be shipped up the river or overseas. When modern shipping practices and the expansion of the port upriver eliminated the need for all that storage space, the Warehouse District was essentially abandoned. From the 1960s to the 1980s it sat empty and ramshackle, an eyesore on the edge of the CBD, with pigeons and bums the only regular residents.

But the 1984 Worlds Fair changed all that, with the development of a massive fair site on the edge of the district. Several warehouses

Sightseeing

The **Confederate Museum**. *See p95.*

in 1976 with the stated mission of providing space for alternative arts in the city, which then had a very conservative art scene. The CAC specialises in modern works by local and national artists and hosts plays in its three small auditoriums. It also houses a popular cybercafé (*see page 281*).

The majority of art galleries in the area are located on Julia Street, which bounds the CAC on one side. The galleries are open to the public and close enough together to be comfortably explored on foot. One of the best ways to see them is on the first Saturday of every month when many hold art openings in the evenings (usually 6-8pm), complete with wine and cheese. Note that on these opening Saturdays, most galleries are closed during the day while setting up their new shows. For details, *see chapter* **Galleries**.

Buried in among the warehouses and galleries is a museum that is aimed at children but great fun for adults. The **Louisiana Children's Museum** (*see page 197*) is jam-packed with hands-on exhibits, most of which are less art than toys. For the littlest tykes there is a play kitchen, a radio station, a grocery store and even a port, all in miniature.

Back on Camp Street are several more art-related shops, while at the corner of Camp and Girod Streets is the city's weekly **Crescent City Market** (*see page 182*). Area farmers and

bakers bring in fresh produce, herb plants, freshly baked bread and jams on Saturday mornings, and the locals crowd in to snatch it all up. Nearby, squeezed in between modern structures, is the soaring form of **St Patrick's Cathedral** (*see page 96*), long the centre of Irish Catholicism in New Orleans.

The Warehouse District is also home to a number of the city's more popular restaurants and bars. At the corner of Poydras and Camp Streets is **Mother's** (*see page 136*), world-famous for its po-boy sandwiches and red beans and rice. At peak times, locals and tourists line up for hours and put up with Mother's counter service just to get some of that fine home cookin'.

The **Mermaid Lounge** (1100 Constance Street) is a popular hole-in-the-wall music bar favoured by the alternative local music scene. Located in a tiny old house surrounded by towering warehouses and the massive underpinnings of the interstate, the Mermaid is a great place for hanging around outside on a hot night, listening to music and drinking cold beer (*see page 221*).

At 828 S Peters Street, you'll find one of the best venues for regional and national bands. The **Howlin' Wolf** club (*see page 221*) offers live music nightly, along with a wide selection of international beers, including a dozen different choices on tap.

For something completely different, head for the very tip of the district in front of the Riverwalk Mall, at the foot of Poydras Street. Between Poydras and Canal Streets on the river is an odd, 1960s-style skyscraper with a round top. This is the optimistically named **World Trade Center** (*see page 96*). While the building houses mainly offices and is due for conversion into a hotel, on the 33rd floor the **Top of the Mart** bar offers a stunning bird's-eye view of New Orleans and the Mississippi River (*see page 157 and page 84* **Viewfinder**).

From the vantage point offered by Top of the Mart you can see the hub of one of New Orleans's top industries: conventions. Past the Riverwalk, the recently expanded **Ernest N Morial Convention Center** (*see page 278*) sprawls alongside the river from Julia Street to the other side of the Crescent City Connection bridge. It's a typical example of undistinguished late 20th-century architecture, strictly utilitarian. The centre is named after the city's first black mayor, the father of current mayor Marc Morial.

Most conventioneers, in their eagerness to get away from business and to the fun of the French Quarter, miss the surrounding

neighbourhood, taking shuttle buses or taxis to and from their hotels. This is a sensible idea at night, but during the day walking is the only way to explore the less obvious pleasures of the surrounding Warehouse District, which lacks the neon signs, barkers and long queues of the Quarter.

Contemporary Arts Center

900 Camp Street, at Howard Avenue (528 3805/ www.cacno.org). St Charles Streetcar. **Open** 11am-5pm Tue-Sun; closed Mon. *Cybercafé* 9am-5pm Mon, Tue; 9am-10pm Wed-Sat; 11am-5pm Sun. **Admission** $5; $3 concessions; free under-5s. **Map** p309 C2.

In 1990 the Contemporary Arts Center found itself in the position of a newly wealthy couple who've just spent megabucks renovating their old house and don't really know what to do with all that glitzy new space. After years of fundraising, the centre found itself with arguably the finest and most innovative interior of any alternative gallery space in the country, with spaces for theatre as well as fine art. Then what? Until recently, theatre seemed to hold the upper hand, providing the majority of the innovation at the 25-year-old institution that had previously thrived on its funkiness and impromptu exhibition spaces. With the

The statue of General Robert E Lee at **Lee Circle** faces north – towards the enemy.

appointment of middle-aged bad-boy David S Rubin as curator of visual arts in early 2000, the centre firmly directed its attention back to its original mission: the display of leading-edge contemporary art and the involvement of the community in its arts programmes.

Confederate Museum

929 Camp Street, at Howard Avenue (523 4522/ www.confederatemuseum.com). St Charles Streetcar. **Open** 10am-4pm Mon-Sat; 10am-3pm Sun. **Admission** $5; $2-$4 concessions. **Credit** MC, V. **Map** p309 B/C2.

This red-stone, Romanesque Revival structure is the oldest history museum in the city. It houses a splendid collection of artefacts from the War of Succession (as the American Civil War was known in the South). Here are all the sinister death-dealing devices, the uniforms and poignant personal mementoes of war that make any such museum interesting to history buffs. The political forces of the war are not discussed, although there is an affecting exhibit about the black Confederate units, a minor but much debated element of the Civil War organised in its final desperate months.

Fold 'em or hold 'em?

New Orleans would seem to be a natural home for high-stakes gambling with its walk-on-the-wild-side image and fondness for raffish characters. The term 'riverboat gambler' was almost an official job description for a large class of 19th-century New Orleanians who played poker for a living on the Mississippi River. Yet the officially sanctioned, heavily regulated type of gambling that developed in the late 20th century has never taken firm root in New Orleans. To the dismay of casino corporations and the Louisiana politicians who promoted gambling as the cure for every public funding ailment, casinos stumbled and fell in New Orleans when they were introduced in 1994.

There are currently four casinos in New Orleans. The biggest is **Harrah's**, located at the foot of Canal Street on the edge of the French Quarter. This is the only 'land-based' casino in Louisiana, meaning it is not locked into a waterside site and required to set sail a designated number of times. The $350 million enterprise opened in late 1999, unveiling a casino of Las Vegas quality with splashy decor, daily indoor Mardi Gras parades and ongoing entertainment. This has not been enough, however, to draw the hordes of high-stakes gamblers that the casino counted on to boost its profits. Saddled with a cumbersome tax deal with the city and state, Harrah's is making loud noises that it's only breaking even, not churning up enormous profits. While it seems incredible that the casino can rake in $16-$20 million a month and only break even, gambling analysts say the 50 per cent tax Harrah's pays may sink the New Orleans franchise (see also page 19). Other riverboat casinos have already sailed away,

finding greater riches in deadly dull Louisiana towns such as Shreveport, Bossier City and Lake Charles.

With the exception of Harrah's, which has a full complement of table games and slots that would do Las Vegas proud, gambling is a minor entertainment form in New Orleans. Other casinos tends to attract novices with slot machines rather than offering skilled games such as poker, blackjack, roulette and craps. Expecting a variety of in-house cafés, à la Las Vegas, many visitors are also surprised at the low-quality of the food served in the casinos. To appease local businesses, the casinos were severely restricted in the types of food service allowed and were prohibited from developing hotels altogether.

Although gambling is probably here to stay in New Orleans it shows no signs of becoming one of the city's prime attractions.

Bally's Casino

Lake Pontchartrain, next to Lakefront Airport, 1 Stars & Stripes Boulevard, New Orleans East (248 3200). Bus 60 Hayne Boulevard. **Open** 24hrs daily.

Boomtown Casino

4132 Peters Boulevard, Harvey, West Bank (366 7711/www.boomtowncasinos.com). **Open** 24hrs daily.

Harrah's Casino

512 South Peters Street, at Canal Street, CBD (533 6777/www.harrahsneworleans. com). **Open** 24hrs daily. **Map** p309 C1.

Treasure Chest Casino

Lake Pontchartrain, 5050 Williams Boulevard, Kenner (443 8000/1-800 298 0711/www.treasurechest.com). Bus Kenner Loop. **Open** 24hrs daily.

Sightseeing

In addition, the Confederate Museum is a time capsule of another era's museum practices and social attitudes. The beautiful 1891 structure, which was purpose-built to house the collection, is a museum piece itself, with long skylights, warm wooden panelling on every wall and rows of built-in display cabinets, all in excellent repair. Today, the Confederacy is commonly viewed as a deeply flawed – if not altogether evil – institution, based as it was on agrarian slavery. Still, the men who fought and died for the South were as often as not simple patriots, not political theoreticians. So, any view of the Confederacy is now an emotional maelstrom of historic chagrin and ancestral pride that can still cause tempers to rise. The Confederate Museum takes no particular stand on these social issues, even as the city it serves has become at least half African-American in population – this in itself makes the museum an anachronism. But that irony only adds to the fascination of a visit to this odd institution – don't miss it.

National D-Day Museum

945 Magazine Street, at Howard Avenue (527 6012/ www.ddaymuseum.org). **Open** 9am-5pm daily. **Admission** $7; $5-$6 concessions. **Map** p309 C2.
The three-storey glass front on Howard Avenue has opened up the drab area around Lee Circle with a bang. This thoughtful, carefully arranged museum presents the D-Day experience through film, exhibits and interactive displays. Opened on 6 June 2000, the 56th anniversary of the invasion, the museum is growing into its space. A full-size replica of a Higgins landing craft, a British Spitfire plane and somewhat smaller World War II hardware are on impressive display. There are also galleries dealing with the American home front and a planned exhibition about the war in the Pacific. The D-Day connection, if you were wondering, is that the famous Higgins landing craft was designed and built in New Orleans.

Ogden Museum of Southern Art

603 Julia Street, at Camp Street (539 9600/fax 539 9602/www.ogdenmuseum.org). St. Charles Streetcar. **Open** 10am-5pm Mon-Fri; closed Sat, Sun. **Admission** free. **Map** p309 C2.
Local entrepreneur and art lover Roger Ogden just couldn't stop buying works by Southern artists for his home. But even in the spacious rooms of his Uptown mansion, the wall space was finally filled, and Ogden had to decide what to do. The answer came in an imaginative gift of the paintings to the University of New Orleans, which was subsequently able to obtain use of a Romanesque Revival building by the noted architect HH Richardson to house the extensive collection. Construction has begun on the new Stephen Goldring Hall, which will house 20th-century works from the collection. Earlier paintings will fill the panelled and vaulted great room of the Taylor Library building. The opening of both buildings is scheduled for the autumn of 2001.

In the meantime, the museum has opened a temporary display in the Julia Street townhouse, where changing exhibitions of works from the collection will be on display. There is a small interpretive library on the premises that gives a taste of what study facilities the permanent facility will offer.

St Patrick's Cathedral

724 Camp Street, at Girod Street (525 4413). Bus 11 Magazine. **Open** *Mass* 11.30am, noon Mon-Fri; 4pm, 5.30pm Sat; 8.15am, 9.45am, 11.30am Sun. *Tours* by arrangement. **Map** p309 C1/2.
When waves of Irish immigrants flooded into the city during the early 19th century, one of their earliest moves was to construct a religious home. Most of the services in the city at that time were conducted in French and the Irish felt – and generally were – unwelcome. Work began on St Patrick's in 1838 to a design by architects James and Charles Dakin; its Gothic style was loosely based on York Minster in England. The building was eventually completed by James Gallier, the respected local architect responsible for Gallier Hall. The interior of the church is impressive, with vaulted ceilings and a dramatic altar. The elaborate murals were painted in 1840 by artist Leon Pomarade.

Sydney & Walda Besthoff Collection

K&B Plaza, 1055 St Charles Avenue, at Lee Circle (586 2007). St Charles Streetcar. **Open** 9am-5pm Mon-Fri; closed Sat, Sun. **Admission** free. **Map** p309 B2.
Now is the time to visit this remarkable collection of outdoor sculpture at Lee Circle, where downtown New Orleans begins to take on residential characteristics. Displayed on the plaza of one of the city's more noteworthy modern buildings, the collection also features works that are on view in the lobby and adjacent ground-floor rooms of the building. Presided over by curator Patricia Chandler, a Parisian with a background in both art and philosophy, the collection is constantly growing; Henry Moore, Barbara Hepworth, Isamu Noguchi and Alexander Calder are among the blue chip artists whose work you can currently enjoy on your own terms. Note, however, that many of the most significant pieces will move to the New Orleans Museum of Art's new sculpture garden, scheduled to open in the autumn of 2001 (*see page 111*).

World Trade Center

2 Canal Street, at the Mississippi River (Top of the Mart 522 9795). Bus 41 Canal. **Open** *Top of the Mart* 10am-11pm Mon-Thur; 10am-midnight Fri; 11am-1pm Sat; 2-11pm Sun. **Credit** AmEx, DC, Disc, MC, V. **Map** p309 C1/2.
It may be unattractive but this international-style high rise offers the best views of the city. From the Top of the Mart bar, on the 33rd floor, the contours of New Orleans and the Mississippi River are clearly visible, making the city's quirky street grid and geography understandable.

Uptown

Head upriver to the zoo and universities via the gracious Garden District to live life like the locals do.

Uptown is the term used to describe the entire area on the other side of the Pontchartrain Expressway from the CBD, an area that stretches upriver as far as the next huge bend in the Mississippi. It encompasses the Lower Garden District, the Garden District – one of the most picturesque neighbourhoods in the city – the student area around Loyola and Tulane Universities, and Audubon Park and Zoo.

People who live Uptown are accused of being snobs, but they came by their snobbery honestly. When Americans from the north-east began to migrate to New Orleans during the first half of the 19th century, they preferred to settle in what is now Uptown rather than in the French Quarter downtown or in the Creole Faubourg Marigny. The Uptown area, which was essentially rural, developed between 1840 and 1900 as the plantations between what is now Howard Avenue and the country community of Carrollton were broken up into suburbs.

The flavour of Uptown is most easily picked up by a drive or streetcar ride down St Charles Avenue. On the lake side of St Charles, dull, boxy buildings from the 1950s stand within a mile of opulent, ornate houses from the mid-19th century. These near-mansions exist as monuments to the wealthy, but stand in close proximity to such working-class institutions as Shoney's, Burger King and Walgreens.

Such franchises and commercial enterprises are found between the Pontchartrain Expressway and Jackson Avenue; the area between Jackson and Carrollton Avenues offers a trip back in time along a street almost untouched by the 20th century. It's worth remembering, however, that wood panelling and rows of beautiful houses do not indicate uniformly wealthy neighbourhoods. In many cases, humble cottages and shotgun houses are less than a block away.

Lower Garden District

Map p309

In the 1830s the area around Annunciation and Melpomene Streets – now known as the Lower Garden District – was a particularly desirable 'American' neighbourhood, but the opening of the Orleans Cotton Press in 1833 on Front Street (between Thalia and Terpsichore Streets) changed that. The combination of industrial activity and European immigrants who settled near the Mississippi kept the area from becoming as fashionable as people hoped. Estates were quickly surrounded by cottages on lots that had been divided and redivided. Working-class immigrants settled near the river because work was available there, just as they did in so many other US cities.

Today, one of the most striking aspects of the Lower Garden District is its treasure trove of beautiful Victorian homes. In the booming economy of the late 1990s these treasures were finally beginning to catch the attention of restoration-minded homeowners and developers. After years of decay, the neighbourhood appears to be on an upswing. Cafés are opening, businesses are sprouting and houses are practically being rebuilt to achieve their former grandeur. Still, the Lower Garden is an uneven neighbourhood with pockets of crime. Stay alert and avoid walking long stretches alone at night. This is one of those neighbourhoods where if it looks like trouble and feels like trouble, you're probably in trouble.

Nonetheless, the area has many attractions. One side effect of the poverty is that rents are low and the young and artistic have flocked here. The neighbourhood was dubbed the 'Hippest Neighborhood in America' a few years ago by a national literary magazine. The area is both beautiful and tawdry, a typical New Orleans state of affairs.

The stretch of St Charles Avenue that runs through the Lower Garden District is generally the most disappointing part of that grand avenue, so start by getting off it. Turn towards the river on any one of the cross-streets (many are named after Greek muses) and head towards **Magazine Street** (*see page 105*), which runs parallel to St Charles about eight blocks away.

Along the way the sidestreets are a lesson in architectural history. The houses were originally built further apart but over time other structures filled the gaps and the original antebellum plantation houses are now surrounded by Victorian and Gothic structures, with dashes of Italianate and Greek Revival style adding a touch of class.

Between St Charles and Magazine is **Coliseum Square**, roughly bounded by Camp and Coliseum Streets, Melpomene and

Felicity, which was the heart of a vital area in the mid-to late 1800s. Writer Grace King owned a house at No.1749 Coliseum Square and lived there until her death in 1932. The area declined in the 20th century and was dealt a near-mortal blow by the construction of a freeway entrance in the 1950s. The unusual twist to this 'old neighbourhood sacrificed to so called progress' story is that preservationists never gave up on the area and finally managed to get the ramp dismantled in 1995. In the few years since, Coliseum Square has made impressive advances in re-establishing itself as a desirable neighbourhood. Walking around the area now, it's hard to believe that the hideous freeway ramp ever existed.

The area may seem familiar to movie-goers. Coliseum Square and the surrounding blocks were used a great deal in the movie *Interview with the Vampire*.

A bit further down on the edge of the Warehouse District, at Camp and Terpsichore Streets, sits the statue of 19th-century philanthropist Margaret Gaffney Haughery. When erected in 1884, it was the first statue of a woman ever dedicated in the US. An Irish immigrant, Haughery was illiterate and widowed as a young woman, but she started her own bakery and dairy business that eventually made her wealthy. Once she was successful, Margaret dedicated her life to helping disadvantaged children and is credited with working with every charitable institution in the city that cared for orphans. When she died, she left her lifetime earnings to the charities she supported, signing her will with an 'X' since she never learned to write. Her statue portrays her seated with a small child at her side and is labelled simply 'Margaret', as the children called her.

Upriver on Constance Street is one of the city's most beautiful churches, **St Alphonsus** (*see below*). Built by the Redemptorist priests in 1858 to minister to the burgeoning Irish community, St Alphonsus is no longer a parish church. It has been saved from ruin by a cadre of devoted volunteers who want this to become a centre for Irish history and neighbourhood culture. With a new roof and structural repairs, the church is open to visitors two days a week and on special occasions. There's also a small museum about the Irish experience in New Orleans.

St Alphonsus Church & Cultural Center

2045 Constance Street, between Josephine & St Andrew Streets (456 5315/www.stalphonsus.org). Bus 11 Magazine. **Open** 10am-2pm Thur, Sat; closed Mon-Wed, Fri, Sun. **Map** pp306-7 B3.

Built in 1855-7 for the Irish Catholics, St Alphonsus is across the street from St Mary's Assumption (2052 Constance Street), home of the city's German Catholics, built in 1858. The absurdity of this situation is one of the interesting facts about St Alphonsus, a massive Romanesque structure. The church's 1866 frescos, though damaged, and stained glass windows are elaborate and impressive. These treasures, as well as the beautiful altars and other decor, were well on their way to total deterioration after the church closed in 1979 and the building was neglected until a group of preservationists toured the church in the 1990s. Now open for tours two days a week, the church's stained glass windows alone (from the German studios of FX Zettler) are worth the trip. The non-profit, all-volunteer group that maintains the church and lobbies for preservation funds has worked hard to build connections to the African-American community around St Alphonsus. The Mardi Gras Indians have performed here and the building has been the site of many community events. St Alphonsus is located hard by the St Thomas Housing Project: be alert to your surroundings and visit only when it's open and staffed.

Garden District

Map p309

While the poor and middle class settled near the river, the more affluent settled around Prytania Street, St Charles Avenue – which was called Nayades in the early 19th century – and Carondelet Street. Areas such as the Garden District – bordered by St Charles Avenue, Louisiana Avenue, Magazine Street and Jackson Avenue – were safely removed from commercial activity and the lots were still large enough to sustain substantial houses and tree-lined streets. The houses here are some of the most remarkable and some of the oldest in Uptown and the best way to see them is on foot. Where possible, walk around the houses to get a sense of their size because some are larger than they first appear, or have interesting features not visible at first glance. (There are a number of good walking tours of the district, including a free one led by rangers from the Jean Lafitte National Park office. For details, *see page 117*.)

On Prytania Street, facing the river and close to the streetcar stop at First Street, is the **Louise S McGehee School** (No.2343), a school for 'proper young ladies' built in 1872 by architect James Freret. Constructed in the Renaissance style, the mansion is notable for its Corinthian columns and for being one of the few houses in New Orleans with a basement (admittedly largely above ground), since the high water table usually makes them impractical. The interior can be seen in the movie *The Kingfish*, which stars John Goodman as flamboyant governor Huey P Long.

Greek Revival mansions line the leafy streets of the **Garden District**. *See p98.*

The oldest house in the Garden District is the **Toby House** (across the street at No.2340 Prytania), a plantation-style home built by a Philadelphian in 1838. Like many of the Garden District's residents, Thomas Toby was subject to the city's cycles of financial boom and bust; at one point, he was so financially strapped that he appealed to the Texas government for repayment of money he had advanced to the state in support of Texan independence.

Intricate ironwork is a particular feature of many Garden District homes. The cast-iron grillework at nearby **1331 First Street**, designed by architect Samuel Jamison, is worth a look, while a few doors down at **No.1315** is a Greek Revival house virtually unchanged from when it was built, down to the oak trees and its lush garden.

On the corner of First and Chestnut Streets is one of the Garden District's most visited sights: **Rosegate**, home of Anne Rice (*see page 40*) – one of several properties she owns in the Uptown–Garden District area.

Further along Chestnut Street (starting at No.2305 and continuing onwards) are the **Seven Sisters**, a row of seven shotgun houses that are dwarfed by the surrounding mansions. Popular legend has it that a father built these houses for his seven daughters to live in side by side, but it's more likely that a land speculator built them hoping someone would want to live in the ritzy Garden District badly enough to move into such small dwellings.

Back on First Street, continuing down towards Magazine, **No.1239** has rose-motif grillework on its gallery and a woven-iron fence – not the more common cast-or wrought-iron version. By today's standards, these houses were steals when they were built; in 1857 this one cost a mere $13,000.

One of the best examples of Greek Revival design in the area is also on First Street, at **No.1134**. Built in 1849, the property has clean, simple lines and a beautiful garden. Jefferson Davis, the president of the Confederacy, died here on 6 December 1889.

One block up from First Street, **1220 Phillip Street** was once the home of Isaac Delgado, founder of the Delgado Community College and an art collector whose bequest began the **New Orleans Museum of Art** in City Park (*see page 111*). The house has a semi-octagonal bay – an unusual feature at the time – and fluted Corinthian columns. **1238 Philip Street** is another Greek Revival house, built in 1853 with 14-foot (4.3-metre) ceilings – typical of the area. Both properties have fabulous gardens.

Peer through the dense shrubbery at **1213 Third Street** to glimpse an Italianate villa, a style that was much more common along the Atlantic seaboard in 1867, when it was built, than in New Orleans. The Italian villa at **1331 Third Street** was built by James Gallier Sr in 1853 for Michael Musson, once the city's postmaster and uncle of painter

Mi New Orleans es su New Orleans

Ask three residents of New Orleans why they live here and chances are at least one will say, 'I came to Mardi Gras [or Jazz Fest] one year and never left.' New Orleans seems to have a powerful pull on visitors that frequently translates into them moving across country to live in the city. This charisma isn't lost on the rich and famous either. They, too, are often swept away by New Orleans, buy a house and become part-time residents.

Trent Reznor, the oversoul of industrial rock, decided to live in New Orleans just as his Nine Inch Nails were hitting the big time in the mid-1990s. He bought a run-down antebellum mansion in the Garden District and

spent tons of money restoring it to its days of glory. Reznor also set up a state-of-the-art recording studio in an old funeral home on Magazine Street, spending two years there putting together his magnum opus, *Fragile* (1999). While he's not really the kind of guy who hangs out at local clubs and sits in on sets with blues guys, Reznor has been an active citizen. He turned over his house to the Preservation Resource Center for a fund-raiser (one of its most successful ever) and throws himself into Mardi Gras with vigour, riding in the Orpheus and Zulu parades. 'The thing about New Orleans is, nobody cares. They leave me alone, and they don't give a shit. It's not about who you are or what you're driving. And that appeals to me.'

Another naturalised New Orleanian is film director Francis Ford Coppola, who decided to buy a French Quarter house in order to break up long airline trips from California to Latin America, but now appears to be spending more time in New Orleans than it takes to change planes.

Uptown is home to the Californian–British couple of director Taylor Hackford and actress Helen Mirren. Hackford began coming to New Orleans to visit his college roommate more than 30 years ago and has been here off and on since. When he and Mirren became a couple Hackford introduced her to the city with positive results. They keep a low profile while in town but have said repeatedly that they consider New Orleans their 'real' home.

Edgar Degas. When he suffered financial reverses after the Civil War, the house was sold and Musson moved his family to a rented house on Esplanade, which his nephew visited in 1897 (*see page 113*). Its cast-iron galleries are among the most impressive in the area and the garden adjoining it is also fine. **No.1415 Third Street** is one of the largest houses in the Garden District. Constructed in the late 1850s for tobacco merchant Walter Robinson, it is also one of the most elaborate, with a wide gallery and central parapet.

Colonel Short's Villa (1448 Fourth Street) – named after its first owner, Robert Short – was built in 1859 for less than $25,000. This showpiece has remarkable ironwork on its columns, framed galleries and a cast-iron cornstalk fence that is its trademark. Walk around both sides to get the full effect. Close by, in the centre of the Garden District, is **Lafayette Cemetery No.1** (*see page 45*), across the street from the **Commander's Palace**, one of the best-known and most expensive restaurants in the city (*see page 142*),

John Goodman, film actor and one-time TV husband on *Roseanne*, lives in New Orleans with his wife and daughter. His wife is co-owner of a children's clothing store and Goodman regularly makes appearances at fundraising events and Louisiana- or New Orleans-oriented public service spots on TV.

Country singer Jerry Jeff Walker has a house in the French Quarter and so does rock singer Lenny Kravitz (pictured left). TV stars Delta Burke (*Designing Women*) and husband Gerald McRaney (*Simon & Simon*, *Promised Land*) have made New Orleans their family seat (Burke is popular locally, often seen walking her dog in the Quarter). Other big names spotted real-estate shopping in recent years include Courtney Love, Mick Jagger (pictured opposite) and OJ Simpson's attorney, Johnnie Cochran (a Louisiana native).

There is also the native son and daughter contingent of stars, most famously Anne Rice. Some high achievers like the Neville Brothers (all of them) have never left the city, while others come back regularly. Harry Connick Jr, one of the city's most famous sons, doesn't own a house here, but with his father, Harry Sr, the city's hard-driving district attorney, and other family members in town, Junior has plenty of options for a place to stay on his frequent visits.

New Orleans is also a place to catch ageing musicians who are coping with life out of the limelight. Barry Cowsill, a member of the teeny-bop '70s band the Cowsills, still pops up at Kerry Irish Pub now and again (see page 216), while Dave Sharp, formerly of the 1980s Welsh band the Alarm, performs with his new band, the Hard Travellers, in clubs around town. Also look out for solo performances by Alex Chilton, former lead singer of the '60s group the Boxtops, and cult figure Tav Falco of the Panther Burns (sometimes called the Jerry Lee Lewis of roots rock).

and the Rink shopping complex. Further down Washington Avenue, at the corner of Magazine Street, is the friendly and fun **New Orleans Fire Department Museum** (*see page 102*).

Back on Prytania Street is a rare Gothic Revival house at **No.2605** – note the pointed arches over the doors and windows of both the house and adjoining guest cottage. While the Gothic Revival style was popular in the North, it never caught on in New Orleans. The house was built in 1849 by James Gallier Sr on a commission from gambler Cuthbert Bullitt;

when Bullitt rejected the house (probably because of financial problems) it was snapped up by Londoner Charles Briggs.

Unfortunately, visiting the inside of a Garden District house is not often possible. There are no historic house museums in the area. House tours are the best bet, when private homes and gardens are opened to the public for a fee. Writer Anne Rice and Nine Inch Nails frontman Trent Reznor are among the civic-minded Garden District residents who have participated.

New Orleans Fire Department Museum

1135 Washington Avenue, at Magazine Street (896 4756). St Charles Streetcar/11 Magazine bus. **Open** 9am-4pm Mon-Fri; closed Sat, Sun. **Admission** free. **Map** p309 A/B3.

A fire station since 1850, this two-storey brick building on a quiet stretch of Washington Avenue now houses an array of vintage firefighting equipment and memorabilia, including an 1838 hand pump and an 1860 hand-drawn truck. Visitors are welcome to wander at will, but friendly, knowledgeable firefighters are on hand to act as guides.

Rosegate

1239 First Street, at Chestnut Street. St Charles Streetcar/11 Magazine bus. **Map** p309 B3.

Called Rosegate after the interwoven design of its striking iron fence, this house, built in 1857, is an official Orleans Parish landmark but the small, reverent crowds who gather on the sidewalks around it aren't interested in architecture. They've come to pay homage to Gothic author Anne Rice. Sadly, the house is not open to he public.

St Charles Avenue

Map pp306-7

The period between the 1860s and the 1880s saw the building of St Charles's signature mansions, such as the **Columns Hotel** (*see pages 64 and 161*), built in 1883 as a home for Simon Hernsheim, then one of the nation's most successful cigar manufacturers. Many houses were built by Northern entrepreneurs who used their business connections and the growth of New Orleans as a port to amass fortunes; as business picked up after the Civil War, so did development. In 1882 St Charles residents –

Streetcars ahead

The New Orleans streetcar is the most famous public conveyance in America. San Francisco has its cable cars but they haven't been immortalised by an artist on the scale of playwright Tennessee Williams. In his 1950 play *A Streetcar Named Desire* the streetcars are a powerful presence in dialogue and the clang-clang background noise. The Desire Streetcar is only a memory now but visitors are rarely disappointed in the New Orleans streetcars. The venerable St Charles line is the best tour bus imaginable for a drive-by look at the city's Garden District, while the smaller Riverfront line links the tourist-driven spots from the French Quarter to the Convention Center.

Locals grumble that the St Charles line has too many breakdowns and that the Riverfront line is so short one can walk it as fast as ride it, but the streetcars are as reliable as most public transport, while providing intangible aesthetic benefits. They look beautiful rumbling down the street, they never belch black smoke and fumes and they are a human-scale, comfortable environment inside. The mahogany seats, brass fittings and old-fashioned styling are a pleasure. Even the lack of air-conditioning is not a problem as the cars have windows that open, a rarity in many modern buses.

The New Orleans streetcar system has been around since 1835. The St Charles line was an important transport artery connecting the city of New Orleans with the surrounding area. In those days it was the New Orleans and Carrollton Railroad and its mule-drawn cars took passengers from New Orleans to the tiny burgs of Lafayette, Jefferson City and Carrollton. That may not seem far today, now that the town of Carrollton is merely part of Uptown and Jefferson City just a suburb, but back then it was a day-long trip. Things continued that way for nearly 60 years, when the railroad line was expanded and converted to electricity in 1893 and the streetcars came into operation. Here and there throughout the city (look along the brick sections of Royal Street), remnants of old car tracks give some indication of how pervasive the network once was.

As with most US cities, streetcars began giving way to buses in the 1920s and '30s, and public transport took a serious dive in the post-World War II era as automobiles became almost universal. New Orleans, as in all things, held on to the old ways longer than most, only giving up the vital Canal Street line in 1964. By that time there was a definite shift in attitudes about the importance and meaning of 'progress' and many citizens started working to reverse the trend away from streetcars and to save what was left. In the 1980s the St Charles line was joined by the Riverfront line, which proved extremely popular. Encouraged, transport planners and quality of life advocates began pushing for reinstatement

tired of the swampy mess created by heavy rain – paid to have the avenue paved; it was one of the first asphalt streets in America.

While New Orleans was expanding towards Carrollton, the Carrollton community was expanding along St Charles Avenue towards New Orleans, although at a slower pace. As the 19th century closed, development from each end had begun to meet and surround **Audubon Park** (*see page 109*).

A good way to explore the avenue is to take the **St Charles Streetcar** from the CBD. You can see how the street developed historically from Canal Street towards Carrollton Avenue, and the streetcar's leisurely pace is ideal for picking out the sights. The whole journey will take about 45 minutes (if you don't get off) and costs $1.25; pay $4 for an all-day pass and you can jump on and off.

The section of St Charles after **Lee Circle** (*see page 91*) is not particularly interesting until you reach Josephine Street, where a glass and iron building looks painfully out of place amid the surrounding mansions. This landmark is, in fact, the restaurant from the Eiffel Tower in Paris, which was broken down, shipped in pieces to New Orleans and reconstructed on St Charles Avenue. It is now the location of the **Red Room** (*see page 222*), a plush music club where both the chi-chi and lounge kids can feel at home.

A couple of blocks later, on the left (at No.4010), is **Sully House**, built by Thomas Sully, one of the city's most prominent architects, in the late 1800s. He built this modest Queen Anne house for his family. Though many of his houses are no longer standing, he was one of the architects who

of the Canal Street line. Happily, they have been successful and streetcars are expected to return to Canal Street late in 2001. They will look like the familiar St Charles cars, having been built in New Orleans by the Rapid Transit Authority, but they'll include modern amenities such as air-conditioning and wheelchair lifts (already in operation on the Riverfront cars). A spur line will run from the end of the Canal Street line to City Park, simplifying travel from the centre of town to the New Orleans Museum of Art and other attractions at the park. There are also plans for reviving the Desire Street line but there's

also a $65 million pricetag ($154 million for the Canal streetcars) to be negotiated.

In the meantime, the St Charles line is still one of the best (and at $1.25 a trip, the cheapest) ways to see great chunks of New Orleans. If you're completely enthralled with the streetcars, you can rent them for a private party (starting at about $200) and cruise down St Charles Avenue with just your friends, or maybe fill up with the characters you meet along the line. The seats will be hard, the breeze will be good and you'll be part of the New Orleans triumph of tradition over 'progress'.

helped create the look that St Charles Avenue is famous for. The grander **Castle's House** (further along at 6000 St Charles) was also built by Sully and is more typical of his work.

At Napoleon Avenue, detour down the street toward the river. At 1314 Napoleon is **St Elizabeth's Orphanage**, an 1860s-era complex. Founded by the Daughters of Charity of St Vincent de Paul, the girls' orphanage operated well into the 20th century. Today, it's owned by writer Anne Rice, who uses it as a gallery and meeting space (*see page 105; see also page 209*). It's one of the few historic buildings in the Uptown–Garden District area regularly open to the public. Here you'll see Anne Rice's enormous doll collection and paintings by her husband, Stan Rice.

Across Napoleon Avenue and on the right is the distinctive **Sacred Heart Academy** (4521 St Charles Avenue). It's a Catholic girls' school and one of the more formal-looking buildings on a very formal street. Further along, on the left, at the junction with Soniat Street, is the **Milton Latter Memorial Library** (*see below*), where one of the biggest second-hand book sales in the city is held every year. One of the more unusual St Charles Avenue houses is at No.5809. Known

as the **Wedding Cake House**, the building barely toes the line between extravagant and over-the-top. No architectural ornament, flourish or geegaw has been left out, with the possible exception of balloons decorated with Disney figures.

Other notable buildings include the **Touro Synagogue** (No.4224), named after philanthropist Judah Touro, son of a Rhode Island rabbi. During Mardi Gras, its steps become a playground for kids waiting for parades to pass (*see page 285*). Also look out for the **Brown House** (No.4717), built in 1905 by cotton magnate WP Brown as a wedding gift for his wife, and the **Orleans Club** (No.5005), which was built just after the Civil War.

Milton Latter Memorial Library

5120 St Charles Avenue, at Soniat Street (596 2625/ www.gnofn.org/~nopl/info/branches/latter/latter.htm). St Charles Streetcar. **Open** 11am-6pm Mon-Thur; 11am-5pm Sat; closed Fri, Sun. **Admission** free. **Map** pp306-7 C9.

A 1907 stone mansion, once the home of pioneer aviator Harry Williams and his wife Marguerite Clark, star of silent films. The neo-Italianate house is now the Uptown branch of the public library. It's a good spot to take a break while exploring the

Magazine Street takes its name from the French 'street of shops', but...

...it's not all spend, spend, spend.

Sightseeing

neighbourhood and is the only grand old house on St Charles with easy public access. The chandeliers and beautiful decorative work are clues to the scale and style of other St Charles homes, although much of the interior has been massively remodelled to accommodate the library's needs.

St Elizabeth's Orphanage

1314 Napoleon Avenue (899 6450/ www.annerice.com). St Charles Streetcar. **Open** *Tours* 11am, 1pm, 3pm daily. **Admission** *Suggested donation* $7; $5 concessions.
Dating from 1865, with additions in the 1880s, St Elizabeth's was a home for orphaned girls operated by Catholic nuns. When Anne Rice aquired it in the 1990s, it was a white elephant. Huge (55,000 sq. feet/5115 sq. metres) but in the middle of a residential district, there didn't seem to be any clear use for the place. Rice and her husband have turned it into galleries for her doll collection (more than 800) and his paintings (a changing selection). Other events have been held here such as Rice's Halloween party, but the Uptown neighbours are leery of crowds and noise and have effectively limited the activities that can be held here. Tours are given daily but are strictly on the specified hour so plan your arrival time.

Magazine Street

Map pp306-7

Translating from the French as 'street of shops', Magazine Street was for many years New Orleans's central street of commerce. Today, it is a long, winding road, banked on both sides with colourful shops from its start

at Canal Street on the edge of the French Quarter all the way Uptown, past the zoo in Audubon Park, to River Road.

The street became the centre of Irish activity in the 19th century, and part of the neighbourhood on the river side of Magazine is still known as the Irish Channel. The homes in the Irish Channel – originally those of the labouring classes – are substantially different from those on the lake side of Magazine Street. They are generally smaller, and narrow 'shotgun' houses are plentiful.

Between the Warehouse District and Sophie Wright Place, Magazine has remained almost unchanged during the last couple of decades. There are signs that this end of the street (in the Lower Garden District) is moving in the gentrification direction. **Rue de la Course** coffeehouse at the corner of Race Street (*see page 140*) and the **Nine Muses Café** (1418 Magazine Street, 527 0088) are charming, small-scale spots (there's a much larger Rue de la Course near Louisiana Avenue). Despite its forlorn spots, there are also little hotels and B&Bs sprouting in the neighbourhood. Many large, fairly intact properties fairly beg rehabbers to turn them into inns. Most noticeable is the former St Vincent's Orphanage, now reworked into **St Vincent's Guesthouse** (*see page 67*).

Serious shopping begins where St Mary and Felicity Streets cross Magazine, running from the 1800 block to Jackson Avenue on the edge of the Garden District. **Jim Russell Records**, at 1837 Magazine Street, is a good place to look for old records and second-hand CDs. No one has seen this much vinyl since disco was king (*see page 186*). **OJ Hooter Furniture** (1938 Magazine Street, 522 5167) is one of those in-between stores where, on a good day, lucky deals can be found. The store rambles over two storeys and tens of thousands of square feet of high quality mahogany and attic junk. **House of Lounge** at No.2044 is a must for anyone with retro-funk taste in lingerie and accessories (*see page178*), while **Jim Smiley Vintage Clothing** at No.2001 has extremely fine pieces, for both men and women, from the Victorian to the 1960s eras (*see page 180* **All dressed up**). Serious antiques are to be found at **Bush Antiques** (No.2109) and **Bep's Antiques** (No.2051; for both, *see page 168*), and at several other stops here. For pure fun, visit artist-raconteur Simon Harteveld, a French chef turned naïve painter, who will sell you one of his signs ('Home Sweet Home'), refinish your furniture or paint whatever you want (2126 Magazine Street, 561 0088).

Unlike the French Quarter, Uptown doesn't have two or three eateries on every block. This area has two very good places for lunch or dinner, **Juan's Flying Burritos** at No.2018, which serves some of the city's best Mexican food (*see page 137*), and **Café Roma** (1901 Sophie Wright Place, 524 2419), where you'll find rich pasta dishes and good salads.

The next concentration of shops begins in the 2900 block skirting the southern edge of the Garden District. **Belladonna Day Spa** (No.2900, 891 4393) is the place of choice for massage, manicures and other kinds of pampering. The atmosphere is California Zen casual with an overlay of Uptown preciousness. A little further up the street, **George Herget Books** (No.3109) is a city landmark, a second-hand bookshop owned and staffed by passionate book lovers, the kind of place that's becoming all too rare in the era of corporate bookselling (*see page 173*). At No.3128 the **Rue de la Course** café is undergraduate central with laptops, study guides and textbooks spread out over almost every table. It's a good place to hang out and it's fairly easy to strike up conversations with the locals, most of whom are eager to take a break from the books. The floor-to-ceiling bulletin board at the rear of the café is one of the best places to find out about music, meetings and cheap apartment sublets (*see page 140*).

In the 3200 block of Magazine, there's a mass of bars and restaurants that makes this area popular with college students and twentysomethings. On many weekend evenings there's a street-party atmosphere as happy people move from bar to bar. **Semolina** (3242 Magazine Street, 895 4260/www.semolina.com)

is a local pasta chain with moderate prices and equally moderate food, but it's full on week nights. Next door is the **Mystic Café** (3244 Magazine Street, 895 7272), a Mediterranean-oriented dining room with a friendly bar. In the same block is the **Bulldog** (*see page 158*), a dive that was renovated into a beers-of-the-world joint. As the night wears on, it becomes more of a college hangout and its narrowness can be a problem for the claustrophobic, but those who want to be where the action is will love it. Diagonally across the street is another newish joint, the **Balcony Bar** (*see page 157*), named, well, after its balcony.

As Magazine Street heads into Uptown, you'll find plenty of small boutiques with very focused points of view. Also on this route, unmarked in any way, is Trent Reznor's **Nothing Studio & Records**. The Nine Inch Nails wizard's studio and offices are in a fortress-looking grey masonry building at the corner of Magazine and Jena Streets, across from Igor's Buddha Belly. The studio was a mortuary in another life and now, naturally, has state-of-the-art security. The building also has the intriguing feature of one-way windows; Reznor and company can look out while no one can see in.

Around the Magazine–Jefferson Avenue crossroads there's another slacker centre with four coffeehouses within a four block area. Representatives of two local chains are in the 5400 block where **PJ's Coffee & Tea** on the river side of the street is faced by **CC's Gourmet Coffee House** on the lake side (for both, *see page 140*). At Magazine and Nashville, **Café Luna** (802½ Nashville Avenue, 899 3723), one of the few independent coffeehouses in New Orleans, looks across at **Starbucks**, which has only recently moved into New Orleans. With a bookstore (**Beaucoup Books**; *see page 172*) and a day spa (**Earth Savers**; *see page 184*) also in the neighbourhood, it's a simple matter for one to drift from coffeehouse to coffeehouse, getting to know the locals and reading New Orleans novels (a speciality of Beaucoup).

Riverbend

Map pp306-7

Riverbend, based around Oak Street and S Carrollton Avenue where the streetcar turns off St Charles Avenue, was originally a cottage community called Carrollton that existed outside the city. Now an area of shops and bars, it caters primarily for Loyola and Tulane university students.

Down where Carrollton meets the levee, **Cooter Brown's** (*see page 160*) is equally known for its wide selection of beers and cheese fries as it is for the number of guys

The majestic Mississippi at **Riverbend**.

wearing baseball caps there. Further up
Carrollton, at St Charles, is the famous
Camellia Grill (*see page 138*), perhaps the
best known diner in the city. When customers
want a slice of pie heated up, it goes on the
grill just like everything else. It's a local
institution not to be missed by those
whose diet and constitution can handle it.

Most of Oak Street, a few blocks up
S Carrollton, feels like small-town America,
with the Whitney bank clock at the corner
as a reminder of the days when people used to
meet under the Whitney clock. Further up the
street is the **Maple Leaf Bar** (*see page 223*), a
watering hole by day but one of the best places
in town for blues and zydeco at night.

The Universities

Map pp306-7

Across St Charles Avenue from Audubon Park,
Tulane University and **Loyola University**
sit next to each other, and because they are so
close together and were built around the same
time, they look like one large campus. Though
the area they occupy might look compact from
St Charles Avenue, this is deceptive: the
campuses reach almost to Claiborne Avenue.

Loyola was founded by the Jesuits, who
opened the College of Immaculate Conception
downtown in 1849. In 1904 the order opened a
second university on the current site on St
Charles and in 1911 united the two schools at
the St Charles address. The campus is
dominated by the Gothic **Holy Name of
Jesus Church**, built in 1914.

Tulane came about through a gift of
wealthy New Orleans businessman Paul
Tulane, in 1883. He wanted to fund a technical
school to train mechanics but in typical
Louisiana style politicians saw this windfall
as a chance to revive the bankrupt University
of Louisiana. Tulane was talked into the deal
and the state university was rechristened
'Tulane' and given a second chance. The
ramshackle downtown campus was
abandoned in 1888 for a more spacious one
Uptown, on the site of a former sugarcane
plantation on the lake side of St Charles
Avenue. Since then, Tulane has expanded
north past Willow Street and the heart of
the campus is now on Freret Street near
Broadway. The campus architecture is
generally undistinguished but a walk
through it is a pleasant diversion.

The most interesting feature of the Tulane
campus is probably its impressive research
collections. The University is home to the
Amistad Research Center, one of the most
important collections of African-American
history in the world. The stacks, with more
than ten million documents, are available only
to scholars but the modest reading room has
changing displays from the collection. Of
equal importance, however, is the Amistad art
collection, which includes major works by
Jacob Lawrence, Henry O Tanner, Elizabeth
Catlett and other important black artists.
Some paintings and sculpture are always on
display and visitors are free to walk through
the offices looking at the work.

Tulane also houses the **Howard-Tilton Memorial Library**. This remarkable collection includes the South-eastern Architectural Archive, dedicated to the architecture of New Orleans and the Gulf South, and the William Ransom Hogan Archive of New Orleans Jazz, devoted to preserving the history of jazz music. The **Newcomb Art Gallery**, located in the Woldenberg Art Center on campus, is a hidden jewel. There are also exhibitions at the nearby School of Architecture, in Gibson Hall, the Romanesque building that greets visitors at the St. Charles Avenue entrance to the campus.

Unlike campus areas in other college cities, the Tulane/Loyola district has not spawned any sort of commercial area catering to the young and groovy. Of the three places where students traditionally waste their student loans – bookshops, record shops and bars – only bars flourish in this neighbourhood, and most of those are party gladiator havens, hardly places for young rebels to cultivate their dissatisfaction with society at large.

Popular among them are **The Boot**, **Phillip's** and **TJ Quills** (for all, *see chapter* **Bars**). What rebels do exist can be found writing in expensive hardback notebooks at the coffeeshops on Maple Street, such as **PJ's Coffee & Tea** (*see page 105*).

Perhaps the only true counterculture outpost is the **Mushroom** record shop (*see page 187*), upstairs from the Boot. Countless second-hand record and CD stores have opened and closed on Maple Street, but only Mushroom has survived.

The **Maple Street Book Shop** (*see page 173*) is the only independent bookstore here, but it lives in spite of students, who show no signs of being interested in reading. It's particularly good on local poetry and its children's shop next door is one of the better places for kids' books in the city. For more on university life, *see page 286*.

Loyola University Campus

Loyola University New Orleans
6363 St Charles Avenue, at Calhoun Street (865 2011/www.loyno.edu). St Charles Streetcar. **Open** *Offices* 8.30am-4.45pm Mon-Fri; closed Sat, Sun. **Map** pp306-7 B/C8.

Loyola University Art Gallery
Collins C Diboll Art Gallery, 4th Floor, Monroe Library, Loyola University Campus, at Loyola & Calhoun Streets (864 7055). **Open** 11am-4pm Mon-Fri; closed Sat, Sun. **Admission** free.

With the opening of the Loyola University Art Gallery in 1999, a trip to the adjoining Tulane-Loyola campuses has become a truly worthwhile venture. Complementing Tulane's Newcomb Gallery, Loyola's new facility, perched high atop the university's stunning new library, offers not only regularly changing exhibitions of faculty, student and local art work, but also an exceptional view over the Uptown landscape through the tall neo-Gothic bay windows that dot the attractive façade. On permanent display is a collection of archival material from the university's Brother Cornet collection, including numerous photographs of his years in the Congo and several of the important African artefacts that he accumulated. The

Newcomb Art Gallery. *See p109.*

university is planning to use this collection as the basis of a growing display of African artefacts donated by local patrons.

Tulane University Campus

Tulane University
6823 St Charles Avenue, at Audubon Park (865 5000/www.tulane.edu). St Charles Streetcar. **Open** *Offices* 8.30am-5pm Mon-Fri; closed Sat, Sun. **Map** pp306-7 B/C8.

Amistad Research Center
Tilton Hall, Tulane University Campus, at St Charles Avenue (865 5535/fax 865 5580/ www.tulane.edu/~amistad). **Open** 9am-4.30pm Mon-Sat; closed Sun. **Admission** free.

Howard-Tilton Memorial Library
7001 Freret Street, at Audubon Street (865 5605). Bus 15 Freret, 22 Broadway. **Open** 8am-12.45pm Mon-Thur; 8-10.45am Fri; 8am-8.45pm Sat; 10am-12.45pm Sun.* **Admission** free.

Newcomb Art Gallery
Woldenberg Art Center, Tulane University campus, at Willow Street (865 5328/ www.tulane.edu/~gallery). St Charles Streetcar. **Open** 10am-5pm Mon-Fri; noon-5pm Sat, Sun. **Admission** free.
Although gallery director Erik Neil is an art historian whose speciality is Renaissance and baroque sculpture, his interests leap from African art to 18th-century French gardens. His tenure promises a wide spectrum of theme-directed exhibitions in the tranquil, naturally lit galleries on the oak-tree-lined Newcomb campus of Tulane University. The entrance to the Woldenberg Art Center's gallery features two large Tiffany windows, and others are on view in nearby Newcomb Chapel. On permanent display are pieces of Newcomb pottery, the art nouveau creations of Newcomb professors and students between the turn of the 19th century and World War II.

Audubon Park & Zoo

Map pp306-7
The area now known as Audubon Park was originally the Foucher plantation, but it was bought by the city and named Upper City Park in 1871. In 1886 it was renamed Audubon Park after the Haitian-born painter and ornithologist John James Audubon, who lived in New Orleans in the 1820s. At the time it extended from the river, through what is now Audubon Zoo and across St Charles Avenue to the current site of Tulane University and Audubon Place. Much of the building and development of the park was carried out for the 1884 Cotton Centennial Exposition, though none of the original buildings has survived.

Today, the park also includes a small golf course, riding stables and the zoo. Winding through these grounds is over a mile of path on which no one ever died of loneliness. Those grim, gaunt runners who seem to embrace their solitude find more emotionally barren places to run because Audubon's path is used by walkers, runners, Rollerbladers and cyclists who like the shade and the fact that there are other people around. Sadly, there is no longer a rental outlet for bikes or skates.

Audubon Golf Course has been a source of controversy at times: some argue that an exclusive sport has no place in such an egalitarian space as a public park and that the land could be better used. But those who complain of elitism cannot have played the course, paid its dirt-cheap green fees or waited behind people who are picking up clubs for the first time and beer for the tenth time that day. Audubon is a part of the wild and woolly world of public golf, where no swing is too shameful and no place is safe (*see page 235*). Even sitting watching the action, from one of the many benches, you're guaranteed some splendid entertainment.

Audubon Zoo, a short walk through the park from the St Charles Streetcar stop, is generally ranked among the top zoos in the US. 'Zoo' here doesn't mean just lions and tigers and bears. The place has wisely adopted a regional focus, promoting Louisiana swamps as a land as exotic as any African savannah. In fact, the meticulously recreated six-and-a-half-acre (two-and-a-half-hectare) swamp installation, complete with alligators and a Cajun fishing camp, has been known to dissuade visitors from bothering to take a fully fledged swamp tour. Also popular are the Embracable Zoo, which encourages visitors to make contact with domestic animals; and the sea lion show in a lovely 1920s outdoor amphitheatre.

Audubon Park
From St Charles Avenue to Mississippi River, between Walnut Street & Exposition Boulevard (information 581 4629/1-800 774 7394/Audubon Park Golf Course 865 8260/Cascade Stables 891 2246/www.auduboninstitute.org). St Charles Streetcar/11 Magazine bus. **Open** 6am-10pm daily. **Admission** free. **Map** pp306-7 A/B 9/10.

Audubon Zoo
6500 Magazine Street, Audubon Park (581 4629/ 1-800 774 7394). St Charles Streetcar/11 Magazine bus. **Open** *Winter* 9.30am-5pm daily. *Summer* 9.30am-6pm daily. **Admission** $9; $4.75-$5.75 concessions. **Credit** AmEx, MC, V. **Map** pp306-7 B9.
A free shuttle bus runs from the St Charles Streetcar stop to the zoo and you can take a riverboat back to the Aquarium and IMAX stop.

Mid City & Beyond

North towards Lake Pontchartrain are the charming City Park and historic-turned-suburban residential areas.

This is one of the sections of the city that most tourists overlook, and more's the pity. The area of town known as Mid City stretches from the edge of the French Quarter to Lake Pontchartrain, and its neighbourhoods are considered by many to be closest in feel to the old New Orleans. Until the mid 19th-century, Mid City was dominated by swamps and a handful of plantations. Bienville established one of the earliest settlements at Bayou St John, which he named after his patron saint. Many of the streets here are built on top of the original dirt trails used by settlers and Indians; Bayou Road, for example, sits on top of an ancient Indian trail that led from Bayou St John to the Mississippi River.

Around the time of the Civil War, plantation owner John McDonough donated his massive property to the city. His one condition was that it be used to provide schools for the city's poor children. To a large extent the city followed his instructions and many schools in town are still named after the antebellum philanthropist, but the city also twisted the law in its own favour, and, with the help of some sympathetic jurisprudence, turned much of McDonough's property into City Park. Once the city had taken over the property, the process of draining the swamps to make the land usable accelerated and over the next half-century more and more property in the area dried out sufficiently to become the residential neighbourhoods that exist today.

Mid City is large, but it's possible to explore sections of it on foot. The most useful bus is 48 Esplanade, which goes from the French Quarter along Esplanade Avenue to the foot of City Park.

City Park

Map p308

City Park (482 4888/www.neworleans.com/citypark) is the fourth largest urban park in the US. Its 1,400 acres (567 hectares) are permeated by streams and bayous crossed with charming, arched bridges under the shade of enormous oaks, many draped in Spanish moss, providing a luxuriant green canopy for most of the park. Some of the trees are believed to be 1,000 years old. Swans and ducks paddle on its waterways,

as do visitors who rent canoes and boats. The network of bayous give the park the feel of an island, a kind of Neverland.

Most of the park's structures and many of its sculptured waterways were constructed as part of the federal Works Project Administration (WPA) put into place by President Franklin Delano Roosevelt to provide jobs during the

City Park, the Neverland of New Orleans.

Depression. WPA artists designed the bridges and details, while hundreds of construction workers put it all together. The WPA insignia can still be seen on many structures and the main drive through the park is still called Roosevelt Drive.

Today, City Park contains riding stables, baseball diamonds and lagoons for boating and fishing, all open to the public. The **Bayou Oaks Golf Course** has four 18-hole courses as well as a driving range, while the **Tennis Center** has lit courts and professional staff who are available for lessons. The **City Park Stables** offer trail rides and riding lessons (for all, *see chapter* **Sport & Fitness**). There's even a tiny amusement park, **Carousel Gardens** (*see page 112*), with a 100-year-old carousel. The lush **Botanical Gardens** adjoin **Storyland**, a colourful children's playground (*see page 112*).

Also inside City Park, on Collins Diboll Circle near the Esplanade Avenue entrance, is the **New Orleans Museum of Art**. While NOMA is not large, it has a good collection, including a valuable Degas completed while the painter was living in New Orleans in 1872. It also hosts touring exhibitions. The 1911 building itself is beautiful and its wide front porch, with massive columns, is a cool place to rest during a walking tour. There aren't many cafés or fast food places around the perimeter of the park, so the museum café is the best place to eat.

Buses 46 City Park, 48 Esplanade and 90 Carrollton all stop at the park. Admission is free, but you have to pay for some of the facilities. For more information about where things are and what to do, visit the Casino Building at the centre of the park near the tennis courts. The park is reasonably safe but night-time visits are not a good idea.

Botanical Gardens

Victory Avenue, southern end of City Park (483 9386/www.neworleans.com/citypark). Bus 46 City Park, 48 Esplanade, 90 Carrollton. **Open** 10am-4.30pm Tue-Sun; closed Mon. **Admission** $3; $1 concessions; free under-5s. **No credit cards. Map** p308 D4.

A ten-acre (four-hectare) plot including a conservatory, gift shop and garden study centre. Visitors are free to walk through the grounds; there are no guided tours but the garden staff and volunteers are friendly, plant-loving types who enjoy talking about the gardens. Especially lovely are the rose garden and the azalea and camellia garden.

New Orleans Museum of Art

1 Collins Diboll Circle, City Park (488 2631/www.noma.org). Bus 46 City Park, 48 Esplanade, 90 Carrollton. **Open** 10am-5pm Tue-Sun; closed Mon. **Admission** $6; $3-$5 concessions; free under-3s. Free to Louisiana residents with ID 10am-noon Thur. **Credit** AmEx, Disc, MC, V. **Map** p308 E4.

The grande dame of the city's art institutions, New Orleans Museum of Art owes its existence to the philanthropist Isaac Delgado, who constructed the building in 1911 but neglected to provide an endowment. Under the leadership of director John Bullard, who is currently approaching his fourth decade in the position, the museum has brought a succession of notable blockbusters to the city, constructed new galleries and built an endowment for the future. Like most metropolitan museums of art, NOMA features a diverse array of arts, including regional furniture; Edgar Degas' portrait of his cousin Estelle Musson, which was painted during a visit to New Orleans in 1872; a representative selection of great European paintings; one of the first museum collections of photography; strong Asian, African and Pre-Columbian galleries; and one of the country's most impressive glass and decorative arts collections. Not to be missed is the museum's Fabergé gallery, based on the spectacular collection of New Orleanian Matilda Geddings Gray. A selection of paintings from the National Gallery of Scotland and an exhibition of works by female Impressionist Berthe Morisot are NOMA's big shows for late 2001 and 2002 and the opening of the museum's new sculpture garden, which will incorporate major pieces from the Sydney and Walda Besthoff Collection (*see p96*), will take centre stage in autumn 2001.

A captivating piece on show at the **New Orleans Museum of Art**.

Sightseeing

Storyland & Carousel Gardens

Victory Avenue, southern end of City Park (483 9381/carousel 483 9356). **Open** *Storyland* 10am-2.30pm Mon-Fri; 10.30am-4.30pm Sat, Sun. *Carousel Gardens* 10am-2.30pm Wed-Fri; 11am-5.30pm Sat, Sun; closed Mon, Tue. **Admission** *Storyland* $2; free under-2s. *Carousel Gardens* $1; free under-2s; plus $8 for unlimited rides. **No credit cards.** **Map** p308 D4.

This pre-Disney children's playground, with its storybook characters and a small amusement park next door with a rare wooden carousel, are great favourites with children. They're attractive to grown-up children, too, who love the tranquil beauty of the carousel (called 'the flying horses' by New Orleanians) and the unfrenzied attitude of Storyland. The kiddie park hasn't been kept up as well as it might have been, but some people actually enjoy the shabbiness as a respite from theme park perkiness.

Top five Monuments

New Orleans is crammed with monuments. The urge to memorialise and adulate began early and continues without pause. Here are some of the most intriguing.

Winston Churchill

Since 1977 a bronze Winston Churchill has presided over the foot of Poydras Street, arm raised, cigar in place. The Churchill statue was a gift from the Hilton Hotel for reasons that remain unclear.

Immigrants

On the riverside at Woldenberg Park a European immigrant family in white marble honours the thousands who poured through the port of New Orleans in the 19th century.

Joan of Arc

The Maid of Orleans is a new French Quarter landmark, refurbished with gold leaf and moved in 1999 to a tiny pocket park where Decatur, North Peters and St Philip Street meet. The statue was a gift from France in 1958.

Professor Longhair

Master of the New Orleans funk piano, the late Henry Roeland Byrd continues to watch over his Uptown music club, Tipitina's (see page 224).

Ignatius Reilly

The slovenly hero of the great New Orleans novel, *A Confederacy of Dunces*, is now permanently anchored to one of his lurking places, 819 Canal Street.

The **Degas House**. *See p113.*

Around Esplanade Avenue

Map p308

From Esplanade Avenue at the foot of City Park, head past the large statue of beloved local Confederate General PGT Beauregard at the park gates to Bayou St John, the inlet that runs along the west side of the park from Lake Pontchartrain. This is the original bayou where early settlers set up camp, where there are now a number of beautiful houses in a variety of local architectural styles. Bayou St John is a pleasant place to linger and is designed for leisurely reflection with regular concrete staircases leading down to the water.

Walk alongside the bayou and after several blocks you will arrive at **Pitot House Museum** (*see page 113*). Constructed in the late 18th century in typical West Indies style, it has period furnishings that offer a realistic look at how the early French residents lived.

Back on Esplanade Avenue, about two blocks away from Bayou St John, is **St Louis Cemetery No.3** (*see page 45*), and nearby is the **Fair Grounds Racecourse**, New Orleans's horse racing track, which opened in 1872 (*see page 233*).

Just a few blocks further along tree-lined Esplanade is a small collection of charming restaurants, coffee shops and boutiques. **Whole Foods Market** (*see page 182*) is a large, progressive health food store with a produce section, freshly baked goods and a deli with an emphasis on vegetarian food. Nearby is **Café Degas**, which specialises in French food at reasonable prices. On sunny days, its patio is a great place to while away an hour or so (*see page 148*). Around the corner is the coffeehouse **True Brew** (3133 Ponce de Leon Street, 947 3948), a good spot to load up with gourmet coffees and pastries.

More beautiful houses may be seen further along Esplanade Avenue, although after about ten blocks the neighbourhood gets noticeably dodgy, and travelling by car or bus is highly recommended. But first, note 2306 Esplanade, known as the **Degas House**, where Edgar Degas stayed during his brief visit to New Orleans in the 1870s (*see page 68; see also* *below*). At the end of the same block, at the intersection of Esplanade Avenue and Bayou Road in a triangular-shaped park, is a monument called *The Goddess of History: Genius of Peace*. The original statue was donated to the city by a wealthy local, George H Dunbar, but was destroyed in 1938. The existing figure is an exact replica.

Degas House

2306 Esplanade Avenue, at Tonti Street (821 5009/ www.degashouse.com). Bus 48 Esplanade. **Open** phone for details of tours. **Map** p308 F5.

The Degas House is an oddity for more than just its famous resident. Built in 1852, the Italianate structure puzzled architectural historians for years because it's substantially different from its representation in paintings at the time. The answer seems to be that the house was split in two at some point and No.2306 is just one wing of the rambling villa that housed an extended family. This was the home of the Mussons, a distinguished French Creole family. Degas' mother was raised in New Orleans but married in France where her son was born. In 1872-3 Degas decided to visit the American branch of his family. His mother had died while he was a child but there were warm ties to her family. In fact, some of the Musson cousins sat out the Civil War in France with their Degas relatives. René, Degas' impulsive younger brother, married their first cousin, Estelle Musson, and settled in New Orleans. Edgar Degas pined for Paris during his whole visit. He felt the semi-tropical sun was bad for his eyes and the city's pleasures were distinctly provincial. He wrote plaintively to his dealer in Paris that there was too much to paint in New Orleans. Their mutual friend Manet, he said, would know what to do with this exotic place. The family solidarity that seemed so hopeful during Degas' visit soon crumbled. Unreliable René abandoned Estelle (who was blind) and their children to elope with another woman to France. Estelle's father (brother of Edgar Degas' mother) adopted her children and changed their name to Musson, wiping out the Degas name in the New World. A local couple bought what was still called the Musson house in the 1990s, restored it and turned it into a B&B (*see p68*). The house is open to the public, although there is little to see directly connected to Degas' visit or even the Musson family. The owners have hung reproductions of Degas' major works in the house, turning it into a kind of Degas gallery.

Fair Grounds Racecourse

1751 Gentilly Boulevard, near Esplanade Avenue (944 5515/www.fgno.com). Bus 48 Esplanade. **Open** Mon, Thur-Sun (phone for details); closed Tue, Wed. **Map** p308 E/F5.

The Fair Grounds isn't one of America's top tracks but in many respects it is one of the most successful. The disastrous clubhouse fire of 1993 didn't put a stop to the racing; a new grandstand was built and opened in 1997. With horse racing marginalised in

many states because of the expansion of the gambling industry, the Fair Grounds fire proved how committed New Orleanians are to their ponies. The importance of the Fair Grounds as an inner-city park and centre has been solidified by the creative use of the complex for Jazz Fest every spring. The racing season, which runs from November to March, offers a haven during stressful times; many locals go to the races on Thanksgiving Day to escape problematic family dinners, and during Carnival season it's a popular respite from the all-encompassing Mardi Gras machine. Parking isn't a problem during the season (with the exception of the opening day). For Jazz Fest it's best to take a taxi or a bus or get dropped off by a friend. *See also p233.*

Pitot House Museum

1440 Moss Street, between Esplanade Avenue & Grand Route St John (482 0312). Bus 48 Esplanade. **Open** 10am-3pm (last tour at 2pm) Wed-Sat; closed Mon, Tue, Sun. **Admission** $5; $2-$4 concessions. **No credit cards. Map** p308 E4.

When Pitot House was built in the late 1790s, Bayou St John was in the country and the land nearby was plantation fields. The bayou, which connected Lake Pontchartrain to the Mississippi River, was lined with plantation houses. Pitot House is the lone survivor of that era, a graceful West Indies-style structure with brick-between-posts construction and a double-pitched roof, built for a family of merchants. It was sold in 1810 to James (formerly Jacques) Pitot, a refugee from the Haitian slave rebellions who resettled in New Orleans and later became mayor. The house was restored in the 1960s and is now furnished with post-Louisiana Purchase, pre-Victorian pieces from the early 19th century. Fitting so naturally into its landscape and painted with the soft reds and yellows favoured by the Creoles, this is one of the prettiest houses in New Orleans.

Lake View & Metairie

Map p308

To reach areas beyond Esplanade Avenue and City Park you will require a car or taxi. Head north, towards the lake, along Wisner Boulevard (which parallels the eastern side of City Park),

The beautiful **Pitot House Museum**.

turn left on to Robert E Lee Boulevard and right on to Lakeshore Drive. Lakeshore is where New Orleans turns into beachfront property. Dotted with palm trees and with a distinctive salt-flavoured breeze, Lakeshore Drive runs along the shores of **Lake Pontchartrain** and its colourful marinas. At 40 miles (64 kilometres) long and 24 miles (39 kilometres) wide, the lake has long acted as beach for New Orleans. But while boating is still a popular pastime, for nearly 20 years the waters of the lake have been deemed too polluted for swimming.

Lakeshore Drive ends at **West End Park**, a popular outdoors area where locals run, walk and cycle. West from here are the suburbs of Metairie and Kenner. One notable spot is at the entrance to the **Lake Pontchartrain Causeway** (*see page 241*), where you'll find a well-marked birdwatching area. In late July thousands of purple martins nest under the bridge; the best time for viewing is sunset, when the birds return for the night.

West of Mid City, **Metairie** – a charming suburb of perfectly manicured lawns and stay-at-home moms driving SUVs – offers good shopping and pleasant cafés (*see chapters* **Shops & Services** and **Restaurants & Cafés**). **Longue Vue House and Gardens**, the carefully constructed estate of a Sears Roebuck heiress and her family, is popular with garden buffs and house museum fans. Tucked into the Country Club landscape, the house is notable for its rich, varied furnishings and the gardens are a showcase of mid-20th century gardening styles.

Longue Vue House and Gardens

7 Bamboo Road, at Metairie Road (488 5488/www. longuevue.com). No public transport. **Open** 10am-4.30pm Mon-Sat; 1-5pm Sun (last tour 4pm). **Admission** $7; $3-$6 concessions. **No credit cards.**
This eight-acre (3.2-hectare) estate on the edge of New Orleans is a monument to people with tons of money and good taste – a rare combination. Edith Rosenwald Stern was an heiress to the Sears Roebuck fortune and her husband Edgar Stern was the scion of an old-line Jewish family of cotton brokers and investors. Married in the 1920s, the Sterns settled in New Orleans. Edith Stern had firm ideas about how to live and commissioned a Greek Revival mansion to be surrounded by a variety of gardens. The house is notable for its intelligent blending of European antiques, Chinese accessories and modern art. Unlike many palatial homes, it's easy to imagine living at Longue Vue, which has many homely amenities such as the 'package room', where the mail was sorted and gifts were prepared and wrapped. The gardens are the estate's most impressive feature. Conceived by garden guru Ellen Shipman as the house took shape, there are examples of almost every garden idea from the 20th century, from a wildflower area to a walled garden to a goldfish pond to a 'yellow garden', inspired by the White Garden of Vita Sackville-West. A children's area with emphasis on learning skills is a recent and well-thought-out addition.

Kenner

Among New Orleanians, suburban Kenner is often used as a shorthand term for all that is plastic, second-rate and boring. 'She got married and moved to Kenner' is the same as saying someone has dropped off the edge of the earth. Yet Kenner, too, has a historic past and some surprisingly interesting mini-museums in its old town area, Rivertown, which occupies the site of an old sugarcane plantation at the edge of the Mississippi River. Among the museums are the **Mardi Gras Museum** (415 Williams Boulevard, Rivertown, 468 7231), the **Saints Hall of Fame** (*see below*) and the **Louisiana Toy Train Museum** (519 Williams Boulevard, 468 7231), which houses several rooms of model trains.

Rivertown is also the home of the **Louisiana Wildlife & Fisheries Museum** (303 Williams Boulevard, 468 7231). Even with Louisiana's relaxed attitude towards the environment, it's a shock to see a scale model of an offshore oil drilling platform and a video praising oil companies as enlightened environmentalists in a museum devoted to the outdoors. The displays also include a giant freshwater tank of marine life.

On the lake side, Kenner houses one of the few surviving casinos in the Greater New Orleans area, the **Treasure Chest Casino** (*see page 95* **Fold 'em or hold 'em?**).

Saints Hall of Fame Museum

409 Williams Boulevard, between Short & Fourth Streets, Rivertown, Kenner (468 7231/www. kenner.la.us). Bus Kenner Loop. **Open** 9am-5pm Tue-Sat; closed Mon, Sun. **Admission** $3; $2-$2.50 concessions; free under-12s. **No credit cards.**
'Saints' and 'Hall of Fame' might be thought contradictory terms, but this museum provides a perhaps unintentional insight into sports fanaticism. The Saints, the local football team, have never won a play-off game and usually have losing seasons, but New Orleans is addicted to the team. The museum takes a wide view of the Saints phenomenon, with uniforms, game balls, photos and installations and even an Aints display (Saints' anti-fans). At the team's lowest points, fans become anti-fans, showing up at the Superdome with paper bags over their heads to show their collective embarrassment. Vintage bags are on display. For more on the Saints, *see p233.*

Greater New Orleans

Bedroom communities dominate New Orleans's fringes, plus a new theme park, Mardi Gras World and some places of historic and natural interest.

New Orleans East

To the east, New Orleans is mostly 20th-century suburbs. Two universities are in New Orleans East, **Dillard** and the **University of New Orleans**, both of which offer typical on-campus events throughout the year; check their websites for particularly interesting plans. Dillard, with its commitment to the African-American history of New Orleans, frequently hosts talks, conferences and performances that are open to the public. The big change in this usually placid landscape is the building of New Orleans's first modern theme park, **Jazzland**. Opened in the summer of 2000, the park combines Disneyesque design and entertainment with New Orleans and regional themes. Sceptics said the park was too far away from the French Quarter to draw tourists, but it opened with a bang and there are plans to continue to add features and attractions.

Jazzland Park

I-10 at I-510, exit 264A Lake Forest Boulevard (253 8000/www.jazzlandthemepark.com). Jazzland shuttle service/73 Oak Island bus. **Open** *Summer* 10am-10pm daily. *Winter* 10am-10pm Fri-Sun; closed Mon-Thur. **Admission** $31; $15-$26 concessions; free under-2s. **Credit** AmEx, MC, V.

Jazzland's promoters boast that it's the largest theme park between Atlanta and Houston. New Orleanians, who tend to be indifferent to imported entertainment, respond that there was no need to fill the gap. Nonetheless, optmistic entrepreneurs have erected a $110-million, 140-acre (57-hectare) park in a bleak, swampy area east of New Orleans off I-10. The park does make a concentrated effort to link itself to New Orleans and Louisiana with daily Mardi Gras parades, Cajun food, live jazz and other touchstones. The park centrepiece is the MegaZeph rollercoaster, modelled on the Zephyr, a much-loved New Orleans institution at the Pontchartrain Beach Park, which closed in 1983. The park offers standard thrill rides and a child-friendly area with much tamer rides. The park is a 20-40 minute trip from the French Quarter, depending on the traffic and whether you travel by car, taxi or bus. A shuttle ($10 for all riders) leaves at 9.40am daily from Tipitina's in the French Quarter (*see p219*).

The West Bank

Thanks to major meanders in the Mississippi, its west bank is in fact to the east and south of New Orleans. The West Bank is made up primarily of sleepy and generally uninviting bedroom communities, but there are a handful of attractions worth a visit.

One of the most pleasant – and free – attractions is the ferry at the foot of Canal Street, which takes riders directly to **Algiers Point** on the West Bank. The ride itself is worth the trip, as passengers watch New Orleans shrink behind them and feel the incredible tug of the river's mighty current as it grabs the ferry and threatens to spin it around. The ferry looks like a toy next to the enormous ships that ply the waterway. On the other side is a charming little neighbourhood of historic homes and wide front porches that looks as though it has been plucked out of Uptown New Orleans and plopped in its current location. During the day, the streets are quiet and make for a pleasant stroll in which to admire the architecture and the gardens upon which many residents pride themselves.

Have a look at **Behrman House** (228 Pelican Avenue), a Queen Anne cottage built in 1896. This was the childhood home of Martin Behrman, who served as mayor of New Orleans from 1894 to 1920. A short distance away, on the corner of Olivier and Pelican Avenues, is the **Mount Olivet Church**. Constructed in 1866, it is the oldest church in Algiers. Also on Pelican Street is the **Algiers Point Public Library**, housed in a charming Italianate structure that was built in 1907 as the community's library; it has served that purpose ever since. Also, notice the very decorative houses on the 300 block of Delaronde Street. These were built in the 1890s, and have been restored to shining Victorian style.

At the foot of the ferry landing in Algiers is a pleasant place to stop for a beer or some lunch. The **Dry Dock Café** (133 Delaronde Street, 361 8240) offers good, inexpensive home cooking and has wide-open windows through which to watch the ebb and flow of ferry riders. On sunny days chairs and tables are set out on the sidewalk. Another spot to consider is the **Old Point Bar** (*see page 224*), a relatively new player on the music club scene. You can hear funk, jazz and brass bands here, in an old saloon that's been beautifully restored.

Perhaps the biggest draw in Algiers is **Blaine Kern's Mardi Gras World** (*see below*), where many of the Mardi Gras floats are designed and built. Shuttle buses take you direct from the ferry terminal to the warehouses. Beat fans also make their way to Algiers to pay homage to the house where **William Burroughs** lived briefly in the 1940s (*see below*).

The other worthwhile West Bank sites are located considerably further afield in the tiny town and large bayou known as **Lafitte**. Located about 30 minutes' drive from New Orleans, Lafitte takes its name from the notorious pirate who once used the thick tangle of the swamp as a hideout. Today, the small town of Lafitte remains a fishing village. Crab nets are frequently spread in backyards that abut the bayou. Houses are perched on stilts that stand a minimum of ten feet (three metres) high, to keep them safe from the floods that occur in any heavy rain. Children here have their own boats by the age of ten, and the water is the most common means of transport. For visitors, too, the water and the swamp are the main attractions.

The town of Lafitte lies south of the **Jean Lafitte National Historical Park & Preserve** (*see below*). About 15 miles (24 kilometres) south of New Orleans, you can wander among exotic swamp trees draped in Spanish moss, while tropical plants that city folk grow a fortune on grow wild all around.

To charter a fishing boat, try **Ripp's Inland Charters** (689 2665), which will introduce you to the wide variety of fish that can be seized from the state's swamps. Charters leave from **Joe's Landing** (689 7966) for reasonable fees that depend upon the size of the boat and the amount of equipment needed. Canoes can be rented from **Bayou Barns** (689 2663) or from **Jean Lafitte Inn** (689 3271, www.jeanlafitteinn.com), where you can also get a beer and advice on where the best wildlife can be found. If all this isn't adventurous enough for you, try an airboat tour, which will show you much the same territory only at great speed and with terrific noise. One of the best can be found in **Des Allemands**, about 30 miles (48 kilometres) from New Orleans off US 90. Captain Arthur Matherne will take you on an informative and occasionally hair-raising trip through the bayous around the old German community, and give you a thorough look at how the state's fishing families make their living today. Phone 758 2365 for bookings.

While you're in the area, though, don't just watch the sea life, eat some, too. Several small, friendly restaurants dot the area, all offering seafood so fresh it's barely dead. In Crown Point, try the **Restaurant des Familles** (corner of US 45 and US 3134, 689 7834). **Boutte's** in Lafitte (Boutte's Street, 689 3889) is another good local find, with an upstairs room that overlooks the bayou.

Algiers Point–Canal Street Ferry

Algiers Point or Canal Street, at the Mississippi River (364 8114). Bus 41 Canal, 108 Algiers Local. **Open** *Canal Street departures* every 30min 6am-midnight daily. *Algiers Point departures* every 30min 5.45am-11.45pm daily. **Admission** free pedestrians; $1 vehicles (paid on the Algiers side). **No credit cards**. **Map** pp306-7 G/H7.

Blaine Kern's Mardi Gras World

233 Newton Street, at Brooklyn Street, Algiers (361 7821/1-800 362 8213/www.mardigras world.com). Bus 108 Algiers Local. **Open** 9.30am-4.30pm daily (tours every hr). **Admission** $11.50; $5.50-$8.50 concessions. **Credit** AmEx, DC, Disc, MC, V.

Blaine Kern is more crucial to Carnival than Rex. Kern's establishment designs floats and oversees more than 40 parades. The complex of warehouses ('dens' in Carnival-ese) and workrooms welcomes visitors. Take the ferry across the river to where a brightly marked Mardi Gras World van picks up visitors for a free shuttle to the den. Visitors enter the eerie world of Carnival make-believe, getting close-up looks at the floats and decorations, sometimes watching the designers at work.

Jean Lafitte National Historical Park & Preserve

7400 US 45 (Barataria Boulevard), Marrero (589 2330/www.nps.gov/jela). No public transport. **Open** *Park* 7am-7pm daily. *Visitor centre* 9am-5pm daily. *Walking tours* 10am daily June-Aug; 2pm daily Sept-May. **Admission** free.

The park offers guided walking tours with a qualified botanist, who tells visitors about the history of the area and its wildlife and plants. Guided canoe treks leave the park every Sunday at 8.30am and, best of all, moonlight canoe treks take off at sunset on nights of the full moon; reservations essential.

William Burroughs House

509 Wagner Street, at Sanctuary Drive, Algiers. Bus 102 Algiers. **Open** closed to the public.

This unassuming little house on the West Bank is a shrine to Beat fans who in turn are a mystery to the family that has lived here since 1951. A historic marker sits in the front yard, paying homage to novelist William Burroughs's 1948-9 residency. Burroughs was visited here by Jack Kerouac, Neal Cassady and others from the Beat circle, as documented in *On the Road*. The house was changed substantially after Burroughs left in a hurry in 1949 to avoid prosecution for drugs offences.

Guided Tours

Entrust yourself to New Orleans's quirky, characterful crew of tour guides.

New Orleans abounds with tours; sometimes it seems as if the city's traffic is made up of lines of tour buses and the streets of the French Quarter are all but impassable for clumps of tourists clinging to a costumed guide. The quality of the tours, however, varies hugely, since although tour guides must be licensed, the requirements are not stringent. Watch out in particular for over-competitive guides in the highly popular vampire tour field, who have been known to literally fight over customers around Jackson Square. As entertaining as this may be to watch, the tours themselves are often highly unreliable.

It's a good idea to reserve the smaller, more specialist tours ahead, as they may not run if there are no bookings.

For swamp tours, *see page 240.*

French Quarter tours

Carriage tours

Every day, usually from 8am to midnight, mule-drawn carriages line up on Decatur Street, in front of Jackson Square. Carriage tours of the French Quarter are a staple of New Orleans tourism but their allure is a mystery. They are smelly, slow, some of the mules wretched and the drivers are notoriously inaccurate – if sometimes captivating – storytellers. If you're determined to see the Quarter by mule, there are several things to bear in mind. Unlike at taxi stands, passengers aren't required to take the first carriage in line, so walk up and down, check out the driver and his beast, and ask about prices; these can vary widely, from $5 a person to $40 for a supposedly romantic tour for a couple. Also ask how long the mule has been out – a fresh animal makes for a much snappier drive.

Walking tours

Friends of the Cabildo French Quarter Walking Tours

Information 523 3939/fax 524 9130/ http://llsm.crt.state.la.us. Tour starts at the 1850 House Museum Store, 523 St Ann Street, on Jackson Square. **Tours** 1.30pm Mon; 10am, 1.30pm Tue-Sun. **Rates** $10; $8 concessions; free under-12s. **Credit** AmEx, DC, Disc, MC, V.

Led by trained volunteers, these two-hour walks around the Quarter are strong on architecture and historical fact.

Gay Heritage Tour

Bienville Foundation 945 6789/fax 945 1586/ Bienvillenola@aol.com. Tour starts at Alternatives bar, 909 Bourbon Street, at Dumaine Street. **Tours** 2pm Wed, Sat only. **Rates** $20 (adults only). **Credit** AmEx, Disc, MC, V.

Roberts Batson, the New Orleans gay history laureate (and writer of our Gay & Lesbian chapter), leads a two-hour walk around the Quarter tracing the lives and struggles of gays and lesbians – including Ellen DeGeneres and Tennessee Williams – from colonial days to the present. A wonderfully funny and poignant experience, but not designed for children. *See also p279.*

Jean Lafitte National Historical Park & Preserve Tours

Information 589 2636/www.nps.gov/jela. Tours start at French Quarter Visitors Center, 419 Decatur Street, French Market. **Tours** 10.30am daily. **Rates** free, but tickets must be picked up in person at the Visitors Center.

Universally called 'the ranger walks', these 90-minute tours of the Quarter by rangers from the Jean Lafitte Park are free and are particularly good on history and architecture. Each walk takes a maximum of 30 people, and passes are handed out at the office in the Visitors Center from 9am each morning. Note that each person going on the tour has to pick up a pass in person.

Literary Tour

Information: PO Box 70495, New Orleans, LA 70112 (949 9805/fax 948 7821). **Rates** $20 (minimum of 3 people). **No credit cards.**

W Kenneth Holditch's tours are legendary. These days he does them only by appointment, but it's often possible to join a group that's already made a reservation. Holditch is the acknowledged expert on Tennessee Williams's French Quarter years and has an outstanding knowledge of the entire literary history of the city. Highly recommended.

Louisiana Scandal Tour

Information 945 6789/fax 945 1586/ Bienvillenola@aol.com. Tour starts at Royal Café, 700 Royal Street, at St Peter Street. **Tours** 5pm daily. **Rates** $15 (adults only). **No credit cards.**

The tour begins with the great New Orleans contribution to civilisation, the cocktail, and takes flight from there. On leaving the Royal Café, walkers are provided with free go cups, to keep them refreshed during the tour. Roberts Batson (*see above* **Gay Heritage Tour**) is a witty, amusing guide who crams three centuries of scandals, disasters and gossip into two swiftly passing hours.

The Authentic Steamboat **NATCHEZ**
New Orleans' Only Steamboat.
Live Jazz Daily on Cruises from The French Quarter

Christened in 1975, the Natchez is one of only six remaining steamwheel steamboats in the country. Passengers can actually tour the steam engine room during the cruise.

The Riverboat **JOHN JAMES AUDUBON,** *a host vessel offering the Aquarium/Zoo Cruise*

NATCHEZ: Daily River Cruises from the French Quarter 11:30 am & 2:30 pm. Featuring the *Steamboat Stompers* Jazz Band. Dinner/Jazz Cruise 7:00pm (boarding begins at 6:00) Featuring the Grammy nominated *Dukes of Dixieland.*

JOHN JAMES AUDUBON: Between the Aquarium of the Americas, IMAX Theatre and the Audubon Zoo! Departs from the Aquarium at 10 am, 12 noon, 2 pm and 4 pm. Departs from the Zoo at 11 am, 1 pm, 3 pm and 5 pm.

Le Monde Creole French Quarter Courtyard Walking Tour

Information 568 1801/fax 528 9426/
creolwrld@aol.com. Tour starts at Le Monde Creole,
624 Royal Street, at Toulouse Street. **Tours**
10.30am, 2.30pm Tue-Sat; 10am, 2.30pm Sun; no tour
Mon. **Rates** $17.50; $15 concessions. **Credit** MC, V.
This tour acquaints visitors with daily Creole life in
New Orleans by following in the footsteps of the
Locouls, a Creole family based at Laura Plantation
(*see p244*). The tour deals with the 'shadow' Locouls
– the white men's black mistresses and children –
with insight and sensitivity.

New Orleans Ghost & Vampire/ Cemetery & History Tours

Information 524 0708/www.ghostsofneworleans.com.
Ghost & Vampire Tour starts at the amphitheatre
between Café du Monde & Jax Brewery, on Decatur
Street, across from Jackson Square. Cemetery &
History Tour starts at CC's Coffeehouse, Royal & St
Philip Streets, Uptown. **Tours** *Ghost & Vampire Tour*
8pm daily. *Cemetery & History Tour* noon Mon-Sat;
10.30am Sun. **Rates** $15; $13 concessions; free under-
12s. **No credit cards.**
Englishman Tom Duran, whose résumé includes
running Jack the Ripper tours in London, has turned
his attention to New Orleans and found, not surprisingly, plenty of skullduggery to investigate.
Dressed in Victorian top hat and cloak, Duran is an
authoritative guide, taking walkers to the alleged
vampire sites and haunted houses. Hannah, the
other guide, is a cheery self-proclaimed 'good witch'.
There are two tours based in the French Quarter:
the night-time 'Ghost & Vampire Tour' and the
morning 'Cemetery & History Tour'.

Garden District tours

Historic New Orleans Walking Tours: Garden District & Cemetery Tour

Information 947 2120/fax 947 2130/
www.tourneworleans.com. Tour starts at Garden
District Bookshop, The Rink, 2727 Prytania Street,
at Washington Avenue. **Tours** 11am, 1.45pm daily.
Rates $14; $12 concessions; free under-12s.
No credit cards.
The Garden District walk hits all the highlights:
architecture, celebrities' homes (from the pavement
only) and a tour of Lafayette Cemetery No.1.

The Literary Garden District Tour

Information 524 0708/www.ghostsofneworleans.com.
Tour starts in the lobby of the Pontchartrain Hotel,
2031 St Charles Avenue. **Tours** 11am Mon-Sat; no
tour Sun. **Rates** $15; $13 concessions; free under-12s.
No credit cards.
Tom Duran and his wife Christie, an Anne Rice
devotee, offer a Garden District tour that uses the
Rice books as its cornerstone. Lafayette Cemetery
No.1 is also included, as well as locations for
Interview with the Vampire, *Double Jeopardy* and
other films.

Cemetery tours

Historic New Orleans Walking Tours: Cemetery & Voodoo Tour

Information 947 2120/fax 947 2130/
www.tourneworleans.com. Tour starts at Café
Beignet, 334B Royal Street, at Conti Street. **Tours**
10am, 1pm Mon-Sat; 10am Sun. **Rates** $15; $13
concessions; free under-12s. **No credit cards.**
Cemetery historian and passionate preservationist
Rob Florence is an expert guide, adroit at balancing
mythic history with the facts. In St Louis No.1, the
city's oldest cemetery, walkers see the grave of
voodoo queen Marie Laveau and a voodoo temple
nearby. The African-American history of New
Orleans is woven into the tour without the usually
insulting sentimentality.

Save Our Cemeteries

Information 525 3377/1-888 721 7493/
www.gnofn.org\~soc. **Tours** *St Louis Cemetery No.1*
10am Sun only. *Lafayette Cemetery No.1* 10.30am
Mon, Wed, Fri; no tour Tue, Thur, Sat, Sun. **Rates**
Lafayette Cemetery No.1 $6; $5 concessions; free
under-12s. *St Louis Cemetery No.1* $12; $6-$10
concessions; free under-12s. **Credit** (advance
booking only) AmEx, MC, V.
This exemplary non-profit group works to preserve
the city's remarkable burial grounds. There are
several, volunteer-led tours of Lafayette Cemetery
No.1 in the Garden District and St Louis Cemetery
No.1 in Tremé each week. Booking is essential.

River tours

New Orleans Steamboat Company

Information 586 8777/1-800 233 2628/
www.steamboatnatchez.com. Tours start at Gray
Line Ticket Booth, Toulouse Street Wharf, at the
Mississippi River. **Tours** phone for a schedule.
Rates $15.75-$44.50; $7.75-$22.75 concessions.
Credit AmEx, DC, Disc, MC, V.
Hear the calliope tooting out old songs? That's the
Natchez, the only steam-powered riverboat regular-
ly plying the waters around New Orleans. The
Natchez always sails with a Dixieland jazz band
aboard. Its sister ship (not a steamboat), the *John
James Audubon*, makes four short trips daily from
the Riverwalk wharf to the Audubon Zoo dock and
back ($14.50/$7.25 return) – a good way to see the
river without spending a whole day on it.

Other tours

Cradle of Jazz Tour

Information 282 3583/http://hometown.aol.com/jazz
tour/cradle.html. **Tours** 10am-1pm Sat; no tours
Mon-Fri, Sun. **Rates** $30 (reservations required).
No credit cards.
Jazz lover and historian John McCusker is an ideal
guide for this three-hour Saturday morning tour into
the heart of New Orleans jazz. The tour visits the

Tours

1850 House
A chance to see the inside of a Pontalba building apartment. See page 78.

Backstreet Cultural Museum
Founder-curator Sylvester Francis explains African-American funeral customs, second line parades, Mardi Gras Indians. See page 86.

Commander's Palace
Not exactly a tour, but book the kitchen table at this world-class restaurant and get a behind-the-scenes look *and* a fabulous meal. See page 142.

Cradle of Jazz Tour
A bus ride through history and culture with jazz enthusiast and historian John McCusker. See page 119.

Gay Heritage Tour
Roberts Batson tells fascinating stories of a hidden and exciting past. See page 117.

Laura Plantation
A trip out to see how the South was really won. See page 244.

Kenneth Holditch's Literary Tour
Legendary for good reason, but you'll have to make an appointment. See page 117.

New Orleans Cemetery & Voodoo Tour
Rob Florence weaves together history and facts without sacrificing the romance. See page 119.

Shotgun House tours
Only in March, alas, when the Preservation Resource Center spotlights the real New Orleans house. See page 120.

Ursulines Convent
The oldest surviving building in the Mississippi River Valley is an oasis of calm and beauty. See page 80.

birthplaces of musicians such as Jelly Roll Morton and Buddy Bolden, plus the cemeteries, old jazz clubs and other music-rich corners of the city.

Preservation Resource Center Tours
Information 581 7032/www.prcno/org.
The PRC, founded in 1974, is a hands-on, creative force in New Orleans preservation. In addition to

implementing innovative schemes such as selling decrepit houses to people who will fix them up, the PRC sponsors several high-profile annual architectural events such as the **Holiday Home Tour** (in December), which opens up showy private homes for public tours; **Shotgun House Month** (in March), which celebrates the archetypal New Orleans dwelling with a number of events; and the **Stained Glass in Sacred Places Tour**, which takes place in spring and autumn and looks at the magnificent windows in New Orleans churches. The PRC will also arrange tailor-made tours; phone for more information.

Spring Fiesta Association Tour of Homes
Information: 826 St Ann Street, New Orleans, LA 70116 (581 1367). **Tours** phone for details.
Since 1937 this pioneering preservation group has opened private homes to the public to spotlight New Orleans culture and raise funds. There are usually three tours in the third week of March covering French Quarter houses, Garden District houses and a bus tour to River Road plantations. These palatial homes are normally only seen in the pages of *Southern Living* or *Architectural Digest*, so it's a big weekend for house-worshippers.

Tour companies

Gray Line of New Orleans
Information 569 1401/1-800 535 7786/fax 587 0742/www.graylineneworleans.com. Tours start at Gray Line Ticket Booth, Toulouse Street, at the Mississippi River. **Tours** phone for a schedule. **Rates** $15-$63; $7.50-$21 concessions. **Credit** AmEx, DC, Disc, MC, V.
Always reliable if rarely exciting, Gray Line offers several tours around New Orleans on bus, boat and foot; phone for a full list.

New Orleans Tours
Information (592 0560/1-800 543 6332/fax 592 0549/www.bigeasy.com). Tours start at various locations around the city. **Tours** 9am-7.30pm daily; phone for a schedule. **Rates** $10-$39; $5-$23 concessions. **Credit** AmEx, MC, V.
Riverboat, bus, foot and combination tours, this company does them all. There are daily walking and bus tours of New Orleans along with bus trips to the plantations and several cruises, including a riverboat trip to the Battle of New Orleans site near Chalmette (*see p88*).

Tours by Isabelle
Information (391 3544/fax 391 3564/ www.neworleans.com). Tours 9am-10pm daily. **Rates** $38-$98. **Credit** AmEx, Disc, MC, V.
While this local tour company offers riverboat and bayou trips, its speciality is small-scale bus tours around New Orleans and to the River Road plantations, with pick-ups from hotels in the French Quarter and Garden District.

Eat, Drink, Shop

Restaurants & Cafés

With a diverse and distinctive culinary tradition and contemporary joints to
compare with the best, New Orleans is a big, fat food fest. You won't go hungry.

Get ready for a food fest, where you roll from
one fabulous meal to the next. New Orleans is
home to some of the best and most interesting
food in the country. It's a beautiful thing when
you can savour beignets and chicory coffee for
breakfast, a muffuletta for lunch, and sautéed
backfin crabmeat with *beurre blanc* for dinner,
all in one day.

The food of New Orleans was originally
influenced by Europeans, Africans and Native
Americans, but after these building blocks were
in place, people from across the globe entered
one of the biggest ports in America and tossed
their two cents' worth of ideas into the mix,
contributing to the crazy mélange of flavours
that characterises New Orleans cuisine.

Whereas the rest of the country has
succumbed to cookie-cutter restaurants that
serve up the same grilled salmon, roast chicken
and pasta, New Orleans has maintained its
down-home joints where the owners don't
believe in remodelling or keeping up with the
times. These are the sorts of places where you
can get the same meal your granddaddy ate 50
years ago. Traditions and rituals are important
to New Orleanians, who staunchly hold on to
the past. Restaurants here attract locals, who
drift in for soul-satisfying cooking.

New York and San Francisco may edge out
New Orleans for creativity in the kitchen, but
the Big Easy has them beat when it comes to
good food at a good price. That's not to say
there aren't superchefs performing their modern
culinary artistry in the city, it's just that you
won't find them on every block. If you dine out
at one of the top spots (whether on Creole at
Galatoire's or haute American at **Peristyle**),
you'll get as fine a meal as in any culinary
capital, but you'll pay a lot less dearly for it. At
Bayona, for example, award-winning chef
Susan Spicer seduces diners with consistently
excellent Mediterranean food, but only three or
four of the main dinner courses cost more than
$20. Eat up, drink your fill and be happy that
you don't have to be rich to enjoy the goods.

The restaurants recommended below ought
to prevent you from running willy-nilly through
a gamut of mediocre meals. The list is by no
means exhaustive of all the possibilities, but it
is representative of New Orleans at its most
creative, zany and authentic.

DRESS CODES

Although New Orleans is a relaxed city, a few
places, such as **Antoine's** (*see page 129*),
Arnaud's (*see page 129*), **Brennan's** (*see
page 129*) and **Galatoire's** (*see page 130*),
stipulate a jacket for men and an equivalent
dress, skirt or trousers for women. In such
places, jeans and trainers will not be welcome.

French Quarter

American

Dickie Brennan's Steakhouse

*716 Iberville Street, between Bourbon & Royal Streets
(522 2467/www.dbrennanssteakhouse.com). Bus 3
Vieux Carré, 55 Elysian Fields, 81 Almonaster, 82
Desire.* **Open** 11.30am-2pm, 5.30-10pm Mon-Fri; 5.30-
10pm Sat, Sun. **Main courses** $6.50-$34.75. **Credit**
AmEx, DC, MC, V. **Map** p316 A2.

A clubby steak emporium, this new Quarter restaurant from the famous Brennan family is giving local
favourite Ruth's Chris Steakhouse (*see p145*) a run
for its money. You'll find the same steakhouse stand-
bys here, such as creamed spinach and stuffed
mushrooms, but the beefy prime-quality steaks,
home-made Worcestershire sauce and excellent
desserts set this restaurant apart from its peers. Try
the huge one-pound bacon cheeseburger with home-
made potato chips at lunch; it's the Quarter's best
bargain at $8.50.

House of Blues

*225 Decatur Street, between Iberville & Bienville
Streets (529 2583/www.hob.com). Bus 3 Vieux
Carré, 55 Elysian Fields, 81 Almonaster, 82 Desire.*
Open 11am-11pm Mon-Sat; 5-11pm Sun. *Gospel
brunch* 9.30am, 11.45am, 2pm Sun. **Main courses**
$5.95-$18. **Credit** AmEx, DC, MC, V. **Map** p316 A3.

On the ground floor of the popular music club, the
House of Blues kitchen turns out lunch and dinner
in a comfortable and fun setting. The Gospel Brunch
($30 adults, $15 children) will fill both your soul and
your stomach, but otherwise, have a drink and an
appetiser while waiting for a show.

Rib Room

*Omni Royal Orleans Hotel, 621 St Louis Street,
at Royal Street (529 7045). Bus 3 Vieux Carré, 55
Elysian Fields, 81 Almonaster, 82 Desire.* **Open**
6.30-10.30am, 11.30am-2.30pm, 6-10pm Mon-Sat;
11.30am-2pm (jazz brunch), 6-10pm Sun. **Main
courses** $26.50-$34. **Credit** AmEx, DC, MC, V.
Map p316 B2.

Be sure to request a table in the window because the Rib Room in the Omni Royal Orleans Hotel is perfectly situated for an all-encompassing view of the incessant comings and goings on Royal Street. Along with a great view, this dark restaurant serves up a sumptuous meatlover's feast. Prime rib is the speciality of the house, but don't overlook the delicious fillet of beef, the lamb T-bone or the excellent poultry and seafood selections. The waiting staff are highly professional and attentive but the overall atmosphere is possibly a little bit too stuffy for the younger set.

What a mouthful!

Get your tongue around some essential New Orleans foodstuffs.

andouille spicy Cajun sausage used in gumbo and other dishes.

beignet square doughnut covered in icing sugar; as served by **Café du Monde** and other cafés. See page 125.

café brulot a flaming Creole coffee concoction that combines lemon and orange peel with cloves, cinnamon, brandy and orange liqueur into a wonderfully boozy after-dinner jolt. It's usually prepared and flamed tableside, right before your eyes. Try **Galatoire's** for the genuine experience. See page 130.

chicory roasted ground chicory roots that were originally added to coffee during the Civil War as an extender. It gives New Orleans or Creole coffee a distinctive flavour.

crawfish Louisiana's official crustacean; also called mudbugs or – outside the state – crayfish.

dirty rice a relation of jambalaya involving a mix of rice and meat (giblets, sausage) and seasoning.

dressed a po-boy (see below) with mayonnaise, lettuce, tomato and pickle. Some places substitute butter for mayonnaise or use both.

étouffée spicy tomato sauce served typically with crawfish or shrimp. It literally means 'smothered'.

filé ground sassafras leaves used to season – typically – gumbo (see below).

grits ground wheat or corn, served like mashed potato (pictured). A staple of the Southern breakfast table, usually served with butter and salt or gravy.

gumbo a soup-stew made with a variety of ingredients that can include shrimp, chicken, okra, tomatoes and rice; seasoned with filé (see above).

jambalaya tomatoes and rice, plus anything the chef feels like tossing in (ham, shrimp,

chicken), flavoured with celery and onions – a Creole pilaff.

maque choux don't let the plethora of spellings fool you: this is (or should be) the dish the Cajuns picked up from the local Chotaw Indians. It's a stewy mix of corn and tomatoes with onion and green bell pepper and, sometimes, crawfish or shrimp. **Uglesich's** (see page 137) makes a fine version with crawfish and the **Pelican Club** (see page 129) loves coming up with new, multicultural approaches to the standard.

mirliton hard-skinned pear-like vegetable usually served stuffed with ham or shrimp.

muffuletta a giant sandwich made with seeded muffuletta bread stuffed with any combination of ham, cheese, sausage and olive salad.

pain perdu French toast. It literally means 'lost bread'.

praline brown sugar and pecans, caramelised into a dentist's worst nightmare of an all-sugar, can't-eat-just-one confection.

po-boy (from 'poor boy') a sandwich made with French bread. It can contain anything from fried oysters or shrimps to roast beef and gravy.

red beans and rice traditional New Orleans Monday-night (washing-day) meal made up of kidney beans with a sauce containing ham or sausage. The pot went on the stove early in the day and the housewife spent the long simmering time getting the household's clothes washed, dried and ironed.

rémoulade a spicy red sauce flavoured with spring onion, cayenne, mustard, lemon, paprika and parsley; usually served cold with shrimp or crabmeat.

roux cooked mixture of butter and flour used for thickening sauces. Central to Creole and Cajun cooking.

tasso smoked and spiced ham.

Eat, Drink, Shop

Cafés

Ben & Jerry's

*537 St Ann Street, at Jackson Square (525 5950).
Bus 3 Vieux Carré, 55 Elysian Fields, 81
Almonaster, 82 Desire.* **Open** 10am-9pm daily.
No credit cards. Map p316 C2.
Sometimes, on a hot afternoon strolling through the
Quarter, nothing is better than rich, creamy ice-
cream. And nobody makes it better than those
peace-loving guys from Vermont. The service is
unusually slow, even for New Orleans.

Café du Monde

*813 Decatur Street, opposite Jackson Square (581
2914/www.cafedumonde.com). Bus 3 Vieux Carré,
55 Elysian Fields, 81 Almonaster, 82 Desire.* **Open**
24hrs daily. **No credit cards. Map** p316 C3.
One of the oldest and greatest cafés in America is
open 24 hours and ready for you when you wake up.
Seat yourself, wait for the server, and then order café
au lait and beignets. Café du Monde brews strong
chicory coffee then adds scalded milk to make a café
au lait that has a distinct New Orleans flavour. The
beignets are squares of deep-fried dough, dusted
with icing sugar. Beignets and coffee can be enjoyed
at any hour of the day or night, but early in the
morning is one of the best times to visit this café: the
streets are quiet, the sun shines softly, locals are
reading the paper and time seems to stand still.
Branches of this stalwart pop up in shopping malls
around the city.

La Marquise

*625 Chartres Street (524 0420). Bus 3 Vieux Carré,
41 Canal, 57 Bourbon, 81 Almonaster, 82 Desire.*
Open 7am-5.30pm daily. **No credit cards.**
Map p316 B2.
Refrigerated cases just inside the front door harbour
pastries, sandwiches and salads. However, the best
bet are the almond croissants. The bakery for La
Marquise also makes birthday cakes, yule logs (complete with meringue mushrooms) and *croquem-
bouche* for special occasions (a French wedding
cake/tower built out of cream puffs and caramelised
sugar). Delicious hot chocolate is served frothed and
sprinkled with chocolate shavings. Coffee, tea and
soft drinks are also available.

Royal Blend Coffee & Tea

*621 Royal Street, at Toulouse Street (523 2716/
www.royalblendcoffee.com). Bus 3 Vieux Carré, 55
Elysian Fields, 81 Almonaster, 82 Desire.* **Open**
7am-midnight daily. **Credit** MC, V. **Map** p316 B2.
Pass through a long carriageway from Royal Street
to enter this courtyard retreat that seems miles away
from the shops, bars and gawking crowds of the
French Quarter. Order a cup of coffee (hot, cold,
frozen, espresso or cappuccino) and grab a big
brownie, and enjoy a rare leisurely moment in a
French Quarter courtyard.
Branch: 244 Metairie Road, at Stella Street,
Metairie (835 7779).

What is New Orleans?

● Red beans and rice on Mondays at
Mandina's (pictured; see page 148).
● Café au lait and beignets at **Café du
Monde** (see left).
● Muffuletta and a Barq's (just ask) at
Central Grocery (see page 180).
● Barbecued oysters at **Uglesich's**
(see page 137).
● Hot spicy crawfish at **Franky & Johnny's**
(see page 144).
● Oysters at **Casamento's** (see page 144).
● Roast beef po-boy at **Domilise Sandwich
Shop & Bar** (see page 144).
● Crawfish étouffée omelette at **Mother's**
(see page 136).
● Jazz Brunch at **Commander's Palace**
(see page 142).
● Hamburger and chocolate freeze at
Camellia Grill (see page 138).
● Fried chicken at **Praline Connection**
(see page 134).
● Café brulot at **Galatoire's** (see page 130).
● Pimm's Cup at **Napoleon House**
(see page 132).
● Soufflé potatoes at **Antoine's**
(see page 129).

Cajun

K-Paul's Louisiana Kitchen

416 Chartres Street, at Conti Street (596 2530/
www.chefpaul.com). Bus 3 Vieux Carré, 55 Elysian
Fields, 81 Almonaster, 82 Desire. **Open** 11.30am-
2.30pm, 5.30-10pm Mon-Sat; closed Sun. **Main
courses** $7-$32.95. **Credit** AmEx, DC, MC, V.
Map p316 B2.

At K-Paul's, chef Paul Prudhomme started the celebration of Cajun cooking that has since spread
around the world. Many other chefs ride his long coat
tails, but no one can match Prudhomme's giant heart,
charming personality and genius for cooking. He's
only rarely seen at the restaurant these days but his
standards continue to rule. K-Paul's is best known
for its blackened fish dishes and its legendary huge
portions, with food dribbling over the edge of the
plates. The menu, which features a wide variety of
Cajun meat, fish and poultry, changes regularly as
the kitchen takes advantage of the freshest ingredients available. Sometimes the more senior waiters
still reward those who eat all of their food with a gold
star on the cheek. Steep prices are the only downside.

Contemporary

Bayona

430 Dauphine Street, at Conti Street (525 4455/
www.bayona.com). Bus 3 Vieux Carré, 57 Franklin.
Open 11.30am-1.30pm, 6-9.30pm Mon-Thur;
11.30am-1.30pm, 6-10.30pm Fri, Sat; closed Sun.
Main courses $13-$30. **Credit** AmEx, DC, MC, V.
Map p316 B1.

Dinner here is a lovely way to spend an evening. In
a relaxed, stylish dining room, you can while away
hours indulging in the delights of chef Susan
Spicer's Mediterranean cuisine. Delicacies at dinner
might include goat's cheese crouton with wild mushrooms, sinfully rich cream of garlic soup, or salmon
with Gewürztraminer sauce. If you come for lunch,
try the smoked duck sandwich with cashew butter
and pepper jelly. And in the evening – as long as the
weather is cooperating – you can dine alfresco in the
courtyard: there is no better place to savour a New
Orleans night out.

Bella Luna

914 N Peters Street, at Dumaine Street (529 1583/
www.belaluna.com). Bus 3 Vieux Carré, 55 Elysian
Fields, 81 Almonaster, 82 Desire. **Open** 6-9.30pm
Mon-Thur; 6-10.30pm Fri, Sat; closed Sun.
Main courses $35. **Credit** AmEx, DC, MC, V.
Map p316 C3.

You've got two reasons to come to Bella Luna: its
beautiful views of the Mississippi and French
Quarter, and its romantic interior, which features
candlelight, soft jazz and cosy booths. The food is
secondary to the surroundings and expensive to
boot. But, if you're planning to propose to your loved
one, do as the rest of New Orleans does and take the
plunge here.

Bistro at the Maison de Ville

Hotel Maison de Ville, 727 Toulouse Street, at Royal
Street (528 9206/www.maisondeville.com). Bus 3
Vieux Carré. **Open** 11.30am-2pm, 6-10pm Mon-Sat;
11am-2pm, 6-10pm Sun. **Main courses** $8-$25.
Credit AmEx, DC, MC, V. **Map** p316 B2.

Café brulot served as it should be at **Galatoire's**. *See p130.*

Eat, Drink, Shop

Cajun or Creole?

So what's the difference between Cajun and Creole food? Ask this question to a handful of locals and you will get a different answer from every one of them and an argument will likely ensue. There are differences among Creole and Cajun for sure, but the line gets muddled in New Orleans, where you get both styles in great quantities.

In simple terms, Creole food is city food influenced by the Europeans who settled here, whereas Cajun is country food that originated from the displaced French-Canadian Acadians ('Cajuns') who made their homes along the bayous and prairies in a large area west and south of New Orleans. Improvising cooks on both fronts created remembered recipes with the ingredients that were available.

In New Orleans itself, well-to-do French settlers demanded food reminiscent of their homeland. Their cooks recreated French dishes using vegetables and herbs that were either native to North America or had been brought here by African and European settlers. The results were versions of French sauces such as rémoulade and béarnaise and dishes like fish meunière that don't quite replicate their classical French counterparts.

By the time the Acadians were kicked out of Canada by the British, they had developed their own distinctive culture. Once established in Louisiana, the Acadians (like the French) made do with the ingredients that grew around them. They learned cooking techniques from Native Americans and African immigrants and, although their ingredients were similar to the ones used in New Orleans, the results were often quite different. Cajun food is usually characterised by hearty, earthy food that is soul warming and often forms a one-dish meal. It is based on rich, dark rouxs, pronounced spices and the rice that the Cajuns were taught to harvest by Native Americans. The perfect example of Cajun cuisine is duck and sausage gumbo over rice. Creole food tends to be flavoured more subtly, with delicately combined spices and herbs as in a bisque or bouillabaisse.

As long as it tastes good you probably won't care whether you're eating Creole or Cajun, and at the following places taste is guaranteed.

For Cajun try **Brigtsen's** (see page 140), **Jacques-Imo** (see page 141) and **K-Paul's Louisiana Kitchen** (see page 126). For Creole try **Antoine's**, **Arnaud's** (for both, see page 129), **Dooky Chase** (see page 146), **Feelings Café** (see page 129), **Galatoire's** (see page 130) and **Mandich** (see page 133).

Waiting for a reservation at Emeril's (*see p135*) to come through? Save yourself the headache and head to the Bistro. The interior is cosy and attractive and the food really dazzles. Chef Greg Piccolo's fresh touch enlivens classic bistro fare. Try such refreshingly simple dishes as bouillabaisse, oysters in filo, and painfully rich chocolate crème brûlée. Patrick, the charming maître d', is one more reason to ditch your reservation at more famous spots.

Mr B's Bistro

201 Royal Street, at Iberville Street (523 2078). Bus 3 Vieux Carré, 41 Canal. **Open** 11.30am-3pm, 5.30-10pm Mon-Fri; 11.30am-3pm, 5-10pm Sat; 10.30am-3pm (jazz brunch), 5.30-10pm Sun. **Main courses** $12-$32. **Credit** AmEx, DC, MC, V. **Map** p316 A2.
Across from the Monteleone Hotel, Mr B's serves progressive Creole cuisine in an elegant restaurant with a comfortable club feel. Rack of lamb, sweet potato and andouille soup, pasta jambalaya, veal chop and chocolate mousse are some of the selections that hold sway over diners. It's known as the place for a business lunch, and is perfect for extended noon meals. Daily specials are a reasonably priced way of tasting world-famous cuisine at a Brennan family restaurant.

Nola

534 St Louis Street, at Chartres Street (522 6652/ www.emerils.com). Bus 3 Vieux Carré, 55 Elysian Fields, 81 Almonaster, 82 Desire. **Open** 11.30am-2pm, 6-10pm Mon-Thur; 11.30am-2pm, 6pm-midnight Fri, Sat; 6-10pm Sun. **Main courses** $9.50-$30. **Credit** AmEx, DC, MC, V. **Map** p316 B2.
More casual than Emeril's (*see p135*) and less romantic than Delmonico (*see p137*), Emeril Lagasse's Quarter restaurant is about loudness and eclectic Louisiana cooking. It helps if you're an Emeril fan like the rest of the customers in the place. That way you can forgive the restaurant's propensity to combine every ingredient on the same plate. The best way to enjoy Nola is to find yourself a seat at the bar for a drink, and choose a tasty morsel from the appetiser menu, or perhaps one of the rich and imaginative desserts.

Palace Café

605 Canal Street, at Chartres Street (523 1661/ www.palacecafe.com). Bus 3 Vieux Carré, 41 Canal. **Open** 11.30am-2.30pm, 5.30-10pm Mon-Sat; 10.30am-2.30pm (blues brunch), 5.30-10pm Sun. **Main courses** $12.50-$29. **Credit** AmEx, DC, MC, V. **Map** p316 A2.

Eat, Drink, Shop

Straddling the border of the French Quarter and the CBD, Palace Café draws a crowd of conventioneers, downtown business people and locals with its well-priced Creole/Cajun cuisine. Another member of the Brennan family empire, the café is located in a former downtown landmark, Weirlein's Music (they've kept the distinctive sign atop the building). The bustling downstairs dining room looks out on Canal Street and there's a comfortable bar at the back of the room. Whatever else you eat at the Palace, order the white chocolate bread pudding, one of the city's finest desserts.

Pelican Club

615 Bienville Street, at Exchange Alley (523 1504/ pelicanclub@earthlink.net). Bus 3 Vieux Carré, 41 Canal. **Open** 5-10pm Mon-Thur, Sun; 5.30-11pm Fri, Sat. **Main courses** $22. **Credit** AmEx, DC, MC, V. **Map** p316 B2.

The Pelican Club serves a contemporary Louisiana menu with international flair. The elegant dining room is reminiscent of New York, with black banquettes, modern art and lots of open space. Chef Richard Hughes is masterfully creative: try the almond and coconut crusted tilapia, the Louisiana cioppino (a Louisiana-style paella) and the must-have profiteroles.

Peristyle

1041 Dumaine Street, at N Rampart Street (593 9535). Bus 3 Vieux Carré, 57 Franklin. **Open** 6-9pm Tue-Thur; 11.30am-1.30pm, 6-10pm Fri; 6-10pm Sat; closed Mon, Sun. **Main courses** $19. **Credit** AmEx, DC, MC, V. **Map** p316 C1.

A fire in November 1999 closed the doors of Peristyle for longer than any food-minded New Orleanian could bear. The remodelled temple to haute-American cuisine will reopen in the autumn of 2000, and is certain to attract more customers than it can accommodate. The decor may be updated, but Anne Kearney's brilliant cooking is sure to remain one of the finest in the country.

Creole

Antoine's

713 St Louis Street, at Bourbon Street (581 4422). Bus 3 Vieux Carré. **Open** 11.30am-2pm, 5.30-9pm Mon-Sat; closed Sun. **Main courses** $19-$29. **Credit** AmEx, DC, MC, V. **Map** p316 B2.

At Antoine's the difference between a good and a great meal depends on your waiter and your choice of food, but that shouldn't keep you away from this 160-year-old New Orleans institution. Come on a Friday or Saturday when the dining rooms are pleasantly bustling (the place can feel as empty as Siberia on Monday evenings, for instance) and stick to any sort of oyster dish to start followed by a fillet steak or pompano with crabmeat. Wander the rooms, where the knick-knacks, photographs and Mardi Gras memorabilia provide heaps of genuine New Orleans character. Proper attire – a jacket for men – is recommended.

Arnaud's

813 Bienville Street, at Bourbon Street (523 5433/ www.arnauds.com). Bus 3 Vieux Carré, 41 Canal, 57 Bourbon. **Open** 11.30am-10pm Mon-Thur; 11.30am-11.30pm Fri, Sat; 10am-2.30pm Sun. **Main courses** $20. **Credit** AmEx, DC, MC, V. **Map** p316 B2.

High ceilings, tiled floors, white tablecloths, professional black-jacketed waiting staff and a chic bar have kept Arnaud's position secure as one of the grandes dames of New Orleans Creole restaurants. Sunday brunch is a lively affair with a three-piece music ensemble travelling the tables. Don't miss shrimp Arnaud – spicy boiled shrimp served with the quintessential rémoulade sauce. Also try shrimp Creole and an appetiser of escargot swimming in garlic butter and topped with puff pastry. At Arnaud's you will experience the opulence of dining on real Creole fare in the city that invented it. Proper attire is recommended.

Brennan's

417 Royal Street, at Conti Street (525 9711/ www.brennansneworleans.com). Bus 3 Vieux Carré, 55 Elysian Fields, 81 Almonaster, 82 Desire. **Open** 8am-2.30pm, 6-10pm daily. **Main courses** $15-$35. **Credit** AmEx, DC, MC, V. **Map** p316 B2.

'What does an Irishman know about French food?', an incredulous friend asked Owen Brennan when he announced he was opening a 'French and Creole' restaurant in 1946. The answer was not long in coming as Brennan's became the premier Creole restaurant in New Orleans. This is the mother ship of the Brennan restaurant dynasty. Other branches of the family have established nouveaux cafés, but Brennan's stands by its classic dishes. The only problem here is making a choice: will it be one of the 20 egg dishes that have made this place famous, or the 'Trout Nancy'? Regardless of what you choose as your main dish, start with superlative turtle soup and end with the signature 'Bananas Foster'. The downside to a meal at Brennan's is that your wallet will weigh considerably less afterwards. Proper attire is recommended.

Broussard's

819 Conti Street, at Bourbon Street (581 3866). Bus 3 Vieux Carré. **Open** 5.30-10pm daily. **Main courses** $18-$35. **Credit** AmEx, DC, MC, V. **Map** p316 B2.

Broussard's menu doesn't stray too far from the Creole formula: shrimp rémoulade, trout meunière, and bread pudding. But the food isn't really the point. Comfort, elegance and romance are the focus here, and Broussard's scores high in these areas. Another bonus is the courtyard, which is an oasis in the heart of the Quarter.

Feelings Café

2600 Chartres Street, at Franklin Avenue (945 2222/www.feelingscafe.com). Bus 57 Franklin, 81 Almonaster, 82 Desire. **Open** 6-10pm Mon, Thur; 11am-2pm, 6-11pm Fri; 6-11pm Sat; 11am-2pm, 6-10pm Sun. **Main courses** $12-$23. **Credit** AmEx, DC, MC, V. **Map** p307 H6.

Eat, Drink, Shop

Set in an old townhouse, Feeling's Café is ever popular with locals for its relaxing ambience, friendly faces and interesting food. Balcony seating is premier real estate at dinner time, when the air is filled with tunes from a pianist tinkling away. The delicious Sunday brunch specials can best be enjoyed in the mimosa-strewn, covered courtyard. Don't leave without a piece of peanut butter pie.

Galatoire's

209 Bourbon Street, at Iberville Street (525 2021/ galatoire@bellsouth.net). Bus 3 Vieux Carré, 41 Canal. **Open** *Bar* 11am-10pm Tue-Sat; 11.30am-10pm Sun. *Restaurant* 11.30am-10pm Tue-Sat; noon-10pm Sun. Closed Mon. **Main courses** $30. **Credit** AmEx, DC, MC, V. **Map** p316 A2.

Yes, the Creole food at this Quarter landmark is excellent (go for the shrimp rémoulade, fried oysters and bacon en brochette, and sautéed crabmeat in *beurre blanc*), but the real reason you're here is the ambience: old-world waiters who remember your name (and your drink), a local society scene and café brulot expertiy performed at your tableside. Proper attire recommended.

Red Fish Grill

115 Bourbon Street, at Canal Street (598 1200). Bus 3 Vieux Carré, 41 Canal. **Open** 5-11pm Mon-Sat; 11am-3pm Sun. **Main courses** $12.95-$25. **Credit** AmEx, MC, V. **Map** p316 A2.

The idea here is fish, and owner Ralph Brennan (yep, another Brennan) has run with it. Fish are painted on the tables, they're hanging from the ceiling, they're on your chairs and on the floor. But despite these distractions, the food is actually enjoyable. The menu consists of fish, fish and more fish: some are simply grilled, while some are gussied up with Creole and Cajun touches. As with most restaurants in the Quarter, the prices reflect the high rent.

Indian

Shalimar

535 Wilkinson Row, at Chartres Street (523 0099/ www.shalimarno.com). Bus 3 Vieux Carré, 55 Elysian Fields, 81 Almonaster, 82 Desire. **Open** 11am-2.30pm, 5.30-10.30pm Mon-Sat; closed Sun. **Main courses** $10-$15. **Credit** AmEx, DC, MC, V. **Map** p316 B2.

Good, reasonably priced Indian food is this restaurant's motto. On an alley half a block from Jackson Square, Shalimar spreads out a terrific lunch buffet where many Indian favourites are available for sampling – hot popadom, tandoori chicken, mint chutney and more.

Italian

Bacco

W Hotel, 310 Chartres Street, at Bienville Street (522 2426/www.bacco.com). Bus 3 Vieux Carré, 41 Canal. **Open** 11.30am-2.30pm, 6-10pm Mon-Sat; 6-10pm Sun. **Main courses** $17-$38. **Credit** AmEx, DC, MC, V. **Map** p316 A2.

Although it's located in tourist central, the food at this stylish restaurant couldn't be further from New Orleans tourist fare. Chef Haley Gambel has created a menu without any Cajun or Creole touches, concentrating instead on strictly Italian ingredients like bresaola, prosciutto, truffles, Reggiano Parmesan and Gorgonzola presented in classic dishes such as bruschetta, gnocchi, ravioli and carpaccio. In fact, the only touristy thing about Bacco are the high prices.

Café Giovanni

117 Decatur Street, at Canal Street (529 2154/ www.cafegiovanni.com). Bus 3 Vieux Carré, 41 Canal, 55 Elysian Fields, 81 Almonaster, 82 Desire. **Open** 5.30-10pm Mon-Thur, Sun; 5.30-11pm Fri, Sat. **Main courses** $15. **Credit** AmEx, DC, MC, V. **Map** p316 A3.

Diners pack this restaurant to taste the Italian creations of Duke LoCicero. Opera-singing waiters deliver delicious goodies, such as grilled Portabella mushrooms, 'Oysters Giovanni', Cajun soft-shell crab with caramelised onions, spicy pork with crawfish mirliton sauce, and tiramisu.

Irene's Cuisine

539 St Philip Street, at Chartres Street (529 8811). Bus 3 Vieux Carré, 55 Elysian Fields, 81 Almonaster, 82 Desire. **Open** 5.30-10.30pm Mon-Thur, Sun; 5.30-11pm Fri, Sat. **Main courses** $13.50-$19.90. **Credit** AmEx, MC, V. **Map** p316 C2.

This dark, small Quarter spot is a time-tested favourite that's consistently packed for dinner. Quirky in an old-Italian-joint kind of way, it has a romantic, cosy dining room that serves robust, homey dishes. Plan on a long wait with the lounge-lizard piano player in the back room and don't forget to bring a monstrous appetite.

Mexican

Country Flame

620 Bienville Street, between Chartres & Royal Streets (522 1138). Bus 3 Vieux Carré, 55 Elysian Fields, 81 Almonaster, 82 Desire. **Open** 11am-10pm Mon-Fri, Sun; 11am-midnight Sat. **Main courses** $3-$8. **Credit** MC. V. **Map** p316 A2.

Our Lady of Guadaloupe watches over diners while they enjoy consistently good and inexpensive Mexican, Spanish and Cuban specialities. Go for the fajitas, empanadas, black beans and rice, yucca and *puerco frito*. The location just inside the French Quarter guarantees an eclectic crowd even at lunch, when hordes of downtowners cross Canal Street and flood the small space.

Neighbourhood

Acme Oyster House

724 Iberville Street, at Bourbon Street (522 5974/ www.acmeoyster.com). Bus 3 Vieux Carré, 41 Canal. **Open** 11am-10pm Mon-Sat; noon-7pm Sun. **Main courses** $5.95-$16. **Credit** AmEx, MC, V. **Map** p316 A2.

Belly up to the raw bar and watch as the quickest shuckers in the South pull apart the fresh beauties. Don't bother with the rest of the food; it's not worth the precious few meals you have in New Orleans.

Clover Grill

900 Bourbon Street, at Dumaine Street (598 1010/ www.clovergrill.com). Bus 3 Vieux Carré, 55 Elysian Fields, 81 Almonaster, 82 Desire. **Open** 24hrs daily. **Main courses** $7.95. **Credit** AmEx, MC, V. **Map** p316 C2.

On the lower end of Bourbon Street, this 1950s-style diner is frequented by a wide variety of local and visiting characters. Loud and often obnoxious customers sing ABBA songs with the jukebox, the cooks dance and sing, and the waiters twist and turn between the bar stools and tables, as they take orders, shout at each other and give customers an earful of good-humoured sarcasm. Burgers and fries, pork chop and egg breakfasts and various club sandwiches are a pleasure to the stomach at any time, but are especially welcome in the wee hours of the morning.

Felix's Seafood Restaurant & Oyster Bar

739 Iberville Street, at Bourbon Street (522 4440). Bus 3 Vieux Carré, 41 Canal. **Open** 10am-midnight Mon-Thur; 10am-1am Fri; 10am-1.30am Sat; 10am-10pm Sun. **Main courses** $10. **Credit** AmEx, MC, V. **Map** p316 A2.

Although it catches a lot of the overflow from Acme *(see p130)*, Felix's is a great oyster house in its own right. A bright neon sign beckons regulars and tourists to the restaurant, with its oyster bar, vinyl-

covered benches and tile floors. Other draws are fresh fish, pizzas with barbecued shrimp, gumbo and green salads topped with fried oysters.

Gourmet Etc

1010 Decatur Street, at St Philip Street (299 0806). Bus 3 Vieux Carré, 81 Almonaster, 82 Desire. **Open** 10am-7pm daily. **Credit** AmEx, DC, MC, V. **Map** p316 C2.

In a wedge of land behind the golden statue of Joan of Arc, Gourmet Etc serves coffee, baklava, gyros and other Mediterranean food. The small space with its outdoor seating offers a welcome respite from the bustle of shopping in the French Market. Order an icy-cold drink or rejuvenating hot coffee and some home-made cookies or a thick slab of cake.

Gourmet Etc also stocks a good supply of Mediterranean groceries that you could use to put together an excellent picnic in nearby Jackson Square or on the Moonwalk.

Maspero's

601 Decatur Street, at Toulouse Street (523 6250). Bus 3 Vieux Carré, 55 Elysian Fields, 81 Almonaster, 82 Desire. **Open** 11am-11pm Mon-Thur; 11am-midnight Fri, Sat; 11am-11pm Sun. **Main courses** $5-$10. **No credit cards**. **Map** p316 B2.

A favourite place for locals to entertain out-of-town guests, Maspero's offers huge sandwiches and seafood platters to satisfy large appetites. Piles of onion rings, mounds of fries, plates loaded with red beans and rice with sausage links, extra-long po-boys filled to the gills. However, after waiting in line for an hour, you'll think you can eat the plate itself, as well as everything on it.

Eat, Drink, Shop

Napoleon House: enjoy Pimms and gumbo in the Emperor's hideaway. *See p132.*

Napoleon House

*500 Chartres Street, at St Louis Street (524 9752/
www.napoleonhouse.com). Bus 3 Vieux Carré, 55
Elysian Fields, 81 Almonaster, 82 Desire.* **Open**
11am-midnight Mon-Thur; 11am-1am Fri, Sat; 11am-
7pm Sun. **Main courses** $4-$10. **Credit** AmEx, DC,
MC, V. **Map** p316 A2.

Sandwiches, gumbo, muffulettas and cheese and
antipasti boards are served on the ground floor of a
house that was supposedly built as a refuge for the
exiled Emperor Napoleon. Paint peels from the
walls, classical music and opera selections are
played by request, and even though Napoleon never
made it, his presence can certainly be felt throughout the building. Try a famous Pimm's Cup for afternoon shopping refreshment. (Ironically, this place's
favourite drink was invented by the punishing
English.) The waiters, though thoroughly professional, mind their own business, sometimes to a
fault. *See also p154.*

Vegetarian

Old Dog New Trick

*307 Exchange Alley, at Bienville Street (522 4569/
www.olddognewtrick.com). Bus 3 Vieux Carré, 55
Elysian Fields, 81 Almonaster, 82 Desire.* **Open**
11.30am-9pm daily. **Main courses** $6.95-$11.95.
Credit AmEx, MC, V. **Map** p316 B2.

Solely vegetarian fare is what you get inside and at
the few tables outside at the Old Dog. A 'Ben
Burger' is the house speciality, an all-vegetable
concoction served up a number of different ways.
Caesar salad, flavoured iced tea and vegetarian
pizza round out the menu.

Marigny & Bywater

American

Café Marigny

*1913 Royal Street, at Touro Street (945 4472/
www.cafemarigny.com). Bus 3 Vieux Carré.* **Open**
11am-10pm Mon-Fri; 11am-3pm Sat, Sun. **Main
courses** $12-$23. **Credit** AmEx, DC, MC, V.
Map pp306-7 G6.

Locals want to keep this place a secret from tourists,
but don't let them. The food is too good and reasonably priced for you to miss out on one of the few
decent places to eat in the Marigny. Bring your own
bottle of wine and dig into steamed mussels with
tomatoes and corn, duck spring rolls and pork with
Asian noodles, or come for a big breakfast.

Elizabeth's

*601 Gallier Street, at Chartres Street (944 9272).
Bus 82 Desire.* **Open** 7am-3pm Tue-Sat; closed Mon,
Sun. **Main courses** $3.50-$7. **No credit cards.**

This small, humble restaurant could expand ten
times over and still draw crowds. Why? Because food
this good is otherwise non-existent in the Bywater.
Fluffy creative omelettes, mountainous po-boys and

Chain reaction

If theme's your scene, New Orleans has
prominent and tourist-packed branches of
all the international theme chains, plus a
couple all its own. If you don't want to eat
the burger without buying the T-shirt, then
head for one of the following.

Hard Rock Café

*418 N Peters Street, at St Louis Street,
French Quarter (529 5617/www.hard
rock.com). Bus 3 Vieux Carré, 55 Elysian
Fields, 81 Almonaster, 82 Desire.* **Open**
11am-11pm daily. **Main courses** $10.99-
$15.99. **Credit** AmEx, DC, MC, V.
Map p316 B3.

New Orleans Planet Hollywood

*620 Decatur Street, at Jackson Square,
French Quarter (522 7826). Bus 3 Vieux
Carré, 55 Elysian Fields, 81 Almonaster, 82
Desire.* **Open** 11am-10pm Mon, Thur, Sun;
11am-11pm Fri, Sat. **Main courses**
$11.95-$19.95. **Credit** AmEx, DC, Disc,
MC, V. **Map** p316 C3.

O'Henry's Food & Spirits

*301 Baronne Street, at Gravier Street, CBD
(522 5242). Bus 41 Canal.* **Open** 11am-
7pm Mon-Fri, Sun; 11am-3pm Sat. **Main
courses** $10.95-$16.95. **Credit** AmEx,
Disc, MC, V. **Map** p309 B1.
Branches: throughout the city.

thick wedges of moist chocolate cake are some of the
simple pleasures that attract a cross-section of blue-
collar workers, artists and young professionals.

Lorenzo's Pizzeria & Bar

*800 France Street, at Royal Street (947 0000). Bus
88 St Claude, 89 St Claude.* **Open** 3-11pm Mon-
Thur, Sun; 3pm-midnight Fri, Sat. **Main courses**
$8-$10. **Credit** AmEx, MC, V.

On a corner, deep in the Bywater, this bar with a few
tables at the back is a neighbourhood secret that
serves some of the best pizza in town. Innovative
daily specials complement a substantial menu of
calzones, sandwiches, pasta and salads. The real
specials are the thin-crust pizzas. Try the Ninth
Ward Pizza made with fresh roasted garlic sauce,
plus mozzarella, Romano, artichoke hearts and
mushrooms. Finish with one of Lorenzo's delicious
home-made desserts.

La Peniche

*1940 Dauphine Street, at Touro Street (943 1460).
Bus 82 Desire.* **Open** 24hrs Mon, Fri-Sun; until 3pm
Tue; from 7am Thur; closed Wed. **Breakfast** $3.95-
$14.95. **Credit** AmEx, MC,V. **Map** pp306-7 H6.

La Peniche cooks breakfast 24 hours a day and is only a short cab ride away from Jackson Square. Every morning the cooks bake pans of their popular Southern biscuits. If your meal doesn't automatically include biscuits, request a couple along with white gravy for smothering the four halves. An eclectic crowd frequents La Peniche, making for good people-watching opportunities, particularly in the early hours of the morning when there can often be a queue of hungry nightfolk.

Snug Harbor

626 Frenchman Street, between Royal & Chartres Streets (949 0696/www.snugjazz.com). Bus 82 Desire. **Open** 5pm-2am daily. **Main courses** $10-$25. **Credit** AmEx, MC, V. **Map** pp306-7 G6.

Just outside the Quarter, Snug Harbor serves filling food and outstanding live jazz every night of the week. Hamburgers are ground fresh daily, steaks are hand-cut, and seafood practically swims to the door. The hamburgers are much the same as those at the Port of Call (*see below*), since the restaurants used to share the same owner, but the menu here is more diverse and the queue is usually far shorter.

Cafés

La Spiga Bakery

2440 Chartres Street, at Spain Street (949 2253). Bus 82 Desire. **Open** 8am-2pm Tue-Sat; closed Mon, Sun. **No credit cards**.

Bring your morning paper and settle in for a homey breakfast of blueberry muffins and coffee at this friendly bakery. Alternatively, come here for lunch and try one of the tasty grilled Italian sandwiches or a substantial soup.

Creole

Mandich

3200 St Claude Avenue, at Louisa Street (947 9553). Bus 88 St Claude, 89 St Claude. **Open** 11am-2.30pm, 5.30-10.30pm Tue, Fri; 11am-2.30pm Wed, Thur; 5.30-10.30pm Sat; closed Mon, Sun. **Main courses** $10.95-$23.25. **Credit** MC, V.

You want old-school, true-blue New Orleans? Then get yourself to Mandich for hammy red bean soup, crisp trout with hollandaise and crabmeat, and oysters bordelaise. The food proves that the downtown scene ain't got nothing on this Bywater gem.

Southwestern

Santa Fe

801 Frenchman Street, at Dauphine Street (944 6854). Bus 3 Vieux Carré, 48 Esplanade. **Open** 5-11pm Wed, Thur, Sat; 11am-11pm Fri; closed Mon, Tue, Sun. Closed 2wks late Dec. **Main courses** $12. **Credit** AmEx, Disc, MC, V. **Map** pp306-7 H6.

At Santa Fe you'll find the customers drinking Margaritas, chatting with friends and having a party. The restaurant serves Southwestern food, and there's always a queue for a table, but the Margaritas are the real reason to visit.

Soul food

Port of Call

838 Esplanade Avenue, at Dauphine Street (523 0120). Bus 3 Vieux Carré, 48 Esplanade. **Open** 11am-1am daily. **Main courses** $10. **Credit** AmEx, MC, V. **Map** p316 D1.

Elizabeth's is the byword for good food in Bywater. *See p132.*

Walk into a dimly lit, South Seas-decorated bar, complete with a fish tank and tropical drinks. Sip on a legendary 'Monsoon', then order the best hamburger or cheeseburger in the world, cooked how you like it, with a big baked potato on the side. Port of Call also offers steak, pizza and big salads, but no chicken, no fish and no French fries.

Praline Connection

542 Frenchman Street, at Chartres Street (943 3934). Bus 3 Vieux Carré, 48 Esplanade, 55 Elysian Fields. **Open** 11am-10.30pm Mon-Thur; 11am-midnight Fri, Sat; 11am-6pm Sun. **Main courses** $5.95-$14.95. **Credit** AmEx, DC, MC, V. **Map** p316 D2.

This is soul food at its finest: fried chicken and chicken livers, stuffed po-boys, greens, corn bread, gravy, daily lunch specials and much more. A dessert case is filled with candy available by the pound, including several kinds of pralines (the best is the delicious chocolate one). During Carnival, sample one of the King Cakes, baked to order. Unlike usual King Cakes, these are wide round cakes filled with praline cream cheese. **Branch: Praline Connection II** 901 St Peters Street, at St Joseph Street, Warehouse District (523 3973).

CBD & Warehouse District

American

Hummingbird Grill

804 St Charles Avenue, at Julia Street (523 9165). Riverfront or St Charles Streetcar. **Open** 24hrs daily. **Main courses** $1.80-$6.80. **Credit** MC, V. **Map** p308 B2.

This hole-in-the-wall (and it isn't much bigger than that) serves bums, cab drivers, police officers, drunk Uptowners and unknowing tourists at any time of the day or night. Sporting a dilapidated Broadway-like sign of huge white bulbs, the joint offers breakfast 24 hours, as well as a number of other 'specials', hardly gourmet stuff but damned cheap. Some tourists would swear the grill is haunted by living spirits on reprieve from the nether world, regulars know the 'colourful' scene as a part of daily life; whatever your take on the other customers, it's a good idea to keep your wits about you, especially late at night.

Mike Ditka's New Orleans

Lafayette Hotel, 628 St Charles Avenue, at Girod Street (569 8989). St Charles Streetcar. **Open** 11.30-2.30pm, 5.30-10pm Mon-Thur, Sun; 11.30-2.30pm, 5.30-11pm Fri, Sat. **Main courses** $7.89-$29. **Credit** MC, V. **Map** p308 B1.

In the same week that he was fired as coach of the hopeless Saints, football god Mike Ditka opened a modestly named restaurant. Unlike the football team, this chop house seems to thrive under Ditka's care. The bar, of course, is cigar friendly and the clubby restaurant is packed with the type of people who can afford the clubby prices: professionals and executives at lunch, and a more diverse well-heeled crowd at dinner. They come for fresh seafood, big salads, double-cut pork chops and generous steaks prepared by Chef Christian Karcher. Ditka, who has two other restaurants in the US, is a fairly regular presence in New Orleans. He's friendly enough, but it's probably a good idea to keep off the subject of his coaching record.

Holy cow and saints alive! Luckily the food is better than the football at **Mike Ditka's**.

The best Alfresco

Bayona
See page 126; pictured.

Broussard's
See page 129.

Café Degas
See page 148.

Café Rani
See page 137.

Feelings Café
See page 129.

Jacques-Imo
See page 141.

Napoleon House
See page 132.

Asian

Lemon Grass Restaurant
International House Hotel, 217 Camp Street, at Gravier Street (523 1200/www.lemongrass.com). St Charles Streetcar/15 Freret, 16 S Claiborne, 19 Nashville bus. **Open** 6-10pm Mon-Thur; 6-10.30pm Fri, Sat; 5.30-9.30pm Sun. **Main courses** $12-$35. **Credit** AmEx, DC, MC,V. **Map** p308 C1.
Bigger and sexier than its Carrollton sibling, the new Lemon Grass in the hip International House Hotel offers a similar menu of dressed-up Vietnamese food. You'll find reliable options such as spring rolls and hot and sour shrimp soup, but be adventurous and try other dishes such as the excellent quail with watercress and lemongrass, or wok-smoked salmon. **Branch**: 216 N Carrollton Avenue, at Bienville Avenue, Mid City (488 8335).

Rock 'n' Sake Bar & Sushi
823 Fulton Street, at St Joseph & Julia Streets (581 7253). Riverfront Streetcar. **Open** 11.30am-2.30pm, 5.30-10pm Mon-Thur; 11.30am-2.30pm, 5.30pm-midnight Fri; 5.30-midnight Sat; 6-10pm Sun. **Credit** AmEx, DC, MC, V. **Map** p309 C2.

Just as the name suggests, you get blaring rock 'n' roll and a great selection of sake at this hip sushi spot, where a young artsy crowd hangs out. The real draw, however, is the impeccably fresh fish. Phat Nguy, the Vietnamese chef, has put together a slew of creative, Americanised sushi rolls: try the Vietnamese-inspired rice paper roll and the tuna sashimi – it's so light you feel you could go on eating it forever.

Contemporary

Cuvee
322 Magazine Street, at Natchez Street (587 9001). Bus 11 Magazine. **Open** 10am-2pm, 6-10pm Mon-Thur; 10am-2pm, 6-11pm Fri; 6-11pm Sat; closed Sun. **Main courses** $19-$29. **Credit** AmEx, DC, MC, V. **Map** pp306-7 F8.
As attractive and comfortable as this new restaurant is, it's the food that really dazzles. Impeccably fresh ingredients – including buttery escolar (white tuna) and vegetables straight from the farm – are the stars of the modern Louisiana dishes. Cuvee is the city cousin of Dakota, the very popular Northshore restaurant (*see p242*). Friendly service and an excellent selection of wines by the glass have made this place an instant player on the New Orleans restaurant scene.

Emeril's
800 Tchoupitoulas Street, at Julia Street (528 9393/ www.emerils.com). Bus 10 Tchoupitoulas. **Open** 11.30am-2pm, 6-10pm Mon-Thur; 11.30am-2pm, 6-10.30pm Fri; 6-10.30pm Sat; closed Sun. **Main courses** $19-$33. **Credit** AmEx, DC, MC, V. **Map** p309 C2.
After making a name for himself at the top of the restaurant industry in New Orleans, Emeril Lagasse made quick work of conquering the TV Food Network and Las Vegas. His original namesake restaurant is guaranteed to please anyone who loves the food icon's over-the-top taste and big Emeril BAM! If you can get a space, sit at the food bar to see all of the culinary works in progress and maybe even catch a glimpse of the chef himself wielding a knife at the butcher's block. To ensure you get a table at Emeril's you'll need a reservation several weeks, if not months, in advance, and don't forget to bring a wallet bulging with green.

Gerard's Downtown
Parc St Charles Hotel, 500 St Charles Avenue, at Poydras Street (592 0200). St Charles Streetcar. **Open** 11.30am-2.30pm Tue-Thur; 11.30am-2.30pm, 5.30-10pm Fri; 5.30-10pm Sat. **Main courses** $18.50-$29. **Credit** AmEx, DC, MC, V. **Map** p309 B1.
At this relaxed, stylish restaurant, chef Gerard Marais spruces up classic French stand-bys with impeccably fresh ingredients, including herbs, fruits and vegetables grown at his farm outside New Orleans. This newcomer was an overnight success on the city's culinary scene thanks to its inspired menu, friendly service and handsome setting.

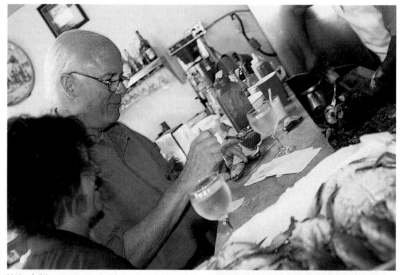

Uglesich's: tongue-twisting name and tastebud-tickling food. *See p137.*

The Grill Room

Windsor Court Hotel, 320 Gravier Street, at Tchoupitoulas Street (522 1992). Bus 3 Vieux Carré, 11 Magazine. **Open** 11.30am-2pm, 6-10pm daily. **Main courses** $20-$25. **Credit** AmEx, DC, MC, V. **Map** p309 C1.

Welcome to the sophisticated world of hotel dining, in all its champagne-walled and cushy-banquette splendour. The soothing decor of the Grill Room lets you savour chef Rene Bajeux's new American-French cuisine in relative peace and exclusive comfort. Like the surroundings, the menu is pretty hoity-toity (read pricey), but it's also very appealing. The house-smoked salmon and the bacony veal chop are real winners, but make sure you leave plenty of room for the delicious desserts, created by the talented Lisa Ligett.

Cuban

Liborio

321 Magazine Street, at Poydras Street (581 9680). Bus 11 Magazine. **Open** 11am-2.30pm Mon; 11am-2.30pm, 6-9pm Tue-Fri; 6-9pm Sat; closed Sun. **Main courses** $10-$23. **Credit** AmEx, DC, MC, V. **Map** p309 C1.

Good food and fair prices make this family-run Cuban eaterie particularly popular with downtown suits looking for a place to lunch. It's hard to go wrong with one of Liborio's daily specials or to fault regular items such as well-seasoned black beans over rice, fried plantains or a Cuban sandwich, which is made of pork, cheese, mustard and pickle on an egg bread.

Neighbourhood

Mother's

401 Poydras Street, at Tchoupitoulas Street (523 9656/www.mothersrestaurant.com). St Charles Streetcar/15 Freret bus. **Open** 5am-10pm daily. **Main courses** $3-$18. **No credit cards.** **Map** p309 C1.

If you're in pursuit of decadent dishes, sink your teeth into one of Mother's debris po-boys (made with beef drippings), one of the most scrumptious, drippiest sandwiches ever created. Make sure you know what you want to eat before you get to the front of the queue; the women behind the counter are an impatient bunch. And come hungry, because besides the debris you have to try the jambalaya, the red beans and the étouffée. The artery-clogging crawfish étouffée omelette served at breakfast is a wonderful way to start the day.

The Pearl

119 St Charles Avenue, off Canal Street (525 2901). St Charles Streetcar. **Open** 10am-9pm Tue-Sun; closed Mon. **Main courses** $6-$15. **Credit** AmEx, MC, V. **Map** p308 C1.

At its home just half a block off Canal Street, the Pearl has been serving New Orleanians since right after World War II and finds its way on to many postcard photographs of the Rex procession travelling down St Charles Avenue on Mardi Gras day. A large neon sign burns bright over a sidewalk decorated with inlaid oysters, marking the entrance to this fine spot. Try a club, a po-boy or oysters. The chances are, if someone you know has visited New Orleans, they will have eaten at the Pearl.

Uglesich's

1238 Baronne Street, at Erato Street (523 8571). St Charles Streetcar. **Open** *Summer* 9.30am-4pm Mon-Fri; closed Sat, Sun. *Winter* 9.30am-4pm Mon-Sat; closed Sun. **Main courses** $10-$13. **No credit cards**. **Map** p309 B2.

Don't leave the city without eating at this true diamond in the rough. In a decaying part of the city on the edge of the CBD, Uglesich's (pronounced 'YOUglesich's') has lured locals and well-informed tourists since opening in 1927. You'd never guess from the rough and rustic dining room that you're in the hands of some very capable cooks, but one bite of the tart fried green tomatoes with boiled shrimp and spicy rémoulade and you'll be convinced. A square of fried grits with creamy white sauce and sautéed gulf shrimp is another winner, and barbecued oysters swimming in garlicky olive oil are not to be missed either. Be sure to come with a big appetite because even that little selection is not even the half of it.

Contemporary

Café Rani

2917 Magazine Street, at 7th Street (895 2500). Bus 11 Magazine. **Open** 11am-9.20pm Mon-Thur; 11am-10.20pm Fri; 10am-9.20pm Sat, Sun. **Main courses** $7-$15. **Credit** AmEx, DC, MC, V. **Map** pp306-7 D9.

This salad and sandwich place has indoor seating and a large courtyard shaded by a huge oak tree. On sunny days the outdoor surroundings at Café Rani provide a pleasant, comfortable place to have a grilled chicken Caesar salad, a glass of iced tea and a relaxing conversation.

Delmonico

1300 St Charles Avenue, at Erato Street (1-800 980 8474/525 4937/www.emerils.com). St Charles Streetcar. **Open** 11.30am-2pm, 6-10pm Mon-Fri; 6-10pm Sat; 10.30am-2pm, 6-10pm Sun. **Main courses** $18-$30. **Credit** AmEx, DC, MC, V. **Map** pp306-7 F8.

The latest effort from celebrity chef Emeril Lagasse, Delmonico is the poshest of his three New Orleans restaurants. It attracts a sea of conventioneers with expense accounts and moneyed locals who don't care that there is better and cheaper food in town. If you're after a chance glimpse of the star chef, you're better off settling at the bar for a drink and an appetiser or salad, rather than forking out for Emeril's standard busy Creole food 'taken up a notch'.

Mexican

Juan's Flying Burrito

2018 Magazine Street, at St Andrew Street (569 0000). Bus 11 Magazine. **Open** 11am-11pm daily. **Price range** $4-$8. **No credit cards**. **Map** pp306-7 E8.

Located in the Lower Garden District, not too far from the St Thomas housing project, Juan's delivers terrific food at a great price. Try one of the wraps on the menu or create your own. The soft tortilla tacos are an excellent choice: the ingredients are fresh; the hot sauce will make you breathe fire; and you will leave nourished for an entire day of shopping.

Neighbourhood

Joey K's

3001 Magazine Street, at 7th Street (891 0997). Bus 11 Magazine. **Open** 11am-10pm Mon-Fri; 8am-10pm Sat; closed Sun. **Main courses** $6.95-$13.95. **Credit** DC, MC, V. **Map** pp306-7 D9.

Eat, Drink, Shop

The best Breakfast & brunch

Arnaud's
See page 129.

Bluebird Café
See page 138.

Brennan's
See page 129.

Camellia Grill
See page 138.

Commander's Palace
See page 142.

Mother's
See page 136.

A chalkboard outside the front door advertises the specials of the day at this simply decorated neighbourhood eat shop. Joey K's also features Southern- and New Orleans-style plate lunches and dinners. If you need a little dessert, try the really delicious blackberry cobbler.

Magazine Poboy & Sandwich Shop
2368 Magazine Street, at 1st Street (522 3107).
Bus 11 Magazine. **Open** 7am-6.30pm Mon-Fri; 10am-6.30pm Sat; closed Sun. **Main courses** $3.75-$7.95.
No credit cards. Map pp306-7 E9.
Just as its name implies, this corner joint turns out a slew of sandwiches. Neighbourhood locals, office workers and Uptowners delight in the airy French bread and fresh seafood used to make all of their favourite po-boys. Don't leave without an order of crunchy French fries.

Uptown

American

Bluebird Café
3625 Prytania Street, at Foucher Street (895 7166).
St Charles Streetcar. **Open** 7am-3pm Mon-Fri; 8am-3pm Sat, Sun. **Main courses** $2.95-$4. **No credit cards. Map** pp306-7 E9.
A seemingly unending queue waits outside the door to this breakfast and lunch spot on Saturday and Sunday mornings, when regular breakfast fare is served as fast as the busy staff can turn it out. Try buckwheat pancakes with cane syrup to fill a bottomless pit, or a portion of *huevos rancheros* if you are hankering for great south-of-the-border flavour. Definitely worth the wait.

Seafood seasons

Granted these seasons can fluctuate dramatically, yet here are the months that these creatures are traditionally at their finest in Louisiana.

Crab The soft-shell crabs are at their best between April and May; hard-shelled blue crabs come into their own from May to October.

Crawfish are in season from March to May.

Oysters are traditionally a cool weather crop, so the best times are late November to April, however, they are generally good all year round.

Shrimp Brown shrimp are in season in May and June; wait until the autumn (Sept-Nov) for white shrimp.

Queuing for brekky at the **Bluebird Café**.

Bud's Broiler
3151 Calhoun Street, at Tonti Street (861 0906).
Bus 3 Vieux Carré, 41 Canal. **Open** 11am-9pm Mon-Sat; 11am-7pm Sun. **Average** $5. **No credit cards.**
Next to Popeye's (*see p139*), this is the best fast food in town. Bud's signature is a burger with serious grill flavour. Get the famous No.5: meat, lettuce, tomatoes, pickles, mustard or mayonnaise served on a squishy bun, along with the consummate companion of school-bus orange cheese fries.
Branches: throughout the city.

Camellia Grill
626 S Carrollton Avenue, at St Charles Avenue (866 9573). *St Charles Streetcar.* **Open** 9am-1am Mon-Thur, Sun; 8am-3am Fri, Sat. **Main courses** $6-$7.
No credit cards. Map pp306-7 A8.
New Orleanians cherish this Uptown landmark. Take a seat at the U-shaped diner counter and watch as white-coated, bow-tied countermen shout your order to the short-order cook at the griddle, who flips eggs, slams burgers down in a row, and drops fries into hissing oil. The grill has a winning way with breakfast, which is served all day and most of the night. The pecan waffle makes a fine dessert or meal on its own; omelettes are the fluffiest and tastiest anywhere, and hamburgers are thin and juicy, on a soft bun. Don't forget a chocolate freeze (milkshake) and a slice of pecan pie heated up on the griddle.

Martin Wine Cellar
3827 Baronne Street, at Napoleon Avenue (899 7411/www.martinwine.com). *St Charles Streetcar.*
Bus 24 Napoleon. **Open** 9am-7pm Mon-Sat; 10am-2pm Sun. **Main courses** $7-$20. **Credit** AmEx, MC, V. **Map** pp306-7 D9.
Martin Wine Cellar is a combination delicatessen, cheese shop, wine store and gourmet speciality shop, where you can pick out bounty for a picnic in Audubon Park or eat in. Busy staff prepare upscale hot plate specials and sandwiches like the Farmer's Delight (vegetarian), the Mouthbuster Burger and the Deli Deluxe (corned beef, pastrami, Swiss cheese, Russian dressing and Creole mustard on an onion roll). Refrigerated cases display home-made salads, pâtés, meats, olives and desserts. Ask wine experts Rick and Brian to help you choose the perfect bottle, and you won't be disappointed.

Popeye's

621 Canal Street, at Exchange Place (561 1021).
Bus 3 Vieux Carré, 41 Canal. **Open** 10am-11pm
Mon-Thur; 10am-1am Fri, Sat; 10am-10pm Sun.
Main courses from $3.79. **No credit cards.**
Map p316 A2.
Although you may well have eaten Popeye's fried
chicken somewhere else in the world, New Orleans
is where Al Copeland began his chicken empire.
Indeed, Popeye's serves the best fried chicken in the
world – at least according to the locals. Try the
Cajun rice, red beans and rice, jalapeños, mashed
potatoes, corn on the cob, jambalaya and battered
fries. Grab plenty of napkins to clean yourself up
after the feast.
Branches: throughout the city.

The Trolley Stop Café

*1923 St Charles Avenue, at St Andrew Street (523
0090). St Charles Streetcar.* **Open** 24hrs daily.
Main courses $2-$12. **Credit** DC, MC, V.
Map pp306-7 E9.
After you've stopped at every Daiquiri shack in the
Quarter and your ears are ringing from the horns
you sat next to at that jazz club, you will be grateful for the Trolley Stop. The soothing comfort food
served 24/7 will make you feel better in just a few
bites. In the early hours, rowdy crowds of late-night
party revellers chow down on eggs with chicken,
fried steak and gravy, a pile of stacked-to-the-
ceiling pancakes, and burgers with fries, while the
friendly waitresses buzz around the yellow-walled
interior of the converted trolley balancing a
coffeepot in each hand.

Asian

Kyoto

4920 Prytania Street, at Jefferson Avenue (891 3644).
St Charles Streetcar. **Open** 11.30am-2.30pm, 5-10pm
Mon-Thur; 11.30am-2.30pm, 5-10.30pm Fri; noon-3pm,
5-10.30pm Sat; closed Sun. **Main courses** $5.95-$15.
Credit AmEx, DC, MC, V. **Map** pp306-7 C9.
This sushi standout is known for its fresh fish and
slow service. But don't despair; if you need a sushi
fix this is the place to satisfy it. Ignore the restaurant,
which is ugly enough to put you off your food, and
instead take a seat at the bar for an order of melt-in-
your-mouth white tuna sushi (escolar). As in all sushi
places worth a damn, the tab adds up quickly.

Cafés

La Madeleine French Bakery

547 St Ann Street, at Jackson Square (568 0073).
Bus 3 Vieux Carré. **Open** 7am-9pm daily. **Credit**
AmEx, DC, MC, V. **Map** p316 B2.
With outlets around the city, these bakeries pack 'em
in. They want to make you feel like you're walking
into a countryside French bakery, but France it ain't.
The croissants and pastries are mediocre and the
bread is of the soft variety, but La Madeleine comes
in handy when you've eaten all the fried food your
stomach can stand and you crave a salad and some-
thing as plain as a tunafish sandwich.
Branches: 601 S Carrollton, at Hampson Street,
Riverbend (861 8661); 3300 Severn Avenue,
Metairie (456 1624).

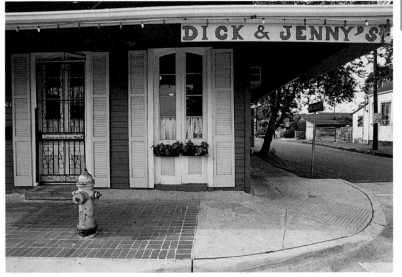

Dick & Jenny's: an Uptown double act. *See p141.*

Eat, Drink, Shop

Café Bayou Bagelry

1907 St Charles Avenue, between St Mary & St Andrew Streets (525 9400). St Charles Streetcar. **Open** 7am-5pm Mon-Fri; 8am-4pm Sun. **Credit** AmEx, MC, V. **Map** p308 A3.

Uptown and downtown, Bayou Bagelry is the place in New Orleans for bagels. For breakfast, lunch or dinner, it's easy to accommodate all tastes with 15 kinds of bagels and nearly as many trademark schmears for spreading. There are also soups, salads and a variety of bagel sandwiches. Eat in or send your other half out for bagels and a tub of honey vanilla walnut schmear for a relaxing morning at your hotel. The CBD location on Gravier Street is open 8am to 2pm Monday to Saturday, but is closed on Sunday.

Branch: 830 Gravier Street, between Carondelet & Baronne Streets, CBD (524 5001).

CC's Gourmet Coffee House

2917 Magazine Street, at 7th Street (891 2115). Bus 11 Magazine. **Open** 6am-11pm Mon-Fri; 6.30am-11pm Sat; 7am-10pm Sun. **Credit** AmEx, MC, V. **Map** p308 A3.

Community Coffee joined the coffee craze with a sophisticated chain of coffeehouses dotted around the city and the state. Rather than just sell the New Orleans Blend Coffee and Chicory that made Community a household name, CC's also offers upscale single-bean and blended bag coffees from around the world to take home and brew yourself. At the bar order drip coffee, espresso, cappuccino, or the chain's signature drink – the Mochasippi – a frozen concoction of espresso, milk and a choice of flavours (the chocolate Mochasippi is terrific). Pastries, pies, cakes and cookies from recipes by TV chef John Folse are also available, as well as teas from the Republic of Tea.

Branches: throughout the city.

PJ's Coffee & Tea Company

5432 Magazine Street, at Jefferson Avenue (895 0273). Bus 11 Magazine. **Open** 6.30am-11pm Mon-Sat; 7am-11pm Sun. **Credit** AmEx, MC, V. **Map** pp306-7 B9.

Each night the brewers at PJ's grind plain and flavoured coffee beans (PJ's avoids flavoured syrups), cover them with cold water and let the mixture brew overnight. The next morning, the coffee is filtered and served over ice with milk. This cold-dripping process produces great-tasting iced coffee – the best in town. Check out the flavour of the day; if you're lucky you will find chocolate raspberry. The original PJ's on Magazine near Jefferson could use a good scrubbing, but that hasn't stopped the owner from franchising this coffeehouse chain around the country.

Branches: throughout the city.

Rue de la Course

1500 Magazine Street, at Race Street (899 0242). Bus 11 Magazine. **Open** 7am-11pm Mon-Thur, Sun; 7am-midnight Fri, Sat. **No credit cards**. **Map** p309 B3.

The **Red Room** is a real Eiffel. *See p142.*

This coffeehouse takes its name from its original location at the corner of Magazine Street and Race Street (*rue de la Course* in French). On entering, customers are greeted by an enticing wall full of teas, a beautifully pressed tin ceiling and straight-backed chairs. Rue de la Course is very popular with undergraduates and others who come here to relax, read or chat with friends. Espresso, cappuccino, chocolate, teas and pastries are available, as well as iced coffee flavoured with syrup.

Branches: 241 Bourbon Street, between Bienville Avenue & Iberville Street, French Quarter (524 0114); 401 Carondelet Street, at Perdido Street, CBD (586 0401); 1128 Magazine Street, at Gaienne Street, Warehouse District (899 0242); 217 Peters Street, between Common & Gravier Streets, CBD (523 0206).

Cajun

Brigtsen's

723 Dante Street, at River Road (861 7610). St Charles Streetcar. **Open** 5.30-10pm Tue-Sat; closed Mon, Sun. **Main courses** $14-$24. **Credit** AmEx, DC, MC, V. **Map** pp306-7 A8.

This charming restaurant, housed in a renovated shotgun house and winner of the James Beard Award for Best Restaurant in the South-east in 1998, is the work of Frank Brigtsen. A champion of local ingredients, Brigtsen combines Creole and Cajun cuisines in exquisite imaginative ways. Picking something from the delicious-sounding items on the daily changing menu is difficult, but a good choice might include baked oysters stuffed with oyster dressing and truffle oil, butternut squash and shrimp bisque, and anything from the list of tempting main courses.

Jacques-Imo

8324 Oak Street, at Camp Street (861 0886). St Charles Streetcar. **Open** 6-10pm Mon-Thur; 5.30-10.30pm Fri, Sat; closed Sun. **Main courses** $13-$18. **Credit** AmEx, DC, MC, V. **Map** pp306-7 A7.

Jacques-Imo's chef Jack honed his skills in Paul Prudhomme's kitchen before opening this terrific little restaurant. It's always bulging at the seams with hungry patrons sampling ample portions of Cajun food with a twist either in the inside dining room at the front or on the rustic covered patio at the rear. Try the fried squash blossoms, shrimp Creole, potato salad, fresh fish specials, maque-choux and fried oysters with garlic sauce. With a full belly, you can walk a few doors down to the Maple Leaf Bar (*see p223*), for a full night of the best music on Oak Street.

Contemporary

Dick & Jenny's

4501 Tchoupitoulas Street, at Jena Street (894 9880). Bus 10 Tchoupitoulas. **Open** 5.30-10pm Tue-Sat; closed Mon, Sun. **Main courses** $12-$19. **Credit** AmEx, MC, V. **Map** pp306-7 C9.

Dick & Jenny's is a recent addition to the New Orleans restaurant scene in an unlikely location, with people waiting over an hour for a seat (you can't book). Before opening this restaurant, Dick, the chef, worked his way around several respectable New Orleans kitchens. Jenny is his wife and she takes care of the front-of-house side of the establishment. Together they offer fantastic modern New Orleans food in a comfortable setting. The menu changes often, but there are always ample duck and pork dishes and quite a few fresh fish dishes from which to choose. At Dick & Jenny's you can guarantee that every morsel of food will be full-flavoured and well presented.

Gautreau's

1728 Soniat Street, between Dryades & Daneel Streets (899 7397). St Charles Streetcar. **Open** 6-10pm Mon-Sat; closed Sun. **Main courses** $40-$45. **Credit** DC, MC, V. **Map** p309 A2.

Michael Saxer is the young chef who has made Gautreau's into a jewel in the city's culinary crown. Situated in residential Uptown, this restaurant has the kind of simple decor that provides a wonderful backdrop for a sophisticated dinner. Do not miss the mussels of the week or the grilled beets for an appetiser. Saxer's seared dry-pack scallops are intensely flavoured and perfectly paired with sautéed spinach and *beurre rouge*. A choice of pork, lamb, fish and beef dishes offers variety enough to please the pickiest diner.

Mat & Naddie's

937 Leonidas Street, at Freret Street (861 9600). St Charles Streetcar/11 Freret, 32 Leonidas bus. **Open** 11am-2pm, 5.30-9.30pm Tue-Fri; 5.30-9.30pm Sat; closed Mon, Sun. **Credit** AmEx, DC, MC, V. **Map** p306-7 A7.

Visit **La Crêpe Nanou** for a pile of crêpes. *See p142.*

Café du Monde
Open 24 hours. See page 125.

Camellia Grill
Open till 3am on Friday and Saturday, and until 1am on all other days. See page 138.

Clover Grill
Open 24 hours. See page 131.

Hummingbird Grill
Open 24 hours. See page 134.

Morning Call Coffee Stand
Open 24 hours. See page 148.

Napoleon House
Open till midnight Monday to Thursday, and till 1am on Friday and Saturday. See page 132.

La Peniche
Open 24 hours. See page 132.

Port of Call
Open till 1am daily. See page 133.

Snug Harbor
Open till 2am daily. See page p133.

The Trolley Stop Café
Open 24 hours. See page 139.

A quaint restaurant in the Riverbend, Mat & Naddie's offers a range of food that will wake up even the most jaded palate. A meal can begin with dishes as different from each other as creamy shrimp bisque, Japanese seaweed salad or Vietnamese spring rolls. Although there is only one vegetarian main course on the menu, vegetables are taken seriously at this restaurant and come straight from local farmers.

Red Room
2040 St Charles Avenue, at Josephine Street (528 9759). St Charles Streetcar. **Open** *Restaurant* 6-10pm Wed-Sun. *Nightclub* 6pm-2am Wed-Sun. Closed Mon, Tue. **Main courses** $20-$30. **Credit** AmEx, DC, MC, V. **Map** pp306-7 E8.

This swank dinner-and-dance club is cloaked in red and tucked into a building made from discarded pieces of the Eiffel Tower. It's popular with a young, hip crowd that is equally at home dancing to the live flamenco, swing bands or smooth crooners. There's no prominent Louisiana influence on the menu, but the Red Room food has garnered national awards. However, if you're conserving your cash, you may want to skip dinner and settle for enjoying late-night dancing and people-watching. For details of live music at the Red Room, *see p222.*

Upperline
1413 Upperline Street, at St Charles Avenue (891 9822). St Charles Streetcar. **Open** 5.30-9.30pm Wed, Thur; 5.30-10pm Fri, Sat; 11.30am-2pm, 5.30-9.30pm Sun; closed Mon, Tue. **Main courses** $17. **Credit** AmEx, DC, MC, V. **Map** pp306-7 C9.

Sick of homogeneity? Then try this intimate eaterie that makes a virtue of originality. The walls of the restaurant are covered with local art and owner JoAnn Clevenger swirls around the dining room lavishing her guests with personal attention. The eclectic Creole menu includes beautifully presented shrimp rémoulade with Creole tomatoes and fillet steak with Stilton and balsamic jus.

Creole

Commander's Palace
1403 Washington Avenue, at Coliseum Street (899 8221). St Charles Streetcar. **Open** 11.30am-1.30pm, 6-9.30pm Mon-Fri; 11.30am-12.30pm (jazz brunch), 6-9.30pm Sat; 10.30am-1.30pm (jazz brunch), 6-9.30pm Sun. **Main courses** $22-$30. **Credit** AmEx, DC, MC, V. **Map** p309 A3.

Thirty years since it opened, Commander's Palace remains one of New Orleans's biggest draws. And that's because the Brennan family knows how to run a restaurant: a talented kitchen, headed by Jamie Shannon, turns out consistent yet inspired Creole food; the service is friendly and professional; and the dining room is festive. Whether you order veal with goat's cheese or real turtle soup, you're in for a treat, and the soufflé bread pudding is the stuff of dreams. On Saturdays and Sundays blend in with the local gentry by coming dressed in a seersucker suit and white buck shoes or a filmy summer frock for a weekend jazz brunch of potent milk punches and grillades and grits. It's worth every penny, and we're talking a lot o' pennies. The dress code requires a jacket for men at brunch and dinner; call for further details.

French

La Crêpe Nanou
1401 Robert Street, at Prytania Street (899 2670). St Charles Streetcar. **Open** 6-10pm Mon-Thur, Sun; 6-11pm Fri, Sat. **Main courses** $7. **Credit** MC, V. **Map** pp306-7 C9.

An enchanting café with a few tables outside, La Crêpe Nanou specialises in crêpes (of course), filled with everything from crabmeat or ratatouille to chocolate sauce and ice-cream. However, you can also start things off with an avocado salad or *salade tropicale*. Nanou is a lively spot for meals with friends, but it can be way too crowded at times.

Italian

Figaro's Pizzeria

7900 Maple Street, at Fern Street (866 0100).
St Charles Streetcar. **Open** 11am-10.30pm Mon-
Thur; 11am-11.30pm Fri, Sat; noon-10pm Sun.
Main courses $5.50-$15. **Credit** AmEx, DC, MC, V.
Map pp306-7 A/B8.

Figaro's is a quiet Italian restaurant on a slow
corner of Uptown. Several tables are set out on the
pavement in front of the restaurant, and the low level
of traffic on Maple Street makes this one of the few
places in New Orleans where it's actually pleasant
to dine outside. Daily specials, pasta, calzones,
salads and Neapolitan-style pizzas make dining
alfresco a pleasure even on the hottest nights of the
New Orleans summer.

Reginelli's

741 State Street, at Magazine Street (899 1414).
Bus 11 Magazine. **Open** 11am-11pm Mon-Thur,
Sun; 11am-midnight Fri, Sat. **Credit** MC, V.
Map pp306-7 B9.

If your legs are aching from going into every dust-
infested antiques shop on Magazine, rest your dogs
at Reginelli's. You won't get the best pizza in your
life here, but the gourmet renditions with goat's
cheese and such aren't bad and will at least get you
refuelled in time to make the rounds at the zoo.
Better yet, sit outside and graze on a designer
focaccia sandwich with prosciutto as you breathe
in the bus fumes.

Mediterranean

Jamila's Café

7808 Maple Street, at Burdette Street (866 4366).
St Charles Streetcar. **Open** 11.30am-2pm, 5.30-
9.30pm Tue-Thur; 11.30am-2pm, 5.30-10.30pm Fri;
5.30-10.30pm Sat; 5.30-9.30pm Sun; closed Mon.
Main courses $10-$15. **Credit** AmEx, MC, V.
Map pp306-7 A7.

Jamila's makes you realise that Tunisian food can
be as forceful and delicious as any Mediterranean
fare. Dig into smoky home-made lamb sausage,
whole grilled fish and perfectly cooked couscous
with fiery harissa. The decor is unspectacular, but
it doesn't matter: the food is the focus here, with the
possible exception of the attractive belly dancer,
who works the room on Saturday nights.

Lebanon's Café

*1506 S Carrollton Avenue, at Jeannette Street (862
6200). St Charles Streetcar.* **Open** 11am-11pm Mon-
Sat; noon-9pm Sun. **Main courses** $3.25-$8.99.
Credit AmEx, DC, MC, V. **Map** pp306-7 A7.

Restaurants have come and gone in this Carrollton
spot, but the simple Lebanon's Café looks like it's
here to stay. Consistently good Middle Eastern food
at cheap prices keeps the punters coming. Did we
mention you can bring your own wine and beer?
Need we say more?

Mexican

Kokopelli's

3150 Calhoun Street, at Claiborne Street (861 3922).
Bus 16 S Claiborne. **Open** 11am-10pm daily.
Main courses $5.80-$7.50. **Credit** AmEx, MC, V.
Map pp306-7 B7.

Kokopelli's choice of hefty, cheap burritos makes it
a favourite spot for slackers who are low on cash.
Choose from the menu's assortment of burritos and
quesadillas, and eat them outside instead of in the
drab dining room.

Superior Grill

*3636 St Charles Avenue, at Antonine Street (899
4200). St Charles Streetcar.* **Open** 11am-10pm Mon,
Tue, Sun; 11am-11pm Wed, Thur, 11am-midnight
Fri, Sat. **Main courses** $5.80-$7.50. **Credit** AmEx,
DC, MC, V. **Map** pp306-7 B8.

'Famosa por fajitas y margaritas' is the logo on the
signs throughout this popular St Charles Avenue
restaurant. On Wednesday nights, a three-for-one
happy hour draws huge after-work crowds that fill
the ample restaurant and spill on to the street. Order
a tart and tasty Margarita as you like it: on the
rocks, frozen, with or without salt, in a pitcher, or
try the excellent Top Shelf Margarita, mixed with
Cuervo Gold and Grand Marnier. The best way to
enjoy Superior is to order some potato chips with
salsa and an ice-cold Margarita and consume them
outside on the patio.

Oyster heaven at **Casamento's**. *See p144.*

Eat, Drink, Shop

Taqueria Corona

5932 Magazine Street, at Nashville Street (897 3974). Bus 11 Magazine. **Open** 11.30am-2pm, 5-9.30pm daily. **Main courses** under $10. **Credit** AmEx, DC, MC, V. **Map** pp306-7 A9.

Everyone in town calls it a Mexican restaurant, although the owner hails from El Salvador. Inside the cantina, order a Margarita on the rocks, sample the *pico de gallo* and guacamole on crunchy chips, and then peruse the menu. Tongue, chorizo and fish are taco choices, while burritos with beef, pork and chicken round out the menu. Order a combination platter if you're really hungry, or try a shrimp flauta served hot from the deep fryer.

Neighbourhood

Casamento's

4330 Magazine Street, at Napoleon Avenue (895 9761). Bus 11 Magazine, 24 Napoleon. **Open** 11.30am-1.30pm, 5.30-9pm Tue-Sun; closed Mon. Closed July, Aug. **Main courses** $6-$12. **No credit cards. Map** pp306-7 C9.

A nostalgic shrine to the local oyster tradition, this is the sort of place where time has stood still. Little has changed in the 80 years of business: the green and white tiles are the same, the old marble oyster bar stands are the same, and the oysters are still only served three ways – raw, fried or stewed. Start with a dozen raw oysters for the essence of the sea; then, test the best oyster sandwich in town: dipped in corn flour and fried in lard, these oysters are ethereally tender and vigorously fresh. Twin with must-have pan-fried French fries.

Clancy's

6100 Annunciation Street, at Webster Street (895 1111). Bus 19 Nashville Express. **Open** 5.30-10.30pm Mon; 11.30am-2pm, 5.30-10.30pm Tue-Thur; 11.30am-2pm Fri; 5.30-11pm Sat. **Main courses** $10.95-$23.95. **Credit** AmEx, DC, MC, V. **Map** pp306-7 E9.

Catering to Uptown ladies who lunch and blue-blazer-sporting residents, this clubby restaurant rarely sees a tourist. It's worth a visit, though, for the smoked soft-shell crab, shrimp rémoulade, lamb chops and home-made peppermint ice-cream. It's hard to find, so take a cab.

Domilise Sandwich Shop & Bar

5240 Annunciation Street, at Bellecastle Street (899 9126). Bus 11 Magazine. **Open** 11am-7pm Mon-Sat; closed Sun. **Main courses** $6.95. **No credit cards. Map** pp306-7 C10.

Domilise is a New Orleans institution. A non-descript building belies the fact that the café inside is a temple to food. This family-owned neighbourhood restaurant serves incredible po-boys to the working class and upper class alike, who generally reckon the roast beef, shrimp and oyster versions hit the top of the po-boy charts. Place your order with the women behind the counter, then order your drink at the adjacent bar and get ready for some great food.

Franky & Johnny's

321 Arabella Street, at Tchoupitoulas Street (899 9146). Bus 10 Tchoupitoulas. **Open** 11am-10pm Mon-Thur; 11am-midnight Fri, Sat; 11am-10.30pm Sun. **Main courses** $5.99-$15. **Credit** AmEx, MC, V. **Map** pp306-7 E9.

Cooking up a seafood frenzy at **Franky & Johnny's**.

Step inside the glass door and into a living history of New Orleans. This neighbourhood bastion on Arabella Street is popular beyond belief during Carnival, Jazz Fest and pretty much any other time of the year. Beyond the bar and the dancefloor-cum-game room, red and white checked tablecloths cover a slew of tables that are the short-lived resting place for crawfish pies, boiled crawfish, po-boys, gumbo, soft-shell crabs, oysters, bell pepper rings and other New Orleans food favourites. To eat at Franky & Johnny's is to capture a part of the soul of the Crescent City; this is particularly the case on big Sunday nights, when older couples take to the dancefloor, the bar is splendidly raucous and the tables are filled with life-loving New Orleanians. Don't miss it.

Hansen's Sno-Bliz
4801 Tchoupitoulas Street, at Upperline Street (no phone). Bus 10 Tchoupitoulas. **Open** *Summer* 2-7pm daily. *Winter* closed. **No credit cards.**
In the summer, New Orleanians will go anywhere for a 'snowball' – a paper cone filled with finely shaved ice and a rainbow of heavily sugared syrups. This no-frills stall in Uptown is the original place that invented the machine that shaves the ice that – you get the picture.

Parasol's
2533 Constance Street, at Magazine Street (899 2054/www.parasols.com). Bus 11 Magazine. **Open** 11am-11pm Mon, Wed-Sun; 11am-8pm Tue. **Main courses** $5.50-$7.50. **Credit** AmEx, DC, MC, V. **Map** pp306-7 E9.
This neighbourhood restaurant and bar is home to one of the biggest St Patrick's Day celebrations in New Orleans. Throngs of revellers flood the streets drinking green beer and meeting new friends all afternoon. During the remainder of the year Parasol's is worth visiting because it serves great po-boys. Enter the Third Street side, order your food at the kitchen door, a drink from the bar window, then sit down and wait for the kitchen staff to call your number.

Pascal's Manale
1838 Napoleon Avenue, at Dryades Street (895 4877). St Charles Streetcar/24 Napoleon bus. **Open** 11.30am-10pm Mon-Fri; 4-10pm Sat; 4-9pm Sun. Closed summer (Memorial Day-Labor Day). **Main courses** $5.95-$10.95. **Credit** AmEx, DC, MC, V. **Map** pp306-7 D9.
Manale's is a crush of drinking, loud talking and breathless oyster eating – and that's before you get anywhere near a table. Sometimes it seems as though everyone in town is standing at Pascal's bar waiting for a seat. The dining room atmosphere verges on raucous, with children running around all over the place and people shouting across to friends at other tables. It's may be an upmarket restaurant, but it's one in the local tradition. Moreover, many locals consider it the true New Orleans home of barbecued shrimp.

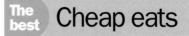

The best Cheap eats

Camellia Grill
See page 138.

Central Grocery
See page 180.

Irene's Cuisine
See page 130.

Jacques-Imo
See page 141.

Kokopelli's
See page 143.

Maspero's
See page 131.

Mona's Café
See page 148.

Taqueria Corona
See page 144.

Mid City

American

Crescent City Steakhouse
1001 N Broad Avenue, at St Philip Street (821 3271). Bus 98 Broad. **Open** 11.30am-11pm Tue-Sun; closed Mon. **Main courses** $16.75-$18.75. **Credit** AmEx, DC, MC, V. **Map** p308 E5.
Look no further than for an incredible steak, cooked to perfection, served in a casual setting, and priced at the reasonable end of the scale. Even with old rivals and new competition, some believe that Crescent City still serves the best steak in town. The one room '50s-style restaurant has a row of partitioned booths that can be made even more secluded by drawing the green privacy curtains. The beef, whether fillet, strip, rib-eye, T-bone or porterhouse, is superb and should be accompanied by spinach au gratin and home-made French fries. No matter how full you are, finish with bread pudding.

Ruth's Chris Steak House
711 N Broad Street, at Orleans Avenue (486 0810/ www.ruthchris.com). Bus 98 Broad. **Open** 11.30am-11.30pm Mon-Fri; 4-11pm Sat; 11.30am-11pm Sun. **Main courses** $24-$30. **Credit** AmEx, DC, MC, V. **Map** pp306-7 E6.
Best steak in New Orleans? Most natives will point you towards Chris's. Hatched in New Orleans, this national chain serves steaks literally sizzling in butter. Go for overkill and begin with home-made potato chips and stuffed mushrooms, followed by

creamed spinach and potatoes au gratin to go with your steak. Wash it all down with a hearty Cabernet, and you'll be in a food coma.
Branch: 3633 Veterans Boulevard, Metairie (888 3600).

Asian

Genghis Khan
*4053 Tulane Avenue, at Carrollton Avenue (482 4044). Bus 39 Tulane, 90 Carrollton.***Open** 5.30-11.30pm Tue-Sun; closed Mon. **Main courses** $12.95. **Credit** AmEx, DC, MC, V. **Map** pp306-7 C6.
At this wacky Korean restaurant waiters are prone to bursting into arias with owner and maître d' Henry Lee joining in on the violin. The endearing waiting staff consists entirely of professional classical musicians, who serve reliable Korean standards such as *bibimbop* and *kimchee*.

Japon
3125 Esplanade Avenue, at Grand Route St John (949 6800). Bus 48 Esplanade. **Open** 11.30am-2.30pm, 5.30-10pm Mon, Wed-Fri; 5.30-10pm Tue; closed Sat, Sun. **Main courses** $15-$25. **Credit** AmEx, MC, V. **Map** p308 E5.
Sushi has long conquered New Orleans, but there remained a sushi-less void around Esplanade Avenue until Japon came along to remedy the situation. The impeccable sushi is made from fish that is FedExed in daily, and you can tell.

Cafés

New Orleans Museum of Art Café
1 Collins Diboll Circle, City Park (488 2631). Bus 48 Esplanade. **Open** 10.30am-4.30pm Tue-Sun; closed Mon. **Main courses** $9. **Credit** AmEx, MC, V. **Map** p308 D5.
When the museum (*see p111*) added a new wing, the designers managed to fit a café into the plan. It's a sun-drenched and relaxing place for refreshment after taking in all the art treasures. The coffee, pastries, desserts and sandwiches will restore your culture-sapped strength.

Caribbean

Palmer's Restaurant
135 N Carrollton Avenue, at Canal Street (482 3658). Bus 43 Canal/Lake Vista, 90 Carrollton. **Open** 11.30am-2pm, 6-10.30pm Tue-Fri; 6-10.30pm Sat. **Main courses** $5.95-$10.95. **No credit cards**. **Map** p308 D5.
This easy-to-miss restaurant looks drab from the street and isn't much more impressive inside for that matter. Nevertheless, it's generally packed with eager diners filling up on spicy Caribbean food. You won't go away hungry with generous portions of jerked fish, curried goat, curried shrimp, meat pies and the like. Palmer's sets up a popular booth at Jazz Fest every year.

Contemporary

Gabrielle
3201 Esplanade Avenue, at Mystery Street (948 6233). Bus 48 Esplanade. **Open** 5.30-10pm Tue-Thur, Sat; 11.30am-2pm, 5.30-10pm Fri. Closed June-Aug. **Main courses** $16.95-$20. **Credit** AmEx, DC, MC, V. **Map** p308 E5.
Gabrielle's chef, Greg Sonnier, comes with many accolades and serves contemporary Creole cuisine from an oft-changing menu that incorporates the freshest ingredients. Duck, rabbit, fish, shoestring sweet potatoes and burned-butter mashed potatoes are always excellent choices in this small restaurant, and the peppermint patti (rich chocolate cake, topped with an intense peppermint-oil flavoured ice-cream) is a must for dessert.

Creole & soul food

Dooky Chase Restaurant
2301 Orleans Avenue, at Miro Street (821 2294). Bus 46 City Park. **Open** 11.30am-10pm daily. **Main courses** $6.50-$25. **Credit** AmEx, DC, MC, V. **Map** pp306-7 F6.
Leah Chase (wife of Dooky) is the reigning queen of her home town's Creole cuisine. In her family restaurant, she serves reliable favourites like grillades, court bouillon and crawfish étouffée. She also adds a generous dose of soul food: barbecued ribs, fried chicken and grilled pork chops. The restaurant is located in a marginal neighbourhood across the street from a housing project. Although the Chases' commitment to their community is to be admired (they've resisted all pleas to move), the best plan for visiting is to take a cab to the front door.

Italian

Angelo Brocato's
214 N Carrollton Avenue, at Canal Street (486 0078). Bus 90 Carrollton. **Open** 9.30am-10pm Mon-Thur, Sun; 9.30am-10.30pm Fri, Sat. **Credit** MC, V. **Map** p308 D5.

Taste the sweet stuff at **Angelo Brocato's**.

When it comes to traditional sweet stuff, it doesn't get any better than this. Tucked away deep in the heart of Mid City, Brocato's is well worth searching out. All its desserts are steeped in old-Italian traditions, and the place itself looks like a Norman Rockwell painting of a turn-of-the-19th-century ice-cream shop. Go directly for the cannoli, the vanilla pudding or the tiramisu.

Mediterranean

Lola's

3312 Esplanade Avenue, at Mystery Street (488 6946). Bus 48 Esplanade. **Open** 6-10pm Mon-Thur; 11.30am-2.30pm, 6-10.30pm Fri, Sat; 11.30am-2.30pm Sun. **Main courses** $6-$12. **No credit cards**. **Map** p308 E4.

Good morning, Vietnam!

So you thought all we had was Creole and Cajun to offer. Perhaps you didn't know that New Orleans has some of the best Vietnamese food anywhere. There's even a Vietnamese farmers market in New Orleans East (a Vietnamese suburb of sorts), complete with weird and wondrous food: long, bitter melon with green nubby skin, orange taro root, mottled squashes, purple basil, water spinach and dried shrimp. And there are plenty of trinkety treasures and all sorts of Asian ingredients to be found at a slew of Vietnamese markets that look like they came straight out of New York's Chinatown.

Most of these ingredients were introduced to Louisiana by the 20,000 Vietnamese-Americans now living in and around New Orleans. (The Crescent City has been a destination for Vietnamese immigrants since the mid-1970s.) Chefs at upscale restaurants have since experimented with Vietnamese ingredients, adding the likes of fish sauce,

rice paper, purple basil and lemongrass into their pantries. At **Mat & Naddie's** (see page 141) in the Riverbend, for example, you'll find shrimp rolls with lime-spiked fish sauce on the menu alongside shrimp bisque. Vietnamese food has become so popular that Minh Bui, chef-owner of **Lemon Grass Restaurant** on Carrollton, was able to open another hipper branch of his successful restaurant in the International House Hotel (pictured; see page 135). Many locals tout this dressed-up Vietnamese spot as the city's best restaurant of any type. Even construction workers who for years have subsisted on po-boys for lunch now frequent places like **Pho Tau Bay** in Gretna (see page 149) for cheap filling bowls of Vietnamese beef noodle soup. And in the CBD, conservative suits have foregone red beans (OK, maybe not every Monday) for com suon (broiled pork chops over Vietnamese crushed rice) at the **Nine Roses** (see page 149).

Eat, Drink, Shop

This hole-in-the-wall across the street from Gabrielle serves authentic Spanish food including vegetarian, seafood and meat paella, garlic shrimp, fish specials, roasted pork tenderloin and big salads. Potent garlic bread is a good filler if you've waited long for a table,which is likely if you come after 7pm. Bring your own wine and prepare for a feast.

Mona's Café

3901 Banks Street, between Canal & Tulane Streets (482 7743). Bus 39 Tulane. **Open** 11am-9pm Mon-Wed; 11am-10pm Fri, Sat; noon-6pm Sun; closed Thur. **Main courses** $5.99-$9.99. **Credit** AmEx, DC, MC, V. **Map** p308 C5.

Mona's good cheap eats, quick service and porch dining make it the most popular Middle Eastern restaurant in town. Choose from decent dips like houmous and baba ganoush, home-made pitta sandwiches and shish kebabs. Walk through the well-stocked Middle Eastern grocery store that shares the premises, and you'll leave with a bagful.

Neighbourhood

Café Degas

3127 Esplanade Avenue, at Ponce de Leon Street (945 5635). Bus 48 Esplanade. **Open** 11.30am-2.30pm, 5.30-10pm Mon-Thur; 11.30am-2.30pm, 6-11pm Fri; 6-11pm Sat; 10.30am-3pm, 6-10pm Sun. **Main courses** $5.95-$17.95. **Credit** AmEx, DC, MC, V. **Map** p308 E5.

For some reason, locals are willing to dismiss slow service and inconsistent food to eat at Café Degas. It must be the patio dining and decent brunches that keep people coming back. You're likely to want to refuel after visiting the New Orleans Museum of Art nearby, anyway, but be wise and stick to the salads and sandwiches.

Mandina's

3800 Canal Street, at N Cortez Street (482 9179). Bus 41 Canal. **Open** 11am-10.30pm Mon-Sat; noon-9.30pm Sun. **Main courses** $6-$13.95. **No credit cards.** **Map** p308 B5.

You need to remember four words at Mandina's: red beans and rice. This New Orleans staple doesn't get any better than this. But to avoid revealing your tourist credentials, don't ask for them on any other day but Monday. The drab dining room hasn't changed since 1932 and neither has anything else – thank goodness. You can still get excellent oyster and artichoke soup, panéed veal and corned beef with cabbage.

Metairie

American

Foodies Kitchen

720 Veterans Boulevard, at Wilshire Street (837 9695/www.foodieskitchen.com). No public transport. **Open** 7am-10pm daily. **Main courses** $2.99-$10. **Credit** AmEx, MC, V.

From the moment you pull open the door, you realise this market-cum-deli is like no other in New Orleans. Jazz blares over the noisy crowd of shoppers at this latest Brennan family creation, a one-stop shop for all kinds of food: the 'hot line' serves grilled-while-you-wait meats, sausages and hot plates; the bakery turns out breads, pies, cakes and cookies; made-to-order sandwiches and salads are served across the aisle from each other; and you haven't even made it to the prepared food section yet, or got anywhere near the wines, fresh produce, coffee or snacks. The friendly staff and buzzing atmosphere make it a tough decision whether to sit and eat right there with the other Foodies or to put together a picnic bag. Be sure to try the chocolate bon bon bread, the wrap du jour, or a single serving of Brennan's famous white chocolate bread pudding. Note, the Kitchen is licensed for wine and beer only.

Asian

Royal China

600 Veterans Boulevard, at Aris Street (831 9633). No public transport. **Open** 11.30am-3pm daily. **Main courses** $2.95-$16.95. **Credit** AmEx, DC, Disc, MC, V.

Royal China is the best place to get away from the boring Americanised Chinese food that has invaded the rest of town. Excellent all-day dim sum, including deliciously delicate shrimp dumplings will make you forget just how far from China you are.

Sake Café

4201 Veterans Boulevard, at Houma Boulevard (779 7253). No public transport. **Open** 11am-10pm Mon-Thur; 11am-11pm Fri; 11.30am-11pm Sat; 11.30am-10pm Sun. **Main course** $15. **Credit** AmEx, DC, MC, V.

With a soothing atmosphere and excellent meals, Sake Café offers the most pleasant and rewarding sushi experience in the New Orleans area. Gentle Japanese music floats through a lofty dining room that is filled with simple, natural wood furnishings to complement elegant trays of the freshest sushi and sashimi imaginable.

Cafés

Morning Call Coffee Stand

Lakeside Plaza, 3325 Severn Avenue, at 17th Street (885 4068). Bus 27 Louisiana, 40, 41 or 44 Canal, 48 Esplanade, then E4 Metairie Road. **Open** 24hrs daily. **No credit cards.**

Morning Call is the Metairie equivalent of Café du Monde (*see p125*). Its location in a strip mall next to a newsstand and across from the Lakeside Mall makes this a popular 24-hour spot in the 'burbs. Morning Call used to be a French Quarter institution to rival Café du Monde but during a long, long renovation of the French Market in the 1970s it decided to follow many of its customers to the other side. The coffee, café au lait and beignets are delicious – made the same as they've been for decades.

Kosher

Kosher Cajun Deli

3520 North Hullen, at West Esplanade (888 2010).
Bus Veterans. **Open** 10am-7pm Mon-Thur; 10am-
3pm Fri, Sun; closed Sat. **Main courses** $2.25-
$10.95. **Credit** AmEx, DC, MC, V.
Once you get over the sterile surroundings, you will
find incredible deli meats that you can have on a
sandwich or order by the pound to go. The completely kosher restaurant also offers soups, salads,
chopped liver, whitefish salad, gefilte fish, potato
latkes and various knishes. A new entrance on busy
Severn Avenue makes this spot a little easier to find,
but at lunch, plan on parking down the street.

Neighbourhood

Drago's Seafood Restaurant & Oyster Bar

3232 North Arnoult Road (888 9254). No public
transport. **Open** 11am-9.30pm Mon-Thur; 11am-
10pm Fri; 5-10pm Sat; closed Sun. **Main courses**
$7.95-$23.95. **Credit** AmEx, DC, MC, V.
Shell out the money to take a cab to Drago's and
you'll be thrilled you did. Its claim to fame are grilled
oysters and its secret lies in smoke from the grill,
incredibly fresh oysters, garlic butter and a sprin-
kling of Parmesan. Is your mouth watering yet?
Swirl the oyster around in the juices and then let the
briny freshness, infused with lemon, garlic and
smokiness, envelop your taste buds. Wipe the shells
clean with bread. Sadly, with only a dozen oysters
in a portion, the experience is over quickly, so forget any notions of sharing and order a dozen all to
yourself. You'll be dreaming about these beauties
for years to come.

R&O's

216 Hammond Highway, at Carrollton Street (831
1248). No public transport. **Open** 11am-10pm Mon,
Wed, Thur; 11am-11pm Fri, Sat; closed Tue, Sun.
Main courses $7-$15. **Credit** AmEx, DC, MC, V.
You have to suffer screaming kids and a long wait
at weekends here, but it's worth it. Forget about the
pizza and start with a rich, dark seafood gumbo,
move on to an oyster or crawfish pie doused with the
local Crystal hot sauce, and finally get your chops
round the pièce de résistance, a roast beef po-boy.
French bread is dipped into pan drippings and then
piled with bits of roast beef in gravy. The resulting
sandwich is incredibly juicy and satisfying.

West Bank

Asian

Kim Son

349 Whitney Avenue, at Westbank Expressway,
Gretna (366 2489). No public transport. **Open** 9am-
9pm daily. **Main courses** $2.50-$25. **Credit** MC, V.

While New Orleanians debate who makes the best
Vietnamese food on the West Bank, Gretna locals
stake their money on this favourite. The decor
doesn't win any points, but the food certainly does.
Ask your Vietnamese waitress to bring you some
salt-baked shrimp and sautéed watercress, and don't
forget to order the Vietnamese iced coffee, which is
brewed at your table.

Nine Roses

1100 Stephen Street (Westbank Expressway),
Gretna (366 7665). No public transport. **Open**
9.30am-9.30pm Mon, Tue, Sun; 9.30am-10.30pm Fri,
Sat; closed Wed, Thur. **Main courses** $6.50-$11.95.
Credit AmEx, DC, MC, V. **Map** pp306-7 G10.
Feeling a little porky after all that rich Creole food?
Venture into the bland strip mall world of the West
Bank and make your way to Nine Roses in Gretna
for some authentic Vietnamese food that is possibly
even better than that served at Kim Son (*see above*).
This place delivers a much-needed break from
Creole and Cajun overkill with such fresh dishes as
shrimp rolls in rice paper, thin slices of raw beef
cooked on your own grill, vermicelli and herb salad,
and shrimp-wrapped sugar cane.

Pho Tau Bay

113C Westbank Expressway, Gretna (368 9846).
No public transport. **Open** 9am-9pm daily. **Main**
courses $5-$17. **Credit** MC, V.
The soup at this Vietnamese caff sets it apart from
its peers. The huge bowls of bubbling fragrant broth
arrive with rice noodles and thin beef slices that cook
as they sit. Topped off with the tastes of coriander,
Vietnamese basil, lime, bean sprouts and jalapeño –
it will make you happy and warm in no time flat.
And you certainly won't find a better cure for the
common cold.

Further afield

Italian

Mosca's

4137 US90 West, Waggaman (436 9942). No public
transport. **Open** 5.30-9.30pm Tue-Sat; closed Mon,
Sun. **Main courses** $10-$24. **No credit cards.**
Its location on the side of the road, across the
Mississippi River and 40 minutes away from the
CBD doesn't deter New Orleanians who love a good
food joint from coming to Mosca's. The restaurant
looks like it came straight out of a Mafia movie –
dim lighting, worn-out floors, a mess of tables – and
the food seems to come out of nowhere. At Mosca's
it's party night every night as old friends magically
appear at your elbow for an impromptu reunion. Get
there early or wait at the bar because once seated,
people don't move in a hurry. The New Orleans
Italian food – oysters Mosca, crab salad, barbecued
shrimp, spaghetti bordelaise and fragrant rosemary-
baked chicken – is memorably tasty and all served
family style, so get down and join the party.

Eat, Drink, Shop

Bars

The world's best place for a pub crawl. Probably.

In a city known for its celebrations, it should come as no surprise that partying is not limited to special occasions. Either as a respite from the stultifying heat and humidity of the summer or for the sheer social pleasure of it, going out in New Orleans invariably includes, at some point in the evening, a stop at one of the hundreds of drinking establishments – or even several of them. Chances are, whatever mood suits you, there's a bar to provide it.

Here is a list of the city's more interesting bars. We've largely ignored the tourist-packed Bourbon Street joints, but they're easy enough to find if that's what you're looking for – just remember that the city has much more to offer. To spend more than one night amid Bourbon Street's strip clubs and karaoke bars would mean missing the real New Orleans, the clubs and hole-in-the-wall places where the city's genuine music and excitements take place.

ALCOHOL AND THE LAW

Local laws make drinking in New Orleans a strange adventure. First and foremost, bars are not required to close or stop serving alcohol at any time, so although only a few stay open 24 hours, there are numerous late-night joints that are open until after the sun comes up. Many have no set closing time and will just keep on serving as long as there are people buying drinks. New Orleans bars have a reputation for relaxed or irregular hours of operation, so it's a good idea to check by phone before making a special trip. This laid-back approach also means a rapid turnover of bars, with some new places going out of business unexpectedly – another good reason for calling ahead. Bars that offer live music may charge admission, but it's rarely more than $5.

The most unusual feature of New Orleans bars is the 'go cup'. It's legal here to walk out of a bar and down the street while carrying your drink, provided you pour it into a plastic cup. Although the bartender or doorman of the next bar will usually make you finish your drink before letting you in, the go cup phenomenon makes traipsing from one joint to the next considerably more enjoyable than in most cities.

The really crucial laws about drinking deal with age limits. For many years New Orleans was alone among US cities in allowing 18-year-olds to drink. Today, the city has joined the mainstream in setting the drinking age at 21.

However, anyone aged 18 or over can enter and hang out in a bar, although they are prohibited from buying or consuming anything alcoholic. This means the crowd, particularly at college bars, tends to be younger than in many other US cities. European visitors should be aware that IDs are regularly checked in bars for proof of age. Only photo identification is accepted, so if you plan on drinking, take your passport or some other official document that shows a photo and birth date. People up to age 30 are regularly checked or 'carded' so take your ID even if you think you look way past 21. Bars with young crowds tend to be especially vigilant as being caught serving drinks to under-21s means big fines and automatic closure.

SAFETY

Since bar- and club-hopping is de rigueur in New Orleans, it's best to take a cab at night, particularly if you're venturing out of the Quarter (and we recommend you do). *See page 275* for a list of local cab companies.

French Quarter

The Abbey

1123 Decatur Street, between Governor Nicholls & Ursulines Streets (523 7150). Bus 55 Elysian Fields, 57 Franklin, 82 Desire. **Open** 24hrs daily. **No credit cards. Map** p315 D3.
Not too long ago, the Abbey had a reputation as the place where visiting sailors went to get falling-down drunk. Since then, under the guidance of a bartender from London, it has reinvented itself as the most interesting and comfortable bar on the Decatur Street stretch. The owner takes pride in the amount of Wild Turkey bourbon consumed here, while the bartenders insist they can keep up with any shot-drinking patron. DJs are scheduled on Sunday nights (usually reggae) and sometimes on other evenings. Drop by and see.

Carousel Bar & Lounge

Monteleone Hotel, 214 Royal Street, at Iberville Street (523 3341/www.hotelmonteleone.com). Bus 3 Vieux Carré. **Open** 11am-2am daily. **Credit** AmEx, DC, Disc, MC, V. **Map** p315 A2.

> ▶ For details of **music clubs** and other venues, see chapter **Music**, and for **gay bars and clubs**, see chapter **Gay & Lesbian**.

Clock in to the **Circle Bar** for Friday night's happy hour. *See p156.*

Bars

Butler's Black Pearl Lounge
A late-night 1970s soul flashback.
See page 160.

Circle Bar
Early evening specials that lead to long nights. See page 156.

Cooter Brown's Tavern & Oyster Bar
New Orleans's mecca for beer fans.
See page 160.

Loa
Upscale and overpriced – for those who enjoy that kind of thing. See page 156.

El Matador
Sip stiff drinks in the hippest seedy bar in the Quarter. See page 153.

Napoleon House
Historical ambience and skilled bartenders.
See page 154.

R Bar
Quirky decor, a hip crowd and a bike behind the bar. See page 156.

St Joe's
Religious icons inside and a voodoo-inspired patio out back. See page 161.

This eccentric bar, located off the lobby of the Monteleone Hotel in the heart of the French Quarter, caters largely to guests and tourists looking for an after-dinner drink. Weirdly, the circular bar is decorated as an antique carousel, and the bar stools and counter revolve around the bartender, taps and bottles. If you don't want to get in a spin, there are tables by the large windows and a back room, where small ceiling lights create a simulated skyscape that usually outdoes the often overcast night sky of New Orleans. Drinks are priced higher than at many places, but not unreasonably so, and while there's no dress code, the crowd tends to be older and smarter than at other places.

The Chart Room
*300 Chartres Street, at Bienville Street (522 1708).
Bus 3 Vieux Carré, 42 Canal.* **Open** 11am-4am daily.
No credit cards. Map p315 B2.
This quiet, dimly lit bar is one of the few in the French Quarter that caters predominantly to a local crowd. Decorated with nautical charts, fishing nets, sextants and other seafaring paraphernalia, it is at its busiest just after work. Both the beer and bar

selections are limited and, without any pool tables or food, there's little reason to visit except for the cheap drinks, which is enough for the middle-aged regulars who call this home.

Club Decatur
*240 Decatur Street, at Bienville Street (581 6969).
Bus 3 Vieux Carré.* **Open** noon-4am daily. **Credit**
AmEx, Disc, MC, V. **Map** p315 B3.
The newest bar on Decatur Street, Club Decatur stands out as the best place for a quality bottled beer in the French Quarter. Only Cooter Brown's, far Uptown, boasts a better selection of Belgian lambics, British ales, German Pilseners and American micro-brews. Like most bars in the area, Club Decatur draws a large service industry crowd, so it is at its busiest late in the evening, when waiters, cooks and bartenders finish their shifts. A small kitchen serves slices of pizza until the early hours to keep patrons fuelled up and thirsty. The bar doesn't have a par-ticularly interesting ambience, but the beer selection alone makes it worth a stop for those with a dis-cerning palate.

Coop's Cajun Kitchen
*1109 Decatur Street, at Ursulines Street (525 9053).
Bus 57 Franklin, 55 Elysian Fields, 82 Desire.* **Open**
11am-4am daily. **Credit** AmEx, DC, Disc, MC, V.
Map p315 C/D3.
Blurring the line between bar and restaurant, Coop's is one of the better places to grab a bite on Decatur Street. The food (served from before noon till 3am) is largely south Louisiana fare and many say the gumbo, thickened with a dark roux, is among the best in New Orleans. But dining here, on the uncom-fortable chairs and rickety tables, is a secondary occupation to drinking, and with about 20 bottled beers and six draughts, along with a pool table and jukebox, Coop's is a good afternoon joint. Evenings can be pretty slow, but that is sometimes a welcome change after the unrelenting bustle of many bars in the French Quarter.

The Dungeon
*738 Toulouse Street, at Bourbon Street (523 5530).
Bus 3 Vieux Carré, 41 Canal.* **Open** midnight-dawn Tue-Sun; closed Mon. **Admission** $3 Fri, Sat.
Credit MC, V. **Map** p315 B2.
The Dungeon is legendary, mainly due to its hours of operation and half-hidden entrance (it's down a narrow alleyway off Toulouse Street). Most tourists are scared away, leaving the red-lit interior and labyrinthine rooms and hallways to a crowd of most-ly younger French Quarter residents. The whole place feels something like a medieval submarine – surrealism is the order of the day here. If there are indeed vampires in New Orleans, it's a good bet that the Dungeon is their preferred hangout.

The Hideout
*1207 Decatur Street, at Governor Nicholls Street
(529 7119). Bus 57 Franklin, 82 Desire.* **Open** 24hrs daily. **Credit** AmEx, Disc, MC, V ($10 min).
Map p315 D3.

Decatur Street is known as a congregation point for New Orleans's seedier characters, from high-school goth kids draped in black satin to bikers bedecked in black leather. And, of all the bars on Decatur that cater to this clientele, the Hideout prides itself on attracting the most extreme cases. The bar smells particularly unsavoury, and when games of pool spin off into arguments, it's common to see the cliché 'Let's take it outside' actually put into use. Most of the skirmishes are between the younger goths and the older bikers, so fear of bar brawls or a few menacing glances shouldn't keep you away. But apart from witnessing this particular side of New Orleans there's not much reason to visit, either.

Lafitte's Blacksmith Shop

941 Bourbon Street, at St Philip Street (523 0066). Bus 3 Vieux Carré, 48 Esplanade. **Open** from noon daily. **Credit** AmEx, Disc, MC, V. **Map** p315 C2.
In any other city in the US, the ancient building that houses Lafitte's would have been taken over by a historical preservation committee years ago. In New Orleans, however, it continues to function as a bar. In fact, it's reputed to be the oldest structure in the country used as a bar and is lit primarily by candles. It's also far enough down Bourbon Street to escape much of the tourist traffic. The beer selection is limited, but the bar is well stocked and the crowd refreshingly local and usually jovial.

El Matador

504 Esplanade Avenue, at Decatur Street (569 8361). Bus 57 Franklin, 82 Desire. **Open** 9pm-2am Mon-Thur; 5pm-2am Fri-Sun. **No credit cards**. **Map** p315 D3.

Vying for top honours as downtown's hippest, nontrendy bar is El Matador, which recently opened in the building that used to house the cabaret-style bar Mint. El Matador is ornately decorated with a pressed tin ceiling that's painted black and gold, red velvet wallpaper, small booths along two walls and a stage at one end featuring local bands on some weekend nights. The bar itself is circular, allowing you to make easy eye contact with fellow drinkers, and has become a haven for late-night imbibers, who are tired of Uptown haunts. The beer selection is rather limited, and cocktails are small but very stiff – perfect for nursing a buzz through the early hours until the sun rises over the Mississippi levee, just a block away.

Molly's at the Market

1107 Decatur Street, at Ursulines Street (525 5169/ www.mollysatthemarket.com). Bus 57 Franklin, 82 Desire. **Open** 10am-6am daily. **Credit** AmEx, MC, V. **Map** p315 C3.
Of all the Decatur Street bars, none goes through as complete a transformation from day to night as does Molly's. Afternoons find it crowded with tourists visiting the French Quarter; in the evening, it's packed with pierced and tattooed twentysomethings. There's a rather homogenised feel to the customers here despite all the effort to look different – think of it as generic eclecticism. The political press clippings on the walls seem completely out of place for the apathetic crowd, but Molly's does offer a decent beer selection and a good choice of music on the jukebox. It's also the kick-off point for the first St Patrick's Day parade.

Take the bull by the horns and try a cocktail at **El Matador**.

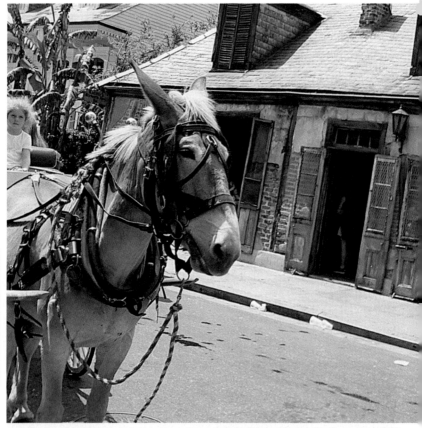

Just like the old days: a regular customer drops in to **Lafitte's Blacksmith Shop**. *See p153.*

Napoleon House

500 Chartres Street, at St Louis Street (524 9752/ www.napoleonhouse.com). Bus 3 Vieux Carré, 41 Canal. **Open** 11am-midnight Mon-Thur; 11am-1.30am Fri, Sat; 11am-7pm Sun. **Credit** AmEx, DC, Disc, MC, V. **Map** p315 B2.

While many French Quarter bars have able bartenders, few employ staff as capable, knowledgeable and commendable as the Napoleon House. It's one of the few bars in town to garnish a Pimm's Cup with a slice of cucumber. The Napoleon House was built at the beginning of the 19th century as the home of the mayor of New Orleans. According to popular myth, it was offered to the then-exiled Napoleon in 1821 by the privateer Jean Lafitte. Napoleon died before attempting his escape, but the building retained his name and now houses a comfortable, dark bar with a large grill menu (*see p131*) and a pleasant outdoor courtyard.

Pat O'Brien's

718 St Peter Street, at Bourbon Street (525 4823/ 1-800 597 4823/www.patobriens.com). Bus 3 Vieux Carré, 41 Canal. **Open** 10am-4am Mon-Thur, Sun; 10am-5am Fri, Sat. **Credit** *Piano bar & patio bar* AmEx, MC, V. **Map** p315 B2.

This is probably the granddaddy of French Quarter bars and few tourists leave the city without stopping here on at least one occasion. Its signature drink is the Hurricane, a saccharine concoction of fruit juices and rum (if the alcohol doesn't give you a hangover, the sugar will) served in a tall glass that you can take home as a souvenir – for a price. There are three bars within the complex: the main patio, with its flaming fountain, draws the biggest crowd, while the piano bar is full of cheesy sing-along types. Drinks are quite expensive, but there are a number of unusual selections to sample. As a landmark, Pat O's is a must-see, but as a cool bar to spend an evening, no way.

Ryan's Irish Pub

*241 Decatur Street, at Bienville Street (523 3500).
Bus 41 Canal, 57 Franklin, 55 Elysian Fields, 82
Desire.* **Open** 11am-3am daily. **Credit** AmEx, Disc,
MC, V. **Map** p315 A/B 3.

Ryan's is a great place to spend your breaks between
sets from music shows at the House of Blues (*see
p216*), just down the street. Prices are a little high,
but the drinks selection is good and so is the company. If drinking's not enough, you can also play billiards here. Paintings and photos of Irish poets and
writers adorn the walls.

La Touché

*621 St Louis Street, at Royal Street (529 5333/
www.omnihotels.com). Bus 3 Vieux Carré, 41 Canal.*
Open 11am-1am daily. **Credit** AmEx, Disc, V.
Map p315 B2.

Part of the Omni Royal Hotel, La Touché is primarily notable for its below sidewalk-level cocktail
lounge. Thanks to the low elevation of New Orleans
and the likelihood of flooding, basements are a rarity. Perhaps playing on this abnormality, La Touché
opens on to Royal Street with the bar itself at street
level, then pours darkly down two tiers to a lower
sitting area. The liquor and beer selection is limited
and prices are average, but the staff are friendly and
competent. While certainly not a destination point,
Touché serves well as a place for a brief respite during an afternoon walk around the French Quarter.
Also in the Omni Royal is La Riviera, a rooftop bar
with great views and a patio.

Turtle Bay Bar & Grill

*1119 Decatur Street, at Ursulines Street (586 0563).
Bus 57 Franklin, 82 Desire.* **Open** 11am-3am daily.
Credit MC, V. **Map** p315 D3.

Extensive beer selections are rare in the French
Quarter, so Turtle Bay is trying to fill the void by
establishing itself as the only beer bar on Decatur
Street. With 24 taps serving US microbrews and a
few imports, it draws a large crowd of waiters on
their way home from restaurants in the Quarter who
aren't quite ready to call it a night. One of the newer
bars on the Decatur Street strip, Turtle Bay still has
a long way to go in matching the funky decor of its
neighbours, but the late-night crowd brings plenty
of atmosphere of its own. The grill serves a standard, if limited, menu until 1am.

Marigny

Apple Barrel

*609 Frenchmen Street, at Chartres Street (949
9399). Bus 82 Desire.* **Open** 11am-2am daily. **No
credit cards. Map** p315 D2.

The Apple Barrel is best used as a break from the
crowds on Frenchmen Street on busy nights. It's
small, often crowded and offers a decent and fairly
priced beer and drinks selection. You can also play
darts. There's a small crowd of regulars, but most
of the business seems to be made up of overspill
from the surrounding music clubs.

Port of Call

*838 Esplanade Avenue, at Dauphine Street (523
0120). Bus 3 Vieux Carré, 48 Esplanade.*
Open 11am-1am Mon-Thur, Sun; 11am-3am Fri, Sat.
Credit AmEx, MC, V. **Map** p315 D2.

Traditionally, one of the French Quarter's least
intimidating dingy, dark bars, Port of Call is best
known for its grill, which many regulars say makes
the best hamburgers and baked potatoes in town
(*see p134*). The bar on Esplanade Avenue attracts
an even mix of locals and tourists. The decor may
be made lighter and brighter, if the interminable
remodelling ever comes to an end, but in the meantime chain bars all over the country spend millions
trying to reproduce Port of Call's shabby interior.
The beer list and drinks selection here are only
average, but it's a comfortable, laid-back hang-out
and a great place for indulging in some random
bar-room conversation.

Eat, Drink, Shop

R Bar

1431 Royal Street, at Kerlerec Street (948 7499/
www.royalstreetinn.com). Bus 82 Desire. **Open** 3pm-
5am Mon-Thur, Sun; 3pm-6am Fri, Sat. **Credit**
AmEx, Disc, MC, V. **Map** p315 D2.
Relatively unknown to Uptown revellers and
students, the R Bar quickly became popular with off-
work bartenders, waiters and other service industry
types. Word spread and the crowds became larger
but remained young and hip. Prices are reasonable,
there's a pool table crammed in one corner and the
decor is film-inspired rather than the aged, dingy
look common in New Orleans bars. Where else can
you sit in an antique barber's chair, sipping a cocktail, or gaze up at a motorcycle perched on top of a
beer cooler above the bar?

Bywater

Saturn Bar

3067 St Claude Avenue, at Clouet Street (949 7532).
Bus 88 St Claude. **Open** 3pm-midnight daily. **No**
credit cards.
The Saturn Bar is one of the city's most out of the
way and unusual drinking holes. Located out on St
Claude Avenue, far away from pedestrian tourists,
it's a locals' place that functions as an air-conditioner
repair shop in the daytime. The beer selection is surprisingly large, but don't try to order any fancy cocktails, or you'll probably be given a severe
dressing-down by the cantankerous bartenders.
Saturn is worth a trip, especially late in the evening,
when it's usually packed with service industry
workers who've just finished their shifts from the
French Quarter bars and restaurants.

CBD

Audubon Hotel

1225 St Charles Avenue, at Erato Street (568 1319).
St Charles Streetcar. **Open** 24hrs daily. **Credit** MC,
V. **Map** p309 B2.
To really view the underbelly of New Orleans's
nightlife, try the Audubon. Despite its location on St
Charles Avenue, mere blocks from some of the city's
swankier restaurants, it's drab, dark and deliciously
hedonistic. Favoured by just-off-duty bartenders and
strippers, the Audubon's melancholy, regulars-only
daytime feel metamorphoses into utter weirdness
after midnight. It's a late-night hang-out, ideal if
you're out for the long haul and looking for a wild
crowd to drink with. The beer selection is pretty
limited, but no matter: if you're at the Audubon at
4am, you'll be on to harder stuff anyway.

The Circle Bar

1032 St Charles Avenue, at Lee Circle (588 2616). St
Charles Streetcar. **Open** 4pm-4am daily. **Credit** MC,
V. **Map** p309 B2.
If Snake & Jake's Christmas Club Lounge (*see p161*)
is the pre-eminent late-night bar for the college
crowd, the Circle Bar (run by the same fine folk) is

Snake's a few years after graduation: the clientele is
a few years older, the room is a little nicer, the drinks
and service are better (although the beer menu needs
improvement) and the crowd isn't quite as big late
in the evening. The bar's location makes it less
accessible to the college crowd than its Uptown
counterpart; the Friday-night happy hour attracts
instead the late-20s singles crowd. Don't miss the
clock from an out-of-business drugstore, hanging
from the ceiling in the main, circular room.

Loa

International House Hotel, 221 Camp Street, at
Gravier Street (553 9550/www.ihhotel.com). Bus 10
Tchoupitoulas. **Open** 5pm-midnight daily. **Credit**
AmEx, Disc, MC, V. **Map** p309 C1.
For everything a typical New Orleans bar is not –
trendy, hip, stylishly chic – visit Loa on a weekend
evening. A dress code and high prices keep out the
riff-raff, leaving a distinctly yuppie crowd with a few
hotel guests interspersed in this light-coloured,
candle-adorned narrow bar. Marble tabletops and
indirect lighting make for one of the more attractive
bars in town, but the atmosphere is sometimes as cold
as the Martinis. Top-shelf brands make the expense
slightly less painful, but socialising is done primarily between old friends, not among new ones.
Altogether, it's a nice place to impress a date or for
an after-dinner nightcap, but not a bar to cut loose in.

Polo Lounge

Windsor Court Hotel, 300 Gravier Street, at
Tchoupitoulas Street (523 6000/www.windsorcourt
hotel.com). Bus 10 Tchoupitoulas. **Open** 11am-
11.45pm daily. **Credit** AmEx, DC, Disc, MC, V.
Map p309 C1.
The Windsor Court is annually selected as one of the
top hotels in the country, and the Polo Lounge undeniably lives up to the hotel's high reputation.
Brightly lit, with paintings of polo ponies on the
walls, a few cocktail tables, couches and a small bar,
the room is right out of the top drawer, from its
liquor to the nuts served with the cocktails. A dress
code is not strictly enforced, but most patrons are
well decked out. Drinks are expensive (average $9),
but you get what you pay for: the signature Polo
Martini comprises gin or vodka, champagne and bitters served in a small pitcher. Fridays and Saturdays
feature a jazz trio of some of the best players in town;
a pianist plays on other nights of the week.

Sazerac Bar

Fairmont Hotel, 123 Baronne Street, at Canal Street
(529 4733/www.fairmonthotel). Bus 3 Vieux Carré,
41 Canal. **Open** 5-10pm Tue-Thur; 5-11pm Fri, Sat;
closed Mon, Sun. **Credit** AmEx, DC, MC, V.
Map p309 C1.
Situated next to the Sazerac restaurant in the lobby
of the Fairmont Hotel, the classy, art deco Sazerac
Bar won international fame after a bartender
concocted the Sazerac cocktail in the early 1900s.
The confident, qualified bartenders expertly spin
glasses in the air to coat them with the local absinthe

substitute used in the cocktail (the other ingredients are rye whiskey, sugar and bitters – definitely worth trying). The Fairmont is across the street from the Orpheum theatre (*see chapter* **Performing Arts**) and only a few blocks from the Saenger (*see p225*), so it's popular with the pre- and post-theatre crowd. Given the opulence of the surroundings, the Sazerac's drinks prices are surprisingly reasonable.

Top of the Mart

33rd Floor, World Trade Center, 2 Canal Street, at the Mississippi River (522 9795). Bus 3 Vieux Carré, 41 Canal. **Open** 10am-11pm Mon-Thur; 10am-midnight Fri; 11am-1am Sat; 2-11pm Sun. **Credit** AmEx, DC, Disc, MC, V. **Map** p309 C1.

Sitting atop the World Trade Center next to the Mississippi, Top of the Mart is a slowly revolving circular room that provides a panoramic view of the French Quarter, the river and Algiers Point on the West Bank. The bar itself doesn't live up to the view, however: drinks are expensive, the menu is limited, the clientele not particularly friendly and the red velvet curtains with gold ties and tassels are reminiscent of a tacky steakhouse in Tulsa. The view alone makes Top of the Mart worth a visit, but limit yourself to one drink or one rotation, whichever comes first. And don't leave your drink on the windowsill, or you'll find yourself chasing it around the room.

Whiskey Blue

W Hotel, 333 Poydras Street, at S Peters Street (525 9444/www.whotels.com). Bus 3 Vieux Carré, 10 Tchoupitoulas. **Open** 4pm-4am Mon-Sat; 4pm-2am Sun. **Credit** AmEx, DC, Disc, MC, V. **Map** p309 C1.

Hotel bars in the CBD have established themselves as the most stylish and trendy of any in New Orleans, and Whiskey Blue is the latest of the bunch. Opened recently by the founders of the famed Sky Bar in Los Angeles, this upscale venue seems out of place in New Orleans, but is just the place for those who like to dress up, strap on a cell phone and drop big bucks on Martinis. The room is exquisitely decorated in dark blue tones, with a back-lit blue panel framing the liquor bottles behind the bar. Although pricey, the excellent Martinis are served with another half-glass worth of cocktail in a small metal shaker.

Warehouse District

Ernst Café

600 S Peters Street, at Lafayette Street (525 8544). Bus 3 Vieux Carré, 10 Tchoupitoulas. **Open** 11am-1am daily. **Credit** AmEx, DC, MC, V. **Map** p309 C2.

This small bar in the Warehouse District generates much of its business by hosting private parties in an upstairs room. Downstairs, Tuesdays and Saturdays are the most popular nights, thanks to Ladies' Night drink specials. The bar's choice of drinks is limited to a few beers and cocktails, although there are free hors d'oeuvres during the Friday happy hour (4-7pm).

Lucy's Retired Surfer's Bar

701 Tchoupitoulas Street, at Girod Street (523 8995/ 523 9198/www.retiredsurfers.com). Bus 3 Vieux Carré, 10 Tchoupitoulas. **Open** from 11am daily. **Credit** AmEx, DC, Disc, MC, V. **Map** p309 C1.

Lucy's is popular with local Warehouse District dwellers and yuppie suburbanites. While weekend nights are the busiest, food (mostly Mexican-inspired) and drink specials keep the bar relatively crowded on most nights throughout the week; it's best as an early evening venue. There's a large dining room at the back and the bar offers a number of fruity, frozen drinks along with a limited beer selection. For reasons apparently only thematic, there are surfboards hanging over the bar and tropical decor reigns throughout.

New Orleans Net Café

Contemporary Arts Center, 900 Camp Street, between Howard Avenue & St Joseph Street (523 0990/www.cacno.org). **Open** 10am-9pm Mon-Sat; 10am-5pm Sun. **Credit** MC, V. **Map** p309 C2.

The Net Café at the Contemporary Arts Center is one of the few cyber cafés in New Orleans. Patrons can order a variety of coffees, teas, beer, wine and mixed drinks while surfing the Internet for free. Reasonable prices and a limited but good selection of wine and local microbrewed beer make hanging out in chat rooms much more enjoyable. Local Latin and jazz bands play most Thursday afternoons. For details of Internet access at the Net Café, *see p281.*

Red Eye Bar & Grill

852 S Peters Street, at Julia Street (593 9393). Bus 3 Vieux Carré, 10 Tchoupitoulas. **Open** 11am-5am Mon-Sat; 6pm-4am Sun. **Credit** AmEx, DC, MC, V. **Map** p309 C2.

Located just half a block from the Howlin' Wolf music club (*see p221*), the Red Eye cashes in on set-break crowds and a noticeably young clientele, who for reasons unknown make this their home. Prices are below average and there is a late-night grill but, as with many bars, the food should only be relied on when you're desperately hungry. Pool is big draw for the younger patrons, and the two tables are always busy.

Garden District

Balcony Bar & Café

3201 Magazine Street, at Harmony Street (895 1600/ 891 2800). Bus 11 Magazine. **Open** 5pm-4am daily. **Credit** AmEx, DC, Disc, MC, V. **Map** p309 A4.

The balcony in question overlooks one of the busier stretches of pedestrian traffic on Magazine Street and provides a pleasant change from New Orleans's standard smoky rooms. Downstairs, 75 taps offer mega- and microbrewed beers from across America and the world. Unfortunately, the compressed air draught system can result in stale and flat beer – definitely ask for a small taste before ordering. A fairly good lunch menu is available. There's a projection TV for larger sporting events, and two pool tables.

Eat, Drink, Shop

The Bulldog

3236 Magazine Street, at Louisiana Avenue (891 1516/www.ultimatebeer.com). Bus 11 Magazine. **Open** noon-2am Mon-Sat; 2pm-2am Sun. **Credit** AmEx, Disc, MC, V. **Map** p309 A3.

One of three New Orleans bars with an extensive beer selection, the Bulldog offers 50 beers on tap, plus a long list of bottles. The draught beer tastes fresher than at the Balcony (*see p157*), but not as good as Cooter Brown's (*see p160*), primarily because the Bulldog's clientele tends to stick to megabrewed swill like Miller and Budweiser. The bar often gets packed later in the evening with suburbanites on their way home from work. On slower nights, a small but loyal group of trivia buffs does battle on a nationally networked trivia game.

Butler's Black Pearl Lounge.
See p160.

The Half Moon

1125 St Mary Street, at Sophie Wright Place (522 0599). Bus 11 Magazine. **Open** 11am-4am daily. **Credit** AmEx, Disc, MC, V. **Map** p309 B3.

Tucked in a relatively empty section of town between the Lower Garden District and downtown, the Half Moon relies on a late afternoon/early evening crowd of young professionals heading home from work; after 1am, it's sparsely populated. The beer selection is surprisingly good, and two back rooms offer pool and football tables, and plastic-tipped darts. There's a great jukebox, too, but the usual customers make some horrible selections; make sure you feed the machine a few dollars to keep AC/DC out of rotation.

Igor's Lounge

2133 St Charles Avenue, at Jackson Avenue (522 2145). St Charles Streetcar. **Open** 24hrs daily. **Credit** AmEx, MC, V. **Map** p309 B3.

This was the first of Australian Igor Margan's four bars and, like the others, it doubles as a laundromat. Exceedingly greasy burgers and French fries are available from the grill, and there are pool tables at the back of the bar and in a small upstairs room. Nestled among three of the larger hotels on St Charles Avenue, Igor's draws crowds of tourists looking for nightcaps. The bar practically exists on the profits made during Mardi Gras, when every Uptown parade rolls by its front doors and both drinks and bathrooms are in huge demand. If you're fond of this Igor's, try his other bars, Lucky's, Buddha Belly and Checkpoint Charlie's (see *p220*).

Branches: Buddha Belly, 4437 Magazine Street (891 6105); **Lucky's**, 1625 St Charles Avenue (523 6538).

Parasol's Restaurant & Bar

2533 Constance Street, at Third Street (897 5413/ www.parasols.com). Bus 11 Magazine. **Open** 11am-10pm Mon-Thur, Sun; from 11am Fri, Sat. **Credit** AmEx, MC, V. **Map** p309 B3.

This small, neighbourhood bar in the Irish Channel is ground zero for St Patrick's Day celebrations. On 17 March the surrounding streets are closed to traffic and when the parade rolls – on the Saturday closest to the holiday – the place is packed until the wee small hours. Parasol's lunch business keeps the place going for the rest of the year, and a regular crowd of older locals maintains a lively, relaxed and comfortable atmosphere.

Rocky's Bar & Pizza Joint

3222 Magazine Street, at Pleasant Street (891 5152). Bus 11 Magazine. **Open** 11.30am-11pm Mon-Thur, Sun; 11.30am-12.30am Fri, Sat. **Credit** AmEx, DC, Disc, MC, V. **Map** p309 A4.

While it could be argued that Rocky's is a so-so restaurant that happens to have a bar, the drink specials would suggest that this is a good bar that happens to serve pizza. In the early evening, the restaurant pulls in most of the business, primarily by attracting the twenty- and thirtysomethings who traverse the coffeehouses, restaurants and bars

along this stretch of Magazine Street. Later on, as the diners thin out, the bar comes alive with drinkers, creating an atmosphere that ranges from relaxed to boisterous.

Samuel's Restaurant & Beer Pub

1628 St Charles Avenue, at Euterpe Street (581 3777/www.samuelspub.com). St Charles Streetcar. **Open** 11am-10pm daily. **Credit** AmEx, DC, Disc, MC, V. **Map** p309 B2.

Located on a section of St Charles Avenue currently experiencing a revival, Samuel's is a prime after-work hangout for young professionals. Although it promotes itself as a big beer bar, the selection pales in comparison to the choice at Cooter Brown's (see *p160*), the Bulldog (see *158*) or the Balcony (see *p157*) – and it's pricey. Still, the beer is better than your average gunk, and there are a few US micro-brews along with established imports. The menu in the adjoining dining room is also better than usual, offering hamburgers, po-boys, salads, pizzas and seafood platters.

Uptown

Le Bon Temps Roule

4801 Magazine Street, at Bordeaux Street (895 8117/www.lebontempsroule.com). Bus 11 Magazine. **Open** 11am-3am daily. **Credit** AmEx, Disc, MC, V. **Map** p306 C10.

A long-time favourite of both college students and locals, Le Bon Temps is one of the most established bars in a city where some places last only a matter of months. Wooden floors and furniture, plus an outdoor patio, provide comfortable surroundings in which to enjoy a wide, if pricey, selection of beers (draught and bottled). In the front room are two pool tables and one of the best jukeboxes in town, while the back room houses a performance space where bands play most Wednesday, Friday and Saturday nights, usually for no cover, and an excellent late-night grill (see *p222*). Nightly specials include cheap Abita beer (a local brew) on Monday nights and free oysters on Friday afternoons.

The Boot Bar & Grill

1039 Broadway, at Zimple Street (866 9008). Bus 22 Broadway. **Open** from 11am daily. **Credit** AmEx, Disc, MC, V. **Map** p306 B8.

Across the street from one of the Tulane University buildings and two blocks from the university library, the Boot is strictly a college bar. Occasionally a professor or three may stop by, but the crowd is predominantly made up of undergrads, who, due to a lack of transport or adventure, stick to the bars near campus. Once in a rare while a band will play inside the bar or outside on the patio, but a music venue the Boot is not. Instead, entertainment is provided by the pool tables and plenty of draught beer, including a dozen choices on tap that are better than the usual college bar swill. Hormone levels run high, but the ensuing meat market is generally limited to classmates.

Bruno's

7601 Maple Street, at Hillary Street (861 7615). Bus 22 Broadway/St Charles Streetcar. **Open** 3pm-3am Mon-Thur, Sun; noon-5am Fri, Sat. **Credit** AmEx, DC, Disc, MC, V. **Map** p306 B8.

Bruno's is across the street from TJ Quills (*see p161*) and about four blocks from Broadway, where many students live. Freshmen usually stick closer to campus, but Bruno's is popular with older undergrads. Drinks are ordinary and the beer list limited, but prices are low and the free popcorn can fill in as a meal for those who miss dinner. Pool tables and dartboards provide an alternative to talking to your classmates, but there are plenty of better places to go, and some are only a couple of blocks away.

Butler's Black Pearl Lounge

140 Millaudon Street, at River Road (861 3444). Bus 22 Broadway, then 10min walk. **Open** 9pm-4am daily. **No credit cards. Map** p306 B8.

New Orleanians like to party long into the night, sometimes staying out until after the sun has come up. Butler's is the latest haven for such all-night revelry. Although it opened in 1999, the bar retained much of the '70s decor from the bar's previous incarnation. With its assortment of old beer advertisements, velvet posters and tacky lamps, Butler's seems caught in an era we'd probably all like to forget. But it's precisely that kitschy feel that makes it worth seeking out. Don't bother stopping by before ten in the evening, even if the bar is open (most likely it won't be). The action doesn't really start until about 2am, when people have already had a few rounds at other bars or music clubs. Note that the door remains locked at all times; patrons are buzzed in by the bartender, who has a closed-circuit television camera fixed on the door.

The Club/Ms Mae's

4336 Magazine Street, at Napoleon Avenue (895 9401). Bus 11 Magazine, 24 Napoleon. **Open** 24hrs daily. **No credit cards. Map** p306 D10.

Popular with older barflies and college students, the Club is one of the few bars to take full advantage of New Orleans's lax liquor laws, staying open 24/7. Wednesday nights are particularly popular with the younger crowd, thanks to a two-drinks-for-a-dollar special. This is also one of the few bars within walking distance (about five blocks) of Tipitina's Uptown (*see p224*), so if it's an exceedingly crowded night at Tip's, this can be a nice place to take a breather, shoot a game of pool or darts and drink cheaply.

Cooter Brown's Tavern & Oyster Bar

509 S Carrollton Avenue, at St Charles Avenue (866 9104/http://turnipseed.com/cooterbrowns). Bus 34 Carrollton Express/St Charles Streetcar. **Open** 11am-2am Mon-Wed, Sun; 11am-4am Thur-Sat. **Credit** DC, Disc, MC, V. **Map** p306 A8.

For beer fans, Cooter Brown's is the mecca of New Orleans bars. It offers a selection of over 65 draught beers (a carbon dioxide tap system keeps it all fresh) and over 350 brands of bottled beer from across the world – if a beer is distributed in New Orleans, you'll find it at Cooter's. It also has one of the best grills in town, a raw oyster bar, two pool tables, a dartboard and numerous TVs for sports fans. The crowd is generally middle-aged and can be annoying, but usually the atmosphere is not too bad.

Dos Jefes Uptown Cigar Bar

5535 Tchoupitoulas Street, at Joseph Street (891 8500). Bus 10 Tchoupitoulas. **Open** 5pm-2am Mon-Thur, Sun; 5pm-4am Fri, Sat. **Credit** AmEx, DC, Disc, MC, V. **Map** p306 C10.

Contrary to the stuffy atmosphere of many establishments that also cater to an older crowd, Dos Jefes is a comfortable place, tucked away in an Uptown neighbourhood along the Mississippi River. There is a large cigar humidor (an excellent ventilation system keeps the room from getting overly hazy), a wide selection of ports, brandies, scotches and bourbons, a good choice of beer, a short wine list and a small menu of appetisers. Other enticements include swings and hammocks, which replace the bar stools on the outdoor patio. You can play a quiet game of billiards in the back room, and jazz musicians play from Thursday to Saturday night.

F&M Patio Bar

4841 Tchoupitoulas Street, at Lyons Street (895 6784). Bus 10 Tchoupitoulas. **Open** 7pm Mon-Thur, Sun; 1pm-6am Fri, Sat. **No credit cards. Map** p306 C10.

For years F&M's was known as the place to go after a show at Tipitina's (*see p224*) and the best place for late-night romantic encounters. The pool table in the front room became so popular as a dance surface that another had to be added on the patio for those actually wanting to play. Crowds can be overwhelmingly dense on weekend nights, but F&M's has a decent beer selection and some of the best bartenders in town. The grill food is not great, but if it's getting close to dawn and your energy is waning, a plate of cheese fries or quesadillas may be the lift you need. Better yet, skip the food and order a Bloody Mary to toast the sunrise.

Fat Harry's

4330 St Charles Avenue, at Napoleon Avenue (895 1045). Bus 24 Napoleon/St Charles Streetcar. **Open** from 9am daily. **Credit** AmEx, Disc, MC, V. **Map** p306 D9.

College students venturing to Fat Harry's for the first time are often warned to bring boxing gloves. This is sage advice, as many of the young local crowd consider this bar to be their territory. Nevertheless, word of mouth has spread Fat's fame far and wide, and the bar draws a large population of local and visiting students. It opens late – weekend nights are particularly busy – and serves grill food until early in the morning. If a large, dense crowd of college students in a dimly lit room is what you're looking for, Fat Harry's is worth a visit. If not, stop by on a sunny afternoon while exploring Uptown.

Madigan's
800 S Carrollton Avenue, at Maple Street (866 9455). St Charles Streetcar. **Open** from 3pm daily. **Credit** AmEx, MC, V. **Map** p306 A8.
Far Uptown near Riverbend, Madigan's is a small bar with a pool table that caters primarily to older college students and young professionals. Despite reasonable prices, there's little to hold people here: it's more a place to meet friends and decide where to go for the rest of the evening.

Phillip's Restaurant & Bar
733 Cherokee Street, at Maple Street (865 1155). Bus 22 Broadway/St Charles Streetcar. **Open** 4pm-2am daily. **Credit** AmEx, Disc, MC, V. **Map** p306 B8.
Long a favourite with Tulane University graduate students, Phillip's has a strict enough door policy to keep drunken undergrads out of the way. The dimly lit, well-staffed bar is supplemented by competent cocktail waitresses. There are pool tables and dartboards for gamers, and a cleverly placed mirror above the bar for those patrons looking for a 'study' partner.

St Joe's
5535 Magazine Street, at Joseph Street (no phone). Bus 11 Magazine. **Open** from 5pm daily. **Credit** AmEx, MC, V. **Map** p306 C9/10.
Formerly Ms Mae's Place, a seedy hangout for local lushes, this bar reinvented itself in 1997 as St Joe's, drastically changing its look and the regular crowd demographics. The bar is still long and narrow, but the ceiling has been raised, making for a less claustrophobic space. The flavoured vodkas and the extensive 'Martini' menu cater to the new clientele – mainly Tulane graduate students and young professionals. There's also a pool table, an above average beer list and a good selection of top quality liquors.

Snake & Jake's Christmas Club Lounge
7612 Oak Street, at Hillary Street (861 2802). Bus 22 Broadway/St Charles Streetcar. **Open** from 9pm daily. **Credit** AmEx, MC, V. **Map** p306 B8.
A tiny neighbourhood bar, Snake's first caught on with the music club crowd due to its late hours – it doesn't open until 9pm and rarely closes before dawn. Soon, word spread about this hole-in-the-wall joint and it grew into a bar that is always busy, especially on weekend nights. The interior is dark, the decor looks like it's been here since the 1950s, the bartenders are notoriously slow, yet everyone who's been at a music show seems to end up at Snake's, comparing notes on that evening's bands. Prices may be average, but the crowd, ranging from students to local journalists and musicians, is not.

TJ Quills
7600 Maple Street, at Hillary Street (866 5205). Bus 22 Broadway/St Charles Streetcar. **Open** 3pm-2am Mon-Sat; 7pm-3am Sun. **Credit** AmEx, Disc, MC, V. **Map** p306 B8.
The last stop on the Tulane/Loyola University stretch, Quills is reputed to be the best place to meet Loyola co-eds. Not surprisingly, it's full of students.

The drinks are cheap and not very good, but specials allow for vast quantities to be consumed on a student budget. Pool tables and video games are provided for the rare few not eyeing up a member of the opposite sex, and, while brief skirmishes among male patrons are common, the bouncers are quick to quell any altercations by throwing people off the patio at the front of the bar.

Victorian Lounge
Columns Hotel, 3811 St Charles Avenue, at Peniston Street (899 9308/www.Columns.com). St Charles Streetcar. **Open** 3pm-midnight Mon-Thur; 3pm-2am Fri; 11am-2am Sat; 11am-midnight Sun. **Credit** AmEx, MC, V. **Map** p306 D9.
The stately, old Columns Hotel houses one of the more comfortable bars in the city. The staff are friendly and knowledgeable. With dark wood, booths, small tables and a large porch overlooking St Charles, the Victorian Lounge is frequented by older students and professionals on their way home from work. It's busiest during the afternoon happy hour. Rumour has it that the hotel is a favourite place for illicit affairs among local politicians, professors and poets, so the bar may be a prime place for snooping.

Waldo's Restaurant & Bar
7130 Freret Street, at Broadway (861 0236). Bus 15 Freret, 22 Broadway. **Open** 6pm-midnight Mon-Thur, 1pm-2am Fri, Sat. **Admission** *Quarter Pitchers* $5 Wed. **Credit** AmEx, Disc, MC, V. **Map** p306 B8.
Second only to the Boot (*see p159*) in its appeal to undergrads, Waldo's is only two blocks from Tulane and in the middle of fraternity/sorority row, otherwise known as Broadway. As well as the main bar, there's a large patio and rooms with pool tables – in one of them, frozen drink machines churn out Daiquiris. Probably the highlight at Waldo's is the occasional Drink or Drown special where patrons pay one price at the door and can then order as much of any drink as they want.

Further afield

Rivershack Tavern
3449 River Road, at Shrewsbury Road, Jefferson (834 4938). Bus Kenner Local to Shrewsbury. **Open** 11am-midnight Mon-Thur; 11am-3am Fri, Sat. **Credit** AmEx, DC, Disc, MC, V.
Stuck way out west on River Road on the Mississippi River levee in Jefferson Parish, the Rivershack is home to metro New Orleans area bikers. On any night, and especially on Wednesdays, the small car park is filled with beautifully chromed and hand-painted motorcycles. Inside is a small stage, where bands play on Wednesday and Saturday nights, a pool table, a good selection of draught beer, one of the city's better grills and the best collection of bizarre barstools and tacky ashtrays anywhere in the state. The crowd is distinctly middle-aged and can be territorial, but if you make it this far out of town, it's worth dropping in.

Shops & Services

Go fossicking for finds in New Orleans's quirky, colourful shops.

New Orleans is not a bargain-shopping kind of city. It's a great shopping city, however: decadent, festive and promising eccentric surprises around every corner. It's high adventure, rather than high fashion or high tech. This is the place to look for the sinful, the impractical, the fun. Shop for Mardi Gras memorabilia, masks and costumes, European antiques, old and new jewellery, voodoo relics, local music and literature, new and second-hand books and records, vintage clothing and local food.

Walking is the best way to shop, especially in the French Quarter and the Warehouse District. You can travel by bus or streetcar to the Riverbend and Magazine Street shopping areas, but you will need a car to visit the suburban malls and discount stores. Rather than driving between different areas, it's more fun to choose one shopping district, then take your time and poke around. You're bound to find something you've never seen before, but just can't live without.

SALES TAX

A hefty nine per cent sales tax is added to the displayed price of most goods and services. Foreigners can recoup this by shopping in any of the stores that display a tax-free sign (there are more than 1,100 of them). Get a voucher and a sales receipt when you make your purchase and obtain a rebate at the **Louisiana Tax Free Shopping Refund Center (LTFS)** at New Orleans International Airport (568 5323) when you leave. Refunds of $500 and less are made in cash; refunds of more than $500 will by paid by cheque and posted to you. Phone 467 0723 for more information.

SHOPPING AREAS

The **French Quarter** is the shopping area that everyone visits. Although thronged with tourists and with more than its share of tacky T-shirt and souvenir shops (especially on Bourbon Street), it also houses antiques shops and art galleries along Royal Street; funky, new and second-hand clothing stores, many along Chartres Street and Decatur Street; a flea market; new and used book and record shops; clothing boutiques and small speciality shops. Be alert: new places spring up all the time.

Canal Street was the place to shop in the mid-20th century, when ladies in hats and

gloves shopped at DH Holmes, Maison Blanche and Krauss – well-known, locally owned department stores that now exist only in New Orleans lore and literature. Today, the historic street caters mostly to tourists. Athletic wear and shoe shops, electronics stores and souvenir shops rub shoulders with long-standing Canal Street merchants like **Adlers & Sons**. It's well worth strolling down Canal Street just to experience the atmosphere of this famous boulevard. A statue of Ignatius Reilly – the hapless intellectual and Lucky Dog-vending hero of *The Confederacy of Dunces* – stands on the sidewalk under the clock at DH Holmes (now the Chateau Sonesta Hotel) waiting for his mama to arrive. Neon aficionados enjoy strolling and window-shopping after dark to see familiar signs like **Walgreen's Pharmacy** or the **Saenger Theatre** (*see pages 225 and 228*). Upscale **Canal Place Shopping Center** is near the foot of Canal, and a new group of shops is slated to open in the Maison Blanche building, which was undergoing renovation in summer 2000.

Magazine Street comprises six miles (9.5 kilometres) of shops and residences that stretch west from Canal Street all the way up to Audubon Park. The spending opportunities keep growing as new and vibrant shops and galleries continue to open. You'll find coffeehouses, bookstores, second-hand clothing, antiques, jewellery, designer shoes and works by local artists, often at prices below those in the French Quarter. The best bargains are on lower Magazine, between Race Street and Jackson Avenue (blocks 1300-2100), while the upper end between Louisiana Avenue and Audubon Park (blocks 3400-6000) is more upmarket. Don't expect to take in Magazine Street in an afternoon: it's way too long and there's way too much to see, so target a certain area instead. The Magazine Street Merchants Association puts out a free helpful brochure that lists the shops and groups them by location. You can pick one up at almost any shop on Magazine Street.

The **Warehouse District** is becoming a new centre for arts in the city, with the **Contemporary Arts Center**, **D-Day Museum**, **Confederate Museum** and soon-to-open **Ogden Museum of Southern Art** all located here (for details, *see chapter*

The French Quarter is thronged with tarot readers and psychics. *See p171.*

CBD & Warehouse District). It's also a hotbed of fine art and craft galleries, including a concentration of glass studios. **Riverwalk**, a covered shopping mall next to the Mississippi, stretches from the foot of Poydras Street in the CBD into the Warehouse District.

Riverbend, often confused with Riverwalk by newcomers, is miles away at the junction of St Charles and Carrollton. This compact, horseshoe-shaped area surrounding a strip shopping centre can be easily walked around and contains a good mix of upmarket clothing and jewellery stores housed in old-fashioned cottages. From Riverbend, walk the eight or so blocks down tree-filled Maple Street, in the heart of the university area. It's lined with bookstores, clothing and accessory shops and coffeehouses catering to the students from nearby Tulane and Loyola Universities.

Old Metairie is a stuffy upper-class neighbourhood that was New Orleans's first modern suburb. The main artery, Metairie Road, is lined with strip shopping centres and speciality shops. Most tourists don't venture out this far, but if you've got a car (travelling by bus is possible, but unreliable), you may pick up some interesting clothes, household items and gifts.

Outside New Orleans, there are discount shops in the suburbs at giant superstores such as Wal-Mart or Sam's Club (where you need a membership card, $35) or at the discount outlet shopping malls in Slidell and Gonzales,

Louisiana, and Gulfport, Mississippi. But they're not really worth the effort of travelling so far.

One-stop

Department stores

Department stores used to be everywhere and used to sell just about everything. No more. With discount giants grabbing big bites in appliances, home furnishings and housewares, you can no longer expect department stores to carry everything from soup to nuts. Department stores still excel, however, in their wide stock of clothes for men, women and children.

Dillard's

Lakeside Shopping Center, 3301 Veterans Memorial Boulevard, at N Causeway Boulevard, Metairie (833 1075/www.dillards.com). St Charles Streetcar/ 16 S Claiborne, 39 Tulane, 90 Carrollton bus, then E5 Causeway bus. **Open** 10am-9pm Mon-Sat; noon-6pm Sun. **Credit** AmEx, DC, Disc, MC, V.
You can outfit the entire family or decorate the home at this regional store, which has four locations in the greater New Orleans area. It's conservative in feel and geared towards conventional tastes, but it does offer reasonable prices in a wide variety of merchandise. Check the *Times-Picayune* for advertised special deals.
Branches: Esplanade Mall, 1401 W Esplanade Boulevard, near Williams Boulevard, Kenner (468 6050); Oakwood Shopping Center, 197 Westbank Expressway, at Terry Parkway, Gretna (362 4800).

JC Penney
Lakeside Shopping Center, 3301 Veterans Memorial
Boulevard, at N Causeway Boulevard, Metairie
(837 9880/www.jcpenney.com). St Charles Streetcar/
16 S Claiborne, 39 Tulane, 90 Carrollton bus, then
E5 Causeway bus. **Open** 10am-9pm Mon-Sat; noon-
6pm Sun. **Credit** AmEx, Disc, MC, V.
An old stand-by in US shopping, offering a decent
selection of clothing and housewares at moderate
prices. A phone ordering service is also available.
Branches: Oakwood Shopping Center, West Bank
Expressway, at Terry Parkway, Gretna (227 2112).

Macy's
New Orleans Centre, 1400 Poydras Street, next
to the Louisiana Superdome, CBD (592 5985/
www.macys.com). Bus 16 S Claiborne. **Open** 10am-
8pm Mon-Sat; noon-6pm Sun. **Credit** AmEx, MC, V.
Map p309 B1.
Macy's basement still yields frequent deals on
housewares, although the legendary bargain basement is a thing of the past. Macy's is good for
moderate to high-end clothing, shoes and make-up,
and also has frequent sales, offering 20% to 40%
discounts on men's and women's clothing.
Branch: The Esplanade Mall, 1401 W Esplanade
Boulevard, near Williams Boulevard, Kenner
(465 3985).

Saks Fifth Avenue
Canal Place Shopping Center, 333 Canal Street,
at Decatur Street, French Quarter (524 2200/
www.s5a.com). Bus 41 Canal. **Open** 10am-7pm Mon-
Sat; noon-6pm Sun. **Credit** AmEx, DC, Disc, MC, V.
Map p309 C1.
This upscale, good-looking store has fine-quality
clothing for men and women, a good shoe depart-
ment and the latest cosmetics from the likes of
Bobby Brown.

Shopping malls: downtown

These three downtown shopping malls are
within walking distance of many hotels and
tourist attractions. They're smaller and easier
to navigate than the suburban malls.

Canal Place Shopping Center
333 Canal Street, at Decatur Street, French Quarter
(522 9200). Bus 41 Canal. **Open** 10am-6pm
Mon-Wed; 10am-7pm Thur-Sat; noon-6pm Sun.
Map p309 C1.
At the foot of 'world-famous Canal Street', this mall
is at the top of the shopping chain in New Orleans,
and has a relaxed and elegant atmosphere. The big
names – such as Saks Fifth Avenue, Laura Ashley,
Pottery Barn, The Limited, Williams Sonoma,
Banana Republic, Gucci and Bally – carry the same
merchandise as in all their other stores nationwide.
Locally owned and operated Weinstein's (*see p175*)
sells fine and hip but expensive clothing for women
(wool sweaters from $300) and an exclusive selec-
tion of wonderful Italian designer labels. Seek out
Linens for a good selection of fine linens and clothes

for infants and children, and RHINO Gallery (*see
p178*) for local contemporary arts and crafts.

New Orleans Centre
1400 Poydras Street, next to the Louisiana
Superdome, CBD (568 0000). Bus 16 S Claiborne.
Open 10am-8pm Mon-Sat; noon-6pm Sun.
Map p309 B1.
Built in the late 1980s and surrounded by office
buildings, this mall caters to business people and
visitors to the Superdome, which is connected to it
by an open-air walkway. The mall is anchored by
national department stores Macy's (*see above*) and
Lord & Taylor, which has a great women's shoe
department. Other shops include the usual suspects
like Gap and Victoria's Secret.

Riverwalk
1 Poydras Street, at the Mississippi River, CBD
(522 1555/www.riverwalkmarketplace.com).
Riverfront Streetcar/3 Vieux Carré, 10 Tchoupitoulas
bus. **Open** 10am-9pm Mon-Sat; 11am-7pm Sun.
Map p309 C1.
Right on the Mississippi, and worth visiting just for
the view of the river, the Riverwalk shopping mall
is best known as the mall that was hit by an out-of-
control Chinese merchant ship in December 1996.
When not watching for runaway boats, you can
shop at more than 100 stores, including Banana
Republic, Gap, Gap Kids and Abercrombie & Fitch.
Curiosity value apart, its linear riverside layout and
frequent crowding make it less than pleasant to
browse through. The shops cater to tourists, so
prices for souvenirs and gifts are higher than elsewhere in town.

Shopping malls: suburban

If you are planning a major shopping trip,
consider visiting the suburban malls in
Jefferson Parish, where the sales tax is slightly
cheaper, at 8.75 per cent, as opposed to nine
per cent in Orleans Parish.

The Esplanade
1401 W Esplanade Boulevard, near Williams
Boulevard, Kenner (465 2161/www.mallibu.com).
Bus Kenner Loop. **Open** 10am-9pm Mon-Sat;
noon-6pm Sun.
The Esplanade is the largest and busiest mall in
town, anchored by Macy's (*see above*) and regional
department stores Dillard's (*see p163*) and
Mervyn's. Mervyn's is the cheaper of the two, without the designer clothes. You will find just about
everything except hardware in the Esplanade's 135
stores. If you're driving, head west on I-10 and take
the Williams Boulevard exit.

Lakeside Shopping Center
3301 Veterans Memorial Boulevard, at N Causeway
Boulevard, Metairie (835 8000). St Charles
Streetcar/16 S Claiborne, 39 Tulane, 90 Carrollton
bus, then E5 Causeway bus. **Open** 10am-9pm Mon-
Sat; noon-6pm Sun.

One of the oldest malls in the country, Lakeside was refurbished in the 1990s. It lacks the larger stores found in the Esplanade, but the pace is less hectic and the layout more straightforward. You'll find the usual chains, including the Gap, The Limited, The Limited Express, Old Navy and Victoria's Secret. Restoration Hardware has new stuff that looks like old stuff from furniture to hardware.

Antiques

For antiques shopping, New Orleans is right up there with Paris. Designers from Los Angeles and New York make the trip for the wide selection and competitive prices; the selection of European antiques is especially good. New Orleans also has many shops full of second-hand collectibles.

Auction houses

If you're seriously interested in furniture buying, the auction houses offer the best bargains. Even if you're not interested in buying anything, auctions are great fun and browsing the previews gives you a chance to check out European and American treasures from the estates of wealthy Southern families. Contact the auction houses below for sales

dates and catalogues (annual subscriptions cost $50 to $300) or check their websites. Remember that a buyer's premium of ten per cent is added to the hammer price, and that US residents pay an additional nine per cent sales tax. The auction companies do not ship or pack goods themselves but will work with you and their regularly used services.

Neal Auction Company

4038 Magazine Street, at Marengo Street, Uptown (899 5329/www.nealauction.com). Bus 11 Magazine. **Open** 9am-5pm Mon-Fri; closed Sat, Sun. **Credit** Disc, MC, V. **Map** p306 D10.
The older of the two local auction houses and strongest in American and English furniture, porcelain, paintings, prints, sculptures, jewellery and oriental rugs. Anything that isn't sold at the Magazine Street showroom goes to a warehouse on Carondolet Street, where no-minimum-bid auctions are sometimes held.

New Orleans Auction Galleries

801 Magazine Street, at Julia Street, CBD (566 1849/www.neworleansauction.com). Bus 11 Magazine. **Open** 9am-5pm Mon-Fri; closed Sat, Sun. **No credit cards. Map** p309 C2.
Opened in 1991, emphasis is on formal French and European antiques, like cypress linen presses. **Branch**: 1330 St Charles Avenue, at Erato Street, Warehouse District (586 8733).

Shopping by area

French Quarter

Accent Annex (branch; see page 184); **Animal Arts Antiques** (see page 166); **Ann Taylor** (see page 174); **Beckham's Book Shop** (see page 173); **Bedazzle** (see page 178); **Bookstar** (see page 172); **Bottom of the Cup Tea Room & Gifts** (see page 171); **Bourbon French Parfums** (see page 183); **Café du Monde Shop** (see page 182); **Canal Place Shopping Center** (see page 165); **Central Grocery Company** (see page 180); **Centuries Old Maps & Prints** (see page 168); **Chi-wa-wa** (see page 187); **Civil War Store** (see page 168); **Creole Delicacies Gourmet Shop** (see page 182); **David's** (see page 171); **A Different Approach** (see page 185); **Dr Mike's Animal House** (see page 187); **Earth Savers** (see page 184); **Eclipse Salon** (see page 183); **Esoterica Occult Goods** (see page 171); **Faulkner House Books** (see page 172); **Feet First** (branch; see page 179); **Fifi Mahoney's** (see page 182); **Le Fleur de Paris** (see page 174); **French Market**

(see page 182); **La Garage** (see page 180); **Gargoyles** (see page 180); **Gentlemen's Quarterly** (see page 181); **Kaboom Books** (see page 173); **The Grace Note** (see page 174); **Hove Parfumeur** (see page 184); **Hula Mae's Tropic Wash** (see page 174); **Jazzrags** (see page 180); **Gerald D Katz** (see page 169); **Keil's Antiques** (see page 169); **Librairie Bookshop** (see page 173); **Louie's Juke Joint** (see page 186); **Louisiana Music Factory** (see page 186); **Lucullus** (branch; see page 169); **Magic Bus**

Antiques at **Manheim Galleries**. *See p171.*

Antiques shops

In New Orleans there is a bar or church on every corner and an antique store in between. Most of the established stores are concentrated on Magazine Street and in the French Quarter; those on Royal Street are highly reputable establishments often run by third- and fourth-generation family members. This high concentration translates into competitive prices,

while the longevity of the establishments is reflected in the range of stock. However grand the surroundings, the staff and owners are usually friendly and knowledgeable.

Animal Arts Antiques
617 Chartres Street, at Wilkinson Row, French Quarter (529 4407). Bus 55 Elysian Fields, 81 Almonaster, 82 Desire. **Open** 10am-5pm Mon-Sat; closed Sun. **Credit** AmEx, Disc, MC, V. **Map** p316 B2.
A veritable menagerie, from dead duck paintings to a live dog on the premises.

Architectural Salvage & Collectibles
3983 Tchoupitoulas Street, between Austerlitz & Constantinople Streets, Uptown (891 6080). Bus 10 Tchoupitoulas. **Open** 9am-5pm daily. **Credit** AmEx, Disc, MC, V. **Map** p306 D9/10.
Chock full of architectural cultural treasures that once adorned old New Orleans homes. Beside the shop itself is a shaded open space that's like being in someone's slightly funky courtyard. Roam among an assortment of cypress shutters and doors, mantels, columns, iron gates and fencing, stained glass windows, corbels and finials. Buy it in the rough or place an order for custom cypress furniture using your choice of architectural details. Prices are reasonable.

(see page 187); **Manheim Galleries** (see page 171); **Mardi Gras Center** (see page 180); **Masquerade Fantasy** (see page 180); **Matassa's Grocery** (see page 181); **Moss Antiques** (see page 171); **MS Rau** (see page 171); **New Orleans Crab Bag** (see page 177); **New Orleans Hat Company** (see page 177); **One of a Kind** (see page 180); **Paisley Babylon** (see page 180); **Pottery Barn** (see page 185); **Progress Grocery Company** (see page 181); **Quarter Moon Gallery** (see page 177); **RHINO Gallery** (see page 177); **Rings of Desire** (see page 184); **Robinson's Antiques** (see page 171); **Rock & Roll Collectibles** (see page 187); **Saint Germain** (see page 178); **Royal Pharmacy** (see page 184); **Saks Fifth Avenue** (see page 165); **Three Dog Bakery** (see page 187); **Tommy's Flower Shop** (see page 179); **Tower Records** (see page 180); **Trashy Diva** (see page 179); **Victoria's Uptown** (branch; see page 179); **Vieux Carré Wine & Spirits** (see page 182); **Virgin Megastore** (see page 187); **Washing Well Laundryteria** (see page 174); **Weinstein's** (see page 175); **Werlein's** (see page 186).

Marigny, Gentilly & New Orleans East
Afro-American Book Stop (branch; see page 172); **American Aquatic Gardens** (see page 185); **Creative Concrete** (see page 185); **Faubourg Marigny Bookstore** (see page 172); **Judy's Collage** (see page 171); **Patrick's Little Shop of Flowers** (see page 179); **Peaches** (see page 187).

CBD & Warehouse District
Accent Annex (branch; see page 184); **Adlers & Sons** (see page 178); **Afro-American Book Shop** (see page 172); **Ann Taylor** (see page 174); **Big Life Toys** (branch; see page 185); **Busta** (see page 183); **Creole Delicacies Gourmet Shop** (see page 182); **Crescent City Market** (see page 182); **DeVille Books & Prints** (see page 172); **Fox Photo** (see page 188); **International Vintage Guitars of New Orleans** (see page 186); **Liberty Camera** (see page 188); **Louisiana Products** (see page 182); **Macy's** (see page 165); **Meyer the Hatter** (see page 177); **New Orleans Auction Galleries** (see page 171); **New Orleans Centre** (see page 165); **Rapp's Luggage & Gifts** (see page 179); **Riverwalk** (see page ▶

As You Like It

3033 Magazine Street, at Seventh Street, Uptown (897 6915/1-800 828 2311/www.asyoulikeitsilver shop.com). Bus 11 Magazine. **Open** 10am-5pm Mon-Sat; closed Sun. **Credit** AmEx, Disc, MC, V. **Map** p309 A3.

An entire store of quality silver flatware, serving pieces and tea services. Sterling silver and silver plate in a variety of designs, eras and prices.

Bep's Antiques

2051 Magazine Street, at Josephine Street, Uptown (525 7726/www.bepsantiques.com). Bus 11 Magazine. **Open** 9.30am-5pm Mon-Sat; closed Sun. **Credit** AmEx, Disc, MC, V. **Map** p309 B3.

Bep's Antiques is a small and charming store packed full of rural American and European pine and oak furniture.

Bush Antiques

2109 & 2111 Magazine Street, between Josephine & Jackson Streets, Uptown (581 3518/www.bush antiques.com). Bus 11 Magazine. **Open** 10am-5pm Mon-Sat; closed Sun. **Map** p309 B3.

French and Belgian antiques, religious artefacts and elaborate antique beds, mirrors and lights.

Centuries Old Maps & Prints

517 St Louis Street, at Chartres Street, French Quarter (568 9491). Bus 3 Vieux Carré, 55 Elysian Fields, 81 Almonaster, 82 Desire.
Open 10.30am-6pm Mon-Thur; 10.30am-6.30pm Fri, Sat; 11am-6pm Sun. **Credit** AmEx, Disc, MC, V. **Map** p316 B2.

In a city that has been governed by five different nations since the 17th century, maps are an important and interesting link to the past. This French Quarter store is a great place for history buffs, but don't rely on the casual staff; if you have a serious question, ask the owner.

Charbonnet & Charbonnet

2728 Magazine Street, at Washington Street, Uptown (891 9948). Bus 11 Magazine. **Open** 9am-5.30pm Mon-Sat; closed Sun. **Credit** MC, V. **Map** p309 A/B3.

Charbonnet & Charbonnet's collection of antique pine and cypress cupboards and tables is complemented by custom-made furniture that is crafted in-house using old Louisiana pine or cypress wood. Single-bed headboards made from old cypress pocket doors start at $375.

Civil War Store

212 Chartres Street, at Iberville Street, French Quarter (522 3328). Bus 3 Vieux Carré, 41 Canal, 55 Elysian Fields, 81 Almonaster, 82 Desire. **Open** 10.30am-6.30pm daily. **Credit** AmEx, Disc, MC, V. **Map** p316 A2.

Sells anything you can think of associated with the American Civil War, from Confederate money to musket balls.

▶ **Shopping by area (continued)**

165); **St Charles Vision** (see page 183); **Victoria's Secret** (see page 179); **Wolf Camera & Video** (branch; see page 188); **Ya-Ya** (see page 186).

Garden District & Lower Garden District

AAA Camera Repair (see page 188); **Colorpix** (see page 188); **Fiesta** (see page 180); **Gallery 2207** (see page 180); **Garden District Book Shop** (see page 173); **Jim Smiley Fine Vintage Clothing** (see page 180); **Mariposa** (see page 180); **MGM** (see page 180); **Mignon** (see page 175); **Mystic Blue Signs** (see page 185); **Ragin' Daisy** (see page 180); **Rite-Aid** (see page 184).

Uptown

Architectural Salvage & Collectibles (see page 167); **Artifacts Gallery** (see page 184); **As You Like It** (see page 168); **Beaucoup Books** (see page 172); **Belladonna** (see page 184); **Bep's Antiques** (see page 168); **Big Life Toys** (see page 185); **Blockbuster Video** (see page 188); **Bush Antiques** (see page 168); **Caveat**

Emptor (see page 181); **Charbonnet & Charbonnet** (see page 168); **Crescent City Market** (see page 182); **Diva Gallery** (see pages 178 and 183); **Earth Savers** (branch; see page 184); **Feet First** (see page 179); **George Herget Books** (see page 173); **Harold Clarke Designs** (see page 175); **House of Lounge** (see page 178); **Jim Russell Records** (see page 186); **Joan Vass of New Orleans** (see page 175); **Langenstein's** (see page 181); **Lucullus** (see page 169); **Magazine Flowers & Greenery** (see page 179); **Martin Wine Cellar** (branch; see page 181); **Ms Spratt's** (see page 175); **Mushroom** (see page 187); **Musica Latina** (see page 187); **Neal Auction Company** (see page 166); **Peter A Chopin** (see page 179); **Pied Nu** (see page 179); **Pippen Lane** (see page 175); **Prytania Liquor Store** (see page 181); **RetroActive** (see page 181); **Rite-Aid** (see page 184); **Ruby Ann Tobar-Blanco** (see page 178); **St Charles Vision** (branch; see page 183); **Scriptura** (see page 185); **Stein Mart** (see page 175); **Uptown Costume & Dancewear** (see page 181); **Utopia** (see page 185); **Video Alternatives** (see page 188).

Gerald D Katz

505 Royal Street, at St Louis Street, French Quarter (524 5050/www.bijous.com). Bus 3 Vieux Carré, 55 Elysian Fields, 81 Almonaster, 82 Desire. **Open** 10am-5.30pm daily. **Credit** AmEx, MC, V. **Map** p316 B2.
The largest collection of antique and vintage jewellery in the US, according to the owners, who, in old-fashioned shopkeeper's style, live upstairs in this beautifully restored 1835 building. Half the collection is Victorian.

Keil's Antiques

325 Royal Street, at Conti Street, French Quarter (522 4552). Bus 3 Vieux Carré, 55 Elysian Fields, 81 Almonaster, 82 Desire. **Open** 9am-5pm Mon-Sat; closed Sun. **Credit** AmEx, MC, V. **Map** p316 B2.
This elegant store with friendly staff and diverse prices specialises in 18th- and 19th-century French and English antiques. New Orleans families have shopped here since 1899. Fine gifts for under $100.

Lucullus

3932 Magazine Street, between Napoleon & Louisiana Streets, Uptown (894 0500). Bus 11 Magazine. **Open** 10am-5pm Mon-Sat; closed Sun. **Map** p306 D10.
From dining tables to porcelain fruit and vegetables, everything here is connected with food and eating. A clever concept and an imaginative collection of culinary antiques, art and objects.

Judy's Collage for collectibles. *See p171.*

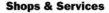

Riverbend

Gae-tana's (see page 174); **Great Acquisitions Books** (see page 173); **Maple Street Bookshop** (see page 173); **Maple Street Children's Bookshop** (see page 173); **Mignon Faget** (see page 177); **The Sun Shop** (see page 185); **Symmetry** (see page 178); **Victoria's Uptown** (see page 179); **Yvonne Lafleur** (see page 179).

Central City, Mid City & Lakeview

Angelo Brocato's (see page 180); **Electric Expressions** (see page 184); **Electric Ladyland Tattoo** (see page 184); **F&F Botanica Company** (see page 171); **Goodwill Retail Store** (see page 175); **Walgreen's** (see page 184); **Whole Foods Market** (see page 182).

Jefferson & Kenner

Dillard's (branch; see page 163); **Esplanade Mall** (see page 165); **Macy's** (branch; see page 165); **PC Tune-ups** (see page 174); **Rapp's Luggage & Gifts** (branch; see page 179); **Salvation Army Thrift Store** (see page 181); **Victoria's Secret** (branch; see page 179).

Metairie

Accent Annex (see page 184); **Adlers & Sons** (branch; see page 178); **Adventure Sports** (see page 188); **Ann Taylor** (branch; see page 174); **Barnes & Noble** (see page 172); **Bennett's Camera & Video** (see page 188); **Borders** (see pages 172 and 186); **Chocolate Soup** (see page 174); **CompUSA** (see page 173); **Computer Shoppe** (see page 173); **Dillard's** (see page 163); **Dorignac's** (see page 180); **Earth Savers** (branches; see page 184); **Foodies** (see page 181); **JC Penney** (see page 165); **Lakeside Shopping Center** (see page 165); **Langenstein's** (branch; see page 181); **Martin Wine Cellar** (see page 181); **Professional Color Service** (see page 188); **St Charles Vision** (branch; see page 183); **Stein Mart** (branch; see page 175); **United Apparel Liquidators** (see page 176); **Victoria's Secret** (branch; see page 179); **Werlein's** (branch; see page 186); **Wolf Camera & Video** (see page 188).

Gretna

Adlers & Sons (branch; see page 178); **Dillard's** (branch; see page 163); **JC Penney** (branch; see page 165); **Prompt Computer Center** (see page 174).

New Orleans
Musical Milestones

1901   Birth of
Louis Armstrong

1970   Start of Jazz &
Heritage Festival

1998   Opening of
Virgin Megastore

Branch: 610 Chartres Street, between Wilkinson & Toulouse Streets, French Quarter (528 9620).

Manheim Galleries
409 Royal Street, at Conti Street, French Quarter (568 1901). Bus 3 Vieux Carré, 55 Elysian Fields, 81 Almonaster, 82 Desire. **Open** 9am-5pm Mon-Sat; closed Sun. **Credit** AmEx, Disc, MC, V. **Map** p316 B2.
This fourth-generation, family-owned business is housed in a building designed by Benjamin Henry Latrobe, one of the architects of the United States Capitol. There are five floors of paintings, porcelain and furniture, and a famous jade room. The master carvers in the store's own cabinet shop have produced custom-made furniture in walnut or mahogany since 1898.

Moss Antiques
411 Royal Street, at Conti Street, French Quarter (522 3981). Bus 3 Vieux Carré, 55 Elysian Fields, 81 Almonaster, 82 Desire. **Open** 9am-5pm Mon-Sat; closed Sun. **Credit** AmEx, MC, V. **Map** p316 B2.
A sister store to Keil's Antiques (*see p169*), offering antique and estate jewellery as well as French and English furniture.

MS Rau
630 Royal Street, at St Peter Street, French Quarter (523 5660). Bus 3 Vieux Carré, 55 Elysian Fields, 81 Almonaster, 82 Desire. **Open** 9am-5.15pm Mon-Sat; closed Sun. **Credit** AmEx, MC, V. **Map** p316 B2.
In business since 1912 and in the present location since the 1930s, this is a third-generation, family-owned outfit. Look out for the Reed and Barton 1920s sterling silver flatware set – 296 pieces for $34,000 – which was originally displayed at Marshall Field's department store in Chicago. There is also an extensive cut glass collection.

Robinson's Antiques
329 Royal Street, at Conti Street, French Quarter (523 6683). Bus 3 Vieux Carré, 55 Elysian Fields, 81 Almonaster, 82 Desire. **Open** 10am-5pm Mon-Sat; closed Sun. **Credit** AmEx, DC, Disc, MC, V. **Map** p316 B2.
Owned by well-known antique dealer Henry Stern until his death in 1993, this shop continues the high quality of merchandise and service for which he was known. You'll find pretty much everything here: French and English furniture, silverware, paintings, chandeliers and rugs.

Collectibles

David's
1319 Decatur Street, at Esplanade Avenue, French Quarter (568 1197). Bus 3 Vieux Carré, 82 Desire, 55 Elysian Fields. **Open** noon-5pm Mon, Thur-Sun; closed Tue, Wed. **Credit** V. **Map** p316 D3.
Located among the funky shops on Lower Decatur, David's has three rooms of knick-knacks, from cookie jars to kooky hats and flash costume jewellery. One

room has a great selection of retro kitchen objects. David himself is a darling.

Judy's Collage
2102 Chartres Street, at Frenchman Street, Marigny (945 0252). Bus 3 Vieux Carré, 55 Elysian Fields. **Open** 10am-5pm daily. **Credit** AmEx, Disc, MC, V. **Map** p316 D2.
A mother-daughter operation that has been in the second-hand collectibles business for two decades. The mama's favourites are lamps, mirrors and jewellery. The place is jam-packed with everything from crooner Bing Crosby's album of cowboy songs to a retro hairdryer that still works. The space gives the feel of being in a dimly lit attic. It's just around the corner from Café Brasil (*see p220*).

Astrology & the occult

F&F Botanica Company
801 N Broad Avenue, at Orleans Avenue, Mid City (482 9142). Bus 46 Canal. **Open** 7.30am-6pm Mon-Sat; closed Sun. **Credit** AmEx, DC, Disc, MC, V. **Map** p307 E6.
Dubbed a spiritual church supply house, this shop has it all, from statues of the saints to a floorwash that's guaranteed to clean out evil spirits. There are rows and rows of candles, and jars of ancient herbs and roots for you to cook up your own concoctions.

Psychic readings

The ancient art of tarot – divining the truth from symbolic images – has been taken up by a small army of psychics and tarot readers who have set up shop around the perimeter of Jackson Square. Anyone who buys a city licence is free to offer readings. Since there's no exam for psychic ability, you won't be able to tell beforehand whether your chosen reader turns out to be an intuitive type or a complete huckster. Readings can be uncannily accurate or completely off the mark. Expect to pay $10 to $30 for a reading that can last from ten minutes up to half an hour, and make sure you agree on a price before you start.

Bottom of the Cup Tea Room & Gifts
732 Royal Street, at St Ann Street, French Quarter (523 1204). Bus 3 Vieux Carré, 55 Elysian Fields, 81 Almonaster, 82 Desire. **Open** 10am-7pm daily. **Credit** AmEx, Disc, MC, V. **Map** p316 C2.
The grandmother of tearooms has been offering tarot and tea leaf readings in the French Quarter since 1929. Audio-taped readings are done in private. A 30-minute consultation costs $30, plus tax, and can be booked in advance. There's also an assortment of tarot cards, crystals and astrological accessories on sale.
Branch: 616 Conti Street, at Camp Street, French Quarter (524 1997).

Esoterica Occult Goods

541 Dumaine Street, at Chartres Street, French Quarter (581 7711/1-800 353 7001/www.onewitch. com). Bus 3 Vieux Carré, 55 Elysian Fields, 81 Almonaster, 82 Desire. **Open** noon-9pm Mon-Thur, Sun; noon-midnight Fri; 10am-noon Sat. **Credit** MC, V. **Map** p316 C2.

Come here for crystal balls, candles, incense, oils and custom-made gris-gris bags (for holding voodoo charms). Self-styled witches give tarot readings ($25 for 30 minutes) or spiritual consultations ($40 for an hour). Walk-ins are welcome, but it's better to make an appointment in advance. The readings aren't recorded, but you're welcome to bring your own tape recorder.

Bookshops

Local branches of the big boys **Barnes & Noble**, **Bookstar** and **Borders** are the places to find discounts on bestsellers and recent hardbacks. All three have in-house cafés. The independents offer the best browsing, unusual finds and expert assistance. Many have a good range of books about New Orleans, including cookbooks. Gift shops in museums and historical houses often have well-chosen selections of books about New Orleans. The **Faubourg Marigny Bookstore**, meanwhile, has the most extensive collection of gay and lesbian literature in New Orleans.

Afro-American Book Stop

New Orleans Centre, 1400 Poydras Street, next to the Louisiana Superdome, CBD (588 1474). Bus 16 S Claiborne. **Open** 10am-8pm Mon-Sat; noon-6pm Sun. **Credit** AmEx, Disc, MC, V. **Map** p309 B1.

An excellent selection of African-American and African books. Author events are held frequently, and the staff are knowledgeable and friendly. **Branch**: Plaza Shopping Center, 5700 Read Boulevard, New Orleans East (243 2436).

Barnes & Noble

3721 Veterans Memorial Boulevard, near Lakeside Shopping Center, Metairie (455 4929/www.barnes andnoble.com). St Charles Streetcar/16 S Claiborne, 39 Tulane, 90 Carrollton bus, then E5 Causeway bus. **Open** 9am-11pm daily. **Credit** AmEx, DC, Disc, MC, V.

New Orleans's largest bookstore, with a full selection of local subjects and authors, including self-published books. It's virtually indistinguishable from all other Barnes & Noble superstores, but considered a good meeting spot for straight singles.

Beaucoup Books

5414 Magazine Street, at Jefferson Avenue, Uptown (895 2663). Bus 11 Magazine. **Open** 10am-6pm Mon-Sat; noon-5pm Sun. **Credit** AmEx, Disc, MC, V. **Map** p306 C9/10.

Beaucoup is a classic neighbourhood bookstore, with excellent author readings. The stock is small

but carefully chosen, heavy on literary fiction and New Orleans and Lousiana authors.

Bookstar

414 N Peters Street, at St Louis Street, Jax Brewery Market Place, French Quarter (523 6411). Bus 3 Vieux Carré, 55 Elysian Fields, 81 Almonaster, 82 Desire. **Open** 9am-midnight daily. **Credit** AmEx, Disc, MC, V. **Map** p316 B3.

Though part of a chain, this is arguably the city's best big bookstore, particularly good on New Orleans and Louisiana subjects, music books and fiction. It also stocks the best selection of US and foreign periodicals in the city (although Borders and Barnes & Noble in suburban Metairie have bigger selections).

Borders

3131 Veterans Memorial Boulevard, at N Causeway Boulevard, Metairie (835 1363/www.borders.com). St Charles Streetcar/16 S Claiborne, 39 Tulane, 90 Carrollton bus, then E5 Causeway bus. **Open** 9am-11pm Mon-Sat; 9am-9pm Sun. **Credit** AmEx, Disc, MC, V.

The most recent of the big-boy chains to open in New Orleans, Borders is giving the others a run for their money in size and selection. The magazine section covers a wide spectrum, including photography, crafts and cars.

DeVille Books & Prints

Riverwalk, 1 Poydras Street, at the Mississippi River, CBD (595 8916). Riverfront Streetcar/3 Vieux Carré bus. **Open** 10am-9pm Mon-Sat; 11am-7pm Sun. **Credit** MC, V ($10 min). **Map** p309 C1.

New Orleans distilled into a bookstore: urbane, charming, eclectic and easygoing. The very knowledgeable staff oversee a shop stocked with local favourites, as well as an excellent history section and a very good collection of regional and local second-hand books. **Branch**: 344 Carondelet Street, at Union Street, CBD (525 1846).

Faubourg Marigny Bookstore

600 Frenchmen Street, at Chartres Street, Marigny (943 9875). Bus 82 Desire. **Open** 10am-8pm Mon-Fri; 10am-6pm Sat, Sun. **Credit** AmEx, Disc, MC, V. **Map** p316 D2.

This is the South's oldest gay, lesbian and feminist bookstore, and it also operates as an informal gay information centre.

Faulkner House Books

624 Pirate's Alley, between St Peter & Orleans Streets French Quarter (524 2940). Bus 3 Vieux Carré, 55 Elysian Fields, 82 Desire. **Open** 10am-6pm daily. **Credit** AmEx, MC, V. **Map** p316 B/C2.

Housed in the building where Nobel Prize winner William Faulkner lived during his 1925 sojourn in New Orleans, this shop specialises, as you might expect, in Faulkner's books, including rare and first editions. There's also a good selection of poetry and

Eat, Drink, Shop

Faulkner House Books. *See p172.*

literature, with a strong emphasis on local and Southern writers.

Garden District Book Shop

2727 Prytania Street, at Washington Avenue, Garden District (895 2266). St Charles Streetcar. **Open** 10am-6pm Mon-Sat; 11am-4pm Sun. **Credit** Disc, MC, V. **Map** p309 A3.
Anne Rice's neighbourhood bookstore is a magnet for Rice fans, who come for the autographed copies, special editions and the author's appearance at special events.

Maple Street Bookshop

7523 Maple Street, at Cherokee Street, Riverbend (866 4916/www.maplestreetbookshop.com). St Charles Streetcar. **Open** 9am-9pm Mon-Sat; 10am-6pm Sun. **Credit** MC, V. **Map** p306 B8.
Maple Street Bookshop's ubiquitous bumper sticker says 'Fight the Stupids', which it has attempted to do since 1964 from a rambling old house in Uptown. It's stuffed with a good selection of fiction and non-fiction books, many of which are autographed by the authors. Next door at No.7529 is **Maple Street Children's Bookshop** (861 2105).

Second-hand

Beckham's Book Shop

228 Decatur Street, at Iberville Street, French Quarter (522 9875). Bus 3 Vieux Carré, 55 Elysian Fields, 81 Almonaster, 82 Desire. **Open** 10am-6pm daily. **Credit** Disc, MC, V. **Map** p316 A3.
Two shabby floors of books, prints and pamphlets. A booklover's haven.

George Herget Books

3109 Magazine Street, at Eighth Street, Uptown (891 5595). Bus 11 Magazine. **Open** 10am-6pm Mon-Sat; 11am-5.30pm Sun. **Credit** MC, V. **Map** p309 A3/4.

At George Herget you'll find second-hand hardback and paperback books, including Southern fiction and non-fiction, plus a few old postcards and sheet music. It's musty, fusty, friendly and fun, with a big black dog named Bear to keep you company while you're browsing.

Great Acquisitions Books

8200 Hampson Street, at S Carrollton Avenue, Riverbend (861 8707). St Charles Streetcar. **Open** 10.30am-6pm Mon-Sat; closed Sun. **Credit** AmEx, Disc, MC, V. **Map** p306 A8.
Great Acquisitions is the place for first editions and rare books. It has sections on art, photography, music, travel and history, and is heavy on Louisiana and Southern literature. The helpful staff provide a free search service.

Kaboom Books

901 Barracks Street, at Dauphine Street, French Quarter (529 5780/kaboombks@aol.com). Bus 3 Vieux Carré, 48 Esplanade. **Open** 11am-6pm daily. **No credit cards. Map** p316 D1.
The character who runs this place will talk your ear off, but if you can tear yourself away, there's a great assortment of classic and contemporary fiction, plus politics, philosophy and drama.

Librairie Bookshop

823 Chartres Street, between Dumaine & St Ann Streets, French Quarter (525 4837). Bus 3 Vieux Carré, 55 Elysian Fields, 82 Desire. **Open** 10am-6pm daily. **Credit** Disc, MC, V. **Map** p316 C2.
The shopkeeper here is a jazz lover. Browse for books on just about any subject to the strains of Miles Davis's trumpet.

Computers

CompUSA

8855 Veterans Memorial Boulevard, at David Drive, Metairie (468 3838/www.compusa.com). Bus 27 Louisiana, 40, 41 or 44 Canal, 48 Esplanade, then E4 Metairie Road. **Open** 10am-9pm Mon-Sat; noon-6pm Sun. **Credit** AmEx, DC, MC, V.
This has the biggest selection (including a few Macs), with aisles of software, books and accessories and good prices. Fine if you know what you want but don't go to get educated about computers; most of the staff lack the knowledge to be of much help. A repair service is available.

The Computer Shoppe

2125 Veterans Memorial Boulevard, between Bonnabel & N Causeway Boulevards, Metairie (833 5100/www.computer-shoppe.com). St Charles Streetcar/16 S Claiborne, 39 Tulane, 90 Carrollton bus, then E5 Causeway bus. **Open** 8am-6pm Mon-Thur; 8am-5pm Fri; 10am-4pm Sat; closed Sun. **Credit** AmEx, Disc, MC, V.
It's hard to find shops that sell or repair Macs in New Orleans, but this is probably the best place; it has been an Apple dealer since 1976.

Eat, Drink, Shop

Repairs

PC Tune-ups

*5614 Jefferson Highway, at Edwards Street,
Jefferson (733 0888/www.afcom-inc.com). St Charles
Streetcar/16 S Claiborne, 39 Tulane, 90 Carrollton
bus, then E5 Causeway bus.* **Open** 10am-7pm
Mon-Fri; 10am-6pm Sat; closed Sun. **Credit** AmEx,
MC, V.

This is a helpful and accommodating mom-and-pop
operation that builds and repairs computers – just
tell them what you want. Prices are competitive.

Prompt Computer Center

*58 Westbank Expressway, at Stumpf Boulevard,
Gretna (362 3922). Bus W-2 Westbank Expressway.*
Open 9am-5.30pm Mon-Fri; closed Sat, Sun.
Credit AmEx, Disc, MC, V.

Offers a 24-hour repair service for IBM-compatibles.
Rentals are also available.

Drycleaning & laundry

In addition to the places listed below, you could
also try **Igor's Checkpoint Charlie** (*see page
219*), a 24-hour music-club-cum-laundromat,
where you can listen to a band, play a game of
pool or grab a burger, all while your clothes
spin and dry.

Hula Mae's Tropic Wash

*840 N Rampart Street, at Dumaine Street,
French Quarter (522 1336). Bus 3 Vieux Carré,
48 Esplanade, 55 Elysian Fields, 57 Franklin,
81 Almonaster.* **Open** 7am-10pm daily. **Credit**
AmEx, MC, V. **Map** p316 C1.

This laundrette is located on the site of Cosimo
Matassa's recording studio; a local legend who
recorded the likes of Little Richard and Fats Domino.
It offers delivery within the French Quarter.

Washing Well Laundryteria

*841 Bourbon Street, at Dumaine Street, French
Quarter (523 9955). Bus 3 Vieux Carré, 55 Elysian
Fields, 81 Almonaster, 82 Desire.* **Open** 7.30am-6pm
Mon-Fri; 7.30am-2pm Sat; closed Sun. **Credit** AmEx,
Disc, MC, V. **Map** p316 C2.

The Washing Well offers same-day pick-up
throughout the city and return of laundry and
drycleaning. Laundry is charged by the load.

Fashion

Go to New York for haute couture. Come to New
Orleans for offbeat and whimsical creations by
local designers often found in small shops on
Magazine Street or in the French Quarter. The
department stores (*see page 163*) carry many of
the major US and European designer labels;
Saks has the most extensive selection. For the
popular fashion chains such as Abercrombie &
Fitch, Gap and Banana Republic, head for the
large-scale malls (*see page 165*).

Harold Clarke Designs. *See p175.*

Ann Taylor

*Canal Place Shopping Center, 333 Canal Street, at
Decatur Street, French Quarter (529 2306). Bus 41
Canal.* **Open** 10am-6pm Mon-Sat; noon-6pm Sun.
Credit AmEx, MC, V. **Map** p309 C1.

Clean lines, good fabrics and neutral colours are the
Ann Taylor trademark. Prices are moderately
expensive (jackets cost between $200 and $300), but
these classics will last forever.

Branches: Lakeside Shopping Center, 3301 Veterans
Memorial Boulevard, at N Causeway Boulevard,
Metairie (835 0843); New Orleans Centre, 1400
Poydras Street, next to the Louisiana Superdome,
CBD (835 0843).

Le Fleur de Paris

*712 Royal Street, at Pirate's Alley, French Quarter
(525 1899). Bus 3 Vieux Carré, 55 Elysian Fields,
81 Almonaster, 82 Desire.* **Open** 10am-6pm daily.
Credit AmEx, MC, V. **Map** p316 C2.

The shop window on Pirate's Alley is an eye-catcher.
Find original pieces, copies of vintage designs by an
in-house designer and custom-designed *My Fair
Lady*-style hats covered in ribbons and flowers.
Check out the made-to-order peignoirs and boned
foundation garments.

Gae-tana's

*7732 Maple Street, between Adams & Burdette
Streets, Riverbend (865 9625). St Charles Streetcar.*
Open 9.30am-6pm Mon-Sat; noon-5pm Sun. **Credit**
AmEx, Disc, MC, V. **Map** p306 A8.

In the university area, this place focuses on upscale but comfortable clothing for twenty- and thirty-somethings. There's a good sportswear selection and some interesting shoes, too.

The Grace Note

900 Royal Street, at Dumaine Street, French Quarter (522 1513). Bus 3 Vieux Carré, 55 Elysian Fields, 81 Almonaster, 82 Desire. **Open** 10am-6pm Mon-Sat; 11am-5pm Sun. **Credit** AmEx, MC, V. **Map** p316 C2.

An unusual selection of clothes and accessories by talented local designers like Libby Brighton, who creates stunning hats inspired by silhouettes from the 1920s and 1930s. There are also wonderful jackets made from vintage fabrics and chibori (Japanese tie-dye) velvet.

Harold Clarke Designs

5234 Magazine Street, at Jefferson Avenue, Uptown (897 0770/www.haroldclarke.com). **Open** 10am-6pm Mon-Sat; or by appointment. **Credit** AmEx, DC, Disc, MC. **Map** p306 C10.

This Jamaican-born designer, who now calls New Orleans home, has a worldwide reputation for designing bridal dresses and glamorous ball gowns that are guaranteed to turn heads. When New Orleans's new first lady, TV reporter Michelle Miller, married dapper mayor Marc Morial, her Clarke-designed dress got almost as much coverage as the event itself. All dresses are made in-house under the practised eye of Iona Clarke, the designer's wife and partner; it's elegant personal service at its best. Delta Burke, of the TV-series *Designing Women*, names this studio as one of her favourite places to shop in New Orleans.

Joan Vass of New Orleans

1100 Sixth Street, at Magazine Street, Uptown (891 4502). Bus 11 Magazine. **Open** 10am-5pm Mon-Sat; closed Sun. **Credit** AmEx, Disc, MC, V. **Map** p309 A3.

This New York designer's signature line consists of cashmere-cotton casual separates for women, in limited colours each season. Pricey but nice.

Ms Spratt's

4537 Magazine Street, at Cadiz Street, Uptown (891 0063). Bus 11 Magazine. **Open** 10am-6am Mon-Sat; 1-5pm Sun. **Credit** AmEx, Disc, MC, V. **Map** p306 D10.

Ms Spratt's sells clothing and accessories with a smart attitude for large women.

Weinstein's

Canal Place Shopping Center, 333 Canal Street, at Decatur Street, French Quarter (522 6278/ wclothing@aol.com). Bus 41 Canal. **Open** 10am-7pm Mon-Sat; 12-6pm Sun. **Credit** AmEx, DC, MC, V. **Map** p309 C1.

Loyal customers return to Weinstein's for its exclusive collection of Italian and Belgian designer clothing for women and men. Prices are high, but then so is the quality.

Children's clothing

All the major department stores have children's departments, with the biggest selection at Macy's in the **Esplanade Mall** in Kenner (*see page 165*).

The malls are also the place to look for branches of Gap Kids and The Limited Too, the pre-adolescent and adolescent version of the women's clothing store The Limited.

Chocolate Soup

2030 Metairie Road, at Bonnabel Boulevard, Metairie (837 8314). Bus 27 Louisiana, 40, 41 or 44 Canal, 48 Esplanade, then bus E4 Metairie Road. **Open** 9.30am-5pm Mon-Sat; noon-5pm Sun. **Credit** MC, V.

This Metairie outlet store has its own line of appliqué clothing as well as designer wear, such as Rachel's Kids. Boys' sizes go up to age seven and girls' up to age 14.

Mignon

2727 Prytania Street, at Washington Avenue, Garden District (891 2374). St Charles Streetcar. **Open** 10am-5pm Mon-Sat; closed Sun. **Credit** AmEx, MC, V. **Map** p309 A3.

This Garden District store carries the kind of kid's clothing you either love or hate: heavy on the lace, appliqué, ruffles and the Little Lord Fauntleroy look from toddler sizes to age four (boys) and age ten (girls). Prices are high (dresses start at $100).

Pippen Lane

2929 Magazine Street, at Seventh Street, Uptown (269 0106/www.pippenlane.com). Bus 11 Magazine. **Open** 10am-6pm Mon-Fri; 10am-5pm Sat; closed Sun. **Credit** AmEx, Disc, MC, V. **Map** p309 A3/4.

Fine quality expensive clothing and accessories for babies and children.

Discount & second-hand

See also page 180 **All dressed up**.

Goodwill Retail Store

123 Robert E Lee Boulevard, at West End Boulevard, Lakeview (282 7655). Bus 40 Canal, then 43 Lake Vista. **Open** 9am-9pm Mon-Sat; noon-6pm Sun. **Credit** Disc, MC, V. **Map** p308 C2.

Off the beaten tourist path, in the affluent Lakeview neighbourhood bordering Lake Pontchartrain, this non-profit charity shop is a must for serious bargain hunters. Many well-to-do Lakeview residents donate their tasteful, barely used clothes for resale; you'll find contemporary stuff for men, women, teens and children, with almost everything under $20.

Stein Mart

5300 Tchoupitoulas Street, at Napoleon Avenue, Uptown (891 6377/www.steinmart.com). Bus 10 Tchoupitoulas. **Open** 10am-9pm Mon-Sat; noon-6pm Sun. **Credit** AmEx, DC, Disc, MC, V. **Map** p306 D10.

Eat, Drink, Shop

Dressing by design

Wearable art has become a cottage industry in New Orleans.

Ellis Anderson

1-228 467 7279.
For 20-odd years, Anderson, once a musician, has been a jewellery designer, creating one-off pendants and rings using amber or lapis, sterling silver and 18-carat gold. Her Mardi Gras Hands earrings and brooches are based on New Orleans architecture (pictured below).
Stockists: Quarter Moon Gallery (see page 177); Symmetry (see page 178).

Gail Kiefer

598 2111.
New Orleans police warned there would be zero tolerance for nudity at Mardi Gras 2000, so the women had to think of another eye-catching way to get their beads. Many marched out and bought Kiefer brassieres, naughty bras loaded with feathers, sequins, beads or anything else that tickles your fancy.

John Abramson

Years ago, Abramson came to New Orleans for the music and decided to stay. Since then, he's successfully made the transition from musician to mask maker, handcrafting leather into jester's faces, horned beasts and devil's masks (pictured right, worn by jewellery designer Ellis Anderson).
Stockists: Quarter Moon Gallery (see page 177).

Libby Brighton

Brighton uses sexy, elegant fabrics to create hat designs inspired by styles from the 1920s and '30s.
Stockists: The Grace Note (see page 175).

Linda Sampson

523 3085.
A theatre designer and stylist for *National Lampoon* magazine, Sampson fashions wearable art from recycled local artefacts such as 1930s glass Mardi Gras beads, porcelain king cake dolls and antique buttons. Some of her pieces incorporate the Victorian art of beading flowers, a popular hobby for Creole ladies during the 1800s. Her hat pins, beaded hairclips, earrings and brooches are intricate pieces, with a whimsical and elegant attitude.

Designer fashions for men and women at rock-bottom prices. Remainders from other retail outlets end up at Stein Mart. You can find some gems among the junk. **Branch**: 2840 Veterans Memorial Boulevard, Metairie (831 0655).

United Apparel Liquidators

3780 Veterans Memorial Boulevard, near Lakeside Shopping Center, Metairie (455 7030). St Charles Streetcar/16 S Claiborne, 39 Tulane, 90 Carrollton bus, then E5 Causeway bus. **Open** 10am-9pm Mon Sat; noon-6pm Sun. **Credit** AmEx, Disc, MC, V.
Good discounts on women's clothing, including well-known labels such as Carol Horne and David Dart.

Fashion accessories

Hats

It's highly recommended that you protect yourself from the ravages of the unforgiving New Orleans sun. Luckily the abundance of talented hatmakers in the city means you can look stylish while you do it. At the low end, you can pick up an inexpensive hat or cap in the French Market or in the souvenir and novelty shops in the French Quarter. Vintage clothing stores (*see page 180* **All dressed up**) usually

Stockists: RHINO Gallery (see page 178); 1850 House Museum Shop, Louisiana State Museum (see page 77).

Kathy Schorr

482 9721.
Schorr's one-of-a-kind designs can be worn or framed and are inspired by local themes: where else can you get a scarf depicting a Barq's Root Beer next to a mound of fresh boiled crawfish?
Stockists: RHINO Gallery (see page 178).

Kathleen Olson Grumich

Delicately beaded, hand-dyed silk chiffon scarves and evening bags inspired by the beaux arts and art deco movements.
Stockists: Diva Gallery (see page 178); Quarter Moon Gallery (see below).

Ruby Moon

908 4427.
Moon is a practitioner of Menhendi, the ancient Middle Eastern art of drawing on the body using a henna dye that stains the skin for a couple of weeks. Call for an appointment.

Susan Gisleson

865 1973.
Gisleson will design just about any kind of speciality garb. The resurgence of masking in the city, especially for Mardi Gras and

Hallowe'en, has caused a big demand for her alternative costumes and exuberant hats.

Tracy Thomson

586 9917.
Thomson's background in the theatrical arts has honed an eye for colour and a feel for fabric. Creator of the Kabuki label, she designs, sews and shapes each hat herself. In cool weather, look for rich taffetas or tasty felts. In warmer weather she fashions comfortable, classy straw hats with generous brims (pictured left). She has her own showroom in the French Quarter (call for an appointment) and several stockists around town – call for details.

Valerie Wozniak

393 7441.
A fibre artist who dyes silk satins, raw silk and velvet fabrics using a centuries-old Japanese technique called 'Shibori' that resembles tie-dye. The luscious fabrics are then sewn to make kimono-style jackets (wearable by both sexes), scarves and shawls.

Stockists

New Orleans Crab Bag

606 Royal Street, at Toulouse Street, French Quarter (552 2722). Bus 3 Vieux Carré, 55 Elysian Fields, 81 Almonaster, 82 Desire. **Open** 9am-9pm daily. **Credit** AmEx, Disc, MC, V. **Map** p316 B2.

Quarter Moon Gallery

918 Royal Street, at Dumaine Street, French Quarter (524 3208). Bus 3 Vieux Carré, 55 Elysian Fields, 81 Almonaster, 82 Desire. **Open** 10am-5pm Mon-Sat; noon- 5pm Sun. **Credit** AmEx, Disc, MC, V. **Map** p316 B2.

have a fun selection of period hats for both men and women. With Hallowe'en in the autumn and Mardi Gras in early spring, outrageous hats are always in demand. Besides vintage and novelty, you'll also find hats for the seriously fashionable by popular local designers like Tracy Thomson and Libby Brighton.

Meyer the Hatter

120 St Charles Avenue, at Canal Street, CBD (525 1048/1-800 882 4287). St Charles Streetcar/ 41 Canal bus. **Open** 10am-6pm Mon-Sat; closed Sun. **Credit** AmEx, DC, Disc, MC, V. **Map** p309 C1.

This dishevelled shop with 1950s decor is a family-run New Orleans institution, where men have been buying top labels such as Dobbs and Stetson since 1894. Old-timers in the hat business provide expert help and can tell a good story to boot: ask about when the Marx Brothers shopped here. Perfect for chaps who like caps.

New Orleans Hat Company

402 Chartres Street, at Conti Street, French Quarter (524 8792/1-877 639 4281). Bus 3 Vieux Carré, 55 Elysian Fields, 81 Almonaster, 82 Desire. **Open** 10am-5pm Mon-Thur; 10am-6pm Fri-Sun. **Credit** AmEx, MC, V. **Map** p316 B2.

This is the place to find classic Panama straw hats, jaunty berets and one-of-a-kind designs for women. It also stocks unusual imported clothing and quirky, handmade jewellery.

RHINO Gallery
Canal Place Shopping Center, 333 Canal Street, at Decatur Street, French Quarter (523 7945). Bus 41 Canal. **Open** 10am-6pm Mon-Wed; 10am-7pm Thur-Sat; noon-6pm Sun. **Credit** AmEx, Disc, MC, V. **Map** p309 C1.
RHINO – 'Right Here In New Orleans' – is an artists' collective that showcases the best of local glassware, pottery, wall hangings, photography, jewellery and hats. Tracy Thomson's wide-brimmed straw creations sell like hot cakes at Jazz Fest. Find them here all year long.

Jewellery

If you're a fan of second-hand family jewellery (usually known as 'estate jewellery'), the French Quarter is your nirvana. Best of all are the antiques shops on Royal Street, but you'll have good luck all over town. Besides older pieces, there are many outlets for contemporary jewellery, from the shudderingly expensive to handmade craft items; **Mignon Faget** (*see below*), for example, is a local jewellery-maker with a national reputation. Most department stores have collections of fine jewellery as well as costume pieces; **Saks** (*see page 165*) is a good place for contemporary designs.

Adlers & Sons
722 Canal Street, at St Charles Avenue, CBD (523 5292). St Charles Streetcar/41 Canal bus. **Open** 10am-5.45pm Mon-Wed, Fri, Sat; 10am-7pm Thur; closed Sun. **Credit** AmEx, DC, Disc, MC, V. **Map** p309 C1.
This highly reputable New Orleans landmark has all kinds of fine jewellery for men and women. **Branches**: Lakeside Shopping Center, 3301 Veterans Memorial Boulevard, at N Causeway Boulevard, Metairie (523 5292); Oakwood Shopping Center, 197 Westbank Expressway, at Terry Parkway, Gretna (523 5292).

Bedazzle
635 St Peter Street, at Royal Street, French Quarter (529 3248). Bus 3 Vieux Carré, 55 Elysian Fields, 81 Almonaster, 82 Desire. **Open** 10.30am-6pm daily. **Credit** AmEx, DC, Disc, MC, V. **Map** p316 B2.
Come here for an unusual selection of bangles and baubles by local designers.

Diva Gallery
1110 Antonine Street, at Magazine Street, Uptown (899 0275). Bus 11 Magazine. **Open** 10am-5pm Tue-Sat; closed Mon, Sun. **Credit** AmEx, Disc, MC, V. **Map** p307 E9.
Reasonably priced earrings, necklaces, pins and other handmade pieces by the best of the region's emerging artists and artisans, including smoked-glass bead necklaces by Wendy Ethridge and freshwater pearl earrings by David Rose. Diva also has sculpture, painting, photography, wall hangings, textiles and stained glass by co-owner Sally Draper, whose studio is on the premises. Her partner, Annie Breaux, runs one of the city's most popular hair salons in the back of the shop (*see p183*).

Mignon Faget
710 Dublin Street, at Maple Street, Riverbend (865 7361/www.mignonfaget.com). St Charles Streetcar. **Open** 10am-5pm Mon-Sat; closed Sun. **Credit** AmEx, Disc, MC, V. **Map** p306 A8.
This New Orleans designer is well known for her nature-inspired designs in silver and gold. The Riverbend shop also sells linens and photo frames. **Branches**: Canal Place Shopping Center, 333 Canal Street, at Decatur Street, French Quarter (524 2973); Lakeside Shopping Center, 3301 Veterans Memorial Boulevard, at N Causeway Boulevard, Metairie (835 2244).

Ruby Ann Tobar-Blanco
3005 Magazine Street, at Seventh Street, Uptown (897 0811/1-800 826 7282). Bus 11 Magazine. **Open** 10am-5pm Mon-Sat; closed Sun. **Credit** AmEx, MC, V. **Map** p309 A3/4.
A local designer who creates elegant, feminine designs with an antique feel, using freshwater pearls, gemstones, coral, wood and sterling silver.

Symmetry
8138 Hampson Street, at Dublin Street, Riverbend (861 9925/www.symmetryjewelers.com). St Charles Streetcar. **Open** *Summer* 10am-5pm Tue-Sat; closed Mon, Sun. *Winter* 10am-5pm Mon-Sat; closed Sun. **Credit** AmEx, Disc, MC, V. **Map** p306 A8.
Handcrafted jewellery by local designers is sold at reasonable prices ; if you have a design in mind, you can get it made here. There's also a small collection of 1930s watches by Bulova and Gruen. Staff are helpful and offer an expert jewellery repair service.

Lingerie

House of Lounge
2044 Magazine Street, between Josephine & St Andrew Streets, Uptown (671 8300/www.houseoflounge.com). **Open** 10am-6pm Mon-Sat; noon-5pm Sun. **Credit** AmEx, Disc, MC, V. **Map** p309 B3.
Some very sexy lingerie that won't fail to leave an impression in or out of the bedroom. There are ostrich-trimmed robes by local costume designer Patti Spinale, custom corsets from Paris, peignoir sets, designer bathing suits, a stylish collection of costume jewellery, handbags and gloves, plus some unusual papier mâché lampshades by local artist Julian Gibson. One of Magazine Street's newest hot spots.

Victoria's Secret
Riverwalk, 1 Poydras Street, at the Mississippi River, CBD (525 6900/www.victoriassecret.com). Riverfront Streetcar/3 Vieux Carré, 10 Tchoupitoulas bus.

Open 10am-9pm Mon-Sat; 11am-7pm Sun. **Credit** AmEx, Disc, MC, V. **Map** p309 C1.
The well-known national chain that caters to gals that love satin.
Branches: Esplanade Mall, 1401 W Esplanade Boulevard, near Williams Boulevard, Kenner (468 2045); Lakeside Shopping Center, 3301 Veterans Memorial Boulevard, at N Causeway Boulevard, Metairie (834 2720).

Yvonne Lafleur

8131 Hampson Street, at Dublin Street, Riverbend (866 9666/www.yvonnelafleur.com). St Charles Streetcar. **Open** 10am-6pm Mon-Wed, Fri, Sat; 10am-8pm Thur; closed Sun. **Credit** AmEx, Disc, MC, V. **Map** p306 A8.
Expensive silk lingerie, including a decent selection in larger sizes, is sold in surroundings that are reminiscent of a classy bordello. Take a look at the cocktail party dresses, imported wedding gowns and custom millinery.

Luggage

Rapp's Luggage & Gifts

604 Canal Street, at St Charles Avenue, CBD (568 1953). St Charles Streetcar/41 Canal bus. **Open** 10am-6pm Mon-Sat; closed Sun. **Credit** AmEx, Disc, MC, V. **Map** p309 C1.
In business since 1865 and located on Canal Street since the 1920s, Rapp's Lugage & Gifts has a wide collection of luggage and leather briefcases as well as a small selection of purses, wallets, belts and gloves. Luggage brands include Hartmann, Tumi, Andimo, French of California, Halliburton and Samsonite. A leather and luggage repair service is also available.
Branches: 17th Street, at Severn Street, Jefferson (885 6536); New Orleans Centre, 1400 Poydras Street, next to the Louisiana Superdome, CBD (566 0700).

Shoes

Feet First

5500 Magazine Street, at Octavia Street, Uptown (899 6800). Bus 11 Magazine. **Open** 10am-6pm Mon-Sat; noon-5pm Sun. **Credit** AmEx, Disc, MC, V. **Map** p306 C9/10.
Designer shoes for women (Kenneth Cole et al) at discount prices, but the selection can be spotty.
Branch: 518 Chartres Street, at St Louis Street, French Quarter (566 7525).

Pied Nu

5521 Magazine Street, at Octavia Street, Uptown (899 4118). Bus 11 Magazine. **Open** 10am-6pm Mon-Fri; 10am-5pm Sat; closed Sun. **Credit** AmEx, Disc, MC, V. **Map** p306 C9/10.
Pied Nu stocks a small but well-selected collection of shoes by Calvin Klein and Robert Clergerie, plus upmarket accessories such as beaded evening bags, and linens and lamps for the home.

Saint Germain

Canal Place Shopping Center, 333 Canal Street, at Decatur Street, French Quarter (522 1720). Bus 41 Canal. **Open** 10am-6pm Mon-Wed; 10am-7pm Thur-Sat; noon-6pm Sun. **Credit** AmEx, DC, Disc, MC, V. **Map** p309 C1.
Sassy shoes from hot designers such as American Donald Pliner and Frenchman Luc Berjen, and hand-made bridal shoes by British star Emma Hope. There is also a small but brilliantly edited selection of accessories, including beaded evening bags.

Victoria's Uptown

7725 Maple Street, at Adams Street, Riverbend (861 8861). St Charles Streetcar. **Open** 10am-6pm Mon-Sat; closed Sun. **Credit** AmEx, MC, V. **Map** p306 A8.
A good range of snazzy labels like Zeitgeist NY, Cynthia Rowley and Enrico Antinori.
Branch: 532 Chartres Street, at St Louis Street, French Quarter (568 9990).

Florists

Magazine Flowers & Greenery

737 Octavia Street, at Magazine Street, Uptown (891 4356). Bus 11 Magazine. **Open** 10.30am-5.30pm Tue-Sat; closed Mon, Sun. **Credit** AmEx, MC, V. **Map** p306 C9/10.
This attractive store offers natural and unpretentious flower arrangements. You'll also find lots of orchids and flowering plants.

Patrick's Little Shop of Flowers

839 Spain Street, at Burgundy Street, Marigny (943 0410). Bus 82 Desire. **Open** 9am-6pm Mon-Sat; closed Sun. **Credit** AmEx, MC, V. **Map** p307 H6.
This tiny, hospitable full-service shop is tucked away in Marigny, an artsy working-class neighbourhood that's minutes by car from the French Quarter. There's no minimum charge, and Patrick, whose parents grew up in this neighbourhood, will work with you to get you anything you could possibly want. Delivery costs from $3 to $15.

Peter A Chopin

3138 Magazine, at Ninth Street, Uptown (891 4455). St Charles Streetcar. **Open** 8am-5pm Mon-Fri; 8am-4pm Sat; closed Sun. **Credit** AmEx, DC, Disc, MC, V. **Map** p306 D10.
The grand master of florists in New Orleans is featured in Anne Rice's books and frequented by the society folk of the Garden District. Arrangements are traditional and formal.

Tommy's Flower Shop

1029 Chartres Street, between Phillip & Ursulines Streets, French Quarter (522 6563). Bus 55 Elysian Fields. **Open** 10am-6.30pm Mon-Sat; 10am-5pm Sun. **Credit** AmEx, MC, V. **Map** p316 B2.
Stop in at Tommy's Flower Shop to pick up a bunch of daisies for your honey.

Eat, Drink, Shop

All dressed up...

In a city that expects you to express yourself, everyone can shed their fashion inhibitions and fulfil their dreams of dressing up. Mardi Gras, Hallowe'en, St Patrick's Day, St Anthony Day and even a raucous and camp celebration of Queen Elizabeth's official birthday all provide an excuse for getting into costume. Dressing up is second nature in New Orleans and if you have the pzazz to enter into the spirit of the city, shopping for a costume is all part of the fun. Both rental outlets and second-hand clothes shops maintain a stock that guarantee you won't have to look dowdy.

In the French Quarter, clustered along a couple of blocks of Decatur Street are several vintage clothing shops: try **Gargoyles** (No.1201, 529 4387) for all things leather (new not vintage), and **Jazzrags** (No.1215, 523 2942), **Paisley Babylon** (No.1129, 529 3696), or **La Garage** (No.1236, 523 4467) for used army gear, khaki coats and old Mardi Gras costumes. This place also usually has old Czech glass Mardi Gras beads from the 1950s.

Masquerade Fantasy (No.1233, 593 9269) sells leather masks decorated with feathers, beads and jewels, in non-traditional, spooky designs, while **One of a Kind** (No.1212, 486 5567) sells second-hand costumes. Just across the street from Fifi Mahoney's (see page 183), there's **Trashy Diva** (829 Chartres Street, 581 4555, www.trashy-diva.net), one of the classiest vintage shops in the Quarter. Come here for high-end vintage suits and dresses, reproduction period clothing from 1860 to 1950, sexy corsets, Asian style jackets, Lucite box purses and costume jewellery.

Elsewhere in the Quarter, the **Mardi Gras Center** (831 Chartres Street, 454 6444) is the place to go for glitter and make-up and to get ideas for costumes. It's small, but packed with everything imaginable to kit you out for a special occasion.

If you've ever longed to dress like Louis XIV or Marie Antoinette, head for **MGM** (1617 St Charles Avenue, at Euterpe Street, Lower Garden District, 581 3999). The stage and movie costumes here cover looks from the Middle Ages to Southern Belle. They were custom-made for a particular actor or actress, so searching for the right fit takes time. Hire prices range from $25 a day for a plain pirate outfit to around $400 for a Mardi Gras Queen's dress, hand-sewn with hundreds of glass beads.

Magazine Street is seventh heaven for vintage clothes lovers. **Jim Smiley Fine Vintage Clothing** (2001 Magazine Street, Lower Garden District, 528 9449) has pricey, glamorous cocktail dresses and exceptional pieces of period clothing from the Victorian era to the 1930s. **Mariposa** (No.2038, at Jackson Avenue, Garden District, 523 3037) sells both men's and women's clothes, mostly from the 1960s and 1970s, at prices ranging from $7 to $100, while **Gallery 2207** (2207 Magazine Street, Garden District, 525 9207) has a large selection of vintage women's clothing at reasonable prices.

Further up the street, **Ragin' Daisy** (3125 Magazine Street, at Ninth Street, Lower Garden District, 269 1960) goes for gothic, rockabilly and vintage pieces: men will find cowboy outfits, Hawaiian shirts and acres of polyester. **Fiesta** (3322 Magazine Street,

Food & drink

Angelo Brocato's

214 North Carrollton Avenue, at Canal Street, Mid City (486 0078). Bus 40 Canal. **Open** 9.30am-10pm daily. **Credit** Disc, MC, V. **Map** p308 D5.

This is a family business that has been around for decades. Generations of New Orleanians have satisfied their sweet-tooth cravings with Brocato's handmade Italian gelato, rich pastries and mouth-watering cookies. Pre-packaged cookies make good gifts or a perfect snack for back at the hotel, and one of the espresso coffees will set you abuzz for quite a while.

Central Grocery Company

923 Decatur Street, at St Philip Street, French Quarter (523 1620). Bus 3 Vieux Carré, 55 Elysian Fields, 81 Almonaster, 82 Desire. **Open** 8am-5.30pm daily. **No credit cards.** **Map** p316 C2/3.

Central Grocery is one of the few remaining Italian groceries in the city, packed to the rafters with edible goodies. It sells great black olives and the city's best muffuletta sandwich, a New Orleans original containing ham, cheese and olive salad. *See also p145* **Cheap eats.**

Dorignac's

710 Veterans Memorial Boulevard, Metairie (834 8216/www.dorignac.com). Bus 41, 42, or 43

Lower Garden District, 895 7877) has a well-chosen, moderately priced selection of vintage garb including satin smoking jackets, flowery Hawaiian-style shirts, Chinese dressing gowns, hand-painted vintage neckties and a small stash of Czech glass Mardi Gras beads. There's also **Uptown Costume & Dancewear** (4326 Magazine Street, at Napoleon Street, Uptown, 895 7969), the spot for costumes, hats, wigs and make-up at prices that will encourage your sense of the outrageous: synthetic wigs cost $10 and packaged costumes start at $20.

Caveat Emptor (4530 Magazine Street, Uptown, 296 4684) is a historical costume emporium: choose your period and Luna, the proprietress, will custom-make a costume or hat for you. **RetroActive** (5418 Magazine Street, Uptown, 895 5054) is jammed with good quality vintage clothes, hats, handbags and costume jewellery from the 1940s to 1970s.

To find the cheapest thrills available in the costume game, travel out to the **Salvation Army Thrift Store** (100 Jefferson Highway, at Dakin Avenue, Jefferson, 837 5914), which sells cheap second-hand clothes and has a large selection of used carnival costumes.

Finally, if you're temporarily in need of a dinner jacket or full evening outfit, **Gentlemen's Quarterly** (232 Royal Street, at Iberville Street, French Quarter, 522 7139) hires out men's formal wear, including shoes, in an extensive range of sizes. Open seven days a week, it offers pick-up and delivery to hotels in the Quarter.

Canal to Cemeteries, then Veterans Memorial Boulevard bus. **Open** 7.30am-9pm Mon-Sat; 7.30am-6pm Sun. **Credit** AmEx, MC, V, Disc.
An old New Orleans supermarket where the assistants call you 'dah-lin' and give you tips on how to cook what you've bought. It stocks lots of local and regional food labels at prices well below what you'll pay in the French Quarter. The deli's corn and crabmeat soup and its stuffed artichoke are zowie.

Foodie's
720 Veterans Memorial Boulevard, Metairie (837 9695/www.foodieskitchen.com). Bus 41, 42, or 43 Canal to Cemeteries, then Veterans Memorial Boulevard bus. **Open** 7am-10pm daily. **Credit** AmEx, MC, V.

The Brennan restaurateur family has done it again, this time with a takeaway 'gourmet foods market', so good your guests will believe you've been working in the kitchen all day. The breads, including the very popular blue cheese walnut bread, are made on the premises and are just about the best in the city. Like Dorignac's (*see above*), its venerable neighbour, Foodies stocks locally made packaged products; it also has a small but respectable wine selection.

Langenstein's
1330 Arabella Street, at Pitt Street, Uptown (899 9283). St Charles Streetcar. **Open** 8am-7pm Mon-Sat; closed Sun. **Credit** MC, V. **Map** p306 C9.
The best meat market in the city. Look for high-end items like leg of lamb and smoked salmon. The deli dishes up a daily selection of high quality but pricey home-made local favourites like crawfish bisque and stuffed mirliton (a local vegetable resembling a pale green pear). The Metairie Road branch is open on Sundays and doesn't close until 8pm in the week.
Branch: 800 Metairie Road, Metairie (831 6682).

Matassa's Grocery
1101 Dauphine Street, at St Philip Street, French Quarter (412 8700). Bus 3 Vieux Carré, 55 Franklin. **Open** 6am-10pm daily. **Credit** AmEx, DC, Disc, MC, V. **Map** p316 C1.
A small, late-opening neighbourhood store with a deli that offers a daily lunch special and sandwiches. Delivery is available within the French Quarter.

Progress Grocery Company
915 Decatur Street, at St Philip Street, French Quarter (525 6627). Bus 3 Vieux Carré, 55 Elysian Fields, 81 Almonaster, 82 Desire. **Open** 9am-5.30pm daily. **Credit** MC, V. **Map** p316 C3.
Another old-fashioned French Quarter grocery, which competes with the Central Grocery (*see above*) for the muffuletta trade. It also sells sandwiches and various speciality foods such as Italian sweets, black olives and the best mozzarella in the city.

Beer & wine

You can buy beer, wine and liquor everywhere in the city – in supermarkets, grocery stores, corner shops, even the major chain drugstores – so there isn't a need for specialist liquor shops. Local beers Dixie and Abita (the latter brewed on the North Shore) are popular, as are beers imported from Britain, Ireland, Australia and Mexico. Unlike in many other US cities, you can buy alcohol on Sundays in New Orleans, but you have to be 21 and you may have to show photo ID.

Martin Wine Cellar
714 Elmeer Street, Metairie (896 7300/www.martin wine.com). Bus 41,42,43 Canal to Cemeteries, then Veterans Memorial Boulevard bus. **Open** 9am-7pm Mon-Sat; 10am-2pm Sun. **Credit** AmEx, Disc, MC, V.

Eat, Drink, Shop

Martin offers the best selection and prices on wine and imported beer, plus a good deli, party foods and an assortment of gourmet treats, such as grapes encased in Roquefort cheese and chopped pecans. There's a speciality gift basket service and the staff are friendly and knowledgeable.
Branch: 3827 Barron Street, at Peniston Street, Uptown (899 7411).

Prytania Liquor Store
1300 Arabella Street, at Pitt Street, Uptown (891 0448). St Charles Streetcar. **Open** 9am-7pm Mon-Sat; closed Sun. **Credit** MC, V. **Map** p306 B9.
A small but well-stocked neighbourhood shop that sells wine, beer and liquor, and glassware for imbibing your drink of choice. Delivery is available.

Vieux Carré Wine & Spirits
422 Chartres Street, at St Louis Street, French Quarter (568 9463). Bus 3 Vieux Carré, 55 Elysian Fields, 81 Almonaster, 82 Desire. **Open** 10am-10pm Mon-Sat; 10am-7pm Sun. **Credit** AmEx, Disc, MC, V. **Map** p316 B2.
Offering the French Quarter's largest selection of wine and spirits, this place is open on Sundays and will deliver to local hotels.

Farmers' markets

Sadly, the **French Market** (located on Decatur Street, at the river) is a shadow of its former self, with souvenir stands now outnumbering the food stalls. However, a few of the vendors stick around all night and you can still get fresh fruit and vegetables, as well as New Orleans spices, hot sauce and pre-packaged seasoned red beans.

The locally popular **Crescent City Market** (700 Magazine Street, at Girod Street, Warehouse District) operates only on Saturday mornings from 8am to noon. This is a true farmers' market, offering regionally produced cheeses from Chicory Farm, locally grown flowers and plants, fruits, vegetables and herbs, fresh fish in season and artisan breads from **La Spiga**, a small bakery in the Marigny (*see page 133*). At around 10am, a local chef (a different one each week) gives a free culinary demonstration. In April 2000, the Crescent City Market added a Tuesday market to its itinerary. The market takes place at the Uptown Square shopping area from 10am to 2pm (rain or shine).

Speciality & gift foods

If you want to take home the flavour of New Orleans, Cajun and Creole spices, sugary pralines, coffee, beignet mix and packaged red beans and rice all travel well. You can find many of these at standard grocery stores, but the speciality shops listed below offer a wider selection.

Visit **House of Lounge** for bags of sexy lingerie. *See p178.*

Café du Monde Shop
800 Decatur Street, at St Ann Street, French Quarter (525 4544). Bus 3 Vieux Carré, 55 Elysian Fields, 81 Almonaster, 82 Desire. **Open** 24hrs daily. **Credit** AmEx, Disc, MC, V. **Map** p316 C3.
Across the street from the famous café (*see p125*), the shop sells the house brand of coffee and beignet mix and will ship overseas.

Creole Delicacies Gourmet Shop
533 St Ann Street, at Chartres Street, French Quarter (525 9508). Bus 3 Vieux Carré, 55 Elysian Fields, 81 Almonaster, 82 Desire. **Open** 9am-5pm daily. **Credit** AmEx, DC, Disc, MC, V. **Map** p316 C2.
This is another place that specialises in gift baskets containing all the mixes and spices you'll need for Creole and Cajun cooking.
Branch: 3rd Floor, Riverwalk Mall, 1 Poydras Street, at the Mississippi River, CBD (523 6425).

Louisiana Products
618 Julia Street, between St Charles Avenue & Camp Street, Warehouse District (529 1666). St Charles Streetcar. **Open** 7.30am-5.30pm Mon-Fri; 8.30am-3pm Sat, Sun. **Credit** AmEx, Disc, MC, V. **Map** p309 B1/2.
The place for Cajun and Creole spices, such as Paul Prudhomme blackening spices or the peppery coating for fried fish made by the local Zatarain family. Choose from pre-packaged gift boxes or get the staff to make one up for you (prices range from $5 to $50).

Natural foods

Whole Foods Market
3135 Esplanade Avenue, at Ponce de Leon Street, Mid City (943 1626/www.wholefoods.com). Bus 48 Esplanade. **Open** 8.30am-9.30pm daily. **Credit** AmEx, Disc, MC, V. **Map** p308 E5.
This small store on Esplanade Avenue is the only full-service natural food supermarket in the city. It sells organic fruit and vegetables, cheese, fresh bread, herbal tea, herbal remedies, food supplements and skincare products.

Eat, Drink, Shop

Health & beauty

Drugstores stock basic, moderately priced cosmetics. For higher-end beauty products head for the large selections in the department stores like **Maison Blanche**, **Macy's** or **Saks Fifth Avenue** (*see page 165*). Day spas (*see page 184*) also sell make-up and have staff who'll show you ways to wear it.

Hairdressers

Busta

752 Tchoupitoulas Street, at Julia Street, Warehouse District (523 4645). Bus 10 Tchoupitoulas. **Open** 9am-7pm Wed-Fri; 9am-6pm Tue, Sat; closed Mon, Sun. **Credit** Disc, MC, V. **Map** p309 C2.
Offers haircuts and body care – including massage (from $55), facial ($40), manicure ($20) and pedicure ($40) – and Aveda skincare products.

Diva Gallery

1110 Antonine Street, at Magazine Street, Uptown (899 0275). Bus 11 Magazine. **Open** 11am-6pm Tue-Fri; 11am-2pm Sat; closed Sun. **No credit cards. Map** p306 A9.
The diva with the scissors, the divine Annie Breaux is an artist who works in many media, including the cutting and colouring of hair. You can trust her to do it right. She's just got the eye for it. *See also p178.*

Eclipse Salon

536 Bienville Street, at Royal Street, French Quarter (522 3318). Bus 3 Vieux Carré, 55 Elysian Fields, 81 Almonaster, 82 Desire. **Open** 9am-6pm Mon, Wed, Fri, Sat; 9am-8pm Tue, Thur; closed Sun. **Credit** AmEx, MC, V. **Map** p316 B2.

This full-service hair salon in the French Quarter provides haircuts for men ($25) and women ($35), makeovers and nail and body treatments. It also sells beauty products such as Aveda and Paul Mitchell. A manicure costs $15, aromatherapy facials start at $35 and body wraps will set you back $55.

Fifi Mahoney's

828 Chartres Street, between St Ann & Dumaine Streets, French Quarter (525 4343). Bus 3 Vieux Carré, 55 Elysian Fields, 81 Almonaster, 82 Desire. **Open** noon-6pm daily. **Credit** MC, V. **Map** p316 B2.
Bustling with action, Fifi Mahoney's is geared towards transvestites, but welcomes customers of either sex looking for a high-energy good time. There are custom make-up services for men and women, and extravagant nail polish and lipstick choices stashed in the racks in the front of the shop.

Opticians

St Charles Vision

138 Carondelet Street, at Common Street, CBD (522 0826). St Charles Streetcar. **Open** 9am-5pm Mon-Fri; closed Sat, Sun. **Credit** AmEx, Disc, MC, V. **Map** p309 B/C1.
An optician with a same-day service and a large selection of designer frames. The Carrollton Avenue branch is especially good.
Branches: 624 S Carrollton Avenue, Uptown (866 6311); Suite 102, 3200 Severn Avenue, Metairie (887 2020).

Perfume

The cosmetics departments in the department stores all carry many of the well-known names in fragrances, while pharmacies stock many of

Crescent City Market. *See p182.*

the less expensive brands for both men and women. For something more in the spirit of the city, try the small shops in the French Quarter.

Bourbon French Parfums

525 St Ann Street, at Decatur Street, French Quarter (522 4480/www.neworleansperfume.com). Bus 3 Vieux Carré, 55 Elysian Fields, 81 Almonaster, 82 Desire. **Open** 9am-5pm daily. **Credit** AmEx, Disc, MC, V. **Map** p316 C3.
In business since 1843, this locally owned shop in the French Quarter makes custom-blended fragrances for men and women.

Hove Parfumeur

824 Royal Street, at St Ann Street, French Quarter (525 7827). Bus 3 Vieux Carré, 55 Elysian Fields, 81 Almonaster, 82 Desire. **Open** 10am-5pm Mon-Sat; closed Sun. **Credit** AmEx, MC, V. **Map** p316 C2.
A New Orleans landmark. The tea olive scent is the quintessential New Orleans fragrance, capturing the smell of the sweet olive trees that bloom in spring and autumn all over the city. Also look out for the vertivier perfumes and soaps for men and women, made from a scented root found in Louisiana.

Pharmacies

Several branches of **Rite-Aid** are open 24 hours daily, including one in the Garden District (3401 St Charles Avenue, at Louisiana Avenue, 895 0344, prescriptions 896 4575) and one Uptown (4330 S Claiborne Avenue, at Napoleon Avenue, 895 6655, prescriptions 896 4570). The Mid City **Walgreen's** branch (3311 Canal Street, at Jeff Davis Parkway, 822 8070) is open from 7am to 11pm daily. The only pharmacy in the French Quarter is the **Royal Pharmacy** (1101 Royal Street, at Ursulines Street, 523 5401), which is open 9am to 6pm Monday to Saturday.

Spas

For **Mackie Shilstone Pro Spa**, *see page 237.*

Belladonna

2900 Magazine Street, at Sixth Street, Uptown (891 4393/www.belladonadayspa.com). Bus 11 Magazine. **Open** 9am-8pm Mon-Fri; 9am-6pm Sat; closed Sun. **Credit** AmEx, MC, V. **Map** p309 A3.
A Japanese-styled day spa offering manicures ($15), massage (one hour $60), facials ($55) and a selection of personalised make-up products. Between treatments, relax with a herb tea in the Japanese garden, or chill out in the jacuzzi, steam room or sauna. Appointments can be hard to come by, so book well ahead. Shop in the retail area for self-indulgent gifts like scented candles or soaps.

Earth Savers

434 Chartres Street, at Conti Street, French Quarter (581 4999/www.earthsaversonline.com). Bus 3 Vieux

Hair is an art at **Diva**. *See p178 and p183.*

Carré, 55 Elysian Fields, 81 Almonaster, 82 Desire. **Open** 10am-6pm Mon-Sat; noon-5pm Sun. **Credit** AmEx, Disc, MC, V. **Map** p316 B2.
Earth Savers has a complete line of 'earth-saving' products for the bath and the body (all are mineral-oil free and have not been tested on animals), including a line of skincare and make-up products for men. A day of relaxation for $160 includes a manicure, pedicure, facial, one-hour massage and a light, healthy lunch. There are several branches.
Branches: 5501 Magazine Street, at Joseph Street, Uptown (899 8555); 3256 Severn Avenue, Metairie (885 5152); 200 Metairie Road, Old Metairie (828 1997).

Tattooing & body piercing

There have long been tattoo parlours around this port city, catering to sailors who come to town looking for fun. Talented tattoo and piercing artists still flourish in small studios scattered about the city: **Electric Expressions** (3421 S Carrollton Avenue, at Bienville Street, Central City, 488 1500); **Electric Ladyland Tattoo** (8106 Earhart Boulevard, at Carrollton Avenue, Central City, 866 3859); and **Rings of Desire** (1128 Decatur Street, at Governor Nicholls Avenue, French Quarter, 524 6147).

Household, furniture & gifts

Accent Annex

2805 N Causeway Boulevard, Metairie (838 8760/ www.accentannex.com). St Charles Streetcar/ 16 S Claiborne, 39 Tulane, 90 Carrollton bus, then E5 Causeway bus. **Open** 9.30am-5pm Tue-Sat; closed Mon, Sun. **Credit** AmEx, Disc, MC, V. **Map** p316 B2/3.
A Mardi Gras supermarket catering to Carnival krewes looking for masses of throws. Check the *Yellow Pages* under Carnival Supplies for other shops.

Branches: Riverwalk Mall, 1 Poydras Street, at the Mississippi River, CBD (568 9000); 633 Toulouse Street, at Cabildo Avenue, French Quarter (592 9886).

American Aquatic Gardens
612 Elysian Fields Avenue, between Royal & Chartres Streets, Marigny (944 0410). Bus 55 Elysian Fields, 81 Almonaster, 82 Desire. **Open** 9am-5pm daily. **Credit** Disc, MC, V. **Map** p307 G6.
A gift shop with everything for the garden: from benches, sculptures, statuary, fountains and plaques for the garden wall, to an entire aquatic garden. There are also interiors items like lamps, wall hangings, mirrors and vases. Outside the gift shop, it's relaxing to stroll through the gardens.

Artifacts Gallery
5515 Magazine Street, at Jefferson Avenue, Uptown (899 5505). Bus 11 Magazine. **Open** 10am-5.30pm Mon-Sat; closed Sun. **Credit** AmEx, DC, Disc, MC, V. **Map** p306 C9/10.
This interiors store-cum-giftshop offers furniture made from vine branches and wooden pyramid cabinets in a primitive country style, plus unusual 'decorative hardware' – doorknobs, drawer handles and so on. Work is often by young Louisiana artists.

Big Life Toys
3117 Magazine Street, between Washington & Louisiana Streets, Uptown (895 8695/www.biglife toys.com). **Open** 10am-6pm Mon-Sat; noon-4pm Sun. **Credit** AmEx, Disc, MC, V. **Map** p306 C9/10.

Fifi Mahoney's.
See p183.

A toy store for adults that sells new and retro pieces. The branch up the road has toys for kids.
Branch: 5430 Magazine Street, at Octavia Street, Warehouse District (899 8697).

Creative Concrete
1700 Benefit Street, at Gentilly Boulevard, Gentilly (949 5195). Bus 90 Carrollton. **Open** 9am-5pm Mon-Sat; closed Sun. **Credit** Disc, MC, V. **Map** p308 F4.
You'll need directions to find this place, tucked under the interstate in old Gentilly. It sells very reasonably priced yard art and statuary, all made on the premises, as well as a collection of Gentilly balls ($29.95-$39.95). Now back in fashion, these decorative silver, gold or blue glass balls got their name in the 1950s because they could be found perched in gardens all over this middle-class neighbourhood.

A Different Approach
824 Chartres Street, at Dumaine Street, French Quarter (588 1978). Bus 55 Elysian Fields, 81 Almonaster, 82 Desire. **Open** 10am-6pm daily. **Credit** MC, V. **Map** p316 B2.
Absolutely fabulous arts and crafts from around the globe. Find silks from Cambodia, carvings from Costa Rica and pottery from the Peruvian rain forest. Part of a fair trade federation, this shop is dedicated to guaranteeing a living wage for artisans.

Mystic Blue Signs
2212 Magazine Street, at Jackson Avenue, Garden District (525 4691). Bus 11 Magazine. **Open** 9am-5pm Mon-Fri; closed Sat, Sun. **No credit cards**. **Map** p309 B3.
One of the few real sign painters, who rejects computer-generated images in favour of classic hand-painted signs. Decide what you want and Eve, the shop's experienced sign painter, will create it. She favours an old-fashioned and whimsical style and does business worldwide.

Pottery Barn
Canal Place Shopping Center, 333 Canal Street, at Decatur Street, French Quarter (568 0011). Bus 41 Canal. **Open** 10am-7pm Mon-Sat; noon-6pm Sun. **Credit** AmEx, Disc, MC, V. **Map** p309 C1.
Part of a nationwide chain, this beautiful store is packed with moderately priced, fashionable home furnishings and decorative accessories. It also has a studio where you can co-ordinate furniture, fabrics, window treatments and floor coverings.

Scriptura
5423 Magazine Street, at Jefferson Avenue, Uptown (897 1555). Bus 11 Magazine. **Open** 10am-5pm Mon-Sat; closed Sun. **Credit** AmEx, MC, V. **Map** p306 C9/10.
The place to find sophisticated, high quality paper products from Italy, London and Paris, including fine stationery, leather-bound journals and exquisite wrapping paper. Venetian glass pens, personalised wax seals made by a local bronze foundry and unusual paper lampshades are but a few of the interesting items available.

The Sun Shop

*7722 Maple Street, at Adams Street, Riverbend
(861 8338). St Charles Streetcar.* **Open** *1.30-5.30pm
Tue, Sat; noon-5.30pm Mon, Wed-Fri; closed Sun.*
No credit cards. **Map** *p306 A8.*

Proprietor Chick Fortner has been at this spot since
1968, selling objects acquired on jaunts to Mexico
and Guatemala. Jewellery, textiles and carved
wooden animals, masks and religious statuary
make up this interesting collection.

Utopia

*5408 Magazine Street, at Jefferson Avenue, Uptown
(899 8488). Bus 11 Magazine.* **Open** *10am-6pm
Mon-Sat; noon-5pm Sun.* **Credit** *AmEx, DC, Disc,
MC, V.* **Map** *p306 C9/10.*

Rummage around this cluttered shop to discover
clothing – including the US family-run Flax label of
simple cotton and linen designs – jewellery, photo
frames and fancifully painted furniture by Texan
designer David Marsh.

Ya-Ya

*628 Baronne Street, at Girod Street, CBD
(529 3306). St Charles Streetcar.* **Open** *9am-6pm
Mon-Fri; noon-5pm Sat; closed Sun.* **Credit** *AmEx,
Disc, MC, V.* **Map** *p309 B1.*

The name stands for 'Young Aspirations, Young
Artists' and it's a non-profit operation that provides
a workspace and shop for local high-school students
and young adults to create and sell hand-painted
furniture. Baby chairs cost $75 to $175; chairs for
adults are $175 to $500. There are also tables, beds
and hand-printed fabrics and pillows.

Music

Musical instruments

International Vintage Guitars of New Orleans

*1011 Magazine Street, at Howard Avenue, CBD
(524 4557). Bus 11 Magazine.* **Open** *noon-6pm
Mon-Sat; closed Sun.* **Credit** *AmEx, Disc, MC, V.*
Map *p309 C2.*

The colours and shapes of the beautiful vintage
guitars in this store mean that walking in here is a
treat. Local and visiting musicians flock here to
check the ever-changing inventory, so you may run
into Eric Clapton or Willie DeVille.

Werlein's

*214 Decatur Street, at Iberville Street, French
Quarter (883 5080). Bus 3 Vieux Carré, 41 Canal,
55 Elysian Fields, 81 Almonaster, 82 Desire.*
Open *10am-6pm Mon-Sat; closed Sun.* **Credit**
AmEx, Disc, MC, V. **Map** *p316 A3.*

Family-owned and operated since 1842, this is a New
Orleans institution. The store in the Quarter has
steel washboards and squeezeboxes for Cajun and
zydeco musicians, while the Metairie superstore
covers everything from all kinds of new and used

Big Life Toys: aimed at adults. *See p185.*

instruments to sheet music, software, sound systems
and accessories.
Branch: 3750 Veterans Memorial Boulevard,
Metairie (883 5060).

Records, tapes & CDs

Considering music is such an important part
of New Orleans life, there is a surprising lack
of good music shops. We've listed the best of
the independent, specialist shops but you'll
probably find the widest selection at the large
chainstores, **Tower Records**, **Virgin** and
the newly arrived **Borders**. **Beckham's
Book Shop** (*see page 173*) is also worth
visiting for second-hand classical recordings,
including old vinyl.

Borders

*3131 Veterans Memorial Boulevard, at N Causeway
Boulevard, Metairie (835 1363/www.borders.com).
St Charles Streetcar/16 S Claiborne, 39 Tulane,
90 Carrollton bus, then E5 Causeway bus.* **Open**
9am-11pm Mon-Sat; 9am-9pm Sun. **Credit** *AmEx,
Disc, MC, V.*

The well-lit second floor has a wide selection of
CDs and is especially strong in world music. Staff
are helpful and knowledgeable, and there are good
discounts on selected CDs.

Jim Russell Records

*1837 Magazine Street, at St Mary Street, Uptown
(522 2602). Bus 11 Magazine.* **Open** *10am-7pm
Mon-Sat; 1-6pm Sun.* **Credit** *AmEx, MC, V.*
Map *p309 B3.*

An extensive, eclectic and strange collection of old
45s and LP vinyls, including some old Neville
Brother albums and other local musicians. There's
also a large selection of rap, soul, R&B, jazz and
blues. Jim Russell Senior, who started the business
30 years ago, is a walking music encyclopedia,
especially about local artists. He's usually around
on Sundays; Jim Russell Junior mans the store the
rest of the time.

Louie's Juke Joint

*1128 Decatur Street, at Ursulines Street, French
Quarter (568 9020). Bus 3 Vieux Carré, 82 Desire,
55 Elysian Fields.* **Open** *10am-9pm daily.* **Credit**
AmEx, Disc, MC, V. **Map** *p316 D3.*

Eat, Drink, Shop

A very cool spot with lots of American roots music, local band music, hard-to-find stuff and vinyls, at good prices. The voodoo altar in the back of the shop adds to the atmosphere. There's also a small selection of herbs for concocting who knows what.

Louisiana Music Factory

210 Decatur Street, at Bienville Street, French Quarter (586 1094/www.louisianamusicfactory.com). Bus 3 Vieux Carré, 41 Canal, 55 Elysian Fields, 81 Almonaster, 82 Desire. **Open** 10am-10pm daily. **Credit** AmEx, Disc, MC, V. **Map** p316 B3.

This French Quarter store is tops for music by New Orleans and regional artists, with extensive jazz and blues selections, bountiful bins of Cajun, zydeco, R&B and gospel, and helpful, knowledgeable staff. Rickety stairs lead vinyl collectors to an attic full of second-hand LPs. On weekends you might catch Tab Benoit, Snooks Eaglin or Ellis Marsalis in a live performance to celebrate a new release; call for the current schedule. The Music Factory was voted best record store by readers of *OffBeat* magazine.

Branch: Old US Mint, 400 Esplanade Avenue, at Decatur Street, French Quarter (524 5507).

Magic Bus

527 Conti Street, at Decatur Street, French Quarter (522 0530). Bus 3 Vieux Carré, 3-6pm Mon, 81 Almonaster, 82 Desire. **Open** 11am-7pm daily. **Credit** AmEx, MC, V. **Map** p316 B3.

The cool English guys who run this place offer some 15,000 titles in new and second-hand CDs and some rare vinyl – mainly rock and pop.

Musica Latina

4226 Magazine Street, at General Pershing Street, Uptown (895 4227). Bus 11 Magazine. **Open** 10.30am-7pm Mon-Sat; 3-6pm Sun. **Credit** AmEx, Disc, MC, V. **Map** p306 D10.

If your taste is for Latin sounds, you'll be thrilled with Musica Latina, which stocks mainstream and hard-to-find salsa, merengue, boleros, flamenco et al.

Mushroom

1037 Broadway, at Zimple Street, Uptown (866 6065). Bus 22 Broadway. **Open** 10am-midnight daily. **Credit** AmEx, Disc, MC, V. **Map** p306 B8.

Shop with the college-aged punters for 'import' CDs of live performances. Mushroom has a decent selection of local releases and indie music and also trades, buys or sells used CDs, LPs and cassettes.

Peaches

3129 Gentilly Boulevard, at Elysian Fields, Gentilly (282 3322). Bus 55 Elysian Fields. **Open** 10am-9pm Mon-Thur; 10am-10pm Fri, Sat; noon-9pm Sun. **Credit** AmEx, Disc, MC, V.

This the best place in town for rap, soul and gospel.

Rock & Roll Collectibles

1214 Decatur Street, at Governor Nicholls Street, French Quarter (561 5683/www.rockcollectibles.org). Bus 3 Vieux Carré, 48 Esplanade, 55 Elysian Fields, *81 Almonaster, 82 Desire.* **Open** 10am-10pm daily. **Credit** AmEx, MC, V. **Map** p316 D3.

This place stocks rock 'n' roll vinyl galore, along with plenty of blues, soul and jazz, including recordings by local musicians.

Tower Records

408 N Peters Street, at Conti Street, French Quarter (529 4411/www.towerrecords.com). Bus 3 Vieux Carré, 55 Elysian Fields, 81 Almonaster, 82 Desire. **Open** 9am-midnight daily. **Credit** AmEx, Disc, MC, V. **Map** p316 B3.

The big daddy of music retail, with two floors offering up an impressive selection in most categories; serious music lovers should plan to spend time and money here. Tower also does a good job in stocking local artists. The video section (on the ground floor) is pretty thorough, too.

Virgin Megastore

Jackson Brewery, 600 Decatur Street, at Toulouse Street, French Quarter (671 8100/www.virginmega. com). Bus 3 Vieux Carré, 55 Elysian Fields, 81 Almonaster, 82 Desire. **Open** 10am-midnight daily. **Credit** AmEx, MC, V. **Map** p316 B3.

It's even bigger and better than the other chain monsters in the scope and depth of its selection, with three floors of CDs, tapes, videos, books and magazines housed in a neon-lit, utilitarian space. When you've found what you're looking for, chill out in the light and airy second-floor coffee shop, which overlooks the Mississippi River.

Pets

Chi-wa-wa

37 French Market Place, at Barracks Street, French Quarter (581 4242). Bus 3 Vieux Carré. **Open** noon-6pm Mon, Wed-Sun; closed Tue. **Credit** AmEx, MC, V. **Map** p316 D3.

Need a gift to take home to your doggie? This place calls itself 'a small store for kinky dogs'.

Dr Mike's Animal House

1120 N Rampart Street, at Governor Nicholls Street, French Quarter (523 4455). Bus 3 Vieux Carré, 57 Franklin. **Open** 8am-6pm Mon-Fri; 8am-noon Sat; closed Sun. **No credit cards. Map** p316 D1.

Expect to pay $40 for a check-up for your pet and $25 for grooming at this vet. House calls are made and the staff are friendly.

Three Dog Bakery

827 Royal Street, at Dumaine Street, French Quarter (525 2253). Bus 3 Vieux Carré, 55 Elysian Fields, 81 Almonaster, 82 Desire. **Open** 10am-6pm daily. **Credit** AmEx, DC, Disc, MC, V. **Map** p316 C2.

The shop looks like a classic old-fashioned bakery and the treats look great, but hungry owners should note that the goodies are custom-made for dogs only. Three Dog celebrates St Joseph's Day (*see p190*) in a big way, creating an awesome canine St Joseph's altar. Home-made dog biscuits cost $4.95 per pound.

Eat, Drink, Shop

Photography

New Orleans doesn't have a great selection of camera equipment, so don't hold out hopes of great buys. Camera shops are usually small, with limited stock and scattered all over the city. Although the string of camera and electronics stores along Canal Street, their windows filled to the brim, look tempting, they don't offer the reliability and expertise available in the smaller shops. If your camera needs mending, visit **AAA Camera Repair** (1631 St Charles Avenue, at Terpsichore Street, Lower Garden District, 561 5822).

Bennett's Camera & Video

3230 Severn Avenue, at 17th Street, Metairie (885 9050/www.bennettscamera.com). St Charles Streetcar/16 S Claiborne, 39 Tulane, 90 Carrollton bus, then E5 Causeway bus. **Open** 9am-6pm Mon-Sat; closed Sun. **Credit** AmEx, Disc, MC, V.
A good selection of many major brands of photographic tackle is stocked, plus darkroom supplies and digital imaging equipment.

Liberty Camera

337 Carondelet Street, at Poydras Street, CBD (523 6252). St Charles Streetcar. **Open** 9am-5.30pm Mon-Fri; 9am-2.30pm Sat; closed Sun. **Credit** AmEx, DC, Disc, MC, V. **Map** p309 B1.
This shop is stuffy but knowledgeable, with the usual brands – Nikon, Pentax, Minolta and Olympus – plus darkroom equipment and a small selection of second-hand cameras.

Wolf Camera & Video

Lakeside Shopping Center, 3301 Veterans Memorial Boulevard, at N Causeway Boulevard, Metairie (837 2665/www.wolfcamera.com). St Charles Streetcar/16 S Claiborne, 39 Tulane, 90 Carrollton bus, then E5 Causeway bus. **Open** 10am-9pm Mon-Sat; noon-6pm Sun. **Credit** AmEx, DC, Disc, MC, V.
A national chain that carries a decent selection of point-and-shoot cameras.
Branch: New Orleans Centre, 1400 Poydras Street, next to the Louisiana Superdome, CBD (581 6905).

Film processing

One-hour photo processing is available at drugstores **Eckerd's** and **Walgreen's** (check the phone book for your nearest branch), at most camera shops (including those listed above) and specialist labs. Check Sunday's *Times-Picayune* for discount coupons that can save you money on film and developing. For custom colour processing, try **Colorpix** (2375 Tchoupitoulas Street, at First Street, Lower Garden District, 522 3164), favoured by Europeans visiting for a few weeks, or **Professional Color Service** in Metairie (604 Papworth Avenue, 835 3551), known among local photographers as a top lab.

Fox Photo

220 Baronne Street, at Common Street, CBD (523 4672/www.wolfcamera.com). St Charles Streetcar/ 41 Canal bus. **Open** 8am-5.30pm Mon-Fri; closed Sat, Sun. **Credit** AmEx, Disc, MC, V. **Map** p309 B1.
One-hour photo developing within walking distance of the French Quarter. This branch is one of the only places, other than professional labs, that processes black and white film on the premises. Check the phone book to find the many other branches.

Sport & fitness

For bicycle and Rollerblading shops, *see chapter* **Sport & Fitness**.

Adventure Sports

333 N Service Road E, at Papworth Street, Metairie (835 1932/www.adventuresportsla.com). Bus 41 Canal. **Open** 10am-6pm Mon-Sat; closed Sun. **Credit** Disc, MC, V.
An outdoors outfitter that will kit you out for Southern weather conditions and wilderness areas. You'll find everything here in all the major brands, from tents, sleeping bags and hiking boots to rock-climbing equipment. There is a good selection of books and hiking maps, and the staff are well informed and helpful.

Ticket agencies

Ticketmaster (522 5555/www.ticketmaster. com) sells tickets for all major sporting and entertainment events in New Orleans. There are outlets in all the **Blockbuster** stores (*see below*).

Video rental

The video selection at **Tower Records** (*see page 187*) is more diverse than at other chain rental stores, and it has a good stock of foreign titles.

Blockbuster Video

5330 Tchoupitoulas Street, at Valmont Street, Uptown (897 9426). Bus 10 Tchoupitoulas. **Open** 10am-midnight daily. **Credit** AmEx, Disc, MC, V. **Map** p306 C10.
This nationwide chain has branches all over town, and stocks all the latest video releases as well as many of the classics. Check the phone book for the location of your nearest branch.
Branches: throughout the city.

Video Alternatives

4725 Magazine Street, at Valence Street, Uptown (891 5347). Bus 11 Magazine. **Open** 11am-10pm daily. **Credit** AmEx, Disc, MC, V. **Map** p306 D10.
An Uptown shop that specialises in rentals of foreign and classic films on video. It's good for hard-to-find US films, too.

Arts & Entertainment

By Season

The New Orleans year is one 365-day party, but if that isn't enough, pump up the volume with a packed events calendar.

Whenever you visit, you are likely to hit one of the dozens of jamborees that fill the Louisiana and New Orleans calendar. New Orleans is collectively uneasy if there isn't some kind of street party going on in town or nearby.

Below we have included an address and phone number for each event, together with a date where possible; for the most up-to-date information on seasonal events, consult the New Orleans Visitors Bureau (566 5011/1-800 672 6124/www.neworleanscvb.com). For out-of-town information, try the Louisiana Department of Culture, Recreation & Tourism (1-800 334 8626).

Spring

St Patrick's Day

Parasol's Bar, 2533 Constance Street, at Third Street, Lower Garden District (897 5413/ www.parasols.com). **Map** p309 B3. **Date** 17 Mar.

St Patrick's Day in New Orleans owes a great deal to Mardi Gras. Like Carnival, the Irish holiday is celebrated with street parties and parades. Parasol's *(see p159)*, a genuine neighbourhood Irish bar, has the most famous party, attracting hundreds (maybe thousands) of dressed-up partyers to the Irish Channel to drink green beer and dance in the street. Due to complaints from some sour neighbours, the party hours have been reduced, but the exuberance remains. The holiday is also marked with a raucous parade on the Saturday closest to the 17th, starting at 1pm at the corner of Magazine and Race Streets and going down Magazine Street through the Irish Channel. There are bands and floats – and danger- ous 'throws'. Instead of plastic beads, riders toss the hefty ingredients of Irish stew to the eager crowds: potatoes, cabbages, turnips, carrots and onions. Molly's at the Market *(see p153)* also hosts a St Pat's party on the Friday night closest to the 17th, with a walking parade through the French Quarter.

St Joseph's Day

Information: American-Italian Renaissance Foundation (522 7294/www.airf.com). **Date** 19 Mar.

The huge Italian-American community of New Orleans is largely assimilated but they nail their colours to the mast on their saint's day. The city's

► For **climate** and other seasonal information, and for a list of **public holidays**, see page 288.

Italian heritage is strongly Sicilian, which accounts for the importance of St Joseph, a major figure in Sicilian culture. Although the historical antecedents are muddy, the local St Joseph tradition has evolved into the assembling of massive altars of food. The altars have become a public event, moving out of pri- vate homes into parish halls, schools and business- es. Altars are usually on display for two days before the 19th. Two good places to see these towering monuments to Italian food are Angelo Brocato's ice- cream parlour Uptown *(see p146)* and St Joseph the Worker Church in Marrero (440 Pine Street, 347 8438). There's usually a parade on the Saturday closest to the 19th, whose route changes each year.

Tennessee Williams New Orleans Literary Festival

Information: Suite 225, 225 Baronne Street, New Orleans, LA 70115 (581 1144/fax 529 2430/ www.Tennesseewilliams.com). **Date** end Mar.

Famous for the hilarious Stella Shouting Contest, the four-day literary festival is fun for scholars and peo- ple who love books and plays. *See also p42.*

French Quarter Festival

Information: French Quarter Festival Office, 100 Conti Street, at the Mississippi River, New Orleans, LA 70130 (522 5730/fax 522 5711/www.french quarterfestivals.org). **Date** early Apr.

The French Quarter Festival is how many people (visitors and locals) like to imagine the French Quarter: bands playing, wonderful-smelling food being cooked in Jackson Square, well-behaved peo- ple dancing in the streets. The festival is a tourism gimmick designed to stir up the slow patch between Carnival and Jazz Fest but it has developed its own personality. The crowds are older than the Jazz Festers and the music is heavily tilted toward trad jazz but it's a fine time in the Quarter all the same.

'Stellaaaah!' **Tennessee Williams Festival.**

Family fun at the **French Quarter Festival**. *See p190.*

Crescent City Classic

Information: Suite 217, 8200 Hampson Street, New Orleans, LA 70118 (861 8686/fax 861 8687/ www.ccc10K.com). **Date** 2nd Sat in Apr.

The New Orleans version of the Boston Marathon is a 10,000m race from Jackson Square through the city. For the first 21 years, runners were routed to Audubon Park but in 2000 the run went to City Park instead. The race draws world-class runners but casual athletes enjoy it, too, and everyone loves the party in the park afterwards.

Ponchatoula Strawberry Festival

Information: PO Box 446, Ponchatoula, LA 70454 (386 6677/www.lastrawberryfestival.com). **Date** 2nd weekend in Apr.

Just 30 minutes north-west of New Orleans, Ponchatoula is a tiny bayou town that is the strawberry capital of Louisiana. Every year the town celebrates its bumper crop with a carnival and a startling variety of foodstuffs made with the berries. Strawberry Daiquiri, strawberry pie, strawberry pizza and strawberry sandwiches. You betcha.

Festival International de Louisiane

Information: PO Box 4008, Lafayette, LA 70502 (1-337 232 8086/fax 1-337 291 5480/www.festival international.com). **Date** last week in Apr.

For anyone who craves a genuine Cajun experience, this festival is Cajun nirvana. Held in Lafayette (*see p257*), the self-proclaimed capital of French Louisiana (about two hours' drive from New Orleans), the four-day event features hundreds of dancers, musicians and artisans from around the world. Great music and terrific Cajun food abound.

Summer

Reggae Riddums Festival

Information: PO Box 6156, New Orleans, LA 70174 (367 1313/www.reggaeriddums.org). Event address: City Park, Mid City. Bus 48 Esplanade. **Map** p308 D/E2-4. **Date** 2nd weekend in June.

This is a mini-Sunsplash (very mini), with three days of sun and music celebrating the culture of the Caribbean. It's held out of doors in the festival area of City Park and the turnout is fairly small, but the crowd is a lot of fun. In addition to reggae music performed by artists from around the world, the festival features art, crafts and food from the islands.

Go 4th on the River

Information: New Orleans Visitors Bureau, 1520 Sugar Bowl Drive, New Orleans, LA 70112 (566 5011/1-800 672 6124/www.bigeasy.com). **Date** 4 July.

New Orleans celebrates the nation's independence with characteristic individuality. Rather than a backyard barbecue, there are jazz bands on Bourbon Street, thousands of people thronging the narrow streets and, at sunset, a huge fireworks show on the river by the French Quarter.

Essence Music Festival

Information: Black Tourism Network, 1520 Sugar Bowl Drive, New Orleans, LA 70112 (523 5652/ www.bigeasy.com/emf). **Date** early July.

In 1995, *Essence*, a slick magazine for African-American women, took its message on the road by organising the Essence Festival. The magazine

New Orleans Jazz & Heritage Festival

The New Orleans Jazz & Heritage Festival, which celebrated its 30th year in 1999, started as a small, four-stage production at Congo Square in Armstrong Park. Since this inauspicious beginning, Jazz Fest has grown into what many consider the premier live music event in the world, featuring more than 4,000 musicians on 13 stages spread out over the New Orleans Fair Grounds.

Held annually over the last Friday, Saturday and Sunday in April and the first Thursday to Sunday in May, Jazz Fest attracts music fans from as far away as Australia and Japan. It draws more visitors to New Orleans than any event apart from Mardi Gras and yet maintains a distinctly local feel thanks to the considerable number of local musicians and supporters who attend every year. Despite some big-name international acts, the festival draws about 80 per cent of its talent from the large and diverse pool of New Orleans and Louisiana musicians.

Since almost 80 bands and musicians are scheduled to play each day between 11am and 7pm, each stage is empty only long enough for one band to remove their gear and the next to set up. There is no lull in the music and usually the big dilemma for fans is not so much finding a good act to see, but working out how to catch a sample of all the great bands playing simultaneously. At a festival where it's possible to see a dozen top bands in the space of eight hours, travelling fast and light is the best choice and is worth the effort of wading through the dense crowds from stage to stage.

The two stages at either end of the Fair Grounds are the biggest, have the largest areas in front of them and typically feature larger-name, nationally touring acts. On the stages between these can be found the WWOZ Jazz Tent, offering contemporary jazz; the Fais Do-Do Stage, which mostly features Cajun and zydeco bands; Economy Hall, for New Orleans traditional jazz; the Gospel Tent, featuring gospel singers, bands and choirs from throughout the south-eastern United States; and Congo Square, showcasing African and Caribbean music. Other stages offer a mixed bag of music ranging from Celtic to klezmer, and the Music Heritage stage is the place for interviews with musicians and short performances highlighting the history of music in New Orleans, Louisiana and throughout the world.

As any Jazz Fest veteran knows, great music is not the only reason to visit the Fair Grounds. It also offers a huge selection of local culinary offerings at dozens of small booths. Portions are small enough (by New Orleans standards) to allow a good serving of crawfish bread, étouffée, cochon du lait, boudin, andouille or any number of other south Louisiana delicacies. A special section associated with Congo Square offers African and Caribbean foods (usually the best port of call for vegetarians). Recent additions in the food fair include booths serving sushi, falafel, houmous, tabouleh and other popular global dishes.

Art exhibitions, storytellers and videos are sprinkled among the music and food, and there's a special kids' tent where weary parents are only too happy to sit down and colour and play with their children. An often overlooked gem is the Book Tent, where local authors give readings, books are sold and

brought in big names in music, bestselling writers, famous personalities for four frothy days of concerts, panel discussions, book signings and shopping sprees. Essence has become an important date on the city's calendar and attracts big crowds. It's *Waiting to Exhale* meets New Orleans and they love each other. The festival might change city in the future.

White Linen Night

Information: Contemporary Arts Center, 900 Camp Street, at Howard Avenue (528 3805/ www.cacno.org). St Charles Streetcar. **Map** p309 C2. **Date** 1st Sat in Aug.

Artists, art lovers and thousands of hangers-on turn out to celebrate the New Orleans art scene at the CAC. The event is a play on Tennessee Williams-style Southern-ness, with everybody draped in white fabric, particularly linen. Live bands, crowded bars, sultry heat and humidity complete the fun.

Original Southwest Louisiana Zydeco Music Festival

Information: Southern Development Foundation Farm, 457 Zydeco Road, Opelousas, LA 70570 (1-318 942 2392/fax 1-318 942 9201/www.zydeco.org). **Date** Sat before Labor Day (1st Mon in Sept).

any musician who has ever written a book is on hand to sign it (and usually not mobbed by fans, making this a terrific spot for a word or two with your idol).

When heading out to Jazz Fest, remember that New Orleans can be hot, humid and sunny in the spring, so dress accordingly. Hats, sunscreen and sunglasses are crucial. Sandals and sneakers are the most appropriate footwear, but if it rains the infield gets muddy and since it's the infield of a horse track, the mud isn't really something you want oozing between your toes. Rain is a regular feature of Jazz Fest so plan accordingly. There's little cover from either the sun or the rain on the field but the recently remodelled Fair Grounds Clubhouse is a godsend. The facilities include air-conditioning, clean bathrooms and comfortable grandstand seats. It's a great place to cool off, rest the feet and plan your next move. There are also several performance areas within the clubhouse so you're still enjoying Jazz Fest even as you recover from it.

Performance schedules are available in the Jazz Fest programme on sale at the Fair Grounds, or pick up a copy of *OffBeat*, distributed free outside the gates, which contains feature stories and interviews with performers as well as complete schedules and club listings for later in the evening. The daily *Times-Picayune* also prints schedules, as does the weekly alternative paper *Gambit*.

New Orleans Jazz & Heritage Festival

Information: Jazz Fest, PO Box 53407, New Orleans, LA 70153 (522 4786/ www.nojazzfest.com). Event address: New Orleans Fair Grounds Racecourse, 1751 Gentilly Boulevard, Mid City. Bus 48 Esplanade. **Map** p308 E/F4/5. **Date** last Fri in Apr to 1st Sun in May.

About two hours from New Orleans, Opelousas is another world and the world is ruled by zydeco. For any zydeco devotee this is *the* festival to attend. Some 13 bands from Texas and Louisiana take to the stage at this one-day outdoor extravaganza in front of crowds of more than 15,000. There are food booths serving Creole dishes, arts and crafts stalls and demonstrations of everything from basket-weaving to storytelling.

Southern Decadence

Information: www.southerndecadence.com. **Date** weekend before Labor Day (1st Mon in Sept).

Just five years ago, this parade and weekend-long party was a tiny, tacky, hysterically funny but local affair. Today, it's an enormous, tacky, hysterically funny event drawing participants from around the globe. Decadence is one of the city's largest gay events and its Sunday afternoon parade – and we mean the whole afternoon – is a spectacle not to be missed. It's really nothing more than a French Quarter-wide drag show, but the costumes are astonishing. Throughout the weekend the city's gay bars are in high fever and dancing continues until everyone passes out. *See also p212.*

Arts & Entertainment

Words & Music: A Literary Feast in New Orleans

Faulkner House Books, 624 Pirate's Alley, between St Peter Street & Orleans Street, French Quarter (586 1612/www.wordsandmusic.org). Bus 3 Vieux Carré, 55 Elysian Fields, 81 Almonaster, 82 Desire. **Map** p316 B/C2. **Date** late Sept.

Evolving from the annual birthday party held for William Faulkner by Faulkner House Books, this autumn literary festival puts its emphasis on music as well, often premiering new works. Well-known writers, local and national, teach classes and talk on panels between cocktail parties and other events. *See also p42.*

New Orleans Lesbian & Gay Pride Festival

Information: New Orleans Alliance for Pride (943 1999). Event address: Louis Armstrong Park, between Orleans Avenue & N Rampart Street, Tremé. Bus 57 Franklin. **Map** pp306-7 F/G6. **Date** end Sept/early Oct.

A small but ever-growing celebration of gay life. In 1998 the festival moved to Armstrong Park, a change of venue from Washington Park, where it had been held for almost two decades.

Art for Arts' Sake

Information: Contemporary Arts Center, 900 Camp Street, at Howard Avenue (528 3805/ www.cacno.org). **Date** 1st Sat in Oct.

The scene: the city streets. The time: end of summer. The shriek: 'Darlin! I love your tan!' Kiss, hug, move on, whisper to companion: 'South of France my ass! She got that tan freeloading at some tacky condo in Gulf Shores!' Art is not just for art's sake at this end-of-summer street party but an excuse to check out who's been where, doing what and with whom all summer long. Galleries go to great efforts to show-case their best and/or splashiest art and the art community organises really good parties. The hotspots are in the Warehouse District around the Julia Street-CAC axis and on Magazine Street between Antonine and Napoleon. There's free food and drink in the galleries and bands in the street, demonstrating that great New Orleans artform, partying.

New Orleans Film & Video Festival

Information: New Orleans Film & Video Society, Suite 1712, 225 Baronne Street, New Orleans, LA 70112 (523 3818/www.neworleansfilmfest.com). **Date** 1 wk in Oct.

Some Hollywood people fly in, tons of independent and documentary filmmakers make their way to the city and dozens and dozens of films are shown. It's not a major film festival where indie films can make a leap to the big time (à la Sundance) but rather an energetic, smalltown gathering where the talk about film is genuine and passionate. It's also the locals' best chance to see some cutting-edge cinema. *See also p201.*

Hallowe'en

Information: Hallowe'ens in New Orleans (945 5546/ Halloween@halloween.com). **Date** Sat nearest 31 Oct.

The city goes full-throttle at Hallowe'en, with a huge variety of options ranging from hanging out with Anne Rice to costume-watching in the French Quarter. Anne Rice's Hallowe'en party (information 897 3983/www.annerice.com), called the Gathering of the Coven, has been an annual event since 1989, with thousands coming from all over the country to meet at one of her many houses. The Vampire Queen herself usually attends, as do various celebrities in disguise. Even larger than that ghoulish happening is the Julia Street Wharf fundraiser for the local AIDS hospice Lazarus House (information www.gayneworleans.com). As many as 10,000 people show up every year for this event, one of the biggest in New Orleans's gay community. Costumes are outrageous, but admission is by invitation only.

Opening Day at the Fair Grounds

New Orleans Fair Grounds Racecourse, 1751 Gentilly Boulevard, Mid City, New Orleans, LA 70119 (944 5515/1-800 262 7983/fax 944 2511/www.fgno.com). Bus 48 Esplanade. **Map** p308 E/F4/5.

Date Thanksgiving Day (4th Thur in Nov).

Only in New Orleans is the country's Thanksgiving holiday, the symbolic anniversary of the pilgrims' first meals on the continent, universally celebrated at a racetrack. Following a 100-year-old tradition, the New Orleans horse racing season opens on Thanksgiving Day and locals turn out in large family groups by the thousands. The mood is festive, the racetrack is beautiful and a good time is had by all horse or gambling lovers. Beats the hell out of TV and family quarrelling all afternoon.

Celebration in the Oaks

City Park, 1 Palm Drive, Mid City, New Orleans, LA 70124 (482 4888/fax 483 9379/www.neworleans. com/citypark). Bus 48 Esplanade. **Map** p 308 E/F2-4. **Date** Fri after Thanksgiving until 1st Sun in Jan.

At Christmas time, the giant oaks in City Park are bedecked with lights, huge luminous displays seem to float over the park's bayous and Christmas music fills the air. This is essentially a drive-through experience, though you can park and walk through the Christmas-tree garden to the amusement park and ride the antique carousel. Christmas lights like you've never seen them before.

Christmas Eve Bonfires along the Levee

Information: St James Historical Society, PO Box 426, Gramercy, LA 70052 (1-225-869 9752/ www.stjamesla.com). Fires begin in Gramercy and continue upriver to Convent, along US 44. **Date** 24 Dec; fires lit 7pm-midnight.

In a tradition dating back to the arrival of European settlers, Christmas Eve fires are lit up and down the Mississippi River levee outside New Orleans. The

Christmas the easy way

December is possibly New Orleans's best 'off season'. There are many who will brave the broiling south Louisiana heat in summer but around Christmas almost everyone is at home. For those who forsake traditional family holidays, New Orleans is a superb place to spend the season. The city is emptied of conventioneers and most tourists, while some of its most endearing traditions are on display.

Bonfires on Christmas Eve are an old custom along the Mississippi River (see page 194). People who live along the river start building bonfires at Thanksgiving, often in fantastical shapes such as castles and animals. At 7pm on Christmas Eve a signal is given by local fire marshals and the fires are lit, making for a thrilling pagan-like event. You can drive up River Road toward Baton Rouge and simply park near the most interesting looking bonfires or book a cruise on a riverboat for dinner and a perfect ringside view.

The Creole tradition of **Reveillon dinners** has been revived by many local restaurants. Instead of dinner at midnight on Christmas Eve,

New Orleans chefs offer elaborate meals all through December, often at a fixed price, built around old-fashioned dishes that emphasise seafood.

Celebration in the Oaks (see page 194) is becoming a major New Orleans event. City Park is covered with millions of tiny white lights, turning it into a fantastical fairyland as night falls.

Music, of course, is a key element. Choirs give free concerts in Jackson Square during the holidays, while churches such as St Louis Cathedral present impressive programmes of sacred music. On the profane side, there's a definite uplift on the club scene because so many touring musicians come home for Christmas.

Spontaneous jam sessions break out as old friends run into each other while making the rounds on the club circuit. For visitors, other winning points of a New Orleans Christmas are the mild weather (sometimes rain but not continuous) and hotel deals that make for a very affordable holiday.

custom is variously attributed to the French 'lighting the way for Papa Noel' and the Germans replicating their winter solstice ritual of bonfires on the Rhine. Whatever the real story, current residents of the River Parishes (St James, St Charles and St John the Baptist) are devoted to the tradition, spending weeks building elaborate structures that they then set ablaze. The atmosphere is festive and the fires lining the slow-moving river under a dark sky are a beautiful sight. The heaviest concentration is in the towns of Gramercy (details given above), Lutcher, Vacherie and Convent, all in St James Parish, about 35 miles upriver from New Orleans.

New Year's Eve

In Jackson Square and throughout the city.
Date 31 Dec.
In a city that will take any excuse for a party, this is a big one. Upmarket hotels and restaurants schedule complete evening festivities, bars are decked out in gaudy decorations, there are fireworks on the river and a Mardi Gras atmosphere centres on

Jackson Square. For years a mostly local event, New Year's Eve is becoming a more organised tourist happening as the city begins to realise that visitors see it as an alternative to New York. Recent festivities have been broadcast live on cable TV.

Sugar Bowl

Louisiana Superdome, 1500 Sugar Bowl Drive, at Poydras Street, CBD, New Orleans, LA 70112 (525 8573/fax 525 4867/www.nokiasugarbowl.com). Bus 16 S Claiborne. **Map** p309 A/B1. **Date** on or near New Year's Day.
One of the plums of American college football, the Sugar Bowl was once held in an old stadium called the Sugar Bowl. Now it's at the Superdome, of course, with two of the leading US collegiate teams fighting it out for post-season glory. One team is always from the south-east. Fans of both teams (usually announced in early December) flood into town wearing their college colours and braying team chants as they roll around the French Quarter. Tickets are impossible to get except from scalpers.

Children

New Orleans is a playground for big kids that has plenty for the littl'uns, too.

In a city where sugar-drenched beignets are considered an appropriate meal at any time of day and adults dress up in profoundly silly costumes at the slightest excuse, children feel immediately at home. They're welcome almost everywhere and, since bad behaviour falls loosely within the city's well-known motto of 'let the good times roll', a temper tantrum is certainly no cause to pass on the bread pudding in the best of restaurants.

The disadvantage of visiting a city governed by the Inner Child is that you can't expect the adults around you to act any more mature than your nine-year-old when it comes to leaping for beads tossed from Mardi Gras floats or selling alcohol to a youngster who could pass for 14. Although the once appalling New Orleans crime rate has been steadily declining in recent times, the only way to be sure of your children's safety is to keep them under close supervision at all times.

Babysitting

You'll have to trust your chosen agency to provide a responsible babysitter, as neither the city nor the state imposes rigorous licensing requirements on babysitting services. Both the agencies listed below claim only to employ sitters over 21, with no criminal records and with prior experience. Nevertheless, careful screening of your sitter is advised. Alternatively, ask your hotel if it either has a babysitting service of its own or, failing that, if it can make a recommendation.

Accent on Children's Arrangements
Information 524 1227/fax 524 1229/ www.accent oca.com. **Open** 8.30am-5pm Mon-Fri; closed Sat, Sun; on call 24hrs daily. **Cost** rates vary; call for more information. **Credit** AmEx, MC, V.
A range of services from daycare to city tours, for large groups only and by prior arrangement.

Dependable Kid Care
Information 486 4001/fax 486 5008/ www.dependaablekidcare.com. **Open** 8am-5pm Mon-Fri; closed Sat, Sun; on call 24hrs daily. **Cost** from $9 per hr depending on number of children; call for more information. **Credit** AmEx, MC, V.
The firm will send a sitter to your hotel or lodging, even if your child is ailing.

Eating out

New Orleans's justly famous cuisine isn't all raw oysters and zesty Cajun spices. There's plenty to please any child's more pedestrian palate. In the French Quarter, sample the beignets at **Café du Monde** (*see page 125*), or, for a more substantial meal, head to **La Madeleine French Bakery** (*see page 139*), which offers wonderful pastries, soups and sandwiches. And if your youngsters won't brave the half-shell at **Acme Oyster House** (*see page 130*) or **Felix's Seafood Restaurant & Oyster Bar** (*see page 131*), then tempt them with a fried oyster po-boy. **The Hard Rock Café** (*see page 132* **Chain reaction**) serves undistinguished fare but kids like the atmosphere and you'll like the prices. The **Louisiana Pizza Kitchen** (French Market Place, 522 9500) uses such delectable toppings as sundried tomato with roasted garlic, and gumbo ya-ya.

In the CBD, **New City Diner** (828 Gravier Street, 522 8198) and **Mother's** (*see page 136*) have cafeteria lines, offering finicky eaters a chance to look at the food before they commit to anything. Uptown, step into a 1950s diner at the **Camellia Grill** (*see page 138*) for the city's best hamburger, an omelette or a slice of pecan pie, or try the enormous plates of pasta at **Semolina** (3242 Magazine Street, 895 4260).

Finally, while fast-food outlets are everywhere, naturally, New Orleans's own **Popeye's** (*see page 139*) does offer a few local specialities – such as red beans and rice and fried chicken – that make for a fine picnic meal if you can stomach the grease.

Entertainment

General

Blaine Kern's Mardi Gras World
For listings, see p116.
Catch the ferry from the bottom of Canal Street to the Algiers side, from where shuttle buses will whisk yoiu to this warehouse where artists work all year round to create the floats for Mardi Gras parades. The fantastic exhibits can be viewed without the accompanying Mardi Gras hubbub and kids can look at the spectacular floats instead of diving under the wheels in search of goodies thrown from them.

Trust in me... snake's alive at **Audubon Zoo**. *See p198.*

Ferry rides

For listings, see p275.

Ferry rides across the Mississippi offer an inexpensive view of the river and are great fun.

IMAX Theater

For listings, see p75.

A five-storey screen and booming digital sound system immerse the viewer in films that are generally about the environment and animals. While these are officially 'educational' films, the bombastic IMAX treatment makes them dramatic enough to hold any kid's attention. It's next door to the Aquarium of the Americas (*see p75 and p198*).

Jazzland Park

For listings, see p115.

Opened in the summer of 2000 with several installations yet to come, Jazzland is New Orleans's first large outdoor theme park.

Louisiana Children's Museum

420 Julia Street, between Magazine & Tchoupitoulas Streets, Warehouse District (523 1357/www.lcm.org). Bus 3 Vieux Carré, 10 Tchoupitoulas, 11 Magazine. **Open** *Sept-May* 9.30am-4.30pm Tue-Sat; noon-4.30pm Sun; closed Mon. *June-Aug* 9.30am-4.30pm Mon-Sat; noon-4.30pm Sun. **Admission** $5. **Credit** AmEx, MC, V. **Map** p309 C2.

The well-conceived interactive exhibits here teach the concepts of maths and science without ever preaching. Kids can create their own news broadcast, encase themselves in giant bubbles or watch the interplay of bones as a skeleton rides a bike. An especially welcome resource on rainy days.

Louisiana Superdome

For listings, see p90.

Shows and athletic events are frequently staged at the Superdome; some are specially geared to children, such as circus shows and Disney on Ice extravaganzas. If nothing is going on, your child might be consoled with a tour of the world's largest indoor arena; TV monitors offer glimpses of many of the events you've missed.

Streetcar rides

The St Charles Avenue streetcar runs from Canal Street to Carrollton and Claiborne Avenues, but the best sights are gone once the tracks turn on to Carrollton. For $4, you can buy a ticket allowing you to get on and off an unlimited number of times (the usual fare is $1.25).

Heading Uptown, disembark at First Street, go left one block to Prytania Street, then head right five blocks for some of the prettiest of all the sights that the Garden District has to offer. At the corner of Washington Avenue and Prytania Street, view the Lafayette Cemetery (*see p45*) and drop into the upscale Rink mini-mall for some well-deserved refreshments and a spot of window-shopping before reboarding the streetcar at Washington and St Charles. If the children need to stretch their legs, disembark again at Audubon Park. If they're wildly energetic, you can even walk the mile to Audubon Zoo at the back of the park (*see p109 and p198*). Reboard, and, finally, disembark at the Carrollton stop for a meal at the Camellia Grill (*see p138*). Another streetcar runs along a short length of the riverfront; *see p102* **Streetcars ahead**.

An angel watches over kids on Royal Street.

Animals & nature

Aquarium of the Americas
For listings, see p75.
The aquatic life of North and South America and the waters in between are explored here, rather effectively. Sharks get star billing. The IMAX Theater is next door (*see p75 and p197*).

Audubon Zoo
For listings, see p109.
Some 1,500 animals are kept in their natural habitats in these beautifully landscaped grounds in Audubon Park, a short walk from the St Charles streetcar stop. The award-winning Louisiana Swamp Exhibit has an impressive array of indigenous species. For the younger and tamer at heart, there's a petting zoo and a nice playground.

Global Wildlife Center
26389 Highway 40, Folsom (1-504 624 9453/1-504 796 3585/www.globalwildlife.com). No public transport. **Open** *Summer* 9am-4pm daily. *Winter* 9am-3pm daily. **Admission** free; wagon tour $10; $9 seniors; $8 2-11s. **Credit** Disc, MC, V.
Admission to the centre is free, but you'll want to take the guided wagon tour around the 900 acres (365 hectares) populated by giraffe, zebra and other African grassland animals. It's about a 75-minute drive from New Orleans.

French Quarter

Although it's most famous for its 24-hour adult entertainments, the French Quarter by day is a fascinating habitat for children. At weekends and on most other fair-weather days, street performers abound in Jackson Square. A walk around the perimeter of the square can occupy several hours if the mime artists, balloon artists, psychics, musicians, tap dancers and portraitists are enjoyed to the full. The balloon artists fashion hats and animals out of balloons for any passing child. They depend on tips more than on set prices. As for the painters and pastel artists, most are amusing to watch and some are even talented. If you want one to do a pastel or caricature of your child, it's probably best to observe a work in progress, rather than relying on the artist's putative samples.

From the New Orleans Welcome Center on the square, brief walking tours head in almost every direction. These will take you down narrow streets overhung with wrought-iron balconies. Even if the kids' stamina is flagging, try at least to coax them down Pirate's Alley, a charming two-block pedestrian walkway along the left side of St Louis Cathedral as you face it. Or cross Decatur and climb the steps to the Moon Walk, which overlooks the Mississippi. From here, you can walk through Woldenberg Riverfront Park, which occupies 17 acres (seven hectares) of green space along the river between the French Quarter and Canal Street, to the Aquarium of the Americas and IMAX Theater.

Along the Decatur Street side of Jackson Square, horse-drawn carriages offer 35-minute tours of the Quarter for about $40 per party (one to four people). The drivers give a brief, shallow but generally interesting commentary on architectural and 'historical' points of interest along the route. The fun of the ride usually keeps children quiet, if not attentive.

Musée Conti Wax Museum of Louisiana
For listings, see p85.
What tourist city would be complete without a wax museum? The Musée Conti takes the usual tabloid approach to history with tableaux that depict Napoleon signing away Louisiana while in his bathtub, frenzied voodoo dancers and slaves being whipped. Kids love it.

New Orleans Historic Pharmacy Museum
For listings, see p80.
This 19th-century apothecary shop has been preserved at its original site. The collection of jars, voodoo powders, gris-gris potions and containers for leeches will appeal to budding scientists, doctors and horror film directors.

Haunts for older children

Haunted History Tour & Voodoo/Cemetery Tour
Tours leave from Rev Zombie's Voodoo Shop, 723 St Peter Street, between Bourbon & Royal Streets, French Quarter (861 2727/www.hauntedhistorytours.com). Bus 3 Vieux Carré. **Tickets** $15; $7 under-12s. **Credit** AmEx, Disc, MC, V. **Map** p316 B2 (departure point).
The Haunted History Tour (2pm, 8pm daily) is a two-hour walking tour led by theatrical, storytelling guides. The Voodoo/Cemetery Tour (10am, 1.15pm daily) takes you to New Orleans's oldest cemetery, St Louis Cemetery No.1, which contains the tomb of legendary voodoo queen Marie Laveau (*see page 46* **Queens of the city**). Reservations are not required if you arrive 15 minutes before the tours start.

Wearing them out

If your little angel has been perfectly attentive to each of the 660 objects at the Cabildo (*see page 78*) or needs an inducement to behave tomorrow, try one of the treats below, all of which are found on the outskirts of the city.

Airline Skate Center

6711 Airline Drive, at David Drive, Metairie (733 2248). Bus 38 Airline. **Open** 1-9pm Mon, Wed, Thur; 1-11pm Fri, Sat; 1-10pm Sun. **Admission** around $6.50. **No credit cards.**
A gigantic new skating rink with rental skates, strobe lights and funky music.

Attack Shak Indoor Paint Ball Arena

1008 Jefferson Highway, at Causeway Boulevard, Kenner (835 8898). Bus Kenner Local. **Open** *Sept-May* 3-10pm Tue-Thur; 3pm-1am Fri; noon-1am Sat; 2-10pm Sun. *June-Aug* noon-11pm Tue-Thur; noon-1am Fri, Sat; 2-10pm Sun. **Admission** $18.50 day pass (includes gun rental, mask & all-day field pass). **No credit cards.**
Takes laser tag one step further. Cloaked in protective gear, kids shoot at each other with paint pellets. The yuck factor usually makes this venue less popular with girls. Note that no under-tens are allowed.

Celebration Station

5959 Veterans Memorial Boulevard, at I-10, Jefferson (887 7888/www.celebrationstation.com). **Open** 10am-11pm Mon-Thur; 10am-midnight Fri, Sat; 11am-10pm Sun. **Admission** $12.99-$16.99 day pass. **Credit** Disc, MC, V.
Video games, pizza-eating, miniature golf, go-karts and batting cages are a few of the many fun things to do at Celebration Station.

Climb-Max

5304 Canal Boulevard, at City Park Avenue, Mid City (486 7600). Bus 42 Canal/Cemeteries or 46 City Park. **Open** *Summer* noon-9pm Mon; noon-11pm Tue-Fri; 9am-11pm Sat; 9am-9pm Sun. *Winter* hours vary; phone for details. **Admission** $15 day pass (includes climbing gear and instruction). **Credit** MC, V. **Map** p308 C5.
An indoor climbing gym where kids can exhaust themselves on rock walls of varying grades of difficulty without much risk of falling.

Laser Tag & Games

8916 Veterans Memorial Boulevard, between David Drive & Williams Boulevard, Metairie (469 7475/ www.ltag.com). Bus E1 Veterans Memorial Boulevard. **Open** *Sept-May* 4-10pm Mon-Thur; 4pm-midnight Fri; 11am-midnight Sat; 11am-10pm Sun. *Summer* 11am-10pm Mon-Thur, Sun; 11am-midnight Fri, Sat. Phone ahead during summer to check hours. **Admission** $4.25 per game; $15 day pass. **No credit cards.**
Kids love laser tag; they're armed with laser guns and dress up in shields that record the 'hits' on them in team warfare. For those aged seven and above and at least 48in (105cm) tall.

Parks

Audubon Park

For listings, see p109.
The Audubon covers 400 acres (162 hectares) in the heart of Uptown. It's closed to traffic; a tranquil lagoon and ancient oaks make it a beautiful place for walking, skating or riding bikes. The zoo (*see p109 and 198*) is a must. There's limited playground equipment at the St Charles Avenue end. Unsafe after dark.

City Park

For listings, see p110.
City Park boasts 1,500 lovely acres (608 hectares) of land. Storyland playground's recreated scenes from nursery rhymes and fairy stories are great for small children, who can sit in Cinderella's pumpkin coach. Nearby, there are scaled-down rides, an old-fashioned carousel, a miniature train and canoe and boat rentals.

Louisiana Nature Center

5700 Read Boulevard, at Nature Center Drive, New Orleans East (246 5674/1-800 774 7394/ www.auduboninstitute.org). Bus 72 Paris Road Express. **Open** 9am-5pm Tue-Fri; 10am-5pm Sat; noon-5pm Sun; closed Mon. **Admission** $4.75; $3.75 seniors; $2.50 3-12s. **Credit** AmEx, Disc, MC, V.
Occasional overnight programmes, hikes and discovery activities are run for kids at this centre (20 minutes by car from the Quarter), which occupies 86 acres (35 hectares) of hardwood bottomland forest and has three miles (4.8km) of trails and a planetarium. In warm months, bring insect repellent.

Swamp tours

Swamp touring companies (*see page 240*) are as plentiful as cypress trees, but children generally appreciate those sites closer to town that can be explored by smaller craft. Most excursions take two hours and include a guide. In summer, when the heat can be brutal, a morning tour is preferable and bug repellent a must. Reservations are required for the tours below, most of which offer transport from the city for an extra fee.

Mr Denny's Voyageur Swamp Tours

55344 US 90 E, Slidell (information 1-504 643 4839). **Tours** 10am, 2.30pm daily. **Tickets** $20; $12 under-12s. **Credit** MC, V.
Groups of six are paddled through Honey Island Swamp in canoes. Overnight and moonlight cruises are also available.

Mockingbird Swamp Tours

Information 1-504 386 7902/1-800 572 3046. **Tours** 10am, noon, 2pm daily. **Tickets** $17; $8 under-12s. **No credit cards.**
Mockingbird runs explorations of the Manchac Swamp, 45 minutes north-west of New Orleans.

Arts & Entertainment

Film

There's little cinema action in New Orleans – unless you're a filmmaker.

New Orleanians spend more time making movies than watching them. Among locals, movie-going finds a place on the list of activities some way below that of partying, dining and partying some more. Per capita film attendance is lower than in most other US cities, and New Orleanians have access to a narrower range of movies than is available in cities of comparable size elsewhere in what Hollywood calls 'Flyover Land' – the great expanse between New York and Los Angeles.

Still, what New Orleans misses is usually missable: second-rate Hollywood fare that performs poorly at the box office elsewhere. All the big US films, in both popular and artistic terms, enjoy a local release. And the city's aggressive arthouses bring in a decent smattering of foreign films, including most of the titles that garner Oscar nominations.

New Orleans is an increasingly popular venue for film production. This is partly because Louisiana is a so-called 'right to work' state, which means production companies can hire non-union employees. Also, the prevailing wages and cost of living are lower in south Louisiana than in almost all other parts of the US. Films can be made for less money than elsewhere, and for decidedly less money than in heavily unionised California.

But, of course, New Orleans and the surrounding area have attractions that go beyond the willingness of its labour force to work cheaply. The architecture of the city is distinctive: in the French Quarter, in the mansions of the Garden District and in the ornate Victorian homes Uptown. Plantations, like the ones at nearby Destrehan and Oak Alley, preserve the 19th century just a short drive up the Mississippi River. And all by itself, the forbidding beauty of the Louisiana swamp has attracted many filmmakers.

Post-production facilities are limited in the New Orleans area, which means that film companies essentially use the city (and Louisiana) as a backdrop. The film community continues to grow, however, with a steady in-migration of filmmakers who move here or establish second homes. Louisiana-born writer-directors Glen Pitre (*Belizaire the Cajun*) and Pat Mire (*Dirty Rice*) continue to live in the area, and they are joined by such distinguished part-time residents as Francis Ford Coppola,

Taylor Hackford and Ron Shelton, all of whom have homes in the city. Perhaps the most powerful film person to live in New Orleans was the late Brandon Tartikoff, one-time president of Paramount Studios and before that head of programming at NBC.

Also contributing to the film-video community are graduates of the University of New Orleans's film school. The New Orleans Video Access Center also supplies resources to local and regional professionals working primarily in video.

New Orleans Video Access Center
913 Magazine Street, at St Joseph Street, Warehouse District, New Orleans, LA 70130 (524 8626). Bus 11 Magazine. **Map** p309 C2.

University of New Orleans Department of Drama & Communications
Lakefront, between Elysian Fields & Robert E Lee Street, Gentilly, New Orleans, LA 70148 (280 6317). Bus 55 Elysian Fields.

Cinemas

Movie-going has a long and interesting history in New Orleans. The first theatre anywhere in America dedicated exclusively to film programming opened in the city in 1896: Vitascope Hall, located at 623 Canal Street (at the corner of Exchange Place, and now occupied by a Burger King). It was the world's second cinema, preceded only by one in France. By the height of the silent era in the 1910s, Canal Street hosted more than a dozen cinemas, while others lined the streets downtown.

By the mid-1920s, the first of the grand movie palaces began to appear. For the first year or so of its existence, the Loew's State (now the **State Palace**) did business as a vaudeville house, showing some films between the acts of its live programme. Across the street the magnificent **Saenger** opened exclusively as a venue for motion pictures, as did the **Orpheum** around the corner. On rare occasions, all three theatres still show movies.

Ironically, all three of these gorgeous old theatres survive today as venues for live performance. The Saenger (*see page 228*) hosts concerts, touring shows of Broadway musicals and other travelling stage productions; the

Prytania Theatre: vintage single-screener.

Orpheum is the home of the Louisiana Philharmonic Orchestra (*see page 226*); and the State Palace (*see page 226*) is booked mainly by music acts. Unrenovated as it is, the State Palace quickly reveals both its decayed splendour and the chilling spectre of the city's segregationist past. The inaccessible second balcony was once reserved for African-American patrons, who had to enter through a small separate entrance off Canal Street and buy their tickets at a separate box office. The other two theatres have been painstakingly renovated: the velvet seats are plush, the brass rails gleam. The Orpheum is beautiful, but the Saenger is nothing less than magnificent, as ornate and glamorous a movie house as was ever built anywhere.

Since the mid-1960s, in a phenomenon typical of mid-sized cities across the US, cinemas in Greater New Orleans have relocated from single-screen theatres downtown to shopping-mall multiplexes in the suburbs. Today, the area has 18 cinema sites. Only two of these are downtown, and only the **Joy** in Canal Street is regularly engaged in mainstream programming. In fact, of these 18 cinemas, only eight, with a total of 29 screens, are located in the municipality of New Orleans. By contrast, there are ten theatre operations with a total of 93 screens in the suburban areas of Jefferson and St Bernard Parishes.

A visitor to the city staying downtown will probably have to travel to one of three multiplexes in Jefferson Parish to view mainstream programming: the **Lakeside Cinema**, **AMC Galleria** or the megaplex

Palace 20. Any of these three is an excellent choice. They are all comfortable, well managed and furnished with state-of-the-art equipment. You can reach them by bus but it's a longwinded process, so it's probably better to go by taxi or car (all have ample parking). The huge Palace 20 features raked stadium seating in each theatre, so sightlines are unimpeded even when screenings are sold out.

For fans of art cinema, the city has four theatres offering US independent and foreign film programming on 11 different screens. Most convenient for downtown is the **Landmark's Canal Place Cinema**. However, there's likely to be more choice at **Movie Pitchers** in Mid City, only two blocks off the Canal Street bus route. It normally offers two independent or foreign titles nightly on each of its four screens.

Other possibilities include the **Zeitgeist** (recently reopened in Central City after a year of reorganisation), which offers a wide range of films from the US and abroad and specialises in pictures with gay and lesbian themes. (It also presents performance art, avant-garde music and hosts art exhibitions.) The Contemporary Arts Center (*see page 228*) also screens movies.

Finally, there's the vintage **Prytania Theatre**, just a short walk from the St Charles Avenue streetcar line uptown. New Orleans's last single-screen cinema, it opened as a neighbourhood movie house in the 1920s. In the 1970s it became the city's leading repertory cinema and in the 1980s the flagship arthouse. It has recently been renovated and currently offers eclectic programming with a speciality in English-language art films.

Daily listings for all areas are available in the *Times-Picayune*. Reviews and other useful information can be found in the weekly *Gambit* and in the *Picayune*'s Friday entertainment tabloid insert *Lagniappe*.

In addition to the city's regular film offerings, each October the New Orleans Film and Video Society (suite 1712, 225 Baronne Street, New Orleans, LA 70112, 523 3818, www.neworleansfilmfest.com) stages the New Orleans Film and Video Festival, a week-long series of premières and screenings focusing on American independent cinema. The festival includes workshops and panel discussions, plus features and shorts on 16mm film and video. Most screenings are held at the Canal Place Cinema and just a few steps away at the Southern Repertory Theater (*see page 229*). Local universities have myriad film offerings but they are unadvertised off campus. For the dedicated cinema buff, obscure film festivals (Latin American movies are big at Tulane and Loyola, African films at Xavier) and weekly free screenings of relatively new commercial films

New Orleans on film (clockwise from left): *Angel Heart, The Big Easy* and *Cat People.*

can be tracked down by checking campus bulletin boards or taking a look at the colleges' websites, which usually include film events on the weekly calendars (for listings of colleges, *see page 286*).

A new spot to see bits of New Orleans-themed movies is the permanent Mardi Gras installation at the Presbytère (*see page 78*). One room in the exhibition is devoted to film posters, photos and a continuous showing of clips from vintage movies with local themes.

AMC Galleria 8 Theatre
Suite 700, 1 Galleria Boulevard, at Causeway Boulevard, Metairie (838 8309/8338). Bus Kenner Local to Causeway Boulevard, then Causeway bus. **Admission** $6.25; $3.50 under-12s, concessions, matinée; $3.50 twilight (4-6pm); seniors $4.25. **No credit cards.**

Joy Theatre
1200 Canal Street, at Elk Place, Tremé (522 7575). Bus 41 Canal, 88 St Claude. **Admission** Noon-5.30pm $3.75. *After 5.30pm* $5.75; $3.75 concessions. **No credit cards.** **Map** p316 A1.

Lakeside General Cinema
3301 Veterans Boulevard, at Severn Avenue, behind Lakeside Shopping Center, Metairie (833 2881). Bus Kenner Local or Veterans Memorial to Causeway Boulevard, then Causeway bus. **Admission** $6.50; $3.75 concessions & matinées. **No credit cards.**

Landmark's Canal Place Cinema
3rd floor, Canal Place Shopping Center, 333 Canal Street, at N Peters Street, French Quarter

(581 5400). Bus 41 Canal, 55 Elysian Fields, 57 Franklin, 82 Desire. **Admission** *Until 6pm* $4.25. *After 6pm* $6.50; concessions $4.25. **No credit cards.** **Map** p316 A3.

Movie Pitchers
3941 Bienville Street, at N Pierce Street, Mid City (488 8881/www.moviepitchers.com). Bus 40, 41, 42, 43 Canal, 90 Carrollton. **Admission** $5; $4 concessions & matinées. **No credit cards.** **Map** p308 D5.

Palace Theatre 20
1200 Elmwood Park Boulevard, at S Clearview Parkway, behind Elmwood Shopping Center, Elmwood (734 2020). Bus Kenner Local to Elmwood Drive, then HP Long minibus. **Admission** $6; $3.50 concessions & matinées. **Credit** MC, V.

Prytania Theatre
5339 Prytania Street, at Leontine Street, Uptown (891 2787). St Charles Streetcar. **Admission** $6; $4 concessions. **No credit cards.** **Map** pp306-7 C9.

Zeitgeist Multi-cultural Arts Center
1724 Oretha Castle Haley Boulevard (formerly Dryades Street), at Polymnia Street, Central City (525 2767/fax 525 6246/www.gnofn.org/~zte). Bus 15 Freret. **Admission** $4-$6. **No credit cards.** **Map** p309 B2.

> ▶ For a **New Orleans filmography**, see chapter **Further Reference**, and for more on **film festivals**, see chapter **By Season**.

Galleries

New openings and expansions are acting as a shot in the art for New Orleans's already-thriving gallery scene.

There are some big changes afoot in New Orleans's art world, with planned museum expansions and the opening of two new arts institutions downtown in 2001-2. The number of galleries ebbs and flows each year, and the range of art on show is establishing areas of diverse interest throughout the city. Three areas are clearly definable: the French Quarter; Julia Street and the emerging museum district in the Warehouse District; and Uptown, with Magazine Street as its anchor. Sandwiched between the Warehouse District and Uptown, Central City is also developing as an art hotspot.

The galleries listed here represent both the grandes dames and the new kids on the block. But this is only a selection. In each neighbourhood, take time to walk and explore, as artists and entrepreneurs open new shops and galleries each month.

A Gallery for Fine Photography. *See p204.*

A Royal Street fixture for many years, the gallery displays realistic and romantic views of New Orleans and environs by both local artists and national figures such as *American Artist* editor Stephen Doherty.

The French Quarter & around

For three other important Quarter galleries, *see page 206* **Primary colours**.

Bassetti Fine Art Photographs
233 Chartres Street, at Bienville Street (529 9811). Bus 3 Vieux Carré, 55 Elysian Fields, 81 Almonaster, 82 Desire. **Open** 10.30am-5.30pm Mon-Sat; closed Sun. **Credit** AmEx, Disc, MC, V. **Map** p316 B2.
Contemporary fine-art photography presented in changing exhibitions.

La Belle Galerie
309 Chartres Street, at Bienville Street (529 5538/ 529 3080). Bus 3 Vieux Carré, 55 Elysian Fields, 81 Almonaster, 82 Desire. **Open** 10am-7pm daily. **Credit** AmEx, DC, Disc, MC, V. **Map** p316 B2.
Walk past the tourist-grabbing posters displayed in the windows and into this visual whirlpool of art and artefacts. Inside, you'll find an array of work by African and African-American artists that runs the gamut from tribal pieces to contemporary prints and sculptural constructions.

Bryant Galleries of New Orleans
316 Royal Street, at Conti Street (525 5584). Bus 3 Vieux Carré, 55 Elysian Fields, 81 Almonaster, 82 Desire. **Open** 10am-6pm Mon-Thur, Sun; 10am-8pm Fri, Sat. **Credit** AmEx, DC, Disc, MC, V. **Map** p316 B2.

Carmen Llewellyn Gallery
240 Chartres Street, at Bienville Street (558 9859). Bus 3 Vieux Carré, 55 Elysian Fields, 81 Almonaster, 82 Desire. **Open** 11am-5pm Mon-Sat; closed Sun. **Credit** AmEx, MC, V. **Map** p316 B2.
A guerrilla fighter in the war to have Latin American art accepted for its quality rather than just for its picturesqueness, Carmen Llewellyn features regular shows by contemporary painters, photographers and sculptors from the region.

Dixon & Dixon of Royal
237 Royal Street & 319 Chartres Street, at Bienville Street (524 0282). Bus 3 Vieux Carré, 55 Elysian Fields, 81 Almonaster, 82 Desire. **Open** 9am-5.30pm Mon-Sat; 10am-5pm Sun. **Credit** AmEx, Disc, MC, V. **Map** p316 B2.
This is the current venture of Dave Dixon, the man generally credited with the creation of the Louisiana Superdome in the early 1970s, is one of the largest dealers in the world in terms of works displayed: almost 1,000. The works in question are 18th- and 19th-century British, French and Dutch paintings and antiques.

Elliott Gallery
540 Royal Street, at Toulouse Street (523 3554/ www.elliottgallery.com). Bus 55 Elysian Fields, 81 Almonaster, 82 Desire. **Open** 9.30am-5.30pm Mon-Sat; 11am-5pm Sun. **Credit** AmEx, DC, Disc, MC, V. **Map** p316 B2.
Can't get enough of Picasso's more accessible Cubist compositions? Don't have a budget like the

Arts & Entertainment

Peligro in the French Quarter.

Metropolitan Museum of Art? This gallery features the work of Max Papart, Theo Tobias and James Coignard at a fraction of the price.

Galerie Lafitte

533 St Louis Street, at Chartres Street (524 0105). Bus 3 Vieux Carré, 55 Elysian Fields, 81 Almonaster, 82 Desire. **Open** 11am-10pm daily. **Credit** AmEx, Disc, MC, V. **Map** p316 B2.

Sinking roots into the site of the 19th-century Lafitte Bank building, Alexandra Monett brings her experience as a gallery director in Paris and Brussels to play on a collection of American artists from the 1960s to the '80s, as well as exhibitions of contemporary art.

A Gallery for Fine Photography

322 Royal Street, at Bienville Street (568 1313/ www.agallery.com). Bus 3 Vieux Carré, 55 Elysian Fields, 81 Almonaster, 82 Desire. **Open** 9.30am-6pm Mon-Sat; 10.30am-6pm Sun. **Credit** AmEx, Disc, MC, V. **Map** p316 B2.

An aptly named space. In the atmosphere of a side-street European gallery, Joshua Mann Pailet has assembled a collection of vintage photographs and books that would make most museums envious. Pailet tempers the traditional atmosphere with exhibitions of work by major contemporary photographers from around the world.

Mann Gallery

713 Bienville Street, at Royal Street (523 2342). Bus 3 Vieux Carré, 55 Elysian Fields, 81 Almonaster, 82 Desire. **Open** 11am-5.30pm Mon-Sat; closed Sun. **Credit** AmEx, MC, V. **Map** p316 B2.

Mann Gallery owner Jake Maguno hit the big time in the 1970s by showing the work of Françoise Gilot, an artist best known as Picasso's mistress. Impressionist-style landscapes now hold place of honour in the gallery.

Peligro

305 Decatur Street, at Conti Street (581 1706). Bus 3 Vieux Carré, 55 Elysian Fields, 81 Almonaster, 82 Desire. **Open** 10am-6pm Mon-Thur; 10am-10pm Fri, Sat; noon-6pm Sun. **Credit** AmEx, Disc, MC, V. **Map** p316 B3.

This gallery takes its cue from the freewheeling style of the nearby House of Blues. There's an intriguing mix of pure folk art and pieces by trained artists who have adopted the style.

Stone+Press Gallery

238 Chartres Street, at Bienville Street (561 8555). Bus 3 Vieux Carré, 55 Elysian Fields, 81 Almonaster, 82 Desire. **Open** 10am-6pm Mon-Fri; 10.30am-5.30pm Sat, Sun. **Credit** AmEx, Disc, MC, V. **Map** p316 B2.

This quiet oasis of the printmaker's art features both classic black and white images by 20th-century lithographers – Thomas Hart Benton and others of the Regionalist school – and colourful images by contemporary artists.

Studio Inferno

3000 Royal Street, at Montegut Street, Bywater (945 1878). Bus 82 Desire. **Open** 10am-5pm Mon-Sat; closed Sun. **Credit** AmEx, MC, V. **Map** p307 H6.

Take the bus named Desire to a metal warehouse in the Bywater neighbourhood downriver from the Quarter. Here the flames of the glass furnaces will remind you of Dante's *Inferno*. It's all very New Orleans, this mixture of decadence and beauty, the latter quality obvious in the vases, pitchers and drinking glasses for which this studio is known. Neon artists, sculptors, painters and photographers also exhibit here.

Nationwide galleries

Two galleries with branches nationwide have exhibition space in the French Quarter, each showing recognised artists such as Peter Max, Adrian Deckbar, Leroy Neiman and Romanian prodigy Alexandra Nechita.

Dyansen Gallery

433 Royal Street, at St Louis Street (523 2902/ www.dyansengallery.com). Bus 3 Vieux Carré, 55 Elysian Fields, 81 Almonaster, 82 Desire. **Open** 10am-6pm Mon-Thur; 10am-8pm Fri-Sun. **Credit** AmEx, DC, MC, V. **Map** p316 B2.

The aptly named **Studio Inferno**.

Herlard-Cimino Gallery. See p207.

Hanson Gallery

229 Royal Street, at Bienville Street (524 8211/ www.hansongallery-nola.com). Bus 3 Vieux Carré, 55 Elysian Fields, 81 Almonaster, 82 Desire. **Open** 10am-6pm Mon-Sat; 10am-5pm Sun. **Credit** AmEx, MC, V. **Map** p316 B2.

Warehouse District

Although Julia Street retains its reputation as the primary venue for upscale art-hopping, the area is bursting at the seams. New galleries are opening on the perimeter, while established galleries are moving away from the river to the area surrounding the Arts Council of New Orleans's new arts centre, scheduled to open in late 2001 on Carondelet Street.

According to Jeanne Cimino, co-owner of Heriad-Cimino Gallery, Julia Street galleries are exhibiting the work of more and more artists with national and international reputations, and are increasingly becoming a hunting ground for collectors from other parts of the US who have discovered the area as a serious centre of contemporary art. With many of the newer, peripheral galleries showcasing works by emerging local artists, the entire Warehouse District–Julia Street corridor is vital and exciting.

On the first Saturday of the month, many contemporary galleries on and around Julia Street are open from 6pm to 9pm in a successful bid to generate public interest in the art scene.

The pick of the bunch

Ariodante Contemporary Craft Gallery

535 Julia Street, at Camp Street (524 3233). Bus 11 Magazine. **Open** 11am-5pm Tue-Sat; closed Sun. **Credit** AmEx, MC, V. **Map** p309 C2.
Ariodante fills its elegant, custom-made display cases with high-end contemporary crafts. In this stylish gallery, you don't have to choose between buying something practical or something beautiful. Almost everything here is both.

Arthur Roger Gallery

432 Julia Street, at Magazine Street (522 1999). Bus 11 Magazine. **Open** 10am-5pm Mon-Sat; closed Sun. **Credit** AmEx, MC, V. **Map** p309 C2.
With the biggest plate-glass windows in the city, Arthur Roger can shout that he represents many of the upper-echelon New Orleans artists and their national counterparts. You won't find bargains here, but you can take home a major work of art that will have your neighbours working hard to keep up with you instead of the Joneses.

Christopher Maier Furniture Design

329 Julia Street, at Commerce Street (586 9079/ www.christophermaier.com). Bus 11 Magazine. **Open** 10am-5pm daily. **Credit** AmEx, MC, V. **Map** p309 C2.
To call Christopher Maier a furniture maker is to miss the point of his massive creations: he's an

Primary colours

'That's right, we've put a paid-in-full tag on the painting, and the dog is yours, bless your heart,' Marsha Ercegovic, director of Rodrigue's Studio, coos into the phone, assuring the purchaser that no one is going to get that Blue Dog but her. 'Hey, why don't you come to a party here Jazz Fest weekend, dear? You know you could just fly in for the day,' she coaxes the client.

Conversations like this reflect the big bucks that collectors such as Whoopi Goldberg and newsman Tom Brokaw are paying for painter George Rodrigue's famous Blue Dogs. As does the lawsuit filed by Rodrigue's ex-wife, who claims that each Blue Dog painting is just a knock-off of an idea they developed together, not a new creation. Try explaining that to someone who's just spent $100,000 for a large, leader-of-the-pack painting of a Louisiana politician or musician with a homely little mutt sitting at his feet.

It didn't make sense to neighbour-artist Jim Tweedy, who decided that a spoof was in order. Rodrigue claims that his long-gone pet dog had appeared to him in a dream, spurring thoughts of the spooky Cajun tradition of the werewolf-type canine who roams the swamps. In the harsh light of day, Tweedy saw the chance to have a good laugh and make a few bucks off a new creation, a Red Cat named Charlie.

But a funny thing happened. Some people were as mad about Tweedy's Red Cat as others had been about Rodrigue's Blue Dog. One collector even claims to have hung his

Red Cat painting between his Peter Max and his Andy Warhol graphics.

Enter artist Martin LaBorde, who took a trip south of the border and found himself at the top of an ancient pyramid one midnight. A trance ensued, and a little magician LaBorde calls Bodo appeared to him in a vision, revealing the secrets of the universe. LaBorde descended from the pyramid transformed. The experience changed his life, and his bank account, forever.

Bodo remains inscrutable, his antics on the canvas not revealing any secrets or hints about how to deal with the universe. But he does seem to love animals, and his current favourite is a yellow pony, upon whose back Bodo balances or does cartwheels.

So, that makes the colour wheel complete: from Blue Dog, to Red Cat, to Yellow Pony, the three primary colours reign in the three-

---

ambience maker whose wooden evocations of past eras – generally in the form of armoires – are the focal point of any room.

docs: A Studio Gallery of Contemporary Arts
709 Camp Street, at Girod Street (524 3936/ www.docsgallery.com). St Charles Streetcar/ 11 Magazine bus. **Open** 11am-6pm Tue-Sat; closed Mon, Sun. **Credit** AmEx, Disc, MC, V. **Map** p309 C1.
docs feels like a trendy modern living room with its curved wooden walls; it's the public space of the owner and the director, both of whom live above the gallery. The gallery specialises in searching out young regional artists who are making a name for themselves on the art scene.

Galerie Simonne Stern
518 Julia Street, at Magazine Street (529 1118). Bus 11 Magazine. **Open** noon-5pm Mon; 10am-5pm Tue-Sat; closed Sun. **Credit** AmEx, MC, V. **Map** p309 C2.
Created by a remarkable French woman who died far too young, the gallery lives up to Simonne Stern's commitment to showcasing the finest Louisiana contemporary artists, interspersed with well-known national artists.

George Schmidt Gallery
626 Julia Street, at St Charles Avenue (592 0206/ www.georgeschmidt.com). St Charles Streetcar. **Open** 12.30-4.30pm Mon-Sat; closed Sun. **Credit** MC, V. **Map** p309 B2.
Painter, musician and singer George Schmidt stays busy creating shows of 'history painting, narrative

block stretch of Royal Street that houses the artists' galleries. There may not be anything truly mystical about the little critters, but they sure do know their colour theory.

Martin LaBorde Gallery
509 Royal Street, at Toulouse Street (587 7111). Bus 3 Vieux Carré, 55 Elysian Fields, 81 Almonaster, 82 Desire. **Open** *10am-6pm daily.* **Credit** *AmEx, Disc, MC, V.* **Map** *p316 B2.*
In addition to LaBorde's signature magician paintings, the gallery also represents local painters and sculptors. LaBorde's prints cost

art and other reactionary works'. He paints seminal moments in New Orleans history, but not as you've ever seen or imagined them before.

Heriard-Cimino Gallery
440 Julia Street, at Magazine Street (525 7300/ www.heriardcimino.com). Bus 11 Magazine. **Open** *10.30am-5.30pm Mon-Fri; 10am-5pm Sat; closed Sun.* **Credit** *AmEx, Disc, MC, V.* **Map** *p309 C2.*
This is a sleek white exhibition space in which minimalist and expressionist art occasionally give way to high-quality figurative pieces. The gallery promotes a minimalist sensibility, featuring abstract works that nevertheless engage the senses with colour. Works by local artists such as Elizabeth Shannon focus on regional images, transforming them into icons.

between $700 and $1,500. His paintings escalate to $75,000 for a wall-size image of Bodo and his pony.

Richard Russell Gallery
641 Royal Street, at St Peter Street (523 0533/www.richardrussellgallery.com). Bus 3 Vieux Carré, 55 Elysian Fields, 81 Almonaster, 82 Desire. **Open** *10am-9pm Mon-Thur, Sun; 10am-10pm Fri, Sat.* **Credit** *AmEx, Disc, MC, V.* **Map** *p316 B2.*
Charlie the Red Cat is hedging his bets, offering Red Cat T-shirts, hats, umbrellas, puzzles, aprons and golf balls, as well as books, cards and, of course, paintings (pictured far left). The interior of the gallery reflects the informal nature of the venture. Graphics go for $700 to $1,500. The most expensive paintings cost $4,000 to $5,000.

Rodrigue's Studio
721 Royal Street, at Orleans Street (581 4244). Bus 3 Vieux Carré, 55 Elysian Fields, 81 Almonaster, 82 Desire. **Open** *10am-6pm daily.* **Credit** *AmEx, MC, V.* **Map** *p316 C2.*
Take a deep breath and exude an air of confidence as you enter the gallery. You do want to be taken seriously. The number of paintings and prints centring on this blue dog (pictured left) is remarkable – doesn't she ever take a day off and go to the vet? Graphics fall into the same price range as those of Bodo and the Red Cat ($700-$1,500); but large tour-de-force images of former Louisiana governor Edwin or jazzman Al Hirt can set a collector back $100,000.

Jonathan Ferrara Gallery
841 Carondelet Street, between Julia & St Joseph Streets (522 5471/www.jonathanferraragallery.com). St Charles Streetcar. **Open** *noon-6pm Tue-Sat; by appointment at other times.* **Credit** *AmEx, MC, V.* **Map** *p309 B2.*
It's hard to know what to expect next from Jonathan Ferrara, and that's the joy of his exuberant attitude toward art. In his new location on Carondelet Street, he wants to be 'a beacon to draw people in' with imaginative and seductive shows.

Lighthouse Glass
742 Camp Street, at Julia Street (529 4494). Bus 11 Magazine. **Open** *11am-6pm Mon-Sat; closed Sun.* **Credit** *AmEx, MC, V.* **Map** *p309 C2.*
Gallery owner Martha Robbins claims that 'you've got to be a bit of a pyro to love this as much as I do.'

Jonathan Ferrara Gallery. *See p207.*

She revels in the 'wonderment of playing with hot glass', a joy that shows in the clean, urbane designs of the utilitarian vessels she creates.

New Orleans School of Glass Works & Print Making
727 Magazine Street, at Julia Street (529 7277). Bus 11 Magazine. **Open** 10am-5pm Mon-Sat; closed Sun. **Credit** Disc, MC, V. **Map** p309 C2.
The gallery houses a veritable wonderland of some of the most sophisticated and imaginative glass that you'll find anywhere. Visitors have the opportunity to view glass blowers at work in the large studio behind the display area.

Rosetree Glass Studio & Gallery
446 Vallette Street, at Opelousas Street, Algiers (366 3602/www.rosetreeglass.com). Canal Street ferry, then 15min walk/101 Algiers Loop bus. **Open** 9am-5pm Mon-Fri; closed Sat, Sun. **Credit** MC, V. **Map** p307 H7.
Combine art with sightseeing by taking the Canal Street ferry (free) across the river to Algiers and enjoy the cool river breezes. Then soak up the atmosphere of the historic Algiers Point neighbourhood as you walk the seven blocks to the Rosetree Glass Studio, where a protected spectators' area overlooks the glass-blowing area.

Stella Jones Gallery
Bank One Center, 201 St Charles Avenue, at Common Street (568 9050). St Charles Streetcar. **Open** 11am-6pm Mon-Fri; noon-5pm Sat; closed Sun. **Credit** AmEx, DC, Disc, MC, V. **Map** p309 C1.

In a city whose arts have been so heavily influenced by African-American culture, it's taken a long time for a gallery featuring exclusively African-American artists to emerge. This place displays sophisticated contemporary art .

The best of the rest

Other Julia Street galleries displaying works by regional artists in changing exhibitions include:

LeMieux Gallery
332 Julia Street, at Tchoupitoulas Street (522 5988/ www.lemieuxgalleries.com). Bus 11 Magazine. **Open** 10am-5.30pm Mon-Sat; closed Sun. **Credit** AmEx, Disc, MC, V. **Map** p309 C2.

Marguerite Oestreicher Fine Arts
720 & 726 Julia Street, at St Charles Avenue (581 9253). St Charles Streetcar. **Open** 10am-5pm Tue-Sat; closed Mon, Sun. **Credit** AmEx, MC, V. **Map** p309 B2.

Suzanne Zinsel Contemporary Fine Art
624 Julia Street, at St Charles Avenue (588 9999). St Charles Streetcar. **Open** 11am-4pm Tue-Sat; closed Mon, Sun. **Credit** MC, V. **Map** p309 B2.

Sylvia Schmidt Gallery
400A Julia Street, at Tchoupitoulas Street (522 2000). Bus 11 Magazine. **Open** 11am-4pm Tue-Sat; by appointment Mon, Sun. **Credit** MC, V. **Map** p309 C2.

Uptown & Central City

Academy Gallery

5256 Magazine Street, at Valmont Street,
Uptown (899 8111). Bus 11 Magazine. **Open** 9am-
4pm Mon-Sat; closed Sun. **Credit** MC, V.
Map p306 C10.
Traditions and techniques of the great European
academies reign supreme here at this appropriately
named institution. The artistic landscape is dominated by the masterfully executed realist paintings
of director Auseklis Ozols.

Barrister's Gallery

1724 Oretha Castle Haley Boulevard, at Euterpe
Street, Central City (525 2767/www.barristers
gallery.citysearch.com). **Open** 10am-
5pm Mon-Sat; closed Sun. **Credit** AmEx, MC, V.
Map p307 F8.
Expect the unusual. You'll find it at this former food
market, a beaux arts landmark in the city's deteriorated black Canal Street shopping district. The
spacious ground floor is filled with ethnographic
material and Southern folk art. Owner Andy Antippas
invited the homeless and controversial Zeitgeist
Multi-Disciplinary Art Center to share the space with
him, ensuring a steady diet of non-mainstream films
and events. The Ashe Cultural Arts Center (1712
Oretha Castle Haley Boulevard, at Euterpe Street, 569
9070, closed Mon, Sun) is nearby.

Carol Robinson Gallery

840 Napoleon Avenue, at Magazine Street, Uptown
(895 6130). Bus 11 Magazine, 24 Napoleon. **Open**
10am-5.30pm Tue-Sat; closed Mon, Sun. **Credit**
AmEx, Disc, MC, V. **Map** p306 D10.
Contemporary New Orleans artists with a realist
flair displayed in a minimalist converted house.

Cole-Pratt Gallery

3800 Magazine Street, at Peniston Street, Uptown
(891 6789/cpgaller@gnofn.org). Bus 11 Magazine.
Open *Oct-June* 10am-5.30pm Tue-Sat; closed Mon,

Pause for thought at **Barrister's Gallery**.

Sun. *July-Sept* 10am-5pm Tue-Sat; closed Mon, Sun.
Credit AmEx, Disc, MC, V. **Map** p306 D9.
The gallery represents 35 Southern artists, featuring a blend of abstraction and realism, with a tilt
towards the former. New Orleans Museum of Art
staff members Paul Tarver, Dan Peirsol and Judy
Cooper exhibit here.

Mario Villa Gallery

3908 Magazine Street, near Constantinople Street,
Uptown (895 8731). Bus 11 Magazine. **Open** noon-
5pm Mon; 10am-5pm Tue-Sat; closed Sun. **Credit**
AmEx, MC, V. **Map** p306 D9/10.
Noted for his imaginative and often humorous metal
furniture, Mario Villa has been featured in numerous
super-glossy design magazines.

Nuance Gallery

728 Dublin Street, at Maple Street, Riverbend (865
8463). St Charles Streetcar/34 Carrollton Express
bus. **Open** 10.30am-5pm Wed-Sat; closed Mon, Tue,
Sun. **Credit** AmEx, Disc, MC, V. **Map** p306 A8.
Glassblower Arden Stuart has added a stable of
Louisiana artists to her studio, which is located in
a quiet neighbourhood near the end of the St
Charles Streetcar line.

Stan Rice Art Gallery

1314 Napoleon Avenue, at Prytania Street (entrance
on Prytania Street), Uptown (897 9966/stanriceart
gal@aol.com). Bus 24 Napoleon. **Open** *Gallery* 11am-
4pm Wed-Sun; closed Mon, Tue. *St Elizabeth's*
Orphanage tours 11am, 1pm, 3pm daily. **Admission**
Gallery free. *Tours* $7; $5 concessions. **No credit**
cards. **Map** p306 D9.
Husband of vampire-queen novelist Anne Rice, Stan
Rice takes refuge in a colourful world that only occasionally features bizarre expressionist monsters
(none of the artwork is for sale). The gallery is on
the Prytania Street side of the Rices' St Elizabeth's
Orphanage, which now serves as home to Anne
Rice's doll collection rather than small children.

Thomas Mann Design

1804 Magazine Street, between Felicity Street &
St Mary Street, Uptown (581 2113). Bus 11
Magazine. **Open** 11am-6pm Mon-Sat; closed Sun.
Credit AmEx, MC, V. **Map** p307 F9.
Whether you're looking for designer-magazine
accoutrements for your home or a stunning high-
tech brooch for your shirt, Thomas Mann's glitzy
metallic designs are sure to please. Excellent quality
makes them the heirlooms of the future.

Wyndy Morehead Fine Arts

3926 Magazine Street, at Austerlitz Street, Uptown
(269 8333). St Charles Streetcar. **Open** 10am-
5.30pm Mon-Sat; closed Sun. **Credit** AmEx, MC, V.
Map p306 D9/10.
Wyndy Morehead moved from Julia Street to a
larger space where she has created a comfortable,
welcoming setting for her eclectic selections of art.
An admitted colour addict, she also leans toward the
representational in art, particularly works that
reflect her addiction.

Arts & Entertainment

Gay & Lesbian

Outlandish and sensual, with bars and parties that never seem to stop, queer New Orleans is a grande dame with a wicked glint in her eye.

Bourbon Pub. *See p211.*

Gay New Orleans in many ways reflects the larger culture of this exciting and historic city. During the early centuries, homosexual activity blended easily into the larger pattern of illicit heterosexual behaviour, where it continued to exist as long as certain conventions were observed. Everyone understood that in the eye of the state, homosexual acts were criminal, and in the eye of the Church, homosexual acts were sinful, so they were kept out of view.

Within this framework of tacit tolerance, a vibrant homosexual culture developed in the French Quarter. Tennessee Williams came to terms with his sexuality there during his first visit in 1938 and found the freedom he needed to create his great body of work. Also seeking asylum in the Quarter were writers Truman Capote and Lyle Saxon, photographer Frances Benjamin Johnston and artist William Spratling. The same society that attracted artists and writers also found a place for homosexual men and women in general.

After 250 years of New Orleans history, the existing concept of homosexual culture was challenged on all fronts by the arrival of the modern gay liberation movement. As elsewhere, the tidal wave of the sexual revolution came crashing down on the old order. Gay people demanded the right – indeed, the responsibility – to be visible, recognised and free from all kinds of discrimination.

But the gay movement was slow to develop in New Orleans. This was due partly to the general culture of the South, which tends to be conservative and slow to change, and partly because New Orleans, despite its sizeable gay population, was not a large city that could provide the anonymity of larger cities such as New York, Los Angeles, San Francisco, Houston, Dallas or Atlanta.

Infamous anti-gay crusader Anita Bryant arrived in New Orleans shortly after her success in overturning Miami's gay rights ordinance in 1977 and her presence provided the flame that ignited local gay political organising. Over the ensuing two decades, gay political activists have became a substantial force in city politics, helping to elect gay-friendly municipal officials.

In the last two decades, police harassment has almost disappeared. In 1991 the New Orleans city council passed an ordinance prohibiting discrimination based on sexual orientation and set up the process for registering same-sex domestic partnerships. In 1997 Mayor Marc Morial ordered spousal benefits for city employees. And in 1998 New Orleans became one of the first US cities to add gender identity to its non-discrimination law.

Today, life is generally good for g/l/b/ts (gay/lesbian/bisexual/transgenders) in New Orleans. While discrimination in the workplace has not evaporated – nor are gay people always safe in public – the liberation movement has created a very different, and much better, world.

Despite the contributions of gay politics, New Orleans lesbian and gay culture is still more social than political. In the old French and Spanish colonial culture, taverns were important gathering places; gay bars have continued the tradition. Likewise, the French custom of masked balls was copied by gay carnival clubs formed in the 1960s. The gay Mardi Gras krewes were tragically diminished by the AIDS onslaught but bravely continued their traditions. No gay krewe has developed the financial clout needed for a parade, but gay balls are some of the most sought-after invitations during Carnival (check out www.gaymardigras.com for information about the krewes and their activities).

A FEW DOS AND DON'TS

Even in a gay-friendly city like New Orleans, it's wise to be aware of the ins and outs of the local culture. This is a very Southern city where good manners are important in every contest. Visitors are expected to be as enthusiastic about the city as locals are.

As in any major city, keep your wits about you while on the streets. Gay bashing is not a major problem in the Quarter, where there's a strong gay presence, but there are always exceptions. Always be wary, particularly if drinking and after dark, and take a cab back if you're staying out of the area.

Never argue with or question the police. Co-operate fully, even if you feel they are out of line. A civil, concerned-citizen demeanour will solve many problems on the spot. If the cops are seriously out of line, note their names and badge number and file a complaint immediately.

Information

There are three publications that will tell you what's going on and where. The oldest is *IMPACT News*, which has been serving the community since 1977. In the last couple of years, a new ownership has turned *Impact* into a

serious, well-edited newspaper. It also publishes *Eclipse*, a fun weekly guide to bars and the like. *Ambush Magazine*, published every other week, is not particularly well organised or written but has a wealth of information about the local scene. For further details of the gay press, *see page 282*.

Staff at the **Faubourg Marigny Bookstore** (*see page 172*) and **Alternatives** are also good sources of information about the gay scene.

Alternatives

909 Bourbon Street, at Dumaine Street, French Quarter (524 5222). Bus 3 Vieux Carré, 48 Esplanade. **Open** 11am-7pm Mon, Wed, Thur, Sun; 11am-9pm Fri, Sat. **Credit** AmEx, Disc, MC, V. **Map** p316 C2.
All manner of gay stuff, such as cards, clothing and toys, is sold at this shop, right in the centre of the Bourbon Street action. Helpful staff will also provide information and directions.

Bars

Gay bars in New Orleans tend to be less specialised than in other cities. Many of the most popular bars are located near each other, and since local laws allow bar patrons to take alcoholic drinks on to the streets, merrymakers like to bar-hop. This means the clientele, dress and attitude can be a complete hodgepodge at any watering hole. However, visitors should take care before walking from one location to another, especially from Quarter bars to Marigny bars. After dark, or if you're alone and/or tipsy, ask the bar staff to call a cab for you.

There's a large number of gay bars and dance clubs, including a few scattered in the suburbs, but the city is light on lesbian spots. Although women are comfortable in men's bars, the closing of Rubyfruit Jungle in the spring of 2000 has created a large vacuum in the lesbian scene. Many of the most popular Quarter and Marigny hotspots listed below are open 24 hours a day and admission is free unless otherwise stated. For a more complete list of bars and clubs, *see chapters* **Bars** *and* **Music**.

Bourbon Pub & Parade Dance Club

801 Bourbon Street, at St Ann Street, French Quarter (529 2107/www.bourbonclub.com). Bus 3 Vieux Carré, 48 Esplanade. **Open** *Pub* 24hrs daily. *Dance Club* from 9pm Mon-Sat; from 5pm Sun. **Admission** *Parade* $2-$5. **No credit cards. Map** p316 C2.
A very popular pub known for its music videos. The Parade, upstairs, is a great dance club and hugely popular. Top sound system and a cruisy balcony hanging over the action on Bourbon Street.

Café Lafitte in Exile & The Corral

901 Bourbon Street, at Dumaine Street, French Quarter (522 8397/www.lafittes.com). Bus 3 Vieux Carré, 48 Esplanade. **Open** 24hrs daily.
No credit cards. Map p316 C2.

Don we now our gay apparel

There's no absolute proof that the party of French explorers who planted their flag in Louisiana were gay but consider this: an all-male group, carrying flags and wearing plumed hats made their discovery on Fat Tuesday, Mardi Gras. It was 1699 and that little band of Frenchmen set the tone for New Orleans, one that it has never departed from. Parties are the New Orleans way and no one has excelled at this more than gay men and women. And when there isn't a celebration in sight, gays have created their own events.

The most famous celebration in New Orleans is, of course, **Mardi Gras**. For years it has provided gay people with the opportunity to wear masks, cross dress and indulge in creative fantasy. While there are no gay parading organisations, four gay carnival clubs – Amon-Ra, Petronius, Armeinius and the Lords of Leather – present elaborate tableaux balls in the weeks preceding Mardi Gras. In the past, attendance at these balls was by personal invitation only, but in recent years all except Amon-Ra have sold tickets to the public. Traditionalists frown on this practice, but it provides visitors with the chance of a glimpse at what was for decades totally private. Ticket information, when available, is published in the gay press in the weeks leading up to Mardi Gras. Be warned, however: each club has a strict dress code for those attending. This varies from club to club, but might include formal evening wear, drag, leather – or a combination of all three.

The madness culminates on Fat Tuesday (Mardi Gras day), which is the only day that costumes are worn in the street. Many of the grandest are those created for the gay balls, and the costume judging at noon is the best place to see the gay finery. The event is still called the **Bourbon Street Awards**, but it now takes place on Burgundy Street in Bywater, in front of Rawhide 2010 (see page 213).

The other major gay craziness is **Southern Decadence**, held on the weekend before Labor Day. Started as a little party for friends in 1972, it is now a major event – and one that is still entirely a gay phenomenon. Mostly, it's an excuse to dress up in genderfuck drag (on the Sunday before Labor Day itself) and careen drunkenly from bar to bar. Although this spectacle is called a 'parade', it has more in common with the running of the bulls in Pamplona.

Other gay celebrations include **Hallowe'en**, which is commemorated with a large circuit party on the Saturday night closest to 31 October, as well as with a number of smaller activities before and after the day. The event is funded by a large group of sponsors and all revenues are donated directly to Lazarus House, an AIDS hospice.

The **New Orleans Lesbian & Gay Pride Festival** is celebrated in autumn (usually late September or early October) with a parade and two days of festival activities in either Washington Park or Armstrong Park. Unlike in other cities with large gay populations, this isn't the premier gay event of the year. There's just too much competition.

For further details of these events, see chapter **By Season**.

Lafitte's, as it is widely known, has been in business at this address since 1953 and is among the oldest gay bars in the country, if not the world. It continues to cater for a predominantly male clientele. The Corral, a popular balcony bar, is located on the floor above.

Good Friends Bar & Queen's Head Pub

740 Dauphine Street, at St Ann Street, French Quarter (566 7191/www.goodfriendsbar.com). Bus 3 Vieux Carré, 48 Esplanade. **Open** 24hrs daily. **Credit** MC, V. **Map** p316 C1.

'Always snappy casual,' they say of the Good Friends Bar. This watering hole in the heart of the Quarter attracts a lot of locals who find it a pleasant place to socialise. The Queen's Head upstairs, which is open at weekends only, is as classy as gay bars get in New Orleans.

Mississippi River Bottom

515 St Philip Street, at Decatur Street, French Quarter (524 2558). Bus 55 Elysian Fields, 57 Franklin, 82 Desire. **Open** 24hrs daily. **Credit** AmEx. **Map** p316 C3.

Shows with male dancers steam up the Mississippi River Bottom, but patrons can cool down in the pleasant courtyard outside.

Oz

800 Bourbon Street, at St Ann Street, French Quarter (593 9491/www.ozneworleans.com). Bus 3 Vieux Carré, 48 Esplanade. **Open** 24hrs daily. **Admission** $3-$5 Fri, Sat and during shows. **No credit cards. Map** p316 C3.

Oz is directly opposite the other very popular dance club, the Parade, so the intersection of Bourbon and St Ann is ground zero for gay nightlife in the city. Oz has been rated one of the top dance clubs in the US.

Down under at **Oz**. *See p212.*

The Phoenix & The Eagle

941 Elysian Fields Avenue, at N Rampart Street, Marigny (945 9264/www.phoenixbar.com). Bus 55 Elysian Fields, 88 St Claude. **Open** *Phoenix* 24hrs daily. *The Eagle* 9pm-5am daily. **No credit cards.** **Map** pp306-7 G6.

Home bar for the local leather club. The upstairs bar, the Eagle, until very recently was called the Men's Room, which says it all.

Rawhide 2010

740 Burgundy Street, at St Ann Street, French Quarter (525 8106/www.rawhide2010.com). Bus 3 Vieux Carré, 48 Esplanade. **Open** 24hrs daily. **Admission** varies. **No credit cards. Map** p316 C1.

Levi and leather males flock to Rawhide, which is also home base for a Bear's Club. The guys can get frisky late at night.

VooDoo at Congo Square

718 N Rampart Street at Orleans Street, French Quarter (527 0703). Bus 88 St Claude, 48 Esplanade. **Open** 24hrs daily. **No credit cards. Map** p316 C1.

Attracts a neighbourhood crowd. The mural on the back wall is filled with local jokes.

Wolfendales

834 N Rampart Street, between St Ann & Dumaine Streets, French Quarter (596 2236). Bus 88 St Claude, 48 Esplanade. **Open** 5pm-5am daily. **Admission** $3 Thur-Sun. **No credit cards. Map** p316 C1.

Dancing and drag shows. Popular with African-American men.

Eating out

Unlike other cities with substantial gay communities, New Orleans doesn't have restaurants with an exclusively gay clientele. However, many restaurants have a very definite gay presence, both in staff and diners. Some informal, gay-owned places in the Quarter and the Marigny include the **Clover Grill** (900 Bourbon Street, at Dumaine Street, 523 0904) for burgers and breakfast, and **House of Bagels**

(718 Orleans Street, between Bourbon & Royal Streets, 525 5007) for bagels, sandwiches and salads. There's a fuller menu at **La Peniche** (1940 Dauphine Street, at Touro Street, 943 1460). **Petunias** (817 St Louis Street, between Bourbon & Dauphine Streets, 524 6440) specialises in crêpes.

Accommodation

New Orleans has a thriving cottage industry in gay-friendly guesthouses and B&Bs. While gay visitors will feel comfortable in most of New Orleans's hotels, the places listed here have a special ambience and warmth that gay men and women love to embrace. Most of the gay spots are in the French Quarter and Faubourg Marigny. For special events such as Carnival, Jazz Fest and Southern Decadence, they are booked months in advance. All New Orleans hotels charge extra during these times, so don't feel you're being taken advantage of. The inns listed here are gay owned but welcome everyone, gay and straight.

Bourgoyne Guest House

839 Bourbon Street, at Dumaine Street, French Quarter, New Orleans, LA 70116 (524 3621/525 3983). Bus 3 Vieux Carré, 48 Esplanade. **Rates** $80.50-$170.50. **Credit** MC, V. **Map** p316 C2.

An 1830s townhouse with antiques-filled rooms and a charming courtyard. The location's great, too: smack in the middle of action, surrounded by Bourbon Street bars.

Southern Decadence. *See p212.*

VooDoo at Congo Square. *See p213.*

The Claiborne Mansion

2111 Dauphine Street, between Frenchmen Street &
Elysian Fields Avenue, Marigny, New Orleans, LA
70116 (1-800 449 7327/949 7327/fax 949 0388).
Bus 3 Vieux Carré, 82 Desire. **Rates** $150-$300.
Credit AmEx, MC, V. **Map** pp306-7 G6.
This is quite a posh place where celebrities often
hide out. The Claiborne boasts some luxurious
furnishings, a beautifully landscaped patio and a
swimming pool. Rooms all have TVs, VCRs and
private telephones with voicemail. Breakfast is
included in the price.

Crescent City Guest House

612 Marigny Street, between Chartres & Royal
Streets, Marigny, New Orleans, LA 70117 (944
8722/fax 945 0904/matlynccgh@msn.com). Bus 82
Desire. **Rates** $69-$89. **Credit** AmEx, DC, MC, V.
Map pp306-7 H6.
Daily maid service and continental breakfasts are
provided at this homey B&B a few blocks from all
the action in the French Quarter. Other amenities
include a hot tub, TV with VCR and direct phone
lines with answering machines.

La Dauphine Guest House

2316 Dauphine Street, at Marigny Street, Marigny,
New Orleans, LA 70117 (948 2217/fax 948 3420/
www.ladauphine.com). Bus 3 Desire, 55 Elysian
Fields. **Rates** $65-$110. **Credit** MC, V.
Map pp306-7 H6.
A bargain. Room prices at La Dauphine Guest House
include airport pickup and free use of bicycles. The
minimum stay is three nights. There's no smoking
and no attitude, and it's very popular with straights
who are lucky enough to have discovered this
Marigny gem.

French Quarter Reservation Service

Suite 263, 1000 Bourbon Street, at St Philip Street,
French Quarter. New Orleans, LA 70116 (523 1246/
1-800 523 9091/fax 527 6327/www.neworleansgay.
com). **Credit** AmEx, DC, MC, V. **Map** p316 C2.
A booking service that offers a range of accommodation, from B&Bs to private condos. The minimum
stay is two nights.

Lafitte Guest House

1003 Bourbon Street, at St Philip Street, French
Quarter, New Orleans, LA 70116 (581 2678/1-800
331 7971/fax 581 2677/www.lafitteguesthouse.com).
Bus 3 Vieux Carré. **Rates** $99-$189. **Credit** AmEx,
DC, Disc, MC, V. **Map** p316 C2.
The location is perfect, the decor is elegant and the
price includes continental breakfast, afternoon wine
and snacks.

Macarty Park Guest House

3820 Burgundy Street, at Alvar Street, Bywater,
New Orleans, LA 70117 (943 4994/1-800 521
2790/www.macartypark.com). Bus 82 Desire.
Rates $59-$115. **Credit** AmEx, Disc, MC, V.
In a lovely quiet setting 25 blocks from the French
Quarter, Macarty Park offers a heated pool, private
gym, cable TV and off-street parking. The rates
include breakfast.

Royal Barracks Guest House

717 Barracks Street, between Bourbon & Royal
Streets, New Orleans, LA 70116 (581 2678/1-800
(529 7269/1-888 255 7269/fax 529 7298/phillips@
getus.net). Bus 3 Vieux Carré. **Rates** $75-$140.
Credit AmEx, MC, V. **Map** p316 D2.
In a quiet part of the Quarter, the Royal Barracks
Guest House features a courtyard with hot tub.
Other amenities include cable TV, private phones
and free coffee and juice.

Sports clubs

Club New Orleans

515 Toulouse Street, between Chartres & Royal
Streets, French Quarter (581 2402). Bus 55 Elysian
Fields, 57 Franklin, 82 Desire. **Open** 24hrs daily.
Admission $20 membership (6 months); $7 day
pass. **Credit** MC, V. **Map** p316 B3.
Club New Orleans is a men's bath with full gym, spa
tub, steam room, sauna and sundeck. Lockers cost
$13 and rooms are between $18 and $35, with
reduced rates from Tuesday to Thursday.

The Country Club

634 Louisa Street, between Chartres & Royal Streets,
Bywater (945 0742). Bus 82 Desire. **Open** 9am-1am
daily. **Admission** $150 annual membership; $5 day
pass. **Credit** AmEx, MC, V.
The Country Club is a relaxed, laid-back swimming
club and bar. Reduced bar rates operate daily from
5pm to 9pm, and swimsuits are optional for both
men and women. The club is about 20 blocks from
the French Quarter in Bywater, and has a fitness
room and pool table.

Music

Music is the beating heart of New Orleans. Get jazzed.

Rock, Roots & Jazz

Music clubs

Few cities in the world are as defined by music as New Orleans. It's appropriate, then, that the number of venues for live music here is extensive and the clubs themselves are wonderfully diverse. Like the bands and musicians, whose sound is often hard to pigeon-hole, New Orleans clubs are difficult to classify. Witness the **House of Blues** (*see page 216*), where, despite its name, blues is usually offered only one day of the week. There are a few clubs that stick exclusively to one format. Check local club listings in *Lagniappe, Gambit* or *OffBeat* magazines, or on the Internet at www.nola.com for details of what type of music will be happening on any given night.

Club patrons more accustomed to canned music or DJs may feel out of place in New Orleans. The club scene here is rooted in live performance and, luckily, the number of talented musicians in town keeps each club booked up with top-notch local talent and the occasional touring band on most nights of the week. Only the House of Blues features regular dance club nights, usually later in the evening after live bands have finished their sets.

Cover charges do not often involve a drinks minimum and are usually very reasonable – $15 is considered expensive here – making visiting more than one club in one night not only feasible but sometimes necessary when trying to take in as many good bands as possible. The best time of the year for music clubs is undoubtedly during **Jazz Fest**, with **Mardi Gras, New Year's Eve** and **Hallowe'en** other big times (for details of these events, *see chapter* **By Season**). But whatever the time of year, whatever the day of the week, there'll be a band playing somewhere in town that you will want to see. For space and taste reasons, our list is selective rather than comprehensive; noticeably absent are music venues on Bourbon Street, but these usually book cover bands and are so close to one another that the prerequisite tourist stroll down Bourbon will give you a taste of what's to be heard (or seen). All clubs listed are accessible by streetcar, bus or taxi from anywhere within New Orleans. Don't

Don't miss Music clubs

Café Brasil
Late-night reggae and Latin music spilling on to Frenchmen Street. See page 220.

Howlin' Wolf
Play pool while the rest of the crowd rocks out. See page 221.

House of Blues
Big-name bands, hefty cover charges and late-night DJs. See page 216.

Maple Leaf Bar
Brass, funk, R&B and zydeco: the epitome of the New Orleans music experience. See page 223.

Mermaid Lounge
Secluded gem hosting a range of experimental music. See page 221.

Mid City Lanes Rock 'n' Bowl
Where even Mick Jagger willingly pays cover to hear rockabilly, R&B, blues and the hottest zydeco in town. See page 224.

Snug Harbor
The epicentre of cutting-edge jazz. See page 220.

Tipitina's Uptown
Legendary shrine to Professor Longhair serving up some of the best live music in town. See page 224.

Arts & Entertainment

overlook smaller, out-of-the-way places, as these are the real gems of the local music scene and often provide the most lasting memories of New Orleans as a *sui generis* city for live music.

French Quarter

Crescent City Brewhouse

527 Decatur Street, at St Louis Street (522 0571/ www.crescentcitybrewhouse.com). Bus 55 Elysian Fields, 57 Franklin, 82 Desire, 92 Express. **Open** 11am-midnight (food served until 10pm) Mon-Thur, Sun; 11am-1am (food served until midnight) Fri, Sat. **Admission** free. **Credit** AmEx, DC, Disc, MC, V. **Map** p315 B3.

One of New Orleans's only two brewpubs, Crescent City offers jazz and Latin combos in the early evening and oldies cover bands later, plus a good, moderately priced menu. The bands play on the ground floor at street level, so the best seats are at the front of the main bar. Because of its French Quarter location, the Crescent City Brewhouse draws more tourists than locals, but the good beers always make it well worth an hour's visit.

Donna's Bar & Grill

800 N Rampart Street, at St Ann Street (596 6914). Bus 3 Vieux Carré, 13 Esplanade, 57 Franklin, 82 Desire. **Open** from 8.30pm Mon, Wed-Sun; closed Tue. **Admission** $5. **Credit** MC, V. **Map** p315 C1.

Donna's Bar & Grill is the city's hotspot for brass bands and hosts performances nightly. Located directly across from the entrance to Louis Armstrong Park on the northern boundary of the French Quarter, it draws a predominantly local crowd. You can order food from the bartenders until late and the cover charge is reasonable, but don't forget to tip the band if the hat is passed around. A word of caution: although the lights outside Armstrong Park make it look inviting in the evening, don't be tempted to visit either the park or the surrounding Tremé neighbourhood outside daylight hours – it can be a bit sketchy.

Funky Butt at Congo Square

714 N Rampart Street, at Orleans Avenue (558 0872/www.funkybutt.com). Bus 31 St Claude. **Open** 8pm-3am daily; noon-3am during Jazz Fest & Mardi Gras. **Admission** free-$15. **Credit** AmEx, MC, V. **Map** p315 C1.

A few doors down from Donna's Bar & Grill, the Funky Butt has, in only a few years, come to rival **Snug Harbor** (*see p220*) as the city's top spot for contemporary jazz. Located in a former restaurant with a refurbished art deco interior and named after the home club of early New Orleans jazz legend Buddy Bolden, Funky Butt serves up hot music and Creole cooking in swanky surroundings with a laid-back atmosphere. Cover charges can be high, but the talent here is top-notch and the setting intimate enough to put spectators only a few feet from some of the city's best jazz players. Free spoken-word events are often held upstairs.

House of Blues

225 Decatur Street, at Iberville Street (529 2583/ www.hob.com). Bus 55 Elysian Fields, 57 Franklin, 82 Desire. **Open** *Music hall* 8pm-3am daily. *Shop* 10am-10pm Mon-Thur, Sun; 10am-midnight Fri, Sat. *Restaurant* 11am-midnight Mon-Thur; 11am-midnight Fri, Sat. *Gospel brunch* 9.30am, noon, 2.30pm Sun (phone for reservations). **Admission** $6-$25. **Credit** AmEx, Disc, MC, V. **Map** p315 A3.

Practically a household name in the US, the New Orleans House of Blues was the second in this music club chain (the first was in Cambridge, Massachusetts). HoB has the largest budget of any local music venue and it shows. Big-name national acts play regularly, as do local hotshots like Dr John, the Neville Brothers and the Radiators. Cover charges are high (often $20 or more), and the club's name and location draw a large number of tourists. Still, great acts play here, from gospel for Sunday brunch to alternative rock and everything in between. The room is comfortable, with the best sound system and live engineer in town. HoB has also cashed in on New Orleans's lack of dance clubs, offering DJs on Monday, Thursday, Friday and Saturday nights from 2am till near-dawn.

Jimmy Buffett's Margaritaville Café

1104 Decatur Street, at Ursulines Street (592 2565/ www.margaritaville.com). Bus 55 Elysian Fields, 57 Franklin, 82 Desire. **Open** 11am-midnight Mon-Thur, Sun; 11am-12.30am Fri, Sat. **Admission** free. **Credit** AmEx, DC, MC, V. **Map** p315 C3.

Fruity cocktail fanatic and pop musician Jimmy Buffett opened this New Orleans club to replicate a similar place in his home town of Key West, Florida. Buffett says there can only be two Margaritaville clubs because Key West and New Orleans are the only two cities that have the right atmosphere. The club offers live music seven days and nights a week. Blues and R&B bands start at 2pm in the club's smaller bar room; bigger acts play in the main room later in the evening. This is not a place to find Jimmy Buffett cover bands. He's made a point of drawing on original, local talent. Admission is always free, and tables and cocktail waitresses in the main room accompany the faux Key West decor. The Jimmy Buffett connection, the Margaritaville gift shop and the club's location, next to the French Market, draw a predominantly tourist crowd, but this is a good place for an afternoon break when touring the French Quarter.

Kerry Irish Pub

331 Decatur Street, at Conti Street (527 5954/ www.kerryirishpub.com). Bus 55 Elysian Fields, 57 Franklin, 82 Desire. **Open** 2pm-4am daily. **Admission** free. **Credit** AmEx, Disc, MC, V. **Map** p315 B3.

One of the better places for acoustic folk music, Kerry Irish Pub offers traditional Irish music and also features ex-Alarm frontman Dave Sharp on Sunday nights (often the most popular). Despite the

Shimmering at **Shim Sham**.
See p219.

Bringing live music back to Bourbon Street at **Storyville District**. *See p219.*

bar's location in the French Quarter, it manages to accommodate a regular local crowd as well as tourists, probably because admission is free every night. A small bar at the front leads to small tables and a pool table at the back; the stage is located along the back wall. Paintings and photos of Irish and Irish-American musicians adorn the walls and ceiling. Bartenders expect a one-drink minimum when a band is playing.

O'Flaherty's Irish Channel Pub

514 Toulouse Street, at Decatur Street (529 1317/ www.CelticNationsWorld.com). Bus 55 Elysian Fields, 57 Franklin, 82 Desire. **Open** noon-3am daily. **Admission** *Ballad Room* $3-$5. *Informer Room* free. **Credit** AmEx, Disc, MC, V. **Map** p315 B2.
O'Flaherty's is in the French Quarter not the Irish Channel, but it is the largest and most Irish-influenced Irish bar in New Orleans, and draws a crowd of expats and visitors. A large complex housing three bars, a small courtyard and a gift shop, it offers a wide selection of British, Irish and Scottish beers and stouts, a number of Irish and Scotch whiskies and Irish food. Traditional Irish ballads are performed for dancers at 8pm in the Informer Room, while the larger Ballad Room features Irish bands later in the evening. On crowded weekend nights the Aengus Lounge, above the Ballad Room, is opened for customers or private parties.

Original Tropical Isle

738 Toulouse Street, at Bourbon Street (525 1689/www.tropicalisle.com). Bus 3 Vieux Carré, 41 Canal. **Open** noon-3am daily. **Admission** free. **No credit cards.** **Map** p315 B2.

With two locations in the French Quarter, the Tropical Isle books blues, folk and cover bands nightly. The Caribbean-influenced decor is tacky and the crowd consists of tourists, plus a few students on weekend nights. The bar's signature drink is the bright green Hand Grenade, which it claims is the strongest in the city. It is certainly the most toxic-looking. There are better places in the French Quarter (let alone the rest of the city), but if you're exploring the Quarter at night it's worth a visit.
Branch: Tropical Isle Bourbon, 721 Bourbon Street, at Orleans Avenue, French Quarter (529 4109).

Palm Court Jazz Café

1204 Decatur Street, at Governor Nicholls Street (525 0200). Bus 55 Elysian Fields, 57 Franklin, 82 Desire. **Open** 7-11pm Wed-Sun (music from 8pm); closed Mon, Tue. **Admission** $5. **Credit** AmEx, Disc, MC, V. **Map** p315 D3.
Second only to **Preservation Hall** (*see below*) as the best place for traditional jazz, the Palm Court (unlike the Hall) offers a full menu and bar, with the restaurant opening at 7pm and music beginning at 8pm. You'll find more tourists than locals, but this isn't a cheesy tourist joint, as the live music attests. An adjoining warehouse sells trad jazz recordings.

Preservation Hall

726 St Peter Street, at Bourbon Street (8pm-midnight 523 8939/after hours 522 2841/ www.preservationhall.com). Bus 3 Vieux Carré, 42 Canal. **Open** 8pm-midnight daily. **Admission** $4. **Credit** AmEx, MC, V. **Map** p315 B2.
As old as the traditional jazz that's played here, Preservation Hall serves as a living testament to

turn-of-the-19th-century New Orleans. Bands play two sets (9pm and 11pm), and a queue usually starts forming outside shortly after 8pm, stretching half a block down St Peter Street to Pat O'Brien's. Inside, amenities are kept to a minimum. There is no bar (bring your own booze), air-conditioning, food or toilets and seating is limited, but that doesn't prevent the musicians (some of whom are well over 80 years old) from playing hot sets. Despite the almost exclusively tourist crowd, to miss Preservation Hall on a visit to the French Quarter is to miss a part of New Orleans history.

The Shim Sham Club & Juke Joint

615 Toulouse Street, between Royal &
Chartres Streets (565 5400). Bus 55 Elysian
Fields, 57 Franklin, 82 Desire. **Open** 2pm-6am
daily. **Admission** varies. **Credit** AmEx, MC, V.
Map p315 B2.
One of the few music clubs in the Quarter that largely ignores the tourist market, the Shim Sham is a haven for retro kids of all flavours. Rockabilly, swing, punk and ska are the genres most often featured at the club, but '80s pop bands sometimes make appearances as well. In the early evening and on slower nights, bands set up in front of the bar in the front room, just off Toulouse Street. Bigger acts play on the main stage, in a mid-sized room that formerly housed a cabaret theatre. Burlesque performances and 'Punk and Porno' nights should be avoided if you're easily shocked. Otherwise, don't miss the sporadic visits by the ShimShamettes, who happily confuse the line between parody and burlesque.

Storyville District

125 Bourbon Street, at Iberville Street (410 1000/
www.storyvilledistrict.com). Bus 3 Vieux Carré, 41
Canal. **Open** 5-11pm Mon-Thur, Sun; 5.30-11pm Fri;
5pm-midnight Sat. **Credit** AmEx, DC, Disc, MC, V.
Map p315 A2.
In an effort to bring original live music back to Bourbon Street, a team of local businessmen launched the Storyville District. Quint Davis, co-founder of the New Orleans Jazz & Heritage Festival, is generally considered the man behind the venture, but he wisely focused on the music at the club, while turning restaurant and bar operations over to Redfish Grill operator and restaurateur Ralph Brennan. This ornately decorated club features three music rooms, often hosting multiple bands on the same evening. The larger Jazz Alley features jazz, brass bands and R&B performers to a crowd of about 200, while the more intimate Jazz Parlor – the real gem of the venue – has small cocktail tables surrounding a performance space that blurs the line between musician and spectator. Music is performed most afternoons and evenings, usually for a nominal cover charge.

Tipitina's French Quarter

233 N Peters Street, at Iberville Street (529 1980/
www.tipitinas.com). Bus 55 Elysian Fields, 57
Franklin, 82 Desire. **Open** 11am-3am daily.
Admission $5-$15. **Credit** AmEx, DC, MC, V.
Map p315 A3.
Faced with the House of Blues' near-takeover of the club scene in the late 1990s, Tipitina's responded with admirable, if unexpected, market savvy. The

Tipitina's French Quarter regularly showcases local bands.

Uptown club (*see p224*) continued as before, a new venue, the **Ruins** (*see p226*), was secured for large shows and this branch was opened in the French Quarter. Rather than siphoning off business from the company's Uptown club, the Quarter club has been a solid addition to the city's music scene. Located on a lively stretch of Decatur, within sight of the Mississippi River and about one block from the **House of Blues** (*see p216*), the main music hall occupies one half of the club; a merchandise shop and restaurant the other. The club has committed itself to booking local bands and musicians almost exclusively, while larger, touring bands play at the Uptown and Ruins venues. Showcase nights are hosted by local music luminaries such as Cyril Neville, and on a Sunday night Tipitina's is the only place downtown that regularly features zydeco bands. A bizarre highlight on the club's schedule is Harry Connick Sr, who sings swing and big band hits every Wednesday night. Not only is Harry the father of the more famous Harry Jr, he's also the elected district attorney of New Orleans, a job that in most cities requires a sense of decorum and unimpeachable propriety. But heh, this is New Orleans, so the DA sings in a nightclub; sometimes he's even joined on stage by the coroner, who plays jazz trumpet.

Marigny, Bywater & Tremé

Café Brasil

2100 Chartres Street, at Frenchmen Street (949 0851). Bus 55 Elysian Fields, 82 Desire. **Open** 6pm-2am Mon-Thur, Sun; 6pm-4am Fri, Sat. **Admission** $5. **No credit cards. Map** p315 G6.

Located in the heart of Faubourg Marigny, three blocks from Esplanade Avenue and the edge of the French Quarter, Café Brasil hops on weekend nights with one of the hipper crowds in New Orleans. Friday nights usually feature Latin bands, while funk, rock, jazz and hip hop bands take to the stage throughout the rest of the week. On more popular nights, the crowd often spills out on to Frenchmen Street, creating a block-party atmosphere. There's an adjoining bar for those unwilling to pack into the main room or pay the $5 cover charge. The beer selection is limited and there's no grill, but if you're in the mood to dance to live music you'll be hard pressed to find a better crowd.

Ernie K-Doe's Mother-In-Law Lounge

1500 N Claiborne Avenue, at Columbus Street (947 1078/www.kdoe.com). Bus 29 St Bernard. **Open** 5pm-4am daily. **No credit cards. Map** p307 G6.

In an area short of music clubs, this small room is owned and run by R&B singer Ernie K-Doe, whose song 'Mother-In-Law' was a hit 30 years ago. The bar is usually open, but live performances are more sporadic, and often feature K-Doe himself. In a town filled with eccentrics, K-Doe is in a league of his own, frequently selling boxer shorts emblazoned

with his face and his catchphrase, 'I'm cocky, but I'm good' from the stage. His wife, Antoinette, manages the bar and Ernie. The couple celebrate Mother-in-Law's anniversary and their own by getting married there every January.

Igor's Checkpoint Charlie

501 Esplanade Avenue, at Decatur Street (947 0979). Bus 55 Elysian Fields, 57 Franklin, 82 Desire. **Open** 24hrs daily. **Admission** free. **Credit** AmEx, MC, V. **Map** p315 D3.

Established by Australian expat Igor Margan, Checkpoint is on the edge of the Faubourg Marigny and presents rock, metal and punk bands nightly. As well as pool tables and a grill that serves hamburgers until about 3am, Checkpoint has a coin-operated laundromat behind the stage, although it's rarely used by the unwashed punk crowd. When all the Frenchmen Street clubs are booked with great bands and large crowds, this is a good place to relax with a beer, even if the music itself isn't relaxing. Resort to the grill only as a last hope.

Snug Harbor

626 Frenchmen Street, at Royal Street (949 0696/ www.snugjazz.com). Bus 82 Desire. **Open** 5pm-3am daily. *Shows* 9pm, 11pm daily. **Admission** $5-$25. **Credit** AmEx, MC, V. **Map** p315 D2.

New Orleans's leading jazz club, Snug Harbor offers the city's best contemporary jazz musicians in an intimate setting, seven nights a week. Cover charges can be high, but are well worth it for fans and even jazz novices. This is the way jazz should be seen and heard. It's a sit-down venue, with tables and benches spread across the floor right up to the stage. Crowds are generally quiet, respectful of the musicians and intense listeners. It's not at all uncommon for unscheduled players to join the band on stage, leading to some of the best impromptu jazz jam sessions you'll hear anywhere in the world. Outside the main music room is a bar and an adjoining restaurant.

Sweet Lorraine's

1931 St Claude Avenue, between Touro & Prauger Streets (945 9654). **Open** 4pm-2am daily. **Admission** varies: phone for details. **Credit** AmEx, Disc, MC, V.

Opened in 1999 in the legendary Ninth Ward ('nint' wourd' in New Orleansese), Sweet Lorraine's is New Orleans's newest spot for jazz and R&B. A small bar area opens on to the club's main room, filled with polished metal tables and comfortable chairs. The sound system is small, but adequate given the intimate size of the room and the types of bands that play. The club attracts a genial crowd of hip, professional African-Americans and middle-aged white bohemians from the surrounding Bywater-Marigny neighbourhoods. The audience here is knowledgeable and appreciative of the music and the kitchen is closed during performances. Drinks tend to be a bit pricey, but the cover charge is usually reasonable.

The best Local talent

Blues	**Jazz**
Bryan Lee	Ellis Marsalis,
	Astral Project
Brass	
Rebirth Brass Band	**Klezmer**
	New Orleans
Cajun	Klezmer All Stars
Beausoleil	
	R&B
Eclectic	Snooks Eaglin,
Royal Fingerbowl	Irma Thomas
Acoustic/	**Rock**
Folk	Radiators,
Gina Forsyth	Cowboy Mouth
Funk	**Zydeco**
funky Meters	Boozoo Chavis

Vaughan's Lounge

4229 Dauphine Street, at Lesseps Street (947 5562).
Bus 82 Desire. **Open** 11am-3am daily. **Admission**
free Mon-Wed, Fri-Sun; $10 Thur. **No credit cards.**
Located way down in the Bywater neighbourhood
and best reached by cab or car, Vaughan's is a small
bar that became a local music lover's haven when it
started booking trumpeter Kermit Ruffins and his
Barbeque Swingers (on Thursday nights). At first,
there was no cover charge, and free red beans and
rice was served at setbreak. Now, with $10 admis-
sion, the place still jumps on Thursday nights,
packed to the street with a decidedly local crowd.
Even such lofty jazz players as Wynton Marsalis
have been known to drop by and play with Kermit
at these intimate sets.

CBD

Le Chat Noir

715 St Charles Avenue, between Girod & Julia
Streets (581 5812). St Charles Streetcar. **Open** 4pm-
2am Tue-Sat; closed Mon, Sun. **Admission** varies.
Credit AmEx, MC. **Map** p309 B2.
This elegant, classy venue on St Charles Avenue is
filling a niche for a crowd too old to hang out at
music clubs until the wee hours of the morning and
too young or too easily bored to spend night after
dreary night at home. One of only two locations that
features regular cabaret shows, Le Chat Noir's bar
is cleanly decorated in black and white, and looks
out on to St Charles. The performance room is small
but not crowded, with cocktail tables around a stage
and small dancefloor. In addition to cabaret shows,
Le Chat Noir also hosts local theatre productions
and the occasional jazz performance. Earlier in the
evening the bar offers a happy hour special that

draws a professional crowd from the CBD offices.
There's an impressive selection of wines by the
glass and some top-shelf liquor, but the beer selection is somewhat limited.

Michaul's Live Cajun Music Restaurant

840 St Charles Avenue, at Julia Street (522 5517/
www.Michauls.com). St Charles Streetcar. **Open** 5-
10pm Mon-Fri; 6-11pm Sat; closed Sun. **Admission**
free. **Credit** AmEx, DC, Disc, MC, V. **Map** p309 B2.
A popular misconception is that New Orleans is
full of Cajun culture and music. In fact, most
Cajuns live in areas of Louisiana south and west
of the city, so it's left to the likes of Michaul's to
cater for tourists looking for Cajun food and music
in New Orleans itself. The restaurant's attempt to
recreate authentic Cajun surroundings – wood
rafters, stuffed and mounted animals and swamp
decor – is as transparent as its plate glass windows and, although Cajun bands play nightly to
an underused dancefloor, the patrons are mainly
here for the dinner.

Warehouse District

Howlin' Wolf

828 S Peters Street, at Julia Street (522 9653/
www.howlin-wolf.com). Bus 3 Vieux Carré,
10 Tchoupitoulas. **Open** from 3pm Mon-Sat; closed
Sun. **Admission** $5-$15. **Credit** AmEx, Disc, MC, V.
Map p309 C2.
Voted 'Favorite Music Club' in a New Orleans
music magazine poll for the last five years, Howlin'
Wolf's success comes from satisfying as many different audiences as possible. That kind of eclecticism
usually spells disaster for a music club, but the
Wolf's hospitable policy means that you'll see
Rickie Lee Jones there one week and an emerging
alternative rock group from East Jesus the next.
The club has an excellent sound system, a pool
table at the back and an impressive (for a music
club) selection of beer. On Monday night, there's an
acoustic open-mike session; on Tuesdays the live
music is replaced by CDs.

Mermaid Lounge

1100 Constance Street, at John Churchill Chase
Street (524 4747/www.mermaidlounge.com). Bus 10
Tchoupitoulas, 11 Magazine. **Open** 9pm-3am Tue-
Sat; closed Mon, Sun. **Admission** $2-$7. **No credit**
cards. Map p309 C2.
Perhaps the most out-of-the-way club in New
Orleans, this hole-in-the-wall is a haven for twen-
ty- and thirtysomething hipsters. There is no real
stage, so bands play in one corner of the L-shaped
club. Expect mostly experimental jazz and funk,
with occasional appearances by rockabilly and
klezmer bands. Bar service is sometimes painfully
slow, but at least the mermaid decor provides some
distraction while you're waiting. There's a small
art gallery in an adjoining room and a sculpture
garden on the lawn.

Arts & Entertainment

Mulate's Cajun Restaurant

743 Convention Center Boulevard, between Howard Avenue & Poydras Street (529 1400/www.mulates. com). Bus 3 Vieux Carré, 33 Tchoupitoulas. **Open** 11am-11pm daily. **Admission** free. **Credit** AmEx, DC, Disc, MC, V. **Map** p309 C2.

Like Michaul's (*see p221*), Mulate's caters to an almost exclusively tourist crowd intrigued by Cajun cuisine and music. The place feels more authentic than Michaul's, though, and usually has higher-calibre Cajun bands, good enough to keep the small dancefloor relatively busy. (Dance instructors are on hand to help out the novices.) There's no cover charge for music, but both restaurant and bar prices are pretty high. A large souvenir shop makes it easy for tourists to take a bit of Mulate's home with them, but this doesn't alter the fact that this is a highly sanitised version of genuine Cajun culture.

Vic's Kangaroo Café

636 Tchoupitoulas Street, at Girod Street (524 4329). Bus 3 Vieux Carré, 33 Tchoupitoulas. **Open** 11.30am-4am daily. **Admission** free. **Credit** AmEx, DC, Disc, MC, V. **Map** p309 C1.

Founded by an Australian expat in 1992, Vic's has managed to escape much of the ultra-hipness of the Warehouse District. This is probably attributable to the club's insistence that only local blues bands are allowed to grace the small corner stage. Bands play on Thursday, Friday and Saturday nights to a mix of local blues fans and occasional conventioneers en route to their hotels. There are some 15 beers on tap, though this may be a few too many given their sometimes poor quality. There are also a few dozen bottled beers, a small grill menu, Australian-theme decor and comfortable chairs and benches in the main room. You can play pool and darts in the upstairs room.

Garden District

Pontchartrain Hotel

2031 St Charles Avenue, at Andrews Street (524 0581/www.thepontchartrainhotel.com). St Charles Streetcar. **Open** 3pm-2am daily. **Admission** free. **Credit** AmEx, Disc, MC, V. **Map** p309 B3.

One of the few true piano bars in New Orleans, the Pontchartrain bar is in the lobby of the hotel, looking out on to St Charles. There is no cover and the bar is a comfortable, intimate and warm space, usually occupied by hotel guests and fans of the piano players. Music is offered early in the evening (starting at 5pm) from Tuesday to Saturday, but the best times to visit are weekend nights when Philip Melancon performs his witty songs about New Orleans characters and celebrities. Drinks are a little pricey but reasonable given the lack of cover charge. Don't forget to tip the piano player, and don't be surprised if you find yourself a character in one of Melancon's songs.

Red Room

2040 St Charles Avenue, at Josephine Street (528 9759). St Charles Streetcar. **Open** 5pm-2am Mon-Sat. **Admission** free. **Credit** AmEx, DC, MC, V. **Map** p309 B3.

The Red Room opened during the '90s revival of '20s- and '30s-style swing clubs, catering to an older crowd waxing nostalgic for times past and a younger crowd looking for something new. The room is decorated in red throughout: red carpet, red chairs, red velvet curtains and red jackets on the waiters. Jazz bands play swing and big band ballads and standards, and the small dancefloor is usually packed with dancing couples. A full menu makes for a dinner club atmosphere, with tables on the main floor, but the bars on either side do good business, too. Prices are high, the crowd is ultra-trendy and the feel is more Los Angeles than New Orleans, but thanks to the supply of great musicians in the city, at least the music is good – even if most of the audience aren't giving it their full attention.

Uptown

Le Bon Temps Roule

4801 Magazine Street, at Bordeaux Street (895 8117/www.lebontempsroule.com). Bus 11 Magazine. **Open** 11am-3am daily. **Admission** free. **Credit** AmEx, Disc, MC, V. **Map** p306 C10.

In the back of the popular Uptown bar (*see p159*) a small stage area presents local jazz, rock and blues bands a few nights a week, usually with no cover. The bar also has one of the better late-night grills in town and, if the music doesn't move you or you need a diversion during setbreak, there are pool tables in the front room. On crowded nights (usually only during Mardi Gras and Jazz Fest), it gets pretty hot and sticky, so don't dress up if this is your destination.

Carrollton Station Bar & Music Club

8140 Willow Street, at Dublin Street (865 9190). St Charles Streetcar. **Open** 3pm-3am daily. **Admission** $5-$8 Fri, Sat. **Credit** AmEx, MC, V. **Map** p306 B7.

Boasting one of the better beer selections of the town's music clubs, Carrollton Station is a relaxed, small room that hosts rock, funk, folk and fusion bands from Thursdays to Sundays. When there are no performances, it's a good place to play darts. Located far Uptown, it's across the street from Jimmy's Music Club and only blocks from the Maple Leaf (*for both, see p223*), so it's perfect for club-hopping. The clientele is usually oldish, and the few tables and benches in front of the stage fill up quickly. With some gentle prodding, the bartenders will tell you about the bar's multiple addresses. Four permanently closed doors attest to the time when illegal numbers games were held here. When one address was shut down, another door would be cut out in the same building under a new address. For more Station mythology, ask about the now-defunct 'Chicken Drop'.

Jimmy's Music Club

8200 Willow Street, at Dublin Street (861 8200). St Charles Streetcar. **Open** 8pm-3am Tue-Sat; closed Mon, Sun. **Admission** up to $20. **Credit** AmEx, Disc, MC, V. **Map** p306 C10.

Now in its 22nd year, Jimmy's is the longest continuously operating music club in New Orleans. The speakers have been pushed a little beyond their years, but the layout is one of the best, with a raised area in front of the bar overlooking the large dancefloor. Expect every type of music, from Latin dance nights to hip hop and even the occasional surprise Nine Inch Nails show (lead singer Trent Reznor lives and has a studio in New Orleans). Crowds and cover charges vary from non-existent and free to jam-packed and expensive. Jimmy's has also become the somewhat unlikely headquarters of the local roots reggae scene, with the New Orleans Reggae Coalition hosting monthly shows at the club.

Maple Leaf Bar

8316 Oak Street, at Dante Street (866 9359). St Charles Streetcar. **Open** 3pm-4am daily. **Admission** $5-$16. **No credit cards**. **Map** p306 A7.

The New Orleans music magazine *OffBeat* once claimed that 'no musical tour of New Orleans would be complete without a stop at the Maple Leaf', and it's true. Inside, there are red-painted, pressed tin walls and a long, narrow dancefloor,

running back to a rear bar, chess and pool tables and an outdoor patio. The place jumps when the city's top brass, funk, R&B and zydeco bands play. Located in Carrollton near Tulane and Loyola Universities, the Maple Leaf draws a perfect black and white mix of college students and older music fans. If there was ever an example of cultural harmony through mutual appreciation of music, this is it. Tuesday nights, when the ReBirth Brass Band plays, are magical and not to be missed. Admission averages $6, but never tops $16. *See chapter* **Performing Arts** for details of the spoken-word events held here on Sundays.

Neutral Ground Coffeehouse

5110 Danneel Street, at Soniat Street (891 3381/ www.acadiacom.net/ngch). St Charles Streetcar. **Open** 8pm-midnight Tue-Thur, Sun; 8pm-1am Fri, Sat; closed Mon. **Admission** free. **No credit cards**. **Map** p306 C9.

Not far from the Tulane and Loyola University campuses, the Neutral Ground is the top spot for acoustic folk, drawing younger kids (who can't get into most bars) and a number of ageing folkies. You can play chess and backgammon when bands aren't playing, but on most nights there are performances by three separate acts, usually local acoustic musicians and performance poets. However, when nationally known folk acts come through town, the Neutral Ground is their most likely choice of venue.

Comparing notes outside **Live Bait**. *See p224.*

Tipitina's Uptown

501 Napoleon Avenue, at Tchoupitoulas Street (895 8477/www.tipitinas.com). Bus 26 Napoleon, 33 Tchoupitoulas. **Open** 5pm-3am daily. **Admission** $5-$12. **Credit** AmEx, DC, MC, V. **Map** p306 D10.

Prior to the opening of the House of Blues in 1995 (*see p216*), Tipitina's was the premier club for both local greats and nationally touring bands. It still offers some of the best live music in the city. Established as a shrine to New Orleans pianist and music legend Professor Longhair (Henry Roeland Byrd) and bearing the name of one of his songs, the club has a bust of the 'Fess' inside the front door and a banner with his picture over the stage. Recent additions to this legendary venue (including a fantastic new PA system and air-conditioning) make it a must on any music lover's itinerary. Everyone from local brass bands to international reggae stars is welcome at Tip's. A large balcony overlooks the stage and dancefloor, and on Sundays there is usually a Cajun Fais Do-Do dance. For details of the other **Tipitina** venues, *see p219 and p226*.

Mid City

Mid City Lanes Rock 'n' Bowl

4133 S Carrollton Avenue, at Tulane Avenue (482 3133/www.rockandbowl.com). Bus 34 Carrollton Express, 39 Tulane. **Open** noon-2am daily. **Admission** $5; $10 special events. **Credit** AmEx, DC, MC, V. **Map** p306 D5.

If Checkpoint Charlie's (*see p220*) distinguishes itself as the only music club in town with a laundromat, the Rock 'n' Bowl ups the ante as the only club in town with a full bowling alley – ten lanes' worth. Located somewhat out of the way (take a cab along Tulane Avenue from downtown) in a strip mall, this is a hidden gem that such rock luminaries as Mick Jagger have sought out. As well as the hottest zydeco night in town (Thursdays), Rock 'n' Bowl offers rockabilly, R&B and blues bands on most nights of the week. The club has expanded on to the floor below the bowling alley, so for one cover charge (usually $5), you can go back and forth between two stages and catch as many as six bands in one night. If you're in town for Jazz Fest (*see p192* **New Orleans Jazz and Heritage Festival**), don't miss the Zydeco Showdown (usually on both Sunday nights of the festival), when Louisiana's hottest zydeco bands vie for the crown of King of Zydeco.

Sandbar

The Cove, University of New Orleans, off Elysian Fields (835 5277). Bus 55 Elysian Fields, 56 Elysian Fields Express, 60 Hayne. **Open** Sept-Dec, Feb-May 8-11pm Wed only. *Jan, June-Aug* closed. **Admission** $5. **No credit cards.**

The University of New Orleans has one of the best jazz studies courses in the world (directed by Ellis Marsalis, the patriarch of the famous Marsalis family), so it should come as no surprise that on Wednesday nights its Sandbar club offers some of the hottest young performers in contemporary jazz, most of whom are students at the school. The college bar ambience is nothing special, but the music is stellar, making the club worth the trek. The best way to find the bar is to get to the UNO campus, look on a campus map for the student centre and then ask. Note that performances are only held during term time.

Further afield

Live Bait Bar & Grill

501 River Road, between Iris Street & Industrial Avenue, Jefferson Parish (831 3070/www.livebait barandgrill.com). No public transport. **Open** 4pm-3am Mon-Fri; noon-3am Sat; closed Sun. **Credit** AmEx, MC, V.

Featuring live local bands most weekend nights, the Live Bait is a large warehouse space across from the Mississippi River levee in Jefferson Parish. On warm and pleasant evenings, the large doors behind the stage are opened on to River Road, providing an unusual backdrop for bands. The back of the performance space opens on to a large patio with tables, chairs and an open-air barbecue pit. The club's relatively long distance from the downtown tourist areas makes it a largely local hangout that draws a more middle-aged crowd than many Uptown establishments. Recent Monday night jam sessions have been a big hit, with members of various local bands showing up for impromptu sets.

Old Point Bar

545 Patterson Street, at Olivier Street, Algiers (364 0950/www.oldpointbar.com). Bus 101 Algiers Loop. **Open** 11am-3am daily. **Credit** AmEx, Disc, MC, V.

This beautifully restored bar and music club lies across the river from downtown New Orleans, keeping it free from those locals and tourists who are only casually interested in local music. Those who do make the short drive or ferry ride to the Old Point are rewarded with intimate sets by local jazz, funk and brass bands. The performance area is at floor level, and patrons are welcome to stand in front of or to one side of the performers. An abundance of wood panelling gives the room warm acoustics, and the bar is well stocked with various imported beers and microbrews.

Larger venues

Tickets for these venues can also be purchased through **Ticketmaster** (522 5555/www.ticket master.com).

Contemporary Arts Center

900 Camp Street, between Howard Avenue & St Joseph Street, Warehouse District (information 523 1216/box office 528 3800/www.cacno.org). **Open** *Box office* noon-5pm Tue; noon-6pm Wed-Sat; closed Mon, Sun. **Tickets** vary. **Credit** AmEx, MC, V. **Map** p309 C2.

Tap while you type. Background music is live at the **Contemporary Arts Center.** *See p224.*

Used as a music venue mainly during Mardi Gras and Jazz Fest, the warehouse space adjoining the Contemporary Arts Center is a hotspot for big-name jazz, funk and rock bands. Amenities are limited to what the production company sets up for each show, but usually include a few full-service bars, food from local caterers and portable toilets in the parking lot. The shows are seasonal, so the crowds are often determined by the event: college-aged revellers for the Mardi Gras funk shows and serious music lovers of all ages and backgrounds for the Jazz Fest concerts.

Louisiana Superdome

Sugar Bowl Drive, at Poydras Street, CBD (box office 587 3800/tour information 587 3808/ www.superdome.com). Bus 16 S Claiborne. **Open** *Box office 9am-4.30pm Mon-Fri; open at weekends for special events.* **Tickets** vary. **Credit** MC, V. **Map** p309 A/B1.

With seating capacity close to 80,000, this is one of the largest venues in the country, hosting only the biggest international rock stars, such as the Rolling Stones and U2. With its covered ceiling and giant size, the cavernous dome can make for some of the worst-sounding shows in the city, but the staging is typically brilliant, and fans of stadium rock rarely complain.

New Orleans Arena

Poydras Street, at the Louisiana Superdome, CBD (tickets 587 3800/24hr information 846 5959/ www.neworleansarena.com). Bus 16 S Claiborne. **Open** *Box office 9am-4.30pm Mon-Fri and 2hrs before performances.* **Tickets** vary. **Credit** AmEx, MC, V. **Map** p309 B1.

Adjacent to the immense Superdome and second to it in size, this brand new arena is home to New Orleans's hockey team, local college basketball teams, and is vying to replace the Lakefront Arena as the city's top spot for large concerts. The arena was rather hastily finished and the lack of polish is obvious to anyone who focuses their attention on the structure rather than the stage. But with the likes of Bruce Springsteen, Britney Spears, Kiss and Nine Inch Nails gracing the stage within a short time span, it's unlikely any fan will pay much attention to their surroundings. The sound, like that in the Superdome, can sound cavernous and muffled in the hands of a less-than-competent engineer, so hope for the best from the crew as well as the band if arena shows are your thing.

Saenger Theatre

143 North Rampart Street, at Canal Street, French Quarter (524 2490/www.saengertheatre.com). Bus 41 Canal. **Open** *Box office 10am-5pm Mon-Fri.* **Tickets** vary. **Credit** AmEx, MC, V. **Map** p316 A1.

Located almost directly across Canal Street from the State Palace Theatre (*see p226*), the Saenger is a more refined, classier version of its neighbour. However, while more genteel performances are regularly staged here, the Saenger also hosts rock, jazz and funk bands that are too popular for area clubs, but not big enough for the arenas and stadiums. Whatever the performance, this exquisitely restored old theatre is almost worth a visit for its ornate decor alone. *See also chapter* **Performing Arts**.

State Palace Theatre
1108 Canal Street, at N Rampart Street, French Quarter (522 4435/www.statepalace.com). Bus 41 Canal. **Tickets** *$5-$8.* **Credit** *AmEx, MC, V.* **Map** *p316 A1.*
This beautifully ornate old theatre reinvented itself as a mid-sized music venue for concerts by nationally touring rock and rap artists. The State Palace seats about 4,000 in four areas: in the orchestra pit in front of the stage, on the main floor and on two balconies. In the past, the theatre has come under fire from local high-school parent groups for hosting large rave parties, but more recently has emerged as the premier venue for multi-band ska and punk tours making stops in New Orleans.

Tipitina's Ruins
1020 S Peters Street, at Howard Avenue, Warehouse District (527 5700/www.tipitinas.com). Bus 3 Vieux Carré, 10 Tchoupitoulas. **Tickets** *vary.* **Credit** *AmEx, DC, MC, V.* **Map** *p309 C2.*
This large, open warehouse space is used by Tipitina's for big-name shows, primarily during Mardi Gras, Jazz Fest and New Year festivities. While amenities leave something to be desired, this is not a regular hangout but instead a place to see a favourite band. Fortunately, the venue is undergoing renovations to enhance sound quality, increase the number of bars and improve the bathroom facilities. Unfortunately, it may end up being used for private events only.

UNO Lakefront Arena
6801 Franklin Avenue, at Leon C Simon Drive, Gentilly (280 7171/http://arena.uno.edu). Bus 14 Franklin, 17 Hayne, 92 Express. **Open** *Box office 10am-6pm Mon-Fri; closed Sat, Sun.* **Tickets** *$15-$65.* **Credit** *MC, V.*
The original New Orleans home of arena rock, Senator Nat G Kiefer University of New Orleans Lakefront Arena (to give it its full name) is like most sports arena/music venues. Lots of cement can make the sound ear-piercingly bright and, with a capacity of over 6,000, it's anything but intimate. But if arena rock is your thing and you'd rather stand in front of an uncomfortable plastic bleacher chair than pack into a club, that's what you'll find here.

Classical & Opera

Performance groups

For details of classical music venues, *see* chapter **Performing Arts**.

Louisiana Philharmonic Orchestra
523 6530/fax 595 8468/www.gnofn.org/lpo.
In the early 1990s the musicians of the New Orleans Symphony rebelled against their own board of directors – composed primarily of local business leaders – over pay and budget structures. The board refused to back down, so, after an extraordinary and public battle of wills, the Symphony disbanded. Within a few months, however, the players reformed, and the Louisiana Philharmonic Orchestra was born. Musician-owned and musician-run, the orchestra struggled financially for several years, but has now become economically sound and rates well compared to similar small city orchestras. Programming is rather conservative, but regular visits by international artists such as Pinchas Zukerman liven things up a bit. The orchestra usually performs at the Orpheum Theatre (*see chapter* **Performing Arts**), but be sure also to check out the free outdoor concerts in City Park, Audubon Park and other venues. Take a picnic, a blanket and enjoy one of the locals' favourite free shows.

New Orleans Musica da Camera
865 8203/www.gnofn.org/~musica.
Concentrating on early music performed on original instruments, this group provides an unusual and beautiful alternative to the city's other classical offerings. Musica da Camera plays in churches and halls throughout the region; for concert dates and venues, check local listings or phone the number above.

New Orleans Opera
information 529 2278/tickets 529 3000/fax 529 7668/www.neworleansopera.org.
Opera and New Orleans go way back. The city was first home to an opera company in the early 1800s, and by the 1890s, the genre had become so popular that a glorious French Opera House was built. Tragically, the building burned to the ground in 1919, effectively ending local opera production until the 1940s, when the Opera Association was formed. It's a testament to the city's love of opera that in these days of astronomical costs and shrinking audiences, the association continues to stage full-scale productions. Performances take place at the Mahalia Jackson Theater of the Performing Arts (*see chapter* **Performing Arts**). Emerging and fading opera stars are usually cast in leading roles and the programming tends to be predictable, although a new administration is attempting to gently lead the audience into more adventurous fare. A new operatic version of *A Streetcar Named Desire* was produced in New Orleans the year after its 1998 world première.

Newcomb College
865 5267/www.tulane.edu/music.
A division of Tulane, Newcomb College stages regular, high quality performances by students, faculty and guest professionals on the Tulane and Newcomb campuses. The Music at Midday programme is a series of classical music concerts performed weekly at noon throughout the school year. The college also has an annual Concert Piano Series and a Classical Guitar Series, which run between August and May, along with a long list of performances by visiting classical players. Check local newspapers for listings, or phone for more information.

The sound system

New Orleans has been a crucible for new musical forms from African chants to jazz to rock and back again.

New Orleans's remarkable musical heritage is drawn from two sources: African call-and-response forms and European classical music and instrumentation. Perhaps nowhere in the history of all art forms has there been such a dramatic convergence of disparate technique and structure resulting in a new art. In the case of New Orleans, that art is jazz.

African-American musical forms, heard only in the fields and black churches, began to edge into the mainstream in the 19th century, as musicians started to perform in the city's numerous brothels and saloons. With a steady influx of sailors through the bustling port, brothels, bars and music halls did a roaring trade. One historian estimates Storyville (the 17-block legal prostitution district) alone employed at least 50 musicians a day. The hot-house environment of competing and co-operating musicians contributed to the rapid development of jazz. When Storyville was closed down by the US War Department in 1917 as a 'danger' to World War I soldiers and sailors, the musicians moved north and took jazz with them.

The elements that conspired in the development of jazz continue to this day. New Orleans combines a rich, diverse community of musicians with an avid audience that is open to a variety of traditional and evolving music. However, far from being stuck in its musical history, New Orleans succeeds in honouring that illustrious past while simultaneously pushing back the genre boundaries, and sometimes changing them completely. On any given night, music fans can go to a club and hear the familiar strains of Dixieland jazz, Delta blues, '50s R&B, Cajun music and zydeco.

And rock in New Orleans is alive and kicking, too. Take the Radiators, for example, stalwart road warriors for more than 20 years and emblematic of the city's rock scene. They draw big crowds during their near-constant tours but their strong connections to home mean they also perform regularly in New

Orleans clubs. Or the Meters, an influential funk band of the late '60s that still performs in various combinations as the funky Meters. Newer developments include a crop of modern rockers such as Better Than Ezra, Galactic and Cowboy Mouth, all of which have made it to the *Billboard* music charts. The steady influx of new college students at Tulane, Loyola, UNO, Xavier and Dillard ensures new music groups with different influences develop every year.

The local musicians with the biggest impact, however, are rappers and producers. New Orleans native Master P has moved from performing to producing and now guides young talent into the professional ranks. His No Limit label has propelled him into rap's top flight and made him enormously rich in the process: in 1999 he was listed as the US's tenth richest entertainer, with an income of $56 million. That's quite a leap from a childhood spent on the BW Cooper public housing project. Cash Money records is another New Orleans rap success story, churning out multi-platinum sales with home-grown performers like Juvenile and Lil' Wayne. The 'South Coast' sound, developed in New Orleans, Atlanta and Houston, is currently the biggest in hip hop.

Happily, New Orleans is more than just a hit-producing town. The local music community is a tight network populated by talented players, many of whom have moved here specifically to be a part of the unique music culture. It's not uncommon to see one musician playing in numerous bands, sometimes ranging in styles from avant-garde jazz, to klezmer, to '50s Cuban music. The New Orleans sound is unmistakeable, but the constant influx of musicians adds textures and flavours to that sound and creates a diverse musical landscape. Music is everywhere in New Orleans from churches to clubs to parades to street corners. The variety, depth and pure joy of the music here mean that New Orleans music isn't a museum piece, it's a story that is evolving every day. Be a part of it.

The Performing Arts

Take a break from the mayhem of the music scene and enjoy the small scale and informality of New Orleans's other performing arts.

The very name 'New Orleans' means music to almost everyone in the world. Certainly most visitors to the city come with the expectation of having a first-class music experience while here. But the performing arts in New Orleans encompass more than music, with interesting theatre, a lively spoken word scene and a variety of dance shows on offer. If one approaches the local performing arts scene with the clear understanding that it is a junior partner to the city's vibrant music scene, there are many pleasures to be had.

Theatre

New Orleans's theatre scene is small and dominated by popular community theatre troupes that offer tried and tested plays and musicals. The touring Broadway shows also tend to be unexceptional, with musical revivals a clear favourite.

Contemporary Arts Center

900 Camp Street, at Howard Avenue, Warehouse District (528 3800/www.cacno.org). St Charles Streetcar. **Tickets** prices vary; phone for details. **Credit** AmEx, MC, V. **Map** p309 C2.
Inside a converted warehouse, the CAC forms the heart of the city's alternative theatre. The ambience is warehouse chic; the building's historic exterior belies its thoroughly modern facilities. Often the CAC is the host rather than the producer of theatre productions. Major events to watch for are the annual New Orleans Black Theatre Festival, usually held in November, and the funky DramaRama festival in January or February. *See also p91.*

Jefferson Performing Arts Center

400 Phlox Street, between W Metairie Avenue & Highway 61, Metairie (885 2000/www.jpas.com). Bus 38 Airline. **Tickets** prices vary; phone for details. **Credit** AmEx, MC, V.
Located in New Orleans's nearest suburb, this venue is home to the Jefferson Performing Arts Society, which programmes a combination of noteworthy travelling productions and its own events. Light opera, musicals, choral groups and ethnic dance are the staples of the schedule. The emphasis is on mainstream performing arts that appeal to a family audience.

Loyola University

Marquette Theatre & Lower Depths Theatre, 6363 St Charles Avenue, at Calhoun Street, Uptown *(box office 865 3824/Department of Drama & Speech 865 3840/www.loyno.edu). St Charles Streetcar.* **Tickets** prices vary; phone for details. **No credit cards. Map** pp306-7 B/C8.
While it stages fewer offerings than Tulane University (*see p229*), Loyola has a vigorous theatre department. The productions at these two theatres are often New Orleanians' best chance to see work by popular playwrights such as Wendy Wasserstein and Tom Stoppard.

Mahalia Jackson Theater of the Performing Arts

Armstrong Park, 801 N Rampart Street, at St Ann Street, Tremé (565 7470). Bus 88 St Claude. **Tickets** prices vary; phone for details. **Credit** MC, V. **Map** p316 C1.
In recent years this theatre has become a valuable alternative to the Saenger (*see p229*), particularly in its staging of innovative local and national ballet and opera productions. It's located in Armstrong Park, adjacent to the Municipal Auditorium and just outside the French Quarter.

North Star Theater

347 Gerard Street, Mandeville (626 1500). Pontchartrain Causeway, then US 190. **Tickets** prices vary; phone for details. **No credit cards.**
Located across Lake Pontchartrain in Mandeville (*see p241*), this little theatre is a major element in the North Shore's cultural life. It offers dinner theatre fare, stylishly presented.

Orpheum Theatre

129 University Place, at Common Street, CBD (524 3285). Bus 3 Vieux Carré, 41 Canal. **Tickets** prices vary; phone for details. **Credit** MC, V. **Map** p316 A1.
This lovely Gothic building, with its grand old lobby, is the home of the Louisiana Philharmonic Orchestra (*see p226*). The building is beginning to crack around the edges and could use a refurb, but the acoustics are good, and the theatre is the perfect environment for any classical performance.

Le Petit Théâtre du Vieux Carré

616 St Peter Street, at Chartres Street & Jackson Square, French Quarter (522 2081). Bus 3 Vieux Carré, 55 Elysian Fields, 57 Franklin, 82 Desire. **Tickets** prices vary; phone for details. **Credit** AmEx, MC, V. **Map** p316 B2.
One of the oldest non-professional theatres in the country, Le Petit defined theatre in New Orleans for decades. In the last few years Le Petit has gone through a renewal, seeking to revitalise itself with

productions of big-ticket musicals such as *City of Angels* and *Grand Hotel*. It sometimes hosts other companies' productions.

Saenger Theatre

143 N Rampart Street, at Canal Street, French Quarter (524 2490/www.saengertheatre.com). Bus 41 Canal. **Tickets** *prices vary; phone for details.* **Credit** AmEx, MC, V. **Map** p316 A1.

First opened in 1927 as a movie palace, the Saenger was considered world class in its time. Even today the building is a beautiful structure, lush with remarkable details. The ceiling in the auditorium is designed to resemble a night sky, with clouds passing twinkling stars. The decor is mostly inspired by Renaissance Florence, with Greek and Roman sculpture, marble statues and cut-glass chandeliers thrown in for good measure. The theatre is generally used for touring Broadway shows and mid-sized, not-too-raucous rock concerts. *See also p225.*

Southern Repertory Theater

3rd Floor, Canal Place Shopping Center, 333 Canal Street, at N Peters Street, French Quarter (861 8163/ www.southernrep.com). Bus 41 Canal, 55 Elysian Fields, 57 Franklin, 82 Desire. **Tickets** *$8-$17.* **Credit** MC, V. **Map** p316 A3.

Southern Rep showcases the works of Southern talent – both playwrights and actors – in a theatre that is intimate and modern. The theatre space is located on the third floor of the ritzy Canal Place Shopping Center, a brilliant move for a theatre when you think about it, as it's centrally located and has plenty of parking. The theatre produces work from young writers in its sporadic New Playwrights series and is the home of New Orleans playwright Rosary O'Neill, who shows new work every season.

Summer Stages

Performances at First Unitarian Universalist Church, 2903 Jefferson Avenue, at S Claiborne Avenue, Uptown (598 3800/Summer Stages office 833 8748). Bus 16 S Claiborne. **Tickets** *$8.* **No credit cards.** **Map** pp306-7 B8.

This group puts on regular performances between June and August. Recently, Summer Stages has offered creative performances of Shakespeare at brilliantly chosen locations in City Park. Past plays have included *Julius Caesar* performed at the Romanesque Peristyle structure, its huge columns providing the perfect backdrop to the drama.

Tulane University

6823 St Charles Avenue, at Audubon Boulevard, Uptown (Dixon Hall 865 5267/McAlister Auditorium 865 5196/www.tulane.edu). St Charles Streetcar/

Le Petit Théâtre: one of the oldest non-professional theatres in the US. *See p228.*

15 Freret, 22 Broadway bus. **Tickets** prices vary; phone for details. **No credit cards. Map** pp306-7 B8. Tulane has a lively schedule of performance events, both university-generated and from touring companies. Unfortunately, none of the events is very well publicised unless you're on campus. During the spring and summer the Tulane Shakespeare Festival presents three Shakespeare plays in repertory, with an excellent professional cast supplemented by the theatre's interns. Tulane is also home to the Summer Lyric Theatre (865 5269/865 5271), which produces plays throughout the summer months.

Zeitgeist Alternative Arts Center

1724 Oretha Castle Haley Boulevard, between Polymnia & Euterpe Streets, Central City (525 2767/www.barristersgallery.citysearch.com). **Tickets** prices vary; phone for details. **No credit cards. Map** p309 B2.

Zeitgeist is an ambitious arts centre that has led a precarious existence. It's had four venues since 1993 but founder Rene Broussard always seems to find a way to keep this theatre-film-art centre going. Invariably worth a visit. *See also p201.*

Dance

Newcomb Dance Program

Newcomb College of Tulane University, Audubon Boulevard, at Freret Street, Uptown (862 8000, ext 1742/www.tulane.edu/~jazz). St Charles Streetcar/15 Freret bus. **Tickets** prices vary; phone for details. **No credit cards. Map** pp306-7 B8.

Until it merged with Tulane University in the 1970s, Newcomb was a separate college for women. It maintains its long tradition of dance with a dynamic department that offers several public performances during the school year. Newcomb Dance runs a comprehensive summer conference/workshop on jazz dance that draws scholars, choreographers and garden-variety dance lovers. It's held every June.

New Orleans Ballet Association

Suite 700, 305 Baronne Street, at Gravier Street, CBD (522 0996/www.nobadance.com). **Tickets** prices vary; phone for details. **Credit** AmEx, MC, V. **Map** pp306-7 D9.

A presenter of dance rather than a dance company, the Ballet Association is the keeper of the flame in dance-impoverished New Orleans. Through judicious selection, the organisation brings significant ballet, modern and ethnic dance companies to venues around New Orleans several times a year, usually for just one performance. Pilobolus Dance and Alvin Ailey are typical of the fare.

Spoken word

Poetry slams and spoken word are the most popular reading events in New Orleans. The audience is sometimes outnumbered by the poets but the atmosphere is always fun and

enthusiastic. Several series of readings have come and gone, moving from bars to coffeehouses to campus and back again. Because the scene is constantly changing, always take a look at listings in the local press (*Times-Picayune, OffBeat* and *Gambit*) before heading out. *See also page 42.*

Community Book Center

217 N Broad Street, at Bienville Street, Mid City (822 2665/www.communitybookcenter.com). Bus 97 Broad. **Open** *Shop* 10am-7pm Mon-Sat; closed Sun. *Open-mike events* every 2nd Fri of mth. **Admission** free. **Map** pp306-7 E6.

An African-American bookstore during the day, this place takes its mission of being a 'community' book centre very seriously. Evenings are packed with poetry readings, writers' groups and other creative writing events, including open-mike evenings.

Flora Café & Gallery

2600 Royal Street, at Franklin Avenue, Marigny (947 8358). Bus 82 Desire. **Open** 6.30am-10.30pm daily. *Poetry readings* 7-10.30pm Mon. **Admission** free.

A wonderfully shabby coffeehouse in Faubourg Marigny, Flora is the haunt of twentysomething artists and self-proclaimed young wits-about-town. The regular Monday-night poetry readings are freeform and friendly.

Funky Butt

714 N Rampart Street, at Orleans Avenue, French Quarter (558 0872/www.funkybutt.com). Bus 31 St Claude. **Open** *Club* 8pm-3am daily. *Poetry readings* 8pm Wed. **Admission** free. **Map** p315 C1.

The Wednesday night poetry at the Funky Butt schedules well-known local writers and poets followed by an open-microphone session. Held upstairs from the nightclub (*see p216*), music floating upwards makes the perfect backbeat for the poetry.

Maple Leaf Bar

8316 Oak Street, at Dante Street, Uptown (866 9359). St Charles Streetcar. **Open** 3pm-4am daily. *Poetry readings* 3pm Sun. **Admission** free. **Map** p306 A7.

The Maple Leaf is a perfect New Orleans landmark. It is physically humble, it has tradition and it comes with its own patron saint. Everette Maddox, whose skills at writing poetry and drinking scotch ran neck and neck, began what is the longest-running regular poetry reading series in the South. Every Sunday afternoon for the past 20 years, people have gathered at the Maple Leaf for beer and poetry. Even before Maddox's death in 1989, the tone of the readings had changed and the days of free-for-alls had largely passed, being replaced with pleasantly informal literariness. Audiences can be very kind and patient, and the poets are similarly moderate in their manner and material; no one is likely to fall to the floor shrieking about the sins of mommy and/or daddy. If someone did, people would applaud politely. For music at the Maple Leaf, *see p223.*

Sport & Fitness

Work off those Cajun calories with some outdoor pursuits.

No major league franchise, but the **New Orleans Zephyrs** always draw a crowd. See p232.

Spectator sports

Like most American cities, New Orleans is wild about professional sports. Unfortunately, because New Orleans isn't a very large television market, pro sports don't return the favour and have little interest in locating teams here. The city lost its basketball team to Utah (of all places), where it was weirdly named the Utah Jazz – a classic contradiction in terms. New Orleans has managed to hold on to the **Saints** football team, but it's a troubled marriage, with the Saints continually in the NFL basement, and the city hoping and praying for a championship team.

INFORMATION

The *Times-Picayune* is the most reliable source of information on local sports and schedules of events. It is not, however, the most comprehensive source of sports information, since sports not played in New Orleans receive

little coverage. Sport junkies will probably want to supplement their morning reading with *USA Today*'s sports page.

Perhaps the number one source for Saints news is Buddy Diliberto, who hosts a nightly sports talk show (6.15-10pm) on **WWL** (870 AM) as well as a show before Saints' games and 'Hap's Point After' after games. Buddy D, as he's known, has been intimately associated with the Saints since he was inspired by yet another loss to suggest that fans wear paper bags over their heads to show the team they were ashamed to be seen at a game. His joke took off, people wore bags and the 'Aints' were born (*see page 114* **Saints Hall of Fame**). Buddy D could only be a celebrity in New Orleans, where his speech impediment and overeager delivery make him a dubious hero. What his callers lack in coherence and logic, however, they make up for in pure mania. There is nothing on the radio quite like it.

TICKETS

Ticketmaster (522 5555) is the giant in New Orleans just as it is everywhere else, so tickets for almost every sporting event in the New Orleans area can be purchased via its ticket line (a service charge is added to the price). Tickets are also generally available from the teams' ticket offices, usually without extra charge.

If you want to get tickets through less official channels, talk to hotel concierges, many of whom act as unofficial ticket brokers. Though this isn't the most reliable way to get tickets and is rarely the most economical, creative concierges can find oversubscribed tickets more easily than lost luggage.

You can also buy tickets from scalpers, but tread carefully and make sure the tickets you are being offered are for the right date and game before handing over any money. And always haggle a little first: if a lot of scalpers are selling tickets, it's a sure indication of a buyer's market, and the patient buyer can get a good deal. Even though there are risks involved in dealing with scalpers, the results can be fruitful: frustrated season-ticket holders can often be found dumping their tickets for below face value in a bad season.

LOUISIANA SUPERDOME

This is the giant home of the Saints football team and also hosts other major events, sporting or otherwise. Tours of the building are available Monday through Friday, and there's a website with more information at www.superdome.com. *See also page 90.*

Baseball

Despite the lack of a major league franchise, New Orleans is a good baseball city. The **New Orleans Zephyrs,** a Triple-A farm team for the National League's Houston Astros, play at Zephyr Field in Metairie, and even though summer isn't a great time to be outdoors in New Orleans, the Zephyrs draw well. The field is as pleasant a place to watch a game as can be found away from an air-conditioner. The beer is cheap, the chairs comfortable and the legroom generous. In 1998 the Zephyrs won the first-ever Triple A World Series, giving New Orleans the dreamed-of Number One team. The team sank like a stone the next season but the city has nevertheless clutched the Zs to its breast.

College baseball, particularly **Louisiana State University** baseball, is a very big deal here. LSU is an hour west of New Orleans in Baton Rouge (*see page 247*), but LSU alumni are everywhere and now that the baseball team has won five College World Series championships since 1990, everybody's proud of their alma

mater. Home games are played at Alex Box Stadium in Baton Rouge. It's a comfortable place to watch a game, but as the Southeastern Conference doesn't allow beer at ball games, thirsty fans may prefer to wait until LSU comes to New Orleans to play the **University of New Orleans (UNO)** or **Tulane,** both of which regularly field competitive teams. The professional season runs from mid-April to early September, the college season from early February to early June.

Louisiana State University

Alex Box Stadium, S Stadium Drive, Baton Rouge (information 225 388 3202/box office 225 388 4148). **Open** *Box office* 8am-5pm Mon-Fri; closed Sat, Sun. **Tickets** $4-$6. **Credit** MC, V.

New Orleans Zephyrs

Zephyr Field, 6000 Airline Highway, between Transcontinental & David Drives, Metairie (734 5155). Bus E2 Airport. **Open** 9am-5pm Mon-Fri; closed Sat, Sun. **Tickets** $6-$8; $1 discount for concessions. **Credit** AmEx, D, MC, V.

Tulane University

Turchin Stadium, Tulane University, at Claiborne Avenue, Uptown (information 862 8239/box office 861 9283). St Charles Streetcar. **Open** 8.30am-5pm Mon-Fri; closed Sat, Sun. **Tickets** $3-$6. **Credit** AmEx, MC, V. **Map** p306 C8.

University of New Orleans

Privateer Park, at Leon C Simon Drive & Press Drive, Gentilly (information 280 6284/box office 280 4263). Bus 58 Franklin Express. **Open** *Box office* 8am-noon, 10am-6pm Mon-Fri; closed Sat, Sun. **Tickets** $2-$6. **Credit** AmEx, MC, V.

Basketball

Now that the New Orleans Jazz professional team is just a fond memory, basketball fans dream of a pro team returning to the city and meanwhile focus on local college basketball. The National Collegiate Athletic Association (NCAA) season runs from early December to early March, when the NCAA Tournament determines the national champion. **LSU,** having produced stars like 'Pistol' Pete Maravich and, more recently, Shaquille O'Neal, commands the most attention, with weekend games usually sold out, but **Tulane** and **UNO** also have strong programmes. Both have appeared in the NCAA Tournament in the 1990s, which is impressive considering that UNO is a commuter school whose players are often junior college transfers, and Tulane's programme, which was ended after a point-shaving scandal, only restarted in the 1990s.

Women's basketball is growing nationwide and, in some places, draws as big a crowd as the men's game. In the past few seasons, both

Tulane and LSU's women's teams have been doing well, but diehard fans might want to take the road trip to Ruston in northern Louisiana, the home of **Louisiana Tech**, a perennial powerhouse in the women's game. Double-headers, featuring a women's and a men's game, are good deals. The basketball season runs from early November to early March.

Louisiana State University

Pete Maravich Assembly Center, N Stadium Drive, Baton Rouge (information 334 4578/box office 388 2184). **Open** *Box office* 8am-5pm Mon-Fri; closed Sat, Sun. **Tickets** phone for details. **Credit** MC, V.

Tulane University

Foggelman Arena, Tulane University, at Freret Street, Uptown (information 865 5505/box office 865 5810). St Charles Streetcar. **Open** *Box office* 8.30am-5pm Mon-Fri; closed Sat, Sun. **Tickets** $8-$16. **Credit** AmEx, MC, V. **Map** p306 B8.

University of New Orleans

UNO Lakefront Arena, 6801 Franklin Avenue, at Leon C Simon Boulevard, Gentilly (information 280 4263/box office 280 6239). Bus 14 Franklin, 17 Hayne, 92 Express. **Open** *Box office* 8am-noon, 1-4.30pm Mon-Fri; closed Sat, Sun. **Tickets** $4-$16. **Credit** AmEx, MC, V.

Football

American football has a heroin-like grip on the nation, so much so that even highlights from high-school games make the TV news. In New Orleans, only **Tulane** fields a college football team, and it plays in the Louisiana Superdome in front of a gathering of fans small enough to learn each others' names. The **Sugar Bowl** (every 1 or 2 January) is an intercollegiate game, part of the end-of-season invitational series that is supposed to determine the best college team in the country. If you're in town for it, it's good fun.

Saints games, also played at the Superdome, are more raucous events, not surprisingly. Fans by necessity possess an inexhaustible supply of dark humour and can find fun and laughs in the midst of the most inept moments. Because they know what it's like to be laughed at, Saints fans are pretty tolerant of other teams' fans. Tickets can be purchased from the Superdome or from the Saints box office, also in the Superdome (on ground level, facing Poydras Street).

The most complete football event in the area is an **LSU** game in Baton Rouge. The LSU campus starts to become RV city on the Friday night before a Saturday game, and by the following day, tents, shelters, barbecues and pick-up trucks are strewn all over campus, surrounded by people preparing for the game. Exactly why a game requires five, even ten

hours of preparation is unclear, but beer and hamburgers seem crucial to fuelling fandom. The scene is impressive in its rawness and enthusiasm, and eventually a football game is played. Tickets are often sold out.

The professional season runs from the end of August to the end of December, the college season from September to December.

Louisiana State University

Tiger Stadium, N Stadium Drive, Baton Rouge (information 225 334 4578/box office 225 388 2184/www.lsusports.net). **Open** *Box office* 8am-5pm Mon-Fri; closed Sat, Sun. **Tickets** $30. **Credit** MC, V.

Saints

Louisiana Superdome, Sugar Bowl Drive, at Poydras Street, CBD (Superdome box office 587 3800/Saints box office 731 1700/www.neworleanssaints.com). Bus 16 S Claiborne. **Open** *Superdome box office* 9am-4.30pm Mon-Fri; open at weekends for special events. *Saints box office* 8.30am-5.30pm Mon-Fri; closed Sat, Sun. **Tickets** $25-$50. **Credit** *Superdome box office* MC, V. *Saints box office* AmEx, D, MC, V. **Map** p309 A/B1.

Tulane University

Louisiana Superdome, Sugar Bowl Drive, at Poydras Street, CBD (information 865 5355/Tulane box office 865 5810/Superdome box office 587 3800/ www.tulane.edu). Bus 16 S Claiborne. **Open** *Superdome box office* 9am-4.30pm Mon-Fri; open at weekends for special events. *Tulane box office* 8.30am-5pm Mon-Fri; closed Sat, Sun. **Tickets** $23. **Credit** *Superdome box office* MC, V. *Tulane box office* AmEx, MC, V. **Map** p309 A/B1.

Horse racing

New Orleans's horse racing fans suffered a tragic loss on 13 December 1993 when the **New Orleans Fair Grounds**' grandstand – at that time the second oldest in the US – burned down. Racing was not affected but the atmosphere of the place was; not that it bothered the real gamblers, many of whom wouldn't mind a bear trap clamped on their leg as long as they were ahead a few bucks. Those who have been to **Jazz Fest** (*see page 192* **New Orleans Jazz and Heritage Festival**) will be amazed at how different the Fair Grounds look during the rest of the year without tents, food booths and tens of thousands of people. The horse racing season runs from Thanksgiving to the end of March, and the opening day of the season is a festive event (*see page 194*).

Fair Grounds Racecourse

1751 Gentilly Boulevard, near Esplanade Avenue, Gentilly (944 5515/www.fgno.com). Bus 48 Esplanade. **Open** Mon, Thur-Sun hours vary; phone for details; closed Tue, Wed. **Map** 5 E/F5.

Runners prepare for the **Crescent City Classic**. *See p236.*

Ice hockey

The **New Orleans Brass** is a part of hockey's great southward migration, and the team is demonstrating what executives everywhere have started to learn: that people don't have to grow up skating on frozen ponds to enjoy ice hockey. The Brass is a minor league team, but its games still sell out regularly. A new stadium next to the Superdome is currently the team's home, but many fans secretly hope the 'Baby Dome' will ultimately be used for a basketball arena, with the longed-for return of an NBA franchise. In the meantime, the hockey season runs from mid-October to early April.

New Orleans Brass
New Orleans Arena, 1660 Girod Street, next to the Superdome, CBD (522 7825/www.brasshockey.com). Bus 16 S Claiborne. **Open** *Box office* 9am-5pm Mon-Fri; noon-5pm Sat; closed Sun. **Tickets** $6-$15. **Credit** AmEx, MC, V. **Map** p309 A/B1.

Participation sports

Louisiana car licence plates announce the state as a 'Sportsman's Paradise'. Archaic, gender-specific name aside, there is a lot the outdoor-minded can do in the New Orleans area, but the heat and humidity do demand respect. During July, August and September

it gets hot early, peaks in the high 90s Fahrenheit (high 30s Centigrade) in the mid-afternoon, then stays hot into the late evening. The heat and humidity are hard to imagine for those who haven't experienced them, so if you're interested in participating in high-exertion activities, take precautions: wear a hat, drink plenty of water and maintain a reasonable perspective.

Cycling

New Orleans is not a particularly good city for cycling, unless you're already an urban expert. Its flatness is appealing, but its potholes and narrow streets aren't. Those who wish to cycle need to be very alert or should head to **City Park** or **Audubon Park**, both of which are safely out of traffic's way. You can rent bikes from **Joe's Bike Shop** and **Olympic Bike Rentals**. In the French Quarter, try **French Quarter Bicycles**, or **Bicycle Michaels** (which also organises tours) in nearby Faubourg Marigny.

Bicycle Michaels
622 Frenchmen Street, between Royal & Chartres Streets, Marigny (945 9505). Bus 3 Vieux Carré, 48 Esplanade, 55 Elysian Fields. **Open** 10am-7pm Mon-Sat; 10am-5pm Sun. **Rates** $16 per day, plus $5 helmet. **Credit** AmEx, Disc, MC, V. **Map** p307 G6.

French Quarter Bicycles

522 Dumaine Street, at Decatur Street, French Quarter (529 3136). Bus 3 Vieux Carré, 55 Elysian Fields, 81 Almonaster, 82 Desire. **Open** 10am-6pm daily. **Rates** $4.50 per hr; $16.50 per business day; $20 per 24hrs. **Credit** MC, V. **Map** p316 C3.

Joe's Bike Shop

2501 Tulane Avenue, at N Rocheblave Street, Tremé (821 2350). Bus 39 Tulane. **Open** 8am-5pm Mon-Fri; 8am-4pm Sat; closed Sun. **Rates** $12 per day; $35 per wk; $25 per weekend. **Credit** AmEx, Disc, MC, V. **Map** p307 E6.

Fishing

The world is divided into three types of people: those who find fishing a colossal bore; those who find the boredom of fishing therapeutic; and those who find every element of fishing quite fascinating.

Those who fear their float going under because it means they'll have to stop drinking and do something will not want to fish in Louisiana, where the bayous and the Gulf of Mexico provide a variety of game fish and a fair amount of action. In the inland waters, you can catch largemouth bass, striped bass, flounder, speckled trout and redfish; in the mouth of the Mississippi you'll find red snapper, amberjack, grouper, copia, tarpon, shark, white trout, barracuda and trigger fish.

Fishing charters are easily arranged. Look in the *Yellow Pages* or ask your hotel concierge. Prices range from $135 to $150 per person per day, depending on the size of the party, services offered, length of journey and demand. Two reputable charters are **Captain Nick's** (361 3004, 1-800 375 3474, www.captnicks.com) and the family-run **Bourgeois Charters** (341 5614, www.neworleansfishing.com).

For information on fishing licences, call the **Louisiana Department of Wildlife & Fisheries** (1-888 765 2602). A three-day non-resident licence usually costs $13, but prices vary depending on the type of fishing.

Golf

During the 1970s oil boom, it was thought that the unconscionably wealthy didn't have quite enough ways to spend their money, so new golf courses were built for them. When the boom ended and the money went to Texas, the New Orleans area was left with a number of fine golf courses. The courses aren't always in the kind of shape they should be due to lack of money for maintenance and the long, hot summers and, inevitably, most of them are outside the city centre, so the best way to reach them is by car.

English Turn, a Jack Nicklaus-designed course on the West Bank, hosts an annual PGA event and is the Cadillac of the area's courses. It is a private club, but hotel concierges can usually get a tee time for those willing to pay the $155 green fees. The fairways are playable for the average club member, but the tricky two- and three-tiered greens will embarrass all but the best putters.

In New Orleans East, **Eastover** (off I-10) is an attractive course that is generally kept in good condition and is more moderately priced. If you don't mind the 30-minute drive to Slidell, **Oak Harbor** has one of the most interesting layouts, where few tee shots are as simple as they look. It is near Lake Pontchartrain and, consequently, the wind is often strong and unpredictable.

Those who don't want to pay a lot of money to discover that their swings are no better in New Orleans than they are back at home will enjoy the **Bayou Oaks Golf Course** in City Park. The prices are very reasonable and both the West and East courses present a fair challenge, the East being a little more interesting. There isn't any rough and each hole could use one more sand trap, but shots that drift too far right or left will end up under very large oaks, forcing players to take shots that resemble Wayne Gretzky more than Tiger Woods. Duffers and those with time constraints may prefer the North course, which is shorter and more open. There's also a very cheap course in **Audubon Park**, but it's not really worth playing.

Bayou Oaks Golf Course

City Park, 1040 Filmore Avenue, near Wisner Boulevard, Mid City (483 9397). Bus 43 Canal. **Open** 6am-8pm Mon-Fri; 5.30am-8pm Sat, Sun; hours vary according to season; usually dawn to dusk. **Rates** *Non-residents* $10-$18 per round; discounts for seniors. **Credit** AmEx, MC, V. **Map** p308 E2.

Eastover

5889 Eastover Drive, at Lake Forest Boulevard, New Orleans East (245 7347). No public transport. **Open** 8am-6pm Mon-Fri; 7am-6pm Sat, Sun (hours vary according to season). **Rates** *mid June-Jan* $95.92 per round. *Feb-mid June* $109 per round. **Credit** AmEx, DC, MC, V.

Rates include golfing cart, green fees and taxes.

English Turn Golf & Country Club

1 Clubhouse Drive, off English Turn Parkway, West Bank (391 8018). No public transport. **Open** *Summer* 6am-7pm Tue-Sun; closed Mon. *Winter* 7am-6pm Tue-Sun; closed Mon. **Rates** $155 per round. **Credit** AmEx, MC, V.

Note that you must be a guest of a member or book a tee time through a hotel concierge to play at this exclusive golf and country club.

Arts & Entertainment

Oak Harbor

201 Oak Harbor Boulevard, at Pontchartrain Drive, Slidell (254 0830). No public transport. **Open** 7am-6pm daily. **Rates** *Non-residents* $79 per round; discounts after 3pm. **Credit** AmEx, Disc, MC, V.

Horse riding

Cascade Stables

700 East Drive, at Magazine Street, Uptown (891 2246). Bus 11 Magazine. **Open** 9am-4pm daily. **Rates** *Trail ride* $20 per person. *Group lesson* $20 per person. *Private lesson* $25 per person. **Credit** MC, V. **Map** p306 B9.

These stables next to Audubon Park offer a 45min trail ride within the park.

City Park Stables

Marconi Boulevard, at Filmore Street, City Park, Mid City (483 9398). Bus 48 Esplanade. **Open** *Office* 9am-5pm Mon-Fri; 9am-6pm Sat, Sun. *Lessons* 3-7pm Tue-Fri; 9am-6pm Sat, Sun; closed Mon. **Rates** *Group lesson* from $25 per 30min. *Private lesson* from $35 per 30min. **No credit cards. Map** p308 D2.

The stables are near the golf course in City Park. Private and group lessons (including jumping) are offered, but there are no trail rides. Book in advance for riding lessons.

Running

Considering New Orleans's drivers, there is something appropriate about residents of the city referring to the grassy traffic medians as 'neutral grounds'. Not only do they keep cars safely separated, but they provide a pleasant place for runners who want to get a feeling for the city. One of the busiest neutral grounds is on **St Charles Avenue**, running Uptown from Lee Circle past Audubon Park and on to Riverbend and Carrollton Avenue. Twice a year, the city hosts the **Crescent City Classic**, a ten-kilometre (six-mile) road race from the French Quarter to City Park. The race is a spring event, usually held on Easter weekend. The **New Orleans Track Club** (482 6682, www.runNOTC.org) administers road races and provides information on upcoming running events. For more detailed listings of running and walking events and organisations, pick up a copy of the monthly publication *Health & Fitness*, which is distributed free around town.

Swimming

New Orleans has few public swimming pools. Residents who want to swim make friends with people who have pools at home, but visitors without such useful contacts should check out gyms (*see page 237*) and the **YMCAs** (*see page 238*) – or, if they have the chutzpah, try to walk into the pool at one of the larger hotels: not all check residents' credentials. Do not go to Lake Pontchartrain for a swim. Although the water is getting cleaner, it is still unsafe for bathing.

Tennis

For the most part, tennis clubs in New Orleans are private, but the **City Park Tennis Center** and the **Audubon Park** courts are open to the public, well kept and well lit.

Audubon Park Tennis Courts

6320 Tchoupitoulas Street, at Calhoun Street, Uptown (895 1042). Bus 19 Nashville Express, or 11 Magazine then 10min walk. **Open** 8am-7pm Mon-Fri; 8am-6pm Sat, Sun. **Rates** $6 per hr. **No credit cards. Map** p306 B10.

City Park Tennis Center

City Park, between Victory Avenue & Dreyfous Drive, Mid City (483 9383). Bus 48 Esplanade. **Open** 7am-10pm Mon-Thur; 7am-7pm Fri-Sun. **Rates** $5.50 Mon-Fri; $6.50 Sat, Sun. **No credit cards. Map** p308 D4.

The best Places to run

Audubon Park
Bypass the walks around the golf course for the riverside area behind the Zoo.

City Park
A pleasant, shady place to run – and shade can be crucial in the summer.

French Quarter
If you're an early riser, the French Quarter is a splendid place to run before 8am. Traffic is minimal and you get to see America's loveliest neighbourhood at its best and most empty.

Lake Pontchartrain
Where West End Boulevard turns into Lakeshore Drive, there are almost two miles of pretty and almost traffic-free road, levee and paths alongside the lake.

Lee Circle YMCA
After dark, or on rainy or oppressively hot days, the indoor mezzanine track at the Y is an excellent option.

St Charles Avenue
Step out on the neutral ground between the streetcar tracks.

A run of good luck: circuit training at Lee Circle **YMCA**. *See p238.*

Watersports

Although boat-owning locals crowd the flat (and still polluted) waters of Lake Pontchartrain, there are limited options for visitors wanting to indulge in some watery sports. **Murray Yacht Sales/Boat Rentals** (283 2507), on the edge of the lake, charters 26-foot (eight-metre) sailing boats and also runs weekend sailing courses ($150 for three hours). Otherwise, you can rent canoes and paddle-boats at weekends and explore the lagoons of **City Park** or try one of the canoe treks offered in **Jean Lafitte National Historical Park & Preserve** (*see page 116*). Outside the city, there are plenty of **fishing** options (*see page 235*) or you can always take a **swamp tour** (*see page 240*).

Fitness

Gyms

The following gyms offer day membership. For spas, *see page 184.*

Downtown Fitness Centers

3800 One Canal Place, at Decatur Street, French Quarter (525 2956). Bus 41 Canal. **Open** 6am-10pm Mon-Fri; 9am-6pm Sat, Sun. **Map** p316 A3.

Le Meridien Hotel, 8th Floor, 814 Canal Street, at St Charles Avenue, CBD (527 6750). St Charles Streetcar/41 Canal bus. **Open** 6am-9pm Mon-Fri; 7am-9pm Sat, Sun. **Map** p316 A2.
Both **Rates** $12 per day (3-day and weekly passes also available). **Credit** AmEx, Disc, MC, V.
The One Canal Place site has free weights, Nautilus and other weight machines, the usual assortment of treadmills, and tanning beds. At Le Meridien there is a swimming pool, a whirlpool, Nautilus machines and a massage therapist. Both venues offer daily aerobic classes.

Elmwood Fitness Center Downtown

701 Poydras Street, at Carondelet Street, CBD (588 1600). Bus 16 S Claiborne. **Open** 5.30am-9pm Mon-Fri; 8am-4pm Sat; closed Sun. **Rates** $10 per day; $35 per wk. **Credit** AmEx, MC, V. **Map** p309 B1.
Offers weights, cardiovascular equipment, a sauna, a whirlpool and aerobics classes.

Mackie Shilstone Pro Spa

Avenue Plaza Hotel, 2111 St Charles Avenue, at Josephine Street, Lower Garden District (566 1212). St Charles Streetcar. **Open** 6am-9pm Mon-Fri; 8am-6pm Sat, Sun. **Rates** temporary membership varies; personal training from $35 per hr. **Credit** AmEx, DC, Disc, MC, V. **Map** p309 B3.
Mackie Shilstone is a legend in the athletics world, developing sport-specific workouts that have pushed boxers to championship level and rehabilitated arm-sore basketball pitchers. Shilstone, a

hyperactive pixie of a man, doesn't limit himself to stars or even professionals: he's happy to work out training programmes for weekend golfers and teenage football players. For anyone serious about a sport, working with Shilstone is like an opera buff being invited onstage at La Scala. To schedule an evaluation and have a personalised workout plan created for you, contact Shilstone well in advance. Alternatively, Shilstone-trained coaches will put clients through a first-rate session on a drop-in basis or clients can work on their own at the impressively equipped gym (all the cardio machines have mini-TVs). Hotel guests at the Avenue Plaza and other local hotels including the Pontchartrain pay a $5 day rate; there are various temporary memberships available.

Rivercenter Racquet & Health Club

New Orleans Hilton, 6th Floor of parking garage, Poydras Street, at Convention Center Boulevard, CBD (556 3742). Bus 16 S Claiborne. **Open** 5.30am-9pm Mon-Fri; 7am-7pm Sat; 7am-5pm Sun. **Rates** $10 1-day pass; $18 2-day pass; $27 3-day pass; $36 4-day pass; $45 5-day pass. **Credit** AmEx, Disc, MC, V. **Map** p309 C1.

The centre has indoor tennis, racquetball and squash courts, Nautilus machines and cardiovascular equipment. There isn't a swimming pool, but there is a sauna, whirlpool and aerobics classes.

Salvation Studio

2nd Floor, 2917 Magazine Street, at Sixth Street, Garden District (896 2200). Bus 11 Magazine. **Open** 8am-10.30am, 4-8pm Mon-Thur; 8am-noon Sat; 4-5pm Sun. **Credit** AmEx, MC, V. **Map** p309 A4.

Salvation Studio is a hip fitness club in the California style with open, clean spaces situated on the second floor of a small shopping centre. Young, enthusiastic trainers lead a variety of workout classes.

YMCAs

There are three YMCAs in New Orleans, two are in the downtown area, one in Metairie. The downtown ones are in novel locations: one is flanked by Lee Circle and the Contemporary Arts Center, and the other is in the Superdome.

Lee Circle YMCA

920 St Charles Avenue, at Howard Avenue, Warehouse District (568 9622). St Charles Streetcar. **Open** 5am-9pm Mon-Fri; 9am-5pm Sat; 12.30-5pm Sun. **Rates** $5 per day. **Credit** MC, V. **Map** p309 B2.

The Lee Circle YMCA offers a host of facilities, including a basketball court, track, sauna, steam room, racquetball courts, free weights, cardiovascular and weight machines, plus aerobics classes. It's a bit dilapidated, but very friendly.

Superdome YMCA

Louisiana Superdome, Sugar Bowl Drive, at Poydras Street, CBD (568 9622). Bus 16 S Claiborne. **Open** 5.45am-7pm Mon-Fri; closed Sat, Sun. **Rates** $8 per day. **Credit** MC, V. **Map** p309 B1.

Smaller than its Lee Circle counterpart, the Superdome site is primarily a workout facility, with different types of weight machines, free weights, cycles, treadmills and stairmasters. There are also aerobics classes.

Exercising religiously at the **Salvation Studio**. *See p238.*

Trips Out
of Town

Getting Started

Let the good times roll you right out of town.

Being at the end of the road, New Orleans isn't the kind of place that lends itself to being a centre for travels. When you're here, you're here. Leaving the city, you leave the New Orleans zone and return to normal life. The good news is, however, that the Big Easy lies within a few hours of several other extraordinary areas. **Cajun Country**, headquartered in Lafayette, is only a of couple hours away. The **Mississippi Delta**, where the blues began, is several more hours away, but it's a place unlike any other on earth, and well worth the trip. Other choices include the fabulous white silver sand beaches of the **Gulf Coast** and waterfront towns such as **Grand Isle**, Louisiana, and **Seaside**, Florida, representing the past and the future of the coast.

PHONE HEX
Phone numbers are given as dialled from New Orleans. However, changes to the 504 area mean that out-of-town 504 numbers (in the area immediately north and west of the city) will be allocated a new code in mid 2001, which was unknown at time of press. A recorded message should operate for a year after the changeover, giving the correct code.

GETTING AROUND
Many travellers like to plan their excursions outside of town as their entry or exit to New Orleans. However, public transport in the region is notoriously poor and making trips, even to nearby destinations, can be problematic without a car.

An **Amtrak** service (1-800 872 7245/528 1614/www.amtrak.com) known as the 'Sunset Limited' runs east–west through New Orleans on its way between Miami and Los Angeles. Westbound trains, which depart from New Orleans on Wednesdays, Fridays and Sundays, call at **Lafayette**. Eastbound trains, which depart on Tuesdays, Thursdays and Sundays, call at the Mississippi Gulf Coast towns of **Bay St Louis**, **Gulfport** and **Biloxi**, before continuing to **Mobile**, Alabama and on to

Pensacola, Florida. For details of all these destinations, *see chapter* **Heading East**.

Greyhound (524 7571/customer services 525 6075/1-800 231 2222/www.greyhound.com) operates an extensive bus network in the area.

Swamp tours

Dr Wagner's Honey Island Swamp Tours
Crawford Landing, at West Pearl River, Slidell (242 5877/fax 643 3960/ honeyislandswamp.com). **Tours** daily; times arranged by reservation. **Rates** *With transport* $40; $20 concessions. *Without transport* $20; $10 concessions. **No credit cards.**
Dr Wagner's tours give you a real feel for the wilderness through which you travel because the small, 12-seater boats used can penetrate far into the tiny bayous and streams where much of the wildlife hides. During spring, summer and autumn you will almost certainly see alligators, bald eagles and herons and possibly otters, deer or black bears.

Jean Lafitte Swamp Tours
Information 689 4186/689 4187/fax 689 2038/www.bigeasy.com. **Open** Tours 10am, 2pm daily. **Rates** *with transport* $38; $23 3-12s; *without transport* $20; $10 3-12s. **Credit** AmEx, Disc, MC, V.

Louisiana Swamp Tours
Information 689 3599/1-888-307 9267/ fax 689 3380/www.louisianaswamp.com. **Tours** 9.30am, noon, 2pm daily. **Rates** *With transport* $38; $20 concessions. *Without transport* $20.50; $16.50 concessions. **Airboat tours** 9am, 11am 1pm and 3pm. **Rates** *With transport* $65. *Without transport* $45. **Credit** AmEx, MC, V.
Both these outfits take visitors through the waters of Lafitte in search of alligators; during the heat of summer you are virtually guaranteed to see some. The guides are usually locals who have both a rapport with the gators and an encyclopedic knowledge of the local flora and fauna.

▶ For tour companies, see chapter **Guided Tours**. For details of New Orleans's airport and train and bus stations, along with car rental companies and driving advice, see chapter **Getting Around**. The Trips Out of Town **map** is on pages 302-3.

Heading North

Track the Mississippi and its history back through commuter suburbs, plantation lands, state capital Baton Rouge and the birthplace of the blues.

The North Shore

Twenty-six miles (41.9 kilometres) across Lake Pontchartrain, the North Shore community is, in urban planning terms, a commuter suburb of New Orleans. But in subjective terms, the North Shore is a whole 'nutha zone' (in Dr John's favourite phrase). In the 19th and early 20th centuries, it was a hot weather retreat for New Orleanians, who cooled off with lake breezes and relaxed in style in summer houses. With the mid-20th century construction of bridges, however, the North Shore became ever more accessible by car. The area is now home to thousands of city workers, who commute daily from their upscale suburban homes to downtown New Orleans.

Beyond suburbia, the North Shore retains its old-fashioned resort mindset and ambience. As a quick and easy side trip to another Louisiana, travelling across Lake Pontchartrain offers a number of rewards. A ride across the awesome 23.87-mile (38-kilometre) long **Pontchartrain Causeway** is a soothing experience in itself and gives you an idea of the vast scale of Lake Pontchartrain. There's a point in the middle where you can barely see either shore.

Immediately across the bridge are **Mandeville** and **Covington**, two small towns almost too cute to bear. Here you'll find boutiques, pleasant coffeehouses, smart shops and the usual attractions of a very rich town's shopping district. While you're in town, check out the **HJ Smith & Son's General Store & Museum**. Dating from 1876, this still-busy hardware store is a window on the North Shore's rural roots. The building is well worn and well maintained, with wooden floors and period appointments. The museum is a free display adjacent to the store, with items from the town's and store's past.

Fans of the late writer Walker Percy (*see page 255*) often make the pilgrimage to Covington to see the town where he lived for most of his adult life. Percy often said he was happy there, even while calling it 'a pleasant non-place'. The bookstore owned by his daughter has now closed but the **St Tammany Library** (310 West 21st Avenue, 871 1220) holds a one-day symposium in his honour during September.

Abita Springs, a tiny but attractive and thriving community of small Victorian houses, is a short drive from Covington on Highway 36. About two miles (3.2 kilometres) before the town look for the **Abita Springs Brewery**. This small, family-owned business makes one of Louisiana's favourite beers, Abita. It also produces Turbodog, Purple Haze, Golden and Amber, as well as root beer and seasonal brews. Free tours are given on Saturdays and Sundays, usually by long-haired young brewers who talk passionately about the virtues and technology of their beer. Tastings follow the tour. The brewery itself is an unassuming industrial jumble of tin-roofed buildings that's easy to miss.

Further afield is **Ponchatoula**, a once-bustling town whose population has since been radically downsized. Luckily, the town has kept its quaint early 20th-century downtown virtually intact and has reinvented itself as a nostalgia town with loads of antiques stores and an annual strawberry festival in April. For the serious shopper, the antiques and second-hand stores can yield treasures, usually at prices lower than in New Orleans.

The most unusual attractions of the North Shore tend to be outside the towns, however. Located about 26 miles (42 kilometres) from Covington in Folsom, the **Global Wildlife Center** is an unlikely wild kingdom. This 900-acre (365-hectare) preserve is home to 40 species, including giraffes, African antelopes, Chinese deer, camels, bison, Texas longhorns, llamas and zebras. Visitors are able to see these animals close up in the covered wagons pulled by tractors. Bizarre, but an undeniable thrill.

For hikers and runners the **Tammany Trace** (follow the signs from Abita Springs) is an old railroad bed that has been converted for recreational use. The 32-mile (52-kilometre) strip winds through pine forests and bayous, crossing 31 bridges. A renovated railcar parked near the entrance is the official information centre, where you can pick up maps and tips on the best way to enjoy the trail.

Abita Springs Brewery

21084 Highway 36, between Covington & Abita Springs (893 3143/www.abita.com). **Open** *Tours* 1pm, 2.30pm Sat; 1pm Sun; closed Mon-Fri. **Admission** free.

The **Pontchartrain Causeway**. *See p241.*

Global Wildlife Center

26398 Highway 40, Folsom (624 9453/
www.globalwildlife.com). **Open** daily; phone for
details. **Admission** $10; $8-$9 concessions.
Credit DC, MC, V.

HJ Smith & Son's General Store & Museum

308 North Columbia Street, Covington (892 0460).
Open 8.30am-5pm Mon, Tue, Thur, Fri; 8.30am-noon
Wed; 8.30am-1pm Sat; closed Sun. **Admission** free.

Tammany Trace Information Center

21411 Koop Drive, Mandeville (867 9490). **Open**
Winter 7am-8pm daily. *Summer* 7am-6pm daily.

Where to stay, eat & drink

In addition to the inevitable chain motels, the
North Shore has a good share of B&Bs. **Trail's
End B&B** in Abita Springs (71648 Maple
Street, 867 9899, rates $75-$115) is a favourite
with Tammany Trace hikers and bike riders.
Tourism offices can suggest other places.

Of note in Covington is **Dakota Restaurant**
(629 North Highway 90, 892 3712, closed dinner
Mon-Fri, lunch Sat, all Sun, main courses $17.95-
$24.95), a restaurant routinely cited as one of
Louisiana's best. You'll also find two noteworthy
restaurants in Abita Springs: Artesia and the
Abita Springs Brew Pub. The **Brew Pub** (72011
Holly Street, 892 5837) has a lively bar scene and
reliable pasta/salad/burger food in the $10-$12.95
range. **Artesia** (21516 Highway 36, 892 1662,
closed Mon, Tue, lunch Sat, dinner Sun, main
courses $9-$15 lunch, $15-$28 dinner) is in what
was once a turn-of-the-19th-century health spa.
It's now the kingdom of hot new chef John Besh,
named one of the US's best new chefs in 1999 by
Food & Wine magazine.

Getting there

By car

This is the simplest way to visit the North Shore.
Take Causeway Boulevard (off I-10 west) north. The
toll for crossing the Pontchartrain Causeway is free
leaving New Orleans and $3.50 on return.

Trips Out of Town

By bus

Public transport is scanty. Information about buses can be obtained from the **St Tammany Tourist Center** (893 0862, 1-800 543 6362). **New Orleans Northlake Excursions** (781 1334, 1-877 821 6749) provides a service in the Slidell area.

Tourist information

New Orleans Northshore/ St Tammany Parish Tourist & Convention Commission

68099 Highway 59, Mandeville, LA 70471 (892 0520/1-800 634 9443/fax 892 1441/ www.neworleansnorthshore.com). **Open** 8.30am-4.30pm daily.

The Great River Road

River Road, the name given to two narrow country roads that run along each side of the river, follows the twisting Mississippi from New Orleans to Baton Rouge. Each road passes dozens of plantation houses, some restored as historic house museums, some still in use as private homes, and a handful slowly rotting to pieces in the hot, wet climate of south Louisiana.

In its prime River Road was one of the most opulent neighbourhoods in America, populated by planter families striving to out nouveau-riche each other with big, bigger and biggest houses, all stuffed with furniture, lamps, rugs, silver, china, crystal and paintings, usually imported from Europe. The wealth was rooted in sugar cane, one of the most profitable crops in the New World but one that was back-breakingly difficult to grow and harvest. High-stakes farming required masses of cheap labour, supplied by slaves until the Civil War, and by their impoverished heirs for many decades thereafter.

Today's visitor still sees the elaborate mansions, but rarely the signs of the forced labour on the collective farm that produced the wealth. Many of the plantation houses stand alone, usually surrounded by beautiful gardens, but no trace remains of the slave quarters that housed the dozens and sometimes hundreds of black people owned by the plantation. The levee that banks the river is a recent addition to the landscape. After a number of devastating floods in the early 20th century, the US Government built what amounts to the Great Wall of Louisiana – an enormous embankment system lining the river throughout the state. The levee is almost never breached and has stopped the seasonal flooding that once destroyed homes and killed dozens of people every year. It has also ruined the view.

Today's plantations are massive petrochemical plants that line the river, often right alongside the historic houses. This far-from-pristine landscape underscores for visitors the reasons for the bitter battle developing between residents of this area and the powerful chemical industry, which has long had free run of the place. Cancer and disease rates are high, and residents have begun fighting the development of new industry, even though they desperately need more jobs.

One way they're doing this is through the promotion of tourism as an alternative to industry. More than a dozen plantations along the river are open to the public, and many are well worth the trip. The plantation buildings are rather scattered about and each tour costs $6-$10, so seeing more than three in a day can get pricey and repetitive. Make a plan before you go, or take a tour (*see chapter* **Guided Tours**).

The closest plantation to New Orleans is the oldest intact structure, though not the most impressive. **Destrehan Plantation** was constructed in 1787 and is unusual in that its builder-contractor was a free man of colour named Charles Pacquet. Commissioned by a French planter, the house shows strong colonial and West Indies influences. It's framed with hand-hewn cypress, and the insulation in its walls is a Louisiana variant of European methods: bousillage, a mixture of Spanish moss and horse hair.

About a mile from Destrehan is **Ormond Plantation**, also an 18th-century West Indies colonial house that has been only recently restored. Note the *garconnières*, the side wings that were built for the young men of the family who had free rein to come and go as they wished. Although relatively small, the house maintains a restaurant and provides B&B accommodation (*see page 246*).

About 30 minutes' drive further on is one of the most fanciful plantations, **San Francisco** (it has no numbered street address, so look out for the signs). Painted in a vivid Victorian azure hue, with two huge, onion-dome topped cisterns on either side, which give it a Middle Eastern look, San Francisco is unique among the state's plantations and was used as a model by the novelist Frances Parkinson Keyes for her book *Steamboat Gothic*. The house's name is a corruption of the moniker originally given to it by its first owner, Edmond Bozonier Marmillion. He was said to be so impoverished by the expense of constructing the building that he labelled it 'sans Frusquin', French slang for penniless. The house was gorgeously and authentically renovated in the 1980s when it was purchased by the Marathon Oil company, which owned a nearby chemical plant (several

House of the spirits

Stories of ghosts are legion in an area already haunted by its own past, but few are more credible than at Myrtles Plantation (see page 251). It is said that somebody from every family that has lived here has been violently killed.

The most horrible story involves the second owners and one of their West Indian slaves. The slave was caught eavesdropping on her owners, who punished her by cutting off her ear. Outraged, she retaliated by feeding the owners' children cake laced with the poisonous juice of the oleander plant at a birthday party. Both children died and the slave was executed for the crime. All three are said to haunt the house today:

the slave in her turban, the little girl in petticoats and the boy in short trousers.

It used to be possible to stay at the Myrtles, but the owners were forced to close the visitor rooms after repeatedly finding their terrified guests were sleeping in their cars. Guests reported hearing noisy parties, complete with string quartets, in the empty main house throughout the night.

Parts of the 1980s US television version of William Faulkner's *The Long Hot Summer* were filmed in the house. On one occasion the crew rearranged the parlour furniture for a scene, only to find on their return that it had been painstakingly moved back into its original place, presumably by upset spirits.

---

of the plantations are now the non-profit, tax-deductible property of major petrochemical corporations). Its elaborately frescoed ceilings and lushly decorated pocket doors are worth the visit alone.

Upriver from San Francisco is **Tezcuco Plantation**, a smaller plantation villa with impressive grounds. It's a sprawling property with original outbuildings including a chapel and a blacksmith shop, which are now an antiques shop, Civil War museum and African-American history museum. The African-American museum is limited in depth but is one of the rare acknowledgements of slave life on River Road. In fact, it is one of the few Southern US sites to deal with the antebellum period at all. The interior of the main house is beautifully furnished. Accommodation is offered in period cottages in the grounds, some of which are brick-between-post construction, providing a personal experience of Louisiana's most important architectural development (*see page 246*).

Less than five miles upriver from Tezcuco is another impressive house that has been immortalised by Hollywood. **Houmas House** starred alongside Bette Davis and Olivia de Havilland in *Hush, Hush Sweet Charlotte*. One of the most beautiful houses on River Road, Houmas House is a classic Greek Revival structure encircled by stuccoed brick columns and a double veranda. The house was restored in the 1940s and '50s by a New Orleans dentist, who made the house and gardens his true life's work. The furnishings are not original to the house but were carefully assembled to match the house's history. One of the surprises of Houmas

House is the charming colonial-era house at the rear of the main building, which dates from 1840. Built in the late 1700s and steadily expanded for many decades, the small, two-storey structure blends beautifully with the main house with a covered courtyard. The gardens are very pleasant, with a grove of mature live oaks and a wide range of native Louisiana plants. (Some of the riverboat tours include a stop at Houmas House on their itineraries.)

From Houmas House, cross the river at the Sunshine Bridge to find **Oak Alley**, perhaps the most famous of the River Road showplaces. Featured in numerous films, TV ads and magazine layouts (most recently in John Travolta's *Primary Colors*), the 1839 Greek Revival house is framed by an alley of live oaks, most of which are a hundred years older than the house. The house was substantially updated in the 1940s, so is more interesting as a mid-20th-century re-creation of plantation luxury than as an authentic replica. Oak Alley offers bed and breakfast cabins and a small restaurant. Take note of the restaurant as it is one of the few places to get a meal on River Road (*see page 247*).

Laura Plantation is practically next door to Oak Alley, just three miles (4.8 kilometres) downriver, and presents an interesting contrast to both its neighbour and most of the other plantations. Laura also offers the best experience on River Road. The main house is modest compared with many of Louisiana's antebellum plantation houses but Laura is a different kind of landmark. Tours of this one-time Creole sugar cane plantation are given by unusually knowledgeable guides. Emphasis is on the day-to-day life of the plantation with proper weight given to the lives of the black workers, during slavery and after. Many of the slave cabins and other outbuildings have been preserved – a rarity among Southern historic house museums.

Founded in the late 18th century, the plantation is also unusual in that it was run primarily by three generations of women. The French Locoul family owned Laura for more than 150 years, and named the plantation after a daughter of the family in the mid-19th century. She was the last person in her family to run Laura, before selling it in order to marry and move to St Louis.

Most significantly, perhaps, Laura is a landmark in the development of American folk tales. The predominantly West African slaves at Laura began to use French, the new language they had learnt in captivity, to recount traditional tales from their homeland. The stories were written down in the late 19th century by the Louisiana folklorist Alcee Fortier and used by his friend, Georgia writer Joel Chandler Harris, as the basis for his 'Uncle Remus' books. These books were written in black dialect so that 'Compair Lapin' became 'Br'er Rabbit'.

Madewood Plantation (follow signs from River Road) is a sumptuous, columned 1846 house in the best *Gone With the Wind* tradition. The estate is a house museum and a B&B, with 21 rooms decorated in period antiques, and is the place for an exceptionally pleasurable plantation stay (*see page 246*).

Almost to Baton Rouge is **Nottoway Plantation**, an enormous, gaudy house that took ten years to build and was completed in 1859 on the eve of the Civil War. The house is enveloped in two storeys of sparkly white Italianate verandas, giving birth to its nickname 'The White Castle' (which is also the name of the nearest town). The interior is notable for its lavish details, which include 200 large glass windows, hand-painted porcelain doorknobs (in 64 rooms!) and chandeliers. Nottoway has overnight accommodation and a large restaurant, both on the pricey side (*see page 246*).

Destrehan Plantation

13034 River Road, LA 70047 (764 9315/www.dest.org.com). **Open** 9am-4pm daily. **Admission** $8; $2-$4 concessions; free under-5s. **Credit** MC, V.

Houmas House

40136 Highway 942/River Road, Darrow, LA 70725 (1-888 323 8314/www.houmashouse.com). **Open** 10am-5pm daily. **Admission** $8; $3-$6 concessions. **Credit** MC, V.

Laura Plantation

2247 Highway 18, Vacherie, LA 70090 (225 265 7690/fax 225 369 9848/www.lauraplantation.com). **Open** 9.30am-4pm daily. **Admission** $8; $4 concessions. **Credit** MC, V.

The plantation houses of **Longwood** (*p253*), **Tezcuco** (*p244*) and **Oak Alley** (*p244*).

Madewood: four-poster boaster. *See p245.*

Madewood Plantation
4250 Highway 308, Napoleonville, LA 700390 (369 7151/fax 369 9848/www.madewood.com). **Open** 10am-4.30pm daily. **Admission** $6; $4 concessions. **Credit** AmEx, DC, MC, V.

Nottoway Plantation
30970 Highway 405, White Castle, LA 70788 (225 545 2730/www.nottoway.com). **Open** 9am-5pm daily. **Admission** $10; $4 concessions; free under-5s. **Credit** AmEx, DC, MC, V.

Oak Valley
3645 Highway 18/River Road, Vacherie, LA 70090 (1-800 442 5539/www.oakalleyplantation.com). **Open** 9am-5.30pm daily. **Admission** $10; $3-$5 concessions. **Credit** *Restaurant & gift shop only* AmEx, DC, MC, V.

Ormond Plantation
13786 River Road, LA 70047 (764 8544/ www.plantation.com). **Open** 10am-3pm daily. **Admission** $5. **Credit** AmEx, MC, V.

San Francisco
535 Highway 44/River Road. Mailing address: PO Drawer AX Reserve, LA 70084 (535 2341/1-888 322 1756/www.sanfrancisco plantation.org). **Open** 10am-4.30pm daily. **Admission** $8; $3-$4 concessions. **Credit** DC, MC, V.

Tezcuco Plantation
3138 Highway 44/River Road, Darrow, LA 70725 (225 562 3929/www.tezcuco.com). **Open** 9am-5pm daily. **Admission** $8; $3-$7 concessions. **Credit** AmEx, DC, MC, V.

Where to stay, eat & drink

Tezcuco offers bed and breakfast accommodation in its 11 period cottages (rates $75-$165), most of which have fireplaces, plus a two-bedroom suite in the main house ($165). If you really want to treat yourself, check in for bed and breakfast at **Madewood**, a little off the River Road path, but worth the diversion. The prices are admittedly high – it costs $225 for a double room – but this family-owned and -operated plantation offers excellent service, comfortable rooms, coffee in bed and a huge Southern breakfast. The emphasis is on relaxation and retreat so there are no telephones or TVs in the rooms. We promise you won't miss them.

Guests at **Nottoway** are offered the chance of sleeping in one of the high-ceilinged bedrooms in the main house but, be forewarned, you have to be up and out by 9am if you arrive any time after 5pm. Other rooms are in newer outbuildings, which have been fitted with antiques. Rooms cost from $125 to $250 per night. The restaurant is pricey – main courses cost between $9 and $15 at lunch, and up to $25 at dinner – and undistinguished but nonetheless, it's a place to keep in mind on eaterie-poor River Road. A better bet, however, is the restaurant at **Oak Valley**, which serves breakfast from 8.30am to 10am and lunch from 11am to 3pm (main courses cost from $5 to $15). The food is standard roadside fare but tastes wonderful when you haven't eaten in hours and would have to drive another hour before finding anywhere else to eat. Visitors who want to stay the night on the plantation can have bed and breakfast in a cottage on site for $95-$125.

Just upriver from San Francisco on the north edge of the tiny town of Convent is one of the area's best seafood restaurants, and a great place to stop for lunch. **Hymel's Restaurant** (8740 Highway 44/River Road, 225 562 7031, closed dinner Tue, dinner Wed, all Mon, main courses $5.59-$18.50) is extremely casual and usually packed with locals, all of whom know each other. When things get busy, some of the customers lend a hand setting and clearing the tables, while others pour their own drinks. Country music trickles out of the jukebox, and the motherly waitress is sure to call you 'dah-lin". The raw oysters here are the biggest and freshest you're ever likely to see – short of a radioactive accident – and are the speciality of the house, along with its fried seafood.

Getting there

By car
From New Orleans head west on I-10 and take the exit marked Geismar/Lutcher Bridge. Follow the road to Highway 44 and the Great River Road. Destrehan Plantation is about 25min from New Orleans.

By bus
Forget public transport for River Road, there isn't any. Bus tours are an option if you're without a car, and actually work out as quite a good deal in the end. You see two to four houses and are spared all the headaches of driving narrow, twisting, two-lane roads with confusing and contradictory road signs. For details, *see chapter* **Guided Tours**.

By water
Several of the riverboat tours out of New Orleans include plantation stops. Usually you only get to stop at one house on a tour but you do get a pleasant trip on the river and glimpses of quite a few houses in places where the levee dips a bit. For details, *see chapter* **Guided Tours**.

Baton Rouge

Poised on the edge of Acadiana, 80 miles (129 kilometres) north of New Orleans, the capital of Louisiana is the centre of the state's infamous and controversial political culture. Baton Rouge was founded in 1699 when an expedition led by two French explorers – Pierre le Moyne, Sieur d'Iberville, and his brother Jean Baptiste le Moyne, Sieur de Bienville – stumbled upon an area of high bluffs on the Mississippi River. The diaries of the two explorers tell of their discovery of a pole stained with animal blood that served as the dividing line between two factional Indian tribes. It is from this bloody 'red stick' that the city got its name.

Today, Baton Rouge is a rapidly growing city with fairly serious traffic problems, especially on the I-10. Luckily, the most interesting parts of the city are in and around its central downtown area, which can easily be explored on foot.

Don't miss the **State Capitol Building**, constructed under the auspices of wild man Governor Huey Long (1893-1935). It is jokingly called 'the house that Huey built', and its phallic shape has led to some less-than-polite comparisons to parts of Long's own anatomy. Whatever his intentions, the building is unique in its art deco styling and size, and considered to be one of the most architecturally significant of the country's state capitols. To reach the building from I-10, turn on to I-110, then take the North Street exit and turn right on to N Fourth Street, which ends at the Capitol.

It is said that Long wanted the Capitol to be the tallest in the country and so it remains to this day, standing 450 feet (137 metres) high. The grand limestone and marble structure with its 34 floors was built in 1932-3, a time when the country was deep in the mire of the Great Depression. The entrance is via a grand staircase with 48 steps (one for each of the US states of the time). Two enormous statues flank the stairs: on the left is *The Patriots*, depicting a soldier and mourners of a warrior slain in battle; on the right, *The Pioneers* represents the state's original settlers. The inside is just as grand as the exterior. There's a great view from the observation deck on the 27th floor: the city, the river and the surrounding countryside open up in a verdant green vista that is unfortunately absolutely destroyed on the north side by dozens of chemical plants.

The greatest attraction of the Capitol is really its greatest tragedy. Long was assassinated as he walked down a main hallway on the first floor in 1935, and most visitors are drawn here, at least partly, to see the murder site. There's a large display case on

Trips Out of Town

the precise location of the shooting, containing articles and photos relating to the incident and showing where Long and his bodyguards were standing at the time. The bullet holes in the marble floors and walls have never been filled in; look carefully and you'll probably find a few. The incident remains clouded in mystery: although a New Orleans doctor was accused of the crime and killed by Long's bodyguards, who shot the governor – and why – has never been fully determined.

Long was buried in front of the Capitol, beneath a massive statue of himself. The local kids are quick to point out that if you stand behind and to the right of the statue it appears that the governor is extending his middle finger. Somehow this seems appropriate.

The **State Governor's Mansion** is only a few blocks from the Capitol. Follow the parking lot as it curves around past the Capitol Lakes – note the 'No Fishing' signs: even these lakes are polluted – and becomes Lake Drive. The mansion is on the right. Despite its antebellum appearance, it was constructed in 1963 and an outside view is probably enough for most visitors (if you want to see inside, tours are conducted by appointment only, except at weekends). Until 1997, the property was ungated and passers-by could stroll to the door if they chose. But the current governor, Mike Foster, disliked the unusual accessibility of the chief executive to the electorate and ordered the erection of a ten-foot (three-metre) high fence around the house. So much for open government.

Return downtown via N Fifth Street and it will take you directly to downtown Baton Rouge's other famous site, the **Old State Capitol**. Until Long built the current Capitol, this was the centre of Louisiana government. It was built in 1847, burned in the Civil War and restored in 1882. Over the years its neo-Gothic architecture has elicited both admiration and ridicule. Mark Twain is supposed to have described the building, which sits on the bluffs above the river, as 'the ugliest building east of the Mississippi', and an unidentified Natchez travel writer in 1855 claimed that 'at a distance, its white appearance and bulk give it the look of an iceberg'. Still, a recent renovation has left it looking its best, with impressive stained glass windows and extensive carved mahogany trim that are as glossy as the day they were built.

At the foot of the bluffs in front of the Old Capitol is the **Louisiana Arts & Science Center**, a small and inexplicably beloved local museum with a permanent exhibition of Ancient Egyptian artefacts. Close by, the USS *Kidd*, a restored World War II destroyer, is now part of the **Louisiana Naval War Memorial**

Museum, which contains some American World War II memorabilia.

If you've had enough history by now, walk a block downriver to a different kind of sea-going vessel: casino boats. Two boats – the **Argosy** (formerly *The Belle of Baton Rouge*) and **Casino Rouge** – sit on the river near the Old State Capitol. Both are busily taking the money of locals, and will undoubtedly welcome yours with hands extended. Try your luck at slots, blackjack and craps 24 hours a day. Nearby is **Catfish Town** (510 St Ferdinand Street), a large, enclosed mall of shops, restaurants and bars that keeps the fun and money flowing.

Also in Baton Rouge is the state's largest university, **Louisiana State University**, which is located on a sizeable campus several miles away from downtown. (To get there, follow St Ferdinand Street away until it becomes Highland Road, which eventually enters the campus at the main gates.) Shaded by huge oak trees, the LSU campus is a pleasant if uneventful place to wander: most of the fun is to be found on the periphery. Do what the students do – hang out at the shops and bars around the intersection of Highland Road and Chimes Street. Park and walk through the stores, coffeeshops and bars that make up college life.

Argosy Casino

103 France Street, off Government Street (1-225 378 5825). **Open** 24hrs daily. **Credit** AmEx, DC, MC, V.

Casino Rouge

1717 River Road North (1-225 381 7760). **Open** 24hrs daily. **Credit** AmEx, DC, MC, V.

Louisiana Arts & Science Center

100 S River Road, at North Boulevard (1-225 344 5272/www.lasc.lsu.edu). **Open** 10am-3pm Tue-Fri; 1-4pm Sat, Sun; closed Mon. **Admission** $1-$3; $1-$2 concessions. Free to all 1st Sun of month. **Credit** MC, V.

Louisiana Naval War Memorial Museum

305 S River Road (1-225 342 1942). **Open** 9am-5pm daily. **Admission** $6; $3.50 concessions; free under-5s. **Credit** MC, V.

Old State Capitol

100 North Boulevard, River Road (1-225 342 0500/www.sec.state.la.us). **Open** 10am-4pm Tue-Sat; noon-4pm Sun; closed Mon. **Admission** $4; $2-$3 concessions; free under-6s. **Credit** AmEx, MC, V.

State Capitol Building

State Capitol Drive (1-225 383 1825). **Open** *Building* 8am-4.30pm daily. *Observation Tower* 8am-4pm daily. **Admission** free.

Baton Rouge's **State Capitol**. *See p247.*

State Governor's Mansion

1001 Capitol Access Road (1-225 342 5855).
Open by appointment only; phone for details.
Admission free.

Where to stay

Accommodation in Baton Rouge is plentiful if
unimaginative – your best bet is probably one
of the major hotels. At the low end, try **La
Quinta Inn** (2333 S Acadian Thruway, 1-225
924 9600, 1-800 531 5900), where a double room
costs $75. At the **Radisson Hotel &
Conference Center of Baton Rouge** (4728
Constitution Avenue, 1-225 925 2244, 1-800 333
3333), expect to pay between $109 and $129 a
night. This has the benefit of more extensive
business facilities, including conference rooms,
fax service and modems.

If you can swing it, however, aim to visit
Baton Rouge during the day and spend the
night at one of the River Road plantations (*see
page 243*) or one of the B&Bs in nearby St
Francisville (*see page 251*).

Where to eat & drink

The student area at the intersection of Highland
Road and Chimes Street is the best place in
town to grab a quick bite to eat or to experience
the local bar scene. Join the local crowd at **The
Chimes** (3357 Highland Road, 1-225 383 1754,
main courses $4.95-$14.95). It's a relaxed,
friendly restaurant with a reliable menu of
sandwiches, crawfish etouffée and a good
selection of beers. Next door is **The Varsity**
(3353 Highland Road, 1-225 383 7018) Baton
Rouge's best live music venue, with nightly
shows from touring bands and local groups.

For a more casual experience, walk down
Chimes Street half a block to **The Bayou** (124
West Chimes Street, 225 346 1765), a favourite
alternative music bar that's famous for being
featured in the film *Sex, Lies & Videotape*
(director Steven Soderbergh has roots here).
The speakers blast non-mainstream music, the
beer is cheap and the pool games never stop.
Mention to the very cool bartenders that you're
from out of town and they will introduce you to
locals who will fill you in on everything you
ever wanted to know about the city.

Directly behind the Bayou is the best 24-hour
diner in the state, **Louie's** (209 W State Street,
1-225 346 8221). After midnight it is crammed
with inebriated partygoers; during the day it's
considerably calmer. The menu is basic – eggs,
sandwiches and hamburgers – but everything
is good and cheap ($3.95-$10.95).

Getting there

By car

From New Orleans, take I-10 west: it's 80 miles
(129km) to Baton Rouge. Take the I-110 north exit,
and then the North Street exit to downtown.

By bus

Greyhound (1-800 231 2222/www.greyhound.com)
offers frequent shuttles to Baton Rouge from the
downtown terminal via Metairie (roundtrip $19.50).
The trip takes 1-2hrs, depending on whether you
catch an express. Note that the Baton Rouge bus
station is not centrally located and cabs can be hard
to find there, especially at weekends. **Amtrak** (1-800
872 7243/www.amtrak.com) runs the Thruway Bus
from 1001 Loyola Avenue in New Orleans (528 1610)
at 12.20pm, 3.45pm, 4.50pm and 10.40pm daily.

Tourist information

Baton Rouge Convention & Visitors Bureau

*730 N Boulevard, between Napoleon & Jackson
Streets (383 1825/1-800 527 6843). Mailing
address: PO Box 4149, Baton Rouge, LA 70821.*
Open 8am-5pm Mon-Fri; closed Sat, Sun.

Playlist Highway 61

However you make the trip from New Orleans to Highway 61, music is a necessary travelling companion. As you leave New Orleans put on '**Spirits of Congo Square**' by the New Orleans Legacy Ensemble to make the transition from the upbeat funk of the Big Easy to the grittiness of the Delta. Move on to *Robert Johnson* (Columbia), the best compilation of the legendary bluesman, and follow with *Mississippi Sheiks, Volume 1* (Document Records), an incredible immersion into the 1930s' Delta dance music that Johnson grew up hearing. BB King, of course, is absolutely essential, and *BB King: Live at the Regal* (MCI) is the ideal road-trip album.

St Francisville

A 45-minute drive north from Baton Rouge, St Francisville is one of Louisiana's true treasures. Once a centre of farming life, today it is a quiet country town, with tourism as its principal trade. The plantations that once thrived on crops of indigo or cotton are now museums and inns, serving as mementos of the state's antebellum past. There's more 200-year-old silver, Sèvres porcelain and French mahogany in these houses than anywhere else in the state. Whereas the River Road plantations are largely part of the state's French history, St Francisville is where the English settled; its architecture, antiques and history are considerably different from those of the old homes downriver.

Driving up US 61 from Baton Rouge, the landscape changes as you move from the city's modern urban accoutrements to the chemical plants at the edge of town; then suddenly you're on a two-lane highway surrounded by thick forest. This is West Feliciana Parish, a peaceful, tree-filled stretch of country, and the site of dozens of plantation houses, many open to the public.

So varied is the wildlife here that the noted naturalist and artist John James Audubon spent nearly two years sketching the flora and fauna, and painting 80 of his famous folios. The town has never forgotten it. The annual **Audubon Pilgrimage** (635 6330), held on the third weekend in March, commemorates the artist with a festival and a tour of those buildings and areas related to his time in St Francisville. Local residents take part, dressed in period costume.

Follow the well-placed signs that direct you off the highway to St Francisville's historic downtown and stop on the main avenue at the **West Feliciana Historical Society Museum**, which doubles as the parish tourist commission. Drop by to stock up on free maps and brochures guiding you to the plantations

scattered throughout the area, as well as historical books and other information.

Head back to the highway, where signs will direct you to the plantations. If you like 'em large, stop first at **Rosedown Plantation**. Its 28 acres (11 hectares) of sculpted gardens frame an enormous white columned house stocked from top to bottom with antiques, china and silver. It is generally considered the most complete of the area's plantations. It is also the most expensive; just getting inside the gate costs $10.80 per person.

If size doesn't matter, just peek at Rosedown through the white arched gateway, then head back up the road to **Catalpa Plantation**. This gracious if small house, located at the end of a long, tree-shaded drive, stands under gnarled oak trees draped in Spanish moss. It is home to descendants of the original owners of Rosedown and is still owned by members of the family that built it. Until 1997, nonagenarian owner 'Miss Mamie' Thompson would personally guide guests through her home, past the priceless silver and china, all the while relating stories of her family and frequently plying her visitors with sherry.

After she died, her daughter Mary Thompson took over the responsibility of handling visitors: 'My mother would have wanted us to keep the house open.' A tour of Catalpa is the most up-close-and-personal look you will get of a plantation: family dogs wander in and out, and you'll get to know Mary Thompson's ancestors as if they were your own. Included in the collection is the still-dented silver, damaged when the family retrieved it from its hiding place in the mud underneath a nearby pond at the end of the Civil War.

Mary, who is also a local schoolteacher, can tie up genealogical loose ends from your visits to other houses in the area and has an encyclopedic knowledge of St Francisville history. She will also offer you a glass of sherry as you tour her dining room.

Another plantation considered crucial to any visit to the area is **Oakley House**, where

Trips Out of Town

Audubon made a living by teaching the family's daughter, Eliza Pirrie, for a brief time in 1821. Although he is supposed to have called the area 'the happy land', that might have been irony on Audubon's part. When Eliza became ill and was unable to take lessons for several months, her father refused to pay the artist and tutor, so he quit. Now part of the State Park system, Oakley House followed the pattern of homes in the West Indies: it is raised to catch every breeze, with a sleeping porch and wide gallery, and it is filled with antiques and portraits.

If you are in St Francisville in the spring or summer, don't miss the **Afton Villa Gardens**, a celebrated and beautifully restored classical garden built around the ruins of a 40-room Gothic mansion. If you're lucky enough to visit in March, you can catch Daffodil Valley at its best, when 100,000 daffodils burst into bloom.

If you've had your fill of nature and the more conventional history of the area, turn into the darkly shaded drive that leads to the **Myrtles Plantation**. This is a completely different kind of plantation house, both in its physical appearance and in its paranormal reputation: for more than 20 years the Myrtles has been known as the most haunted house in America (*see page 244* **House of the spirits**). The exquisite plaster frieze work, for which Myrtles is renowned, is more than 200 years old and has apparently never been renovated. It matches the blue colour of the lacy wrought ironwork on the porch, and contributes to the house's atmosphere of eerie perfection. The tour itself is spooky and lively, with an entertaining mix of rumour and history.

The weird theme continues if you turn off US 61 on to the road simply marked 'Angola'. This is Highway 66 and in about 15 miles (24 kilometres) it will take you directly to the gates of the infamous **Louisiana State Prison Farm** (655 4411). The prison, which is surrounded on three sides by swamp and river and on the fourth by massive fences, is said to be inescapable.

During the early part of this century the prison was among the most brutal in the nation and became known as 'the bloodiest prison in the South' due to both inmate and guard violence. Its most inhumane practices have since been banned or alleviated under federal court order, but inmates are still required to work in the fields, escorted by mounted guards toting rifles. The prison was used in the Susan Sarandon/Sean Penn film *Dead Man Walking* (1995) and also in Oliver Stone's *JFK* (1991). Bizarrely in the circumstances, every Sunday in October inmates compete in the Angola Prison Rodeo, which is open to the public.

For a less intimate but still informative look at the prison, visit the **Angola Museum**, just outside the prison gates. It houses everything from log books from the 1940s listing prisoners' crimes and sentences to the actual electric chair used in the prison until it was replaced by lethal injections several years ago. The prison's dark history is outlined in startlingly honest fashion. The fascinating prison records on display include the admission papers for the blues singer Leadbelly, with a notation indicating he was arrested for manslaughter and released after writing a song for the prison warden.

Afton Villa Gardens
9247 US Highway 61 North, St Francisville (1-225 635 6773). **Open** *Mar-June & Oct-Nov* 9am-4.30pm daily. *July-Sept, Dec* closed. **Admission** $5; free under-12s. **No credit cards.**

Angola Museum
Louisiana State Prison Farm, Highway 66, Angola (1-225 655 4411). **Open** 8am-4.30pm Mon-Fri; 9am-5pm Sat; 1-5pm Sun. **Admission** free.

Catalpa Plantation
Highway 61 North, St Francisville. Mailing address: *PO Box 131, St Francisville, LA 70775 (1-225 635 3372).* **Open** 1-4pm Mon, Wed, Fri-Sun; closed Tue, Thur; phone for reservations. **Admission** $6; $3 concessions. **No credit cards.**

Myrtles Plantation
7747 Highway 61, St Francisville, PO Box 1100, LA 70775 (1-225 635 6277). **Open** 9am-4.15pm daily. *Evening tour* 8pm Fri, Sat. **Admission** $8; $4 concessions. *Evening tour* $10. **Credit** AmEx, MC, V.

Oakley House Plantation
11788 Louisiana Highway 965, St Francisville, LA 70775 (1-225 635 3739). **Open** 9am-5pm daily. **Admission** $2; free children & seniors. **No credit cards.**

Rosedown Plantation
12501 Highway 10, St Francisville, LA 70775 (1-225 635 3110). **Open** 9am-5pm daily. **Admission** $10; $8.95 concessions; free under-10s. **No credit cards.**

West Feliciana Historical Society Museum
11757 Ferdinand Street, at Feliciana Street, St Francisville (1-225 635 6330). **Open** 9am-5pm Mon-Sat; 9.30am-5pm Sun. **Admission** free.

Where to stay

After a day of touring, there's no reason to leave St Francisville – the area has some of the best B&Bs in the state; contact the **West Feliciana Parish Tourist Commission** (*see page 252*) for a complete list, and expect to

Trips Out of Town

pay $60 to $110 for a double. One of the most unusual and relaxing is the **Shadetree Inn** (1818 St Ferdinand Street, 1-225 635 6116, rates $145-$195). Owner KW Kennon has restored this once-abandoned house to splendid, rustic beauty. Three private suites, each with its own separate entrance, are decorated in an elegant, simple style, with polished wooden floors, stained glass and dozens of windows overlooking the bluffs that lead down to the river. No detail is overlooked: the toiletries are self-indulgent, the porches are generous, each with their own rocking chairs, and there's even a spot where visitors are allowed to build their own campfire.

Shadetree offers a relaxing view of the bluffs but for an even higher perspective, walk about a block down Ferdinand Street to Our Lady of Mount Carmel Catholic Church, which is perched on the highest hill in the area and offers a really great view. Nearby is a larger B&B, the **Butler Greenwood Plantation** (8345 US 61, 1-225 635 6312, rates $110-$160), which has five modern cottages scattered around the grounds and a peaceful pond complete with rather decorative ducks. Each cottage is decorated differently, and most have fireplaces. A tour of the main house, which is conducted by owner Anne Butler, a seventh-generation plantation resident, is included in the price.

Where to eat

St Francisville is a small town, so eating opportunities are somewhat limited and generally based around seafood – generally fried or boiled. The locals gather for lunch at **Magnolia Café** at the corner of Ferdinand and Commerce Streets (1-225 635 6528, main courses $3-$14), which has friendly, no-frills service and familiar, home-made food such as soups, meatloaf and turkey divan. If you're after more upmarket dining, try the **Keane's Carriage House** restaurant at the Myrtles Plantation (1-225 635 6276, closed Mon, Tue, lunch Wed-Sat, dinner Sun, main courses $17-$22). Advance reservations are recommended.

Getting there

By car

From New Orleans, take I-10 west to Baton Rouge (80 miles/129km). Exit on to I-110 north, then follow it until it turns into Highway 61 north. Follow the signs to St Francisville.

By bus

Greyhound (1-800 231 2222/www.greyhound.com) runs 2 buses a day. A return ticket costs about $39 weekdays, $41 weekends.

Tourist information

West Feliciana Parish Tourist Commission

West Feliciana Historical Society Museum, 11757 Ferdinand Street, St Francisville, LA 70775 (1-800 789 4221/www.saint-francisville.la.us). **Open** 9am-5pm Mon-Sat; 9.30am-5pm Sun.

Mississippi

About 30 minutes north of St Francisville over the Mississippi border in Wilkinson County is the Clark Creek Natural Area, known locally as **Tunica Falls**. Popular with local outdoor types, it is made up of steep hills and ravines, walking trails and several beautiful waterfalls. The area is vast and a good map is essential (pick up one at the **West Feliciana Historical Society Museum**; *see above*). The area is known for its wildlife as well as its beautiful trails, but the hiking can be difficult, so wear proper footwear.

A somewhat easier, if less wild, alternative is the **Mary Ann Brown Nature Preserve**, a 109-acre (44-hectare) preserve in the Tunica Hills run by the Nature Conservancy of Louisiana. A two-mile (3.2-kilometre), well-blazed trail passes through a hardwood forest dominated by magnolia and beech trees, and traverses shallow ravines. The preserve also includes butterfly and humming bird gardens.

Natchez

Sixty miles (96.5 kilometres) north of St Francisville on US 61 in Mississippi lies the historic town of Natchez. This small, distinctly Southern community sits like a jewel on the high, hazy bluffs overlooking the Mississippi River.

Unusually, the integrity of Natchez's historic neighbourhoods has been largely preserved, with new construction relegated to the outskirts of town. The community lies on the site of an ancient village belonging to sun-worshipping Natchez Indians. Bienville, the same pioneering Frenchman who settled New Orleans, established Fort Rosalie on the bluffs above the river in 1716. The Indians fought for their home, taking the fort in 1729 and killing or capturing most of the colonists, but France sent the full strength of its army to put down the tribe, destroying them in the process. Eventually, the town took the name of the tribe it had displaced.

Natchez residents made their huge wealth during the early 1800s, when the town was the only port on the Mississippi between the mouth of the Ohio River and New Orleans and the development of the steamboat trade made fortunes for local speculators. Most people come to Natchez to see the results of that money.

The most famous event is the **Natchez Spring Pilgrimage** (1-800 647 6742), which is held annually in March. You can visit the historic houses as well as a number of private homes not usually open to the public. The locals participate enthusiastically, dressing in antebellum clothes and guiding visitors on a variety of tours.

Start your visit at the **Natchez Convention & Visitors Bureau** (*see page 254*), where you can collect maps and brochures. There are so many extraordinary houses to see here it is best to do some research first and then pick and choose which you want to see. Any trip to the area, however, should include some of the following houses.

Rosalie was built in 1820 on the Mississippi near the site of Fort Rosalie. It's a modest, redbrick mansion with white columns built in a restrained style; the ribbon-like wrought-iron fence that surrounds it adds most of the frills. It is easy to see why the site attracted armies: from its perch high above the river you can see for miles in every direction. Appropriately, Rosalie was the headquarters of the Union Army during the Civil War.

Dunleith is a magnificent Greek Revival mansion built in 1856. It sits on 40 acres (16 hectares) of landscaped parkland. You will pass it as you come into town. It is one of the most striking houses in the area, completely surrounded by colonnaded galleries, and includes an 11-room B&B (*see below*).

Stanton Hall is worth touring because of its sheer size. Original owner Frederick Stanton constructed four enormous Corinthian columns in the front gallery, imported Italian marble for the fireplaces, built 19-foot (5.8-metre) ceilings into the ground floor and developed a vast hallway as the grand entrance. The huge, bronze Gothic chandeliers in each of the downstairs rooms are rare and detailed enough to merit the $6 tour fee.

The house with possibly the oddest history in the South is **Longwood**, a tragedy in brick. Built in the Byzantine style, the eight-sided structure is topped with an onion-shaped dome, making it a rarity among the forests of Greek Revival mansions in the South. Its original owner, cotton magnate Haller Nutt, planned the house in 1859 as a permanent home for his family. Nutt's timing was disastrous. Work began on the house in 1860 and stopped a year later at the outbreak of the Civil War. Most of the artesans he had hired to build his dream

house were from Pennsylvania and they left on the last boat out of Mississippi before the war.

The house was intended to have six storeys and 32 rooms, encircling a massive central gallery. Nutt, who had a weakness for gadgetry, designed an intricate system of mirrors and windows to bring light to the rooms on the inside of the circle. But the house was never finished and, by the middle of the war, Nutt was ruined financially. Although he was a Union sympathiser, the Yankees took no pity on him and destroyed his farms. He died a few years after the war, a broken man. His family lived in the shadow of his overweening dreams for many years to come, with several generations of Nutt descendants living in near poverty on the ground floor of the extraordinary, unfinished house. In 1970 the family finally donated Longwood to the Pilgrimage Garden Club (which also owns Stanton Hall). The tour includes the impressive (though incomplete) portion of the house that still contains the tools left behind by the fleeing Northern workers. Both Stanton Hall and Longwood are on the route of **Natchez Pilgrimage Tours** (1-601 446 6631/1-800 647 6742).

Dunleith
84 Homochitto Street, at Duncan Avenue, LA 39120 (1-800 433 2445/www.dunleithplantation.com). **Open** 7am-10pm daily. *Tours* 9.30am-4.30pm Mon-Sat; 12.30-4pm Sun. **Admission** $6; $3 concessions. **Rates** $110-$225 single/double. **Credit** MC, V.

Longwood
140 Lower Woody Road, at John R Junkin Street (1-800 647 6742/www.natchezpilgrimage.com). **Open** 9am-4.30pm daily. **Admission** $6; $3 concessions. **Credit** AmEx, MC, V.

Rosalie
100 Orleans Street, at Canal Street (1-601 445 4555/www.rosalie.net). **Open** 9am-4.30pm daily. **Admission** $6; $3 concessions. **Credit** MC, V.

Stanton Hall
401 High Street, at Pearl Street (1-601 447 6282/Pilgrimage tours 1-800 647 6742). **Open** 9am-4.30pm daily except during Pilgrimages. **Admission** $6; $3 concessions. **Credit** AmEx, MC, V.

Where to stay

The best accommodation is to be found in the crush of B&Bs in historic houses (such as **Dunleith** – *see above*) throughout the area. Most are affordable, with rooms costing between $110 and $225 a night, although you can certainly spend much, much more if you want to. The **Natchez Convention & Visitors Bureau** (*see below*) has a brochure listing the B&Bs (with a photo of each). Reservations are required at all, so plan ahead.

Trips Out of Town

One of the most sought-after B&Bs is at **Monmouth Plantation** (36 Melrose Avenue, at John Quitman Parkway, 1-601 442 5852, 1-800 828 4531, rates $155-$250), which has 28 rooms and suites in the main house and the surrounding outbuildings. Its lush gardens, blue ponds dotted with wooden bridges, gazebos, marble statuary and lovely, croquet-friendly lawn will explain why it has been named one of the most romantic places to stay in the US by several newspapers and magazines. Rates include the house tour and a large Southern breakfast.

Harper House (201 Arlington Street, at State Street, 1-601 445 5557, rates $80 double, $130 quadruple) is a smaller B&B, with just a few guest rooms inside a large owner-occupied Victorian house. Prices include a tour of the house and breakfast, served in the gazebo. For a less expensive option, try the chain hotel **Howard Johnson Lodge** (45 Sargent Prentiss Drive, at John R Junkin Drive, 1-601 442 1691, rates $35-$69).

Where to eat

When you ask locals for advice on a good place to eat, notice how they hesitate. This is because there is really not much in the way of good food in Natchez: most of the dining options here run the very short gamut between heavy and fried. For dinner, head to Under the Hill, the area under the bluffs at the very edge of the Mississippi River. The restaurants here are touristy, but the food is hearty and the views are great. The **Wharf Master's House** (57 Silver Street, 1-601 445 6025, closed lunch Mon-Sat, main courses $5-$25) specialises in charbroiled steaks and seafood.

For upscale dining, **Monmouth Plantation** (*see above*) offers a five-course dinner every evening in its grand dining room ($46 per person, not including wine). The menu changes daily and places are limited, so book in advance for a unique treat.

Getting there

By car

From New Orleans, take I-10 west to Baton Rouge (80 miles/129km). Exit on to I-110, which turns into Highway 61 and leads directly to Natchez. Follow the signs to downtown. It's a 2hr-long drive from New Orleans.

By bus

Greyhound buses (1-800 229 9424/www.greyhound.com) run twice daily between Natchez and Baton Rouge. A return costs $41 and the journey takes 2hrs. The trip from New Orleans takes over 5hrs and costs $74 return.

Tourist information

Natchez Convention & Visitors Bureau

640 S Canal Street, by the river, Natchez, LA 39120 (1-601 445 4611/1-800 647 6724). **Open** 8.30am-5pm/6pm daily.

The Blues Highway

The stretch of US 61 between Natchez and Memphis is known as the 'Blues Highway'. It won the name through hard use, as the most direct route leaving the Mississippi Delta heading north. The Delta was the birthplace of many of the country's greatest blues players and for many the first stop beyond the insular, cotton-growing Delta was Memphis, the nearest large city, where there was some possibility of playing music and getting paid for it. Such greats as BB King, Muddy Waters, Howlin' Wolf, James Cotton, Willie Dixon, Son House, Elmore James, Bukka White and Robert Johnson all came from the Delta and made their way to Memphis, St Louis, Kansas City, Chicago and beyond.

Just driving through the Delta, long considered the single most impoverished section of the US, gives you a feeling for how the blues evolved. Things change, but somehow the Delta stays the same. Tarpaper shacks have been replaced by rotting wooden shacks; the antebellum plantations have been replaced by simple farms and factories, but there remains the quintessential Mississippi sense of melancholy, and a beauty that belies the poverty. Seeing the Delta first hand helps even casual visitors to develop some sense of how Mississippians have lived the blues for centuries – and why it gives them the blues.

At the centre of it all is **Clarksdale**, a Delta town that most blues aficionados believe is the true heart and soul of the blues. But before and after Clarksdale, the road winds through small towns and farms where the masters of the blues lived out their youth, and past the small roadhouses where they honed their skills. The route is geared toward blues travellers: sites are generally clearly marked and the Mississippi Visitors Centers, located on major highways at all the state borders – including the one outside St Francisville – offer helpful maps and brochures to guide blues-hunting visitors.

There's not much to interest the music fan in Vicksburg and Natchez (*see page 252*), which have their share of Old South history and sites. Sticking strictly to Highway 61, the first important stop on the pilgrimage is **Greenville**, a town inextricably intertwined with the local arts: blues and literature. Pick up

Riverside roadtrip: drive the blues down **Highway 61**.

information at the **River Road Queen Welcome Center** at the intersection of US 82 and Reed Road in Greenville. You won't miss the building – it's the only one designed to resemble a paddle-wheeler steamboat. Greenville is the site of the annual **Delta Blues & Heritage Festival** in September (1-601 335 3523/1-888 812 5837). This is the quintessential Mississippi blues festival, packed with the best music the region has to offer and plenty of greasy, calorific and fabulous food dished up by locals. Other than the festival, the best spot for music is the **Flowing Fountain**, which showcases local and touring musicians.

The **Greenville Writers' Exhibit** is also worth visiting. Greenville produced an impressive group of writers (almost all white and upper middle class) during the 20th century. Civil War historian and novelist Shelby Foote, crusading journalist Hodding Carter and novelists Walker Percy, Ellen Douglas and Beverly Lowry are all among the remarkable members of the Greenville School of White Southern Angst.

From Greenville, the next stop is the main blues destination on the route: Clarksdale, a mecca for blues lovers throughout the world. Start at the **Delta Blues Museum**, which is jam-packed with memorabilia and minutiae related to the blues. You'll see videos, photographs and sound-and-slide shows as well as sheet music and instruments used by some of the old blues stars.

The Delta is still learning how to deal with the blues heritage, which most whites completely dismissed and many middle-class blacks saw as a vulgar lower class form. Other than the Delta Blues Museum there are no large-scale institutions or sights to see in Mississippi, but blues devotees seek out a number of spots associated with the greats. Muddy Waters lived with his family in a modest frame cabin on the **Stovall Plantation**, six miles (nine kilometres) outside Clarksdale (US 6 west to Highway 322, then south on to US 1). You'll find the spot marked by a plaque, but the cabin has gone: an archivist for the House of Blues was sent to the Delta to scout out treasures and he scooped up the entire cabin. It was dismantled and is now 'on loan' to the HoB chain. Reportedly, the House of Blues man also bought an entire cotton gin, which was taken apart and rebuilt as part of the Los Angeles club.

Another home without a home is that of WC Handy (1873-1958), who is regarded by many as the 'Father of the Blues'. He composed 'Memphis Blues', 'St Louis Blues' and countless other songs but, almost as importantly, he wrote and published song sheets for his music, thereby giving African-American music widespread visibility and publicity for the first time. A plaque at 317 Issaquena Avenue, Clarksdale marks the location of the vanished house where Handy lived with his family from 1903 to 1905. Handy was a highly trained musician whose early bands played waltzes and classical music. One night at a dance in Clarksdale the affluent white audience asked him to play his 'native music' instead. Handy was baffled at what they meant but agreed to let a local trio of ragged black musicians perform. Handy was amazed to see the audience go wild for the 'outlandish' music. He was even more agitated when the crowd showered the three with silver dollars, far more than his nine-piece orchestra's fee for the evening. 'Then,' he later wrote in his autobiography, 'I saw the beauty of primitive music.'

Finally, there's the inevitable question of 'The Crossroads'. Robert Johnson's seminal blues song ('I went down to the Crossroads/Fell on my knees') has intrigued and plagued blues followers for decades. Well, the meeting between Johnson and the Devil on a dusty Delta crossroads could have been anywhere. *Living Blues* magazine even did an investigative story several years ago trying to nail down the exact spot. Most popular choice is the intersection of US Highway 61 and US Route 49 in the centre of Clarksdale, probably because it's the easiest to find and makes for a cool photograph to show off later.

Clarksdale is also the site of two popular festivals: the **Delta Jubilee** (1-662 627 7337/ www.clarksdale.com) held in June and the **Sunflower River Blues & Gospel Festival** (1-601 627 6820) in August. Both are centred around two local favourites: music and food.

Delta Blues Musuem

1 Blues Alley, Clarksdale (1-662 627 6820/ www.deltabluesmuseum.org). **Open** 9am-5pm Mon-Sat; 1-5pm Sun. **Admission** free.

Flowing Fountain

816 Nelson Street, Greenville (1-662 335 9836). **Open** from 7pm Thur-Sat. **Admission** $3. **No credit cards.**

Greenville Writers' Exhibit

William Alexander Percy Memorial Library, 341 Main Street, Greenville (1-662 335 2331). **Open** 9am-7pm Mon-Wed; 9am-6pm Thur, Fri; 1-5pm Sat; closed Sun. **Admission** free.

Where to stay

There isn't a highly developed travel culture in most of Mississippi, which means the best bets for accommodation are the reliable, no-surprises chain hotels. In Clarksdale try the **Hampton Inn** (710 S State Street, at Highway 61 (1-662 627 9292, 1-800 426 7866, rates $64-$74) or the **Days Inn** (1910 N State Street, 1-662 624 4391, rates $69.95). In Greenville there's a **Comfort Inn** (3030 Highway 82 East, at Highway 1, 1-662 378 4976, 1-800 228 5150, rates $65). There are a few B&Bs in the Delta

but they tend to go in and out of business. Check with the local tourist office for up-to-date accommodation suggestions.

Where to eat

Sad to say, the best places for a meal are the chain eateries, with names such as **Western Sizzler** (a steakhouse), that have made their way into even the desolate towns of the Delta. Vegetarians should bring supplies with them. The most famous restaurant in the entire Delta is **Doe's Eat Place** in Greenville (502 Nelson Street, 1-662 334 3315, closed Sun, main courses $15-$60), an idiosyncratic café (you enter past the kitchen) that serves up fabulous steaks and tamales among other dishes. Ask the locals for other recommendations.

Getting there

By car

This is the only practical way to tour the Delta, and offers several options. The obsessive traveller might want to start Highway 61 at its terminus in Louisiana north of St Francisville and follow the meandering road north through Vicksburg, Natchez and countless other small towns. A more rational plan is to take I-10 west out of New Orleans, then I-55 north to Mississippi. Head east at Jackson on I-20 to Vicksburg or continue on I-55 to Winona then east on Highway 82 to Greenville.

By bus

Greyhound buses (1-800 229 9424, www.greyhound.com) do travel to the Delta (allow 9-12hrs New Orleans–Greenville), but once you arrive, local transport is very spotty. Weekday return is $114; weekend return $117.

Tourist information

Clarksdale–Coahoma County Chamber of Commerce

PO Box 160, Clarksdale, MS 38614 (1-662 627 7337/fax 627 1313/www.clarksdale.com). **Open** 8.30am-5pm Mon-Thur; 8.30am-4pm Fri; closed Sat, Sun.

Greenville–Washington County Convention & Visitors Bureau

410 Washington Avenue, Greenville, MS 38701 (1-662 334 2711). **Open** Phone for details.

Mississippi State Office of Tourism

Box 1705, Ocean Springs, MS 39566 (1-800 927 6378/www.visitmississippi.org). **Open** 7am-7pm daily.

River Road Queen Welcome Center

119 S Theobald Street, at Main Street, Greenville, MI 38701 (1-662 335 3523/1-888 812 5837). **Open** 8.30am-5pm Mon-Fri; closed Sat, Sun.

Heading West

A couple of hours from the Big Easy, you can experience the unique sights, sounds and tastes of Cajun Country.

Step back in time in **Vermilionville**.

Lafayette & Cajun Country

French-speaking Acadians, known worldwide as Cajuns, are the cultural heart of Louisiana and consider Lafayette their de facto capital. Located about 120 miles (193 kilometres) west of New Orleans, it's a booming oil town surrounded by swamps, farms and crawfish ponds. It is the centre of Cajun activity and where you must go to find what some consider to be the 'real Louisiana'.

Throughout the 20th century the local government went to lengthy efforts to wipe out the French language here (Cajuns over 40 will tell you stories of being beaten for speaking French in school). But now a massive movement is under way to restore the language to prominence. Cajuns today are revelling in their history. They've received support from a new, more culturally aware America and from the Government of France. Cajun music, food and art is now known the world over, and the intensive tourist interest in Acadiana has bolstered their self-confidence. These days, Cajuns are so proud to be Cajuns it's almost annoying.

Most Cajuns from the rural communities surrounding Lafayette still speak French in their homes, and recently local restaurants and shops have begun offering weekly 'L'états Françaises' – morning or evening sessions during which only French is spoken. Particularly in the small villages, you're almost as likely to hear 'bonjour' as 'hello' from passing strangers. Tourists with passable French skills could find themselves warmly embraced and invited to a local *boucherie* (basically a pig slaughter and barbecue). Cajuns are that friendly.

Once you've got your bearings on this Cajun business, start with the past and work your way forward: **Vermilionville** is a perfect first stop. It's a living history museum of Cajun culture in the form of a recreated Acadian village. Sprawling over 23 acres (nine hectares), Vermilionville invites visitors to experience Cajun life as it was a century ago. The town has homes, a one-room schoolhouse, church, bakery and blacksmith shop. The buildings, with steeply peaked roofs and stairways from the front door to the upstairs, are typical examples of Acadian architecture. Workers and guides wander about in costume and French is widely spoken. Regular activities include Cajun bands and cooking, art and dance instruction. The whole experience is very leisurely and well put-together, with no trace of Disneyism.

Just outside Vermilionville is the **Acadian Cultural Center**, which puts the whole Cajun experience into context. Galleries grouped by era use photos and artefacts to trace the Acadian diaspora and the development of Cajun life in Louisiana. A beautifully composed film narrates the story of French settlers in Acadiana. Be advised, however, that the film's point of view is fanatically anti-British, which skews the whole endeavour. ' Oh yes,' said one staff member when the film was mentioned, 'English visitors usually get up and walk out long before it's over.'

After absorbing the big picture of Cajun history and culture, head downtown to wander among the old buildings, restaurants and shops. Lafayette is a largely utilitarian place, but it has charming touches and winding streets. The best nightclub in town, **Grant Street Dance Hall**, is in the middle of downtown, presenting local and regional acts nightly.

Although central Lafayette is pleasant, the best sites lie in the surrounding territory, so head about 15 miles (24 kilometres) south to Iberia Parish to see the mini-kingdom of one of the area's more quixotically successful families, the McIlhennys. **Avery Island**, off US 90 (follow the signs), is a barrier island in the Louisiana wetlands and has long been the home of the McIlhenny and Avery families, creators of Tabasco sauce and collectors of unusual animals.

The areas of Avery Island that are open to the public are actually a tiny percentage of the space and activity on the island. The rest is home to the family and its pepper farms and factories. The island itself is an oddity, sitting as it does on a salt mountain (known as a salt dome) hundreds of feet tall. The public cannot visit the salt mines on the island, which are said to contain tunnels more than 100 feet (30.5 metres) high and a mile (1.6 kilometres) wide, but you can tour the factory and see the process by which Tabasco is made, with bushels of salted peppers mashed and set in oak barrels to age.

The island's other attraction is its 200-acre (81-hectare) gardens that are ablaze in spring and summer. They encompass a wildlife park,

Jungle Gardens, which is refuge to hundreds of species of birds – another fixation of early 20th-century patriarch Edmund McIlhenny. The park is walled with bamboo, and features alligator ponds and bird-nesting platforms crowded with endangered species. McIlhenny saw himself as a naturalist but his goofy experiments led to lasting problems.

He imported nutria, a large South American swimming rat, to the island many years ago in a misguided attempt to balance his ecosystem. Some of the animals escaped during a hurricane and spread like wildfire. Today, these voracious vegetarian creatures are blamed for devouring the area's wetlands and are considered a menace to the conservation of the state's marshes and swamps. Attempts to popularise nutria fur and meat in order to encourage hunters to kill the huge rats have so far been unsuccessful, and the critters are gradually munching their way through southern Louisiana.

Head back on US 90 toward Lafayette and stop off at another salt dome island. **Jefferson Island** is famous for its breathtaking gardens, which trail around the top and sides of the salt dome that rises out of Lake Peigneur. The island was established as an estate by the famous actor Joseph Jefferson (1829-1905), who constructed a handsome house there in 1870. Perched at the island's highest point, the house has wide porches and Moorish details in a light version of Steamboat Gothic. Jefferson used the house as his winter hunting camp and it was later taken over by a wealthy family as their retreat. The estate is called **Rip Van Winkle Gardens** in honour of Jefferson's most famous (and lucrative) theatre role and is open for tours. B&B accommodation and an excellent waterside restaurant are also available.

Beyond its beauty, however, there's a strange and mysterious story about Jefferson Island. In 1980 an oil rig on the lake somehow punctured the ceiling of the vast salt mine that lay underneath it, triggering a massive whirlpool that swallowed the drilling rig, 11 barges, several tugboats, houses, 65 acres (26 hectares) of land and all the water in the lake. Miraculously, no one was killed but the

Some like it hot. Visitors to Avery Island can tour the **Tabasco** factory.

Playlist Cajun country

Buckweat Zydeco Story

(Tomorrow Records)
When he played 'Jambalaya' during the
closing ceremonies for the Atlanta Olympics,
Stanley Dural Jr (aka Buckwheat Zydeco)
made this melange of R&B and Cajun dance
music internationally famous.

Beausoleil: La Danse de la Vie

(Rhino Records)
Brothers David and Michael Doucet led the
Cajun revival with their band Beausoleil.

Allons en Louisiane

(Rounder Records)
An anthology that comes with a CD-rom
providing cooking lessons, dancing tips (not
while your driving!) and even some French.

Alligator Stomp: Cajun & Zydeco Classics, Vol. 2

There's a series of three, but volume two
gives a good overview and includes
wonderful tunes like 'Toot Toot' by Doug
Kershaw and Fats Domino.

landscape was changed forever. Years of
litigation followed, but who or what was to
blame for the disaster was never determined.
The event remains a mystery to scientists and
a vivid memory to local residents.

To sample the natural world of swampy
Cajun country, the **Atchafalaya Swamp
Basin** is a must. You'll see great chunks of it
while travelling on the elevated section of I-10
outside of Baton Rouge. For closer inspection,
there are numerous swamp tours and alligator-
watching events. The best idea is to check
adverts in the weekly *Times of Acadiana*
newspaper, pick up current brochures at a hotel
or make direct enquiries at the **Lafayette
Convention & Visitors Commission**.

A few miles out of Lafayette, **Breaux
Bridge** is a charming town that retains its
original downtown buildings along with
elevated sidewalks and old wooden shopfronts.
Restored Victorian homes in the surrounding
neighbourhood make for a pleasant drive
through town and there are several antiques
stores in downtown that are worth a browse.
The most important reason to stop here,
though, is to try out the food at **Café des
Amis** (*see page 260*).

After leaving Breaux Bridge, head south on
Highway 31 about 12 miles (19.5 kilometres) to
St Martinville, another quaint bayou town
with historic charm. This little community is
home to several legends. It is central to
Longfellow's poem *Evangeline*, which tells the
tale of star-crossed Acadian lovers Evangeline
and Gabriel. Part of the forced migration of
French Canadians from Nova Scotia, the two
lovers were pushed on to different ships and
were only reunited in middle age when
Evangeline had become a nun and Gabriel was
dying. The poem ends in Louisiana with
Gabriel dying in Evangeline's arms. The story
was so popular that the line between fiction and

reality has been erased, and although historians
roll their eyes, everyone in St Martinville will
tell you that the 'real' Evangeline and Gabriel
met at last under the Evangeline Oak in the
middle of St Martinville. You'll find it behind
the **Presbytère of St Martin de Tours**
church on the banks of Bayou Teche. Nearby is
a statue of Evangeline, modelled on early
Hollywood film star Dolores del Rio, who
played the Acadian heroine in the 1928 silent
film *The Romance of Evangeline*.

St Martinville was also a favoured refuge for
French aristocrats fleeing the French Revolution.
Many of its more impressive homes were
constructed during that period, when the town
was so elegant that it became known as 'Petit
Paris'. For more information, visit the **Petit
Paris Museum** next door to the church, which
offers visual and written information on the
history of the town.

Acadian Cultural Center

501 Fisher Road, Lafayette (1-318 232 0789). **Open**
8am-5pm daily. **Admission** free.

Grant Street Dance Hall

113 West Grant Street, Lafayette (1-318 237 2255).
Open Fri, Sat; phone for details. **Admission**
phone for details.

Jungle Gardens

Highway 329, Avery Island (1-337 369 6243). **Open**
8am-5pm daily. **Admission** $5.75; $4 concessions.
Credit MC, V.

Petit Paris Museum

131 S Main Street, St Martinville (1-318 394 7334).
Open 9.30am-4.30pm daily. **Admission** $1; 75¢
concessions. **No credit cards.**

Rip Van Winkle Gardens

*5505 Rip Van Winkle Road, Jefferson Island, New
Iberia (1-800 375 3332/www.ripvanwinkle.com).*
Open 9am-5pm daily. **Admission** $9; $6-$7
concessions. **Credit** AmEx, DC, MC, V.

Trips Out of Town

Tabasco Plant

329 Avery Island (1-318 365 8173). **Open** 9am-4pm daily. **Admission** free.

Vermilionville

1600 Surrey Street, Exit 103A Evangeline Thruway, Lafayette (1-318 233 4077/www.vermilionville.org). **Open** 10am-5pm daily. **Admission** $8; $5-$6.50 concessions. **Credit** AmEx, DC, MC, V.

Where to stay

Tourism is still a relatively recent phenomenon in Acadiana, so the selection of places to spend the night is limited. However, a handful of B&Bs have opened in recent years, providing a welcome alternative to the mainstream hotels.

One of the best is **Alida's Bed & Breakfast** (2631 SE Evangeline Thruway, 1-318 264 1191, rates $85-$125), located in a pleasant historic house off the busy central road through Lafayette. Run by Tanya and Douglas Greenwald, it has four large guest rooms, furnished with antiques, a TV and telephone. If you want to talk to locals and get their insight into the community, this is the place to stay. Breakfast is a sit-down affair with all the guests together, and conversation is lively.

Alternatively, try the **Old Castillo Hotel** in St Martinville (220 Evangeline Boulevard, at Highway 31, 1-318 394 4010, 1-800 621 3017, rates $50-$80), a large B&B on the banks of the Bayou Teche directly under the branches of the Evangeline Oak. The 19th-century building was formerly a girls' school, and provides spacious, comfortable rooms that offer the best view in town. Photos of past pupils line the walls in the small restaurant (main courses $8.95-$15.95). For an upscale, mainstream hotel, the **Courtyard by Marriott** in Lafayette (214 E Kaliste Saloom Road, Lafayette, 1-318 232 5005, rates $75-$89) has everything you could hope for, including a location near downtown. Those on a budget should head for **Motel 6** (2724 NE Evangeline Thruway, near the I-10/I-49 Exchange, 1-318 233 2055, rates $38-$42), which offers nondescript but serviceable rooms with televisions.

Where to eat

Café des Amis (140 East Bridge Street, Breaux Bridge, 1-318 332 5273, closed dinner Mon-Wed & Sun, main courses $15-$22) is one of the best restaurants in the region. The small dining room is often packed and for good reason. The food is excellent and at about $15 per person, reasonably priced. Catfish, crawfish and shrimp with creative sauces are a speciality and the fried eggplant (aubergine) is the best in the South. The atmosphere is festive, with wide windows thrown open on warm days, wooden floors, antique furniture and local art decorating the walls.

Another excellent restaurant to keep in mind is located 15 minutes' drive north of Lafayette in the tiny burg of Grand Coteau. **Catahoula's** (234 Martin Luther King, Grand Coteau, 1-318 662 2275, 1-888-547-2275, closed dinner Fri, Sun, all Mon, main courses $12.95-$21.95) is located at the only traffic light in town, directly across the street from Grand Coteau's biggest attraction, the peaceful, historic convent **Academy of the Sacred Heart**. Elegant and creative versions of local cuisine are served, accompanied by a surprisingly good wine list and a pleasant atmosphere. The walls are decorated with large photos of the restaurant's namesake: the strange-looking Catahoula, who is the official state dog. It's a welcome change from the sometimes overly enthusiastic Cajun restaurants that predominate in the area.

If you don't feel like making the drive to Grand Coteau, **Evangeline Seafood & Steakhouse** (SE Evangeline Thruway, Lafayette, 1-318 233 2658, closed lunch Sat, main courses $7.95-$17.95) offers great food in the middle of town. Main courses include fried tilapia with crabmeat sauce.

Getting there

By car

From New Orleans, follow I-110 west through Baton Rouge, over the spectacular Atchafalaya Swamp and take exit number 103A, which will deposit you on the Evangeline Thruway. The **Lafayette Convention & Visitors Commission** is a couple of miles down the road.

By bus

Greyhound (1-800 229 9424/www.greyhound.com) runs frequent daily services to Lafayette from New Orleans. A return ticket costs $33 and the journey takes 3-4hrs.

By train

For **Amtrak** services (1-800 872 7245/www.amtrak.com), *see p240.*

Tourist information

Iberia Parish Convention & Visitors Bureau

2704 Highway 14, New Iberia, LA 70500 (1-318 365 1540/www.iberiaparish.com). **Open** 9am-5pm daily.

Lafayette Convention & Visitors Commission

1400 NW Evangeline Thruway, off I-10, Lafayette, (1-800 346 1958/www.lafayettetravel.com). Mailing address: PO Box 52066, Lafayette, LA 70505. **Open** 8.30am-5pm Mon-Fri; 9am-5pm Sat, Sun.

Heading South

At the seaward tip of Louisiana, Grand Isle is the nearest beach to town.

Grand Isle

Many people who know Grand Isle's reputation through literature often take the trouble to seek out this barrier island at the tip of Louisiana, 110 miles (177 kilometres) from New Orleans. In Kate Chopin's 1889 novel *The Awakening*, a conventional 19th-century wife begins to find herself during a summer on Grand Isle. Famous New Orleans writer Lafcadio Hearn wrote a lyrical novel and many adoring articles about the place 'where finally all the land melts down into desolations of seamarsh'. Today, the sandy, six-mile (9.7-kilometre) long island bears little resemblance to the languid resort described by earlier writers, but Grand Isle is still an entertaining side trip from New Orleans – in some ways the trip itself is more interesting than the destination.

The drive to Grand Isle from New Orleans is a pleasant tour of the most watery part of Cajun Country, where farms give way to the maritime world of commercial fishing, offshore oil work, charter boats, shipbuilding and ship repair. At Raceland, 50 miles (80 kilometres) south-west of New Orleans on US 90, the Grand Isle tour truly begins when you turn due south on Highway 1. This two-lane road runs alongside Bayou Lafourche (pronounced 'La Foosh'), a busy navigable waterway that runs down to the Gulf of Mexico. The bayou is known as 'the longest street in the world' because it is the main thoroughfare and point of reference for this part of south Louisiana.

While Highway 1 runs on the west side of Bayou Lafourche, Highway 308 runs parallel to the east side. The area is thickly populated, with the towns of Lockport, Larose, Cut Off, Galliano, Golden Meadow and Leeville blending into one another. Large Catholic churches are the dominant municipal structures, a reminder that Cajun Country, for all the tourism hoopla, is a very real place, firmly rooted in family and church. Points of interest along the way include religious shrines, stores and restaurants.

In Cut Off, there's the **Louisiana Catalogue Store**, a combination bookstore and Louisiana emporium run by filmmaker Glen Pitre (maker of *Belizaire the Cajun*). It sells a wide range of Louisiana items such as records, food, spices, crafts, souvenirs and folk art.

For large-scale folk art, look out for an impressive, handmade, outdoor shrine to the Virgin Mary in Golden Meadow. Located on the Highway 1 side of Bayou Lafourche, beside the Golden Meadow police department, this is a pocket park of Catholic devotion with a larger-than-life Mary in a glass refrigeration unit (so that fresh flowers won't wilt), whitewashed cement pews and guest books and prayer lists thoughtfully sheltered in purpose-built cases. After Leeville, the land really begins to 'melt down' and the rest of the drive is rather bleak.

Look for a tiny church on the east side of Highway 1. Measuring a scant 10 by 14 feet (3 by 4.3 metres), **Smith's Chapel** was built by a local couple as a memorial to their two sons, one who died of a childhood disease and one in a knife fight. It's never locked (if the door is closed, lift the bolt and go in) and there are always candles burning at the minuscule altar. Paper and pens are left for visitors to write messages to God ('thank you God!! Clean and sober for 24 hours!'; 'Please tell my Mom hello up there.'). Mrs Noonie Smith, who built the chapel, lives across the road and operates an 'adult novelties' business in a trailer. She sees no contradiction between her X-rated adult videos and the chapel, and is happy to greet visitors at either site.

Grand Isle floats off the tip of Louisiana like a footnote, connected to the mainland by the causeway-like highway and sheer determination. In 1893 one of the worst hurricanes on record swept the island clear of hotels, fishermen's cottages and the landscape that gave Lafcadio Hearn heart palpitations ('imposing groves of oak, its golden wealth of orange trees, its odorous lanes of oleander, its broad grazing meadows yellow starred with wild camomile… its loveliness is exceptional'). Alas, Grand Isle's great beauty has faded, but not its seaside allure. Despite Louisiana's considerable coastline, there's hardly a beach in the state. When New Orleanians want real beach, they go east to Mississippi, Alabama or Florida. When they want an immediate beach or fishing beach, they head to Grand Isle.

The island is home to a small group of year-round fishermen, oil rig workers and their families, but the population increases significantly as the weather gets warmer. Most summer visitors come for the excellent fishing

Grand Isle, six miles of sand and sea.

from piers or by boat. The island is full of modest summer homes, usually simple frame cabins on stilts, painted garish colours and given humorous names.

Oddly for a place that promotes itself as a seaside playground, access to the water is limited. For those who aren't staying in a summer house or a motel, just about the only way to get to the water is through the **Grand Isle State Park** at the eastern tip of the island. Relatively new, the park has very good facilities and is a favourite with those who enjoy no-frills camping. The beach is reached by a long, elevated walkway past the scrubby landscape; while this isn't the sparkling white sand beaches of the rest of the Gulf Coast, it does have sand, picnic tables and a mile of beach. The 400-foot (122-metre) fishing pier is the main draw but a small beachside campground is popular, too.

Though Grand Isle is mostly a laid-back resort with no nightlife, things change dramatically during the annual **Tarpon Fishing Rodeo** in August, when thousands of fishing fanatics and a young redneck party crowd flood the island. The 'rodeo' is best avoided except by extreme party animals. It's not a good time to fish, either, with the waters overcrowded and raucous.

Grand Isle State Park

PO Box 745, Grand Isle, LA 70358 (787 2559/1-888 787 2559/www.crtpstate.la.us). **Open** 7am-9pm Mon-Thur; 7am-10pm Fri, Sat; 7am-9pm Sun. **Admission** *Up to 4 people* $2; $1 children. *5 or more people* 50¢ each. **No credit cards**.

Louisiana Catalogue Store

14839 W Main Street, Cut Off (693 4100/1-800 375 4100/www.lacat.com). **Open** 9am-5pm Mon, Tue, Thur, Fri; closed Wed, Sat, Sun. **Credit** DC, MC, V.

Where to stay, eat & drink

Randolph's Restaurant (806 Bayou Drive, Golden Meadow, 475 5272, closed Mon, Tue, main courses $11-$17) is a local landmark, dating back to the 1930s. It's famous for its

moderately priced seafood dishes, cooked in the local Cajun style. Depending on the season, there are also fruit stands along the way.

On Grand Isle itself **Cigar's Cajun Cuisine** (1119 Highway 1, 787 2188, main courses $9.95-$17.95) offers seafood and a bar and is open seven days a week. Year-round residents and weekend visitors gather in the compound, which includes a marina and a motel (787 3220, rates $69-$89).

Campers can rough it at the **Grand Isle State Park Campground** (1-877 266 7652) for $10 per night. It's primitive – meaning no running water or electricity – and all facilities are a five-minute walk away. For a more civilised stay, **Seabreeze Cottages** (3210 Highway 1, 787 3180, rates $80-$105) is a pleasant compound of small, two-bedroom cottages with kitchenettes. There's a two-night minimum during summer. If you want to rent a private fishing camp (usually a summer house with water access), the **Grand Isle Tourist Commission** keeps a list.

Getting there

By car

A car is the only way to get to Grand Isle as there is no bus service or other public transport. From New Orleans take US 90 west. At Raceland turn south on US 1, which ends at Grand Isle.

Tourist information

Grand Isle Tourist Commission

Mailing address: PO Box 817, Grand Isle, LA 70358 (787 2997/wwwsportsmansparadise.com). **Open** 8am-4pm Mon-Fri; closed Sat, Sun.
Phone or write for tourist information about the island; there isn't an office to visit.

Lafourche Parish Tourist Commission

Mailing address: PO Box 340, Raceland, LA 70394 (537 58001/cajun@lafourchetourism.org). **Open** 9am-4pm Mon-Fri; 10am-3pm Sat; closed Sun.
This very handy tourist office is at the junction of US 90 and US 1 in Raceland, and is clearly signposted.

Heading East

The further you go, the better the beaches – and the bigger the casinos.

'I'm going to the coast,' say New Orleanians as the weekend approaches, their faces softening and their voices taking on a happy lilt. The weekend exodus out of the city (year round) is a mystery to New Orleans-bound travellers who can't wait to get here. But the residents of New Orleans need a respite from the endless parties – and party-planning – of the Big Easy. Carnival and Jazz Fest may only last for a few weeks each year, but locals spend hundreds of hours in meetings, conferences, costume-fittings and working lunches planning the damn things: the 'coast' is their release from the pressure of having fun in New Orleans.

The 'coast', as defined in New Orleans terms, means the seaside areas of the Gulf of Mexico that are within a day's drive of the city. They stretch from the almost-suburb of Bay St Louis, Mississippi, to the quintessential southern beach town of Panama City, Florida. For New Orleans visitors the coast is an alluring trip, too, since the city is an easy drive from some of the best beaches in North America. Travelling east, the mossy, laid-back seaside towns of Mississippi give way to 'the poor man's New Orleans' of old coastal cities Mobile and Pensacola, and then on to the gorgeous beaches of the Gulf of Mexico. From roughly Mobile Bay to Panama City, the coast is a paradise of white, sugary sands edged by warm, blue-green waters.

Of course, no paradise is complete without its serpent, and the Gulf Coast, alas, has several. Once the coast was practically a secret playground for Southerners. Until fairly recently it was a collection of lightly populated waterside towns characterised by old-fashioned guesthouses, lazy fishing villages and untouched beaches. Today, the Mississippi coast sometimes seems to be one big gambling casino, while the magnificent beaches of south Alabama and north-western Florida have been discovered by condo-crazed developers.

Yet the beauty and the charm of the Gulf Coast somehow overwhelm the tawdriness that has been inflicted upon it by mega-casinos and appalling holiday architecture. From the arty little towns in Mississippi to the pure white sand beaches of the Florida Panhandle, the coast offers rich rewards to travellers. And it's not just a summertime place. With the mild semi-tropical climate, swimming is possible from March to October and beach walking, bird watching, fishing and boating are year-round activities.

Travel by car is the best way to see the Gulf Coast. There is train and bus transport from New Orleans to Mobile, Pensacola and Mississippi coast towns (*see page 240*), but local public transport (when there is any) doesn't tie into the train or bus routes. Amtrak schedules are incredibly inconvenient, putting east-bound travellers into Mobile and Pensacola in the early morning hours when long waits for taxis are the norm. Once in Mobile or Pensacola, the local bus systems

Arts & Entertainment

Vegas-style luxury awaits at the $650-million **Beau Rivage** casino resort. *See p265.*

The pristine beaches of **Ship Island**.

are poorly organised and limited in scope. Hitchhiking among younger travellers isn't unknown, but neither is it recommended.

Mississippi Gulf Coast

If your priority is beaches, keep going. While there are some pleasant public beaches along Highway 90, they are poor substitutes for the sparkling white sands another hour to the east. The barrier islands that line the Mississippi coast intercept the best sand and the clearest water, making the state's 80-mile (130-kilometre) coastline a pale imitation of the better coastal spots.

But the Mississippi coast has its attractions, from the wannabe-Las Vegas casinos to the likeable little beach towns, nicely summarised by **Bay St Louis**, 60 miles (96 kilometres) east of New Orleans on US 90 (and several exits off I-10). Bay St Louis has a big casino, **Casino Magic**, but it is thankfully located outside the village beside the quiet waters of the bay that gives the town its name. The old town is centered around Beach Avenue and Main Street, both heavily populated with antiques shops, second-hand stores, art galleries and cafés. Of particular interest is the **Serenity Gallery**, which specialises in local and regional artists.

Gambling is growing rapidly here: there are more than a dozen large casinos along the coast, with more on the horizon. Mississippi is welcoming the gambling world, warts and all, with open arms. And why not? Even crime is down, as residents find that well-paying casino jobs offer better deals than petty theft.

The Mississippi Coast attempted to move into the big league casino ranks with the opening of **Beau Rivage**, a $650 million casino-hotel-resort that opened in 1999. With

12 restaurants, a full-service spa, excellent fitness centre, 13 shops and 1,780 rooms, the casino has been a tremendous hit with Southerners. However, although it's often filled to capacity, Beau Rivage has not been an unqualified success for its Las Vegas planners. Like every other gambling centre outside Las Vegas and Atlantic City, the Mississippi Coast hasn't been able to attract the critical mass of high rollers who pad the casino's bottom line. Nevertheless, regional travellers flock to the Biloxi resort, eager to roll the dice and catch the Cirque du Soleil show; a neo-circus of humour, European performers and dazzling effects that is sold out for weeks at a time.

Other casinos along the coast have had a dip in business with the arrival of Beau Rivage but still remain healthy. The gambling revenues from Mississippi casinos amount to $1.72 billion a year: third in the nation after Nevada and New Jersey.

For those in search of beach-oriented fun, Mississippi has a 26-mile (42-kilometre) man-made beach stretching from Pass Christian, just over the Louisiana border, to Ocean Springs. But the biggest surprise of Mississippi beach life isn't to be found on the main shoreline; instead, it is a ferry ride away from Gulfport Yacht Harbor. The ferry takes travellers 12 miles (19 kilometres) across the Gulf to **Ship Island**, a barrier island that is part of the Gulf Islands National Seashore.

A wooden boardwalk crosses the island, linking the swamps with a wide, breezy beach. The best area of beach, which is pristinely maintained, is on the far side of the island where the sand is as white and the water as blue as any in Florida. The row of barrier islands blocks the muddy water of the Mississippi River from sullying the ocean, as

Built in the 1840s, **Fort Morgan** kept out the Union navy during the civil war. *See p268.*

it does elsewhere, creating an oasis that verges on a tropical paradise. Note that visitors are only allowed on the island between March and October from morning until sunset.

Unexpected by most visitors, the Mississippi Gulf Coast offers two remarkable small museums, both devoted to eccentric local artists. The **Ohr–O'Keefe Museum of Art** in Biloxi displays the work of the turn-of-the-19th-century 'Mad Potter of Biloxi'. Ohr (1857-1918) was known for his two-foot (60-centimetre) long moustache as well as his idiosyncratic approach to pottery. His work is designed to look as though it is constantly in motion: teapots with impossibly curling handles seem to jig, while bowls twist and turn in oddly graceful ways.

Ohr was never appreciated in his lifetime, and it is said that one day he just up and quit; packed large crates with his favourite work, hauled them out to Biloxi's back bay and buried them in the mud. He then gave up pottery forever. Nobody has ever found the buried pottery, which is a particular shame given that a quality Ohr pot now sells for about $35,000 at auction.

Another magnificent lone artist, Walter Anderson, is showcased in the nearby **Walter Anderson Museum of Art** in Ocean Springs. Ranked as one of the best small museums in America, the Walter Anderson Museum deftly blends world-class art and

small-town intimacy. Anderson (1903-65) was a classically trained artist turned visionary, who painted an intensely personal world of sun, sky, sea, wildlife and light. Anderson rarely sold or exhibited his work during his lifetime, which was punctuated by bouts of mental illness. He lived a hermit's life in the midst of his artistic family, often avoiding his wife and children and working at his brothers' famous art pottery workshop only when he needed money. The extent of Anderson's work and vision was discovered after his death when his family was finally free to look through his work. They discovered Anderson's masterwork, a dazzling mural of the earth's creation that covered the walls, ceiling and floor of one locked room of his small cottage.

The 'Little Room' is now a room within the museum, painstakingly taken apart and reassembled right down to the latched door. Its panoramic vision is echoed in the community hall in the museum, which Anderson volunteered to paint during a period of clarity in 1951. This second masterpiece describes the Mississippi Gulf Coast's flora and fauna, as well as its Indian past and European conquest, in vivid, powerful colours and forms. The Anderson family's **Shearwater Pottery**, just a few minutes' drive from the museum, is still in operation and is also well worth a visit.

Beau Rivage

875 Beach Boulevard, Biloxi, MS 39530 (1-888 567 6667/www.beaurivage.com). **Open** 24hrs daily. **Credit** AmEx, DC, Disc, MC, V.

Casino Magic

711 Casino Magic Drive, Bay St Louis (1-800 562 4425/www.casinomagic.com). **Open** 24hrs daily. **Credit** AmEx, MC, V.

Ohr–O'Keefe Museum of Art

136 George Ohr Street, Biloxi (1-228 374 5547/ www.georgeohr.org). **Open** 9am-5pm Mon-Sat; closed Sun. **Admission** $3; $2 concessions. **No credit cards**.

Serenity Gallery

126 ¹⁄₂ Main Street, Bay St Louis (1-228 467 3061). **Open** 10am-5pm Mon-Sat; noon-5pm Sun. **Admission** free.

Shearwater Pottery

102 Shearwater Drive, Ocean Springs (1-228 875 7320). **Open** 9am-5.30pm Mon-Sat; 1-5pm Sun. **Admission** free. **Credit** MC, V.

Ship Island Excursions

Gulfport Yacht Harbor, Hwy 90 & 49 (1-228 864 1014/www.msshipisland.com). **Departures** *Mar-mid May, Sept, Oct* 9am (outbound), 2.30pm (return) Mon-Fri; 9am, noon (outbound), 2.30pm, 5pm (return) Sat, Sun. *Mid May-Sept* 9am, noon (outbound), 2.30pm, 5pm (return) daily. **Rates** $16; $8-$14 concessions. **No credit cards**.

Walter Anderson Museum of Art

510 Washington Avenue, Ocean Springs (1-228 872 3164). **Open** 10am-5pm Mon-Sat; 1-5pm Sun. **Admission** $5; $2-$4 concessions. **Credit** DC, MC, V.

Where to stay

For a splurge, **Beau Rivage** (*see above*) has the most glamour and amenities (room rates are between $99 and $299 depending on the time of year), while the **Grand Casino Biloxi Hotel** (245 Beach Boulevard, Biloxi, 1-228 432 2500, rates $49-$200) has many flourishes.

B&Bs abound on the coast. Two very pleasant spots are the **Father Ryan House** (1196 Beach Boulevard, Biloxi, 1-228 435 1189, rates $100-$175) and the **Bay Town Inn** (208 North Beach Boulevard, Bay St Louis, 1-228 466 5870, rates $90-$105). For more B&Bs, check out the Gulf Coast B&B Guild's brochure (1-800 237 9493, www.msgulfcoastbnbs.com).

Where to eat & drink

Plenty of restaurants, mostly chains, dot the area, but a careful search can turn up a few good ones. The number of worthwhile eateries is growing as tourism and gambling bring in more visitors.

Old rock 'n' rollers will want to stop at **Dock of the Bay** restaurant (119 North Beach Boulevard, Bay St Louis, 1-228 467 9940, closed

The **USS Alabama**. *See p268.*

Arts & Entertainment

Mon, Tue, main courses $14.95-$18.95), owned by former Blood, Sweat & Tears guitarist Jerry Fisher. He still keeps a hand in the music biz, playing great old blues and rock songs with a pick-up band most Saturday nights. Food at the Dock, by the way, is some of the best on the Mississippi coast, particularly the grilled fish.

For an upmarket experience, **Mary Mahoney's Old French House** in Biloxi (110 Rue Magnolia, off Highway 90, 1-228 374 0163, closed Sun, main courses $18.95-$35.95) specialises in seafood, particularly shrimp dishes. In Ocean Springs, the **BlowFly Inn** (1201 Washington Avenue, Gulfport, 1-228 896 9812, main courses $4.75-$22.95) offers a pleasant view of a nearby bayou and traditional Southern cooking – barbecue ribs are the mainstay. Also in Ocean Springs, **Aunt Jenny's Catfish Restaurant** (1217 Washington Avenue, 1-228 875 9201, closed all Mon, lunch Sat, main courses $8.45-$12.95) is a down-home place in a beautiful historic house on the shores of the back bay. All-you-can-eat specials of seafood and chicken cost under $13.

Getting there

By car

From New Orleans, take I-10 east (about 45min). Large signs indicate the exits to Biloxi and Gulfport.

By bus

Greyhound (1-800 231 2222/www.greyhound.com) runs daily buses to Biloxi from New Orleans; a return costs $41. Several area casinos also provide shuttle services for New Orleans gamblers.

By train

For **Amtrak** services, *see p240.*

Tourist information

Mississippi Gulf Coast Convention & Visitors Bureau

135 Courthouse Road, at 161 Steel, Gulfport (1-601 896 6699/www.gulfcoast.org). Mailing address: PO Box 6128, Gulfport, MS 3950-66128. **Open** 8am-5pm Mon-Fri; closed Sat, Sun.

Mobile, Alabama

Older than New Orleans by more than a decade, Mobile, Alabama is often looked on as the poor man's New Orleans. Located 120 miles (193 kilometres) east of New Orleans on the deepwater port of Mobile Bay, the city was founded by the same French Le Moyne brothers (Iberville and Bienville) who were to be the mainstays of early New Orleans. Mobile (pronounced 'MOE-beal' – citizens will correct anyone saying 'Mo-bull') underwent the same

chaotic French and Spanish colonial history but was also in the hands of the British for long stretches, which gave it a more Anglo character than New Orleans. Although the city has many of the same street names (Conti, St Ann, Royal, Dauphin, Iberville, Bienville and so on), its own fully fledged Mardi Gras and even flashes of the same colonial architecture, the city is far more conservative, Protestant and American Southern than New Orleans.

Visitors interested in the city will find plenty of written information and plenty of Southern hospitality at the visitor centre at **Fort Conde**, a reconstructed 1711 French fort.

Two of the Mobile area's biggest tourist draws are interesting enough to merit stopovers. **Bellingrath Gardens & Home**, 20 miles (32 kilometres) south of Mobile, has more than 800 acres (324 hectares) of carefully designed gardens and woodlands, with changing seasonal displays. The estate started out as a hunting camp in 1917 for Coca-Cola magnate Walter Bellingrath and his wife Bessie, and evolved into their full-time home. The vaguely Mediterranean manor house is stuffed with antiques that the Bellingraths bought off Southern gentry who had been impoverished by the Depression.

The battleship **USS Alabama**, which is permanently anchored in Mobile Bay, was one of the workhorse ships of World War II. It's now a walk-through museum and is today a favourite with kids. It was used as a location in the 1992 Steven Segal–Tommy Lee Jones movie *Under Siege.*

Civil War buffs will certainly be interested in the two historical sites at the tip of Mobile Bay. **Fort Gaines** (on the west side) occupies Dauphin Island, a barrier island that is connected to the mainland by bridge (located at the east end of Bienville Boulevard). Its mirror image across the bay is **Fort Morgan**, at the end of Highway 180. They are among the coastal fortifications that the US built in the 1840s, many of which were in use throughout World War II. As Confederate strongholds, they kept out the Union navy until Admiral David Farragut overwhelmed them with his 1864 assault and famous battle cry: 'damn the torpedoes! Full steam ahead!' Both forts regularly host Civil War re-enactments. A car ferry runs daily between Fort Gaines and Fort Morgan, but though fun, it is notoriously unreliable.

Bellingrath Gardens & Home

12401 Bellingrath Gardens Road, US 90, Theodore (1-334 973 2217/www.bellingrath.org). **Open** 8am-5pm daily. **Admission** $8; $5 concessions; free under-5s. **Credit** AmEx, MC, V.

Fort Gaines
51 Bienville Boulevard, Dauphin Island (1-334 861 6992). **Open** *Summer* 9am-6pm daily. *Winter* 9am-5pm daily. **Admission** $3; $1 concessions; free under-12s. **Credit** MC, V.

Fort Morgan Historic Site
180 West Highway 51, Gulf Shores (1-334 540 7125). **Open** *Fort* 8am-7pm daily. *Museum* 8am-5pm Mon-Fri; 9am-5pm Sat, Sun. **Admission** $3; $1 concessions; free under-6s. **No credit cards.**

Mobile Bay Car Ferry
Embark at Fort Morgan, Gulf Shores Highway 180 (1-334 540 7787). **Open** 8.45am-7.15pm daily. **Rates** $10 car; $3 passenger. **No credit cards.**

USS Alabama
Battleship Parkway, off I-10 (1-800 426 4929). **Open** 8am-6pm daily. **Admission** $8; $4 concessions; free under-6s. **Credit** MC, V.

Where to stay
Mobile has all the usual US chains, most of them strung along I-10 and I-65. Try the **Admiral Semmes-Radisson Hotel** (251 Government Street, 1-800 333 3333), a stately old downtown hotel, refurbished to its pre-World War II glory, or the **Battleship Inn-Best Western** (2701 Battleship Parkway, 1-334 432 2703), an unexceptional roadside motel with great views, perched on Mobile Bay alongside the USS *Alabama* battleship museum. The **Holiday Inn Downtown** (301 Government Street, 1-334 694 0100, 1-800-692-6662) is a standard chain motel in one of those god-awful circular towers. However, it does offer a convenient location and good views from the top-floor rooms.

Where to eat
Like many Southern cities, Mobile is not a good restaurant town. To have a really superior meal you have to dine in someone's home. Nevertheless, local favourites are **Rousso's** (166 S Royal Street, 1-334 433 3322, closed Sun, main courses $6.75-$30), next to Fort Conde, where the seafood is reliable and the service fast, and **Wintzell's Oyster House** (605 Dauphin Street, 1-334 432 4605, main courses $9.95-$19.95), a colourful, ramshackle downtown seafood restaurant.

Getting there
By car
The fastest method is to take I-10 east. It's almost a straight line from New Orleans to Mobile and the 120-mile (193-km) trip should take less than 3hrs. Alternatively, you can take the scenic route via US

90. Take Broad Street/Gentilly Boulevard east. The old highway goes through suburban Gentilly and out along the Chef Menteur highway, finally dwindling to two lanes winding through fishing camps and small towns. US 90 hits all the populated areas along the Mississippi Gulf Coast before going into Mobile through the back door.

By bus
Greyhound (1-800 231 2222/www. greyhound. com) runs several buses a day. The journey takes 3-4hrs and the return costs $43.50 on weekdays and $46.20 at weekends. **Amtrak** (1-800 872 7245/www. amtrak.com) runs a bus service to Mobile on days when there are no trains *(see p240)*. The journey takes 3¾hrs and a one-way ticket costs about $20.

By train
For **Amtrak** services (1-800 872 7245/ www.amtrak.com), *see p240*.

Tourist information
Visitor Center
Fort Conde, 150 South Royal Street, Mobile, AL 36602 (1-800 252 3862). **Open** 8am-5pm daily.

The Alabama Gulf Coast
Alabama has a minuscule coastline compared to Florida, but for the New Orleans-based traveller, it's an attractive alternative because it's very easily accessible without giving up any beach quality.

The beachside town of **Gulf Shores** is the orientation point for the Alabama coast. US 59 (exit off I-10 east of Mobile) dead-ends in Gulf Shores, where it intersects with the 'Beach Highway', US 180. The main public beach is located at the end of US 59. There is plenty of free parking, good facilities and an excellent beach, with lifeguards on duty during the summer. The beach is ground-zero for teenagers and college students on spring break or summer vacation, so the atmosphere is usually 'Party down, dude!' in thick Southern accents. A public fishing pier lies a mile or so east of the public beach on Highway 182. There are also several public access areas along this road, with parking areas an easy walk from the beach.

Shopping is a major draw for the area because of the **Riviera Center Factory Stores** in nearby Foley. Riviera has more than 100 outlet shops, where prices are said to be cut by 20 to 70 per cent.

East of Gulf Shores is **Perdido Key** (regularly voted one of the best beaches in the US; *see page 270* **White silver sands**) and the Florida state line. The area on both sides of the line is called Perdido Key, but the Alabama side seems to have the bigger and uglier condo resorts.

White silver sands

It's a well-kept secret that America's best beaches are on the Gulf of Mexico. Beach specialists such as geologist Dr Stephen Leatherman (fondly known as 'Dr Beach') routinely rate Gulf Coast beaches above West Coast Pacific beaches. **Grayton Beach** and **Perdido Key** make regular appearances in the 'top ten' list alongside the best Hawaii has to offer.

In fact, unscientific beach lovers often rate the Gulf Coast over Hawaii, pointing to the width and depth of Southern beaches, which are rarely plagued by the yucky seaweed and such that wash up on Hawaii's pretty shores. California, with its rocky coast, damp sand and freezing water, remains notably absent from discussions of 'best beaches'.

The beaches of the Gulf Coast are the result of millions of years of earth works. The beautiful white sands started off aeons ago as quartz rocks in the Appalachian Mountains. Over thousands of years, post-Ice Age flooding moved bits of quartz through the rivers into what is now the Gulf of Mexico. As the current coastline began to form about 5,000 years ago, the quartz chips, now ground down to shining bits of blindingly white sand, were deposited along the shoreline. The sand is so fine that it actually squeaks when it's walked on.

For beach camping, nothing on the Gulf Coast is better than **Rosamont Johnson Beach** (information 1-850 492 1595),a white-sand paradise on the Florida side of the Key, off the Beach Highway (Highway 292) and part of the Gulf Islands National Seashore. While there's a lovely daytime beach, the real jewel in the crown of the park is the seven and a half miles (12 kilometres) of untouched island that is open to primitive camping. That means you have to hike in with all your supplies, but the bonus is a pristine beach with no cars, no condos, no noise.

Riviera Center Factory Stores

2601 Highway 59 South, Foley (1-334 943 8888/ 1-888 3333). **Open** 10am-9pm Mon-Sat; 11am-6pm Sun. **Credit** varies.

Where to stay

Renting a beach house for a few days or a week is the best way to visit the Gulf. There's a huge word-of-mouth network but newcomers can usually find a place through agencies such as **Kaiser Realty** (1-800 225 4853/ www.kaiserrealty.com); **Bender Realty** (956 West Beach Boulevard, Gulf Shores, 1-800 528 2651, condos only); and **Meyer Real Estate** (1-800 824 6331/www.gulfbeach.com). Minimum stay is almost always one week.

Hotels and motels tend to be big, impersonal and dominated by chains. The **Gulf State Park Resort Hotel** (21250 East Beach

Boulevard, near Highway 59, 1-334 948 4853, rates $49-$214) is a low-rise development to the east of Gulf Shores. For information on camping on **Rosamont Johnson Beach**, phone 1-850 492 1595.

Where to eat & drink

Gulf Shores has little of the raffishness associated with most beach towns, in part because of Alabama's Deep South prudery. For years it was illegal to call drinking establishments bars or saloons and bizarre laws made serving mixed drinks a legal maze. Nevertheless, the area has two of the most famous bars on the Gulf Coast. On the beach, the **Pink Pony Pub** (1-334 948 6371) has live music, an unapologetic pick-up scene and reasonably good seafood (main courses $5-$10.95). The **Flora-Bama** (17401 Perdido Key Drive, 1-850 492 3048), predictably located on the Alabama–Florida state line, is a beach bar crossed with a country juke joint. Pick-up trucks usually outnumber convertibles, but the free-flowing spirits, loud music and its reputation for outrageousness have kept customers coming for more than 30 years.

The **Oar House Café** (Mile Marker 2, Fort Morgan Road, 1-334 967 2422, closed Sun, main courses $10.95-$18.95) on Fort Morgan Marina is a casual waterside eatery, more a convenience for the fishermen and boaters who dock their vessels here than a commercial restaurant. It does good grilled fish. You could also try **Live Bait** (24281 Perdido Beach Boulevard, Orange Beach, 1-334 974 1612, main courses $10-$20) on the east of Gulf Shores, which has live music on Thursday, Friday and Saturday. **Doc's Seafood Shack & Oyster Bar** (161 Canal Road, US 189, Orange Beach, 1-334 981 6999, main courses $8-$11), east of Gulf Shores, caters to the unrepentant consumers of traditional Southern-cooked seafood. As the sign at the door says: 'If it ain't deep-fried, it ain't worth eating.'

Getting there

By car
Gulf Shores is about 40 miles (64km) south-east of Mobile, via Highway 59.

Tourist information

Gulf Shores & Orange Beach Alabama Gulf Coast Tourism
3150 Gulf Shores Parkway (Highway 59), Gulf Shores, AL 36542 (1-800 982 8562/ www.gulfshores.com). **Open** 8am-5pm Mon-Fri; closed Sat, Sun.

Pensacola & North-west Florida

The north-west corner of Florida, usually called the Panhandle, was long seen as the state stepchild, more hick Alabama and Georgia than sophisticated Palm Beach and Miami. But now that south Florida is excessively built up and crime continues to be a major worry, the Panhandle is coming into its own: residents like to call it the 'real' Florida. The Panhandle also suffers from overbuilding but a large military (mostly naval) presence has kept many prime waterfront lands in government hands, making for far more unspoiled coastline than other parts of the state.

Pensacola, 60 miles (96 kilometres) east of Mobile on I-10, is another Gulf Coast city with colonial roots similar to Mobile and New Orleans. While there are some museums and restored houses in Pensacola, the two main places of interest for the passing traveller are **Pensacola Beach** and the **National Museum of Naval Aviation**.

The Navy Museum, as most locals call it, is a well-designed, airy building that will interest even non-militarists. Restored aircraft and vintage navy memorabilia are on display. In addition, an IMAX cinema adds a powerful visual experience with a programme that practically puts viewers in the cockpit of an F18 fighter jet. The museum is on the grounds of the Pensacola Naval Air Station: take exit 2 off I-10, or follow Navy Boulevard south.

Pensacola Beach is actually separate from the city; it's on Santa Rosa Island, the barrier island in Pensacola Bay. From the city, take US 98 east across the three-mile (five-kilometre) Pensacola Bay Bridge to the neighbouring community of Gulf Breeze, then follow signs marked 'Beaches' to the toll bridge to the island. The beach has plenty of public access and even some traces of its old beachcomber personality, with a handful of family-owned, one-storey motels and non-theme bars. There's plenty of parking for daytrippers and good facilities such as bathrooms and showers.

Santa Rosa Island also has two other beaches which are worth exploring. **Navarre**, a less crowded but beautiful beach, is on the east end of the island, while **Fort Pickens**, a National Seashore Park, is at the western tip. Fort Pickens has drive-up camping spots and the old fort is famous for being the prison of Geronimo, the American Indian guerrilla leader. The jetties off Fort Pickens are a prime spot for Gulf Coast snorkelling.

From Santa Rosa Island to Panama City, the coast is an almost unbroken development of condos, villas, resorts and strip malls. Two places stand out in the frenzy for tourist dollars. The village of **Grayton Beach**, 50 miles (80 kilometres) south of Pensacola off Alternate US 98 (also called Florida Road 30A), is the Gulf Coast answer to Brigadoon. This sleepy little town of modest cottages, beach houses and shacks is a throwback to the 1950s that has somehow managed to opt out of the modern development maw. While a few gaudy villas have begun to rise at the edge of the beach, Grayton Beach is a town firmly committed to the past.

A couple of miles down 30A, **Grayton Beach State Park** offers good daytime facilities, a campground and several miles of perfect, whitesand beaches and beautiful blue-green Gulf waters (*see also page 270* **White silver sands**).

Just south of Grayton Beach, also on 30A, is the most influential beach town in America, **Seaside**. Begun in the 1980s as a revolt against high-rise condoism, Seaside – the inspiration for Seahaven in *The Truman Show* – is a planned community that keeps a firm grip on design, mandating a 19th-century look. Approaching the thickets of pastel neo-Victorian houses and picket fences is like driving into a Walt Disney movie. Innovative in its beginnings, Seaside now has a rather precious feel about it. Yet the shops, cafés and services are very good and it's an easy place to spend some time.

Fort Pickens

1400 Fort Pickens Road, Santa Rosa Island, Pensacola (1-800 365 2267). **Open** dawn to dusk daily. **Admission** $6 per car. **Credit** DC, MC, V.

Grayton Beach State Park

357 Main Park Road, US 30A, Santa Rosa Beach (1-850 231 4210/www.dep.state.fl.us/parks). **Open** 8am-dusk. **Admission** $3.25 per vehicle (up to 8 people). **No credit cards**.

National Museum of Naval Aviation

Navy Base, 1750 Radford Boulevard, Pensacola (1-800 327 5002/www.navalair.org). **Open** 9am-5pm daily. **Admission** free.

Where to stay

At Pensacola Beach, the **Best Western** motel (16 Via De Luna, Pensacola Beach, 1-800 934 3301) on the beach side has its own pools, comfortable rooms and good prices ($59-$79 winter, $119-$159 summer). **Tiki House** (17 Via De Luna, Pensacola Beach, 1-850 934 4447, rates $50-$105) is an old-fashioned, one-level motel. Some rooms on

the less desirable north side, facing Santa Rosa Sound, have kitchenettes. For condo and beach house rentals, contact **Gulf Coast Accommodations** (22 Via De Luna Drive, Pensacola, 1-800 239 4334) or **Tristan Realty** (1020 Fort Pickens Road, Pensacola, 1-800 445 9931). There are no hotels or motels at Grayton Beach, but rentals are available through **Rivard Realty** (15 Pine Street, Santa Rosa Beach, 1-800 423 3215). A central agency in Seaside (1-850 231 4224/www.seasidefl.com) has about 250 cottages available in the town.

Where to eat

Boy on a Dolphin (400 Pensacola Beach Boulevard, Pensacola, 1-850 932 7954, main courses $14.95-$22.95) offers seafood with a Greek emphasis and is a long-standing favourite among Pensacola citizens. There's also **Flounder's** (800 Quietwater Beach Road, Pensacola Beach, 1-850 932 2003, main courses $15-$19), which has good seafood, an attractive outdoor beach bar and a dancefloor.

Since 1949, hearty Southern meals have been served at **Hopkins Boarding House** in Pensacola (900 North Spring Street, at West Street, 1-850 438 3979, closed Mon, dinner Sun, main courses $6.95-$7.95), a rambling old house near downtown. It's an unpretentious place and the food is marvellous.

Getting there

By car

If you're coming from Mobile, Pensacola is 60 miles (96km) east on I-10. If you're travelling from Gulf Shores, you can take US 59 and US 98 or go along the coast on smaller roads.

By bus

Greyhound (1-800-231-2222/www.greyhound.com) runs several buses a day between New Orleans and Pensacola. The journey takes just over 5hrs and a return costs $49.50 Mon-Thur, $52.50 Fri-Sun.

By train

For **Amtrak** services (1-800 872 7245/www.amtrak.com), *see page 240*.

Tourist information

South Walton Tourist Development Council

2577 US 331 South, Santa Rosa Beach. Mailing address: PO Box 1248, Santa Rosa Beach, FL 32459 (1-800 822 6877/www.beachesofsouth walton.com). **Open** 8am-5.30pm daily. The Tourist Development Council provides information on Grayton Beach and Seaside.

Directory

Directory

Getting Around

By bus

Greyhound services to and from destinations throughout the US arrive and depart from the **Union Passenger Terminal** at 1001 Loyola Avenue in the CBD.

Greyhound Lines
524 7571/customer service 525 6075/1-800 231 2222/ www.greyhound.com.

By train

Three **Amtrak** (1-800 872 7245) services arrive at and depart from the **Union Passenger Terminal** (528 1610). The 'City of New Orleans' service runs daily between Chicago and New Orleans; the 'Crescent' runs threes time a week from New York and Washington, DC, to New Orleans. Visitors who want to explore Louisiana and the surrounding regions will find 'Sunset Limited' the most useful route, though departures are infrequent. For further details, *see page 240.*

By air

New Orleans International Airport (464 0831) is located to the west of the city in Kenner and is served by the following major international airlines. For domestic and other international airlines, consult the *Yellow Pages.*

AirTran 1-800 825 8538/ www.airtran.com.
American Airlines 1-800 433 7300/www.aa.com.
British Airways 1-800 247 9297/ www.britishairways.com.

Continental Airlines 1-800-523 3273/www.continental.com.
Delta Air Lines 1-800 221 1212/ delta-air.com.
Northwest Airlines Domestic 1-800 225 2525 International 1-800 447 4747 www.nwa.com.
Southwest Airlines 1-800 435 9792/ www.southwest.com.
Trans World Airlines (TWA) Domestic 1-800 221 2000 International 1-800 892 4141 www.twa.com.
USAirways (USAir) 1-800 428 4322/ www.usairways.com.
United Airlines 1-800 241 6522/ www.ual.com.

By bus

Louisiana Transit (818 1077, weekdays only) provides a bus that runs from the airport to the CBD, two blocks away from the French Quarter. You'll need the exact fare ($1.50) and only carry-on luggage is allowed. Buses run daily to and from the airport from 6am to midnight, departing every ten to 15 minutes from 6am to 9am and between 3pm and 6pm, every 20 minutes at other times.

The bus will take you to Tulane Avenue and Elk Place – which is about four blocks from the heart of the CBD and just above the French Quarter – until 6.30pm. After 6.30pm, it stops at Carrollton and Tulane Avenues, about 15 blocks from Tulane and Elk, where you can catch an RTA bus (39 Tulane-CBD).

Buses to the airport from Tulane and Elk run from 6am to 6.30pm. From 6.30pm to midnight, the bus picks up at Carrollton and Tulane. There is no service between midnight and 6am.

By shuttle

The airport provides an excellent shuttle service (465 9780), which costs $10 (cash or credit card) per person one-way to most downtown hotels. The service is available as soon as planes arrive at the airport, and runs until the last plane has arrived. Shuttles depart from the airport every ten minutes. If you want the shuttle to collect you from your hotel and take you to the airport, phone 522 3500 the day before your departure and make a reservation.

By taxi

There is always a long queue of taxis at the airport waiting to whisk you into the city. Expect to pay $21 from the airport to almost anywhere in New Orleans for up to two passengers. For three or more passengers, the cost is $8 per person ($24 for three people, $32 for four people). Taxis are probably the quickest and most efficient way of getting to and from the airport – although not the cheapest.

The public transport system in New Orleans is run by the **Regional Transit Authority** (www.regional transit.org). RTA operates all the Orleans Parish buses and streetcars, including the famous St Charles Streetcar, the longest continuously operating railcar line in the nation (*see page 100* **Streetcars ahead**). Public transport – generally used only by those who don't have a car – is fairly dependable, although if there is a breakdown you might have to wait 30-60 minutes for a bus, even on a heavily used route.

The fare for all lines, except express buses and the Riverside Streetcar, is $1.25, plus 25¢ for a transfer. Transfers must be purchased at the same time as the ticket when you board the first bus and cannot be used on the same bus route from which they are purchased. The fare for express buses and the Riverfront Streetcars (known as the Red Ladies) is $1.50.

For bus schedule information, phone the **Regional Transit Authority's RideLine** (248 3900).

Travel passes

Travel passes, known as **VisiTour Passes**, can be used in place of tickets and transfers on any RTA vehicle, and are an excellent bargain if you plan on being out and about most of the day. The one-day pass for Orleans and Jefferson Parishes costs $4 and can be bought on the bus. The one-day pass for Orleans Parish ($5), the three-day pass ($12) and the 30-day pass ($55) are available from most hotel concierges and tourist information booths.

Ferries

As a river city, New Orleans does have a workhorse ferry system, but visitors are not likely to find it very useful for sightseeing as it is planned around commuting needs. However, the trip itself is a marvellous way to get on the

river, see the New Orleans skyline and get a feel for the city's water-dictated geography. On the sightseeing agenda, the ferry is helpful in getting to **Blaine Kern's Mardi Gras World** on the West Bank, in Algiers (*see page 116*). There are three ferries: all are free to pedestrians. There is a charge of $1 for vehicles, which is collected on the West Bank side. For more information about the ferries, call 364 8110.

Canal Street– Algiers Ferry

Departs from the foot of Canal Street, between the Aquarium of the Americas and Riverwalk Mall, every 15 minutes from 5.45am to midnight daily.

Chalmette– Algiers Ferry

Departs from Chalmette at the intersection of Paris Road and St Bernard Highway (about a mile and a half east of the Chalmette Battlefield) and runs to Patterson Road in east Algiers every 15 minutes, 5.45am to 9.30pm daily.

Jackson Avenue– Gretna Ferry

Departs from the foot of Jackson Avenue, at the intersection of Tchoupitoulas Street, and runs to Huey P Long Avenue and First Street in Gretna every 15 minutes, 5.45am to 9.30pm daily.

Taxis & limos

Taxis are a great way to get around New Orleans if you don't have a car. They are, without a doubt, the safest way to travel late at night, and as a rule, the taxi drivers are friendly and helpful: the city even sent most of them to a special school recently, to make sure that they understood the concept of good customer service.

If you are downtown during the day, you won't have a problem finding a cab. You can flag down a taxi on Decatur Street, other parts of the

Quarter and on Canal near the large hotels; otherwise, your best bet is to find a big hotel and go to the first taxi in line outside. If you are in Uptown, Mid City or Carrollton, just call the local number and one will arrive shortly. Driving a cab in New Orleans is a pretty good way to make a living, so there isn't any shortage of available hires. If you are at a bar, restaurant or store, ask the staff to call one for you. Regular meter fares begin at $2.50 and increase 20¢ every one-sixth of a mile or 40 seconds. There is an additional charge for each extra passenger. A tip of $1 is the norm; if you have packages, tip a dollar more. In the unlikely event that you have any complaints about a cab, driver or the service provided, phone the **Taxicab Bureau** (565 6272).

Local taxis

United Cabs 522 9771.
White Fleet 948 6605.
Checker-Yellow Cabs 943 2411.

Limousine services

New Orleans Limousine Service 529 5226.
Orleans Limousines 288 1111.

Driving

Driving a car in New Orleans can be a thrill, especially if you are from a place where driving rules are obeyed and enforced. In New Orleans few local drivers even pay much heed to traffic lights, so always look both ways before pulling into an intersection, even if your light is green. There will almost always be some fool blasting through their red light at the last second.

American Automobile Association (AAA)

3445 N Causeway Boulevard, at 14th Street, Metairie (838 7500/ 1-800 222 7623/www.aaa.com). **Open** 8.30am-7pm Mon, Wed; 8.30am-5.15pm Tue, Thur, Fri; closed Sat, Sun.

Directory

Useful bus routes

New Orleans's bus system is a tad impenetrable: even the RTA doesn't have a city-wide bus map. Visitors will find the services below most useful for covering the city, but bear in mind that some are very long routes that travel from the safety of the French Quarter to questionable areas such as the Desire Housing projects. Always ask the driver if you are unsure of your destination.

3 Vieux Carré

These small buses dressed up to look like trolleys circle the French Quarter, predominantly along Dauphine and Chartres Streets. The loop continues west to Poydras Street in the CBD and east to Elysian Fields Avenue in Marigny. (The line is being experimentally extended to Bywater's Poland Avenue from 10am to 3pm weekdays only.)

11 Magazine

The outbound service runs the entire length of Magazine Street, from the intersection with Canal Street as far as Audubon Park. The inbound service turns off Magazine Street at St Andrew Street (where it becomes one-way) and continues on Camp Street (parallel to Magazine) to Canal Street.

12 St Charles Streetcar

The route stretches from Carondelet Street at Canal Street in the CBD to the intersection of N Carrollton and Claiborne Avenues on the northern edge of Uptown. It passes along the entire length of St Charles Avenue and serves the CBD, the Warehouse District, the Garden District, Audubon Park, Tulane and Loyola universities and the Riverbend area.

46 City Park

This service runs from the intersection of Marconi Avenue and Central Park Street down Orleans Avenue, skirting the edge of Armstrong Park and turning into Basin Street, a block from the edge of the French Quarter. The route ends on Canal at a major bus stop. (The cross-street is Crozat, a small one-way street.) This route is best for Delgado Community College and St Louis Cemeteries Nos.1 and 2. It's also back-up for 48 Esplanade (see below) as a route to City Park and the New Orleans Museum of Art.

48 Esplanade

This route starts from the intersection of Canal Street and North Rampart Street, on the lake side of the French Quarter and covers the length of Esplanade Avenue as far as the intersection with N Carrollton Avenue. It continues along City Park Avenue as far as Canal Street. Use this route for City Park and the New Orleans Museum of Art, the Fair Grounds, the Pitot House Museum and St Louis Cemetery No.3.

The AAA has piles of maps and state-by-state guidebooks, plus a treasure trove of travel tips – all free to members, including those belonging to affiliated clubs such as the British AA.

Car rental

You will need a valid driver's licence and a major credit card (American Express, Discover, MasterCard, Visa) to rent a car in New Orleans. Since the car rental business is very competitive, it's worth phoning two or more agencies to compare prices.

National rental companies

Avis 1-800 331 1212/ www.avis.com.

Budget 467 2277/ www.drivebudget.com.

Enterprise 1-800 736 8222/ www.enterprise.com.

Hertz 1-800 654 3131/ www.hertz.com.

National 1-800 227 7368/ www.nationalcar.com.

Breakdown services

AAA Emergency Road Service

1-800 222 4357. **Open** 24hrs daily.

Members – including members of affiliated clubs such as the British AA – receive free towing and roadside service.

The Auto Clinic

Recorded information 349 0800. The Clinic offers a free tow and delivery service included in the price of repairs.

Doody & Hank's

522 5391/524 0118. **Open** 7.30am-5.30pm Mon-Fri; closed Sat, Sun.

Doody & Hank's provides road service in the CBD and surrounding areas.

Expert Auto Service

895 4345. **Open** 9am-5pm Mon-Fri; closed Sat, Sun. Uptown service.

Parking

Although finding a car parking space is fairly easy – except in the CBD and the French Quarter – there are countless rules about street parking in New Orleans, and

55 Elysian Fields

From N Peters Street, this route runs along the river side of the French Quarter and then travels the entire length of Elysian Fields Avenue as far as the University of New Orleans. It's good for the French Market, Marigny and UNO.

57 Franklin

This service loops the French Quarter from the corner of Decatur Street, north up Canal Street and then east along N Rampart Street as far as Franklin Avenue in Marigny. It runs the length of Franklin as far as Leon C Simon Drive before terminating at the Southern University at New Orleans. The inbound service returns south down Franklin Avenue as far as Royal Street and re-enters the French Quarter on Decatur Street.

81 Almonaster

The outbound service runs along N Peters Street from Canal Street in the French Quarter and then north up Elysian Fields as far as St Claude Avenue. It continues north along Franklin Avenue and Almonaster as far as Higgins Street, where it turns east. At Desire Parkway, the route loops south to Florida Street and then north up Louisa Drive back to Higgins Street. Note that this area is close to the unsavoury Desire Housing project and

should be avoided. The inbound service follows the same route as far as Franklin and St Claude Avenues where it continues south on Franklin to Royal Street. It re-enters the French Quarter on Decatur Street.

82 Desire

From the corner of N Peters Street this route runs north up Canal Street and then right along N Rampart Street as far as Esplanade Avenue. At Esplanade it turns on to Dauphine Street, continuing downriver as far as Desire Street in Bywater. It travels the length of Desire Street north terminating at the intersection with Florida Street (an area to be avoided). The inbound service runs from Florida Street south down Mazant Street and France Street. At Royal Street the bus heads back towards the French Quarter turning on to N Peters/Decatur Street at Esplanade.

89 St Claude

From the intersection of Canal Street, this route travels east along N Rampart Street and St Claude Avenue, through Marigny and Bywater, across the Industrial Canal to the Holy Cross and Arabi neighbourhoods and into St Bernard Parish. At Aycock Street it heads south towards the river, turning on to N Peters Street and terminating near the Chalmette Battlefield. This route is also handy for visiting Jackson Barracks.

the city makes a tidy profit from issuing tickets and impounding cars.

If you park your car on any street near downtown or the French Quarter, look carefully for signs telling you when and where you can park: the parking authorities know where they are and will tow your car away in a heartbeat. Never waste your time or energy arguing with a meter maid. They are made of stone and will not pay attention.

The bad habits of New Orleans drivers mean your vehicle will be much safer in an off-street lot, and luckily New Orleans has plenty of them, even during high season. There are several parking lots

in the French Quarter where you can expect to pay in the region of $3 an hour and $18 for 12 hours – quite reasonable compared to many congested US cities. During the hot months consider paying a bit more to park in an indoor lot. In the French Quarter you can find easy parking in the Canal Place shopping complex and within the Quarter itself.

Louisiana Superdome

Sugar Bowl Drive, at Poydras Street (587 3805/www.superdome. com). **Map** p309 B2.
There are four garages at the Superdome, where you pay a flat rate of $5 from 6am to 2pm, then an hourly rate until 9pm. Daily, weekly and monthly rates are also available.

Cycling

Cycling around New Orleans is quite possible and easier than in many cities because of the flatness of the landscape. But beware: not only do many local cyclists complain of the attitude of local drivers toward the rules of the road, but New Orleans is seventh highest in the nation for bicycle fatalities. The huge potholes everywhere don't help, either. Maps are available from bike shops with suggested bike routes, though these routes are designed more for recreational biking than getting from A to B. For more information, contact the New Orleans bicycle club at www.gnofn.org/~nobc/.

Resources A-Z

Business

The convention industry is one of the city's primary sources of revenue. It's also one area where New Orleans excels. There are dozens of businesses devoted to keeping conventions and meetings running smoothly, from meeting planners to sound engineers to coat-check concessions. For expert guidance in connecting with these kind of support businesses, the **New Orleans Metropolitan Convention & Visitors Bureau** is invaluable (*see page 279* **Tourist Information**).

Ernest N Morial Convention Center

900 Convention Center Boulevard, at Julia Street, Warehouse District (582 3027/www.mccno.com). Bus 3 Vieux Carré, 10 Tchoupitoulas. Closed to the public. **Map** p309 C2. This ever-expanding complex is the fourth largest in the US and is capable of handling up to two million conventioneers, who pour into the city every year for more than 2,000 conventions and meetings.

Courier services

Local and national messenger and delivery services include:

A Plus Courier Service
467 1080.

Provides a 24-hour daily 'hot shot' service.

Federal Express
1-800 463 3339.
Phone for opening hours and pick-up places.

United Cab
522 9771.
A taxi company with desk-to-desk delivery 24 hours a day.

UPS
1-800 742 5877/www.ups.com.
Phone for the opening hours and pick-up places of this national service.

US Postal Service
1-800 222 1811/www.usps.gov
Priority mail service to 27 countries.

Office services

Kinko's
762 St Charles Avenue, at Julia Street, CBD (581 2541/ www.kinkos.com). St Charles Streetcar. **Open** 24hrs daily. **Map** p309 B2.
Services include on-site use of eight computers, Internet access (20¢ per minute), typesetting, printing, photocopying and faxing. Check the phone directory for the location of other branches.

Consulates

All embassies are located in Washington, DC; however British nationals visiting New Orleans may also contact the **Honorary British Consulate** in the city for information and advice. The nearest consular offices for all other English-speaking countries are in Washington. Phone directory assistance on 1-202 555 1212 for their location and phone numbers.

Honorary British Consulate
10th Floor, 321 St Charles Avenue, between Union & Perdido Streets, CBD, New Orleans, LA 70130 (524 4180). St Charles Streetcar. **Open** 9.30am-2.30pm Mon-Fri; closed Sat, Sun. **Map** p309 C1.
In case of emergency outside office hours, British passport holders should contact the Consulate General in Houston (713 659 6270/www.britain usa.com/houston). All visa enquiries should be directed to the Consulate General in Los Angeles (310 477 3322/ www.britainusa.com/la).

Consumer information

Better Business Bureau
24hr information line 581 6222.
The BBB has information on almost every company in the city. If you have a complaint about a product or service, give the BBB a call and it will make a report. If you want to know if a complaint has already been registered, the BBB will tell you.

Consumer Product Safety Commission
1-800 638 2772/www.cpsc.gov

Louisiana Attorney General's Office of Consumer Protection
1-800 351 4889.
Call this office to make a complaint regarding consumer law enforcement or any other agency.

Emergencies

Ambulance, Fire Brigade or Police 911 (toll-free from any payphone). 911 also works from mobile phones.
Bell South (telephone) Automated hotline 557 7777/557 6500.
Entergy Corporation (gas & electric) Information hotline 1-800 368 3749.
Poison Control Center 1-800 256 9822.
Sewerage & Water Board of New Orleans 942 3833.

Directory

Tourist information

Visitor information hotline
566 5003. **Open** 24hrs daily.
Recorded information about the city.

New Orleans Metropolitan Convention & Visitors Bureau
1520 Sugar Bowl Drive, at Poydras Street, CBD (566 5011/1-800 672 6124/ www.neworleanscvb.com). Bus 16 S Claiborne. **Open** 8.30am-5pm Mon-Fri; closed Sat, Sun. **Map** p309 B1.

French Quarter office
529 St Ann Street, at Jackson Square, French Quarter (566 5031). Bus 3 Vieux Carré, 55 Elysian Fields, 81 Almonaster, 82 Desire. **Open** 8.30am-5pm daily. **Map** p316 C2.
This is a beautiful little office, located in the heart of the French Quarter opposite Jackson Square. Maps, general directions, tour information, local history and hotel and restaurant recommendations can all be obtained here.

Disabled access & information

New Orleans is very lax when it comes to the disabled. Many of the federally mandated accessibility laws seem to have been ignored here and the historic nature of most buildings precludes making structural changes. More restaurants and hotels are becoming 'friendly' to people with disabilities, but, with many located in old buildings, it is always wise to phone your destination first to check on the facilities. When finding a hotel room, the best solution for anyone with impaired mobility is one of the newer hotels, most of which are now designed with a barrier-free mindset.

Getting around the city is a little easier. All regional city buses on fixed routes are equipped with lifts, can 'kneel' to make access easier and have handgrips and spaces designed for wheelchair users. RTA technically provides customers who are mobility-impaired with a special pick-up service, **Paratransit** (827 7433). But the conditions of use make it a long shot for visitors: you must book two weeks in advance and provide medical certification of your condition to be eligible to use it.

Availability of the Paratransit system is best during non-rush hours (10am-3pm weekdays). For full details of the Paratransit system, as well as information concerning just about any aspect of navigating New Orleans if you have a disability, contact **Citizens With Disabilities**.

Citizens With Disabilities
Katherine Hoover, Disability Affairs Specialist, Suite 306, 1221 Elmwood Park Boulevard, Jefferson, LA 70123 (736 6086/fax 731 4520/www. jeffparish.net).

Deaf Action Center
Catholic Charities 523 3755. **Open** *Phone line* 8am-4.40pm Mon-Fri; closed Sat, Sun. Information on interpretation and local resources. Catholic Charities will pick up the phone and then connect you to the Deaf Action Center – there is no direct line.

National Federation of the Blind of Louisiana
1-800 234 4166/www.lcb-ruston.com. **Open** *Phone line* 8am-5pm Mon-Fri; closed Sat, Sun. The Federation can provide resource information such as a guide to restaurants with Braille menus.

WRBH (88.3 FM)
899 1144/www.wrbh.org
This radio station reads the daily newspaper for the blind

and print-handicapped (7-10am, 6.30-8pm daily). On Saturdays (8-9.30am), the *Times-Picayune*'s Friday entertainment guide, *Lagniappe*, is read.

Electricity

Rather than the 220-240V, 50-cycle AC used in Europe, the United States uses a 110-120V, 60-cycle AC voltage. Except for dual-voltage, flat-pin plug shavers, you will need to run any small appliances you bring with you via an adaptor, available at airport shops, pharmacies and department stores. Bear in mind that most US videos and TVs use a different frequency from those in Europe: you will not be able to play back camcorder footage during your trip. However, you can buy and use blank tapes.

Gay & lesbian

Resources

Check out the **Faubourg Marigny Bookstore** (*see page 172*) for an extensive selection of gay and lesbian books and friendly, well-informed staff. For details of the gay press, *see page 282* **Media**.

Gay Heritage Tour
Alternatives, 909 Bourbon Street, at Dumaine Street, French Quarter (information 945

*6789/Alternatives 524 5222/
bienvillenola@aol.com). Bus 3
Vieux Carré, 48 Esplanade.*
Rates $20. **Credit** AmEx, MC,
V. **Map** p316 C2.
Now in its sixth year, the
acclaimed two-and-a-half-hour
French Quarter walking tour
illuminates the vibrant lesbian
and gay history and culture of
New Orleans. It departs from
Alternatives – a shop selling an
eclectic mix of gay cards,
clothing and toys – twice
weekly. Advance reservations
are required.

Lesbian & Gay Community Center of New Orleans

*2114 Decatur Street, at
Frenchmen Street, French Quarter
(945 1103/fax 945 1102/www.gay
neworleans.com/The_Center). Bus
82 Desire.* **Open** noon-7pm Mon-
Fri; 9am-5.30pm Sat, Sun. **Map**
p316 D2.
Although the centre is a small,
volunteer-based organisation,
it provides current details on
social, cultural, health,
religious, political and
recreational activities.

Health

The NO/AIDS Task Force

*Suite 500, 2601 Tulane Avenue,
at Dorgenois Street, Tremé
(821 2601/statewide hotline 1-800
992 4379/www.crescentcity.
com/noaids). Bus 39 Tulane.*
Open *Centre* 8.30am-5pm Mon-
Fri; closed Sat, Sun. *Phone line*
noon-8pm daily. **Map** p307 E6.
The Task Force provides
information and a full range of
educational, prevention, testing
and client services.

Emergency care

In New Orleans, the Charity
Hospital system provides
access to medical care in
almost every imaginable area.
Charity's Trauma Care Unit is
rated the best in the country. In
the unlikely event that you are

on the receiving end of a
gunshot, Charity's Emergency
Room is the place you want to
wind up. You will have to pay
for emergency treatment, so if
you are a foreign national, try
to contact your insurers before
seeking treatment, and you will
be directed to a hospital that
will deal directly with them.
For referral to a doctor, contact
the **Tulane University
Professional/Physicians
Referral Group** (588 5800).

Charity Hospital Campus

*Louisiana State University
Medical School, 1532 Tulane
Avenue, CBD (568 3723/
www.lsu.edu). Bus 39 Tulane.*
Open *Emergency Room* 24hrs
daily. **Map** p309 B1.

Children's Hospital

*200 Henry Clay Avenue, at
Tchoupitoulas Street, Uptown
(899 9511/www.chnola.org). Bus
10 Tchoupitoulas.* **Open** *Clinic*
8.30am-4.30pm Mon-Fri; closed
Sat, Sun. *Emergency Room* 24hrs
daily. **Map** p306 B10.

Clinics

Acupuncture Clinic

*4212 Teuton Street, off Houma
Boulevard, Metairie (288 1303).
Bus E5 Causeway.* **Open** 8am-
3pm Mon, Wed, Fri; closed Tue,
Thur, Sat, Sun.

Daughters of Charity Health Center

*3900 S Carrollton Avenue, at
Palmetto Street, Central City (482
0084). Bus 90 Carrollton.* **Open**
8am-6.30pm Mon-Fri; 10am-2pm
Sat; closed Sun. **Map** p306 C6.
Care for the entire family, includ-
ing a pharmacy and counselling.
A sliding fee scale is operated.

Dentists

NO Dental Association

834 6449/nodental@aol.com.
Open *Phone line* 9am-5pm Mon-
Fri; closed Sat, Sun.
The place to call for referrals to
a dentist; outside office hours, a
recorded message will direct you
to an emergency number.

Pharmacies

For pharmacies, including
those open 24 hours daily,
see page 184.

AIDS/HIV

See also above NO/AIDS
Taskforce.

AIDS/HIV Hotline

821 6050. **Open** *Phone line*
10am-8pm Mon-Fri; 10am-4pm
Sat; closed Sun.

Alcohol/drug abuse

Alcoholics Anonymous Central Office

779 1178/www.gnofn.org/~aagno.
Open *Phone line* 9am-4.45pm
Mon-Fri; closed Sat, Sun.
Outside office hours, an
answering service will take
your phone number and a
counsellor will call you back
as soon as possible.

Narcotics Anonymous

899 6262. **Open** *Recorded
information* 24hrs daily.
Call for a recorded list of
meeting times and locations.

Child abuse

Child Protection Hot Line

680 9000/fax 680 9172. **Open**
Phone line 24hrs daily.

Psychiatric emergency services

DePaul-Tulane Behavioral Health Center

*DePaul-Tulane University, 1040
Calhoun Street, Uptown (899
8282/www.depaultulane.com). Bus
15 Freret.* **Open** 24hrs daily. **Map**
p306 B8.
This excellent psychiatric
hospital provides outpatient and
evening treatment. A sliding
scale is operated for fees.

Rape

Rape Crisis Line
483 8888. **Open** *Phone line*
24hrs daily.

Suicide

Suicide Prevention
523 2673. **Open** *Phone line*
24hrs daily.

Immigration & Customs

Few international flights arrive in New Orleans: you will usually have to transfer to a domestic flight at another US city, and will go through Immigration and Customs there. This means that you also have to reclaim your baggage at the transfer airport, take it through Customs and then check it in again. The airlines try to make this a painless process by having a transfer check-in desk just outside Customs at most major transfer airports; however, you will have to make your own way to the domestic departures terminal. Connection times do take account of this, and the fact that you may have to queue at Immigration, but we recommend that you get through the transfer process and check in for your New Orleans flight before you take any time to relax.

Standard immigration regulations apply to all visitors. During your flight, you will be handed an immigration form and a Customs declaration form to be presented when you land at the airport. Fill them in very carefully, and ask for another if you make a mistake – nothing less than perfection will do. Be prepared to wait for up to an hour when you arrive at Immigration. Expect to explain the nature of your visit (business and/or pleasure). If you don't have a return ticket

and are planning a long visit, you will be questioned closely. Usually, you will be granted an entry permit to cover the length of your stay. For information on visas, *see page 287*.

US Customs allows visitors to bring in $100 worth of gifts ($400 for returning Americans) duty free, 200 cigarettes or 50 cigars and one litre of spirits (liquor). No plants, fruit, meat or fresh produce can be taken through Customs. For more detailed information, contact your nearest US embassy or consulate.

UK Customs & Excise allows returning travellers to bring in $145 worth of gifts and goods and an unlimited amount of money, as long as they can prove it's theirs.

Insurance

It's advisable to take out comprehensive insurance cover before arriving in the United States: it's almost impossible to arrange once you are there. Make sure that you have adequate health cover since medical expenses can be high. *See page 280* **Health & medical** for a list of New Orleans hospitals and emergency rooms.

Internet access

One of the chief charms of New Orleans is its insistent otherworldliness. Visitors are initially pleased and intrigued but often end up frustrated when trying to use normal 21st-century amenities such as the Internet. You'll find fewer computer-friendly zones in New Orleans than probably any other city of its size in the US. Hotels have begun to work harder at becoming computer- and Internet-friendly, with many of the established hotels refitting rooms with dataports and dual phone lines. The newer places, of course, are

built with these business-crucial tools. For hotels that offer modem or dataport facilities (listed under Room services), *see chapter* **Accommodation**.

Beyond the hotels and convention halls, however, Internet access is thin. The cybercafé trend has barely touched New Orleans, so the best low-cost Internet linkage is through the public library. Although scandalously underfunded, the **New Orleans Public Library** has made heroic efforts to go online and provide computer access to everyone. There are a number of branches, but your best bet is to head to the main library (*see page 282*). There are more computer stations here than in the satellite libraries and the staff are well trained and helpful about computer and online issues.

If you have contacts or new friends connected with any of the colleges or universities, you may be able to gain access to the excellent computer labs on campus. Other options include the CBD branch of **Kinko's** (*see page 278* **Office services**) or the **New Orleans Net Café** at the Contemporary Arts Center.

New Orleans Net Café
900 Camp Street, at Howard Avenue (523 0990/
www.cacno.org). St Charles Streetcar. **Open** 7am-8pm Mon, Tue, Sun; 7am-11pm Wed-Sat.
Map p309 B/C2.
The Contemporary Arts Center houses the city's best cybercafé. It provides free Internet access from five computer kiosks with Windows-based computers equipped with mini-speakers. There's a full coffee bar selling pastries and light lunches and a bar (this is New Orleans) complete with happy hour. You can also listen to poetry readings by local writers, receive tips on buying a computer or learn how to build a website. Free parking for patrons is another plus.

Directory

Libraries

New Orleans Public Library (main library)

219 Loyola Avenue, at Tulane Avenue, CBD (596 2570/ www.nutrias.org). Bus 39 Tulane. **Open** 10am-6pm Mon-Thur; 10am-5pm Sat; closed Fri, Sun. **Map** p309 B1.

Keller Library

4300 S Broad Avenue, at Fontainebleau Street, Central City (596 2675/www.gnofn.org/~nopl). Bus 21 Fontainebleau. **Open** 11am-8pm Mon, Wed; 1-5pm Sun; closed Tue, Thur-Sat. **Map** p306 C7.

Gentilly Library

3000 Foy Street, at Gentilly Boulevard, Gentilly (596 2644). Bus 51 St Bernard/Lake Terrace. **Open** 11am-8pm Mon, Wed; 11am-6pm Tue, Thur; 11am-5pm Sat; closed Fri, Sun.* **Map** p308 F4.

Latter Memorial Library

5120 St Charles Avenue, at Soniat Street, Uptown (596 2625). St Charles Streetcar. **Open** 11am-6pm Mon-Thur; 11am-5pm Sat; closed Fri, Sun.* **Map** p306 C9.

Nix Library

1401 S Carrollton Avenue, at Willow Street, Uptown (596 2630). Bus 34 Carrollton Express/St Charles Streetcar. **Open** 11am-6pm Mon-Thur; 11am-5pm Sat; closed Fri, Sun.* **Map** p306 B7.

Media

Despite its talkative, engaging nature, New Orleans is a town short on media. Like many US cities, it only has one daily newspaper, which severely limits public discourse. To balance the New Orleans-centric view in the local media, many residents pick up the *New York Times* every day. Other national newspapers including *USA Today* and the *Wall Street Journal* are widely available – and widely read – here, too.

Newspapers & magazines

Ambush

www.ambushonline.com
A monthly gay newspaper with spotty news judgement and amateur writers. It's a good window on the New Orleans gay scene, if you can make your way through the unedited verbiage.

City Business

www.neworleans.com/citybusiness
Fortnightly tabloid devoted to New Orleans and regional business. Bland and uncritical but a good source of information on the tourism, oil and sugar industries.

Eclipse

A lively weekly guide to gay bars and nightlife, published by the people behind *Impact* (*see below*).

Gambit Weekly

www.bestofneworleans.com
An alternative paper, distributed free to cafés, coffeehouses and other spots. Centrist in its politics (which means slightly to the left in New Orleans, definitely to the right everywhere else), it's non-committal in most reviews but the entertainment and events listings are the most comprehensive you'll find.

Impact

www.impactnews.com
Fortnightly gay newspaper; very professional and crisp in its survey of local and national issues.

New Orleans Magazine

A glossy monthly that delivers uncritical stories on local personalities and surveys such as the Top 50 doctors, entrepreneurs, whatever. It also has good restaurant reviews and interesting snippets of little-known local history.

OffBeat

www.offbeat.com
A nearly comprehensive monthly magazine on New Orleans music, with a detailed calendar of gigs, interviews, album reviews and lively columns. Distributed free at cafés, bars, clubs and other likely spots.

Times-Picayune

www.nolalive.com
Cock of the walk. The *Times-Picayune* not only has no major competition, it doesn't even have any small suburban dailies to worry about as is the case in most US metro areas. The paper is professionally written and well edited but takes a complacent, if not wilfully obtuse, attitude towards the enduring New Orleans problems of race, crime, political malfeasance and lack of leadership. The exceptions are columnists Lolis Eric Elie, Bill Grady and James Gill, who try to take the readers into the complexities of New Orleans. Columnist Chris Rose is the fun guy, who enjoys tweaking social and civic noses now and again. The newspaper periodically pours massive resources into high-profile series in transparent attempts to win big prizes such as the Pulitzer Prize for Journalism. And it succeeds.

Radio

WRBH (88.3 FM)

Radio for the blind and 'print impaired'. Volunteers read the daily paper, magazines, children's books, bestsellers and even romance novels. The readers are uneven but the pros who read the book selections are a delight.

WTUL (91.5 FM)

Tulane University student-run station is unpredictable, but usually interesting.

WWNO (89.9 FM)

The public radio station broadcasts National Public Radio's stellar news programmes: 'All Things Considered' and 'Morning Edition'. It's light on local news but a crucial pipeline to intelligent reporting on national and world news. The majority of the programming is devoted to classical music, with spots for jazz and opera.

WWL (870 AM)
Talk radio.

WWOZ (89.9 FM)
Music heaven. WWOZ is a public radio station devoted to New Orleans and roots music. Volunteer DJs broadcast incredibly knowledgeable programmes about jazz (in all its varieties), '50s R&B, zydeco, Cajun, blues, gospel, Latin, Caribbean, world music and almost everything else that isn't Top 40. Local musicians are regularly interviewed and the music scene is discussed in detail. *See also page 293* **Websites**.

WYLD (98.5 FM & 940 AM)
The largest African-American station has mainstream music and popular DJs who invite comments from the community.

TV

Like most US cities, national networks dominate the airwaves. There is some public access TV but it is largely devoted to government meetings and school events – all rather boring.
WGNO, Channel 26, ABC
WDSU, Channel 6, CBS
WWL, Channel 4, NBC
WYES, Channel 12, PBS
WLAE, Channel 32, PBS and Catholic programming
WHNO, Channel 20, religious programmes

Money

The US dollar ($) equals 100 cents (¢). Coins range from copper pennies (1¢) to silver nickels (5¢), dimes (10¢), quarters (25¢) and half dollars (50¢). In 2000 the US Mint issued a new 'golden' dollar coin. Embossed with a portrait of Sacagawea, a Native American woman who acted as

a guide to early 19th-century explorers Lewis and Clark, the coin has been so popular with collectors that very few have made their way into general circulation. Most vending machines are not yet set up for them. Very rarely you may also come across the smaller 'Susan B Anthony' one-dollar coin, recognisable by its extra weight and rimmed edges; however, these will go out of circulation in a year or so.

Paper money 'bills' come in denominations of $1, $5, $10, $20, $50 and $100, which are confusingly all the same size and colour. Moreover, the US Treasury is currently issuing redesigned bills with larger portraits on them, so you may well end up with bills of the same denomination that look slightly different.

Since counterfeiting of $50 and $100 bills is a booming business, many small shops will not accept them. If you have to use a $50 or $100 bill, ask first, especially if your payment is only a few dollars. On the whole it is best to restrict your paper money to denominations of $1, $5, $10 and $20.

Banks & bureaux de change

Most banks are open from 9am to 5pm Monday to Friday. Some banks stay open until 6pm and most are open from 9am to noon on Saturdays. You will need some kind of photo identification, such as a passport, to transact any business such as cashing travellers' cheques or obtaining cash from a credit card. Note that there aren't as many bureaux de change (exchange offices) in New Orleans as in other tourist meccas such as San Francisco and New York. If you arrive in New Orleans after 5pm, change money at the airport or, if you have US dollars travellers'

cheques, buy something in order to get some change. If you want to cash travellers' cheques at a shop, ask first if a minimum purchase is required. Most banks and shops in New Orleans accept travellers' cheques in US dollars. You can also obtain cash on a credit card account from certain banks. Check with your credit card company before you leave, and be prepared to pay interest rates that vary daily.

American Express Travel Services
201 St Charles Avenue, at Canal Street, CBD (586 8201/ www.americanexpress.com). St Charles Streetcar/41 Canal bus. **Open** 8.30am-5pm Mon-Fri; closed Sat, Sun. **Map** p309 C1.

Bank One
201 St Charles Avenue, at Canal Street, CBD (623 8413/www.bankone.com). St Charles Streetcar/bus 41 Canal. **Open** 8am-4pm Mon-Fri; closed Sat, Sun. **Map** p309 C1.

Hibernia National Bank
12th Floor, 313 Carondelet Street, at Gravier Street, CBD (533 5471/ www.hibernia.com). St Charles Streetcar. **Open** 9am-5pm Mon-Fri; closed Sat, Sun. **Map** p309 B1.

Regions Bank
541 Charters Street, at Toulouse Street, French Quarter (584 2185/www.regionsbank.com). Bus 3 Vieux Carré, 55 Elysian Fields, 81 Almonaster, 82 Desire. **Open** 9am-4pm Mon-Fri; 9am-noon Sat; closed Sun. **Map** p316 B2.

Travelex America
465 9647. **Open** 6am-7pm daily. Handy for when you arrive, this bureau de change is located in the main lobby of the airport.

Western Union
1-800 325 6000/ www.westernunion.com Western Union has been around for what seems like forever, but it still works if you are in need of cash. You can get advice on how to get money wired to you and where to pick it up at one of the dozen or so locations in New

Directory

Orleans. You can also wire money to anyone outside the state over the phone using a Visa or MasterCard. Phone the number above, or check the phone book for the location of the nearest branch.

ATMs

Automated Teller Machines (ATMs or cashpoints) are everywhere – and that includes in shops and, rather more worryingly, bars. Most accept American Express, MasterCard, Visa and selected international debit and cash cards – tap in your usual PIN number. There is a fee, of course – cash on demand has its price. You can get directions to the nearest ATM location by calling **Plus System** (1-800 843 7587) or **Cirrus** (1-800 424 7787). If you have forgotten your PIN number or have de-magnetised your card, most banks will dispense cash to card holders; try **Bank One** (*see above*), which offers advances at any of its branches. You can also get cashback at supermarkets if you pay with a card bearing the Cirrus or Plus logo (with your usual PIN).

Credit cards

Less disastrous if you're robbed, and accepted almost everywhere, credit (and not debit) cards are required by almost all hotels, car rental agencies and airlines. They are also accepted by restaurants, petrol stations, many taxi cabs and, of course, shops. Without a doubt, your stay will be made much more pleasant if you 'don't leave home without them'. The five major credit cards most often accepted in the US are American Express, Discover, Diners Club, MasterCard and Visa. If you lose your credit card (or your travellers' cheques), call the appropriate number below.

Lost or stolen credit cards

American Express 1-800 992 3404.
Discover 1-800 347 2683.
MasterCard 1-800 307 7309.
Visa 1-800 336 8472.

Lost or stolen travellers' cheques

American Express 1-800 221 7282.
Thomas Cook 1-800 223 7373.
Visa 1-800 227 6811.

Postal services

Most post offices are open from 8.30am to 5pm Monday to Friday, with limited hours on Saturday. Contact the **US Postal Service** (1-800 725 216/www.usps.com) for information on your nearest branch and mailing facilities (be ready with a zip code). Stamps can be bought at any post office as well as at many hotels, grocery stores and convenience stores. **Western Union** (1-800 325 6000) will take a telegram over the phone and charge it to your phone bill (not available from payphones). For money transfers, *see page 283* **Money**.

Central Post Office

701 Loyola Avenue, at Girod Street, CBD (1-800 275 8777). Bus 88 St Claude. **Open** 7am-11pm Mon-Fri; 7am-8pm Sat; noon-5pm Sun. **Map** p304 B1.
The CPO is open later than any other post office in the city, and is by far the best place for sending foreign mail. If you need to receive mail in New Orleans and you're not sure where you will be staying, have it marked General Delivery and posted to the Central Post Office, where it will be kept for ten days. Present photo ID to collect it.

Vieux Carré Post Office

1022 Iberville Street, between Burgundy & N Rampart Streets (1-800 275 8777). Bus 3 Vieux Carré, 40 Canal. **Open** 8.30am-4.30pm Mon-Fri; closed Sat, Sun. **Map** p316 A1.

Royal Mail & Parcel

828 Royal Street, between St Ann & Dumaine Streets, French Quarter (522 8523). Bus 10 Vieux Carré. **Open** 8.30am-6.30pm Mon-Fri; 9.30am-5.30pm Sat; closed Sun. **Map** p316 C2.
This French Quarter shop is experienced in packing and shipping objects large and small, from the teapot you've bought for grandmother to the wing chairs you want to ship home. Royal Mail rents post office boxes, sells mail and package supplies and offers a number of other services.

Public toilets (restrooms)

Finding a toilet has been a problem for visitors to New Orleans for ever and a day. During Mardi Gras hundreds of people, male and female, are arrested for public urination. In the French Quarter, especially during a big event such as Mardi Gras or Jazz Fest, you will see signs in almost every establishment to the effect that only customers can use the facilities. Buy a drink from a café or restaurant so that you can use their toilet without restraint. There are public toilets opposite Jackson Square on Decatur Street.

Religion

New Orleans is a predominantly Catholic city; however, there is no lack of places to worship regardless of your faith or beliefs. For a complete list, check the *Yellow Pages* and read the religion page in the Saturday *Times-Picayune*.

Buddhist

Zen Center of New Orleans

748 Camp Street, at Julia Street, Warehouse District (523 1213). St Charles Streetcar. **Map** p306 C2.

Christian (Catholic)

St Louis Cathedral

725 Chartres Street, on Jackson Square, French Quarter (525 9585/www.stlouiscathedral.org). Bus 55 Elysian Fields, 82 Desire. **Map** p316 C2.

A beautiful church at the heart of the French Quarter.

St Patrick's Catholic Church

724 Camp Street, at Julia Street, Warehouse District (525 4413). St Charles Streetcar. **Map** p309 C2.

Christian (other)

First Unitarian Universalist Church

5212 S Claiborne Avenue, at Jefferson Avenue, Central City (866 9010). Bus 16 S Claiborne, 32 Carrollton. **Map** p306 B6.

Cerebral, intellectual, friendly.

Greater St Stephen Full Gospel Baptist Church

2308 S Liberty Street, at Simon Bolivar Avenue, Central City (244 6800/www.greater ststephen.org). Bus 15 Freret. **Map** p309 A2.

One of the largest churches in the nation, Greater St Stephen is a powerhouse with three locations and several thousand members. Its African-American congregation welcomes all visitors.

The Hispanic Apostolate

3368 Esplanade Avenue, at Maurepas Street, Mid City (486 1983). Bus 48 Esplanade. **Map** p308 E5.

St Mark's United Methodist Church

1130 N Rampart Street, between Governor Nichols & Ursulines Streets, French Quarter (523 0450). Bus 57 Franklin, 88 St Claude. **Map** p316 D1.

Located on the edge of the French Quarter, this modern congregation strives for racial integration with an agenda of social justice.

Jewish

Congregation Anshe Sephard

2230 Carondelet Street, at Jackson Avenue, Central City (522 4714). St Charles Streetcar. **Map** p309 B3.

Orthodox/traditional.

Touro Synagogue

4238 St Charles Avenue, at General Pershing Street, Uptown (895 4843). St Charles Streetcar. **Map** p306 D9.

The second oldest reform *schul* in the USA.

Safety

Common sense is your most important ally in a safe visit to New Orleans. The once-staggering crime rate has been steadily declining, but as in most US cities, there's still a problem. Because the cityscape can change block by block in New Orleans, your level of security can change quickly. Be aware of your surroundings and always retreat from any situation that feels in the least bit uncomfortable. Never wander around alone after dark, especially if you aren't completely sure where you are or where you are going. (Mardi Gras, happily, is the exception, when the maxim of 'safety in numbers' is writ large on the streets.) And never take all your wealth with you: make use of the hotel safe.

The most unstable areas are, of course, the poorest places. Public housing projects are often at the epicentre of crime districts, and they are liberally scattered throughout New Orleans (not just at the urban edge). The Lafitte Housing Projects, surrounding the ancient St Louis Cemeteries Nos.1 and 2, for example, are just a couple of blocks from the French Quarter. Note that the cemeteries themselves should also never be entered alone. Some travellers, perhaps lulled into a false sense of security by the declining crime statistics and the general friendliness of New Orleans, have been lured to public housing to buy drugs. Setting aside all questions about the legality of drug use, it cannot be overemphasised how foolhardy it is to do a drug deal with strangers on their home ground.

The French Quarter, with its 24-hour timetable and police protection for tourists, is probably the safest neighbourhood in the city. But that doesn't mean that crime is not a problem here. The tourist-thronged Quarter provides rich pickings for robbers, muggers and car thieves who are alert to the straggler alone on an empty street in the wee hours.

St Charles Avenue and Magazine Street are usually cheerful places, but there are dicy neighbourhoods within a few blocks of these streets and it's not always easy for an outsider to recognise them. If you're veering more than a block or two off the main road, ask a shop clerk, passer-by or a bus driver for the best route.

Thieves tend to be young and/or drugged – these are not the cool pros of crime you see in the movies – and crime tends to be woefully low-tech. The basic approach is armed robbery: sticking a gun in someone's face and demanding the goods. Should you be confronted by an armed thief, give up everything immediately and with no protest. No camera, passport or any amount of cash is worth your life. Always dial 911 and report the crime to the police immediately. You will need a police report for any insurance claims and it's even possible the cops might actually find the perpetrators.

For details of safety issues particularly relevant to women travellers, *see page 288* **Women**.

Directory

Smoking

According to anecdotal evidence, the citizens of New Orleans smoke a lot of tobacco. Except in hospitals, federal buildings, large shopping malls and a few upmarket restaurants, you are free to light up at will. Most small restaurants have smoking and no-smoking sections.

Study

With five well-known universities, New Orleans has a large and diverse student population. Although the city doesn't have the campus neighbourhoods that one associates with some university towns, it more than makes up for it with music clubs, coffeehouses, shops and laissez-faire attitude. It's also a favourite destination for vacationing students.

Delgado Community College

501 City Park Avenue, at Bienville Street, Mid City (483 4216/ www.dcc.edu). Bus 46 City Park. **Map** p308 C5.
Mostly working-class students follow two- and four-year technical programmes. The college also offers non-credit courses such as pottery, local history, ballroom dancing and even barbecuing.

Dillard University

2601 Gentilly Boulevard, at Elysian Fields, Gentilly (283 8822/www.dillard.edu). Bus 97 Broad.
Founded in 1869 to educate former slaves, Dillard is one of the old-line African-American universities. Its green, relaxed campus in Gentilly, populated by some of the South's top black students, reminds many of the TV sitcom *A Different World*.

Loyola University

6363 St Charles Avenue, at Broadway, Uptown (865 2011/ www.loyno.edu). St Charles Streetcar. **Map** p306 B8.

Located adjacent to Tulane on St Charles Avenue, Loyola's Jesuit heritage is apparent in a strong student bent toward social justice causes and activism. Loyola is known for its law school, business school, sociology and theology faculties.

Southern University at New Orleans

6400 Press Drive, between Chef Menteur & Leon C Simon Streets, Gentilly (286 5000/ www.suno.edu). Bus 57 Franklin, 59 Congress.
Developed as a branch of Southern University in Baton Rouge, SUNO opened in 1959 when Louisiana colleges were still segregated by race. It's primarily a black institution but has become increasingly multiracial. Strong on education and night-school courses.

Tulane University

6823 St Charles Avenue, at Calhoun Street (865 5000/www.2tulane.edu). St Charles Streetcar. **Map** p306 B8.
Rich, old and social, Tulane is the school of choice for Eastern students who think it will be easier than Ivy League schools and Southerners who want to live here. The law school is sought after for its networking opportunities, while the business school, Latin American studies and architecture faculties are nationally recognised.

University of New Orleans

Lakefront, between Elysian Fields & Robert E Lee Street, Gentilly (280 6000/www.uno.edu). Bus 55 Elysian Fields.
The classic commuter school success story, UNO was originally a branch of Louisiana State University but is now the largest college in New Orleans with an enrolment of 16,000. It's popular with returning students, people who work full-time and non-New Orleanians who want cheap tuition and a Big Easy degree. UNO has developed some first-class studies, including writing, jazz (headed by Ellis Marsalis) and World War II.

Xavier University

1 Drexel Drive, between Carrollton Avenue & Washington Street (486 7411/www.xula.edu). Bus 34 Carrollton, 39 Tulane. **Map** p306 C6.
Xavier is the only Catholic university (as opposed to college) founded for African Americans in the US. It has found a niche in the healthcare field, with a very competitive pharmacy degree programme and a hugely successful pre-med programme. The small campus hosts many African, Third World and black cultural events.

Telephones

Dialling & codes

The area code for the city of New Orleans, Orleans Parish, Jefferson Parish and St Bernard (Chalmette) Parish is 504. If you are making a local call within this area, you don't need to dial the area code. The listings in this guide do not include the 504 area code, so if you're phoning from outside New Orleans but within the US, dial 1 + area code 504 before the seven-digit numbers listed. All other area codes are included in the listings, where appropriate.

From December 2000 the North Shore, Grand Isle and surrounding areas (*see section* **Trips Out of Town**) will have a new area code (unknown at press time). However, this will not come into full effect until June 2001.

When calling New Orleans from abroad, dial the international access code of the country from which you are calling (00 from the UK), followed by the US country code (1), the area code and the number as before. Note that toll-free calls generally start with 1-800 or 1-888, while expensive pay-per-minute calls usually start with 1-900 or 1-976. However, many hotels add a surcharge on all numbers.

Making a call

The telephone system in New Orleans is cheap and reliable. A local call costs 35¢, and operator, directory and emergency calls are free. Public payphones only accept nickels, dimes and quarters – not ideal for long-distance calls. To make a call from a public phone, pick up the receiver and check for a dial tone before parting with your money; some phones require you to dial the number first and wait for an operator or recorded message to tell you how much change to deposit. To make a collect (reverse charge) call, dial 0 for the operator followed by the area code and phone number. For help, dial 0 for an operator.

One of the most convenient ways of making a call is to use a phone card. These can be purchased at almost any retail outlet and range in price from $5 to $50, with a cost as low as 3¢ per minute. Read the card info carefully before buying; some have a 'connection charge', which deducts up to 75¢ from your card every time you use it. To use, dial the 1-800 number given from any phone and follow the instructions.

European-style prepaid phone cards that you insert directly into public phones instead of coins can be used in some special phone booths. Alternatively, you can charge calls to your MasterCard with **AT&T** (1-800 225 5288) or **MCI** (1-800 269 2255).

Telephone directories are available at most public phones and in hotels. If you can't find one, dial directory assistance (555 1212 for local numbers) and ask for your listing by name.

Useful numbers

Operator assistance 0.
Emergency (police, ambulance, fire) 911.

Directory assistance 1 + area code + 555 1212. Calls are free from pay phones.

International calls

To phone abroad from New Orleans dial 011 followed by the country code, followed by the area code and phone number. Country codes include: UK 44, Australia 61, New Zealand 64. The *White Pages* has a full listing of city and country codes.

Moblie phones

Whereas in Europe mobile phones work on the GSM network at either 900 or 1800mHz, the US does not have a standard mobile phone network that covers the whole country. Some of the major urban centres such as New York and Los Angeles offer access to the GSM network at 1900mHz but the rest of the country, including New Orleans, uses a variety of other digital and analogue networks. This means that European handsets will not work in New Orleans, and travellers from Europe will have to rent a handset and service once they arrive. Try **Cellular Rentals** (2601 Tulane Avenue, at S Dorgenois Street, Tremé, 822 7770) or **Solid Communications** (710 Poland Avenue, at Dauphin Street, Bywater, 943 1888), both of which rent mobile phones on a daily, weekly or monthly basis. US visitors to New Orleans should check with their service provider whether they will be able to use their mobile phone.

Coverage in the city is good, but storms are often fierce enough to disconnect both land lines and cell phones.

Local service providers

Nextel 1-800 639 8359.
PrimeCo 891 9006.
SunCom 1-877 786 2661.

Time & date

New Orleans is on Central Standard Time, which is one hour behind Eastern Standard (New York and Washington) and six hours behind GMT. It is one hour ahead of Mountain Time (Denver and the Rocky Mountains) and two hours ahead of Pacific Standard Time (California). Daylight Savings Time (which is almost concurrent with British Summer Time) runs from the first Sunday in April to the last Sunday in October. During this period the clocks are put forward one hour.

In the US, dates are written in the order of month, day, year; therefore, 2.5.01 is the fifth of February 2001, not the second of May.

Tipping

The tourism industry in New Orleans employs a large proportion of the local labour force. Many employees depend on gratuities for part of their income: tip accordingly. Here are some rough guidelines:
Bellhops & baggage handlers $1-$2 per bag
Hotel maids $1 a night
Hotel concierges $3-$5
Bartenders 15% of the bill
Cabbies, waiting staff, hairdressers & food delivery staff 15%-20% of the bill
Valets, counterstaff $1-$3, depending on the size of the order and any special arrangements
Wait staff 15%-20% if no service is included in the bill

Visas

Under the Visa Waiver Program, citizens of the UK, Japan, Australia, New Zealand and all Western European countries (except Portugal, Greece and the Vatican City) do not need a visa for stays in the United States of less than 90 days (business or pleasure) – as long as they have a passport that is valid for the

Directory

Average monthly climate

	High temp	Rainfall	% poss sunshine	Relative humidity
Jan	69°F (20°C)	4.97in (11.9cm)	49%	67%
Feb	65°F (18°C)	5.23in (13.3cm)	51%	64%
Mar	71°F (21°C)	4.73in (12cm)	57%	60%
Apr	79°F (26°C)	4.50in (11.4cm)	65%	59%
May	85°F (29°C)	5.07in (12.9cm)	69%	59%
June	90°F (32°C)	4.63in (11.8cm)	67%	60%
July	91°F (32°C)	6.73in (17.1cm)	61%	62%
Aug	90°F (32°C)	6.02in (15.3cm)	63%	63%
Sept	87°F (31°C)	5.87in (14.9cm)	64%	62%
Oct	79°F (26°C)	2.66in (6.8cm)	72%	59%
Nov	70°F (21°C)	4.06in (10.3cm)	62%	60%
Dec	64°F (18°C)	5.27in (13.4cm)	48%	66%

full 90-day period and a return ticket. An open stand-by ticket is acceptable. Canadians and Mexicans do not need visas but must have legal proof of their residency. All other travellers must have a visa. Full information and visa application forms can be obtained from your nearest US embassy or consulate. If you require a visa urgently, apply via the travel agent when you book your ticket.

US Embassy Visa Information Line

Recorded information in the UK 0891 200 290.

When to go

New Orleans is located in the subtropics, but that doesn't even begin to sum up just how miserably hot and humid the summer and autumn can be. A favourite local cry is, 'It's not the heat, it's the humidity'; yet this does so little to describe the breathless, dripping summers that the saying has morphed into, 'It's not the heat; it's the stupidity'.

No matter what the meteorologists say, summer lasts from March to October. In April temperatures are in the 80°F (27°C) range and, with humidity factored in, during July, August and September

they can hover well above 100°F (38°C): suddenly, you understand why Tennessee Williams's characters are so neurotic and grumpy.

It is also worth bearing in mind that mosquitoes swarm as soon as the weather gets warm, particularly from about 5pm until dark. Use a repellent regularly if you're vulnerable, especially on outdoor forays such as a swamp tour.

And yet despite these annoyances, for those who can cope with the heat, summer is the best time to visit. A steamy New Orleans summer night is sensual and oppressive, almost physically heavy. It's hard to breathe, or to think, and that's sort of what it's all about. On a night like this, with a long, cold cocktail in your hand, you'll really be experiencing the Big Easy. There's also the economic factor: summer is the off-season for New Orleans, which means almost everywhere is having a sale or offering cheaper rates. Crowds are much smaller, so it's far easier to get into popular restaurants and music venues.

For the best weather, stick to autumn (fall) and spring. Even winter is comfortable for most of the time, as the temperature rarely drops below 55°F (12°C) and in

spring the days are warm and breezy and the city blooms with tropical flowers.

Take the heat seriously, especially if you're not used to subtropical climates. Hats and sunglasses are a good idea during the day and sunblock essential. During the hottest months, try to avoid being outdoors between 11am and 3pm except for short bursts. The heat and humidity will sap your energy more quickly than you can imagine. Do like the locals and pace yourself.

See also page 289 **Hurricane watch** and *above* **Average monthly climate**.

Public holidays

New Year's Day (1 Jan).
Martin Luther King Day (third Mon in Jan).
Presidents' Day (third Mon in Feb).
Memorial Day (last Mon in May).
Independence Day (4 July).
Labor Day (first Mon in Sept).
Columbus Day (second Mon in Oct).
Veterans' Day (11 November).
Thanksgiving Day (last Thur in Nov).
Christmas Day (25 Dec).

Directory

Women

New Orleans is a comfortable city for women, retaining enough of its old-fashioned manners to soften the edges of its mostly unapologetic male supremacy. Feminist consciousness may not be a major element here, but the cult of the Scarlett O'Hara-style Southern belle with a will of iron persists. New Orleans has consistently elected strong women to represent it, including former US Representative Lindy Boggs and current US Senator Mary Landrieu (daughter of the last white mayor of New Orleans), and has several female city councillors. Women are also making headway in most career fields, including the professions. Yet New Orleans retains a definite masculine feel, smelling strongly of Stanley Kowalski underneath its Blanche DuBois frills.

In terms of crime and safety, the usual caveats apply (*see*

page 285). However, women seem to be no more at risk than men, and despite the high crime rates, incidents of rape are relatively low. Women going to bars and clubs alone or in groups will not find it difficult to blend in, especially where there is a younger crowd.

Newcomb College Center for Research on Women

200 Caroline Richardson Hall, Tulane University, at Audubon Boulevard, Uptown (865 5238/fax 862 8948/www.tulane.edu/~wc). St Charles Streetcar. **Open** *Sept-May* 9am-9pm Mon-Sat; closed Sun. *June-Aug* 9am-5pm daily. **Map** pp306-7 B8.

One of the leading academic centres on women's issues, Newcomb has a fascinating library, changing exhibits, a full schedule of talks and meetings. The friendly staff are happy to welcome visitors.

Planned Parenthood

4018 Magazine Street, between Napoleon & Louisiana Avenues, Uptown (897 9200). Bus 11

Magazine. **Open** 8am-5pm Mon; 10am-7pm Tue, Wed; 9am-5pm Thur; noon-5pm Fri; 9am-noon Sat; closed Sun. **Map** pp306-7 D9. Under siege in Catholic Louisiana, Planned Parenthood is still the best source of birth control and abortion info.

Rape Crisis Center

Information 482 9922. **Open** *Hotline* 24hrs daily.

Work

The employment situation in New Orleans is unstable at best. There is little in the way of a middle-income population, making decently paid employment scarce. To work legally, non-US citizens must obtain a 'green card' from the US embassy in their home country. UK students should check out **Study Abroad** (020 7801 9699/www.studyabroad. com) to see if they qualify for a work/study programme.

Under-the-table (illegal) work is not unknown but is low-paying and insecure.

Hurricane watch

A hurricane coming out of the Gulf of Mexico is a serious business. Although New Orleans is far enough inland to escape the very worst of the weather, the storm can cause flooding and considerable material damage. Usually, the hurricane season lasts from May to November, with most activity occurring between August and October. A Scale 1 hurricane involves sustained winds of 74 to 95 miles (119-153 kilometres) per hour, while a Scale 5 hurricane (the severest and fortunately very rare) yields winds of over 155 miles (250 kilometres) per hour. There are two distinct warning stages. If you hear a Hurricane Watch (issued when a hurricane may strike within the next 36 to 48 hours), fill up your car's tank, secure loose items and, if flooding threatens, leave the area if you can. If a Hurricane Warning is issued (meaning a storm is expected to strike within 24 hours), monitor a TV or radio for information and stay indoors.

You will have three options if a hurricane hits the city during your visit.
● Stay where you are. If you are in a large hotel, you will be directed to a place of safety by the staff and management.
● Follow the evacuation signs directing you out of town. These signs are located on all the roads designated as major evacuation routes. Follow the directions of the state police and local law enforcement officials manning the routes. Listen to them – they know what they are doing.
● Listen to the radio or tune into the TV for directions to the nearest shelter. Go immediately to the shelter when directed.

American Red Cross

586 8191. **Open** 24hrs daily.
Provides information on disaster preparedness.

Weather Information

24hr recorded information 828 4000.

Glossary

For a list of culinary terms, *see page 123*, and for notes on street-name pronunciation, *see page 70* **How do you say that again?**

bayou (pronounced 'bye-yew') Marshy tributary of a river or lake.

Cajun
A descendant from the Acadians – French exiles from Nova Scotia who settled in Louisiana in the 1760s; also used to describe the French dialect, the food and the music they popularised.

crawfish
Freshwater crustacea, also known as mudbugs. Sometimes spelled as 'crayfish'.

Creole
A descendant of European (especially French and Spanish) settlers of the Caribbean basin; 'Creole of colour' was used for those with black ancestors. The term is beginning to re-emerge in local vocabulary, in cooking for example.

debris
Served with your roast beef po-boy; all the delicious bits and pieces of meat and gravy that pile up during preparation. Always say 'yes' when asked in a café, 'You want debris wit dat?'

Dixie
Geographically, the Old South; as an adjective for anything of the South. The term may have come from *dix*, the French word for ten, which appeared on the first $10 bills issued by the Citizen's Bank of Louisiana, or may have been derived from the Mason-Dixon Line, the surveyors' 1767 line between Pennsylvania and Maryland that became the demarcation of North and South between the states.

Faubourg
Means 'suburb' in French and 'neighbourhood' in New Orleans.

go cup
Plastic cups handed out at bars for patrons to take their drinks away with them.

gris-gris
Powders used in the voodoo charms; a spell.

king cake
Traditional ring-shaped oval pastry, decorated in Mardi Gras colours (purple, green and gold) and containing a small plastic baby Jesus.

krewe
Mardi Gras parade organisation or 'club'.

lagniappe
A baker's dozen – something extra thrown in for nothing. Also the title of the *Times-Picayune*'s weekend entertainment supplement.

laissez les bons temps rouler
Let the good times roll: a popular Cajun expression.

levee
Embankments built up along the Mississippi River to control or, at least, limit flooding.

makin' groceries
Shopping for groceries.

Mardi Gras
While the term can be used to mean both the pre-Lenten season and 'Fat Tuesday' itself (the last day of celebration before Ash Wednesday, the first day of Lent), native New Orleanians usually use Mardi Gras to mean Fat Tuesday and Carnival to denote the season.

neutral ground
The strip of land that divides the lanes of a street or highway (the median). Usually grassy or landscaped.

New Orleans
Get your pronunciation right. With Orleans, when referring to the parish, it's pronounced 'Or-leens'; when it's the city, it's always 'Noo Or-lins'.

pirogue (pronounced 'pee-roe')
Cajun flat-bottomed boat, ideal for the shallow waters of the bayou.

quadroon
An archaic, romanticised term for a person of mixed black and white parentage, meaning they are one-quarter black. There are similar terms such as octoroon, meaning one-eighth black.

second line (noun and verb)
The friends and family members who follow behind the coffin and band in a jazz funeral.

shotgun house
Small, wood-frame house built with rooms one behind another, with no hallway. So called because a shotgun (supposedly) could be fired through the front door and out of the back without ever hitting anything. A **double shotgun** is a duplex (maisonette) and a **camelback shotgun** means a partial second storey (usually bedrooms) has been added at the back of the structure. *See also chapter* **Architecture**.

streetcar
In New Orleans the public transport electric cars are always 'streetcars' and never 'trolleys' or 'trams'.

throw
The largesse of Mardi Gras; the trinkets thrown from the parade floats – plastic beads, cups, toys, candy.

Vieux Carré
Literally the 'old quarter', the French name for the French Quarter.

where y'at?
Typical New Orleanian greeting. Native Orleanians who speak with the local Brooklynesque accent are known as Yats from this greeting.

yeh, you right
Yat small-talk response to almost any comment.

zydeco
Dance music of south-western Louisiana's black, French-speaking Creoles; thought to be a corruption of the first two words of the old dance tune 'les haricots n'est pas salé'.

Further Reference

Books

Non-fiction

John M Barry: *Rising Tide*
Gripping and elegantly written account of the great Mississippi flood of 1927.

Christopher Benfey: *Degas in New Orleans*
Degas' stay on Esplanade Avenue in 1870s New Orleans.

Jason Berry, Jonathan Foose & Tad Jones: *Up From the Cradle of Jazz: New Orleans Music Since World War II*
Insights into the succeeding generations of musicians such as Fats Domino and the Neville Brothers who took New Orleans music in new directions.

John Broven: *Rhythm & Blues in New Orleans*
History of R&B in the city.

John Churchill Chase:
Frenchmen, Desire, Good Children and Other Streets of New Orleans
Definitive and delightful history (written in the 1950s) of the city through its streets, by a former *Times-Picayune* cartoonist.

Randolph Delahanty: *New Orleans: Elegance and Decadence*
A satisfying examination of New Orleans through its houses and cultural history.

Joy Dickinson: *Haunted City: An Unauthorized Guide to the Magical, Magnificent New Orleans of Anne Rice*
The who, what, when and where of New Orleans in Rice's books

Robert Florence: *New Orleans Cemeteries: Life in the Cities of the Dead*
History, myth, culture and the present are interwoven in this beautifully illustrated volume.

James Gill: *Lords of Misrule: Mardi Gras and the Politics of Race in New Orleans*
British transplant Gill turns a sharp yet not unsympathetic eye on the intertwined history of Mardi Gras and New Orleans's identity.

Lafcadio Hearn: *Creole Sketches*
Hearn's plummy tales of 1880s New Orleans are probably more invented than fact-based – history the way life should have been.

Walter Johnson: *Soul by Soul: Life Inside the Antebellum Slave Market*
Johnson presents New Orleans as a fulcrum for the slave trade in an impeccable cultural history.

John R Kemp: *New Orleans: An Illustrated History*
Large illustrated overview of New Orleans's history.

Richard S Kennedy (ed): *Literary New Orleans*
A scholarly but engaging study of major New Orleans writers and the city's literary community.

Susan Larson: *The Booklover's Guide to New Orleans*
Times-Picayune book editor Susan Larson covers all the bases for literary tourists.

Kerri McCaffety: *Obituary Cocktail*
Affecting and affectionate photographic documentation of New Orleans bars.

Tim Pickles: *New Orleans 1815*
Part of the Osprey Military Campaign Series: illuminates the Battle of New Orleans and the War of 1812. Superb maps and illustrations.

Henri Schindler: *New Orleans Mardi Gras*
Lavishly illustrated discussion of the Carnival tradition by one of the most knowledgeable Mardi Gras historians.

Michael P Smith: *Mardi Gras Indians*
The first book to examine the culture of the black Indians of New Orleans. Superb photos.

Mary Ann Sternberg: *Along the River Road: Past and Present of Louisiana's Historic Byway*
Useful for visitors exploring the River Road and its plantations.

Jerry E Strahan: *Managing Ignatius: The Lunacy of Lucky Dogs and Life in the Quarter*
The real-life 'Confederacy of Dunces', by the over-educated manager of the Lucky Dog hotdog carts. Very funny.

Michael Tisserand: *The Kingdom of Zydeco*
Authoritative and entertaining history and culture of zydeco.

Roulhac Toledano: *National Trust Guide to New Orleans*

Architectural and Cultural Treasures
Toledano's 1996 guide is small and portable. An excellent companion to walks and rides around the city.

Christina Vella: *Intimate Enemies: The Two Worlds of the Baroness Pontalba*
Masterful biography of one of New Orleans's mythic women and one of the best histories of colonial New Orleans available.

New Orleans Architecture Series
A seven-volume set, written by various architects, writers and preservationists. Lavishly illustrated, each volume is devoted to a different district of the city.

Fiction

Nelson Algren: *A Walk on the Wild Side*
Wonderfully tawdry American novel set in the French Quarter.

Poppy Z Brite: *Exquisite Corpse*
Fantasy writer Brite's vivid tale of a French Quarter serial killer.

Robert Olen Butler: *A Good Scent From a Strange Mountain*
The New Orleans of immigrant Vietnamese, told in short stories.

George Washington Cable: *Old Creole Days*
Cluttered with Creole and black dialect, slowed down by the elaborate descriptive style of the Victorian era, Cable's 1879 stories are nevertheless entertaining tales.

Kate Chopin: *The Awakening*
Chopin's 1899 novel of a sexually and spiritually frustrated Creole wife is told with dreamlike softness but is startlingly contemporary in its understanding of gender roles.

Tony Dunbar: *Shelter from the Storm*
The best of a series of mysteries by a New Orleans attorney, featuring hapless lawyer-cum-gourmand Tubby Dubonnet.

William Faulkner: *Pylon*; *Absolom, Absolom!*; *The Wild Palms*
New Orleans is a marginal but significant setting for many of Faulkner's books. Only his apprentice novel *Pylon* is completely set in the city.

Ernest Gaines: *A Gathering of Old Men*
The old men are black, and they gather on decrepit porches in rural Louisiana to recount stories shot through with wisdom.

Ellen Gilchrist: *Victory Over Japan; In the Land of Dreamy Dreams*
Stories of bored Uptown divorcees, sexually ravenous teenagers and Irish Channel adventurers. The early books are best.

Shirley Ann Grau: *Keepers of the House; The House on Coliseum Street*
A Pulitzer Prize winner delves into post-World War II, pre-Civil Rights movement New Orleans.

Everette Maddox: *American Waste; Bar Scotch; The Everette Maddox Songbook*
Maddox was a poet whose books of romantic barfly poetry capture life in the Riverbend area.

Walker Percy: *The Moviegoer*
Troubled Catholic Bix Bolling retreats to lower-middle-class Gentilly and searches for meaning in movies.

Anne Rice: *Lasher; The Feast of All Saints; Interview With the Vampire*
New Orleans is the stage for Anne Rice's fertile imagination.

John Kennedy Toole: *A Confederacy of Dunces*
Definitive and hilarious tale of New Orleans that won the author a posthumous Pulitzer Prize.

Tennessee Williams: *A Streetcar Named Desire*
Read the play or watch a production, but don't miss the Marlon Brando/Vivien Leigh film.

Margaret Woodward: *No Place Called Home*
A suspenseful walk on the darker side of New Orleans in the company of a seven-year-old boy.

Film

A Streetcar Named Desire (1951)
Filmed in Hollywood but infused with a New Orleans ambience.

Angel Heart (1987)
Erotic gothic on the bayou, a confusing noir tale with Mickey Rourke and Robert De Niro.

The Big Easy (1996)
Natives groan at Dennis Quaid's Cajunesque accent but it's an entertaining mystery-love story that has a good feel for the New Orleans view of corruption.

The Buccaneer (1958)
Anthony Quinn as pirate Jean Lafitte and Charlton Heston as Andrew Jackson.

Cat People (1982)
Natassia Kinski slinks round town.

Down by Law (1986)
Jim Jarmusch's quirky tale of three losers who bond in jail then break out for a loony road trip.

Easy Rider (1969)
How everyone expects their road trip to New Orleans to turn out.

Hard Times (1975)
Charles Bronson, James Coburn, bare-knuckled fighters in Depression-era New Orleans.

The Flame of New Orleans (1941)
Marlene Dietriech drives New Orleans men crazy.

Interview With the Vampire (1994)
Anne Rice's word made flesh.

JFK (1991)
Admire Stone's impassioned filmmaking but keep in mind that this is pure historical fantasy.

Double Jeopardy (1999)
Framed for a murder she didn't commit, Ashley Judd tracks down and confronts the husband who framed her in the French Quarter.

Jezebel (1938)
Once thought to be the story of an emasculating woman getting her just desserts, Bette Davis's complex Southern belle is clearly a case of a woman being persecuted for exercising her intelligence, nerve and sexuality. Terrifically entertaining.

King Creole (1958)
Elvis Presley sings in a French Quarter club and gets involved with the Mob.

Kingfish: A Story of Huey P Long (1995)
Beautifully photographed bio of Louisiana's enigmatic madman governor. John Goodman makes a creditable Huey.

Mardi Gras (1958)
Mindless musical has military school straight arrow Pat Boone and pals finding true love at Carnival.

New Orleans (1947)
Sanitised version of the birth of jazz; at least Billie Holliday (as a maid) sings 'Do You Know What it Means to Miss New Orleans' accompanied by Louis Armstrong.

Obsession (1976)
Brian de Palma thriller about New Orleans businessman Cliff Robertson who loses his wife and child to kidnappers.

Panic in the Streets (1950)
This manhunt to find a gangster carrying the plague makes the ideal travelogue of mid 20th-century New Orleans. With Richard Widmark.

Pretty Baby (1978)
Brooke Shields's infamous turn as a 12-year-old virgin auctioned by prostitute mother Susan Sarandon. Louis Malle's oblique view of New Orleans decadence.

Tightrope (1984)
Clint Eastwood in kinky form as a New Orleans cop chasing a killer.

Undercover Blues (1993)
Kathleen Turner and Dennis Quaid are retired spies who become embroiled in a caper in New Orleans.

Walk on the Wild Side (1962)
Smug morality tale about women forced to become prostitutes in a lush French Quarter bordello.

Wild at Heart (1990)
Sleaze to the nth degree in David Lynch's ode to dysfunctional lovers on the run.

WUSA (1970)
Paul Newman's alcoholic DJ sobers up to a right-wing conspiracy.

Music

Albums are in italics, tracks in inverted commas.

Louisiana

Alex Chilton: *High Priest* (1987); *A Man Called Destruction* (1995)

Charlie Daniels Band: 'Sweet Louisiana' (1976)

Dr John: 'Louisiana Lullabye' (1979)

Emmylou Harris: 'Leaving Louisiana in the Broad Daylight' (1978)

Gil Scott Heron: 'Angola, Louisiana' (1978)

Maria McKee: 'This Property's Condemned' (1989)

NRBQ: 'Boozoo, That's Who!' (1989)

A tribute to zydeco's Boozoo Chavis.

Kid Ory: *Kid Ory's Creole Jazz Band* (1954)

Tom Petty & the Heartbreakers: 'Louisiana Rain' (1979)

Paul Revere & the Raiders: 'Louisiana Redbone' (1969)

Muddy Waters: 'Louisiana Blues' (1950)

Victoria Williams: *Happy Come Home* (1987).
Williams is an art-folkie whose songs have a feel for smalltown life.

New Orleans

Louis Armstrong: *The Hot Fives, Vol 1* (1988)
Satchmo's earliest work from 1925 and 1926; *Let's Do It* (1995) – a collection of his later vocal work, much of it with Ella Fitzgerald.

Sidney Bechet: *New Orleans Jazz*; *Spirits of New Orleans*.

Freddy Cannon: 'Way Down Yonder in New Orleans' (1957)

Fats Domino: 'Walking to New Orleans' (1960)

Dr John: *Gris Gris* (1968); *The Night Tripper (The Sun, Moon and Herbs)* (1971); *Gumbo* (1972); 'I Thought I Heard New Orleans Say' (1979)

Gottschalk: *Classics of the Americas Vol 4: Piano Works* (Georges Rabol, piano).

Donald Harrison Jr: 'Indian Blue: featuring the Guardians of the Flame Mardi Gras Indians and Dr John'

Invisible Cowboy: *Unsafe Trigger (at the White Trash Discotheque)* (1996)

John Kay: 'Down in New Orleans' (1978)

Led Zeppelin: 'Royal Orleans' (1978)

The Meters: *Funkify Your Life: The Meters Anthology* (1995)

Jelly Roll Morton: *The Complete Jelly Roll Morton 1926-1930*

The Neville Bros: *Treacherous: A History of the Neville Bros Vols 1 & 2* (1986, 1990)

Maceo Parker: *Southern Exposure* (1993)
James Brown's sax player with New Orleans bands.

Elvis Presley: 'New Orleans' (1958)

Professor Longhair: 'Mardi Gras in New Orleans' (1950); *New Orleans Piano* (1972); *Crawfish Fiesta* (1980); *The Last Mardi Gras* (1982); *Rock 'n' Roll Gumbo* (1985)

Michael Ray & the Cosmic Krewe: *Michael Ray & the Cosmic Krewe* (1994)

Redbone: 'Witch Queen of New Orleans' (1971)

REM: 'New Orleans Instrumental No.1' (1992)

Silver Jews: 'New Orleans' (1994)

Shirley and Lee: *The Legendary Masters Series* (1990)

Swingin' Haymakers: *For Rent* (1995)

Thousand $ Car: *Big Shot* (1997)

The Tractors: 'Trying to Get to New Orleans' (1995)

Tom Waits: 'I Wish I was in New Orleans' (1977)

Wild Magnolias: *They Call Us Wild* (1975)

Wild Tchoupitoulas: *The Wild Tchoupitoulas* (1976)

Compilations: *Cajun Dance Party: Fais Do-Do* (1994); *The Mardi Gras Indians Super Sunday Showdown* (1992)

Websites

Bywater Neighbourhood Association
www.Bywater.org
Good source of local and civic news.

Cashmoney Records
www.cashmoney-records.com
Rap millionaire Master P's hip hop, entrepreneurial empire (anchored in New Orleans, his hometown) is showcased here.

Flo magazine
www.flo.com
An online magazine put together by a coalition of post-college New Orleanians.

Greater New Orleans Free Net
www.gnofn.org
Many local non-profits have their home pages here; excellent guide to arts, culture, fun stuff.

Gumbo news
www.gumbopages.com
New Orleans expat Chuck Taggart publishes a Big Easy-Acadiana homepage from Los Angeles. A

mixed bag of recipes, news and some good travel tips.

Magazine Street
www.magazinestreet.com
A big ad for members of the merchants' organisation but a good place to check on events and changes in the shops.

Mayor Marc H Morial
www.neworleans.com/government/morial.html
The mayor's picture and a welcome message.

MoJo New Orleans
www.mojono.com
News and calendar listings for locals and visitors with a bohemian viewpoint. Good links, updated on a spotty basis.

City of New Orleans
www.new-orleans.la.us
City's official site. Much happy talk but you can find facts and reliable info as well.

New Orleans City Council
www.nocitycouncil.com
Check on the antics of local politicos.

New Orleans East
www.neworleanseast.com
Focuses on the largely middle-class, African-American area that is hoping for a boost with the opening of Jazzland Theme Park.

New Orleans Police Department
www.new-orleans.la.cnoweb/nopd
Crime stats.

New Orleans Public Library
www.gnofn.org/~nopl/
Excellent site with emphasis on how to find local news, history and useful information.

New Orleans Weather
www.neworleans.com/weather.html
Get a four-day forecast.

Nola LIVE – New Orleans Home Page
www.nolalive.com
The web arm of the *Times-Picayune* is less fusty and great for listings.

Superfly Productions
www.superfly.com
Hip music production/events group.

WWOZ
www.wwoz.org
The sounds of New Orleans from its best radio station, with excellent links to other music sources and perhaps the most comprehensive links to New Orleans sites in general.

Directory

Index

Note: Numbers in **bold** indicate where key information is to be found; *italics* indicate illustrations.

Advertisers' Index

Please refer to the relevant sections for
addresses/telephone numbers

Maps

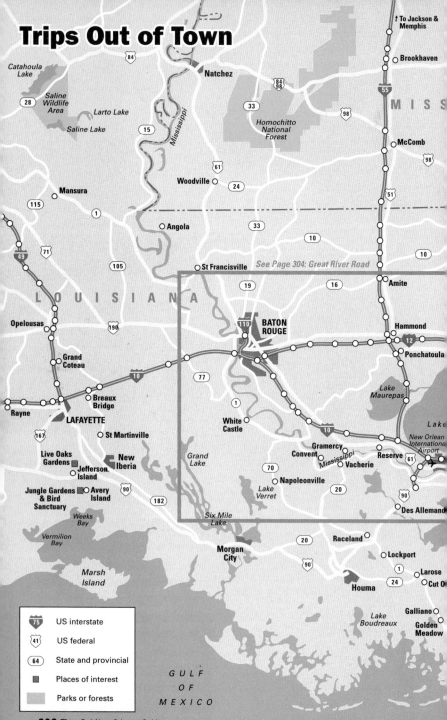

Trips Out of Town

See Page 304: Great River Road

† To Jackson & Memphis

Brookhaven

Natchez

Catahoula Lake

Saline Wildlife Area

Larto Lake

Saline Lake

MISS

Homochitto National Forest

McComb

Woodville

Mansura

Angola

Mississippi

Amite

St Francisville

Hammond

LOUISIANA

BATON ROUGE

Ponchatoula

Opelousas

Grand Coteau

Lake Maurepas

Breaux Bridge

LAFAYETTE

Rayne

White Castle

Lake

St Martinville

New Orlean International Airport

Live Oaks Gardens

Grand Lake

Gramercy

Convent

Reserve

Jefferson Island

New Iberia

Mississippi

Vacherie

Jungle Gardens & Bird Sanctuary

Avery Island

Napoleonville

Lake Verret

Weeks Bay

Six Mile Lake

Des Allemand

Vermilion Bay

Raceland

Morgan City

Lockport

Marsh Island

Larose

Houma

Cut O

Galliano

Lake Boudreaux

Golden Meadow

	US interstate
	US federal
	State and provincial
	Places of interest
	Parks or forests

GULF

OF

MEXICO

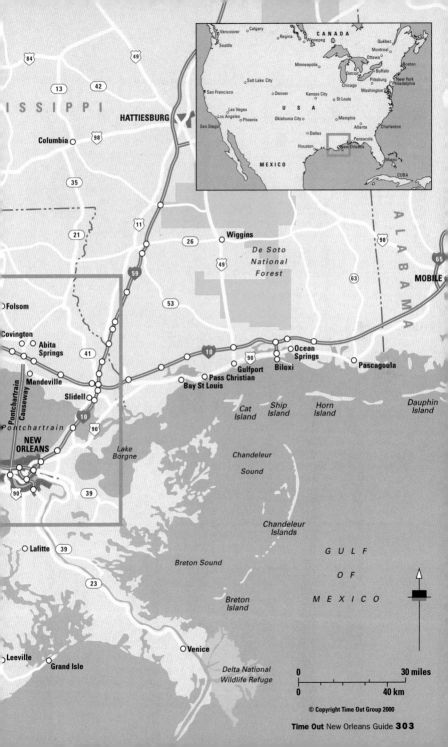

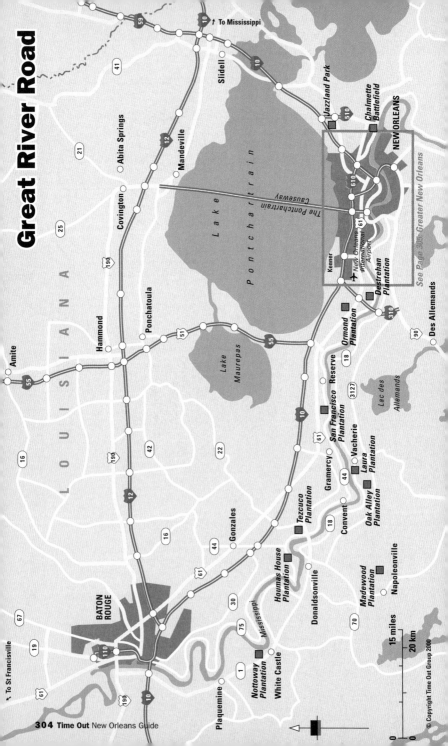

Great River Road

↑ To Mississippi

59

70

41

Slidell

12

Mandeville

Abita Springs

21

25

Covington

190

Ponchatoula

Hammond

Amite

55

16

42

190

12

16

LOUISIANA

BATON ROUGE

67

19

110

61

190

10

↑ To St Francisville

Plaquemine

Mississippi

75

White Castle

Nottoway Plantation

1

30

44

61

Gonzales

22

51

55

Lake Maurepas

10

Lake Pontchartrain

The Pontchartrain Causeway

See Page 305: Greater New Orleans

Jazzland Park

510

Chalmette Battlefield

NEW ORLEANS

610

Kenner

61

New Orleans International Airport

Destrehan Plantation

Ormond Plantation

310

18

90

Des Allemands

Lac des Allemands

3127

Reserve

61

San Francisco Plantation

Gramercy

44

Vacherie

Laura Plantation

Oak Alley Plantation

18

Convent

Tezcuco Plantation

Napoleonville

Madewood Plantation

70

Donaldsonville

Houmas House Plantation

61

44

15 miles

20 km

© Copyright Time Out Group 2000

0

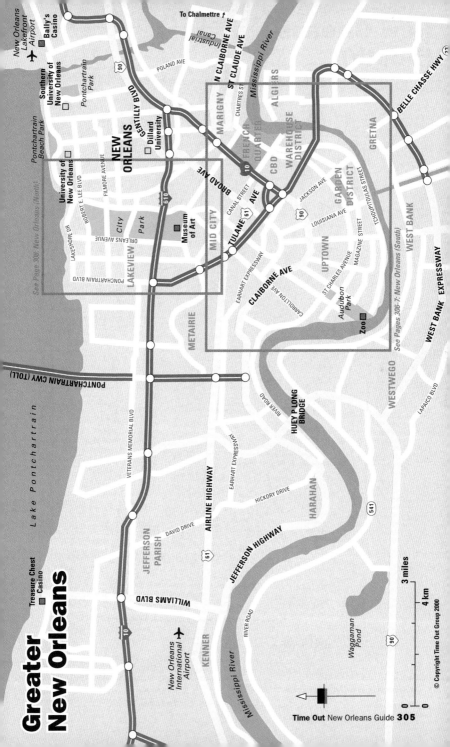

Greater
New Orleans

New Orleans
Lakefront
✈ Airport

Bally's Casino

Southern
University of
New Orleans ☐

Pontchartrain Park

POLAND AVE

To Chalmettre ↑

Industrial Canal

CHARTRES ST

N CLAIBORNE AVE

ST CLAUDE AVE

Mississippi River

BELLE CHASSE HWY

90

GENTILLY BLVD

Pontchartrain Park

Dillard
University

Pontchartrain Beach Park

NEW
ORLEANS

MARIGNY

FRENCH QUARTER

ALGIERS

GRETNA

See Page 306: New Orleans (North)

University of
New Orleans ☐

FILMORE AVENUE

ROBERT E. LEE BLVD

City
Park

BROAD AVE

CBD

WAREHOUSE
DISTRICT

610

Canal Street

TULANE AVE

61

90

JACKSON AVE

GARDEN
DISTRICT

WEST BANK

LAKESHORE DR

ORLEANS AVENUE

Museum
of Art

MID CITY

TULANE AVE

LOUISIANA AVE

UPTOWN

WEST BANK EXPRESSWAY

PONTCHARTRAIN BLVD

LAKEVIEW

Earhart Expressway

CLAIBORNE AVE

CARROLLTON AVE

ST CHARLES AVENUE

MAGAZINE STREET

TCHOUPITOULAS STREET

See Pages 306-7: New Orleans (South)

METAIRIE

Audubon
Park

Zoo ☐

WESTWEGO

PONTCHARTRAIN CWY (TOLL)

Lake Pontchartrain

VETERANS MEMORIAL BLVD

RIVER ROAD

HUEY P LONG BRIDGE

Earhart Expressway

HICKORY DRIVE

HARAHAN

541

JEFFERSON
PARISH

DAVID DRIVE

AIRLINE HIGHWAY

61

JEFFERSON HIGHWAY

WESTWEGO

LAPALCO BLVD

Treasure Chest
☐ Casino

WILLIAMS BLVD

New Orleans
International Airport ✈

10

KENNER

Mississippi River

RIVER ROAD

Waggaman
Pond

90

3 miles

4 km

© Copyright Time Out Group 2000

Time Out New Orleans Guide 305

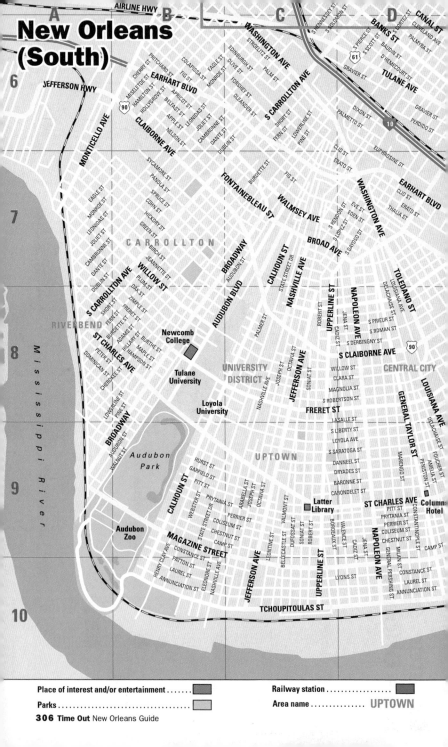

New Orleans (North)

Lake Pontchartrain

LAKESHORE DR

LAKESHORE

LAKE VISTA

City Yacht Harbour

N ROADWAY ST
S ROADWAY ST

Orleans Marina

LAKE MARINA DR

AMETHYST ST
TOPAZ ST
CRYSTAL ST
JEWEL ST

TURQUOISE ST
EMERALD ST

ROBERT E LEE BLVD

ROBERT E LEE BLVD

PARIS AVE

PERLITA ST

CHATHAM DR
CHAMBERLAIN DR

CONRAD ST
WALKER ST

CATINA ST
WUERPEL ST

CANAL BLVD

MOUTON ST

CHAPELLE ST

ORLEANS AVE

City Park

ST BERNARD AVE

CARTIER AVE

CRESCENT DR
MITHRA ST

FILMORE AVE

LAKEVIEW

FILMORE AVE

GENERAL HAIG ST

VICKSBURG ST

City Park Stables

Golf Club House

GARDENA DR

RIVIERA ST
GRANADA DR

MIRABEAU AVE

PONTCHARTRAIN BLVD

WEST END BLVD

MILNE BLVD

PORTEOUS ST

COLBERT ST
LOUISVILLE ST
LOUIS XIV ST
BRAGG ST

MEMPHIS ST
GENERAL DIAZ ST

MARSHALL FOCH ST

ARGONNE BLVD

FLEUR DE LIS DR

HARRISON AVE

FRENCH ST

GERMAIN ST

WISNER BLVD

OWENS BLVD

DUPLESSIS ST

PERLITA ST

MANDOLIN ST

HARRISON AVE

SENATE ST

GIBSON ST

HAMBURG ST

PARIS AVE

POLK AVE

CATINA ST

VICKSBURG ST
HARRISON CT

GENERAL HAIG ST

ORLEANS AVE

MARCONI BLVD

BROOKS ST

KENILWORTH ST

DIAGONAL DRIVE

CADILLAC ST

MILTON ST

SERE ST

610

FLORIDA BLVD

FLORIDA BLVD

ZACHARY TAYLOR DR

FLORIDA AVE

10

CATINA ST
MILNE ST

HOMEDALE ST
WOODLAWN PL

ST BLVD

VICKSBURG ST
HIDALGO ST
NAVARRE ST

VISION DR

MARCONI BLVD

Tad Gormley Stadium

City Park

R WILLIAMS ST

DESAIX BLVD

TRAFALGAR ST

GENTILLY BLVD

ST BERNARD AVE

Greenwood Cemetery

GENERAL DIAZ ST

ORLEANS AVE

Botanical Gardens

Storyland

New Orleans Museum of Art

St Louis Cemetery No 3

CASTIGLIONE ST
BELFORT AVE

N GALVEZ ST
N DUPRE ST

O'REILLY ST

AUBRY ST

D'ABADIE

Metairie Cemetery

CITY PARK AVE

ST ANN ST

CONTI ST
ST PETER ST
TOULOUSE ST

MOSS ST

MYSTERY ST

Fair Grounds Race Track

PAUL MORPHY ST

ONZAGA ST

LAPEYROUSE ST

BIENVILLE ST

MID CITY

Pitot House Museum

FORTIN ST
MAUREPAS ST
PONCE DE LEON ST
ST JOHN ST

ESPLANADE AVE

LEPAGE ST

N GAYOSO ST

N DORGENOIS ST

LAHARPE ST

COLUMBUS

CANAL ST

N CARROLLTON AVE

ORLEANS AVE

MOSS ST

N BROAD AVE

CLEVELAND AVE
PALMYRA ST
IBERVILLE ST

CONTI ST

ST PHILIP ST

DUMAINE ST

N ROCHEBLAVE ST

BANKS ST

HAMILTON ST
HOLLYGROVE ST

PEACH ST
PEAR ST

MARKS ST

BAUDIN ST

N PIERCE ST

SCOTT ST

ST ANN ST

See Page 306-7: New Orleans (South)

Place of interest and/or entertainment ....

Parks ....

N

0   0.5 mile

0   800 m

© Copyright Time Out Group 2000

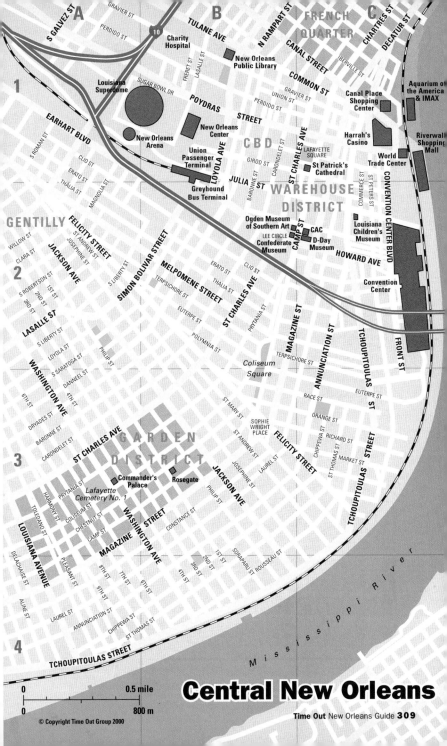

Central New Orleans

0   0.5 mile
0   800 m

A

GRAVIER ST
S GALVEZ ST
PERDIDO ST
10
TULANE AVE
Charity Hospital
Louisiana Superdome
Sugar Bowl Dr
POYDRAS
EARHART BLVD
S ROMAN ST
CLIO ST
ERATO ST
THALIA ST
MAGNOLIA ST
New Orleans Arena
Union Passenger Terminal
LOYOLA AVE
Greyhound Bus Terminal
JULIA
STREET

GENTILLY
FELICITY STREET
WILLOW ST
CLARA ST
JACKSON AVE
ST ANDREW ST
JOSEPHINE ST
S ROBERTSON ST
1ST ST
2ND ST
3RD ST
S LIBERTY ST
LASALLE ST
SIMON BOLIVAR STREET
S LIBERTY ST
LOYOLA ST
S SARATOGA ST
PHILIP ST
WASHINGTON AVE
6TH ST
4TH ST
DANNEEL ST
DRYADES ST
BARONNE ST
CARONDELET ST
MELPOMENE STREET
TERPSICHORE ST
EUTERPE ST
POLYMNIA ST

GARDEN DISTRICT
ST CHARLES AVE
Commander's Palace
Rosegate
Lafayette Cemetery No. 1
PRYTANIA ST
HARMONY ST
COLISEUM ST
CHESTNUT ST
CAMP ST
CONSTANCE ST
MAGAZINE AVE
WASHINGTON STREET
JACKSON AVE
PHILIP ST
JOSEPHINE ST
LAUREL ST
ST ANDREW ST
ST MARY ST

LOUISIANA AVENUE
TOLEDANO ST
DELACHAISE ST
ALINE ST
PLEASANT ST
8TH ST
9TH ST
7TH ST
6TH ST
4TH ST
2ND ST
3RD ST
1ST ST
SORAPARU ST
ROUSSEAU ST
LAUREL ST
ANNUNCIATION ST
CHIPPEWA ST
ST THOMAS ST
TCHOUPITOULAS STREET

B

TULANE AVE
N RAMPART ST
CANAL STREET
New Orleans Public Library
FRERET ST
LASALLE ST
COMMON ST
GRAVIER ST
UNION ST
PERDIDO ST
New Orleans Center
CBD
ST CHARLES AVE
CARONDELET ST
LAFAYETTE SQUARE
GIROD ST
St Patrick's Cathedral
BARONNE ST
JULIA ST
WAREHOUSE DISTRICT
Ogden Museum of Southern Art
LEE CIRCLE
Confederate Museum
CAC
CAMP ST
D-Day Museum
ERATO ST
CLIO ST
THALIA ST
ST CHARLES AVE
PRYTANIA ST
MAGAZINE ST
TERPSICHORE ST
Coliseum Square
ANNUNCIATION ST
RACE ST
ORANGE ST
SOPHIE WRIGHT PLACE
FELICITY STREET
CHIPPEWA ST
RICHARD ST
ST THOMAS ST
MARKET ST

C

FRENCH QUARTER
CHARTRES ST
DECATUR ST
CANAL STREET
IBERVILLE ST
Aquarium of the America & IMAX
Canal Place Shopping Center
Harrah's Casino
Riverwalk Shopping Mall
World Trade Center
ST CHARLES AVE
COMMERCE ST
ST PETERS ST
CONVENTION CENTER BLVD
Louisiana Children's Museum
HOWARD AVE
TCHOUPITOULAS STREET
Convention Center
FRONT ST
EUTERPE ST
TCHOUPITOULAS STREET

1
2
3
4

Mississippi River

New Orleans Transport

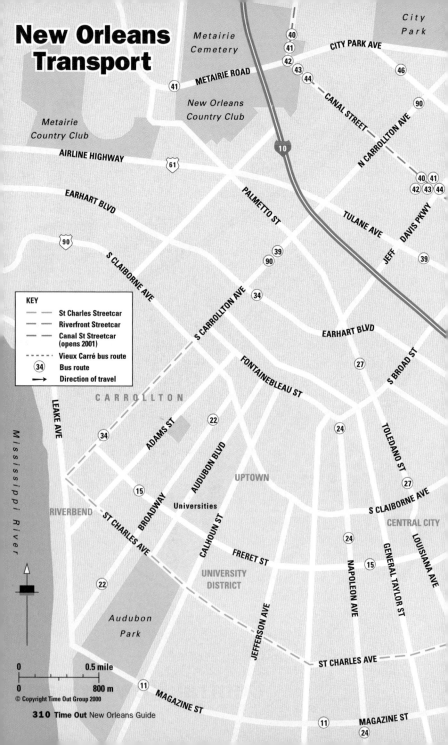

KEY

– – –	St Charles Streetcar
— —	Riverfront Streetcar
– –	Canal St Streetcar (opens 2001)
········	Vieux Carré bus route
(34)	Bus route
→	Direction of travel

Metairie Cemetery

City Park

Metairie Country Club

New Orleans Country Club

CITY PARK AVE

METAIRIE ROAD

CANAL STREET

N CARROLLTON AVE

AIRLINE HIGHWAY

EARHART BLVD

PALMETTO ST

TULANE AVE

JEFF DAVIS PKWY

S CLAIBORNE AVE

S CARROLLTON AVE

FONTAINEBLEAU ST

EARHART BLVD

S BROAD ST

CARROLLTON

UPTOWN

ADAMS ST

AUDUBON BLVD

Universities

BROADWAY

CALHOUN ST

FRERET ST

TOLEDANO ST

S CLAIBORNE AVE

CENTRAL CITY

NAPOLEON AVE

GENERAL TAYLOR ST

LOUISIANA AVE

LEAKE AVE

RIVERBEND

ST CHARLES AVE

UNIVERSITY DISTRICT

Mississippi River

Audubon Park

JEFFERSON AVE

ST CHARLES AVE

MAGAZINE ST

MAGAZINE ST

0   0.5 mile

0   800 m

© Copyright Time Out Group 2000

310 Time Out New Orleans Guide

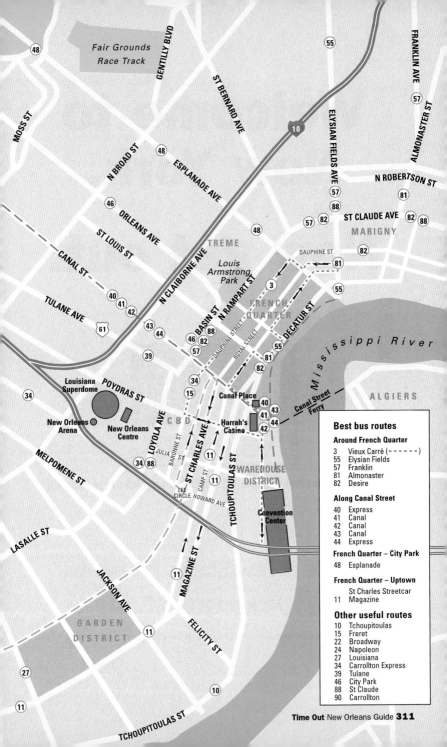

Welcome to New York.

Now get out.

The obsessive guide to impulsive entertainment

On sale at newsstands in New York
Pick up a copy!

To get a copy of the current issue or to subscribe, call *Time Out New York* at 212-539-4444.

Street Index

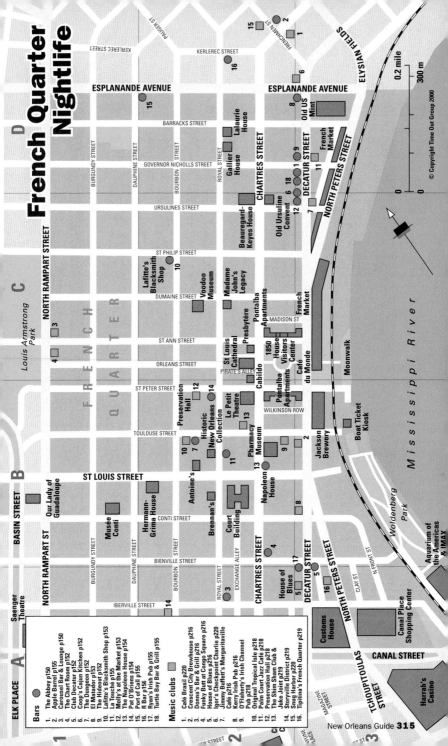

French Quarter Nightlife

Bars

1. The Abbey p150
2. Apple Barrel p155
3. Carousel Bar & Lounge p150
4. The Chart Room p152
5. Club Decatur p152
6. Coop's Cajun Kitchen p152
7. The Dungeon p152
8. El Matador p153
9. The Hideout p152
10. Lafitte's Blacksmith Shop p153
11. La touche p155
12. Molly's at the Market p153
13. The Napoleon House p154
14. Pat O'Briens p154
15. Port of Call p155
16. R Bar p156
17. Ryan's Irish Pub p155
18. Turtle Bay Bar & Grill p155

Music clubs

1. Café Brasil p220
2. Crescent City Brewhouse p216
3. Donna's Bar & Grill p216
4. Funky Butt at Congo Square p216
5. House of Blues p217
6. Igor's Checkpoint Charlie p220
7. Jimmy Buffett's Margaritaville Café p216
8. Kerry Irish Pub p216
9. O'Flaherty's Irish Channel Pub p218
10. Original Tropical Isle p218
11. Palm Court Jazz Café p218
12. Preservation Hall p218
13. The Shim Sham Club & Juke Joint p218
14. Storyville District p219
15. Snug Harbor p220
16. Tipitina's French Quarter p219

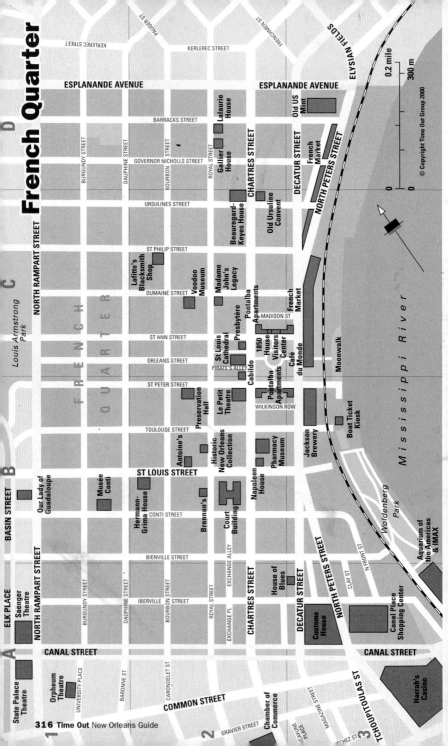

French Quarter

ELYSIAN FIELDS

0.2 mile
300 m

© Copyright Time Out Group 2000

ESPLANANDE AVENUE

ESPLANANDE AVENUE

Old US Mint

Lalaurie House

BARRACKS STREET

KERLEREC STREET

KERLEREC STREET

PAUGER ST

FRENCHMEN ST

BURGUNDY STREET

DAUPHINE STREET

BOURBON STREET

Galier House

CHARTRES STREET

DECATUR STREET

French Market

NORTH PETERS STREET

GOVERNOR NICHOLLS STREET

ROYAL STREET

URSULINES STREET

Beauregard-Keyes House

Old Ursuline Convent

St PHILIP STREET

Lafitte's Blacksmith Shop

Voodoo Museum

Madame John's Legacy

DUMAINE STREET

Presbytère

Pontalba Apartments

French Market

NORTH RAMPART STREET

MADISON ST

F R E N C H   Q U A R T E R

St ANN STREET

St Louis Cathedral

1850 House

Visitors Center

Café du Monde

ORLEANS STREET

PIRATE'S ALLEY

Cabildo

Louis Armstrong Park

St PETER STREET

Preservation Hall

Le Petit Theatre

Pontalba Apartments

WILKINSON ROW

Moonwalk

TOULOUSE STREET

Antoine's

Historic New Orleans Collection

Jackson Brewery

Boat Ticket Kiosk

M i s s i s s i p p i   R i v e r

Musée Conti

St LOUIS STREET

Pharmacy Museum

Our Lady of Guadaloupe

Hermann-Grima House

Brennan's

Court Building

Napoleon House

CONTI STREET

BASIN STREET

BIENVILLE STREET

BURGUNDY STREET

DAUPHINE STREET

BOURBON STREET

ROYAL STREET

EXCHANGE ALLEY

EXCHANGE PL

House of Blues

CHARTRES STREET

DECATUR STREET

NORTH PETERS STREET

CLAY ST

N FRONT ST

Woldenberg Park

Aquarium of the Americas & IMAX

IBERVILLE STREET

Customs House

Canal Place Shopping Center

ELK PLACE

Saenger Theatre

NORTH RAMPART STREET

CANAL STREET

CANAL STREET

State Palace Theatre

Orpheum Theatre

UNIVERSITY PLACE

BARONNE ST

CARONDELET ST

COMMON STREET

Chamber of Commerce

MAGAZINE STREET

TCHOUPITOULAS ST

Harrah's Casino

316 *Time Out New Orleans Guide*

GRAVIER STREET

LAFAYETTE PLACE

NATCHEZ ST

A   B   C   D

1   2   3